HOUSEHOLD DYNAMICS

HOUSEHOLD DYNAMICS

Economic Growth and Policy

William A. Lord

Department of Economics
University of Maryland, Baltimore County

New York   Oxford
OXFORD UNIVERSITY PRESS
2002

Oxford University Press

Oxford   New York
Athens   Auckland   Bangkok   Bogotá   Buenos Aires   Calcutta
Cape Town   Chennai   Dar es Salaam   Delhi   Florence   Hong Kong   Istanbul
Karachi   Kuala Lumpur   Madrid   Melbourne   Mexico City   Mumbai
Nairobi   Paris   São Paulo   Shanghai   Singapore   Taipei   Tokyo   Toronto   Warsaw

and associated companies in
Berlin   Ibadan

Copyright © 2002 by Oxford University Press, Inc.

Published by Oxford University Press, Inc.
198 Madison Avenue, New York, New York, 10016
http://www.oup-usa.org

Oxford is a registered trademark of Oxford University Press

Library of Congress Cataloging-in-Publication Data
Lord, William A., 1954–
     Household dynamics : economic growth and policy / William A. Lord.
         p. cm.
     Includes bibliographical references and index.
     ISBN 0-19-512900-8 (alk. paper) — ISBN 0-19-512901-6 (pbk. : alk. paper)
     1. Family—Economic aspects. 2. Households—Economic aspects. 3. Finance, Personal.
   4. Consumption (Economics) I. Title.

HQ518 .L67 2001
332.024—dc21   2001021208

Printing number: 9 8 7 6 5 4 3 2 1

Printed in the United States of America
on acid-free paper

For mother Elizabeth,
whose example always demonstrates the primacy of love

And daughter Sarah,
whose presence makes gratitude my natural sentiment

CONTENTS

PREFACE

It is my belief that all important personal economic decisions made by individuals or families are conditioned by the past and take future implications into account. This book makes this intertemporal or dynamic perspective its organizing principle. The core models of life-cycle and household behavior, including intergenerational relations, are developed in depth. Economic implications of these models are stressed and then evaluated in light of empirical findings. These same models constitute the modern microeconomic foundations of aggregate physical and human capital accumulation, and of population growth. I take full advantage of this by developing extensive applications of the core models to macroeconomic growth. Further, the welfare of individuals, families, and successive generations is best assessed from the longer term perspective this book affords. For this reason, the book is full of policy applications at both the household and macroeconomic level. The topics covered are among the most important and interesting in economics, if not all of social science. (Contributions of seven current Nobel Laureates figure prominently in the text.) My contribution is integrating a heretofore diffuse literature into a readily accessible form. The interplay of modeling, empirical assessment, and application to policy and growth made this book wonderful to write, and I hope to read.

Chapter 1 develops the basic theory of life-cycle consumption and saving decisions. Special emphasis is accorded to saving for retirement, the role of future earnings, and credit market imperfections. The second chapter offers important extensions, such as the implications of earnings and life span uncertainty. It also includes an extended discussion of the efficacy of saving incentive plans, such as IRAs and 401(k)s. In Chapter 3 an overlapping-generations version of the theory of neoclassical economic growth is developed, emphasizing physical capital accumulation. The roles of human capital accumulation and technical change are also considered, although in this chapter they are not modeled as the outcomes of optimizing behavior. The fourth chapter employs a simplified version of Chapter 3's framework to address important fiscal policies, such as Social Security and income tax reform.

Chapter 5 examines the motivations for, and implications of, financial transfers between parents and their grown children, such as the leaving of financial bequests. Determining what motivates these transfers is shown to be crucial to understanding the implications of various government policies. This chapter also assesses the contribution of intergenerational transfers to aggregate wealth accumulation. The sixth chapter focuses on investments made by parents in their children's human capital development while they are still dependents. Such investments are seen to have important implications for inequality and economic growth. Chapter 7 considers accumulation of human capital later in life. Significant applications are made to earnings inequality, economic growth, and the effect of taxation on human capital accumulation.

The allocation of time between market employment, household production (including child care), and leisure is the subject of Chapter 8. One goal of that chapter is to explain the increase in female labor market participation in the twentieth century. This requires some discussion of the gains from marriage and the risks of divorce. The final chapter considers the economics of fertility decisions, emphasizing the roles of income, the value of women's time, and family structure. It also includes an application to long-term economic growth, emphasizing the changing relationship between income and fertility.

My intent was to present the implications of dynamic household behavior in depth, but to minimize the technical difficulty of obtaining that depth. This enables readers from a broad range of preparation to benefit from the text, although the amount of assistance needed, and speed with which the materials may be covered, varies appreciably over that range. Every chapter presupposes that the reader is comfortable with intermediate microeconomic theory. An exposure to intermediate macroeconomic theory would ease the journey through Chapters 3 and 4, and the macro sections of several other chapters. However, since the macroeconomics always follows directly from the microeconomic foundations, such exposure is only recommended. Mathematics is employed sparingly, although some chapter sections contain a fair number of equations. I do routinely use derivative notation to indicate slopes and other rates of change. However, readers need not recall the rules of differentiation (although the "exponent rule" is explained and used in the context of Cobb-Douglas utility and production functions). The standard one-semester course in calculus required of majors in most economics departments is more than adequate mathematical preparation for reading this book.

Household Dynamics, Economic Growth and Policy may be adopted for courses at the advanced undergraduate level. I have used these materials at this level with success at the University of Maryland, Baltimore County, where the average student scores in excess of 1,150 on the SAT. In such courses the lectures need to adhere rather closely to the text, and no more than four full chapters (or *parts* of more) can comfortably be covered in a semester. Significantly, these chapters certainly need not be the first four, as I explain below. Some sections, such as the uncertainty material in Chapter 2, prove relatively more challenging for students at this level.

As the principal text to be used in (much of its) entirety, the book is ideally suited to courses in master's degree programs in economics or public policy. Master's degree students find the conceptual and technical level a good fit. They could easily complete a total of seven chapters, especially if lectures emphasize the readings. Doctorate degree students could benefit most from having this text assigned as supplementary reading in article-based courses covering these topics at a higher technical level. Other Ph.D. students may find this treatment a useful complement (antidote?) to the highly technical sequence of courses necessary to prepare for a career as an academic or research economist. Academics and policy practitioners should find the volume to be a valuable reference for their personal libraries: The book contains an accessible, yet close-to-the-research-frontier exposition and integration of a large important literature. The book is obviously well suited to serve as a reference volume in libraries.

End-of-chapter review questions and problems provide valuable reinforcement of each chapter's main lessons. Problems preceded by an asterisk are more challenging. An *Instructor's Manual* which includes solutions to the chapter problems is available from Oxford University Press for those who adopt the text for classroom use.

Household Dynamics, Economic Growth and Policy is designed to be flexible enough for use in a variety of courses. This feature is a result of the fact that many chapters may be read independently; the integration with other chapters is accomplished with as little carry-over of jargon or significant reliance on previous results as possible. Below I list several sample course syllabi, referencing section numbers in the Table of Contents. Optional sections are listed in parentheses.

Undergraduate Household or Family Economics: 1.1–1.3, (2.3), 5.1, 5.2, (5.3), 6.1, (6.2), (7.1), (7.2), 8.1–8.3, 9.1–9.3. Policy applications may be omitted, and it is possible to omit Chapter 1. Graduate Household or Family: All of the above, plus the option of Chapter 2.

Undergraduate Consumption/Savings: 1.1–1.5; 2.1, 2.2, 2.3, (2.4), (3.1.2), (4.2), (4.4), (4.5), 5.1, 5.2, (5.3), 5.4, (7.1), (7.2). Graduate Consumption/Savings: All of the above, plus the rest of (3.1), (3.2), (3.3).

Undergraduate Growth: 1.1, 1.2, (1.3), Ch. 3, (Ch. 4), 6.1, 6.3, (7.1), (7.4), (8.3), 9.4. Graduate Growth: All of the above, plus (6.2), (7.2), (7.3), (9.1), (9.2). It is possible for most graduate students to omit Chapter 1.

Undergraduate Public Finance: 1.1–1.5, 2.1c, (2.2), (4.1), 4.2, 4.4, 4.5, (5.1), (5.5), 7.1, 7.5, 8.1, 8.5, (9.1). Graduate Public Finance: All of the above plus 2.1.1, 2.1.2, 2.1.3, (6.2), (6.4), (7.2), (9.2), (9.3).

Undergraduate Labor (featuring labor supply, income distribution, and policy): 6.1, 6.2, (6.4), 7.1, 7.2, (7.3), (7.5), 8.1–8.5, 9.1–9.3 (9.4). Graduate Labor: All of the above, plus (6.3), (7.4).

Graduate Macroeconomics: 1.1–1.5, (2.3), 3.1–3.6, 4.1–4.5, (4.6), (5.1–5.6), (6.1–6.6), (7.1–7.5), (8.3), (8.4), (9.4).

ACKNOWLEDGMENTS

Many people assisted in the preparation of this manuscript. Ken McLeod, then at Oxford University Press, shared my vision for the book, got me a contract, and procured for me an excellent set of chapter reviewers. Mia McIver of Oxford shepherded the project to completion. I am grateful to Justin Collins and other members of the production department at Oxford who quite wonderfully converted my submitted manuscript into the bound volume.

My principal debt is to three senior scholars who read the manuscript in its entirety and made many valuable suggestions for its improvement. Peter Rangazas and I have collaborated on many articles over the years and I have learned much from him in the process. Pete could have written this book better and faster. Instead, he volunteered to test a rough draft of this manuscript in his master's course in macroeconomics and provided detailed guidance for improvements on the basis of that experience. On at least a dozen occasions I called him when confused about technical, other substantive, or stylistic issues. In each case he received my call graciously and offered unusually insightful advice. He insisted that the microeconomic models be assessed empirically and their macroeconomic implications be pursued vigorously. Although this made for a lengthy volume, I believe it also describes the main contributions of the book.

Jim Davies and Larry Seidman have supported my efforts in many ways over the years, even though I have not been in a position to reciprocate in kind or, indeed, have much contact with them. Jim read every chapter carefully and made extensive comments on most. He caught more mistakes than he should have needed to and simultaneously saw the project in its best light. Larry also made extensive, useful comments on several chapters. His unique contribution was to see clearly how materials should best be organized to aid students' understanding. I am grateful to have attracted these wonderful mentors.

Chris Carroll allowed me to sit in on his graduate courses in 1994, which greatly stimulated my interest in, and deepened my understanding of, consumption and savings. Saul Hoffman and Jonathon Skinner provided encouragement and useful advice at an early stage of the writing. My colleagues at UMBC, especially Dave Greenberg, Dennis Coates, and Bonnie Wilson, also read one or more chapters and provided useful comments.

The writings of several economists furthered my understanding of issues in this book beyond their representation in the bibliography. Especially important in this regard are Gary Becker, Chris Carroll, Jim Davies, James Heckman, Larry Kotlikoff, and Pete Rangazas. Lou Maccini allowed me to launch the writing of the manuscript in a course at Johns Hopkins in the fall of 1995. My departmental chair at UMBC, Alan Sorkin, also supported my efforts in various ways. I am grateful to my students in various courses who endured successive drafts of the manuscript. Zongxiang Luo, with help from Ryan Mutter, prepared the many figures, for which I am *immensely* grateful. My thanks also to Freda Vaughn for her help typing the references.

On a personal note, I thank Jessica Dibb and others in the Inspiration Community for supporting my development of Essence. Finally, my daughter Sarah has been a constant source of joy. I could not have completed the project without our creative playfulness (which often included her friends Michele and Alica).

HOUSEHOLD DYNAMICS

Chapter 1 | CONSUMPTION AND SAVING, I

> *"It is hard to think of economic issues that are more important than the accumulation of capital, and the means by which citizens, either individually or collectively, make provisions for their futures."*
>
> —ANGUS DEATON, P. VII, 1992

Young adults start out with a time "endowment" of several decades, a set of skills, and perhaps a little money. These resources are used to earn income, guide family decisions, and acquire cars, houses, and other consumer goods. This chapter develops the implications of one simple fact: In any particular year, the income received and the consumption desired need not be equal. We develop a theory of life-cycle consumption and saving decisions, taking as given the stream of income received over the life cycle. Implications of that theory are evaluated in the light of empirical evidence. Understanding the consumption and saving behavior of households is important. For example, understanding how households prepare for retirement is crucial to assessing Social Security. At the macroeconomic level, consumption is roughly two-thirds of gross domestic product (GDP), and savings from personal income are an important source of funds for capital accumulation and growth. This makes consumption and saving behaviors crucial inputs into the formulation of policies designed to affect the aggregate demand and/or stimulate economic growth.

Consumption occurs when resources are used to confer current satisfaction and are depleted in the process. *Saving* is the accumulation of assets for future use. Clearly, a meal at a restaurant is consumption, while adding to one's financial reserves is saving. The purchase of a new car provides consumption benefits in both the current and future periods. The purchase of such *durable goods*, then, entails both consumption and saving. The expenditure of current resources on training to bolster future wages, or *human capital investment*, is another important form of saving. This type of investment is the subject of a separate chapter. Another form of consumption, that of *leisure* time, will be examined as part of a general discussion of time allocation decisions.

Figure 1.1 illustrates some trends in saving rates and wealth in recent decades. The top profile is the gross of depreciation national saving rate. This rate is the sum of the public and private sector's total savings as a percent of GDP. From the mid-1960s through

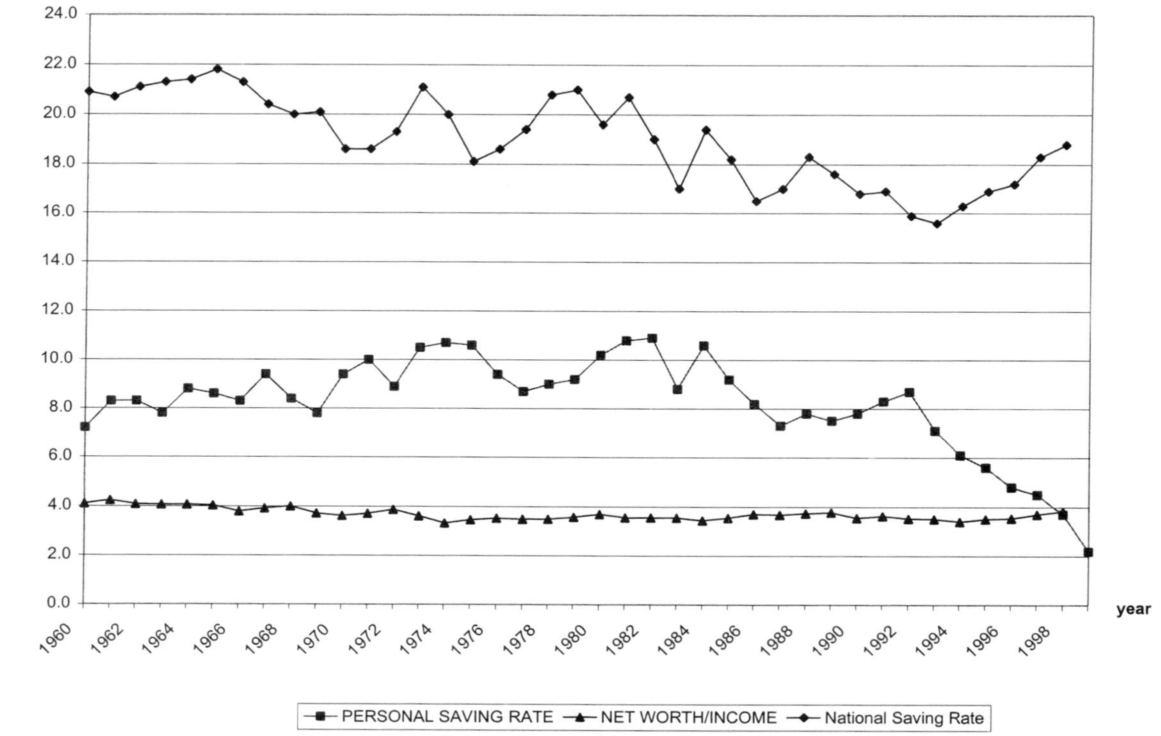

* Reflect 1999 NIPA revisions
**Both net worth and income have been adjusted for changes in the distribution of age and marital status

Figure 1.1 Trends in saving rates and wealth, 1960–2000

the mid-1990s this rate declined appreciably. More dramatically, the *net* of depreciation saving rate (not shown) fell by half over this period: The net saving rate averaged 11.9 percent between 1960 and 1964 but only 5.73 percent between 1995 and 1998.[1] As discussed in Chapters 3 and 4, a lower rate of saving implies slower capital accumulation, which may, in turn, reduce growth in worker productivity. The rise in the gross national saving rate in recent years reflects the elimination of large federal government budget deficits and the emergence of surpluses.

In the National Income and Product Accounts the personal saving rate is defined as personal disposable (or after-tax) income minus consumption.[2] Figure 1.1 reveals that this saving rate has declined precipitously over the past fifteen years, from 10.6% in 1984 to 2.2% in 1999. (It was negative in 2000.) This rate gives an indication of the flow of savings from the household sector that are available for investment in business capital. Significantly, this rate does not include capital gains on stock holdings, and thus omits the wealth generated from the bull market of the late 1980s and the 1990s. These gains may be particularly relevant when assessing whether households are saving adequately for their retirement years. In fact, as Figure 1.1 shows, the ratio of household wealth to household income has risen slightly in recent years, even as the personal saving rate has plummeted.[3] In fact, since stock market gains are not included in personal income but may increase consumption, capital gains on stocks may explain the rapid growth in aggregate consumption in the late 1990s, the low personal saving rate, and the increasing wealth to income ratio. These links are discussed in greater detail later in the chapter.

This chapter models the saving decisions of households; the book returns to aggregate savings in Chapters 3 and 4. Our perspective is that consumers or households are rational, forward-looking agents who attempt to maximize the utility from consumption over the life cycle. This approach with its implications was most prominently developed by Nobel Laureate Franco Modigliani and his coauthors beginning in the 1950s. Also in the 1950s, Nobel Laureate Milton Friedman developed the Permanent Income Hypothesis. Modigliani stressed the issues surrounding the finiteness of life and planning for retirement. Friedman, on the other hand, gave greater emphasis to issues surrounding income fluctuations, or dynamics. Both emphasized the connection between own earnings and own consumption. Thus, they largely neglected inheritances and bequests, which are also likely important (see Chapters 5 and 6).

As did Modigliani, we emphasize behavior over the life cycle. However, in recent years the life-cycle model has been enriched to incorporate uncertainty regarding, as examples, future income and the age at death. Augmented in this fashion, the life-cycle model incorporates much of the income dynamics so central to Friedman's Permanent Income Hypothesis. The modern versions of these models have many similarities and, though not identical (cf. Deaton, 1992), are often collectively termed the Life Cycle/Permanent Income Hypothesis.[4] This perspective is employed to explain the basic facts regarding consumption and savings over the life cycle.

In this chapter we assume that income is given (i.e., is exogenous to the model), received with certainty, and that utility depends only upon the quantities of market goods consumed in different periods. Subsequent chapters generalize the theory along these dimensions or develop macroeconomic extensions. Section 1.1 lays out the basic model of intertemporal choice. Then, in section 1.2, the implications of this framework are evaluated in the light of empirical evidence. Section 1.3 further examines the relationship between income and savings, stressing the roles of future earnings and credit markets. The following section, 1.4, is devoted to policy applications. A final section summarizes what we have learned and previews related chapters.

1.1 THE BASIC MODEL OF INTERTEMPORAL CHOICE

1.1.1 Preferences

The consumer or household utility maximization problem is formulated in terms of preferences and opportunities. We begin by describing preferences. Supposing the consumer lives for two periods, life cycle utility U is given by

$$U = U(C_1, C_2) \tag{1.1}$$

where C_1 and C_2 are the aggregate household consumptions in periods one and two, respectively. Assuming the first period begins with the onset of economic independence, period one corresponds, roughly, to ages 20 to 50, and the second period to ages 50 to 80. After developing intuition in the two-period context, the discussion is extended to the many-period, or annual, context.

When considering a household headed by more than one adult, it is reasonable to ask whether their distinct preferences can be meaningfully aggregated into a common utility function. If not, then the standard approach of maximizing a unified household utility function subject to a household budget constraint is not appropriate; some type of bargaining model would be better.

In fact, there is evidence that the proportion of family expenditures exclusively benefiting a particular spouse (a *Sports Illustrated* subscription?) *within a period* increases with that spouse's contribution to family income (Browning et al., 1994). However, if we limit attention within a period to the aggregate of consumption, it is not clear how this affects the allocation of expenditures *across periods*. Consequently, in the absence of a convincing alternative, we assume the common family utility function in (1.1).[5]

More so than the general utility function of (1.1), we emphasize implications of the popular Cobb-Douglas specification,

$$U = C_1^\theta \, C_2^{1-\theta} \tag{1.2}$$

where θ is a taste parameter, and where $0 < \theta < 1$. As shown below, this specific functional form for utility yields a simple explicit solution to the utility maximization problem. That solution allows us to highlight important mechanisms easily, makes for easy numerical application, and is suitable for many of the issues addressed in this chapter. However, limitations of the Cobb-Douglas form make it less useful for some topics. These limitations and an important generalization are taken up in Chapter 2.

A representative indifference curve consistent with both (1.1) and (1.2) is shown in Figure 1.2. It is drawn in the usual way, convex to the origin. Convexity implies consumers prefer "balanced" consumption bundles over extreme allocations. The slope of an

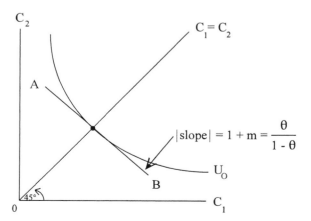

Figure 1.2 Time preference

indifference curve (in absolute value) at any point is termed the *marginal rate of substitution* $MRS_{1,2}$ of C_1 for C_2. Since utility is constant along the indifference curve, the $MRS_{1,2}$ is the maximum amount of C_2 the consumer would trade or pay for another unit of C_1. Convex indifference curves imply diminishing $MRS_{1,2}$; the consumer values C_1 less in relation to C_2 the larger is C_1's share of the consumption bundle.

The $MRS_{1,2}$ may also be conceived of as the ratio of first- and second-period marginal utilities. For the general utility function of (1.1) we denote these marginal utilities u_1 and u_2, respectively. For example, if $u_1 = 2$ and $u_2 = 1$, the $MRS_{1,2} = u_1/u_2 = 2$, and the consumer is willing to trade up to two units of C_2 for an additional unit of C_1.

Applying these concepts to the Cobb-Douglas utility function (1.2), it can be shown (note 6 explains how) that[6]

$$MRS_{1,2} = \theta C_2/[(1 - \theta)C_1] \tag{1.3}$$

Equation (1.3) shows that the convexity property holds: as the consumer moves down the indifference curve, C_2 falls and C_1 rises, lowering the $MRS_{1,2}$.

Since the $MRS_{1,2}$ varies along an indifference curve, an "anchored" measure of the consumer's relative preference for present compared with future consumption is desired. To this end, the pure *rate of time preference* is defined as

$$m \equiv MRS_{1,2} - 1 \text{ (with the } MRS_{1,2} \text{ evaluated where } C_1 = C_2)$$

Thus, m tells us how much more or less than 1 unit of C_2 we would be willing to give up for another unit of C_1 *when we consume equal amounts of each*. Intuitively, m is the rate at which the consumer *subjectively* discounts future satisfactions. Most economists believe that m is positive, meaning that with everything else the same, people prefer present to future satisfactions. (This preference is obvious and strong among young children.) The higher m is, the stronger the relative preference for current consumption is. In the Cobb-Douglas case when $C_1 = C_2$, equation (1.3) gives us $MRS_{1,2} = \theta/(1 - \theta)$, so that $m = \theta/(1 - \theta) - 1$. Thus, an increase in θ (the exponent on C_1) increases the relative desirability of first-period consumption.

Time preference is illustrated in Figure 1.2. Along the 45-degree line, $C_1 = C_2$. Therefore, the slope of the line tangent to indifference curve where it crosses the 45-degree line reflects the $MRS_{1,2}$ when consumption is equal in the two periods. So, AB has slope $-(1 + m)$. The larger is m, the more impatient we are, and the steeper is an indifference curve as it crosses the 45-degree line. If $m = 0$, we would be willing to trade C_1 and C_2 on a one-for-one basis if we had the same amount of each. Below we discuss empirical evidence concerning time preference, provoking a brief discussion of its determinants.

Given that $1 + m = \theta/(1 - \theta)$ in the Cobb-Douglas case, the MRS *at any point* on the indifference curve may be expressed in terms of time preference, using (1.3), as

$$MRS_{1,2} = (1 + m)C_2/C_1 \tag{1.4}$$

From (1.4) we see that the amount of future consumption we would trade for current consumption increases with m. This version of the $MRS_{1,2}$ proves helpful below in isolating the different influences on optimal consumption over the life cycle.

1.1.2 Consumption Opportunities

Consumption is limited by the consumer's resources, or budget constraint. In the simplest case, the household works full-time in period one, receiving labor (or wage) income of E_1 at the start of the period. The second period (old age) is devoted to retirement. The consumer allocates the wages of youth between C_1 and C_2. For convenience, units of consumption are chosen such that the current period price is 1, making expenditures in a period equal to the number of units consumed. Any monies saved, or "invested," for second-period consumption are assumed to earn interest at rate r. This is the interest rate for an entire period (perhaps 30 years). Consequently, if the interest rate for a single year is 3 or 4 percent, r would be above 100 percent, or greater than 1.

The budget constraint may be written as

$$C_1 + C_2/(1 + r) \leq E_1 \tag{1.5}$$

By this expression, the consumer is free to choose any combination of C_1 and C_2 having present value equal to (or uninterestingly less than) E_1.[7] The budget line is depicted in Figure 1.3, letting $E_1 = 20$ and $r = 1$. Budget line AE_1 is every combination of C_1 and C_2 costing E_1 in present value. The horizontal axis intercept reveals that one possibility is simply to consume everything while young, setting $C_1 = E_1$. At the other extreme, if all is put aside for retirement consumption, then C_2 would equal first-period earnings plus the interest earned on those savings, $E_1 + rE_1 = (1 + r)E_1$. More generally, every dollar saved increases period-two consumption by principal plus interest, or $1 + r$. Thus, the slope of the budget line is $-(1 + r)$. Viewing preferences in light of budget opportunities, we now consider the consumer's optimal life-cycle consumption choices.

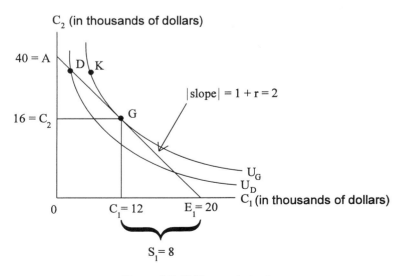

Figure 1.3 Utility maximization

1.1.3 Optimal Consumption Choices

The consumer's utility maximization problem can be stated as

$$\text{Maximize } U = U(C_1, C_2)$$

by choice of C_1 and C_2, subject to

$$C_1 + C_2/(1 + r) \leq E_1$$

The solution is portrayed in Figure 1.3. Utility is maximized at consumption bundle G, where the indifference curve U_G is tangent to the budget line. For the general preferences of (1.1), tangency requires

$$MRS_{1,2} = u_1/u_2 = 1 + r \tag{1.6a}$$

Viewing Figure 1.3, all other consumption bundles along the budget line yield less utility than does G. For example, at point D the amount of C_2 the consumer is willing to trade for another unit of C_1—the $MRS_{1,2}$—exceeds the $1 + r$ unit reduction in C_2 that the "bank" requires when we increase C_1 (reduce savings) one unit.

We are accustomed to thinking of the tangency condition (1.6a) as equating the $MRS_{1,2}$ to the ratio of prices. According to this logic, $1 + r$ must equal the price ratio. How so? The opportunity cost—or price—of an additional unit of C_2 is the amount of C_1 that must be foregone to obtain it. This is simply $1/(1 + r)$ because, if C_1 is reduced by that amount, the additional savings will grow to equal 1 at the start of period two. Thus, the "price" of C_2 is $1/(1 + r)$; the amount of current consumption we must forego in order to increase future consumption falls as the interest rate rises. As noted above, the period-one price of C_1 is simply \$1 of life wealth. Therefore, the ratio of the price of C_1 to that of C_2 is $1/[1/(1 + r)] = (1 + r)$; this is also called the relative price of C_1. Since the consumer makes the life-cycle plan at the start of period one, we typically express both prices and resources in terms of period-one dollars.

If preferences are Cobb-Douglas, the tangency condition (1.6a) becomes

$$\theta C_2/[(1 - \theta)C_1] = 1 + r \tag{1.6b}$$

or, substituting in $1 + m$ from (1.4) and rearranging,

$$C_2/C_1 = (1 + r)/(1 + m) \tag{1.6c}$$

From (1.6c) we see that consumption grows (falls) over the life cycle if $r > m$ ($r < m$); if the rates of interest and time preference are equal, consumption should be flat over the life cycle. This makes good intuitive sense. Recall that the higher is r, the less expensive is future consumption, which pushes consumption into the future. The higher is m, on the other hand, the more impatient is the consumer, which encourages earlier consumption. Equation (1.6c) summarizes this tug of war. Below, equation (1.6b) is used to derive the levels of optimal consumption.

Although the tangency condition pins down the slope of an indifference curve when utility is maximized, to learn which indifference curve the consumer lands on—and thus the actual consumption bundle—we must utilize the budget constraint. To determine consumption in the two-period Cobb-Douglas case, first solve the tangency condition (1.6b) for C_2 in terms of C_1, producing

$$C_2 = C_1(1 - \theta)(1 + r)/\theta \tag{1.7}$$

Next, use (1.7) to eliminate C_2 from the budget constraint (1.5), giving us a single equation in C_1

$$E_1 = C_1 + \frac{C_1(1 - \theta)(1 + r)}{(1 + r)\theta} = C_1\left(1 + \frac{1 - \theta}{\theta}\right)$$

so that

$$C_1 = \frac{E_1}{1 + \dfrac{1 - \theta}{\theta}} = \frac{E_1}{\dfrac{\theta}{\theta} + \dfrac{1 - \theta}{\theta}}$$

which simplifies to

$$C_1 = \theta E_1 \tag{1.8}$$

Equation (1.8) tells us that consumers with Cobb-Douglas preferences simply devote the proportion θ of their life wealth—here labor earnings while young—to consumption in the first period of life. Since m increases with θ, (1.8) confirms that less patient consumers do consume more of life wealth when young. With Cobb-Douglas utility, the proportion of life wealth devoted to C_1 is determined solely by preferences, being independent of the structure of relative prices—as determined by the interest rate. In Chapter 2, we show that this result does not survive in the presence of a more general utility function.

First-period savings may be measured as income minus consumption. In terms of the optimal consumption rule for C_1, savings when young are

$$S_1 = E_1 - C_1 = E_1 - \theta E_1 = (1 - \theta)E_1 \tag{1.9}$$

Notice that the supply of savings is explained rather indirectly, as the residual between income and consumption demand. (*Warning:* In some later settings, first-period income will include interest income and life wealth will include second-period earnings. Thus, while savings may always be measured as income minus consumption, it will not always equal the fraction $(1 - \theta)$ of life wealth, let alone of first-period labor income.)

With the second period devoted to retirement, consumption in the second period is limited to what was saved when young, plus interest earned.

$$C_2 = S_1(1 + r) \tag{1.10}$$

Second-period consumption may also be found by substituting optimal C_1 from (1.8) into (1.7) and then rearranging. Households dissave in the second period what was saved in the first, dying (exactly) penniless: Savings in the second period equal interest income rS_1 minus C_2, or $-S_1$.

Equations (1.8) and (1.10) provide explicit solutions for the utility-maximizing consumption bundle in terms of the model's parameters E_1, r, and θ. Working through a numerical example helps fix ideas. To that end, suppose $\theta = .6$, $E_1 = \$20,000$, and $r = 1$. An interest rate of 1 means one unit of C_2 costs one-half unit of C_1, or 50 cents. Using equations (1.8–1.10), $C_1 = (.6)(\$20,000) = \$12,000$, $S_1 = (.4)(\$20,000) = \$8,000$, and $C_2 = \$8,000(1 + 1) = \$16,000$. These parameter values and optimal choices are depicted in Figure 1.3.

1.1.4   Many Periods

The many-period version of this model offers additional insight. Suppose, therefore, the consumer lives T periods, each lasting one year. She maximizes a T-period Cobb-Douglas utility function that depends on consumption in each year. As seems reasonable, suppose the degree of impatience between any two adjacent years is equal and given by m. Similarly, the one-period interest rate is constant at r throughout life. The optimality condition governing consumption growth between periods one and two remains

$$C_2/C_1 = (1 + r)/(1 + m)$$

while the relationship between first- and third-period consumption, for example, becomes

$$C_3/C_1 = [(1 + r)/(1 + m)]^2$$

More generally, consumption in any period t is related to first-period consumption by

$$C_t/C_1 = [(1 + r)/(1 + m)]^{t-1}$$

As in the two-period story, consumption rises (falls) if $r > m$ ($r < m$). Figure 1.4 plots consumption in each year t of economic life, C_t, for each relative magnitude of r and m. These "age-consumption" profiles further illustrate that consumption is predicted to be "smooth" over the life cycle, with r and m determining the slope.

The process of asset accumulation for retirement is also clarified by reference to the many-period context. To that end, now assume the consumer retires after R periods. To focus on retirement savings, assume that the interest rate $r = 0$, which enables us to avoid the complications associated with interest income. To further simplify, we consider the case where $r = m$, so that utility maximization requires constant consumption across periods, $C_t = C$. Finally, let earnings be constant each year until retirement, so that $E_t = E$. To be concrete, suppose the consumer retires after $R = 40$ years, while living for a total of $T = 50$. Earnings each year are $E = \$20,000$. Under these assumptions, life wealth is simply the product of years worked and earnings per year, $W = ER = \$800,000$. Con-

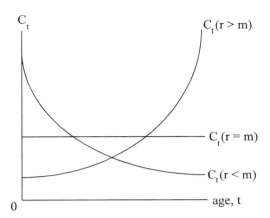

Figure 1.4 The age-consumption profile

sumption per year is wealth divided by the number of years of adult life, C = ER/T = $16,000. The consumption and earnings profiles are illustrated in Figure 1.5.

Since consumption continues throughout retirement, assets must be accumulated during the working years. With E and C being constants, so also is saving over the working years, $S_w = E - C = \$20,000 - \$16,000 = \$4,000$. The age-asset profile A_t increases throughout the working years, peaking at the start of retirement, where $A_{R+1} = RS_w = \$16,000$. Consumers dissave C each year of retirement, $S_R = -C$, so that at the time of death assets are zero. Figure 1.5 shows how these annual saving patterns translate into asset holdings in each year, A_t.

Figure 1.5 illustrates the life-cycle theory of saving, according to which most saving is done to provide for retirement consumption. Asset holdings during the peak years are sometimes referred to as "hump wealth." Modigliani (cf. 1988) is the most prominent proponent of the life-cycle theory of savings. According to Modigliani, perhaps three-quarters of all wealth holdings throughout the economy result from this motive for saving. His position is controversial. Indeed, other economists have argued that life-cycle

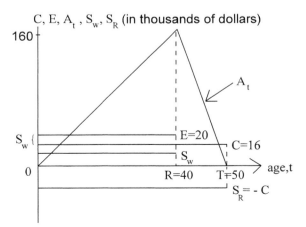

Figure 1.5 Life-cycle saving and asset profiles

savings are but a fifth of the total, intergenerational transfers accounting for the rest (cf. Kotlikoff, 1988). As Modigliani notes, "knowledge of the relative contributions is important to assess the effectiveness of measures designed to affect saving and wealth as well as the effects on wealth of measures intended to achieve other goals, such as estate taxation designed to reduce economic inequalities" (p. 17). We examine these relative contributions in Chapter 5 when discussing intergenerational accumulation.

1.2 EMPIRICAL IMPLICATIONS OF THE BASIC MODEL

The optimal solutions derived above have important implications. First, households should build up a stock of assets before retirement. Second, during retirement, the household should spend all those assets—plus any interest earned on them—to die penniless. Third, households differing only in their earnings levels should behave essentially the same. Specifically, assuming all households have identical tastes and face the same interest rate, all households should consume at the same *rate* from life wealth. Finally, equation (1.6c) suggests that whether consumption rises or falls over the life cycle depends upon the relative magnitudes of r and m. The evidence related to these predictions is now assessed.

1.2.1   Asset Holdings over the Life Cycle

First we consider whether asset accumulation before retirement and decumulation during retirement are consistent with the basic pattern of Figure 1.5. Preretirement accumulation is driven largely by the rate of saving during the prime working years. For most people, housing equity, Social Security, and private pension plan benefits constitute the core retirement assets. Despite this, the saving measure most frequently reported by journalists (the personal saving rate) is current disposable income minus consumption. This measure omits capital gains in stocks and home values and distorts the roles of Social Security and pensions. Using much better household level data, careful measures of life-cycle saving and how such saving varies with life resources are only recently appearing.

Carefully measured saving rates are provided by Dynan, Skinner, and Zeldes (1996, 2000). These authors employ data from the Panel Study of Income Dynamics (PSID), an elaborate study that has followed the same set of families since 1968 and features quality information on annual income. Total asset holdings are measured well less frequently, but good estimates were obtained in 1984 and 1989. In the 1996 paper, Dynan et al. adjust these data in several ways. First, annual income is rather volatile and not very useful for determining how households save from their average, or as Friedman would say, "permanent," income. For this reason, Dynan et al. average each household's annual earnings over several years to obtain an estimate of average or "permanent" income. They further adjust savings to reflect that portion of Social Security contributions which, under current legislation, increases one's Social Security retirement pension (rather than being redistributed to older or poorer households). A similar modification is made to account for contributions to private pension plans. Saving is calculated as the change in household wealth between 1984 and 1989 for households (divided by 5).[8] These revised

Table 1.1 Median Saving Rates, Adjusted for Social
Security and Pension Accumulation, by Lagged
Labor Earnings Quintile and Age Group (PSID)*

Ages	1	2	3	4	5
30–39	7.4	11.5	14.5	14.5	14.9
40–49	10.0	12.4	12.9	21.4	20.8
50–59	11.0	18.8	21.2	23.3	19.6

*PSID, Panel Study of Income Dynamics.
Taken from Dynan, Skinner, and Zeldes (1996), Table 7.

figures are used to examine how saving rates vary over the life cycle and by household's "permanent" income. Dynan et al. group households by age into those in their 30s, 40s, and 50s. A further partitioning splits those in an age group into quintiles on the basis of permanent income.

Table 1.1 (see Dynan et al.'s Table 7, 1996) reports the median saving rates from "permanent" income for each age and permanent income grouping. Clearly, households during these prime working years are accumulating significant assets, with substantial rates of saving in each cell. In fact, for all but the poorest households in their 30s, this comprehensive saving rate exceeds 10%. Comparing the 30–39 and 50–59 age groups reveals a tendency for saving rates to increase over this portion of the life cycle. Altogether, this evidence supports the model's prediction of significant asset accumulation before retirement. Further confirmation is obtained below by a viewing of wealth holdings near retirement.

The sum of each year's saving up to some age equals, by definition, the household's wealth position as of that age. The vast majority of workers retire at or before age 65 (cf. Costa, 1998). For this reason, households whose heads in their 50s and early 60s should have completed much of their retirement accumulation. Gustman et al. (1999, Table 3) use Health and Retirement Study Survey data to determine the net wealth of households with members aged 51 to 61 in 1992. The wealth measures are quite comprehensive, including estimates of the present value of expected Social Security and private pension benefits (expected future earnings, or human wealth, are omitted). The average value of assets for the middle, or median, 10% of households is almost $340,000. Since the average income of those same households is about $36,000, wealth is nine times income. The importance of imputing Social Security and pension values is clear: Social Security accounts for 43% of wealth and private pensions for another 18%. Housing equity contributes an additional 20 percent. Wealth holdings of the affluent explain why average or mean wealth for the entire sample is about 50 percent above the median value (or about $500,000). Indeed, Poterba (2000) notes that the "one percent of U.S. households with the greatest net worth hold roughly one-third of the assets in the U.S. economy. The least wealthy four-fifths of households, by comparison, hold roughly 20 percent of the assets" (p. 101). The wealth position of households whose members are nearing retirement also varies with household structure. Gustman et al. (their Table 6) report the average couple had wealth of about $610,000. This is almost twice that for single males ($359,122) and almost three times that for single females ($212,641).

As predicted by the model, households do in fact build up often sizeable nest eggs before the onset of retirement. Is the magnitude of such assets consistent with our framework? As one might suspect, this is difficult to answer definitively. On one hand, consumption appears to drop somewhat upon retirement and continues to fall until death. For example, Hurd (1997) examines panel data from the Retirement History Survey on the consumption of the same retirees between 1969 and 1979. He finds that on average their consumption fell by a total of 38% over that decade. In contrast, as seen below, consumption tends to rise over the working years. Falling consumption during retirement has helped motivate some natural extensions to the current framework. In one such extension, as explained in Chapter 2, a declining consumption profile in retirement is consistent with rational decumulation when households face uncertainty about the age at death: Intuitively, the *expected* marginal utility of future consumption declines with age, due to the reduced probability of being alive to consume. Further, as discussed in Chapter 8, if goods and leisure are substitutes, the increase in leisure upon retirement would reduce consumption of market goods. Summarizing, consumers do accumulate significant resources before retirement and, from a broader perspective, it is difficult to conclude they are accumulating "too little."

Is observed asset decumulation during retirement consistent with our simple model? In general, people do not die penniless, and a small minority of consumers die with substantial assets. In the aggregate, bequests exceeded $100 billion in 1986 (see Chapter 5). In part, positive wealth at death may reflect an optimal response to uncertainty about the age at death, given a desire to maintain suitable consumption should life prove long. Such "accidental" bequests are discussed in Chapter 2. However, accidental bequests cannot account for the saving behavior of affluent retirees. In the same study discussed above, Dynan et al. also examine median saving rates by income for those age 70 to 79 using a variety of savings definitions and data sets. Taken together (see their Table 12), the evidence is that saving rates remain *positive* among the more affluent even at this late age. Since the wealthy, on average, appear to have positive saving rates until (at least) quite late in life, we conclude that a large proportion of them *intentionally* die with positive wealth. This motivates our discussion of *intentional* bequests in Chapter 5.

1.2.2   Consumption and Saving over the Life Cycle

Our model potentially allows households to differ in their preferences (m or θ), r, and E_1. Initially we assume all households face the same interest rate and have identical preferences. This leaves differences in earnings as the only potential source of variability in household behavior. The model predicts that these differences in the magnitude of earnings should affect only the height and not the shape of the consumption and saving profiles. (In section 1.3 we will see that differences in the timing of income do affect saving rates by age.)

Once again we refer to the comprehensive saving rate from the permanent income measure in Table 1.1. The table reveals that in general the saving rate is positively related to permanent income throughout the working years. Considering those age 40 to 49, for example, this saving rate is 10% for the lowest but 20.8% for the highest quintile.[9] Thus, saving rates do not appear to be independent of life earnings. Dynan et al. (2000) confirm that this finding is robust across several data sets and definitions or proxies for permanent income. Significantly, even the figures of Table 1.1 understate the contribution of the affluent to *total* savings, as their higher saving rates are applied to a larger income base. Thus, understanding the high saving rates of the rich is crucial to understanding aggregate savings.

Does our framework offer clues as to why saving rates increase with life resources? Continuing to assume r is constant across households, we first relax the assumption of identical preferences across households. Equation (1.6c) shows that variation in the rate of time preference m across income groups would cause consumption to grow at different rates. Consumption growth and assets relative to income upon retirement would be higher for the affluent if they are more patient (lower m).

Samwick (1998) presents evidence consistent with this hypothesis. He constructs a large simulation model of household behavior in which consumers face serious earnings risk. From the Survey of Consumer Finances, he obtains household measures of wealth and earnings information. He combines this information with estimates of earnings risk, income growth, asset returns, and risk aversion found in the consumption literature. His strategy is for each household to determine the rate of time preference that would induce that household to accumulate its actual amount of wealth. Of course, higher time preference leads to less wealth accumulation. Households are arrayed by income and partitioned into income deciles. The 10% of households in the lowest decile were estimated to have an average discount rate of about 8%, while those in the top quintile had an annual rate of time preference of about 4% (see his Figure 5). Lawrance (1991), using entirely different methods, also finds the affluent are more patient.

Becker and Mulligan (1997) argue on *theoretical* grounds that time preference is inversely related to life wealth. To them, patience among the affluent is an *implication* of rational behavior. They argue that consumers are able to reduce the extent to which they discount the future, m, by investing in "future oriented capital." For example, one can study enticing brochures about retirement resorts, helping one appreciate possibilities for that period of life, enabling one to discount it less heavily. Further, when wealth is high, the marginal utility of current consumption is low, since consumption is relatively high. This reduces the utility cost of investing in future-oriented capital when young. Finally, since future consumption flows and thus total future utility are high for the affluent, their benefit from lowering the rate of time preference is also high. Consequently, the affluent invest more in future-oriented capital, which makes them more patient. To support their arguments, Becker and Mulligan informally review evidence consistent with their thesis.[10] In summary, empirical and theoretical arguments have been made that the affluent discount the future less heavily than do those less well off. Lower time preference among the affluent is therefore one reason they have faster consumption growth when young and higher rates of preretirement savings.

Another reason the affluent save more and experience faster consumption growth is that they may obtain a higher rate of return on their savings. From the tangency condition (1.6c), even if m is constant across households, those facing higher r will experience faster consumption growth. Kotlikoff and Summers (1981) calculate a portfolio-weighted real (or inflation-adjusted) after-tax rate of return for the entire economy of 4.5% between

1900 and 1974. However, the return to stocks has been above 8%. Since rich households hold a disproportionately large share of all stocks, their average return exceeds 4.5%. The poor hold much less stock (even taking employer-provided pension plan contributions into account). For them, the real after-tax rate of return on treasury bills of less than 1% (which nevertheless exceeds that for passbook savings accounts) may be a more appropriate benchmark.

Variation in the rate of time preference and the interest rate *may* explain why the affluent save at higher rates when young. Another potential explanation is the incentives associated with Social Security. Social Security benefits replace a larger portion of the poor's preretirement earnings, reducing the rate at which they must save to maintain some preretirement consumption level (see section 1.1.4). However, neither of these explanations is consistent with the fact that the affluent don't dissave more rapidly than the less affluent in retirement: It appears as though the rich do not consume all of their life wealth.

Dynan, Skinner, and Zeldes (2000) argue that differences in asset holdings across income groups can be understood as responses to poverty programs, uncertainty over medical outlays in old age, and differences in the value of bequests. They note that in old age the costs of medical care (such as nursing care) may be quite large, especially in relation to the life wealth of the poor. However, eligibility for many income-support programs is conditioned on low asset holdings. This is true, for example, of eligibility for public assistance to pay for nursing home care. These programs therefore reduce the incentive of poor households to accumulate much in the way of assets (see also Chapter 2). On the other hand, though affluent households also fear large medical outlays when old, they may find the living standard associated with public assistance unattractive. Consequently, they may accumulate a large nest egg "just in case" large medical outlays are necessary. Thus, even if households have identical preferences and face identical interest rates, government policies may induce more affluent households to save at higher rates. Further, as explained in Chapter 5, the satisfaction in leaving a bequest is predicted by some prominent models to be greater when life earnings are high relative to children's (which is more likely for rich parents). Consequently, the rich feel less as if their resources were used poorly if they should die with substantial wealth. Their model is *consistent* with the observed savings patterns; it is less clear at this point whether it in fact *explains* them.

Saving rates also vary appreciably *within* earnings classes. Venti and Wise (2000) demonstrate that even among households with similar lifetime wealth, there exists considerable dispersion in the level of assets brought into retirement. Further, most of this dispersion within lifetime earnings classes persists even after the authors control for other potentially important determinants of wealth upon retirement, such as the number of children, large health outlays, or differences in how assets were invested. This leads them to conclude that there may be substantial heterogeneity in the "tastes for saving," or rate of time preference, even among those with similar life wealth. While the analysis of Becker and Murphy discussed above models differences in time preference across life wealth classes, economists currently lack thoughtful models of why tastes may vary within income groupings. There appear to be cultural differences across countries in the propensity to save, and one might expect there also to be intergenerationally transmitted family values and propensities that affect saving. Some evidence of this is seen in Chapter 5 where, controlling for other determinants, the amount of wealth bequeathed to children increases among households that benefited from an inheritance. Alternatively, the finding of substantial variability in saving behavior within income classes is a relatively new result. Subsequent research is bound to explain more of the "residual" in terms of economic factors, thereby reducing the perceived need for theories of preference formation.

In summary, as predicted, households accumulate substantial assets for retirement. In contrast to the predictions of our simple framework, asset decumulation during retirement is incomplete. However, we noted that intuitively appealing extensions to the framework, to be developed in later chapters, will prove consistent with the asset holdings observed at death. Rates of saving from permanent income and consumption growth rates are higher among more affluent than poorer households. These savings patterns may be explained by (1) government policies that encourage saving by the affluent and discourage saving by the poor and (2) a greater interest in leaving a bequest among the affluent. Alternatively, the faster consumption growth among the affluent may be a consequence of their facing higher rates of return or their being relatively more patient.

1.2.3   Comparative Statics in the Basic Model

A central purpose of our modeling is to explain how consumption and savings respond to changes in the consumer's economic environment. In the current framework this environment is characterized by first-period earnings (the wage) and the interest rate. The analysis of such responses is termed *comparative statics*.

First-Period Earnings

We begin by considering the effect of changing earnings E_1. Figure 1.6 shows that when the consumer has resources of E_1^0, the optimal consumption bundle is given at point A. Suppose instead the consumer anticipates that earnings before retirement will be E_1^1. This increase in resources shifts the budget line out in parallel fashion. Since C_1 and C_2 are surely both normal goods, consumption will be higher during both the working and re-

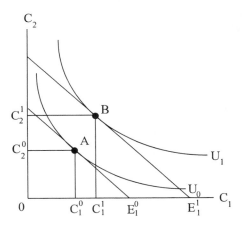

Figure 1.6 The effect of higher earnings on consumption

tirement years, such as at point B. Assuming preferences are Cobb-Douglas, we can say more. In that case, the comparative statics effect of a change in earnings on first-period consumption is just the derivative of (1.8) with respect to E_1,

$$dC_1/dE_1 = \theta \qquad (1.11a)$$

so that

$$dC_1 = \theta dE_1 \qquad (1.11b)$$

Equation (1.11a) says that the marginal propensity to consume in period one is θ (in fact, from (1.8), θ is also the average propensity to consume).

As a simple illustration, assume households devote 40% of life wealth to first-period consumption, $\theta = .4$. Now, suppose a tax cut increased net of tax earnings E_1 by some small amount, say 5. Then first-period consumption would, from (1.11b), increase by $dC_1 = (.4)(5) = 2$. More generally, an increase in earnings is spread over both periods, rather than being entirely consumed upon receipt. This result also obtains for all plausible specifications of the general utility function (1.1).[11] Notice that the role of savings is to "smooth" consumption over the life cycle, arranging resources to coincide with desired consumption. In section 1.3 the model is extended to include earnings in the second period of life. At that time, the theory and evidence concerning earnings and consumption are addressed in more depth.

Interest Rate

Many policy proposals, such as tax-preferred savings plans (like IRAs) or reducing the rate of tax on capital income, are motivated in part by an assumption that savings are positively related to the net-of-tax interest rate. To assess that premise we first develop some theoretical points. Recall that the tangency condition for optimal consumption, equations (1.6), reveals that consumption growth is faster the higher is r. This does not require that an increase in r must reduce C_1, and thus increase savings $S_1 = E_1 - C_1$. To see this, suppose savings were positive at the initial, lower, interest rate. Then, holding C_1 constant, C_2 would be higher—and thus consumption growth faster—due to greater interest earnings. In fact, the response of C_1, and thus of savings, to a change in the interest rate is ambiguous.

In the current setup, life wealth derives solely from first-period earnings. Consequently, the *sources* of lifetime wealth are independent of r. Conversely, changes in r do affect the *uses* of income. This occurs as a higher interest rate lowers the price (opportunity cost) of C_2, which we have seen to equal $1/(1 + r)$.

Suppose that, before the initial consumption plans can be implemented, the interest rate rises. In Figure 1.7, this pivots the budget line from E_1F based on r_0 to E_1G after r increases to r_1. That is, since the sources of income, measured in period-one dollars, are unaffected, the budget line continues to emanate from E_1 on the horizontal axis. But since the price of second-period consumption has fallen, the C_2 axis intercept is now higher. Intuitively, the budget set increases more the larger is the share of wealth devoted to the

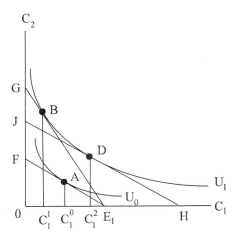

Figure 1.7 Income and substitution effects of raising r

now cheaper C_2. Utility maximization is initially at A, where first-period consumption is C_1^0 and savings are $S_1 = E_1 - C_1^0$. At the higher interest rate, utility is maximized at B, and consumption falls to C_1^1. As drawn, C_1 falls and savings rise. However, this is not a general result.

Since r determines the price of consuming at different points in time, changing r alters the structure of those prices. As with other price changes, additional insight is obtained by a decomposition into income (or wealth) and substitution effects. In Figure 1.7, the higher interest rate expands the budget set, enabling utility to rise from U_0 to U_1. In theory, an equal increase in utility could be produced through higher wealth alone, leaving r at the initial level. The wealth that would achieve utility U_1 produces the budget line HJ (the increase in wealth is E_1H units of C_1). The increase in first-period consumption from C_1^0 to C_1^2, due to higher wealth alone, is called the *wealth or income effect.*

However, r did of course rise, thereby lowering the price of C_2. This induces a utility maximizer to substitute away from the now relatively more expensive C_1. Specifically, *if* utility is fixed at U_1, the optimal consumption bundle moves from point D to B, following the increase in the interest rate. The associated movement from C_1^2 to C_1^1 is the *substitution effect.* The substitution effect of an increase in r always serves to reduce C_1, since its relative price has risen. Thus, the wealth and substitution effects conflict for C, making the relationship between *saving* and the interest rate ambiguous. As drawn, the substitution effect dominates.

As detailed in Chapter 2, the substitution effect is naturally larger the closer substitutes are C_1 and C_2. The wealth effect is greater the more one consumes of the good whose price has fallen, here C_2. Thus, relatively patient (low m) consumers spend more on C_2 and benefit more from an increase in r. Since the affluent and better educated are more patient, they would benefit more from the higher r *relative to their life wealth* than would the poor.

With Cobb-Douglas preferences and assuming all life wealth derives from first-period earnings, savings are independent of the interest rate. In this case, recall, savings are first-period earnings minus C_1. From (1.8), C_1 is independent of r, so that the income and substitution effects exactly offset one another. In Chapter 2 we consider more general preferences and budget sets to gain better understanding of what determines the size of the income and substitution effects.

We have not addressed *why* the interest rate rose. One obvious possibility is a reduction in the rate of interest income taxation. If this is why the (after-tax) r rose, the analysis above assumes that any reduction in tax revenues did not require other taxes to be levied on the consumer (which would counteract the wealth effect). Another interesting policy is where lump-sum taxes are used to "compensate" households (keep them on the initial indifference curve) following the interest income tax cut. Then only substitution effects remain, so that the compensated supply of savings is unambiguously positively sloped. Section 1 of Chapter 2 addresses the taxation of interest income in detail.

Theory identifies conflicting wealth and substitution effects from fully anticipated changes in the interest rate. This makes even the qualitative response of saving to the interest rate an empirical matter. The empirical evidence is inconclusive, but suggests that the response of savings is probably positive, but small. Estimates of the interest elasticity of saving—the percentage change in saving per 1% change in r—hover slightly above zero, with upper-bound empirical estimates of around .4 (Boskin, 1978). However, many difficulties are associated with the empirical estimation of that elasticity: Was an observed change in r anticipated? Does the consumer expect it to be permanent or temporary? Did whatever caused r to change also affect expectations of future earnings prospects? Because of the difficulty of discerning answers to the questions, many recent studies have turned to computer simulation where, at least, the information set may be fully specified. Lord and Rangazas (1992) simulate that elasticity for a permanent change in r in a framework that incorporates the responses of human capital accumulation and intergenerational transfers and also holds constant the timing of taxes over the life cycle. At the household (or partial equilibrium) level, they find elasticities in the same range as the empirical estimates discussed above (usually between .2 and .4).[12]

Examples and Implications of Movements in Rates of Return

Many assets have uncertain returns, and occasionally the realized rate of return varies significantly from what may have been expected. A case in point concerns the returns realized on stock market investments. Returns were unexpectedly high for the average stock market investor in the United States between 1980 and 2000. Recently, the Dow Jones Industrial Average rose from 5,000 in November of 1995 to over 11,000 in May of 1999. These capital gains averaged over 22% per year, far exceeding historical norms and thereby creating trillions of dollars of largely unexpected stock market wealth. Poterba (2000, p. 101, Table 1) reports that measured in 1999 dollars, the value of equities rose from about $3.7 trillion in 1989 to approximately $13.3 trillion in 1999. Stock appreciation therefore accounts for almost two-thirds of the rise in households' real net worth from about $27 trillion to $42 trillion over that same period. In our two-period model, all of this wealth accrues to the old who would consume it. In reality, both working and retired households hold stock, many through their employer-provided retirement plans.

The "wealth effect" from these capital gains may account for the rapid growth in consumer spending observed in the latter part of the 1990s and the decline in the personal saving rate (recall Figure 1.1). Since personal saving equals disposable income minus consumption, it requires some active decision to save. In contrast, increases in wealth associated with capital gains on stocks, for example, require no specific action and are in that sense "passive" saving. An important issue is the extent to which stock market gains increase consumption, thereby displacing measured active savings.

Juster et al. (1999) employ the PSID to assess the impact on consumption of capital gains. As discussed in section 1.2, the PSID measures wealth at 5-year intervals. They find that, over a 5-year interval, "a dollar of capital gains in stocks reduces active saving by about seventeen cents" (p. 17). This estimate overstates the actual impact for a couple of reasons. First, the PSID does not sample the super-wealthy, who own much stock and may have lower consumption propensities; including their consumption responses would lower the average. Second, the PSID wealth measure does not include changes in defined contribution employer-provided pension plans. Many households have such plans, and the value of these plans rises with the stock market. Consequently, the observed rise in consumption was induced by a larger increase in the households' stock holdings than the PSID data suggest. Thus, the increase in consumption per dollar were all stock market gains accounted for would be lower. Nevertheless, their estimates suggest a powerful link between the bull stock market and the rise (fall) in consumption (active savings). Further, they show that their estimated response, coupled with the huge gains in stock market wealth through the late 1990s, is capable of explaining the entire decline in the personal saving rate of this period. And, recall from Figure 1.1, this consumption binge was accompanied by a rise in the ratio of household assets to household income. Thus, vigorous consumption of stock market gains has not been associated with deteriorating balance sheets for the average of American households. It is important to keep in mind, though, that stock market wealth is highly concentrated. Thus, an improving aggregate balance sheet is less informative about effects on the median household. Stock market wealth declined in 2001, perhaps presaging a rise in the personal saving rate.

As another example, consider the implications of changing interest rates for homeowners. One common way to finance the home purchase is by a fixed-rate mortgage, which fixes the monthly payments until the loan is paid off. The largely unexpected decline in home mortgage interest rates that occurred at several points between the mid-1980s and late 1990s enabled households to refinance their homes, obtaining new mortgages at lower rates. Many homeowners realized housing payment savings in excess of $1,000 per year. Households with adjustable-rate mortgages also benefit when rates decline. Falling mortgage rates further fueled nonhousing consumption expenditures in the 1990s.

The same decline in interest rates that lowered housing costs and, by increasing the present value of future corporate profits, contributed to the stock market boom, affected many retirees adversely. As they attempted to reinvest the principal from maturing higher interest bonds, they were faced with unexpectedly low yields on new bond offerings. This lowered their income and consumption. Overall, then, unanticipated changes in the rate of return on assets entail a variety of sometimes conflicting effects on wealth, consumption, and savings. And, since aggregate wealth is substantial, so can be the effects of changes in asset earnings.

1.3 THE ROLE OF FUTURE EARNINGS: AN INTRODUCTION

The model developed thus far reserves the second period for retirement, limiting earnings to the first period of life only. In fact, future earnings are an obviously important consideration in life-cycle planning. Future earnings also highlight the role of credit markets and affect the response of saving to the interest rate. Clearly, future earnings are not known with certainty. Issues surrounding the response of current consumption to changes in the amount of future income uncertainty are considered in Chapter 2. This section addresses the certainty case, developing implications for consumption and evaluating them in light of the empirical evidence.

We now also allow the household to enter the first period with real property and financial wealth (not ruling out the possibility of school debts, say). For simplicity, we focus on the monetary value of the consumer's overall asset position, terming it initial financial wealth A_1. In our model, interest is paid at rate r at the start of the period on assets brought into the period. Thus, first-period interest income, also called capital income, is rA_1. Of course, if A_1 is positive it enhances life-cycle consumption opportunities compared with what earnings alone would afford. Similarly, bringing debt into the first period limits C_1 and C_2.

First- and second-period earnings, denoted by E_1 and E_2, are received at the start of periods 1 and 2. Total first-period income is then $rA_1 + E_1$. In the presence of second-period earnings and initial assets, life wealth W becomes

$$W = A_1(1 + r) + E_1 + E_2/(1 + r)$$

The present value of life-cycle earnings, $E_1 + E_2/(1 + r)$, is termed *human wealth*. Thus, W is the sum of financial wealth, $A_1(1 + r)$, and human wealth. Poterba (2000, p. 102) reviews the literature to conclude that the aggregate value of human wealth in the economy exceeds that of financial assets. Human wealth is lowered by an increase in the interest rate r, or by a downward revision of expected future earnings. In a many-year version of the model, human wealth is typically high and financial wealth low when people are young. As they work, consume, and save for retirement, human wealth falls and financial wealth increases. Financial assets fall during retirement. At the end of life, human and financial wealth would each equal zero.

Assuming credit markets enable one to borrow or lend at rate r, the consumer is free to choose any combination of C_1 and C_2 with present value (less than or) equal to W.

$$C_1 + C_2/(1 + r) \leq A_1(1 + r) + E_1 + E_2/(1 + r) = W \qquad (1.12)$$

These budget opportunities are shown in Figure 1.8.[13] Point G shows the income endowment, which remains given (or exogenous) to the consumer. We may now think of saving in two distinct ways. As before, subtracting first-period consumption from income leaves saving, $S_1 = rA_1 + E_1 - C_1$, the only innovation being the allowance for interest income. Second, saving is the change in financial wealth between periods, $S_1 = A_2 - A_1$.

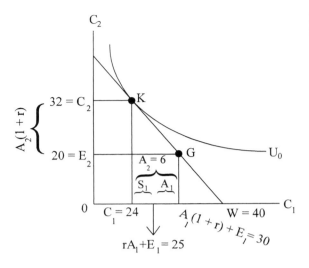

Figure 1.8 Numerical solution to utility maximization problem

Thus, if I bring $10,000 into the start of the second period, A_2, that is my first-period savings only if I began period one with a clean slate, $A_1 = 0$.

In the Cobb-Douglas case, the consumer's utility maximization problem is to maximize (1.2) subject to (1.12). As before, the consumer devotes the fraction θ of life wealth to first-period consumption. That is,

$$C_1 = \theta W = \theta A_1(1 + r) + \theta E_1 + \theta E_2/(1 + r) \tag{13a}$$

Since the rest of wealth is devoted to C_2, we have

$$C_2 = (1 - \theta)W(1 + r) \tag{13b}$$

so that the present value of expenditures on C_2 equals $(1 - \theta)W$.

We again solve the consumer's problem numerically. For example, suppose we let $\theta = .6$, $r = 1$, $A_1 = 5$, and $E_1 = E_2 = 20$ (where the values for income and assets may be thought to be in thousands of dollars). From the definition of wealth, we have $W = 5(2) + 20 + 20/2 = 40$. Using (13a), first-period consumption is $C_1 = (.6)40 = 24$, and from (13b), $C_2 = (.4)40(1 + 1) = 32$. Consequently, savings are $S_1 = rA_1 + E_1 - C_1 = (1)5 + 20 - 24 = 1$. This makes for total assets brought into period two of $A_2 = A_1 + S_1 = 6$. Note that second-period consumption can also be expressed as $C_2 = A_2(1 + r) + E_2 = (6)(2) + 20 = 32$. This example is illustrated in Figure 1.8.

1.3.1 Income Dynamics in the Cobb-Douglas Case

From the first equality in (13a), if wealth increases by $1, first-period consumption rises by θ cents. Thus, θ is the *marginal propensity to consume* from wealth in period 1; that is, $dC_1/dW = \theta$. From the second part of (13a), θ is also the marginal propensity to consume from an increase in E_1, since changes in first-period earnings produce equal changes in wealth. These comparative static results just repeat that of equation (11a) when $W = E_1$. Similarly, from (13b) the marginal propensity to consume in period 2 from wealth is $dC_2/dW = (1 - \theta)(1 + r)$.

The new results concern second-period earnings. The rate at which first-period consumption changes from a fully anticipated change in second-period earnings is

$$dC_1/dE_2 = \theta/(1 + r) \qquad (14a)$$

so that, for small changes in second period earnings,

$$dC_1 = \theta dE_2/(1 + r) \qquad (14b)$$

This makes good intuitive sense: when young the propensity to consume from W is θ, and a dollar increase in second-period earnings increases life wealth by $1/(1 + r)$ cents. Further implications of (1.14) are taken up below.

First, though, appreciate that this marginal propensity assumes the change in E_2 is fully anticipated at the start of period one. In contrast, suppose that *after* having committed to some level of C_1, second-period earnings *unexpectedly* fall by \$1. Since the reduction in wealth cannot be spread over both periods, C_2 would fall by the full dollar. The propensity to spend from second-period windfalls is 1. This result generalizes to the many-period context in a meaningful fashion: Everything else the same, the older a household is upon the receipt of a windfall, the higher is the marginal propensity to consume in the current period. In the case where $r = m$, this propensity is just 1 divided by the number of years of life remaining. These results imply that the economy-wide average marginal propensity to consume increases with the proportion of young households, and thus with the population growth rate.

This has important implications for government tax and transfer policies. At any given time, there will be alive both young and old consumers. Suppose the government unexpectedly transfers \$1 from a young to an old person. While the young person will spread the reduction in consumption over periods one and two, the old person will consume the entire dollar. Consequently, this government transfer between the generations will increase aggregate consumption, thereby lowering aggregate savings. The full aggregate implications of such policies are detailed in Chapter 4.

As noted earlier, the net national and personal saving rates have fallen significantly in recent decades. Gokhale, Kotlikoff, and Sabelhaus (1996) argue that this is a consequence of government policies providing benefits to the old which they had not anticipated when young. They note that Medicare and Social Security both became appreciably more generous in the 1960s, 1970s, and for Medicare, into the 1980s. Since these increases were not foreseen several decades before, the consumption of the old rose dramatically. (Chapters 4 and 5 draw out the macroeconomic implications of such policies.)

The marginal propensity to consume from a temporary rise in income is expected to be less than that for a permanent increase. In our two-period model, the marginal propensity to consume from an increase in first-period income alone is θdE_1. If instead there is a permanent increase in income, so that both first- and second-period income rises the same amount, $dE_1 = dE_2$, the increase in C_1 would be θ percent of the increase in life wealth, which exceeds the increase in E_1 alone. In fact, empirical research provides convincing evidence that the marginal propensity to consume is less from temporary wind-falls than from permanent income changes. One significant example of a temporary wind-fall is the one-time restitution payments from Germany to Israeli citizens in 1957–1958. These payments were large, roughly equal to the average family's annual income. Com-menting on studies of this episode, Mankiw (1997) concludes that "the typical family's consumption expenditure during the year of the windfall rose by no more than 20% of the amount received" (p. 121). Carroll (2000) notes that findings of marginal propensi-ties of at least 0.2 are common throughout the consumption literature. This poses a bit of a problem for our basic model. To see why, suppose that $r = m = 0$ and that the average consumer is 45 years old, with 30 years of life remaining. In this case, the average mar-ginal propensity to consume should equal $1/30 = .033$, or only 3.3%. Extensions to the basic model that incorporate limitations on borrowing (below) and income uncertainty (Chapter 2) prove consistent with higher marginal propensities among some consumers.

Mankiw concludes that "the marginal propensity to consume out of permanent changes in income is large and not much different from one" (p. 121). This finding is also obtained by Carroll (1999) in the context of a large simulation model in which house-holds face both transitory and permanent shocks to income. Thus, even our basic model enjoys success on some points. First, the marginal propensity to consume from perma-nent shocks is quite large, and close to 1. Second, the marginal propensity to consume from permanent shocks exceeds that from temporary windfalls.

This discussion has assumed the consumer can maximize utility subject only to life wealth, borrowing and lending as necessary to match available resources to desired con-sumption. Below, it is seen that credit markets sometimes limit the amount of borrowing by consumers. When these restrictions bind, the propensities to consume derived above no longer apply. We return to this below.

1.3.2 Saving in the Presence of Future Earnings: The Life Wealth Hypothesis

One of the more important, and controversial, implications of the simple life-cycle model of consumption is that the *timing* of consumption is independent of the *timing* of income. Graphically, in Figure 1.8 utility is maximized at point K, regardless of where the earn-ings (or, more generally, resource) endowment lies along the budget line. We term this fundamental implication the *life wealth hypothesis* (LWH): consumption choices depend only upon life wealth W, not upon when income is received.

The LWH implies that the role of savings is to enable life-cycle consumption to be "smooth," regardless of the time path of income. To illustrate, suppose a cardiologist and a professional football player have the same life-cycle wealth and utility function. The football player, with earnings high in the first period but low in the second, is predicted to save when young. Conversely, the cardiologist, whose earnings profile is just the op-posite, is expected to rely heavily on borrowing to finance first-period consumption.

There is general agreement that households do smooth consumption over short peri-ods of time. Thus, people consume on weekends, even if they earn no income over that period. As a more meaningful test, in years when households have higher than average, or "permanent," income, saving should be greater in order to finance consumption in years when income is below average. The same Dynan et al. (1996) paper discussed previously offers support for consumption smoothing over at least a year. As above, households are arranged into income quintiles, but now the grouping is based on *annual* income. For each household, consumption is subtracted from current year disposable income. Dynan et al. find an appreciable divergence between consumption and income over the course of a year. For example, among those aged 40 to 49, the median saving rate is -24% in the bottom 20% of the income distribution and 46% for the most affluent quintile. These saving rates are much more volatile than when based on permanent income. This is seen by reference back to Table 1.1. For that same age group when saving was from *permanent* income, the poorest quintile had a saving rate of 10% while that for the most affluent was 20.8%. This comparison suggests that some of those households with a low current-year income earn more in the "average" year, and are dissaving only because income is temporarily (or transitorily, as Friedman phrased it) low. Symmetrical remarks help explain the incredibly high saving rates of those in the upper quintile when based on annual income. This evidence supports the contention that over short and moderate-length intervals the timing of consumption is largely independent of the timing of income.

However, even over short periods there is some "excess" sensitivity of consumption to current income. One example concerns the response of consumption to tax refunds. People who overpay taxes during the year may anticipate with some accuracy the amount of their tax refunds. Even if forecast errors are moderate relative to the size of the refund, they would be quite small relative to life wealth and, in the aggregate, should largely cancel out. Nevertheless, Souleles (1999, p. 953) finds "for each extra dollar of refund received, total consumption rises by 18 cents." The question really is whether there is so much excess sensitivity that the LWH is not a useful benchmark. As now seen, this has proven especially controversial when applied to long intervals (low frequencies) of the life cycle.

Influential evidence of the relationship between life-cycle consumption and income presented by Carroll and Summers (1991) casts significant doubt on the independence of income and consumption. To examine this relationship, they employed data from the Consumer Expenditure Survey (CEX), which contains detailed individual family consumption—and less detailed income—data over the course of a year. Since the CEX does not follow the same families through time, the authors consider consumers of different ages at a given point in time (i.e., they look at the cross section). Figure 1.9 from Carroll and Summers presents their findings for the different occupational groups in the 1972–1973 CEX.[14]

The striking feature of these profiles is the strong positive correlation between consumption and income when households are grouped by occupations. Clearly, consumption is not simply equal to income. However, just as clearly, consumption never strays too far away from income, either. Further, in a careful empirical analysis using household and cohort data, Carroll (1994) shows that current income plays a much larger, and expected future income a much smaller, role in determining current consumption than is consistent with the LWH.

Gathering results, the tangency condition for utility maximization with Cobb-Douglas preferences (1.6c) makes the slope of the age-consumption profile increase with r and decline with m, with the height of the profile determined by W. That is, consumption should be smooth and independent of the shape of the income profile. In contrast,

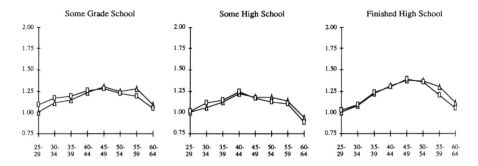

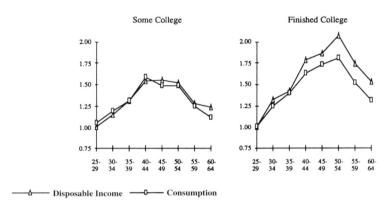

Figure 1.9 Ratio of annual disposable income and consumption to age-25 values. *Source:* Reprinted with permission from Carroll and Summers (1991), Figure 10.7a, p. 322

Figure 1.9 indicates that consumption tracks income closely over the life cycle, suggesting the timing of income does affect consumption. However, this evidence against the LWH is far from conclusive. This close tracking of income by consumption is based on *family* consumption and, since family size changes over the life cycle of the household, such tracking is silent about how consumption per family member (or "adult equivalent") varies over the life cycle. In particular, since family size and family consumption both grow while the household is young, the tracking of family income by family consumption need not imply that the consumption of adults is also tracking family income.

Attanasio and Browning (1995) employ cohort data from the United Kingdom that also indicate that *family* consumption tracks income. Unlike Carroll and Summers, however, they do not disaggregate into occupational or educational groups. Rather, they examine how family consumption varies with the number of adults and children in the household, or with family composition. They find that "family size adjusted" consumption across birth cohorts does not track income, but is basically flat. However, their result has not proven robust. Gourinchas and Parker (1999) revisit this issue employing CEX data from 1980 to 1993. Like Attanasio and Browning, they employ a set of controls for family size. In addition, as did Carroll and Summers, they partition by occupational group. And, they (alone) adust income and consumption to account for cohort effects. Even after adjusting for family size, their profiles indicate that during the early portion of the life cycle consumption tracks income closely, as in Carroll and Summers unadjusted data. Though consumption and income are both hump-shaped over the life cycle, Gourinchas and Parker find only weak tracking later in the life cycle. They develop and test a model based on earnings uncertainty that proves consistent with the empirical profiles. We discuss such models in depth in Chapter 2.

It is reasonable to be persuaded by the results of Gourinchas and Parker that, even adjusting for family size, there remains some positive correlation between the shapes (as opposed to just heights) of the income and consumption profiles, especially early in the life cycle. Also, in Chapter 9 we argue that the number, expenditures on, and (to some extent) the timing of children are all choice variables. To the extent expenditures on children are a choice variable, even the close tracking of income by total family consumption cannot be dismissed as "an accident of demographics." Altogether, this evidence casts some doubt on the validity of the LWH over long intervals.

Whether or not the LWH applies is crucial to assessing many fiscal policies. To appreciate this, we need to be more precise about what constitutes a change in the timing of income. By definition, wealth is constant along the budget line. Consequently (letting $A_1 = 0$), changes in income timing must satisfy $dW = dE_1 + dE_2/(1 + r) = 0$. This imposes the restriction that $dE_1 = -dE_2/(1 + r)$. For example, if $dE_2 = \$20,000$ and $r = 1$, $dE_1 = -\$10,000$.

Many fiscal policies involve redistributing taxes and transfers over the life cycle. Such policies include temporary tax cuts, Social Security, and changes between consumption and wage income tax bases. To be concrete, consider the following temporary tax cut: In the consumer's first period, taxes are cut by $x (forcing the government to borrow $x). In the second period, taxes are to be raised by $x(1 + r)$, just enough to pay interest on and then retire the debt issued in period one. Since the present value of the tax hike just offsets the tax cut, this policy satisfies the definition of a change in income timing. Therefore, by the LWH, it should have no effect on consumption—the household should simply save the tax cut in period one. If, instead, current consumption is excessively sensitive to current income, a temporary tax cut would increase current consumption, thereby stimulating aggregate demand and proving to be an effective countercyclical policy. (Of course, many fiscal policies also alter the *magnitude* of taxes over the life cycle. Chapter 4 treats tax policy from an aggregative perspective.)

The controversy surrounding the LWH has motivated a variety of extensions to the basic model. To account for the apparent excess sensitivity of current consumption to current income, these extensions must increase the role of current income in determining current consumption. One quite plausible route is to explicitly model earnings uncertainty. If future income is uncertain, already realized income naturally carries more weight. We develop the theory of consumption under future income and length of life uncertainty in Chapter 2. Another possibility, developed below, is that credit markets impose an additional constraint on choices beyond satisfaction of the life wealth budget constraint.

1.3.3   The Life Wealth Hypothesis and Liquidity Constraints

The LWH will fail if the consumer is unable to borrow and lend freely at rate r, subject only to life wealth. For then savings cannot be used to transfer income from when it is not needed to finance current consumption to other periods when it is. An important in-

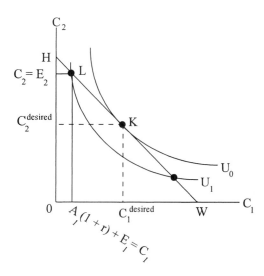

Figure 1.10 Liquidity-contrained household

stance is when a consumer desires to borrow against expected future earnings to finance current consumption, but can't find anyone to lend him or her the money. When such dissaving is prohibited, the consumer is said to be credit or *liquidity constrained*. As developed below, restrictions on borrowing are another reason consumption may track income "too closely" over the life cycle. In our model, a liquidity-constrained household has a desired C_1 that exceeds first-period resources, $E_1 + A_1(1 + r)$. This is illustrated in Figure 1.10, where the desired C_1,C_2 combination—point K—lies to the right of the endowment point L. This is more likely the higher is the rate of time preference m, the higher is E_2 relative to E_1, and the lower is A_1. A young cardiologist, for example, may have school debts (negative A_1), earn relatively little as an internist (E_1 low), but expect tremendously high future earnings. Even if the cardiologist is moderately patient, he or she would still prefer a C_1 in excess of first-period resources.

But wouldn't lenders gladly lend to the young cardiologist? Perhaps not. The reason is that even though E_2 is on average high for cardiologists, it may prove low in this case. The physician could die, have his or her license revoked, leave the country with the loan proceeds, and so on. Couldn't the banker just compensate for the risk of default by charging a higher interest rate? Not necessarily. On one hand, doctors who strongly suspect they won't repay the loan will not care as much about the interest rate. Conversely, some of those doctors most likely to repay at the initial rate will no longer be interested in borrowing should rates be increased. Assume, as may be reasonable, that the bank can't tell which doctors are likely to repay and which are not. Then, if the bank offers loans at a somewhat higher rate, they may still lose money, since a larger proportion of the remaining borrowers will default. This response of the customer base to the risk premium is termed *adverse selection*.

Due to adverse selection, among other problems, consumers are rarely able to borrow much against expected future earnings. Of course, many households borrow on credit cards and carry balances at high interest rates. And, as witnessed by the large number of personal bankruptcies annually, households can become overextended. What is important, though, is that there is some ceiling to borrowing (cf. Carroll, 2000). To simplify the story without materially affecting conclusions we pick a particularly convenient ceiling; we assume consumers can't borrow against future earnings at all. Notice that this is not inconsistent with widespread borrowing by consumers for home mortgages or other durable goods. In the case of the home mortgage, for example, the house itself serves as collateral. Further, if the household's equity in the home is less than 20% of the home's value, homeowners typically must purchase mortgage insurance, providing further protection for the bank. What we are ruling out are loans backed *only* by the consumer's promise to repay out of future earnings.

Returning to Figure 1.10, if the consumer can't borrow to finance consumption at combination K, what will he or she do? The consumer will maximize utility subject to the budget constraint available, segment HL, along which assets brought into the start of period two are nonnegative. Faced with this opportunity set, he or she consumes at point L. With basket L, the $MRS_{1,2} > 1 + r$, so that *if* the consumer could trade $1 + r$ units of C_2 for another unit of C_1 he or she would—but it can't be done.

For liquidity-constrained consumers, changes in the timing of income *do* affect consumption. For example, with $r = 1$ and starting at L, suppose a tax cut in period one increases E_1 by 1, but that a tax increase is scheduled to reduce E_2 by 2. This maintains life-cycle wealth at its initial level, but moves the after-tax income endowment closer to (but still above) point K. Under the LWH there should be no change in consumption. However, the liquidity-constrained individual will happily increase C_1 by 1. Here the change in the timing of income enables the consumer to do what the credit markets won't—increase C_1 at the expense of C_2. Consequently, the LWH fails among liquidity-constrained households. Another implication is that the propensities to consume when the LWH holds are no longer valid if the household is liquidity constrained.

As seen above, the marginal propensity to consume from changes in first-period resources is 1 for liquidity-constrained households, making the second-period change equal 0. Conversely, marginal changes in second-period earnings, anticipated at the beginning of period 1, have no effect on first-period consumption.

Notice that binding liquidity constraints increase the rate of growth of consumption for young consumers: in the two-period model, C_2 is forced to be higher and C_1 lower than if the consumer could borrow against future earnings. Such constraints may thus help explain the rapid growth in consumption in young households for most occupational groups seen in Figure 1.9. However, it has been estimated that no more than 20% of households are liquidity constrained at any given time (cf. Hall and Mishkin, 1982). Nevertheless, when we allow for income uncertainty in Chapter 2, we will see how the *possibility* of facing liquidity constraints in the future predicts rapid consumption growth when young for a much larger proportion of the population.

1.4 POLICY APPLICATIONS

This section applies the theory developed above to two important policy issues. The first application indicates that Social Security may help explain the positive relationship between saving rates and permanent income. The second application compares consumption and wage income taxation from a life-cycle perspective.

1.4.1   Why Social Security Causes the Rich to Save More

The Social Security system in the United States redistributes intragenerationally from those with higher to those with lower incomes. This may help explain the higher saving rates—and therefore lower consumption propensities when young—among the affluent. That is, their Social Security benefits replace a lower proportion of what they earned while working. Consequently, the rich require a higher private saving rate to achieve the same relationship between retirement consumption and earnings during the working years as that obtained by the poor. To see this clearly, consider some basic features of the financing and benefit structures for Social Security.

The payroll tax for Social Security is a flat percentage of a worker's gross earnings, up to some maximum amount (that is indexed for inflation, and was $68,400 in 1999). Half of the tax, or 6.2%, is paid by employees and half by employers. This total tax of 12.4% does not include the further levies for Medicare. Most evidence suggests that the employers' share is largely shifted to employees via lower wages.

The benefit structure is more complicated and is much more progressive (in the equity sense of providing greater benefits relative to contributions at lower than higher income levels). The Social Security benefit, termed the *primary insurance amount* (PIA), is based on the highest 35 years of earnings preceding retirement. Earnings in each year are indexed for inflation. The total across all years is then converted into a monthly sum called *average indexed monthly earnings* (AIME). For a person turning 65 in 1993, the primary insurance amount was calculated as 90 percent of the first $401 of AIME, plus 32% of AIME between $402 and $2,420, plus 15 percent of AIME above $2,420 until the ceiling (based on the maximum income subject to the Social Security tax). Depending upon the recipient's retirement income (inclusive of Social Security), some of the Social Security benefits are subject to tax. This increases the progressivity, since those with higher retirement income typically have higher AIME. Clearly, the rate of return to participation in the Social Security system is, ceteris paribus, higher for those with lower incomes.

An example illustrates how the progressive benefit structure translates to higher replacement rates for relatively low earners. Define the *replacement rate* as the PIA/AIME. Suppose Dot, a waitress, had AIME of $800, for annual (reported) earnings of $9,600. Karen, a CPA, had AIME of $5,000, or $60,000 per year. The PIA for Dot is .9($401) + .32($399) = $488.58, giving a replacement rate of almost 62% (488.58/800). Karen's PIA is .9($401) + .32($2019) + .15($2580) = $1521.66. This produces a replacement rate of 1521.66/5000 = 30.4%. Clearly, the saving rate from wage earnings to reach a given consumption replacement rate is much lower for Dot than for Karen. Although there is some agreement that these effects may be important, Dynan et al. (2000) argue it is unlikely that these features of Social Security can account for all of the increase in saving rates across income levels. Thus, there appears to be some role for the social safety net and bequest motives described in section 1.2.

It is worth noting that the numerical example above overstates the extent of progressivity of Social Security (i.e., the extent to which it redistributes from rich to poor within a generation). For, though omitted from our example, life expectancies increase with income. Thus, while Social Security replaces income at a lower rate among the affluent, their payments may continue for more years.

1.4.2 Equivalence of Wage and Consumption Taxation in Partial Equilibrium

In the United States, the federal government imposes heavy taxes on wage income, while consumption taxation is primarily limited to user's fees. There has long been substantial interest among both academics and policymakers regarding how the implications of taxation may differ across these tax instruments. This application contrasts wage and consumption taxation in a partial equilibrium context, where the pretax wage and interest rate facing a household is invariant to the tax employed. However, in Chapter 4 we stress that resource prices may well differ across the tax bases, depending upon the particulars of how the taxes are imposed.

Popular wisdom suggests that taxing wage income is more progressive or equitable than is taxing consumption. For in a given year, a low-income or "poor" person on average spends all of his or her income on consumption, whereas a "rich" person saves some income, which is thus spared from the consumption tax. In fact, Dynan et al. (1996) report the saving rate from income among the lowest annual income quintile is negative and large while for the upper income quintile it is positive and large. Thus, consumption taxes hit the poor harder than the rich, making these taxes regressive. However, this simple argument breaks down when looked at from a life-cycle, as opposed to an annual, perspective.

How might we compare the tax bases from a life-cycle perspective? A reasonable point of departure is to require the consumer to pay the same fraction of his or her life wealth in taxes under either tax base. When the present value of taxes raised is held constant, the two tax bases would differ "only" in the timing of the tax collections. Although the timing of after-tax income would differ across the bases, life wealth would be the same. Then the life wealth hypothesis is applicable, and we should expect no difference in consumption behavior. In this case, the choice between consumption and payroll tax bases affects only the pattern of savings over the life cycle, but not consumer welfare.

However, these differences in household savings between consumption and wage income taxes may be appreciable. For whereas consumption—and thus consumption taxation—continues throughout life, wage income taxation ceases upon retirement. To finance consumption taxation during the retirement years, consumers need to accumulate a larger retirement nest egg than if wage taxation were employed. Since the timing of taxes over the life cycle differs between the two tax bases, so will the stream of aggregate tax revenues. (As discussed in Chapter 4, if the government must raise the same revenues each year under either tax base, it will not be possible to keep the present value of life-cycle taxes equal under the two bases. Under such a "balanced budget" assumption, the partial-equilibrium analysis proves to be quite misleading. Chapter 4 discusses important general-equilibrium differences between the tax bases. For example, under the balanced budget assumption, national savings and income are higher under a consumption tax base.[15])

In the partial-equilibrium context, why do consumption taxes appear to hit the poor harder? In our model, both "rich" and "poor" consume all their earnings over the life cycle. However, in any given year, a person whose earnings are *temporarily* higher than the person's average earnings must save to finance consumption in the years when income is *temporarily* lower. Thus, when a person is temporarily "rich," savings will be positive, and not all earnings would face immediate taxation under a consumption tax. This is perhaps why a consumption tax gives the impression of being regressive.

One might well counter, "The rich bequeath much of their wealth so that their earnings partly escape taxation under a pure consumption tax." This is true (though their heirs would be taxed when they consume the inheritance). However, if the consumption tax is extended to include bequests and, similarly, the wage tax is extended to cover inheritances, the equivalence of tax bases is restored. We shall say more about the taxation of inheritances and bequests in Chapter 5.

The base for the personal income tax includes both wage earnings and interest income. As discussed in section 1.2, taxation of interest income alters the *slope* of the budget line, and thus the opportunity cost of consumption choices. The incentive effects of interest income taxation create important differences between income and consumption bases. Suppose, though, that under an income base *all* savings enjoyed the same tax-preferred status as traditional IRAs and 401(k)s (both discussed in section 2.1). If all savings were tax deferred and there was tax-free accrual of interest, the personal income tax *would* be equivalent to a consumption tax base. To see this, suppose in our two-period model the consumer saves a portion of wage earnings when young. Since the savings escape immediate taxation, taxes would be applied only to income minus savings, or consumption. Now, in period two, taxes would be paid not only on second-period earnings but also on savings plus interest. But this sum is just second-period consumption. Thus, the tax base is simply consumption. Thus, one may get to a consumption base either by abolishing the income tax or less directly by extending tax-preferred treatment to all forms of saving.

Details for the Diligent in the Partial-Equilibrium Case

Somewhat more formally, we now show that a proportional tax on wage earnings at rate t_w has an identical effect on consumption opportunities, and raises the same revenues, as does a consumption tax at rate $t_c = t_w/(1 - t_w)$. Assuming the individual works only in period one and that there are neither inheritances nor bequests, the pretax budget constraint is that given in equation (1.5), repeated here (assuming all life wealth is consumed)

$$E_1 = C_1 + C_2/(1 + r) \tag{1.5}$$

Now impose a tax on wage income at rate t_w, which alters the budget constraint to

$$(1 - t_w)E_1 = C_1 + C_2/(1 + r) \tag{1.5'}$$

Dividing both sides of (1.5′) by $(1 - t_w)$ produces

$$E_1 = C_1/(1 - t_w) + C_2/[(1 + r)(1 - t_w)] \tag{1.5''}$$

Suppose that, instead of taxing wages, we impose a tax on consumption at rate t_c. This consumption tax leads to the constraint

$$E_1 = (1 + t_c)C_1 + (1 + t_c)C_2/(1 + r) \tag{1.5'''}$$

Here, $(1 + t_c)$ is the tax-inclusive current period price of goods. Comparing (1.5″) and (1.5‴) we see that the consumer faces an identical budget set under the wage and consumption bases so long as $1 + t_c = 1/(1 - t_w)$. Solving for t_c implies equivalence of wage and consumption taxes so long as $t_c = t_w/(1 - t_w)$, as claimed. For example, a 25% tax on wages or payrolls would be equivalent to a 33.3% tax on consumption. In the former case you retain 75 cents on the dollar earned; in the latter, the price of a good costing $1.00 rises to $1.33.

1.5 SUMMARY[16]

In this chapter we examined a simple model of life-cycle consumption and savings that assumed earnings are exogenous and certain and that consumers care only about their own consumption of market goods over the life cycle. We stressed how the consumer's consumption demand over the life cycle provides insights into saving behavior. This framework makes several important predictions including:

1. Consumption is a function of lifetime wealth and should not follow short-term fluctuations in annual income nor the longer-term pattern of earnings over the working years. That is, the pattern of consumption over the life cycle should be "smooth." A specific prediction was termed the *life wealth hypothesis*; the timing of income does not affect the timing of consumption.
2. Individuals should save enough for retirement so that consumption after retirement is consistent with preretirement consumption (this is just a corollary of 1).
3. Savings during retirement should be reduced gradually, with no planned bequest to children, and zero assets at death.
4. The rates of consumption should not vary significantly across households with different lifetime earnings *levels* (no account taken for systematic variations in preferences across households).
5. The response of saving at the household (or partial-equilibrium) level to changes in the interest rate is theoretically ambiguous. Tax policies that alter the interest rate and simultaneously compensate the consumer for changes in wealth induce a positive relationship between private saving and the interest rate.

Let us now review how these predictions fared in light of the empirical facts. First, annual income definitely varies much more than annual consumption, suggesting at least some consumption smoothing over short intervals of time. In general, though, there does appear to be some excess sensitivity of current consumption to current income. For example, consumption increases following the receipt of predictable tax refunds. Also, consumption tends to parallel earnings, especially early in the life cycle. Such evidence suggests the LWH is, at best, an imperfect benchmark. Any deviation from the LWH may be consistent with far-sighted, rational behavior if consumers face restrictions on how much they can borrow or if, as will be discussed in Chapter 2, households are exposed to substantial earnings risk. Better results are associated with the response to windfalls: As predicted, the current consumption response is greater when a given shock to income is expected to be recurring (or permanent) than when it is understood to be temporary.

Predictions 2 and 3 may not be consistent with the data on more affluent households, as their saving rates remain high at very old ages. This fact may be explained by precautionary saving associated with health or nursing home expenses (Chapter 2) and intergenerational transfer motives (Chapter 5). Positive assets at death also occur naturally when there is length-of-life uncertainty (Chapter 2).

Prediction 4 is brought into question by the higher observed saving rates of the rich and estimates suggesting that m varies inversely with wealth. However, at least some of the differences could be due to intragenerational redistribution associated with Social Security. This type of explanation is reinforced by policy-precautionary saving interactions (see Chapter 2).

Prediction 5 is difficult to validate directly in the data (the reason for the popularity of the simulation approach). However, most economists believe there is a positive, though perhaps weak, relationship between saving and the rate of return. Additional evidence will be considered in Chapter 2.

Chapter 2 enriches the model by allowing for uncertainty over future earnings and the length of life. That chapter also generalizes preferences in important ways, enabling a deeper examination of the response of savings to tax incentives. Chapter 3 shows how to aggregate the household-level decisions of Chapter 1. These aggregates are then joined to a model of aggregate production, contributing to a model of economic growth. A simpler version of the Chapter 3 framework addresses macro fiscal policy issues in Chapter 4. Subsequent chapters enrich the life-cycle perspective by consideration of human capital investment decisions, intergenerational transfers, time allocation, and fertility.

ENDNOTES

1. The net saving rate figures are based on the 1998 measures of saving in the National Income and Product Accounts. Thus, unlike the figures in the graph, they do not include the 1999 revisions to personal savings rates. Also, they are defined as a percent of net national product (NNP), rather than of GDP. Paul Lally of the Bureau of Economic Analysis calculated the net saving rate.

2. Disposable income is roughly equal to NNP minus all taxes, plus government transfers and interest on the debt, minus the retained earnings of corporations. Some believe that since households are the ultimate owners of corporations, retained earnings should be included in the measure of personal savings.

3. This time series was computed by Juster et al. (1999) using data from the Federal Reserve on household balance sheets. They compute several versions of the wealth and income variables, most showing a faster increase in the ratio of wealth to income in recent years than that shown in Figure 1. Compared with the benchmark Federal Reserve figures, the series in Figure 1.1 omits pension fund reserves and adjusts for changes in the age and marital composition of the household. Juster and colleagues' income measure, unlike that used in personal saving rate, employs gross rather than disposable income.

4. Not all theories of saving rely on rational, farsighted behavior (cf. Thaler, 1994). Our stance is that while current models based on rationality cannot explain all facets of consumption and saving behavior, the implications of the rationality approach are not yet fully developed—and that it remains the best paradigm available.

5. For a discussion of bargaining within marriage see Lundberg and Pollack (1996).

6. It can be shown that the current-period marginal utilities are

$$u_1 = \theta C_1^{\theta-1} C_2^{1-\theta}$$

and

$$u_2 = (1 - \theta)C_1^{\theta}C_2^{-\theta}$$

so that

$$MRS_{1,2} = u_1/u_2 = \theta C_1^{\theta-1}C_2^{1-\theta}/(1-\theta)C_1^{\theta}C_2^{-\theta} = \theta C_2/[(1-\theta)C_1].$$

To appreciate how these marginal utilities are found, consider u_1, the rate at which life-cycle utility rises when C_1 is increased and C_2 is held constant. Mathematically, this is the partial derivative of the total utility function with respect to C_1, $\partial U/\partial C_1$. For those familiar with calculus of a single variable only, this is essentially the same as regarding U as a function of C_1 alone and computing the (regular) derivative, dU/dC_1, using the simple exponent rule for differentiation. That rule, used again in later chapters, states that if $y = ax^b$, where a and b are constants, the derivative is $dy/dx = bax^{b-1}$. This is the rate at which y changes for a small change in x.

7. The present value, or PV, of an amount to be received in the future is the magnitude financial markets would give you *now* in exchange for your claim on that future sum. Suppose one has claim to amount F_1 to be received one period from now. Assuming financial markets pay interest at rate r on assets held one period, the present value of F_1 is $F_1/(1 + r)$. This makes sense because, if the amount $F_1/(1 + r)$ were invested now at rate r, it would grow to $[F_1/(1 + r)](1 + r) = F_1$ in one period. Thus, $PV = F_1/(1 + r)$. Similarly, were an amount F_2 to be received two periods hence, $PV = F_2/(1 + r)^2$.

8. Stock prices fluctuate a fair amount from year to year, making saving rates inclusive of capital gains on stocks sensitive to the years in which valuations are measured.

9. A further possible adjustment to savings would include capital gains on, as examples, corporate stock and housing. Since those more affluent hold most of the stocks and homes, such an adjustment might well reinforce the positive relationship between saving rates and income.

10. Extending the utility maximization model to make the rate of time preference a choice variable (on a par with C_1 and C_2) may be viewed by some as unjustified in the absence of more convincing empirical support. On the other hand, there does appear to be appreciable heterogeneity in the taste for saving both within and across income groups (even after accounting for pensions, marital status, health, number of children, etc.). Thus, theories of preference formation may prove important to explaining this "residual" variation in saving behavior.

11. All that is required is that C_1 and C_2 are normal goods. One obvious way to ensure normality is to assume that both goods have diminishing marginal utility and that they are neither substitutes nor complements for each other with respect to the utility function. Although these conditions are surely sufficient, they are not necessary.

12. They also simulate a model of the entire economy, taking into account the effect of savings on the return to capital and the wage rate (i.e., the general equilibrium steady state response, see Chapter 3). In that context they find the interest elasticity of savings to be somewhat higher. We revisit this topic in chapters 2 and 4.

13. The budget equation may be derived a bit more formally. In the first period, income is used for either first-period consumption or savings,

$$C_1 + S_1 = A_1r + E_1 \qquad \text{(1N)}$$

The total resources available for consumption in the second-period are: second-period earnings, plus the assets ($A_2 = S_1 + A_1$) brought into the start of period two, plus the interest earned on those assets

$$C_2 = (S_1 + A_1)(1 + r) + E_2 \qquad (2N)$$

Solving (1N) for savings and substituting into (2N) yields, after some rearrangement, equation (1.12).

14. Summers and Carroll partition the CEX samples of the different years by education and occupational groups. Then within these groups they partition by age. Next, the consumption and income of everyone with common age and occupational status (or education) is averaged. They make no adjustment for cohort effects, which may be important. For example, the consumption of those 60 years old in 1972 may be quite different from those 60 years old in 2002; and it is the latter that is relevant for those 30 years old in 1972.

15. Note that we are here excluding leisure consumption. As discussed in Chapter 8, a great source of inefficiency with respect to wage and consumption taxes is the inability to tax leisure consumption. Even though the equivalence of wage and consumption taxation is retained once allowance for leisure consumption is made, those valuing leisure more highly work and consume less, and pay less tax.

16. Peter Rangazas (personal communication) provided an overview on which this summary is based.

QUESTIONS AND PROBLEMS

▶ REVIEW
QUESTIONS

1. **A.** What are the stylized microeconomic facts about the relationship between household savings and (a) annual income, (b) average or "permanent" income, and (c) age?

   B. Why is the distinction between median and mean asset holdings important when discussing the adequacy of savings for retirement by representative households?

2. During the 2000 presidential campaign, then Vice President Al Gore proposed a savings incentive plan for households in which the government would match dollar for dollar savings by households in certain types of retirement accounts (the match rate would fall at higher household incomes). Would this policy have increased private savings? Public savings? Defend your answers, but recognize that the actual response is unclear. Suppose savings are viewed as important by the government to (a) provide for households needs, especially in retirement, and (b) allow for plentiful capital accumulation (investment). Does this policy work equally well for each goal? Explain. Given Figure 1.1, does there seem to be a pressing need for such a policy? (There may be other attractions of the policy, unrelated to the current question.)

3. **A.** Graph a consumer's budget line and endowment point assuming $E_2 > E_1 > 0$, $r = 0$, and $A_1 = 0$. Relative to this initial position, how would the budget line and endowment point look were (a) $A_1 > 0$, (b) there was an increase in E_1, (c) $dE_2 > 0$, $dE_2 = -(1 + r)dE_1$?

B. Define, graph, and interpret preferences associated with positive and neutral time preference. Intuitively explain how m, C_1, and S_1 vary with θ.

4. Suppose $E_2 = A_1 = 0$. Envision that the government increases the rate of tax on interest income, with any change in government revenues used to finance government consumption.

A. Intuitively explain the effects for first-period savings. Use the language of income and substitution effects and a clearly labeled graph.

B. Graph savings as a function of the interest rate, assuming first that the substitution effect dominates, second that the income effect dominates, and third that it is a Cobb-Douglas case.

C. In words, how would your answer to part A change if all revenues raised from the tax were returned to the same households in lump-sum fashion.

5. Figure 1.9 (and other studies that find the same pattern) is considered strong evidence against the LWH, as well as against the prediction from the optimality condition for utility maximization that consumption should either rise or fall smoothly over the life cycle, depending upon the relative magnitudes of r and m.

A. How and why does adjusting the household's age-consumption profile for family size affect the interpretation of Figure 1.9 as evidence against the LWH?

B. Many government policies involve shifting resources over the life cycle, such as Social Security. Suppose the economy is in a recession and Congress contemplates passage of a temporary tax cut, to be repaid through higher taxes once the economy recovers. Explain how the implications of this policy would differ, depending upon whether the LWH is true. (If the LWH fails, assume it is because of binding liquidity constraints.)

6. A. Why does the marginal propensity to consume from remaining life wealth in the current period vary between the young and old?

B. Why does the effect of a tax cut when young vary depending upon whether it is expected to be temporary (i.e., in period 1 only) or permanent (i.e., repeat in period 2)?

7. Why doesn't it make sense to measure poverty in terms of annual income? It is often argued that switching from an income tax base to a consumption tax base would hurt the poor and help the rich. What assumptions is this conclusion based on and why is this not necessarily correct?

▶ PROBLEMS

1. Consider the two-period problem where consumers have Cobb-Douglas preferences. Suppose $r = 1$, $\theta = .6$, $E_1 = 10$, $E_2 = 30$, $A_1 = 2$.

A. Determine the initial value of W, say W_1. Graph the budget line, showing magnitudes for axis intercepts. Find and interpret the slope of the budget line.

B. Draw an indifference curve on the graph from A consistent with the optimality condition, assuming the life wealth hypothesis holds. What are the utility maximizing values of C_1, C_2, and S_1? Label these on the graph.

C. Suppose there is a tax cut of 2 in the first period. What effect will this have on C_1, C_2, and S_1, assuming the life wealth hypothesis holds? Determine the new values for C_1 and C_2.

D. Repeat part C assuming instead that there is a reduction of 5 in Social Security benefits in period 2.

E. Suppose instead that there are first-period taxes of 5 and second-period transfers of 10. Show the effect on the budget line and the consumption choices, continuing to assume the life-wealth hypothesis holds.

F. Now suppose that credit markets do not allow one to borrow against first-period consumption. Returning to the parameter values at the start of the problem, again solve for C_1, C_2, and S_1.

G. Under the assumptions of part F, again let first-period taxes be 5 and second-period transfers equal 10. Determine the effect of this tax policy.

2. A. Suppose retirement after $R = 40$ years, and death after $T = 50$ years. Let $r = m = 0$. Suppose earnings are constant during each working year at $E = 100$. Solve for consumption and saving in each year. What is the amount of assets at the start of retirement (at the start of period of $R + 1$)?

B. Suppose at the start of economic life you correctly anticipate that you will receive an inheritance of 2,000 after 30 years of life. You also plan to leave a bequest of 2,000 upon death. Again solve for consumption in each period and assets at the start of retirement. Sketch the age/asset profile and compare with the profile in the absence of inheritances and bequests (without numbers if you prefer). If inheritances are important, do you think life-cycle saving motives (saving from own earnings) explain most of aggregate savings?

3. Suppose that $r = m = 0$ and that each consumer has *three* periods of adulthood. Also, assume there is no population growth so that there are equal numbers of consumers of each age. What is the marginal propensity to consume (mpc) from remaining life wealth for someone beginning period 1? Period 2? Period 3? What is the average population mpc for equal windfalls received by everyone? Now suppose that population growth is such that each successive birth cohort is double the size of the preceding one. What is the average mpc for the adult population now?

* 4. Assume that $W = E_1$ and consider the general utility function

$$U = u(C_1) + u(C_2)/(1 + m)$$

A. Assume the within-period u functions are identical. So, if $C_1 = C_2$, what does this imply about the "within period" marginal utilities of C_1 and C_2, $du(C_1)/dC_1 = u_1$ and u_2? What if instead, $C_2 > C_1$ (recall there is diminishing marginal utility)?

B. Set up the consumer optimization problem and derive the tangency or optimality condition. (Use Lagrangian methods if possible.) If $r = m$, what does the optimality condition imply about C_2 relative to C_1? What if $r > m$?

* 5. Suppose that $W = A_1(1 + r) + E_1$ and that the utility function is

$$U = \theta \ln C_1 + (1 - \theta) \ln C_2$$

A. Set up the consumer optimization problem and derive the tangency or optimality condition. (Use Lagrangian methods if possible.)

B. Solve for C_1, C_2, and S_1.

C. Compute the comparative statics results on these solutions of a change in (a) r, (b) E_1, and (c) A_1. How do these results compare with those for the Cobb-Douglas utility function discussed in the text? Why is that?

D. Now suppose that $W = A_1(1 + r) + E_1 + E_2/(1 + r)$. Again solve for the variables in b. Compute the comparative statics results on these variables for (a) E_2 and (b) r.

Chapter 2 | CONSUMPTION AND SAVING, II[1]

This chapter develops further the theory and evidence regarding consumption and saving over the life cycle. Section 2.1 is devoted to deepening understanding of the response of saving to the rate of return. First, the implications of preferences more general than the Cobb-Douglas utility function emphasized in Chapter 1 are developed. That section then addresses the roles of future earnings and saving incentive programs for household saving. The extensions of sections 2.2, 2.3, and 2.4 provide more satisfactory answers to the puzzles of Chapter 1 posed by the excess sensitivity of consumption to current income and the shape of the age-consumption profile. In Chapter 1 future economic variables were assumed to be known with certainty. This unrealistic premise is discarded in sections 2.2 and 2.3. Section 2.2 explicitly addresses the issues that arise—and the consumer's response—when there is uninsurable earnings risk. Chapter 1 assumed the consumer knew exactly when he or she would die. The consumer doesn't know this, and section 2.3 considers the implications for consumption and asset decumulation during retirement. Finally, in section 2.4 we acknowledge that the enjoyment of consumption in one period may depend upon consumption in other periods. That is, we allow for the possibility that consumption patterns are, in part, habitual.

2.1 THE RESPONSE OF SAVING TO THE INTEREST RATE

2.1.1 The Constant Elasticity of Substitution (CES) Utility Function

In Chapter 1 we relied heavily on the Cobb-Douglas utility function to illustrate many important concepts, especially regarding income dynamics. Cobb-Douglas preferences are less illuminating when we address the substitution effect associated with a change in the interest rate. For although the magnitude of the substitution effect is an unresolved empirical question, Cobb-Douglas preferences restrict the ease of substituting between consumption in different periods to a particular (and perhaps unrealistic) value.

In contrast, the degree of substitutability is a free parameter in the following utility function

$$U = C_1^{1-1/\sigma}/(1 - 1/\sigma) + C_2^{1-1/\sigma}/[(1 - 1/\sigma)(1 + m)] \tag{2.1}$$

The new parameter, σ, is the *intertemporal elasticity of substitution,* defined as the percentage change in the consumption ratio C_2/C_1 following a 1% change in the relative price of C_1. Since that price is $1 + r$, σ measures the ease with which the consumer can substitute between C_2 and C_1 when the interest rate changes. Since σ can assume any (non-negative) value, (2.1) generalizes the Cobb-Douglas case, making it preferable for both theoretical and empirical research. This utility function does restrict σ to be constant across periods and independent of the level of consumption. For this reason, it is termed a *constant elasticity of substitution* (CES) utility function.

Intuitively, σ is bigger the closer substitutes are consumption in the two periods. This may be seen graphically. When goods are close substitutes, indifference curves are shallow, so the $MRS_{1,2}$ changes only slowly. Then, as in Figure 2.1, an increase in the interest rate, such as from r_0 to r_1, will produce a large increase in the consumption ratio, here from bundle A to bundle B. Were C_1 and C_2 poor substitutes, the same change in r would produce only a small change in the consumption ratio. If σ were zero, indifference curves would be L-shaped and the consumption ratio would be independent of the interest rate.

This elasticity also affects the rate at which consumption grows over the life cycle. Recall that the tangency condition for optimality equates the slopes of the indifference curve and budget line, $MRS_{1,2} = 1 + r$. For the CES preferences of (2.1), the marginal rate of substitution is

$$MRS_{1,2} = u_1/u_2 = C_1^{-1/\sigma}/[C_2^{-1/\sigma}/(1 + m)] = (C_2/C_1)^{1/\sigma}(1 + m)$$

Consequently, optimality implies

$$(C_2/C_1)^{1/\sigma}(1 + m) = 1 + r$$

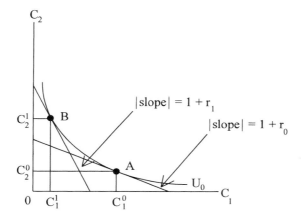

Figure 2.1 Effect of changing r when the elasticity of substitutions is large

This expression is usefully rearranged as

$$C_2/C_1 = [(1 + r)/(1 + m)]^\sigma \qquad (2.2)$$

Notice that when σ equals 1, equation (2.2) reduces to the tangency condition for the Cobb-Douglas case, reproduced below

$$C_2/C_1 = (1 + r)/(1 + m) \qquad (1.6c)$$

This suggests, correctly, that $\sigma = 1$ in the Cobb-Douglas case. Thus, Cobb-Douglas preferences are also CES, but less general. This expression also reveals that Cobb-Douglas preferences are behaviorally equivalent to the more general CES preferences when σ is equal to 1. In both cases consumption growth over the life cycle increases with r and declines with m. However, with general CES preferences, the consumption growth associated with a given positive difference between r and m increases with σ. As seen in section 2.2, σ also influences the consumer's response to income uncertainty.

Attanasio and Weber (1995) estimate a value for σ of around .6, while older surveys of the literature suggest σ may not be much above .25 (cf. Auerbach and Kotlikoff, 1987). Consequently, it appears Cobb-Douglas preferences overstate the extent of substitutability. Attanasio and Weber also question whether the constant elasticity assumption is appropriate. For they find σ increases with the level of consumption. Intuitively, affluent households are found to consume more "luxuries" in their later years. Almost by definition, the consumption of luxuries can be more readily timed to when their price is lowest. Due to the time value of money, luxuries are less expensive later in the life cycle. If further results support this finding, the CES formulation will need to be replaced by a yet more general utility function.

The CES case provides ready closed-form solutions that may then be differentiated to yield comparative statics information. To solve for the consumption levels, use (2.2) to solve for C_2, then substitute for C_2 in the budget constraint (see equation 1.5). Solving for optimal first-period consumption yields

$$C_1^* = \frac{W}{1 + \left(\dfrac{1 + r}{1 + m}\right)^\sigma \left(\dfrac{1}{1 + r}\right)} \qquad (2.3)$$

Finally, using (2.3) in (2.2) one can solve for C_2^*.

2.1.2   More on Interest Elasticity of Saving and Taxation of Interest Income

As in Chapter 1, we motivate an increase in the interest rate by supposing there is a reduction in the rate of tax on interest income. We assume that any change in government receipts is reflected in government consumption and does not affect the consumer's plans. Thus, in terms of the impact on consumer behavior, this policy is effectively just an uncompensated increase in the interest rate. (In the general equilibrium setting of Chapter 4, the effects on the pretax wage and pretax interest rate of changing taxes are addressed.)

The explicit solution for first-period consumption with CES preferences, equation (2.3), makes it relatively easy to obtain comparative statics results for that case. In particular, the comparative statics response of C_1^* with respect to r is simply the derivative of equation (2.3) with respect to r. If wealth derives from first-period income only, this will be positive if $\sigma < 1$, so that *saving* when young rises with r (see problem 2.3). As noted above, σ may well be less than 1. If it is, the income effect dominates the substitution effect and saving falls. This is unsurprising, since the substitution effect exactly offsets the income effect in the Cobb-Douglas case, where more substitutability was assumed. When life wealth also depends on future earnings, it is again possible for savings to rise with r, even when $\sigma < 1$.

The Human Wealth Effect

In Chapter 1 we studied the response of saving to the interest rate when wealth consists of first-period income only. An important extension addresses the role of future labor earnings. Recall that the present value of life earnings is termed human wealth. When labor income is received in the first period of life only, changes in the interest rate do not affect human wealth. However, when future earnings are positive, an increase in the interest rate lowers their present value, reducing human wealth. The effect this has for consumption and saving, which we now develop, is termed the *human wealth effect*.

With earnings in both periods, life wealth becomes $W = E_1 + E_2/(1 + r)$. The initial budget line MW_0 is shown in Figure 2.2 where the income endowment is given by point K. Now, letting the interest rate rise, the budget line rotates *through* the endowment point K. The new budget line LW_1 intersects the C_1 axis closer to the origin, reflecting reduced wealth. Wealth falls as the higher interest rate lowers the present value of second-period earnings, and therefore human wealth. Thus, when second-period earnings are positive, the *sources* of income from the perspective of period 1, are reduced from W_0 to W_1. This reduction in human wealth lowers consumption relative to when $E_2 = 0$, making it more

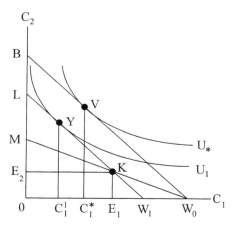

Figure 2.2 The human wealth effect on consumption

likely that an increase in r will increase saving. Following the increase in r, the consumer maximizes utility at point Y with first-period consumption of C_1^1.

To isolate the human wealth effect graphically, suppose instead that initial wealth derives solely from first-period income, but continues to equal W_0. Then the same increase in the interest rate would produce budget line W_0B. Continuing the thought experiment, utility would then be maximized at point V, with first-period consumption of C_1^*. This hypothetical budget line lies everywhere above the initial constraint MW_0 due to the positive wealth effect on the *uses* of income—higher r lowers the price of C_2—discussed in Chapter 1. Now comes the new twist: Compared with the budget line following the r increase when E_2 was positive, W_1L, the *hypothetical* constraint is higher by the amount higher r lowered human wealth. Ceteris paribus, this reduction in human wealth lowers first-period consumption from C_1^* to C_1^1; this is the human wealth effect.

The negative human wealth effect on the sources side and the positive wealth effect on the uses side exactly offset each other at the endowment point K. To the left of the endowment point the "lower price effect" dominates and utility is increased by higher r. Thus, the overall wealth effect is positive for households with positive savings at the initial interest rate. Intuitively, for savers higher r increases interest income, making them better off. Conversely, if the household is initially in debt—operating to the right of the endowment point—higher r implies greater interest expense, so that utility falls. Thus, the greater is E_2 relative to E_1, the more likely it is that the overall wealth effect will be negative. (An implication is that the human wealth effect and the interest elasticity of saving are predicted to be higher in economies anticipating rapid growth.)

Figure 2.3 illustrates the full effect of higher r for a household with positive savings. Utility is initially maximized at D on budget line AW_0. Following a tax cut which increases r, the budget line becomes BW_1 and utility is maximized at F. Thus, as drawn, consumption falls from C_1^0 to C_1^1, and saving increases with the interest rate. The overall wealth effect incorporating both the human wealth and price effects is here positive, from C_1^0 to C_1^2 (D to G). The substitution effect is the movement along U_1 from G to F, or reduction in C_1 from C_1^2 to C_1^1.

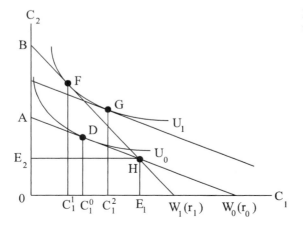

Figure 2.3 Effect of changing the interest rate on consumption

Suppose, instead, that at the initial r, utility is maximized with borrowing, somewhere on budget line segment HW_0. Further, assume that interest expense on debt is tax deductible. Then after the reduction in capital income taxation, the interest expense tax deduction would be worth less, and utility is lower on budget line segment HW_1. Thus, in this case both the wealth and substitution effects favor lower C_1, so that saving would unambiguously rise with r.

Continuing to let the household be a debtor, assume now that interest expense is *not* tax deductible. Under current U.S. tax law, home mortgage (and home equity loan) interest expense is tax deductible, but other forms of interest expense, such as on credit card debt, are not. Consequently, interest income is not deductible for households who rent, rather than own. For these households, the tax cut would not affect the budget line, so there is no effect on saving.

Using computer simulations, Summers (1981) demonstrates that the interest elasticity of saving is appreciably increased by the human wealth effect when future earnings are certain. The magnitude of his simulated response has proven controversial. One reason, as seen in section 2.3, is that the human wealth effect is smaller when future income uncertainty is taken into account. Recall from Chapter 1 that empirical estimates of the interest elasticity of saving are typically positive, but small.

Initial Wealth

Another worthwhile extension incorporates the asset position at the start of period one, A_1. An interesting case is where A_1 is positive and large, perhaps reflecting an inheritance. Life wealth W becomes $(1 + r)A_1 + E_1 + E_2/(1 + r)$. Now an increase in r also raises current interest income. This creates an additional wealth effect—this one positive—which shifts the budget line rightward. However, since the first-period marginal propensity to consume from an increase in wealth is below 1, the increase in C_1 from this effect will be less than the increase in disposable income of A_1dr. Thus, saving would increase with r, considering positive A_1 in isolation. The overall effect on saving (i.e., including the substitution effect) remains ambiguous.

As noted in Chapter 1, the distribution of financial wealth is quite unequal. A reduction in the rate of interest, or more generally capital, income taxation would further translate the wealth inequality to income inequality. For this reason, proposals to cut capital income taxes are viewed by many as calls for tax breaks for the rich. "Conservatives" respond by noting that, if savings increase as a result of the tax cut, investment in physical capital will increase, raising the productivity and wages of all workers. This mechanism is often termed the "trickle down effect." This and other general equilibrium implications of capital income taxation are developed in Chapter 4.

Interest Rate Uncertainty

We have assumed the interest rate on savings is known with certainty. In fact, there are many types of assets and they vary by both expected return and variance of returns. Suppose there is but one type of asset. Define an increase in the riskiness of that asset as an increase in the variance of the rate of return when there is no change in the expected rate of return. Sandmo (1970) points out that such a change has an ambiguous effect on savings. "An increase in the degree of risk makes the consumer less inclined to expose his resources to the possibility of a loss. . . . On the other hand, higher riskiness makes it necessary to save more in order to protect oneself against very low levels of future consumption" (pp. 358–359). In section 2.2 we briefly consider portfolio decisions when assets vary in their risk characteristics.

2.1.3   Tax-preferred Saving Incentive Programs

While changes in the rate of interest income taxation affect returns on the broad class of interest-bearing assets, other government policies raise the after-tax return only for monies placed in *designated accounts*. These include Individual Retirement Accounts (IRAs) and 401(k) plans. Between 1982 and 1986 any worker could deposit up to $2,000 per year in a qualified IRA account. Such accounts include most of the usual forms of saving, such as savings accounts, and money and stock market mutual funds. IRAs were made less generous in 1986 and contributions to them fell accordingly. Currently, contributions are capped at $3,000 per year, with limits falling as income rises. The 401(k)s, named for the section of the Internal Revenue Code that authorizes their use, are employer-provided plans utilized by many employees. They have higher contribution limits than IRAs ($11,000 in 2002) and contributions to them have risen rapidly in recent years. Engen and Gale (2000, p. 1) note that by 1995 "the number of active participants had increased to 28 million, contributions had reached $87 billion—accounting for 29 percent of personal saving and 55 percent of all pension contributions—and balances had reached $864 billion."

Traditionally, contributions into such plans have been tax deductible. Then, both the contributions and interest earnings are subject to tax upon withdrawal. However, in 1998 the Roth IRA became available. Contributions to Roth IRAs are made with after-tax dollars. Since these assets also feature tax-free accrual, there are no further taxes due upon withdrawal. All IRAs impose additional taxes or penalties on withdrawals before age $59\frac{1}{2}$ except for "qualified special purposes," such as costs of acquiring a first home. We assume monies deposited are left until retirement. The deductibility of contributions is beneficial if the tax rate is lower when the funds are withdrawn than when the contributions are made. Since withdrawals are most often made during retirement when income is low, this condition is usually met (since marginal tax rates rise with income).[2] However, the Roth IRA has other features that make it preferable to conventional IRAs for some investors. For example, with Roth IRAs, unlike traditional IRAs, there is no age at which the investor *must* begin to take disbursements. If a retiree can draw on other funds, Roth funds can continue to accrue tax free. Also, Roth IRAs eliminate record keeping for tax purposes: Contributions are after-tax and all withdrawals are tax free; with traditional IRAs the investor needs to report the initial contribution and, upon withdrawal, isolate the portion associated with the contribution.

The tax-free accrual of interest income feature of these plans confers advantages even if taxation at rate μ is constant over the life cycle. To see this, suppose $1 is contributed to a fund now and will be withdrawn after T years. After T years of tax-free accrual this will have grown to $(1 + r)^T$. Subtracting the $1 initial investment, interest earnings will be $(1 + r)^T - 1$. Since taxes are paid when money is withdrawn, the net-of-tax interest earnings will be $[(1 + r)^T - 1](1 - \mu)$. If the \$1 were instead placed into a regular, taxable account, the net-of-tax interest earnings after T years would be $[1 + r(1 - \mu)]^T - 1$. (Capital gains on homes and stocks are also taxed only upon realization, rather than accrual.)

Effectively, tax-free accrual constitutes an interest-free loan on taxes otherwise due. Thus, there is no advantage if withdrawal is just one year away (taxes are μr either way). After two years benefits are positive, but small. However, these advantages compound, so that when the number of years until retirement becomes large, so do the benefits of tax-free accrual. For example, suppose $r = .1$, $\mu = .4$, and that the consumer withdraws the funds after 40 years. Now, in a regular savings account the amount of interest earned after tax will be \$9.29. Under tax-free accrual, there is \$26.56 left after taxes. Thus, the advantage per dollar contributed is \$17.27—start your tax-preferred contributions today! Unfortunately, if the interest rate you face is below 10%, or the number of years until withdrawal is less than 40, so will be the advantages compared with a regular account.

Notice that an expansion of deductibility and tax-free accrual to all forms of savings would effectively convert the income tax into a consumption tax base: In a given year taxes would be paid on income minus any increment to savings; however, this is just consumption. Suppose instead that all forms of saving receive the treatment of assets in Roth IRAs—active additions to saving would be with after-tax dollars and asset earnings would be tax free. This, effectively, would constitute a system of wage income taxation.

Everything else the same, tax-free accrual means tax revenues lost to the government. Thus, if the goal of such tax incentive plans is to increase national—private plus public—savings, the increase in private savings must exceed the revenues lost to the government. However, we know that the effect on private savings of a higher net-of-tax return is theoretically ambiguous, so that this may be a difficult hurdle for such a policy to clear. A further complication is that one cannot immediately equate personal retirement plan contributions with *new* savings. A household with preexisting financial holdings could simply reshuffle its assets out of "regular" accounts and into the tax-preferred plans, without increasing its total savings.

The effectiveness of saving incentives plans remains controversial, though the range of dispute has recently narrowed. Poterba, Venti, and Wise (1996) conclude that the bulk of contributions to personal retirement programs constitute new savings. They point out that the other financial savings of contributors have not declined as their personal retirement plan contributions have grown. This, they argue, is evidence that the saving for these plans was not at the expense of other forms of saving. Further, in their view these new savings far exceed the loss of government revenues from their favored tax treatment. Hubbard and Skinner (1996) believe that each dollar of tax-preferred contributions increases national savings by about 26 cents, taking the lost government revenues into account. They note, though, that this does not necessarily imply that these programs increase welfare, for such plans push consumption to later in the life cycle when, due to positive time preference, it is less highly valued.

Conversely, Engen, Gale, and Scholz (1996) conclude that such programs may have reduced national saving. They marshall substantial evidence that contributors to these plans are on average families with high saving propensities. Consequently, they argue that nondeclining holdings of other financial assets need not imply that 401(k) eligibility increased their overall savings. More recently, Engen and Gale (1997) point out that among homeowners, mortgage debt rose along with IRA contributions. Since mortgage interest payments are tax deductible, the ability to increase IRAs at the expense of higher mortgage debt creates an opportunity for "tax arbitrage." To appreciate this, suppose the pretax rates at which one can borrow and lend are each 10% and that a household is in the 28% tax bracket. Since the mortgage interest is tax deductible, one could borrow at 7.2% by increasing mortgage debt and lend at 10% to fund an IRA. To the extent IRAs (or 401(k)s) slow the rate at which mortgages are paid off, deposits into tax-preferred accounts constitute a reshuffling of household assets rather than an increase in wealth.

Quite recently, Engen and Gale (2000) address how 401(k) eligibility effects on household wealth differ across earnings classes. Their results provide some reconciliation of the divergent findings reported above. They employ data from waves of the Survey of Income and Program Participation (SIPP), focusing on the 1987 and 1991 data. These SIPP waves contain information on 401(k) eligibility and wealth, as well as on important demographic controls. Eligibility and participation are positively related to income: in 1991, 14 percent of families with earnings between $10,000 and $20,000 participated in a 401(k), whereas 51% of households with earnings above $75,000 did so. Among households earning more than $40,000, Engen and Gale find little effect of 401(k)s on wealth. Thus, affluent households tend to fund 401(k)s principally by reducing housing equity (as suggested by Engen and Gale, 1997) and holdings of other financial assets (which previous researchers had found unchanged when viewing *all* eligible households). For households with earnings below $40,000, eligibility for 401(k)s does appear to induce new saving (as suggested by the aggregate analyses of Poterba, Venti, and Wise). Since more affluent households make the bulk of 401(k) contributions, the effect of 401(k)s on aggregate private saving would not exceed 30 percent of all contributions (even if all contributions among lower earning households constitute new saving). The effect on national savings would be lower, since 401(k) contributions reduce taxes paid.

2.2 UNCERTAIN INCOME AND PRECAUTIONARY SAVING

2.2.1 Theory

To this point we have assumed the consumer knows the entire path of future earnings with certainty. This is patently false, as uncertainties regarding health, market luck, general economic growth, and ability all subject future earnings to substantial risk. Even among consumers with similar education, there is great variability in earnings, and this variability increases with age.

Of course, some earnings variability over the life cycle is fully anticipated, or even planned, by the household. For example, some women fully intend to, and then do, withdraw from the labor force for an interval following the birth of a child. Unfortunately, it is difficult for an econometrician to know which fluctuations in income are surprises to the consumer and which are fully anticipated. On the basis of observed fluctuations, Carroll and Samwick (1997) report that in a given year about one-third of households experience "permanent" shocks to income exceeding 14% of their average income; one-third also experience "transitory" shocks exceeding 21% of average income. Even granting that not all of this variation represents uncertainty to the household, these figures suggest earnings uncertainty may be substantial.

Further, much of the uncertainty surrounding future earnings is uninsurable. Temporary unemployment benefits, welfare, and disability insurance are important exceptions, but would not nearly replace full time earnings. Notice that if one *could* fully insure earnings—guaranteeing their magnitude no matter what—the negative effect on work effort could be sizeable: Why work hard if earnings are independent of your actions? This effect on effort is an example of *moral hazard,* whereby insuring against an outcome reduces the care taken to prevent that outcome (here low earnings) from occurring. Work incentives are emphasized in Chapter 8.

Moral hazard is one important reason private insurance against earnings risk is largely unavailable. In the absence of market insurance, consumers may be expected to self-insure in some way. One way would be to undertake some *precautionary saving* that could help smooth consumption should earnings prove low. Other less formal "insurance networks" involving friends and family could also be developed. This section develops the theory and discusses the evidence regarding the effect of uninsurable earnings uncertainty on consumption and saving. The theory is taken up first. (The appendix to this chapter offers an introduction to the economics of uncertainty, which some readers may find helpful.)

Unsurprisingly, the effects of uncertainty on consumption and saving depend upon the consumer's preferences, particularly attitude toward risk. The relevant points can be made using the following simple utility function:

$$U \equiv u(C_1) + u(C_2) \tag{2.4}$$

Life-cycle utility U is the simple sum of the first-period utility from period-one consumption and the second-period utility from period-two consumption. The CES preferences of section 2.1 are an important example of such preferences. The little u functions are identical, so that if $C_1 = C_2$, then also $u(C_1) = u(C_2)$. We assume the consumer is risk averse, which simply requires there to be diminishing marginal utility. With diminishing marginal utility, an $x loss reduces total utility by more than an $x gain would increase it. Thus, a risk-averse consumer would turn down a bet offering an equal chance of gaining or losing $x.

Before proceeding, it is helpful to develop a bit more notation. As in Chapter 1, the marginal utilities of first- and second-period consumption are u_1 and u_2, the first derivatives of the single-period utility functions with respect to consumption in that period. Diminishing marginal utility requires marginal utility to decline as consumption rises, or $du_1/dC_1 \equiv u_{11} < 0$ and $du_2/dC_2 \equiv u_{22} < 0$. Thus, the second derivatives of the single-period utility functions are negative. Diminishing marginal utility by itself does not tell us how the consumer will respond to uncertainty. As we shall see, the effect on consumption and saving depends upon whether marginal utility declines at a constant rate, in which case $du_{11}/dC_1 \equiv u_{111} = u_{222} = 0$, or at a decreasing rate, so that u_{111} and $u_{222} > 0$. Both possibilities are shown in Figure 2.4 for u_2, since it is second-period consumption that is uncertain.

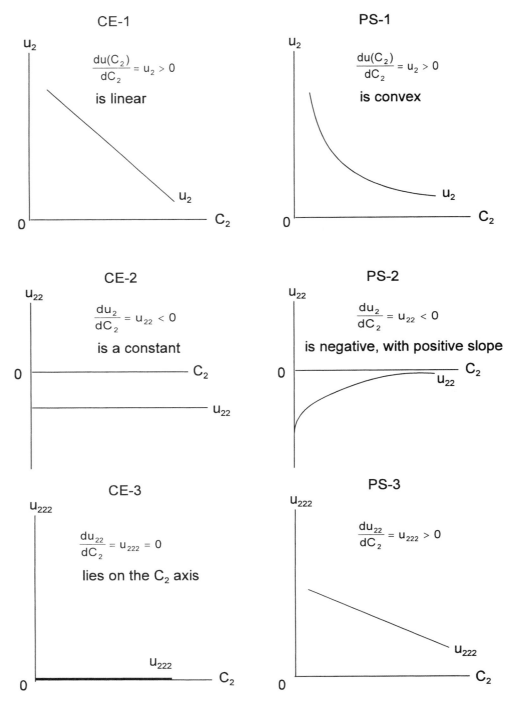

Figure 2.4 Certain equivalence (CE) and precautionary saving (PS)

For reasons made clear below, the panels labeled CE will correspond to *certainty equivalence*. Those labeled PS connote the presence of a *precautionary saving* motive. In panel CE-1, marginal utility u_2 is a negatively sloped straight line. The negative slope guarantees risk aversion. That the function is a straight line tells us that marginal utility falls at a constant rate, or that u_{22} is constant, as shown in panel CE-2. Since u_{22} is a constant, its rate of change is zero, $du_{22}/dC_2 = u_{222} = 0$, as plotted in CE-3. (The most prominent explicit preferences associated with certainty equivalence are those of the quadratic utility function, $U = a + b(C_1 + C_2) - d(C_1^2 + C_2^2)$, where b and d are both positive.)

By contrast, in panel PS-1 marginal utility is a negatively sloped *convex* function of C_2. Since it is negatively sloped, $u_{22} < 0$; since it is convex, marginal utility falls at a decreasing rate, making u_{22} less negative as C_2 rises. Panel PS-2 shows this general pattern for u_{22}.[3] Since the slope of the u_{22} function is positive, so is u_{222}, as drawn in PS-3.

There are perhaps two questions in your mind: Which assumption for marginal utility is most plausible? What difference does it make? Most economists believe marginal utility is convex. One reason is that if marginal utility is linear, it becomes negative at some finite value of consumption. In fact, if there is substantial risk aversion, the consumption level at which marginal utility becomes negative need not be all that high. No one would consume beyond where marginal utility crosses the consumption axis. This implies an upper limit to the amount any person would consume, regardless of his or her wealth. However, although the rich do have higher saving rates, greater wealth does in general induce greater consumption. With convex marginal utility, marginal utility crosses the consumption axis at a much higher consumption level, if at all. This is a strong argument in favor of convex marginal utility.

As to the second question posed above, it is important whether u_{222} is positive or zero. If it is zero, C_1 will not change if E_2 becomes less certain, holding expected income constant. In that case, consumers exhibit *certainty equivalence*—their first-period consumption and saving are not affected by uncertainty. On the other hand, if $u_{222} > 0$, consumers have a *precautionary saving motive*. In this case, an increase in income uncertainty that leaves expected income unchanged will reduce first-period consumption. Saving is increased as a form of self-insurance against low income states of the world. These implications of precautionary saving are developed below.

To focus on the issues at hand, assume that $r = 0$ so that life wealth is simply $W = E_1 + E_2$. Recall from Chapter 1 that when earnings are certain, optimal consumption equates the $MRS_{1,2}$, here u_1/u_2 to $1 + r$. With $r = 0$ this simplifies to $u_1 = u_2$ and, with the superscript c denoting the certainty case,

$$u_1(C_1^c) = u_2(C_2^c)$$

Thus, in the absence of uncertainty, marginal utilities are equated and consumption is equal in each period, $C_1^c = C_2^c$. This solution is illustrated in Figure 2.5 for convex marginal utility. The intersection of the marginal utility schedules occurs where C_1^c and C_2^c each equal $W/2$. First-period consumption is measured to the right from the origin. Second-period consumption is measured to the left from point A. If E_2 is uncertain, how would C_1 and S_1 be affected?

Denote second-period earnings in a certain world by E_2^c. To model earnings uncertainty in a simple way, suppose $E_2 = E_2^c + x$ or $E_2 = E_2^c - x$, each with probability .5.

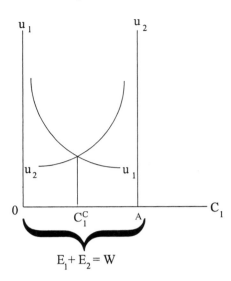

Figure 2.5 Marginal utilities equated in absence of uncertainty

Since we have increased the risk symmetrically around E_2^c, *expected* earnings remain E_2^c. With certain income, choice of C_1^c completely determines second-period consumption, $C_2^c = E_1 + E_2^c - C_1^c$. With uncertain second-period earnings, that same choice of C_1 is associated with two possible values for second-period consumption, $C_2^c + x$ or $C_2^c - x$. (The expected value of C_2 is unaffected.)

This means second-period marginal utility is uncertain; it will exceed u_1 if E_2 proves low, or be below u_1 if earnings are high. For this reason, consumers can no longer choose C_1 to equate the marginal utility of consumption in each period. Consequently, a new decision rule is required. In the presence of uncertainty it is most often assumed that consumers maximize *expected utility*,

$$\mathbf{E}_1 U = u(C_1) + \mathbf{E}_1 u(C_2)$$

where $\mathbf{E}_1$ denotes the expectations at the start of period 1 regarding aspects of the world— here earnings—in period 2. As the expression makes clear, in period 1 we can choose and receive certain utility from C_1. On the other hand, for a given choice of C_1, both C_2 and second-period utility are uncertain. The optimality condition for maximizing expected utility is that *expected* marginal utility be equated across the two periods,

$$u_1(C_1) = \mathbf{E}_1 u_2(C_2) \tag{2.5}$$

Here, $\mathbf{E}_1 u_2$ is the expected marginal utility of period 2 consumption.

Below we show for convex marginal utility that, holding C_1 constant, expected marginal utility in period 2, $\mathbf{E}_1 u_2$, exceeds the marginal utility when C_2 is certain, $u_2(C_2^c)$. This means that with earnings risk, first-period consumption must be reduced relative to the certainty case, in order to satisfy (2.5). Notice that lowering C_1 entails an increase in first-period savings. Also, depressing C_1 increases *expected* second-period consumption.

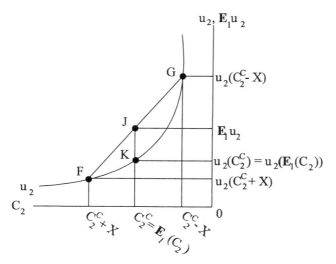

Figure 2.6 Expected marginal utility

Consequently, uncertainty increases the average growth rate of consumption over the working years (among a cohort of households). We now develop these claims.

Consider $E_1u_2(C_2)$ when earnings are uncertain but where, for comparison's sake, C_1 equals the amount optimal when there is certainty, $C_1 = C_1^c$. Then

$$E_1u_2 = (.5)[u_2(C_2^c + x)] + (.5)[u_2(C_2^c - x)]$$

Now view Figure 2.6. Since the probability of each earnings outcome is .5, E_1u_2 lies on chord GF exactly half-way between $u_2(C_2^c + x)$ and $u_2(C_2^c - x)$. This is indicated by point J. In contrast, when C_2^c is to be received with certainty, its marginal utility is shown by point K. Since J lies above K, it follows that

$$E_1u_2 > u_2(C_2^c)$$

so that, as claimed above, expected marginal utility exceeds the marginal utility under certainty. Intuitively, convexity implies that as we move down the u_2 schedule from $u_2(C_2^c - x)$, the rate of descent is initially quite rapid. Consequently, by the time C_2 equals C_2^c, having increased half of the way to $C_2^c + x$, u_2 will have completed more than half of the total decline between $u_2(C_2^c - x)$ and $u_2(C_2^c + x)$.

With convex marginal utility, uncertainty raises the expected marginal utility of second-period consumption. The reason is that symmetrical risk around an arbitrary C_2 value will increase marginal utility by more in the bad state than it is reduced in the good state, increasing the average. Because of diminishing marginal utility, higher expected marginal utility requires that C_1 be reduced relative to the certainty case. The lower C_1 raises u_1, while the higher savings raise expected C_2, driving down E_1u_2.

This is illustrated in Figure 2.7. The equilibrium with certain earnings is where $u_1 = u_2$ and $C_1^c = C_2^c$. With uncertainty, $u_1 = E_1u_2$ occurs where first-period consumption is C_1^u. *The reduction in C_1 due to the uncertainty is the amount of precautionary savings:*

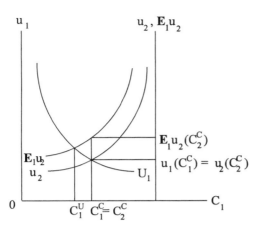

Figure 2.7 Expected utility maximization

This is $C_1^c - C_1^u$. Notice that with uncertainty, C_2 can no longer be read directly from the graph. Second-period consumption will be savings plus second-period earnings, which will equal either $E_1 + E_2^c - x - C_1^u$ or $E_1 + E_2^c + x - C_1^u$.

If we don't reduce the value of C_1 in the face of uncertainty, we run the risk of ending up with distressingly low consumption in period two. If earnings in period two are low, the last few dollars are very meaningful to our welfare, so that $u_2(C_2^c - x)$ is high. Since there are no insurance markets allowing us to shift consumption from the good state of the world to the bad one, we self-insure against low C_2 the only way we can, by increasing the financial reserves we take into period two.

On the other hand, with *linear* marginal utility, the chord connecting $u_2(C_2^c - x)$ and $u_2(C_2^c + x)$ would coincide with the u_2 schedule for certain amounts. For this reason, the expected marginal utility equals the marginal utility of certain amounts. This is the case of certainty equivalence. That is, first-period consumption and saving are uninfluenced by the uncertainty, $C_1^c = C_1^u$. Consequently, unless there is convex marginal utility ($u_{222} > 0$), there is no precautionary saving motive.

Implications of Precautionary Saving Motive

In Chapter 1 we saw that, in apparent contradiction to the life wealth hypothesis, there is a strong positive correlation between annual consumption and annual income. Even after making adjustments for variation in family size, this correlation remains relatively strong in the early years of the life cycle. In that chapter the existence of young, liquidity-constrained households was proposed as one explanation for the correlation. As we now explain, earnings uncertainty has similar implications. Suppose for now that there are no restrictions on borrowing, other than the life wealth constraint. In the two-period model above we saw that earnings uncertainty depresses consumption in the young household relative to the certainty case. Thus, *on average*, households have higher consumption in the second period than were there no uncertainty. Thus, in the two-period model uncertainty increases consumption growth.

Similar results obtain in the annual or many-period version of the model (which draws heavily from Carroll (cf. 1997a, 2000). Suppose there is a fixed period of retirement and that the age at death is known with certainty. It helps to recall equation (2.2), repeated below, which shows that with CES preferences and *no uncertainty*, the ratio of consumption between periods one and two is

$$C_2/C_1 = [(1 + r)/(1 + m)]^\sigma \qquad (2.2)$$

It can be shown that with many periods, consumption growth between each period is likewise governed by the right-hand side of (2.2). Suppose that the growth rate of earnings is also constant, producing an earnings ratio equal to, say G. Carroll refers to consumers for whom

$$[(1 + r)/(1 + m)]^\sigma < G \qquad (2.6)$$

as *impatient*. Inspection of (2.6) reveals that consumers expecting higher earnings growth and/or having a higher rate of time preference are more likely to be impatient. The impatience condition implies that if income were known with certainty, the consumer would like to borrow when young. To see this, first note that when the condition is satisfied, consumption would grow less rapidly than earnings throughout the life cycle. Combined with the life wealth budget constraint, this means the consumer would like to borrow when young. (If consumption grows less rapidly than earnings and is below earnings early in life, assets would increase each year of life if there is no retirement.)

Now, suppose that consumers are impatient but also face serious earnings risk. In particular, there is some low probability that earnings will be at or near zero for many years. For example, the consumer may become disabled. At the start of economic life, it is then *prudent* for the consumer to build up some reserves to guard against the possibility of low earnings (and therefore quite low consumption into the future). Over this interval, despite the consumer's impatience, consumption must be lower than earnings in order to build up a "buffer stock" of assets. Assets are then growing for the average household, since the average household doesn't experience unusually bad luck. This reduces "prudence" relative to "impatience" in the average household. So long as prudence dominates impatience, assets are rising, and consumption grows faster than income. When some asset target has been reached, say around age 30, prudence and impatience are roughly in balance, so that consumption grows at about the same rate as, or tracks, earnings. As the years pass, more of the life-cycle earnings uncertainty is resolved. At some point, perhaps in the mid-40s, the consumer begins to behave more as if the world were certain. Consequently, consumption growth slows almost to the rate associated with equation (2.2), and the consumer begins to accumulate "hump wealth" for retirement. In retirement, consumption growth satisfies (2.2) exactly.

The predicted age-consumption profile for the average across consumers is illustrated in Figure 2.8, under the assumption that the impatience condition (2.6) is satisfied, with both sides positive. The consumer achieves adulthood at age 21, retires at age 65, and dies at age 75. Notice that this figure produces a fairly close tracking of earnings by consumption, until roughly late middle age. Thus, this story is broadly consistent with the empirical consumption and income profiles discussed in Chapter 1. Note also that households beginning adulthood with positive assets (not shown) would have less need of precautionary savings and should experience slower consumption growth early in life.

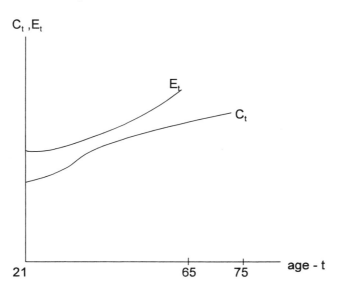

Figure 2.8 Age-consumption profile with uncertain earnings

This model also has implications for the life-cycle pattern of the marginal propensities to consume from current-period windfalls. Following Deaton (1992), we term the sum of current-year earnings and assets (all financial and relatively liquid real assets) cash-on-hand. With a precautionary saving motive, there is a strong negative relationship between cash-on-hand and the marginal propensity to consume. Cash-on-hand is low for most households early in the life cycle. At that time, intense precautionary motives serve to keep consumption painfully low out of the fear of an unfavorable income draw in the next period(s). However, while the marginal utility of current consumption is quite high, the marginal utility of future consumption in the low-probability "bad states of the world" is much higher: Should the worst earnings possibilities occur, future consumption would be minuscule since, to date, very few assets have been accumulated. In this context, a positive windfall can be largely consumed and still satisfy a many-period version of (2.5). The marginal propensity to consume is high because, with convex marginal utility, saving even a little will dramatically lower the marginal utility in those potential future contexts in which the worst earnings luck has transpired.

Since consumption rises quickly early in life, the marginal utility of current consumption falls rapidly. For this reason, the marginal propensity to consume falls as well. The consumption propensity ceases to decline once the target buffer stock of assets is achieved, and consumption growth moderates. Then, the forces associated with the finiteness of life begin to dominate. Recall from Chapter 1 that, when earnings are certain, the marginal propensity to consume is 1 divided by the number of years of life remaining (abstracting from interest and pure time preference). Thus, with twenty years of remaining life, a household would spend an extra 5 cents in the current year if it unexpectedly received an extra dollar. The marginal propensity to consume in the last year of life, assuming death is certain that year, is 1. The pattern of marginal propensities to consume associated with this story is depicted in Figure 2.9. Naturally, consumers beginning life with positive assets enjoy more cash-on-hand and are expected to have lower consumption propensities when young.

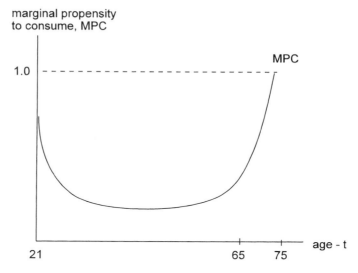

Figure 2.9 Marginal propensity to consume (MPC)

2.2.2 Empirical Evidence Concerning Precautionary Saving

In Chapter 1 we stressed that households accumulate assets during the working years, then use that "hump wealth" to finance retirement consumption. Above we noted that households facing serious earnings risk engage in precautionary saving to self-insure against the possibility that future earnings prove low. Economists attempting to estimate the contribution of precautionary saving to total wealth accumulation face numerous problems. First, since some variability in earnings is surely anticipated, it is difficult to know how much uncertainty the consumer faces. Further, informal support networks of friends and family provide a measure of insurance that is hard for the researcher to gauge. Another problem is that the theory doesn't automatically imply that those with greater earnings uncertainty should have higher precautionary savings. This is because those with riskier earnings, such as the self-employed, may have self-selected into those professions on the basis of a higher tolerance for risk in general (cf. Skinner, 1988). And, unfortunately, there is little consensus among economists regarding the determinants of consumer preferences. Finally, if one is examining how wealth levels vary with objective measures of uncertainty, which measure of wealth should be employed? For example, does the existence of home equity loans mean housing wealth should be included? Does the substantial penalty for early withdrawal mean that IRAs should be excluded?

Carroll and Samwick (1998) examine the empirical relationship between observed income variability and wealth. They estimate that much of the wealth held by prime working-age consumers may be attributable to precautionary saving. According to their estimates, precautionary motives may account for up to 40 percent of aggregate wealth holdings. Since observed income variability overstates true uncertainty, their estimates surely constitute an upper bound. In fact, most empirical studies conclude that precautionary saving plays a far less important role in aggregate wealth accumulation. To overcome the problem of not knowing what part of observed earnings variability is truly uncertain, some researchers have employed subjective measures of earnings variability. Viewing observed wealth as a function of such measures, Lusardi (1997) concludes that the precautionary motive explains 13% of wealth accumulation. Using yet other empirical approaches, some researchers (cf. Skinner, 1988) find little evidence of precautionary saving.

The empirical problems noted above have prompted some economists to employ simulation methods. Initially, one might think that the contribution of precautionary savings to total savings should increase strongly with the strength of the precautionary motive in the consumer's preferences. However, general-equilibrium simulations by Lord and Rangazas (1998) employing the CES preferences of section 2.1 find that the effect of uncertainty on *total* savings doesn't vary much (at a bit less than 2% of GDP) regardless of the extent of risk aversion. This is in spite of the fact that when risk aversion is higher, so is the *proportion* of total savings owed to the precautionary motive. The reconciliation of these findings is due to the inverse relationship between tolerance for risk and the intertemporal elasticity of substitution of consumption, σ, for CES preferences. In fact, the link between σ and one measure of the tolerance for risk is exact: the coefficient of relative risk aversion is exactly $1/\sigma$. (Since σ is a parameter in the CES utility function, those preferences exhibit constant relative risk aversion (CRRA)).

To appreciate that relationship, recall equation (2.2), which shows that consumption growth with certain earnings depends only upon r, m, and σ (which mediates the tug of war between r and m). With uncertainty, consumption growth increases with the strength of the precautionary motive. For CES preferences, when risk aversion—and thus the precautionary saving motive—is strong, σ is low. If σ is low, the marginal utility of consumption falls rapidly, requiring a relatively flat consumption profile under certainty—there is a large utility cost if consumption is not kept "smooth." Viewing uncertainty alone, to avoid those costs requires significant precautionary saving, which produces faster consumption growth. Thus, the implications of low σ for consumption growth under certainty are the opposite of those under uncertainty.

This is why the total saving rate in Lord and Rangazas' simulations is not much affected by the value of σ. For a given excess of the interest rate over the rate of time preference, the lower is σ, the slower is consumption growth over the life cycle under certainty. This entails lower planned retirement consumption, which reduces desired hump wealth. Conversely, low σ implies high risk aversion, higher precautionary savings, and faster consumption growth while working (in a large cross section of households where luck averages out). Consequently, the lower is σ, the higher are precautionary savings but the lower are retirement savings. For this reason, that elasticity affected primarily the shares of saving due to each saving motive, and had much less impact on the total saving rate.

Precautionary Saving and/or Liquidity-constrained Households?

We now have two explanations regarding the tracking of earnings by consumption in the early portion of the life cycle, the precautionary saving motive, and, as discussed in Chapter 1, liquidity constraints. Unfortunately, as Carroll (2000, p. 19) notes, "(t)he implications of precautionary saving and liquidity constraints for consumption growth are virtually indistinguishable. The reason is that the precautionary motive reduces consumption in precisely the same circumstances as a liquidity constraint would: when cash-on-hand is low. Precautionary saving is in essence like a self-imposed, "smoothed" liquidity constraint" (p. 19). However, an exogenous increase in the supply of credit would seem to increase consumption by more if consumers are liquidity constrained than if they are voluntarily restricting current consumption. Along these lines, Gross and Souleles (2000) employ a data base containing credit report information on a representative sample of consumers. They find that exogenous increases in households' credit limits lead to similarly sized increases in the households' debt burdens. This particular study therefore suggests that at least some of the tracking of earnings by consumption early in the life cycle may be associated with borrowing restrictions. A model featuring both precautionary saving and explicit borrowing constraints may be more realistic than models featuring either in isolation (cf. Deaton, 1991).

Again viewing precautionary saving in isolation, changes in the extent of earnings variability households have faced over time should affect the amount of such saving. Along these lines, family labor supply and composition have undergone dramatic changes in recent decades. As a consequence of the rise in female labor force participation, examined in Chapter 8, more families have two earners, which reduces the variability of family income. Conversely, the increase in the probability of divorce over this same period has made family income (and especially family consumption) less certain, perhaps increasing precautionary saving (cf. Cubeddy and Ríos Rull, 1997). Government programs such as Unemployment Insurance, Social Security, Medicaid, and Medicare all reduce uncertainty over consumption, reducing precautionary saving. The rapid growth in such programs since the 1960s provides one explanation for the decline in savings discussed in Chapter 1. We now consider such interactions between government policy and precautionary saving in more detail.

2.2.3 Policy Applications of Precautionary Saving

The existence of a precautionary saving motive has important implications for tax and transfer policies. By offering a degree of earnings insurance, such policies reduce the amount of precautionary saving. We also explain why the response of saving to the interest rate, and thus interest income taxation, is altered by earnings uncertainty.

Tax and Transfer Policies

Many government tax and transfer programs provide "social insurance," because they redistribute income from some people's realized good state of the world to other people's realized bad state of the world. For this reason, welfare programs are plagued by the problem of moral hazard. That is, since the household knows the bad income state is partially insured, it may take actions—such as increasing leisure or otherwise reducing effort—which end up increasing the probability of the bad income state occurring. To illustrate, suppose there is no moral hazard problem and that everyone is identical in period 1. Then consumers differ only with respect to their "market luck" in period 2, when they gain or lose $x. Under these assumptions, the optimal social policy would be full insurance: The government should simply impose a tax of $x on those in the good state and transfer it to those in the bad state. Then second-period income (net of taxes and transfers) would be guaranteed; earnings would be effectively fully insured. The fact that this policy proposal sounds disastrous suggests that work incentives must be taken seriously in the design of transfer programs. We address these issues in Chapter 8. In this section we simply assume private insurance is unavailable.

Even in the absence of work-incentive problems, redistributive programs affect behavior in the presence of a precautionary saving motive. The full insurance policy considered above, for example, eliminates earnings uncertainty, and thus the need for precautionary saving. In fact, many tax and transfer policies offer a measure of earnings insurance, thereby reducing precautionary saving and increasing expected utility.

Notably, both progressive and proportional income taxation have an insurance component whenever the tax proceeds are redistributed equally. This point warrants a specific example. Assume there are initially no taxes and that first-period income is $E_1 = 15$. Second-period earnings are uncertain; they equal $E_2^B = E_2^c - x = 15 - 6 = 9$ in the bad state of the world, or $E_2^G = E_2^c + x = 15 + 6 = 21$ when luck is favorable. With the probability of each state equaling .5, expected second-period earnings are just $(.5)9 + (.5)21 = 15$. Assuming the interest rate is zero, expected life wealth is just 30, the sum of the certain first-period earnings and the expected second-period earnings.

Now suppose taxes are cut on those currently young by 5, with the cut financed by newly issued government bonds. In the next period taxes are to be raised on those old (the same cohort receiving the tax cut) by just enough to retire the newly issued bonds. Assume the taxes levied on the old are *proportional* to second-period earnings. Notice that if each person's income risk is independent of the luck of others, aggregate second-period pretax income will average each person's expected earnings of 15. Then a second-period tax rate equal to one-third of income raises taxes by an average of 5 per person, as required to pay off the bonds. The tax cut raises first-period after-tax income to 20. Second-period after-tax income becomes $9(1 - 1/3) = 6$ in the bad state, or $21(2/3) = 14$ when market luck is good. Expected second-period after-tax income is therefore 10. (Notice that expected life wealth is unchanged at 30.) Nevertheless, precautionary saving will fall since the variability of second-period consumption has been reduced.

To see this, suppose the household just saves the tax cut, leaving C_1 unchanged. The effect on C_2 in each state is then the difference between the increased savings and the second-period tax liabilities. Bad-state income rises: Second-period taxes are $(1/3)9 = 3$ but, since savings increased by 5, second-period resources and consumption are higher by 2. On the other hand, taxes are $(1/3)21 = 7$ in the good state so, net of the additional savings, good-state consumption *falls* by 2. Thus, holding C_1 constant, the variability in C_2 has been reduced. Facing less risk, the consumer will reduce precautionary saving and C_1 will rise.[4] At the macroeconomic level, this policy is initially expansionary in the sense that aggregate consumption rises in the period of the tax cut. Effectively, this tax plan shifts resources from the good to the bad state, providing a measure of insurance unavailable from the private sector. Alternatively expressed, the policy increases the portion of expected life wealth that is received with certainty.

As a second example, proportional taxes are again levied on earnings in period two, making taxes paid lower in the bad state than in the good state. Suppose now, though, that the tax revenues raised are simply redistributed equally in lump-sum fashion in period two (that is, those with high and low income get the same transfer). Browning and Johnson (1984) refer to this as a demo-grant policy, and argue that it is a pretty good description of the government's operations.[5] Under this policy, lump-sum transfers exceed taxes paid for low income or bad-state households, while the opposite is true for good-state households. This policy also narrows the distribution of second-period earnings, net of taxes and transfers. Once again, the tax system has provided insurance that will lower precautionary saving.

The policies above are based on *income* levels. Almost all transfer programs are means tested in this sense. Many types of social insurance, such as Medicaid and (the now eliminated welfare program) Aid to Families with Dependent Children, also base eligibility on *asset* holdings. For example, in 1993 to be eligible for AFDC, tangible assets, excluding a home and car, could not exceed $1,000. The benefit rules tax the accumulated assets of those with bad market luck, discouraging such accumulation. To see this, consider a consumer who suffers a bad "shock" to earnings that may be expected to persist (the onset of a chronic back problem, for example). Earnings now will be low, but assets may remain high due to accumulation when earnings were better. Suppose that further bad luck (failed back surgery) would qualify the consumer for Medicaid on the basis of income alone, but that current assets are too high for eligibility. Contemplating his or her plight, the consumer recognizes the incentive to run down assets so the asset test can also be satisfied.

Hubbard, Skinner, and Zeldes (1995) employ such arguments to explain why many poor people are not pure life-cycle savers in the sense that their assets remain low even as retirement approaches. They simulate a life-cycle model that features both uncertainty and social insurance programs, including the asset test for eligibility. Hubbard et al. find that consumers with average to good income behave much as the life-cycle model would predict, with assets increasing appreciably before the onset of retirement. On the other hand, those with poor earnings accumulate few assets before retirement (even relative to their lower earnings). The authors argue that the poor's low accumulation is due to the very high penalty or tax on accumulated wealth for those ultimately entering welfare programs. For a person would have to spend down assets to $1,000 immediately, rather than smooth consumption optimally, if he or she wanted to enter these programs. Since the probability of entering a program may be fairly high if one is currently poor, it makes more sense to keep wealth low and spread consumption across time than to splurge just before entering the program, should further bad luck arise. Significantly, this test applies to all family assets. Consequently, a dependent teenager could not, for example, save much money from a part-time job for college tuition without sacrificing family eligibility for welfare aid.

Interest Income Taxation, Saving, and Uncertainty

Relative to certainty models, precautionary saving models predict a weaker positive response of saving to the interest rate. There are two reasons for this. First, consider someone with positive savings at the initial interest rate. A higher interest rate will increase highly valued bad-state interest income, reducing the need for precautionary saving. This effect, relative to the certainty case, implies a lower response of saving to a reduction in interest income taxation. As discussed in Chapter 1 where earnings were certain, an increase in r lowers the present value of earnings (human wealth), thereby reducing C_1 and increasing saving. As we now explain, this human wealth effect is diminished by earnings uncertainty, which is the second reason uncertainty weakens any positive response of saving to the interest rate.

The precautionary saving motive induces young households to consume less when earnings are uncertain than when expected earnings are received with certainty. Alternatively expressed, the same C_1 chosen in the presence of uncertainty would also be chosen if income was certain but life wealth was somewhat lower. We shall label as the *certain lifewealth equivalent* (CLE) that certain wealth that leads to the same C_1 as that chosen in the presence of uncertainty.[6] Intuitively, the CLE is below expected wealth because the consumer effectively discounts good-state income at a higher rate than under certainty, focusing more on the bad-state possibilities. Thus, an increase in the variability of earnings (with expected earnings unchanged) lowers both first-period consumption and the CLE. This has clear implications for the response of saving to the interest rate. Relative to the certainty case, distant uncertain earnings are heavily discounted, so that current consumption is based primarily on financial assets and current earnings. Since future earnings are only a modest part of the consumer's effective portfolio, reductions in human wealth from an increase in r do not lower the CLE by very much. Consequently, there is little effect on C_1 or saving. (In the unrealistic case where the consumer completely disregards uncertain future earnings when choosing C_1, the human wealth effect is zero!) More generally, the human wealth effect is lowered by earnings uncertainty, weakening the positive response of saving to the interest rate.

For the two reasons discussed above, the positive influences on saving of a higher interest rate are weakened by a precautionary saving motive. Consequently, uninsurable earnings risk reduces any increase in private saving that may result from lowering the rate of tax on interest income. Engen (1992) demonstrates these results using an extensive simulation model that includes earnings uncertainty. His model produces interest elasticities of saving that are much lower than in otherwise similar models where income is certain.

2.2.4   Earnings Uncertainty and Life-Cycle Portfolio Decisions

Suppose that in addition to earnings uncertainty, the household must decide how to allocate its financial assets over the life cycle between a risk-free and a risky asset. In doing so, the household takes into account that future labor earnings are another asset type that has its own risk characteristics. If labor income is broadly defined to include unemployment compensation and other social insurance programs, there is a nontrivial floor to labor income. This floor constitutes a riskless asset and tends to make labor earnings altogether somewhat less risky than stocks. Cocco, Gomes, and Maenhout (1999) note that as the consumer ages and the remaining years of employment decline, so does the magnitude of safe earnings. This induces the rational consumer to reduce the share of equities (stock) in his or her financial portfolio later in the life cycle.

Carroll (2000) points out that models incorporating both earnings uncertainty and portfolio choice have difficulty simultaneously matching stylized facts regarding the age-consumption and age-portfolio profiles. In particular, "unless one assumes an enormous coefficient of relative risk aversion, a model which matches consumption facts over the life cycle reasonably well implies that 100 percent of the household's portfolio of liquid assets should be held in stocks" (p. 29). He notes that this is just the microeconomic manifestation of the extremely large historical gap between returns to safe assets, such as short-term government debt, and the stock market. The inconsistency of the size of that gap with empirical estimates of risk aversion has come to be known as the *Equity-Premium Puzzle* (Mehra and Prescott, 1985). To appreciate the puzzle, recall that the coefficient of relative risk aversion is $1/\sigma$ for CES preferences. On the basis of the estimates of σ discussed in section 2.1, suppose that $\sigma = .5$. This produces a coefficient of relative risk aversion equal to 2. In contrast, D. Romer (1996) reviews the literature and suggests that in order to reconcile the historical equity premium, the coefficient of relative risk aversion must equal *at least* 25.

In the framework developed thus far, individuals concerned only with their own life-cycle consumption have two distinct saving motives. When young, they engage in precautionary saving, building up a buffer stock of assets to hedge against financial misfortune. As they age, they become more concerned about retirement and build up hump wealth to finance retirement consumption. These considerations imply rapidly rising consumption among those in the early working years, with consumption later tracking income closely until perhaps the early 40s. Then retirement saving commences in earnest, driving consumption somewhat below income. We now consider how uncertainty about the length of life affects consumption and asset holdings in retirement.

2.3 UNCERTAINTY ABOUT AGE AT DEATH

In the models discussed so far, assets are brought into retirement to finance a given number of years of retirement consumption. However, the age at death is not known with certainty. This may have important implications for consumption and asset holdings late in life. We first review the certainty results. Consider again the multiperiod consumption problem where income is certain and the rates of time preference and interest both equal zero, making for constant annual consumption. The individual retires at age R and dies at age T. If assets at the start of period $R + 1$ are A_{R+1}, then optimal consumption over the rest of life would simply be A_{R+1} divided by the number of retirement years, $T - R$ (continuing to assume $r = m = 0$). Thus,

$$C_t = A_{R+1}/(T - R) = C^* \text{ for } t = R + 1, \ldots, T \tag{2.7}$$

Suppose instead that the length of retirement is uncertain but that the expected life span is T (cf. Davies, 1981). Now, if one continued to follow the policy described in (2.7), consumption would fall to zero if one were lucky enough to live beyond T. Conversely, if death occurred at the end of period $R + 1$, say, most of the retirement assets would go unconsumed. Assets at death would be an "accidental bequest" to heirs of the descendant (intentional bequests are addressed in Chapter 5). In section 2.2 we saw that consumers confronted with uncertainty maximize expected utility. How would an expected utility maximizing agent improve upon C^* when the length of life is uncertain?

Before answering, we need to know whether the uncertainty is insurable. Suppose consumers can insure against the possibility of outliving their assets. Such insurance would take the form of an end-of-life annuity. That is, it would pay the retiree a constant amount, or *annuity*, each year until the person dies, regardless of age at death. To see how this might work, suppose an insurance company is willing to just break even on the coverage. Such a policy would then be a "fair bet" or actuarially fair. If actuarially fair rest-of-life annuities were available, the constant consumption C* of (2.7) could be achieved regardless of life's length. To appreciate this, assume everyone has an expected lifetime of T years. Then on a policy costing the consumer A_{R+1}, the insurance company could provide C* each year, with the money made on those dying young just offsetting the losses on those living to old ages. In this way, one could insure against the possibility of living "too long" (relative to one's resources) and annual consumption of C* would remain optimal.[7]

Private rest-of-life annuities are available but are somewhat more expensive than if actuarially fair. In fact, they are purchased by few individuals (cf. Hurd, 1997). Possible reasons include adverse selection (only those with high life expectancies would purchase policies, which drives up their price), utility from bequests left to heirs (which reduces their attractiveness), and the fact—discussed below—that Social Security and private pensions already imply a substantial amount of annuitization of retirement resources.

Consequently, we now examine the optimal age-consumption and age-wealth plan assuming market insurance is unattractive. First, simplify the problem by assuming that the longest one can possibly live is T* periods, and that the consumer is starting period T* − 1 now. Thus, the only question is whether the consumer will die at the end of period T* − 1, or live through period T*. Suppose the consumer knows the probability of dying at the end of period T* − 1 is p, making the probability of living until the end of period T* equal to 1 − p. Further, since the probability of dying within a year generally rises with age, p < 1 − p.

Recall from section 2.2 that the optimality condition in the presence of uncertainty equates the expected marginal utility of consumption across periods. Here, the certain marginal utility in T* − 1 must be equated to the expected marginal utility of consumption in T*

$$u_{T*-1}(C_{T*-1}) = \mathbf{E}_{T*-1}u_{T*}(C_{T*}) = (1-p)\,u_{T*}(C_{T*}) + p(0) = (1-p)u_{T*}(C_{T*}) \quad (2.8)$$

where $\mathbf{E}_{T*-1}$ are expectations at the start of period T* − 1.

There are several things to note about this expression. First, the utility from consumption in T* − 1 is certain; we have already made it to the start of T* − 1 and the earliest we can die (by assumption) is at the end of T* − 1. Second, if we are dead in period T*, with probability p, we get no utility from the assets carried into T*. Thus, with diminishing marginal utility C_{T*} must be less than C_{T*-1} in order that $u_{T*-1} = (1-p)u_{T*}$. That is, consumption is predicted to fall during retirement. Intuitively, we make a consumption plan for which consumption is highest when we are most likely to be alive, but which preserves some assets so that consumption doesn't get "too low" if we live to a ripe old age. Thus, an increase in the probability of death at a future point will lead to increased current consumption. In this sense mortality risk affects choices between present and future consumption the same way the rate of pure time preference does.

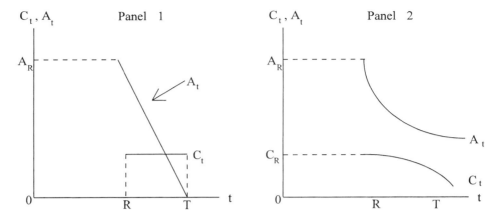

Figure 2.10 Retirement consumption: when age at death is known (Panel I) and when age at death is not known (Panel 2)

The multiperiod story is now easily told. Panel 1 of Figure 2.10 graphs the optimal solution when the age of death is certain: Assets A_t decline at a constant rate from R to T and C_t is constant. In Panel 2 with uncertainty, optimal consumption contingent upon surviving to each age declines with age. In fact, consumption declines at an increasing rate. This faster decline in old age is due to increasing probabilities of death at old ages. For the probability that a 65-year-old will be alive when 66 greatly exceeds the probability that an 85-year-old will be alive when 86; thus the relative decline in consumption between 85 and 86 is predicted to exceed that between 65 and 66. This implies that wealth decumulation slows as one ages. (In practice, with positive interest rates, private pensions, and Social Security, the shape of the age-wealth profile is harder to discern.) Recall Figure 2.8 that showed the predicted age-consumption profile in the presence of earnings uncertainty and certain age of death. The results above indicate that uncertainty of time of death causes this profile to grow less rapidly, or tilt downward, in the later years of life. This improves the fit of the predicted profile with empirical profiles. Figure 2.9, which shows the marginal propensity to consume from windfalls at each age, is now revised to stay below 1 at every age, since a person usually does not know which year will be the last. Similar reasoning suggests the marginal propensity to consume at all advanced ages is lower than suggested by the figure.

The empirical evidence on wealth and consumption during retirement is in broad agreement with these predictions. For example, Hurd (1997) examines panel data for the consumption of retirees from the Retirement History Survey. He finds that on average their consumption fell by a total of 38% over a 10-year period, 1969–1979. Using the same data set he finds total dissaving over the 10 years of 36% for singles and 15% for couples. One reason couples decumulate less rapidly may be that the effective horizon for a couple (when the surviving spouse dies) exceeds that for a single person.

As noted in Chapter 1, Dynan et al. find that the affluent do little, if any, dissaving even in old age. This suggests that many affluent households plan to leave a bequest. In contrast, Hurd (1999) constructs an explicit model of wealth holding for couples facing uncertain mortality and concludes that observed decumulation is consistent with an absence of intentional bequests. We consider this further in Chapter 5.

2.3.1 A Rationale for Social Security?

The U.S. Social Security system has redistributed large amounts of money from those now young to those now old and to those who have died within the last several decades (see Chapter 4). The current configuration of the program also significantly redistributes from the more to the less affluent within a generation (see section 1.4). These significant redistributions could well be accomplished by other programs.

One justification for a fully funded, actuarially fair Social Security system derives from its ability to provide something the private sector can't. We noted above that due to problems of adverse selection, privately supplied rest-of-life annuities are not available at anything near actuarially fair prices. Social Security payments continue until death, and thus payroll taxes effectively purchase the consumer an annuity (often at poor rates of return). Since Social Security is a national program with compulsory participation, there is virtually no adverse selection problem.[8]

2.4 HABIT FORMATION

The satisfaction derived from current consumption may depend upon the consumption level to which one is accustomed. For this reason, we develop a simple model of habit formation and examine the implications for the optimal life-cycle consumption plan; we also discuss the limited empirical evidence.

We continue to abstract from market interest and time preference, $r = m = 0$, so that the age-consumption profile would be flat without "habits." Recall the consumer's preferences employed in the precautionary savings story, repeated here:

$$U = u(C_1) + u(C_2) \qquad (2.4)$$

In this additively separable case, the enjoyment received from consumption in one period is independent of the amount consumed in any other period. (Formally, $du_1/dC_2 = u_{12} = u_{21} = du_2/dC_1 = 0$.)

There are many ways in which habitual preferences can and have been modeled (cf. Deaton, 1992). We pursue a simple specification that has proven useful in recent empirical work (Dynan, 2000). Here second-period utility depends positively upon C_2 but negatively upon C_1:

$$U = u^1(C_1) + u^2(C_1, C_2) = u^1(C_1) + u^2(C_2 - \gamma C_1) \qquad (2.10)$$

where γ is positive.[9] The amount consumed in the first period now affects the enjoyment of second-period consumption. In contrast, the amount consumed in the second period does not affect the enjoyment from consumption in the first period. For this reason, the "within-period" utility functions are no longer identical, and are superscripted by the period. Since first-period consumption imposes a drag on second-period satisfactions, the "effective consumption" in period two is $C_2 - \gamma C_1$. The within-period utility functions *are* identical in effective consumption. That is, if $C_1 = C_2 - \gamma C_1$, then $u^1 = u^2$. Due to diminishing marginal utility in effective consumption, the u^1 and u^2 functions increase at a decreasing rate.

The first-period utility function is the same whether or not there are habits. However, habits reduce the marginal effect of C_1 on life-cycle utility by lowering the second-period utility associated with any amount of C_2. Intuitively, my first-period consumption level has conditioned me to a particular lifestyle that spoils my experience of a low second-period consumption level.

This is formalized by denoting the (life-cycle) marginal utility of C_1 by $MU_1 = u^1_1 + u^2_1$. Here, u^1_1 is the positive effect of C_1 on first-period satisfactions while u^2_1 is the negative effect, or drag, of C_1 on second-period satisfactions. Note that the higher is γ the stronger is the effect of habits. (If $\gamma = 0$ we just have a fancy way of writing (2.4)).

We previously assumed that u^2 is concave, or has diminishing marginal utility in effective second-period consumption, $C_2 - \gamma C_1$. Since this effective consumption is lower the higher is C_1, the marginal utility of second-period consumption measured in natural units, C_2, increases with C_1. Intuitively, if my early years are gluttonous, moderate consumption in later life will seem like deprivation, making me very desirous of a few more amenities while old.

Summarizing, habits lower the marginal utility of first-period consumption MU_1 and raise the marginal utility of second-period consumption u^2_2. Since the $MRS_{1,2}$ is the ratio of these marginal utilities, MU_1/u^2_2, it is reduced by habits. Graphically, this makes indifference curves with habits less steep than those without habits. This is illustrated in Figure 2.11 where at consumption bundle A the MRS is smaller along the indifference curve with habits U_H than along U_N without habits.

Fortunately, the preceding makes it easy to determine the effect of habits on the utility-maximizing consumption bundle. Suppose the consumer's budget line is given by BD. Then, when there are no habits, utility is maximized at N. Since preferences are identical in each period, consumption is equal at $C^N_1 = C^N_2$. However, if preferences embody

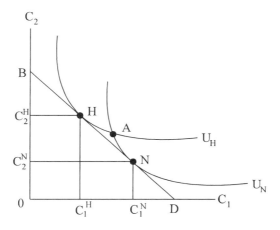

Figure 2.11 Effect of habits on marginal utility of consumption

habits, utility is maximized at H where $C_2^H > C_1^H$. Thus, when the consumer is young, habits postpone consumption so as to cushion the damaging effect on utility later in life.

Clearly, increasing the number of periods would not affect the basic argument. Consequently, habits steepen the life-cycle consumption profile. In this way, habits have an effect similar to *reducing* the rate of time preference. Also, with certain income and no borrowing constraints, habits will not lead to a violation of the life wealth hypothesis: the timing of consumption will remain invariant to the timing of income. Recall that one challenge to the life-cycle model is the close tracking of income by consumption over the life cycle. Since income typically rises rapidly while one is young, so does consumption. Since habits, liquidity constraints, uncertainty, and increases in family size all increase consumption growth, there is certainly no shortage of explanations for why consumption growth is rapid among young households.

Research aimed at determining the importance of habits has begun only in recent years. In one prominent study, Dynan (2000) estimates a model of habit formation based on preferences like those of (2.10). Using household data on life-cycle food consumption from the Panel Study of Income Dynamics (PSID), she finds little evidence of habit formation. However, her important results are far from conclusive: The popular estimation procedure she employs (based on the Euler equation) has recently been subject to substantial criticism (cf. Carroll, 1997b); it is unclear that total consumption has the same structure of habits as food consumption; and, if there is any systemic measurement error of food consumption in the data, her estimates are biased against finding evidence of habits. It may be that many goods physically consumed within a year nevertheless have durable goods features: The memories of a pleasant vacation, for example, may last a lifetime. Then, the combined effect of "memory goods" and habitual consumption may balance out in the aggregate, though each is important within its class of goods.

Less formally, Carroll, Overland, and Weil (2000) marshal evidence that fast macroeconomic growth within a country induces an increase in the saving rate. This is somewhat puzzling if households have the standard CES preferences since, if earnings growth over the life cycle is expected to be fast, human wealth is large relative to earnings when young. Higher wealth increases the consumption and reduces the saving of the young, which implies that expected growth should decrease saving. However, Carroll et al. show that a growth model featuring consumers with habitual preferences is capable of explaining causation running from growth to savings. In conclusion, although intuition and informal evidence suggest a role for habits, early econometric analysis has found little evidence of habits.

2.5 SUMMARY

This chapter has tied up several loose ends from Chapter 1. First, we have shown how use of more general CES preferences allows for a greater range of substitutibility between consumption in different periods, enabling a fuller account of the relationship between the interest rate and saving. This relationship was also studied in more general environments (initial assets and future earnings) and in light of specific policies. Another major extension considered how uncertainty alters the optimal consumption plan. Earnings uncertainty was found to increase the weight placed on current income, increase saving when young, and increase the rate of growth of consumption over the life cycle (in a cross section of consumers where luck has averaged out). Therefore, earnings uncertainty provides an alternative explanation for the fast growth of consumption in the early years of the life cycle, when it appears to track income "too closely" to be consistent with the simple certainty model of Chapter 1. Tax and transfer policies were shown to have insurance effects that may alter the amount of precautionary saving. Similarly, consumption decay and incomplete asset decumulation are easily understood once it is acknowledged that length of life is uncertain. A final section showed that the observed fast consumption growth of the young may also be, in part, due to preferences for a habitual level of consumption.

The amount of assets left at death by affluent households appears inconsistent with simple planning for a retirement of uncertain length. To better understand these estates, in Chapter 5 we consider intentional bequests. More generally, to this point we have paid little attention to the economic consequences of family units. Nor have we considered any form of consumption aside from market goods. Beginning in Chapter 5, the consumer's problem is gradually expanded to include other family members and goods beyond those for sale in conventional markets.

ENDNOTES

1. My understanding of the materials in this chapter was deepened by interactions with Chris Carroll, to whom I am grateful.

2. Let μ_0 be the tax rate in the year contributions are made. Suppose Y pretax dollars of income are put into a Roth IRA (i.e., $(1 - \mu_0)Y$ after-tax dollars of income). If these monies are withdrawn upon retirement T years later, the amount of after-tax assets would be $[(1 - \mu_0)Y](1 + r)^T$. Conversely, in a qualified account with deductibility, after T years there would be $[Y(1 + r)^T](1 - \mu_\tau)$, where μ_T is the individual's rate of income taxation in the year of withdrawal. If $\mu_T < \mu_0$, deductibility reduces taxes.

3. I have drawn u_{22} concave, which maintains risk aversion ($u_{22} < 0$) at high C_2, but a positively sloped linear u_{22} function would also have worked.

4. Consider the implications for national savings, the sum of private and government, or public, savings. Since C_1 increases, private savings rise by less than the tax cut, with the difference being the reduction in precautionary savings. On the other hand, government savings are reduced by the entire tax cut. Consequently, national savings fall. Lower savings slow capital accumulation and, consequently, the wages of workers. Therefore, although the micro-level effect of insurance is to increase welfare, this may be overturned once the effects on capital accumulation are taken into account.

5. Equivalently, suppose that government programs, goods and services, are perfect substitutes for private sector goods, and that all income brackets get the same amount of government services.

6. Note this differs from the certainty equivalent discussed in the appendix to this chapter for timeless risk. There the certainty equivalent was the certain current wealth producing the same *utility* as the lottery. The CLE is the certain intertemporal wealth producing the same first-period *behavior* as the uncertain earnings prospect.

7. We usually think of insurance as converting an uncertain financial prospect into a certain one; an insurance policy is purchased that promises to rebuild a house if it burns. With a rest-of-life annuity, though, a certain sum of money is exchanged for an uncertain prospect: the up-front premium purchases a policy that pays little if death is soon but a large amount if the insured lives a long time. Thus, in one sense life annuities are "reverse insurance." Nevertheless, they are clearly insurance in the decisive sense that the risk of living too long relative to one's resources is eliminated.

8. Bernheim (1991) explains that if parents desire to leave a bequest to their children, Social Security may force some parents to *over*annuitize their retirement wealth. That is, if there were perfectly functioning private annuities markets and no Social Security, the amount of wealth some parents would choose to annuitize would be less than that required by the Social Security program. Such parents would prefer to retain more of their assets in liquid form, so that their heirs would benefit upon their death. One way to increase bequests would be to increase purchases of term life insurance. Since the elderly have little income risk, such purchases of insurance would indicate a desire to leave more assets at death. The premiums for these policies would effectively reduce annual annuity income. However, Auerbach and Kotlikoff (1998, p. 420) report that life insurance protection among the elderly relative to remaining life resources declined between 1960 and 1990—even though the proportion of total resources that are in annuitized form, such as Social Security and many private pensions, increased.

9. It is worth noting that letting $\gamma < 0$ produces a model of durable goods. Durable goods purchased in period one increase the second-period utility associated with any amount of purchases in the second-period. A car is clearly a durable good, while a great vacation may qualify if meaningful memories prove persistent.

QUESTIONS AND PROBLEMS

▶ REVIEW
QUESTIONS

1. **A.** Why is the value of elasticity of substitution in consumption important to discussions regarding changing the rate of income taxation and/or altering the features of personal retirement savings plans, such as IRAs?
   B. How and why does the value of the interest rate affect human wealth?
   C. Summarize briefly the effects for the interest elasticity of savings of (a) increasing the elasticity of substitution, (b) allowing for future earnings, (c) allowing for initial assets.
   D. Why does the magnitude of the overall wealth effect of an interest rate change depend upon the timing of income over the life cycle and on the rate of time preference?

2. Summarize the recent research regarding the effects on private saving, national saving, and welfare of tax-preferred saving plans. For private saving, does the effect seem to differ by income level? Do the effects on private portfolio composition seem to vary by income level?

3. **A.** What is precautionary saving? What assumptions are necessary to produce a precautionary saving motive?
   B. Explain how various government policies might affect saving by changing the degree of individual income uncertainty.

C. Why might the magnitude of the human wealth effect differ in the presence of uncertainty, as opposed to when earnings are certain?

4. A. The simple life-cycle model (unadjusted for family demographics) has difficulty explaining the close parallel between average consumption and average earnings over much of the working life. Does acknowledging that future earnings are uncertain help in this regard?

B. For policy purposes, does it matter whether family demographics or earnings uncertainty is the true explanation for that parallel?

C. The simple life-cycle model has difficulty explaining the observed level of aggregate saving. Does introducing precautionary saving help to explain aggregate saving?

5. It is possible that in some working years income equals, or is close to, zero. With risk aversion, marginal utility approaches infinity in year t as C_t approaches zero. Let $A_1 = 0$ and consider an age-earnings profile with a positive slope throughout the working years. Assuming $r = m = 0$, what will the optimal consumption profile look like when the life wealth hypothesis holds? How about if one can't borrow against future income to finance current consumption? Sketch the C_t profile (for an average of households) in the presence of not only borrowing constraints, but also uncertain earnings and $u_{222} > 0$. Explain your picture.

6. A. If parents derive utility from their children's consumption, how might that affect the size of parent's optimal actuarially fair retirement annuity?

B. A retirement annuity takes a certain sum of money, say A_R, and converts it into an uncertain amount, since the number of years payments will be made is uncertain. In that sense it is "reverse insurance." In what sense is this insurance?

7. Assume $r = m = 0$ and that there is life span uncertainty.

A. Why would one choose *not* to follow the same constant consumption plan that would be chosen were the date of death known for sure?

B. Why would the average retiree be made better off if private actuarially fair end-of-life annuities were available?

C. Explain the predicted shape of the age-consumption profile when the date of death is uncertain and end-of-life annuities are not available. Is this supported by the evidence? How does this predicted profile compare with that if life's length is certain?

D. How would sizeable Social Security and private pension plans affect your answer to C)?

8. At the household level, savings need to be adequate to finance retirement consumption, smooth consumption in the face of uneven income, or provide a buffer against unexpected negative shocks to income or necessary expenditures. At the macroeconomic level, as developed in Chapters 3 and 4, savings finance business investment in plant and equipment, thereby increasing worker productivity. This chapter has mentioned several policies that might increase private saving. Summarize these policies and discuss their strengths and weaknesses.

▶ PROBLEMS

1. A. Consider the quadratic utility function, $U = a + b(C_1 + C_2) - d(C_1^2 + C_2^2)$, where b and d are both positive. Recall that $u_{22} < 0$ was sufficient for risk aversion and for people to purchase actuarially fair full insurance. Precautionary saving required further that $u_{222} > 0$. Show that quadratic preferences are consistent with risk aversion, but not with a precautionary saving motive.

B. Consider the CES preferences of equation (2.1). Show that this utility function is characterized by both risk aversion and a precautionary saving motive.

2. Consider tax-preferred savings accounts. Suppose that $\tau_T = \tau_0 = \tau = .25$, $Y = 100$, $T = 35$, and the pretax rate of return is $r = .08$ (8%).

A. What is the tax savings associated with an account offering tax-free accrual relative to a regular savings account?

B. Assume there is no tax-free accrual. Once again, $T = 35$, $Y = 100$. What is the advantage of a program with tax-deductible contributions (but where withdrawals are taxed), compared with a regular savings account? Assume $\tau_T = .2$ and that $\tau_0 = .30$.

*3. A. Suppose that all life wealth derives from first-period earnings, $W = E_1$. Differentiate the expression for optimal first-period consumption C_1^*, equation (2.3), with respect to r. Show that this implies that the response of savings in the first period, S_1, to r is positive whenever $\sigma > 1$. (What happens to C_1?)

B. Repeat part A under the assumption that W consists of both first- and second-period earnings. Why does the result from A no longer obtain?

*4. Set up the Lagrangian for the consumer's utility-maximization problem associated with the preferences of equation (2.1). Derive the first-order necessary conditions for utility maximization. Use these to determine optimal first- and second-period consumption.

5. This question reviews the material in the appendix. Suppose $U = x^{1/2}$. Also suppose that with probability $p = 7/12$ you will suffer a loss of 48. Otherwise, your wealth with no loss is $x_n = 64$. Use this information to calculate the

A. expected wealth if uninsured.

B. expected utility if uninsured.

C. certainty equivalent. Explain this concept intuitively.

D. risk premium. Explain this concept intuitively.

E. utility of $E(x)$.

F. expected loss.

G. cost of actuarially fair insurance.

H. maximum amount you would be willing to pay for full insurance.

I. wealth in the loss state, if insured at actuarially fair premium.

J. wealth in the no loss state, if insured at actuarially fair premium.

K. increase in expected utility from purchase of actuarially fair full insurance.

L. increase in expected utility from purchase of full insurance equal to the maximum you would pay for full insurance.

M. Show each of these answers on a clearly labeled graph.

Appendix: Uncertainty and Insurance

Uncertainty

Most people face substantial uncertainty concerning health, employment status (not to mention income), marital status, and other issues. Individuals dislike large risks and take extensive measures to insure against bad outcomes through the purchase of market insurance or self insurance or through implicit arrangements with others. This appendix introduces basic concepts of probability theory, discusses attitudes toward risk, and considers decision-making in the presence of uncertainty.

If a fair coin is flipped, it randomly will come up either heads H or tails T. The probability of coming up H is one-half and of coming up T is one-half, and the sum of the probabilities of these two outcomes is 1. These simple notions capture much of what we need to know of probability theory. More formally, suppose a random trial has n mutually exclusive and exhaustive outcomes. In our example, a "random trial" is a single flip of the coin; $n = 2$, H or T; mutually exclusive means there is no overlap between the outcome H and outcome T; exhaustive means H and T cover all possible outcomes. Suppose the likelihood, or probability, of each outcome is determined. Then the sum of the probabilities across all outcomes is 1.

Often, the outcomes of a trial have numerical values attached to them. Then it may prove of interest to the decision-maker to know what the average, or expected, numerical value of the trial is. The *expected value* of a trial is found by multiplying each outcome's numerical value by its probability, and then adding the products. Suppose in the flipping of a fair coin $1 will be given to the flipper if an H occurs and $2 if a T occurs. The expected value of the coin flip is $(.5)(\$1) + (.5)(\$2) = \$1.50$. If we denote the numerical outcome of a trial by x, the expected value is often denoted, $E(x)$. If, in the previous example, it costs $1.50 (i.e., $E(x)$) to be the flipper, this would be a *fair game*.

A second game with the same expected value gives the flipper $1,000 if an H occurs but has the flipper *pay* $997 if a T occurs. Intuitively, this second game is riskier, and we should not expect people to be indifferent between it and the first. The additional risk arises as the possible outcomes in the second game are more disperse, even though the expected value is the same. A common measure of dispersion is the *variance*. Intuitively, for a given expected value, the greater the variance of a trial, the greater the risk. The variance is the sum of the squared deviations between the possible outcomes in a lottery and the expected value of the lottery, each multiplied by its respective probability. Thus, the variance of the first coin toss game is:

$$(2 - 1.5)^2(.5) + (1 - 1.5)^2(.5) = .25$$

while that of the much riskier second game is:

$$(1{,}000 - 1.5)^2(.5) + (-997 - 1.5)^2(.5) = 997{,}002.25$$

In the presence of uncertainty, any particular choice ultimately will lead to but one from the range of possible outcomes. However, since at the time the decision is made the individual does not know which outcome will occur, he or she does not know how much utility will result from any decision made. Consequently, the best a person can do is make a decision in a fashion that maximizes *expected utility*. Shortly, we will see how expected utilities are calculated. First, though, we need to develop some language and intuition regarding people's attitudes, or preferences, toward risk.

Economists believe that, especially when the amounts of resources involved are significant, people are *risk averse*. Technically, risk aversion requires an individual to prefer receipt of some amount with certainty to a risky lottery, or game, having the same expected value. That is, a risk-averse person would turn down the offer to play a fair game. Thus, if an individual was offered the opportunity to play either of the coin toss games described above at a cost of $1.50, he or she would refuse. Risk aversion is consistent with the common assumption of diminishing marginal utility. Letting x be income, $dU/dx = U'(x)$ is the marginal utility of income. This first derivative of the total utility function is positive, since with additional income one can purchase more, or higher quality, market goods.

Diminishing marginal utility means that the rate at which (total) utility increases with income, $U'(x)$, decreases as income rises. This is illustrated by the concave total utility function $U(x)$ in the top panel of Figure A2.1. Intuitively, an extra dollar increases utility by more when income is low than when it is high. (The belief in diminishing marginal utility of income surely underlies many government programs transferring monies from rich to poor.) At any x, $U'(x)$ is just the slope of the $U(x)$ schedule. Diminishing marginal utility requires that this slope be falling, or that the second derivative of the utility function be negative, $d^2U/dx^2 = U''(x) < 0$. Graphically, as shown in the bottom panel of Figure A2.1, the marginal utility function is positive, but negatively sloped.

The top panel of Figure A2.1 helps motivate the link between diminishing marginal utility and risk aversion. Consider a lottery that pays you x_2 with probability p and x_1 with probability $1 - p$. The expected value of the lottery is $E(x) = (1 - p)x_1 + px_2$. Similarly, the expected utility is $E[U(x)] = (1 - p)U(x_1) + pU(x_2) = U(x_1) + p[U(x_2) - U(x_1)]$ where the last equality shows that expected utility increases linearly with p, the probability of the good outcome's occurrence. On the other hand, consider the utility a person would derive if he or she received the expected value of the lottery for certain. (The expected utility of a sure thing x_i, say, is $pU(x_i) = (1)U(x_i) = U(x_i)$.) Denoted $U[E(x)]$, this is the height of the $U(x)$ function at $E(x)$. With risk aversion, $U[E(x)] > E[U(x)]$. That is, the utility from certain receipt of the expected value of a lottery exceeds the expected utility of playing the lottery.

Suppose, for example, you are one of two finalists with a chance to win a million-dollar lottery. If the other contestant wins, you get zero. If your chance of winning is 50%, the expected value of the lottery would be $500,000. Risk aversion implies that if they give you the choice between playing the lottery or getting $500,000 for sure, you will pocket the 500K.

A related question is, "What is the minimum amount of money for which I would sell my prospect in this lottery?" If your answer is less than $500,000, you are by definition risk averse. The specific numerical response is called your *certainty equivalent* for that lottery. Technically, the certainty equivalent of a lottery (game, risky venture) is the amount received for sure that makes one indifferent between that sure amount and taking

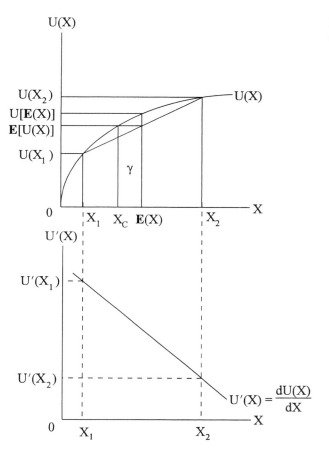

Figure A 2.1 Risk aversion and diminishing marginal utility

the risk of the lottery. In the top panel of Figure A2.1 the certainty equivalent is denoted x_c. It is the x such that U(x) equals the expected utility of the lottery, $E[U(x)]$. Graphically, find where the height $E[U(x)]$ crosses the U(x) function, then drop down to the x axis to determine x_c.

The difference between the expected value of a lottery and its certainty equivalent is called the *risk premium*, γ. Thus, $\gamma = E(x) - x_c$. If, for the lottery described above, your certainty equivalent is \$240,000, the risk premium is $\gamma = \$500,000 - \$240,000 = \$260,000$.

People who are risk averse desire to convert risky prospects into certain ones, so long as the cost of doing so is not too high. The following example illustrates the interplay between risk aversion and the demand for insurance. Let L denote the magnitude of a loss and p the probability of the loss. Then the expected loss, $E(L) = pL$. If the loss "state of the world" does not occur, wealth is x_n, whereas wealth is but $x_1 = x_n - L$ should the loss transpire. Thus, expected wealth is $E(x) = p(x_n - L) + (1 - p)x_n = x_n - pL = x_n -$

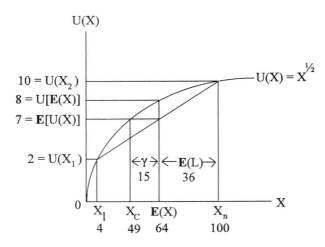

Figure A 2.2 Insurance and risk premium

E(L). That is, without insurance, the individual's expected wealth is simply wealth in the "no loss state," minus the expected loss. This is indicated in Figure A2.2.

Consider now an insurance policy that reimburses you for the full amount of the loss, should the loss state of the world occur. If the cost, or premium, of this policy is equal to the expected loss, the policy is said to be *actuarially fair*. (Note the similarity between actuarially fair insurance and what we previously called a fair game.) Suppose actuarially fair insurance is purchased, at cost $pL = E(L)$. Then, after paying the insurance premium, wealth is $x_n - pL = E(x)$ if no loss occurs. It is also $E(x) = x_1 - pL + L = x_n - pL - L + L$ *if* the loss occurs, taking the loss, premium, and reimbursement all into account. With full insurance, all risk is eliminated, and wealth is $E(x)$ regardless of the state of the world.

Since the (expected) utility of receiving $E(x)$ for certain exceeds $E[u(x)]$, the expected utility without insurance, the opportunity to purchase actuarially fair full insurance increases individual welfare. Again, see Figure A2.2. The individual is willing to pay somewhat more than the expected loss to fully insure. What is the most the individual would pay for full insurance? Now, we know the individual is indifferent between no insurance, with expected wealth of $E(x)$, and the certainty equivalent of $E(x)$, which is x_c. Thus, the individual will pay up to $x_n - x_c$ for full insurance. From the graph, this maximum is simply the sum of the expected loss, $E(L)$, and the risk premium, γ.

Assuming a specific functional form for $U(x)$, we can illustrate many of the uncertainty and insurance concepts numerically. Let $U(x) = x^{1/2}$, and assume that in the absence of a loss wealth is $100. Suppose, however, that with probability of 3/8 you suffer a loss of $96, leaving you with only $4. If you aren't insured against the loss, your expected wealth is $E(x) = (3/8)(\$4) + (5/8)(\$100) = 512/8 = \$64$. Note that $U(100) = 100^{1/2} = 10$ and that $U(4) = 4^{1/2} = \$2$. Thus, the expected utility is $E[U(x)] = (5/8)(10) + (3/8)(2) = 56/8 = 7$. To find the certainty equivalent, determine the x such that $U(x) = x^{1/2} = E[U(x)] = 7$. Therefore, $x_c^{1/2} = 7$, or $x_c = 7^2 = \$49$. The risk premium is thus $E(x) - x_c = \$64 - \$49 = \$15$.

The expected loss $E(L) = pL = (3/8)(96) = \$36$ is the cost of actuarially fair full insurance. The maximum amount you would pay for full insurance is $E(L) + \gamma = \$36 + \$15 = \$51$. If you pay this amount, you are left with your certainty equivalent of $49. All of these calculations are shown in Figure A2.2.

Many types of insurance policies, such as health insurance, are more complicated than what we have discussed, incorporating deductibles and co-payments. Further, we have treated the probability of a loss as being outside the control of the agent. This is not always true. When the agent can influence the probability of states of the world occurring, this creates *moral hazard* problems for the insurance company. For example, an individual who is fully insured against auto theft may increase the probability of theft by failing to lock the car, even though he or she would lock it if uninsured.

Chapter 3

NEOCLASSICAL GROWTH THEORY

"In the history of humankind, the era of modern economic growth is the width of a golf ball perched at the end of a football field."
—CHARLES JONES, 1988, P. 81

For many thousands of years there was no *sustained* rise in living standards, anywhere. Only in the past few centuries have even the richest countries experienced ongoing increases in per capita income (cf. Galor and Weil, 2000). As these advanced economies have grown, both the quantity and quality of goods consumed by their inhabitants have increased dramatically. To appreciate the distance traveled, consider the United States in the late eighteenth century. Although already among the richest countries in the world, its population was still 95 percent rural. Brady (1972) and Easterlin (2000) paint pictures of life at that time that underscore the subsequent economic progress. Brady writes that housing consisted of "(o)ne story log houses and frame houses with one or two rooms and an attic under the rafters. . . . Cellars and basements were practically unknown and frequently there was no flooring except the hard earth. The fireplace with a chimney provided heating and cooking . . ." (p. 64). Easterlin notes that "(t)oilet facilities consisted of outdoor privies. Water and wood had to be fetched. A few windows with shutters but no glass provided ventilation and daylight; candles supplemented the fireplace for light in the evening. The only methods of food preservation were curing and pickling. Transportation consisted of a horse and wagon" (pp. 11–12). Clearly, contemporary Americans have not only more income but, as well, higher quality consumption options.

Rural households at that time produced on the farm a large share of what they consumed, making a comparison of their money incomes with those of contemporary Americans of questionable value. A century later this was less of a problem, as the share of the population that was rural had declined dramatically (though it remained above the current proportion). Taking 1870 as a benchmark, per capita growth in GDP has increased at an average annual rate of about 1.8% (Jones, 2000). Consequently, per capita income is roughly 10 times that of 130 years ago. One goal of the chapter, then, is to understand the sources of persistent increases in living standards over long periods.

Other issues important to growth may be illustrated by contrasting the recent experience of different countries. This is the point of Table 3.1, adapted from Jones (1998).

Table 3.1

Country	GDP per capita in 1990	GDP per worker in 1990	LFPR	Annual Growth Rate, 1960–1990
"Rich Countries"				
USA	$18,073	$36,810	.49	1.4
Japan	$14,317	$22,602	.63	5.0
"Poor countries"				
China	$1,324	$2,189	.60	2.4
India	$1,262	$3,230	.39	2.0
"Growth Miracles"				
Taiwan	$8,067	$18,418	.44	5.7
South Korea	$6,665	$16,003	.42	6.0
"Growth Disasters"				
Venezuela	$6,070	$17,469	.35	−.5

LFPR, labor force participation rate.

Countries are grouped by their relative incomes ("Rich" and "Poor") and growth experiences ("Miracles" or "Disasters"); incomes are expressed in 1985 U.S. dollars.

GDP is reported on both per capita and per worker basis. These measures sometimes differ appreciably across countries. For example, under the heading of "Rich Countries," 1990 GDP per capita in the United States was about 26% higher than in Japan. However, when the comparison is made on the basis of GDP per worker, the gap is a much larger 63%. This differential is explained by column three, which shows a far higher labor force participation rate in Japan than in the United States. Since those outside the formal labor market engage in, as examples, the "household production" of parental child care, meal preparation, shopping, and cleaning, GDP per worker is perhaps the better welfare measure. (Because there are also differences in hours worked per week, output per hour would be better yet.) Significantly, other welfare measures, including infant mortality and life expectancy, are highly correlated with both GDP per capita and per worker. Consequently, these summary output measures may proxy well for overall living standards.

Using Table 3.1 to compare the incomes of people in Japan and the United States with those of people in China and India reveals that *at a point in time there is enormous variation across countries in income per capita or per worker.* For example, GDP per worker in 1990 in India was about 9% of that in the United States and India is more affluent than many African countries. Below we address the question, "Why are we so rich while they are so poor?"

Neither the relative nor absolute income differences across countries are immutable. Inspection of the last column of Table 3.1 shows that *over a given interval of time, rates of economic growth vary substantially across countries.* For example, between 1960 and 1990 GDP per worker in the United States grew at an average annual rate of 1.4%, causing living standards to rise about 52% over that period. The comparable rate in Japan was a robust 5%, enabling real GDP per capita to rise by over 330 percent! As a good rule of thumb, the number of years it takes for an economy's GDP to double is 70 divided by the country's average percentage growth rate. Thus, annual growth of 5% allows a doubling of GDP every 14 years, while a rate of 1.4% produces a doubling about every 50 years. Consequently, had these growth rates persisted, in just a few generations U.S. citizens would have been relative paupers compared with the Japanese. Of course, Japan's rapid expansion did not survive into the 1990s, a strong growth period in the United States.

More generally, the fact that growth rates vary across countries and through time means that a country's relative position in the world distribution of per capita incomes is subject to change. A prominent example of this phenomenon is Great Britain;the world economic leader at the end of the nineteenth century is behind many countries as the twenty-first century dawns. Similarly, Table 3.1 understates China's position, as China has grown explosively in recent years.

Note the rapid growth enjoyed by South Korea and Taiwan (and other newly industrialized economies, or NICs), whose average expansion rates were 6% and 5.7%. Crucially, is there a set of policies that the governments of growth laggards, such as Venezuela and India, could adopt to promote that same growth? Are such periods of rapid expansion inevitably followed by an interval of consolidation, as with the Asian currency crisis? To organize our thinking regarding these and other questions requires some sort of general framework.

This chapter introduces some standard theories of economic growth and considers how well they perform empirically. Several subsequent chapters generalize these theories along important dimensions. Section 3.1 develops a model of balanced, or steady state, growth. Section 3.2 complements that discussion with an analysis of the economy's behavior when it is away from its balanced growth path. The following section discusses the role of capital in growth models more generally. Section 3.4 attempts to explain productivity differences across countries, and addresses whether such differences might persist. In a fifth section, the concepts developed earlier are employed to address the slowdown in productivity that plagued the United States and other economies from the 1970s until recently. A short summary concludes the chapter.

3.1 STEADY STATE GROWTH IN A NEOCLASSICAL GROWTH MODEL[1]

3.1.1 Aggregate Supply and the Demand for Inputs

As Keynes stressed, over short periods of time the level of aggregate demand relative to an economy's productive capacity exerts a powerful influence on the pace of economic activity. In contrast, an economy's growth over a long period of time is largely determined by the "supply-side," or productive capacity, of the economy. Thus, the sources of growth include greater quantities and higher quality of resources and better recipes, or technologies, for their combination in the production process. Also important, perhaps especially in developing economies, are advances in social, political, and economic institutions. These structures affect the incentives to work, save, and innovate. If poor incentives keep returns to investments or effort sufficiently low, a country may linger in a "development trap" in which there is no (or even negative) growth.

Among the broad classes of resources, modern growth theory stresses the aggregate quantities and qualities of labor and capital (including 'land'). Long-term, or ongoing, increases in the labor resource are obtained through population growth and growth in the *human capital* or skill level of the workers. Shorter term, or transitional, increases in market labor arise when the labor force participation rate or market hours per week increase. Physical capital accumulation rises with the supply of savings. The quality of capital rises as older vintages are replaced by their more productive successors.

Much of the expansion of an economy's productive capacity is attributable to technical progress, the creation of better recipes for the combining of inputs in production. Pure technological improvements are *disembodied*, and those new ideas can be used by many firms simultaneously. Examples of technical change include production innovations (such as the assembly line for mass production and "just in time" inventory practices) as well as design advances (as for a new computer chip or Napster). In contrast, improvements in the quality of capital and/or labor are *embodied* in, or tied to, the particular resource. For this reason, an electrician's expertise contributes to output only when he or she puts those ideas to work. Similarly, a new laser-based surgical instrument can be used by only one surgical team at a time. Below we address the relative contributions to growth of "resources" and "technology."

We begin our analysis by assuming the economy's aggregate production function has the following multiplicative (or Cobb-Douglas) form

$$Y_t = K_t^{\alpha}(\mathbf{A}_t L_t)^{1-\alpha} \tag{3.1}$$

where Y_t is the economy's aggregate output or real GDP in year or period t. This homogeneous, all-purpose output may be consumed or used as physical capital. K_t is the stock of physical capital in period t, which is assumed never to depreciate. $\mathbf{A}_t$ is the stock of ideas available for use in the economy. Below we consider interpretations under which these ideas are disembodied (a computer manual) or embodied as human capital (the computer operator). Use of the bold $\mathbf{A}$ distinguishes the state of technology from the notation for financial assets, A_t, used in other chapters. L_t is the number of workers in t. The product $\mathbf{A}_t L_t$ is termed *effective labor*. By this formulation, a unit of natural labor is made twice as productive by a doubling of $\mathbf{A}_t^2$. An interesting special case is if $\mathbf{A}_t = 1$ in every period, which makes effective labor and the quantity of labor identical. Interpretations of the technical parameter α in equation (3.1), which is restricted to be positive and less than 1, are provided below.

In much of this chapter the only resource determined within the model (endogenously) is the stock of physical capital. Such models were standard until the mid-1980s. More recent or "new" growth models endogenize one or more of technical change, population growth, and human capital accumulation. Later in this chapter, we consider a model in which human capital accumulates endogenously but is not based on utility maximization. Subsequent chapters model fertility and human capital in terms of optimizing behavior; the stock of ideas will be modeled as a function of fertility and human capital decisions.[3]

The time paths of ideas and labor supply are determined by exogenous parameters. In particular, the labor force (and as explained below, population) is assumed to grow exogenously at rate n. For this reason

$$L_t = (1 + n)L_{t-1} \tag{3.2}$$

Given the labor force at one point in time and n, the labor force is known at every time. Similarly, the evolution of ideas is governed by

$$\mathbf{A}_t = (1 + v)\mathbf{A}_{t-1} \qquad (3.3)$$

where v is the rate at which ideas grow.

Our principal interpretation of $\mathbf{A}_t$ will be as the state of disembodied technology. However, when invented, currently disembodied ideas (such as the calculus) were embodied in the inventor. And, such ideas often continue to produce benefits only to the extent that they are embodied in workers as human capital. This encourages us to consider for a moment a model by Lucas (1988) in which $\mathbf{A}_t$ (which he labels h_t) is the human capital per worker in t. In Lucas' formulation, v may be viewed as the proportion of time parents—or more generally adults—spend teaching children.[4] Equation (3.3) implies that so long as the share of time devoted to teaching is unchanged, human capital can grow exponentially at rate v through time. If that proportion of time is influenced by government policy or private rates of return, this growth rate could be made endogenous to the model. The Lucas model is important because it reminds us that the transmission and progression of embodied knowledge, or human capital, is an intergenerational phenomenon that depends upon the amount of time elders devote to it. A strong assumption of his model, embedded in equation (3.3), is that if the human capital of teachers $\mathbf{A}_{t-1}$ is doubled, so will be the increase in human capital in the next generation. We show that this assumption may not be warranted in Chapter 6, which focuses on the intergenerational transmission of human capital.

For the rest of this chapter $\mathbf{A}_t$ will be interpreted as the state of disembodied technology—the stock of "general knowledge." This is not to imply that we have seen the last of human capital in this chapter. In section 3.3 we consider a formulation that includes both the state of technology and human capital. Equation (3.3) stresses that the creation of disembodied technologies is also importantly related to past discoveries. Or, as Sir Isaac Newton famously expressed, "If I have seen farther than others, it is because I was standing on the shoulders of giants." As above, (3.3) implies that if the giants' shoulders (i.e., magnitude of $\mathbf{A}_t$) are twice as high, so will be the increment to new knowledge. This assumption is challenged in Chapter 7 where a more general "discovery function" for ideas is considered.

The production function (3.1) is characterized by constant returns to scale in effective labor and capital. That is, for a given set of ideas, if we double the amounts of both capital and the number of workers, output will double:

$$(2K_t)^\alpha (\mathbf{A}_t 2L_t)^{1-\alpha} = (2)^\alpha (2)^{1-\alpha} K_t^\alpha (\mathbf{A}_t L_t)^{1-\alpha} = 2Y_t$$

Intuitively, replicating an existing plant and its usage of resources yields the same output from each plant. In the Cobb-Douglas case, constant returns results as the exponents on capital and effective labor sum to 1; if their sum exceeds (is less than) 1, there are increasing (decreasing) returns to scale. Notice that if both ideas $\mathbf{A}$ and the quantity of labor L are doubled, effective labor will not just double, but quadruple. For this reason, doubling each of $\mathbf{A}$, L, and K more than doubles GDP—there are increasing returns to scale in ideas, effective labor, and capital.

Constant returns in capital and effective labor mean there are diminishing returns to capital or effective labor alone. Thus, doubling only capital will increase GDP by less than double. Diminishing returns to capital are shown below to constrain capital's role in long-term growth. These characteristics, constant returns overall and diminishing returns to capital and labor, are the core of *neoclassical growth models*. Robert Solow was awarded the Nobel Prize for his contributions to neoclassical growth theory (cf. 1956, 1957). This chapter emphasizes the neoclassical approach.

The simplification that there is only one type of output makes it natural to assume that firms in the economy are perfectly competitive and identical. However, assuming but one type of output and perfect competition glosses over the invention of new products and the incentives compatible with product development. For example, Microsoft is willing to create the next version of Windows only if it can enjoy exclusive rights to the sale of that product, at least until a profit can be turned. This protection requirement is the basis for the system of patent and copyright laws, which vests exclusive property rights in the inventor of a product for an extended interval of time. Indeed, economic historians argue that the development of a system of legal property rights over inventions was a necessary precondition to the era of modern growth. However, patents provide a measure of monopoly power to firms, making them inconsistent with the model of perfect competition. An important line of research (cf. Jones, 1998; Romer, 1990) develops models of imperfect competition in which technical change results from intentional, profit-seeking behavior. Our current focus is on resource accumulation (later chapters do develop links between resource accumulation and knowledge creation). To keep our story tractable, we abstract from the issues associated with patenting new ideas, which allows us to assume markets are perfectly competitive.

When a competitive industry is in equilibrium, firms earn zero *economic* profit (i.e., all factors of production receive their opportunity cost). Firms take the state of technology as given. Since we have assumed constant returns to scale in K and **AL**, a given firm can earn zero profits at *any* level of output. This makes the size of any particular firm indeterminate. Also, though, it means the production function of individual firms looks just like the aggregate production function (3.1). Thus, we refer to (3.1) when discussing either firm or aggregate production.

Input Demands

Under perfect competition firms can sell all the output they produce at the going price. We normalize this price to 1. This eliminates the need for output price notation; it also makes total revenues equal to output. Similarly, firms can hire any amounts of effective labor at the going wage per unit of effective labor w_t, or $w_t \mathbf{A}_t$ per full-time worker. Capital is paid the market interest rate, or rental rate on capital, r_t. The firm's profits π are the difference between output and payments to the factors of production. The firm's profit maximization problem is

$$\text{Maximize } \pi_t = K_t^\alpha (\mathbf{A}_t L_t)^{1-\alpha} - w_t \mathbf{A}_t L_t - r_t K_t$$

With the price of output equal to 1, an input's marginal product is also its contribution to total revenues—its marginal revenue product. Diminishing returns to capital mean its marginal product falls as more capital is hired, with labor held constant. Mathematically, the marginal product of capital is the "partial" derivative of the production function with respect to capital,[5]

$$dY_t/dK_t = \alpha K_t^{\alpha-1}(A_tL_t)^{1-\alpha}$$

while that for effective labor is given by

$$dY_t/d(A_tL_t) = (1 - \alpha)K_t^{\alpha}(A_tL_t)^{-\alpha}$$

To maximize profits, the firm hires capital until its marginal product falls to equal the rental rate. Similarly, effective labor is hired until its marginal product has fallen to the wage rate. This marginality (or "first-order") condition for effective labor is

$$(1 - \alpha)K_t^{\alpha}(A_tL_t)^{-\alpha} - w_t = 0$$

so that

$$w_t = (1 - \alpha)[K_t/(A_tL_t)]^{\alpha} = (1 - \alpha)k_t^{\alpha} \tag{3.4}$$

In (3.4), k_t is defined as the *capital to effective labor ratio* ($K_t/(A_tL_t)$). The right-hand side of that equation is the marginal product of effective labor. In the special case where $A_t = 1$, k_t simplifies to the *capital-labor ratio* K_t/L_t and therefore earnings per worker are simply w_t. Because of diminishing returns to effective labor, (3.4) could be rearranged to reveal the familiar result that the demand for labor is a negatively sloped function of the wage (holding capital constant).

The analogous expression for a firm's profit-maximizing capital is

$$\alpha K_t^{\alpha-1}(A_tL_t)^{1-\alpha} - r_t = 0$$

or

$$r_t = \alpha k_t^{\alpha-1} \tag{3.5}$$

Equation (3.5) states that firms maximize profits by hiring capital until its marginal product falls to equal the interest rate. This makes the demand curve for capital a negatively sloped function of the rental rate of capital. Constant returns to scale is why the marginal products of capital and effective labor can be expressed in terms of the capital-labor ratio alone, rather than in terms of the absolute quantities of capital and labor.

In developing the conditions for simultaneous, or general, equilibrium in the input and output markets, our effort is reduced if we think of firms as having a demand for a capital-effective labor ratio as a function of the input prices. Rearranging (3.5) a bit, we may express the firm's demand for the capital-labor ratio in terms of the interest rate as

$$k_t^d = [\alpha/r_t]^{1/(1-\alpha)} \tag{3.6}$$

Below, an analogous expression for the supply of the capital-effective labor ratio is developed from an analysis of the household sector.

Output per worker is perhaps the best summary statistic of an economy's state of economic development. However, it is easier to solve for and work with the model in terms of output per unit of effective labor. This can then be multiplied by the effectiveness of labor to recover output per worker. Dividing aggregate output from (3.1) by effective labor, output per unit of effective labor is

$$Y_t/(A_tL_t) = K_t^\alpha(A_tL_t)^{1-\alpha}/(A_tL_t) = K_t/(A_tL_t)^\alpha,$$

or more compactly,

$$y_t = k_t^\alpha \tag{3.7}$$

Equation (3.7) is known as the *intensive form* of the production function. This relationship, depicted in Figure 3.1, reveals that output per unit of effective labor y_t increases with k_t. It is concave because of the diminishing returns to capital alone. After developing interpretations for the parameter α, we can be more precise about the link between y and k.

One interpretation of α is found by multiplying both sides of (3.5) by k_t and then using the definition of y_t to obtain $r_t k_t = \alpha y_t$. Upon rearranging we have

$$\alpha = r_t k_t/y_t$$

or in terms of aggregate capital and output,

$$\alpha = r_t K_t/Y_t$$

In this latter expression, the numerator is the economy-wide payments to the capital input, making α the share of GDP paid to capital, or "capital's share." That our Cobb-

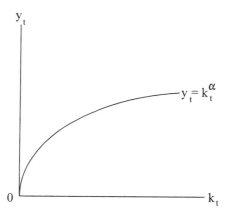

Figure 3.1 Output per unit of effective labor

Douglas production function forces capital's share to be constant is actually a selling point: capital's share has fluctuated only little about its average value of .30 over the last hundred years.(Beginning with (3.4), it is easy to see that $1 - \alpha$ is labor's share of GDP.)

The parameter α is also the elasticity of y_t with respect to k_t. This percentage change in y_t per 1% change in k_t, can be written as

$$\frac{dy_t/y_t}{dk_t/k_t} = (dy_t/dk_t)(k_t/y_t) = \frac{(\alpha k_t^{\alpha-1})k_t}{y_t} = \frac{r_t k_t}{y_t}$$

where we differentiated (3.7) to obtain $dy_t/dk_t = \alpha k_t^{\alpha-1}$, which from (3.5) equals r_t. The last term is capital's share, previously shown to equal α.(This interpretation assumes capital's contribution to output is completely captured by its contribution to the firm that owns it; there are no positive externalities to other firms from capital. We revisit this assumption in section 3.3.) This elasticity interpretation for α means that capital's share of GDP is *the* critical determinant of the contribution capital deepening can make to growth. This important fact is developed in detail below.

On many occasions we will naturally be more interested in output per worker than output per unit of effective labor. Multiplying both sides of (3.7) by the state of technology, output per worker is

$$y_t^w = A_t k_t^\alpha \tag{3.8}$$

A closely related concept is *labor productivity*, which is output per hour. Since all laborers work full-time in our model, output per worker is just labor productivity times the hours worked per year. As these are perfectly correlated, we refer to them interchangeably. The wage earnings *per worker* are just labor's share of GDP, or $1 - \alpha$, times output per worker. Since labor's share has been fairly constant over the past century, our framework predicts that wages should rise in lock step with labor productivity. Substantial evidence indicates this link is in fact quite strong (cf. Auerbach and Kotlikoff, 1998, Fig. 1.7).

3.1.2   The Supply of Inputs with Overlapping Generations

So far we have modeled the supply of output and the demand for inputs. We now consider the supply of inputs and the demand for output. These are based on the simplest version of the two-period life-cycle model of Chapter 1, which provides a natural link between household and aggregate behavior. At any point in time, there will be both old households living out their retirement and young households—their children—toiling in the labor market. Since two generations are alive simultaneously, growth models based on the life-cycle framework are termed *overlapping generations (OLG) models* (cf. Samuelson, 1958; Diamond, 1965). We first review the saving decisions of representative households, from which we derive aggregate saving and the stock of physical capital. Similarly, aggregating the effective labor supply across households yields the aggregate supply of labor. Attaching this specification of factor supplies to that of factor demands from above enables us to characterize general equilibrium at a point in time.

To keep track of calendar time and generations we introduce a second subscript for household variables that indicates when activity takes place. For example, $S_{1,t}$ is savings in the first period of life for a member of the generation young at time t. Similarly, $C_{2,t}$ is the consumption at time t of an old household, which began economic life at time $t - 1$.

All those currently young are assumed to work full-time, while every old person is retired. For this reason, the number of young equals the size of the labor force, and the rate of growth in labor supply, n, is also the rate of population growth. Under these assumptions, the life wealth of someone beginning economic life in t is simply $w_t A_t$. In the notation of Chapters 1 and 2, this is just earnings in the first period of economic life E_1 for someone alive at time t. However, we employ the new notation in order to distinguish the separate effects of labor market conditions and technology.

A consumer starting economic life in period t has the Cobb-Douglas preferences of Chapter 1,

$$U_t = C_{1,t}^\theta \, C_{2,t+1}^{1-\theta}$$

With Cobb-Douglas utility, recall, the constant proportion θ of life wealth is devoted to consumption when young. Further, with life wealth equal to first-period earnings, first-period consumption, and therefore savings, are independent of the interest rate. This simplifies our development of growth theory without compromising the qualitative results (implications are discussed in the context of fiscal policy in Chapter 4).

With these assumptions we can readily derive consumption, savings, and labor supply at both the household and aggregate level. The consumption of a young person in t is

$$C_{1,t} = \theta w_t A_t,$$

Savings when young are labor earnings minus consumption, or

$$S_{1,t} = w_t A_t - \theta w_t A_t = (1 - \theta) w_t A_t \tag{3.9}$$

so that $(1 - \theta)$ is the marginal propensity to save while young from life wealth. Since the second period is devoted to retirement, consumption by the old is limited to their savings and interest earned on them, $C_{2,t} = (1 + r)S_{1,t-1}$. Aggregate consumption at any time is just the consumption per young person times the number of young, plus the consumption per old person times the number of old. Savings when old, equal to interest income minus consumption, is simply the negative of savings when young

$$S_{2,t} = r_t S_{1,t-1} - C_{2,t} = r_t S_{1,t-1} - (1 + r_t)S_{1,t-1} = -S_{1,t-1} \tag{3.10}$$

That is, if I save \$10 when young, I will dissave \$10 when old.

Aggregate private savings at time t, $S_{P,t}$, are simply the savings of the young plus the (negative) savings of the old.

$$S_{P,t} = L_t S_{1,t} + L_{t-1} S_{2,t}$$

or, using equations (3.9) and (3.10),

$$S_{P,t} = L_t(1 - \theta)w_t A_t - L_{t-1}(1 - \theta)w_{t-1}A_{t-1} \tag{3.11}$$

Thus, if the young and old are equal in number, $L_t = L_{t-1}$, and have the same earnings when young, $w_t A_t = w_{t-1}A_{t-1}$, aggregate savings would equal zero. If the young are more numerous and/or have higher earnings when young than their parents had, savings are positive.[6]

The savings of one period are ultimately invested in physical capital (banks and other financial intermediaries are assumed to work efficiently, but are not explicitly modeled). Since we do not consider international trade or (until Chapter 4) government savings, private savings equal investment. Similarly, the sum of current and past savings, or aggregate household wealth, equals the sum of current and past investments in physical capital, the economy's stock of capital (recall we ignore depreciation). U.S. wealth in 2000 exceeded $40 trillion, including business's plant and equipment, the stock of residential housing, cars, and so on. This diverse stock of productive assets is made trivial by our two-period life-cycle setup. By assumption, the old die with no assets and the young bring no assets with them into the start of economic life. Consequently, *the supply of capital in t + 1 is simply the assets the young of period t bring into the start of t + 1, that is, their savings in t.* Multiplying savings per young person by the number of young yields

$$K_{t+1} = S_{1,t}L_t = (1 - \theta)w_t A_t L_t \tag{3.12}$$

Dividing K_{t+1} by the effective labor supply of $t + 1$ yields an expression for the household supply of the capital to effective labor ratio

$$k_{t+1}^s \equiv K_{t+1}/(A_{t+1}L_{t+1}) = (1 - \theta)w_t A_t L_t/(A_{t+1}L_{t+1}) \tag{3.13}$$

$$= (1 - \theta)w_t/(1 + n)(1 + v)$$

Consider first a special case of (3.13) in which there is neither population nor effective labor growth, $n = v = 0$, and where knowledge A is equal to 1. The value of this case is that it isolates the core intuition. With these simplifications, k_{t+1}^s becomes the supply of capital per worker and is just equal to the portion of a young worker's wage that is saved, $(1 - \theta)w_t$.

It is easy to build on that intuition while restoring population and knowledge growth. With population growth at rate n, there are n% more workers to be equipped in $t + 1$, so capital per worker in $t + 1$ is n% less than the amount a young worker saved in t. Allowing for growth in labor effectiveness, v is positive and A_t no longer equals 1. Now k_{t+1}^s is no longer simply capital per worker, but again capital per unit of effective labor. However, the same intuition applies as when we added population growth: Since the effectiveness of each worker is v% higher in $t + 1$ than in t, the savings per young person in t translate to v% less capital per unit of effective labor in $t + 1$.

Factor Market Equilibrium

Equation (3.6) provided an expression for the demand for capital-effective labor ratio in terms of the interest rate in period t. This inverse relationship is readily updated to time

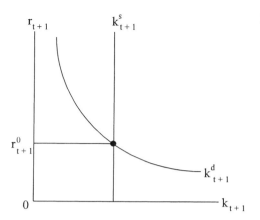

Figure 3.2 Factor market equilibrium

t + 1 and is depicted in Figure 3.2. On the other hand, the household's supply of the capital-effective labor ratio is determined once the wage of *time t* is known. It is therefore independent of the interest rate in t + 1.[7] Consequently, the supply curve for the capital-effective labor ratio in t + 1 shown in Figure 3.2 is vertical, or completely inelastic. The intersection of these schedules determines the factor market-clearing interest rate and capital-effective labor ratio. Notice that an increase in the supply of the capital-effective labor ratio will lower this general equilibrium interest rate. Of course, one reason that ratio would rise is if there is an increase in capital. *In general equilibrium, there is an inverse relationship between the supply of capital (or k^s) and the interest rate.*

Given the equilibrium k, the marginal product of labor, and therefore the general-equilibrium wage, is determined by equation (3.4). This reveals an important macroeconomic implication of that equation: *The higher is k_t—or the more tools a worker has at his or her disposal—the greater is worker productivity and the market wage.* The role of savings in increasing the capital per worker, called capital deepening, is one of the central themes of this chapter. More generally, since w_{t+1} increases with k_{t+1} and r_{t+1} falls with k_{t+1}, equilibrium dictates that factor prices increase with the factor's relative scarcity.

With both the factor markets clearing, the output market must be clearing also. That is, the aggregate demand for output—the sum of aggregate consumption and investment (equal to savings)—must equal GDP (see problem 3.3).

3.1.3   How the Economy Moves Through Time

The general-equilibrium factor prices of one time need not carry over to the next. Nevertheless, it is easy to track through time the evolution of the capital-effective labor ratio, and therefore of the entire economy. To do so, substitute the wage from equation (3.4) into the capital-effective labor ratio supply equation, (3.13). The resulting expression, called the *transition equation*, links the capital-effective labor ratio in successive time periods, here t and t + 1.

$$k_{t+1} = \frac{(1 - \theta)(1 - \alpha)k_t^\alpha}{(1 + n)(1 + v)} \qquad (3.14)$$

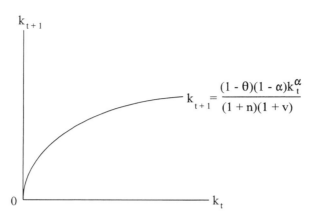

Figure 3.3 Transition equation diagram

However, since there is nothing special about times t and t + 1 we can, for given values of θ, α, n, v, and the current capital-effective labor ratio, trace that ratio into the indefinite future. And, since the (exogenous) effective labor force is known as of any period t, one can determine the aggregate stock of capital in t from k_t. Significantly, this means that if you are given the capital-effective labor ratio in time t you can solve for every economic variable in our model into infinity!

Because of the diminishing returns to capital alone—α less than 1—the transition equation is concave, as shown in Figure 3.3. (In fact, k_{t+1} is just the concave y_t function of Figure 3.1 multiplied by a constant.) This equation is first used to motivate a type of long-term balanced growth path, or "steady state" equilibrium. Once the balanced growth path is well understood, we return to the transition equation to examine the economy's behavior when it is away from that path.

3.1.4 Steady State Growth

Does the economy we have described stabilize about a constant growth rate? If so, what is it, and what does it depend upon? In fact, this economy converges to a *steady state* or *balanced growth path*, in which some variables grow at constant rates while others remain constant. Along a balanced growth path, GDP, the stock of capital, and the quantity of effective labor all grow at a common rate. This keeps constant the capital-effective labor ratio and, thus, the wage per unit of effective labor and the interest rate. The constancy of the interest rate means the model satisfies at least one plausibility test, since the real interest rate in the United States has fluctuated only modestly, and without trend, for at least the last century (even though the U.S. has presumably not been in steady state throughout that time).

The transition equation diagram may be modified to identify the constant, or steady state, capital-effective labor ratio. In Figure 3.4 we have added a 45-degree line, along which $k_{t+1} = k_t$. This straight line crosses the transition curve only once. We denote this steady state capital-effective labor ratio by k*. Using the fact that $k_{t+1} = k_t = k^*$ in the

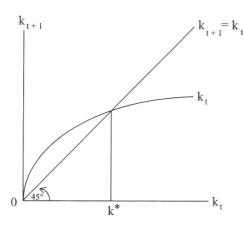

Figure 3.4 The steady state capital-effective labor ratio

steady state, we can use the transition equation to solve for k* in terms of the model's parameters. Making this substitution in (3.14) produces

$$k^* = \frac{(1-0)(1-\alpha)k^{*\alpha}}{(1+n)(1+v)}$$

Collecting terms and rearranging, the explicit solution for k* is

$$k^* = \left(\frac{(1-\theta)(1-\alpha)}{(1+n)(1+v)} \right)^{1/(1-\alpha)} \tag{3.15}$$

Once we are in possession of k*, many characteristics of the steady state may be found. For example, using k* in (3.4), (3.5), and (3.7) we find the steady state wage w*, interest rate r*, and output per unit of effective labor y*. These are unchanging along the balanced growth path. To determine scale values at a particular time along the steady state path we first find the effective labor supply, using the exogenous growth rates and initial values for technology and size of the work force. Then all other variables, including consumption and the stock of capital, could be determined.

At what rates do variables grow along the steady state path? The constancy of the capital-effective labor ratio in steady state requires that the stock of capital grow at the same rate as the effective labor supply, which we know to be n + v. Since the interest rate is constant in the steady state, aggregate capital income must also grow at rate n + v. *Since the wage per unit of effective labor is constant, wage earnings per worker, or worker productivity, increase at the rate of labor effectiveness growth v.* Thus, the "engine of growth" in the *steady state*, technical change, is determined by forces exogenous to our model. (We model the roles of human capital and fertility in determining technical change in Chapters 7 and 9). Aggregate wage income grows at rate n + v. Further, since GDP is just the sum of aggregate wage and capital income, it also increases at rate n + v. More generally, all variables relating to the scale of the economy grow at rate n + v, while all household, or standard of living, variables grow at the same rate that labor effectiveness grows, v. (Scale variables actually grow at rate $(1 + n)(1 + v) - 1 = n + v + nv \simeq n + v$.)

Steady state output per worker is found by substituting k* into (3.8)

$$y_t^{w*} = (k^*)^\alpha \mathbf{A}_t \tag{3.16}$$

$$= \left[\frac{(1 - \theta)(1 - \alpha)}{(1 + n)(1 + v)} \right]^{\frac{\alpha}{(1-\alpha)}} \mathbf{A}_0 (1 + v)^t$$

From the first line of (3.16), output per worker is higher when more advanced technology is employed—high $\mathbf{A}_t$. No surprise there! The second line of (3.16) reexpresses the current state of technology in terms of the rate of technical growth, $\mathbf{A}_t = \mathbf{A}_0(1 + v)^t$. This makes clear that output per worker is higher the faster technology has grown.

Output per worker also increases with $1 - \theta$, the propensity to save from wealth when young. This makes good sense; the more households accumulate assets for retirement, the more "tools per worker" there will be. This is portrayed in Figure 3.5. An initial transition equation k_{t+1}^0 produces the steady state capital-effective labor ratio k_0^*. Following an increase in the propensity to save, the transition equation shifts upward to k_{t+1}^1, which results in greater capital intensity in the new steady state k_1^*. And, from (3.16), more capital per worker means more output per worker. The process by which this capital deepening comes to pass is discussed in detail in section 3.2.

Equation (3.16) further reveals that y_t^{w*} is lower the faster population grows. Intuitively, the faster the work force grows, the more capital is required each period just to maintain the existing amount of tools per effective worker. Figure 3.5 illustrates the downward shift in the transition equation and the associated decline in capital intensity when there is an increase in the rate of population growth. In section 3.4 we employ an equation similar to (3.14) to explain the distribution of world income.

Is the U.S. economy in steady state? On one hand, the rise in GDP per capita over long intervals has averaged about 1.8 percent per year since 1870 (cf. Jones, 2000). On the other hand, many important changes have occurred during this period, suggesting the importance of transitional considerations. For example, below we argue that human capital and research and development expenditures are important to growth. The share of the life cycle devoted to schooling and the proportion of the labor force devoted to R&D have increased dramatically in recent decades, suggesting the economy has not been in steady state.

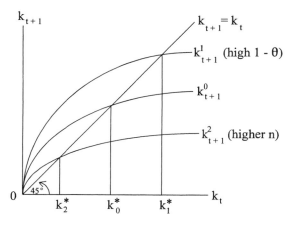

Figure 3.5 Comparison of steady states

3.2 TRANSITIONAL GROWTH AND THE PRINCIPLE OF TRANSITION DYNAMICS

We now discuss the economy's behavior away from the steady state, termed *transitional dynamics*. These dynamics are readily conveyed using the transition diagram. For by construction, for any time t the transition diagram provides the value of k_{t+1}, given k_t. To illustrate this approach, consider in Figure 3.6 an initial capital-effective labor ratio k_0, which is appreciably below k^*. Since the transition diagram lies above the 45-degree line when capital intensity is less than the steady state amount, the value for k_1 will exceed k_0. Significantly, since we are now in possession of k_1, we can again utilize the transition diagram to determine k_2. To use the graph, extend a horizontal line from k_1 to the 45-degree line; then simply dropping down, pinpoint k_1 on the horizontal axis. Given k_1, the transition diagram provides k_2. Proceeding in this fashion, the capital-effective labor ratio follows the path indicated by arrows. The path eventually converges to k^*. Thus, an important implication of our model is that countries that are away from their steady state will converge to it. That is, economies will neither implode nor explode if they are temporarily knocked from their steady state path.

A second important implication is that an economy's growth rate is higher the further below the steady state the economy is. To appreciate this, first notice that the further an economy is below its steady state, the larger is the increase in k—and thus y—from one period to the next. Visually, this follows from the fact that the vertical distance between the transition equation and the 45-degree line is bigger the more k falls short of k^*; the increase from k_0 to k_1 exceeds that from k_1 to k_2. The prediction that economies grow faster the further below the steady state they are is termed the *principle of transition dynamics*.[8] Notice that this implies that, among countries with the same steady state, relatively poor countries should grow faster on average than rich countries. In section 3.4 this principle is used to help explain differences in growth rates across countries.

As capital intensity rises, so do wages and income per capita. Thus, during a time of transitional growth, wages and income per capita grow above the steady state growth rate

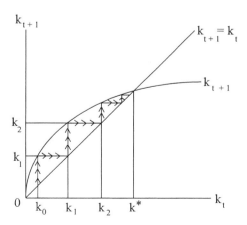

Figure 3.6 Transitional dynamics

v. Since savings of the young are proportional to earnings, they also rise more rapidly than in steady state, fueling the increases in the capital-effective labor ratio. However, due to the diminishing returns to capital alone ($\alpha < 1$), transitional growth cannot continue forever. For with diminishing returns, each increase in the capital-effective labor ratio yields a smaller rise in the wage. This in turn produces a smaller increase in capital per effective worker in the subsequent period. Eventually, transitional growth winds down, and we are left with steady state growth alone.

What do we know about the rate at which economies converge to their steady state levels? Barro (1997, p.17) addresses this issue using data for a large number of countries and across several time periods (he employs the Summer-Heston World tables). His results suggest an annual rate of convergence of about 2.5%. These findings imply that convergence to the balanced growth path is slow; it would take approximately 27 years for the economy to converge half-way to the steady state, and 89 years to converge 90% of the way.

3.2.1   Application to Post-World War II Growth in Japan and Germany

The principle of transition dynamics helps explain the post-World War II experiences of the United States, Germany, and Japan (cf. Auerbach and Kotlikoff, 1998, p. 68). All three countries suffered tragic loss of life. However, unlike the United States, Japan and Germany experienced dramatic declines in physical plant and equipment as a consequence of the Allied force's saturation bombing near the conclusion of the war. To frame the issues in the context of our model, suppose all three economies were in steady state just prior to the onset of the war. Due to the bombing, at war's end the capital-labor ratio was further below steady state in Germany and Japan than in the United States. Consequently, our model predicts faster growth for Germany and Japan than for the United States. Why? Because of diminishing returns, the initial x% decline in tools per worker produces a smaller than x% reduction in the wage (see equation 3.4). For this reason savings of the young also decline by less than x%. With savings falling by a smaller percentage than capital, the capital-labor ratio rises in the next period, inducing growth. Unfortunately, due to diminishing returns, faster-than-steady state-growth must eventually cease. In fact, income per capita in those countries did rise relative to income in the United States for many years. For example, in 1950 the GDP per capita in Japan and Germany were 14 and 36 percent, respectively, of that in the United States. By 1988, per capita incomes in Japan and Germany had reached 66 and 68 percent of the U.S. level.

Consistent with this transitional growth being driven by physical capital accumulation, the saving rates in Germany and Japan exceeded the rate in the United States throughout the recovery period. As predicted by the principle of transition dynamics, the strong economic performances of Japan and Germany following World War II may be understood as a process of catching up with the United States through restoration of their capital-labor ratios.

3.2.2   The Effect of Increasing the Saving Rate

This subsection analyzes the implications of a change in the saving rate. Since our model highlights transitional capital deepening as a source of growth, it is important to spell out the mechanism in depth. To focus on that process, we now abstract from population growth and technical progress. This is accomplished simply by setting $n = v = 0$ and $A_t = 1$. With these simplifications the transition equation (3.14) becomes

$$k_{t+1} = (1 - \theta)(1 - \alpha)k_t^\alpha = (1 - \theta)w_t = S_{1,t} \qquad (3.14')$$

Since the technology index A is set, or "normalized," to 1, k_{t+1} simplifies to "tools per worker" in $t + 1$ and, similarly, w_t is wage earnings of a young worker in t. Equation (3.14′) shows the capital per worker in $t + 1$ is just the portion of the wages saved per worker in t, $S_{1,t}$.

In this context, consider an increase at time 0 in the fraction of wage income saved from $1 - \theta_0$ to $1 - \theta_1$. Although economists usually do not resort to changes in preferences to explain economic phenomena, the mechanisms illustrated here are common to policy-induced changes in savings emphasized in Chapter 4, and previously in Chapters 1 and 2. Figure 3.7 graphs k_{t+1} as a function of k_t for the two saving propensities. Initially, the economy is in steady state at $k*_0$. However, the increase in the young's saving rate shifts the capital accumulation function upward. The arrows track the economy's transition path toward the new steady state at the higher capital-labor ratio k_1*.

Clearly, the rise in the propensity to save increases savings of the young at time 0, and thus k_1. In turn, higher capital intensity increases output per worker y_1 and the wage per worker w_1. The capital-labor ratio will continue to rise in $t = 2$, $t = 3$, and so on, but because of diminishing returns the process eventually stops at k_1^*. We now explain why the steady state rise in k is larger the higher is α.

Since α is the output elasticity of capital, it measures the returns to capital alone. As long as α is below 1 there are diminishing returns. This parameter was also shown to equal capital's share of GDP, historically about 0.3. In the absence of population growth, labor supply is unchanging from period to period. Consequently, the increase in k_{t+1} equals that in the savings of the young in period t. Then if savings of the young rise 10% at time 0, both the aggregate stock of capital and the capital to labor ratio will be 10% higher in period one. With $\alpha = .3$, the 10% increases in K_1 and k_1 translate to 3% increases in out-

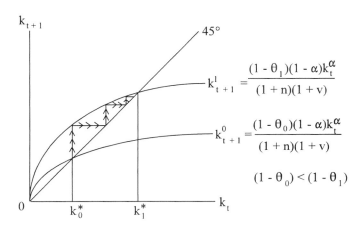

Figure 3.7 Effect on steady state of increasing the saving rate

put and output per worker in period one. Since the wage is just labor's share of output times output per worker, $w_1 = (1 - \alpha)y_1 = (1 - \alpha)k_1^\alpha$, it also rises by 3%: more tools per worker, higher labor productivity, higher wages.

To complete the intuition, recall the link between the wage at time 1, w_1, and the savings per young worker at time 1

$$S_{1,t} = (1 - \theta_1)w_1$$

(where the **A** has been omitted because it now equals 1). Compared with time 0, savings of the young are also higher by 3% at time 1, as are the capital stock in period 2 and k_2. Repeating the chain of reasoning from above, y_2^w, w_2, $S_{1,2}$, and k_3 each rise by $(.3)$ 3% = .9% compared with their period 0 values. More generally, in each subsequent period the percentage increases in capital intensity, worker productivity, and capital all fall. Eventually, the increases in labor productivity cease when the capital-labor ratio achieves its new steady state level k_1^*. Rephrasing, a given change in k produces a smaller percentage increase in w, and since savings are proportional to wages, a smaller percentage increase in savings, and therefore k in the subsequent period. Eventually, the capital accumulation process tapers off.

Although a permanent increase in the young's saving rate produces higher steady state output, capital, and consumption per unit of labor, *it does not alter the rate of steady state per capita growth.* This is a direct consequence of diminishing returns to the produced input capital. However, an increase in the saving rate does raise the growth rate during the transition between steady states. Thus, it is important to assess the size of the steady state increase in output per worker.

The steady state percentage increase in $(y^w)^*$ per 1% *initial* increase in k is $\alpha/(1 - \alpha)$. The intuition is just as with Keynesian multipliers. Letting k_1 exceed k_0 by 1, the first-period increase in y^w of α leads to a second-period increase of α^2, or an ultimate rise of $\alpha + \alpha^2 + \alpha^3 + \cdots = \alpha/(1 - \alpha)$. With $\alpha = .3$, a 1% increase in the saving rate would increase steady state output per worker by .43%. To better appreciate the magnitude, suppose a higher saving propensity initially increases the aggregate saving rate 10%, from 5 to 5.5%. The increase in steady state output per worker would be 4.3%. Assuming output per worker is $40,000 per year, this is $1,720.

3.3 CAPITAL'S SHARE AND THE IMPORTANCE OF TRANSITIONAL GROWTH

In neoclassical growth models the saving rate does not influence the steady state growth rate. Also, all growth associated with technical change is modeled exogenously. Consequently, the significance of neoclassical models hinges upon their ability to explain transitional growth, and on transitional growth being an important component of historical growth. King and Rebelo (1993) assess whether the type of framework developed above is consistent with significant transitional growth. They performed computer simulations that show that transitional growth based on physical capital deepening cannot account for much growth without generating counterfactual implications for capital accumulation and interest rates.

In their simulations, each period equals 1 year. When they require physical capital accumulation to explain half of the growth in output per worker over a 100-year period, they find this implies an interest rate for 100 years ago of over 100%! This proves to be the model's downfall, as King and Rebelo find little evidence that interest rates were much, if any, higher then than now. More generally, they conclude that if physical capital is the only resource that accumulates endogenously, transitional growth can explain only a small portion of the rise in living standards in the United States over the past century. Similar reasoning shows that differences in physical capital accumulation in such models are incapable of explaining observed current cross-country income differences. They suggest that growth theorists turn their attention to models based on either human and physical capital accumulation or on an endogenous formulation for the evolution of technology.

3.3.1 Details for the Diligent

We can illustrate their points in our two-period setup. Let $y_1^w = k_1^\alpha A_1$ be output per worker currently and $y_0^w = k_0^\alpha A_0$ be that of 100 years ago (they actually refer to the period from 1870 to 1970, assuming the economy is in steady state in 1970). Real per capita income in the United States is somewhat less than seven times the level of 100 years ago. Supposing transitional growth is quantitatively important, let's attribute *half* of that growth to transitional capital deepening. The other half then would be due to growth in A. Current output per worker may be rewritten in terms of the capital-labor ratio and the state of technology as

$$y_1^w = (K_1/L_1)^\alpha A_1^{1-\alpha}$$

If increases in the capital-labor ratio and technology are to each contribute half of the growth in y^w, then each of $(K_1/L_1)^\alpha$ and $A_1^{1-\alpha}$ must be $7^{1/2} = 2.65$ their levels a century earlier (since they enter the expression for output per worker *multiplicatively*).

For the capital to labor ratio this requires

$$(K_1/L_1)^\alpha/(K_0/L_0)^\alpha = 2.65$$

so that with $\alpha = .3$,

$$(K_1/L_1)/(K_0/L_0) = 2.65^{3.33} = 25.74$$

Tools per worker must be currently almost 26 times the level of 100 years before.

To quantify the implications for the interest rate, recall that

$$r_t = \alpha k_t^{\alpha-1} = \alpha(K_t/L_t)^{(\alpha-1)}A_t^{1-\alpha}$$

so that

$$\frac{r_1}{r_0} = \frac{\alpha(K_1/L_1)^{(\alpha-1)}A_1^{1-\alpha}}{\alpha(K_0/L_0)^{(\alpha-1)}A_0^{1-\alpha}}$$

$$= (25.74)^{(\alpha-1)}(2.65) = 0.273$$

This implies that the initial-period interest rate was roughly four times that currently.[9]

3.3.2 The Role Of Human Capital

In our current model, physical capital accumulation cannot explain a large share of historical growth. The model would perform better if increases in capital had a larger effect on output. This would be true if capital's share of GDP—and thus the elasticity of output with respect to capital—were larger than the historical value of .3. Then, smaller increases in physical capital could account for a given amount of growth, implying smaller (and therefore less counterfactual) declines in the interest rate.

In fact, the total returns to "capital" probably do exceed physical capital's share of GDP, α. In particular, if we think of capital as any durable input that may be produced, the conception of capital should be expanded to include human capital. This broader view of capital has considerable empirical justification. The production of human capital requires schools, parent's time and money, and student's time. In fact, the value of resources devoted to human capital accumulation exceeds that invested in physical capital accumulation (cf. Davies and Whalley, 1991). It is reasonable to assume that the share of human capital in GDP is .4. Again associating the GDP share with the output elasticity, this would imply an output elasticity for human capital of .4, exceeding that for physical capital. Thus, adding human capital increases the total returns to produced inputs to about .7.

How does a capital share of .7 alter the analysis? Consider again an increase in the rate of saving for physical capital in period 0. As in the earlier model, the immediate effect is a 10%, say, increase in k_1, producing an α10% increase in y_1^w. Assume that in each period s_h% of GDP is saved in the form of human capital. Consequently, a new effect is that higher y_1^w increases human capital investment per worker in period 2 by its saving rate s_h times the increase in output per worker α10%, for a total of $s_h\alpha$10%. Consequently, in period 2 and later, y^w increases because of greater physical capital, as before, but also from a higher stock of human capital.

Such an augmented model is capable of explaining a large share of historical and cross-country income differences by "capital deepening," without counterfactual implications. To illustrate this, now use a value of .7 for "capital's share" α in the expression for the increase in steady state output per worker when the saving rate rises. This yields $\alpha/(1-\alpha) = .7/.3$, or that $(y^w)^*$ increases by 2.33% per each 1% initial increase in "capital" (requiring, for example, that the saving rate for each of human and physical capital rises 1%). In the King-Rebelo experiment, the size of the initial capital stock can be much higher and the marginal product of capital (or interest rate) much lower—largely eliminating the counterfactual implications discussed above.

Another reason the returns to "capital" may exceed α is that physical capital may generate positive externalities, making its social marginal product exceed its private marginal product. Suppose, for example, that as a firm installs new capital, its workers learn, in the normal course of production, new production techniques (a process called *learning by doing*). As workers migrate between firms, these ideas spread throughout the economy. For this reason, the benefits to an individual firm from installing new capital are less than to the economy as a whole (cf. Arrow, 1962). Some economists believe such externalities are sufficiently large that there are constant returns to capital alone, $\alpha = 1$. In these models (often called **AK** models since the exponent on capital is 1) *an increase in the saving rate permanently increases the economy's growth rate*. For x% higher capital in one period would produce x% more output and, with the new saving rate, x% more capital in the next period; the contributions of capital to output would not decline each period as with diminishing returns. In these models the economy's growth rate is determined *endogenously* as a function of the saving rate and other model parameters. The magnitude of such externalities is largely unknown, making the **AK** assumption problematic (see Chapter 7).

Summing up, the returns to "capital" determine the importance of transitional capital deepening. A good argument can be made that capital should be defined broadly enough to include the skills accumulated by workers, or human capital. Also, the returns to capital may exceed capital's share of GDP, measured as payments to capital as a proportion of GDP. The reason is that capital accumulation may entail positive externalities that increase the productivity of capital in all firms (though capital is not directly compensated for these "spillover" effects).

3.4 DEVELOPMENT ACCOUNTING: EXPLAINING THE CROSS-COUNTRY DISTRIBUTION OF INCOME

One of the oldest and most important questions addressed by economists is, "Why are some countries so poor, and others so rich?"Explaining the global state of economic development is no small task, requiring an understanding of history, geography, political institutions, and economic incentives, among other influences. Attempts to explain the current distribution of income across countries are termed *development accounting*. In this section we add human capital to the steady state framework of section 3.3, and then see how well the neoclassical model fares in explaining economic development. First we examine the distribution of income across countries at a given point in time. Then we consider differences in the rates at which countries grow.

3.4.1 Differences in Steady State Labor Productivity

Households invest in the future by acquiring education and on-the-job training. Such human capital acquisition presumably increases the effective labor supply and output per worker. In the preceding section we supposed there is a human capital saving rate from GDP, just as with physical capital. Mankiw, Romer, and Weil (1992) conduct development accounting using this approach. Here we follow Jones (1998), who focuses on years of schooling as a proxy for the broader human capital accumulation process. Of course, since time spent schooling is certainly an investment, the two approaches do not differ all that much.

To allow for human capital we rewrite the aggregate production function as

$$Y = K^{\alpha}(\mathbf{A}H)^{1-\alpha}$$

where H is human capital. There is a broad literature from labor economics concerned with estimating the impact of an additional year's schooling on earnings. Overall, it appears as though an additional year's schooling increases earnings by about 10%, or the proportion .1 (cf. Bils and Klenow, 2000).[10] Employing this value, the human capital per worker h becomes

$$h = (1.1)^u$$

where u is the number of years of schooling. Multiplying h by the number of workers yields aggregate human capital,

$$H = hL = (1.1)^u L$$

where L has been implicitly adjusted to reflect the time a worker withdraws from the labor force to accumulate skills. Using this expression we write aggregate production as

$$Y = K^\alpha [A(1.1)^u L]^{1-\alpha}$$

This model may be solved for output per worker in exactly the same fashion as our baseline model. Effective labor is now $A_t h L_t$. Capital per unit of effective labor becomes $k_t = K_t/(A_t h L_t)$. Redefining k_t in this fashion, the steady state value k* is again given by (3.15).[11] Further, the term for h, $(1.1)^u$, enters into the aggregate production function the same way as A in the production function equation (3.1). For this reason, h also enters the expression for output per worker the same way as A. Thus, analogous to equation (3.16), the output of a worker devoting u years to schooling is

$$y_t^{w*} = y^* A_t (1.1)^u = (k^*)^\alpha A_t (1.1)^u$$

$$= \left[\frac{(1-\theta)(1-\alpha)}{(1+n)(1+v)} \right]^{\frac{\alpha}{(1-\alpha)}} A_t (1.1)^u$$

$$(3.18)$$

This equation constitutes our explanation of the distribution of income across countries. As in the model without human capital, output per worker increases with the state of technology and the saving rate of the young. And, as before, countries with a rapidly growing population require more investment just to equip the larger numbers of new workers. The new implication is that countries in which workers devote more years to education are also expected to be more affluent.[12] Rich countries like the United States enjoy relatively advanced technology, have relatively slow population growth, and have historically high rates of investment in physical and human capital. In contrast, the less developed economies use primitive technologies, save little in the way of physical and human capital, and have high population growth rates.

Our discussion in the previous paragraph ignored α and the rate of technical advance v. When we implement the model below, both will be taken to be equal across countries. The role of α was discussed above, but a few further remarks regarding v are in order. First, growth in knowledge is hard to measure, so assuming that v is constant across countries is certainly a convenient starting point. This assumption is also plausible. Presumably the *level* of technology and the contribution to *new* knowledge differ a great deal across countries. However, because of technology diffusion, the growth rates of technical know-how within a country may be similar across countries. That is, although the "leading edge" economies probably develop most of the new ideas and utilize a higher level of technology, the "assimilating" economies may adapt technology at about the same rate, thereby keeping unchanged their *relative* technology levels.

Neoclassical models explain growth as a function of resource accumulation (they do not model **A** endogenously). Following Mankiw et al., we want to see how much of the differences in living standards can be explained by these neoclassical considerations. Consequently, we examine how much of the income variability can be explained by the growth in and quality of the labor force, n and u, and the saving rate, $1 - \theta$. Technology **A** is assumed to be constant across countries. This assumption is surely counterfactual, and we consider the implications of variation in the state of technology below. Holding **A** constant, we use information for the remaining parameters and then compare for pairs of countries the predicted *relative* GDP per worker with the actual GDP differences.

To illustrate our approach, we use the model to explain the relative GDPs of the United States and India in 1990. The GDP per worker in India was $3,230 in 1990, or about 10% of that in the United States. Assuming specific values for the model's parameters allows us to solve the steady state numerically. As noted above, in the United States, physical capital's share of GDP has averaged about .3 for some time; we set $\alpha = .3$ for both countries.[13] From 1980 to 1990 the annual U.S. population growth rate was a bit below 1 percent, at .009. Since each period of our model corresponds to 30 years, annual growth at .9 percent for thirty years would make $L_{t+1}/L_t = 1 + n = (1.009)^{30} = 1.31$, so $n = .31$. Population growth in India was appreciably faster, averaging about 2.1 percent annually. This produces a value of $n = .87$ in that country. Assuming the United States was in a steady state from 1960 to 1990, the annual rate of technical change v equals the growth rate of GDP per worker. This averaged about 1.1 percent from 1960 to 1990 in the United States. For a 30-year period this makes $v = [(1.011)^{30} - 1] = .39$. Recall we model v as equal across countries due to technology diffusion.

The gross of depreciation investment share averaged 21% of GDP in the United States from 1980 to 1990, so we set $1 - \theta = .21$.[14] India's saving rate is appreciably lower, $1 - \theta = .144$. Finally, in 1985 the adult U.S. population had completed 11.8 years of formal schooling, so $u = 11.8$. For India, average schooling was only 3 years, $u = 3$.

Under these assumptions, using (3.18), output per U.S. worker is predicted to be

$$y_t^{w*} = \left[\frac{(1 - \theta)(1 - \alpha)}{(1 + n)(1 + v)} \right]^{\alpha/(1-\alpha)} \mathbf{A}_t(1.1)^u$$

$$= \left[\frac{(.21)(.7)}{(1.31)(1.39)} \right]^{43} \mathbf{A}_t(1.1)^{11.8} = 1.05\mathbf{A}_t.$$

The similar calculations for India produce

$$y_t^{w*} = \left[\frac{(1 - \theta)(1 - \alpha)}{(1 + n)(1 + v)} \right]^{\alpha/(1-\alpha)} \mathbf{A}_t(1.1)^u$$

$$= \left[\frac{(.144)(.7)}{(1.87)(1.39)} \right]^{43} (1.1)^3 \mathbf{A}_t = .33\mathbf{A}_t$$

Thus, even ignoring the large differences in the level of technology across India and the United States, our model predicts that the GDP per worker in India relative to the United States should be

$$.33/1.05 = .314$$

or about 31% of that in the U.S.

In fact, the actual relative income is about .10. If our model had no explanatory power, it would have predicted equal relative incomes, or a ratio of 1.0. A perfectly performing model would have explained the entire difference between 1.0 and .10. Consequently, our model explained about 77% of the income differences between the two countries: $(1 - .31)/(1 - .1) = .69/.9 = .77$. Thus, although the model doesn't account for the entire income difference between the United States and India, it does perhaps surprisingly well in light of all the cultural, political, and historical differences between the countries *and* the fact that we assumed the level of technology **A** was the same in both countries. The vast differences in technology across the countries would seem capable of explaining the remaining 23%.

When differences in technology are less important, the model performs better. To see this, we contrast the United States with Belgium, a relatively advanced economy, in 1990. Population growth was quite slow in Belgium, averaging .001 annually from 1980 to 1990. This produces a value of $1 + n = 1.034$. The investment rate was quite similar to that in the United States, equaling .207 of GDP. Finally, average educational attainment as of 1985 was 9.2 years. Overall, the two countries had nearly identical saving rates, while in the United States educational attainment was higher and population growth slower. Using these values for Belgium produces

$$y_t^{w*} = \left[\frac{(.207)(.7)}{(1.034)(1.39)} \right]^{43} (1.1)^{9.2} \mathbf{A}_t = .896 \mathbf{A}_t.$$

Thus, the predicted income of Belgium relative to the United States is $.896/1.05 = .853$, or 85.3 percent. The actual GDP per worker was 86 percent. In this case, where the "common technology" assumption is more accurate, the model performs brilliantly.

The neoclassical model explains economic growth and the wealth of nations as capital accumulation (human and physical) per worker. The model predicts that long-run worker productivity is determined by three variables: investment in physical capital, investment in human capital, and population growth. Mankiw, Romer, and Weil (1992) examine almost 100 countries and show that these three variables explain, on average, almost 80% of the per capita income differences.[15] Given the vast differences in the cultural, political, and institutional features of these countries, few could have expected the neoclassical model to prove such a success.

Jones (1998) points out a weakness in the neoclassical approach. Using essentially the same approach as Mankiw et al., he plots the predicted values of labor productivity against the actual values for about 120 countries. For the richer half of the countries, the neoclassical predictions are remarkably accurate. However, for the poorer half, the neoclassical model systematically overpredicts worker productivity. The estimation bias stems, of course, from the assumption that all countries in the world share a common production technology. While this drastic, and therefore useful, simplification works for the richer half, if clearly fails for the poorer half.

3.4.2 Conditional Convergence

Table 3.1 indicates that some countries remain mired in both relative and absolute poverty. Poor economies can catch up to their rich counterparts only if they grow faster. However, Table 3.1 makes clear that poor countries such as India sometimes grow slower than more affluent countries such as Taiwan and South Korea. Other examples indicate that relatively poor countries can grow faster (again consider Taiwan and Korea, but now in comparison with the U.S.). Our neoclassical model can explain both high and low growth rates at a given income level.

The neoclassical explanation of why countries grow at different rates focuses on differences in resource accumulation. That model rejects the notion of *absolute convergence*, by which all countries eventually converge to a common income level. Instead, each economy is predicted to converge to its *own* steady state level, depending upon the rates of saving from physical and human capital, and the rate of population growth. This more modest proposition is known as *conditional convergence*.

The key to understanding conditional convergence is to combine the facts that countries have different steady states with the principle of transition dynamics. If all countries in the world share the same steady state, the principle of transition dynamics would predict faster growth among those relatively poor currently, since they would be further below their steady state. However, since countries differ appreciably with respect to their predicted steady states, it is possible for a poor country to be at or close to its steady state while a more affluent country remains some distance below its steady state. In this case, the principle of transitional dynamics predicts the rich country would grow faster, leading to a greater divergence of incomes. Thus, our model appears capable of explaining differences in growth rates, but how does it fare in light of the data?

With some qualification, the evidence is quite supportive of conditional convergence. Barro and Sali-i-Martin (1992) and Mankiw et al. (1992) demonstrate that this prediction is capable of explaining differences in growth rates across countries of the world. Although poor countries do not necessarily grow faster, countries that are "poor" in comparison with their own steady states do tend to grow faster. Jones (1998) finds the same result: He calculates for many countries the deviation of the economy from its predicted steady state, and then plots this relationship against the economy's actual growth rate between 1960 and 1990. Jones finds the further an economy was below its steady state in 1960, the faster was its subsequent growth. Other prominent examples of this phenomenon are the economies of Japan, Korea, Hong Kong, and Singapore circa 1960; they were below their projected steady states at that point, and grew rapidly over the next 30 years.

The neoclassical model explains differences in growth rates in terms of the principle of transition dynamics. There are many reasons countries may not be in steady state. These include changes in the saving rate in the form of human or physical capital, a war that destroys much of an economy's capital stock, or a change in the population growth rate. Any of these create a gap between an economy's current income and its steady state income, causing transitional growth rates to differ from the steady state rate.

3.4.3 Further Considerations

An important area of research in economics is to explain what factors limit a poor country's ability to adopt the technology common to rich countries. The ideas underlying advanced technology are most often nonrival. For example, the ideas underpinning advanced molecular biology do not need to be reinvented by each scientist. With some lag, these ideas make their way into relatively inexpensive scientific journals that anyone, in any country, can purchase. However, to read and digest the contents of the technical journals requires a significant investment of time studying the journal, not to mention a degree of "readiness" conditioned by years of prior human capital investments.

Building on these notions, Jones (1998) presents a model of steady state technology diffusion in which countries with a more educated work force are better able to assimilate the technology of the leading-edge economies. Balanced growth paths in his model are characterized by equal growth rates of human capital and technology in the "adopting" and "leading-edge" economies. Therefore, in steady state, all countries grow at the same rate; poor countries never catch up. In his framework, the wealth of a nation depends on human capital accumulation in two ways. First, as developed in this chapter, the effective labor supply of educated workers is higher. Further, educated workers better assimilate advanced foreign-produced technology into the economy.

Jones' conclusion that poor countries will never catch up assumes that the determinants of steady state GDP other than technology—saving rates, fertility, and educational attainment—differ across countries *and are immutable*. Suppose, though, that the inhabitants of all countries are fundamentally alike. Then, as the technologies of more affluent economies are assimilated, why shouldn't the saving rates, fertility, and educational attainment of assimilating countries change as well? If they do change, there will eventually be a greater degree of absolute convergence of living standards.

Later chapters argue that such mechanisms are operative. In Chapter 6 a model by Rangazas (2000b) is presented in which, for an interval of history, educational attainment rises with income until parents become affluent enough to make the efficient investments in their children. As income continues to rise, educational attainment levels off (barring changes in the rate of return on such investments). Chapter 8 explains how economic development may induce increased labor force participation among married women. Also, as countries develop they undergo a demographic transition in which increases in life expectancy precede dramatic declines in the fertility of the average woman. This suggests the rate of population growth is not an unchanging parameter (see Chapter 9).

The foregoing suggests that the story of conditional convergence may be incomplete. Countries further below their steady states—as implied by relatively recent values for n, θ, and u—will grow faster due to the principle of transition dynamics. However, *viewed over longer periods*, there may also be convergence among n, θ, and u. Should this occur, inequality across countries may ultimately fall. These predictions are consistent with those of Nobel Laureate Robert Lucas (2000), who presents a simple model in which countries begin to develop at different points in time. Late entrants to development grow faster than early entrants. However, the faster growth of late entrants declines as they close the income gap with the early developers. Ultimately all economies in his model grow at the same rate and enjoy similar living standards. World inequality is eventually reduced to preindustrial levels, but with all countries much richer. Given the abject poverty in many parts of the world, this scenario is certainly a hopeful one. But it remains a theoretical prediction. In fact, world inequality has risen since the onset of the Industrial Revolution and several countries in sub-Saharan Africa, for example, do not seem ready to join the club of developed economies.

3.5 GROWTH ACCOUNTING: THE PRODUCTIVITY SLOWDOWN (AND ITS REVIVAL?)[16]

The level of and growth in labor productivity are perhaps the single most important measures of an economy's performance. This section attempts to account for fluctuations in productivity and aggregate output growth. Production functions, such as (3.1), link inputs to output. They may also be used to link *changes* in output to *changes* in inputs. This technique is the basis of *growth accounting*, developed and first implemented by Nobel Laureate Robert Solow (1957). To appreciate his approach, first notice that the percentage contribution to GDP growth of capital over some period may be expressed as the elasticity of output with respect to capital, times the percentage change in capital. For the Cobb-Douglas production function (3.1), that elasticity is α, which is also capital's share of GDP. Likewise, the elasticity of output with respect to effective labor is labor's share of GDP, $1 - \alpha$. Since a change in effective labor can arise from a change in L or $\mathbf{A}$, the growth in output using (3.1) may be expressed as

$$\%\Delta Y = \alpha\%\Delta K + (1 - \alpha)\%\Delta L + (1 - \alpha)\%\Delta \mathbf{A}$$

A somewhat different expression is typically utilized in empirical applications.[17] Production function (3.1) views all technical change as increasing the effectiveness of labor. In contrast, empirical implementations are typically more agnostic about the effects of technical change, allowing it to affect capital and labor effectiveness directly. The level of technology is then termed *multifactor productivity* or *total factor productivity*. A simple production function of this sort is $Y = BK^{\alpha}L^{1-\alpha}$, where B is multifactor productivity. (Actually, this formulation is essentially the same as (3.1), just letting $B = \mathbf{A}^{1-\alpha}$.) For this case, reasoning similar to that above enables us to write the percentage change in GDP as

$$\%\Delta Y = \%\Delta B + \alpha\%\Delta K + (1 - \alpha)\%\Delta L \qquad (3.19)$$

where α and $(1 - \alpha)$ continue to have the same elasticity and GDP-share interpretations. The empirical implementation of growth accounting first measures the observed factor shares, along with the growth in capital, labor, and GDP. Then the growth unexplained by factor accumulation—termed the *Solow residual*—is attributed to technical change. Significantly, this procedure credits to B any increases in output deriving from qualitative improvements in capital and labor (such as more human capital per worker).

This procedure is illustrated using data from the Bureau of Labor Statistics for the period from 1948 to 1973. This interval begins just as the economy has settled down somewhat following the war, and ends just before the OPEC oil embargo. Over that span, annual (real) GDP growth averaged approximately 4%, while the increases in the capital and labor inputs were 3.8% and .6%. Capital's share of GDP was about .3%. Rearranging (3.19) we solve for multifactor productivity as

$$\%\Delta B = \%\Delta Y - \alpha\%\Delta K - (1 - \alpha)\%\Delta L = 4.0 - (.3)(3.8) - (.7)(.6) \approx 2.5$$

Thus, multifactor productivity accounted for roughly 62% ($= (2.5/4) \times 100$) of the growth in GDP over this period. (What were the relative contributions of labor and capital?)

We are particularly interested in changes in labor productivity (output per hour worked), since they produce equal percentage changes in hourly wages, so long as labor markets are perfectly competitive. Labor productivity growth is found by subtracting the percentage increase in labor from that in GDP, $\%\Delta y^w \equiv \%\Delta Y - \%\Delta L$. This measure grew at a robust average annual rate of $4.0 - .62$, or about 3.4% over the 1948 to 1973 period, dramatically raising the standard of living. Using (3.19) we can express labor productivity growth in terms of multifactor productivity growth and the capital-labor ratio,

$$\%\Delta y^w = \%\Delta B + \alpha\%\Delta k \tag{3.20}$$

This expression will prove useful below.

Unfortunately, labor productivity growth slowed appreciably after the post-World War II period. In fact, from 1973 to 1994, labor productivity grew only at a 1.2% annual clip. Much of this decline resulted from a slowing of multifactor productivity growth. This measure increased but .6% annually, compared with 2.5% in the earlier period. The effects of this slower growth differed significantly across skill or educational groups. Beginning in the 1980s, the real wages of the college educated increased, while those of the less skilled stagnated, or fell. For this reason, wage inequality grew rapidly in recent years. One prominent explanation is that the technical change that occurred during this period was "skill-biased," or complementary to skill and/or ability. This phenomenon is examined in Chapter 7.

The pace of productivity growth has picked up significantly in recent years. Between 1995 and 1999, average labor productivity growth grew at a rate of 2.65 percent (Gordon, 2000, Table 1). Further, for the year ending with the second quarter of 2000, productivity rose more than 5%. However, even the rate between 1995 and 1999 is below that of the post-World War II years, and it is difficult to know if this recent acceleration can be sustained.

This *productivity slowdown* was cause for real concern. To put it in perspective, first note that in a recession, real income per capita falls by perhaps a few percent relative to its "usual" path—and often makes up part of the loss during the next expansion. In contrast, had labor productivity grown as fast between 1973 and 1994 as it did between 1948 and 1973, real hourly wages in 1994 would have been over 50 percent larger! Thus, until quite recently, the productivity slowdown appeared to be the most important economic issue confronting us. Was the slowdown a consequence of bad economic policy or of deep structural factors—such as demographics—which are less amenable to policy intervention? Similarly, what are the sources of the recent revival in productivity growth? Unfortunately, although much progress has been made, there remains disagreement concerning the reasons behind the slowdown, its magnitude, and whether it is temporary or permanent. Similarly, there is no consensus on whether the recent gains in productivity can be sustained. We now consider factors relevant to each.

Some economists view the slowdown as being, at least in part, an artifact of improper measurement. A couple of examples illustrate the problem. Until October of 1999, the Bureau of Economic Analysis assumed that banking output rises at the same rate as hours worked by bank employees. This practice ignored the impact of ATM transactions, electronic funds transfers, and other banking innovations that have improved efficiency. Another change made in October of 1999 is to treat computer software purchases by business as investment (which contributes to measured GDP and therefore output per worker) instead of as a nondurable input, as before. These and related revisions boost productivity growth by around two-tenths of 1% compared with the figures discussed above—hardly enough to alter the character of the slowdown.

More generally, Griliches (1994) notes that productivity growth is easier to measure in some sectors (such as agriculture and manufacturing) than in others (such as medical care and finance). According to his estimates, the "hard-to-measure" sectors—for which productivity growth will be underestimated—grew from 51 to 69% of total output between 1947 and 1990. Further, he finds that over three-quarters of computer investment has gone into hard-to-measure sectors. The potentially substantial productivity effects of these investments are therefore largely invisible in the data.

Although there is undoubtedly some validity to Griliches' arguments, they do not seem to explain the fact that real wage growth was as tepid as labor productivity growth from the early 1970s to the early 1990s. In fact, real wage growth was flat, at best, for less skilled workers over this entire interval (see Chapter 7). If worker productivity was rising faster than measurable output, wages would be bid up by firms, who would find such "inexpensive" labor profitable. However, computations of real wage growth are only as reliable as the price indices they employ. And, many economists believe the Consumer Price Index (CPI), which is used to convert nominal wages into real wages, overstates inflation. In 1996 a commission established by the U.S. Senate concluded that in recent years the CPI has overstated inflation about 1.1% per year. As examples, the CPI does not adequately account for adjustments by consumers when prices change, nor does it reflect fully the cost savings associated with the growth in large retail discounters. Consequently, real wage (and therefore labor productivity) growth may have been much faster than reported. On one hand, in order for this mismeasurement to explain the slowdown, the bias in the CPI would have had to be substantially greater following 1973 than in the earlier period. On the other hand, this bias may have increased in sectors such as medical care in recent years. Although costs have risen dramatically in that sector, so has the quality of care, as measured, for example, by increased cancer survival probabilities.

Other economists see the slowdown as quite real, but argue that it might be temporary (so that recent productivity gains may be expected to persist). At the microeconomic level, worker productivity is typically modeled as increasing with education and experience. Two phenomena caused a decline in average worker experience in the 1970s and 1980s, perhaps contributing to the productivity slowdown. First, there was a rapid increase in the labor force participation of women with young children. For instance, just between 1970 and 1980 the proportion of women age 20 to 24 with children who were employed increased from 23 to 38% (see Chapter 8). Also, the large number of baby boomers born in the 1950s and early 1960s began swelling the ranks of the employed in the 1970s and 1980s. Neither the young mothers nor young boomers had much, if any, work experience, serving to dilute the average experience in the labor force. This effect is believed to dominate the effect of somewhat higher education among these entrants. In terms of the equation for labor productivity growth (3.20), lower average experience reduces multifactor productivity growth. Also, this rapid influx of workers slowed capital deepening which, by (3.20), also translates into slower productivity growth. That is, although capital grew at roughly the same clip as before, labor grew faster, reducing the capital-labor ratio and worker productivity.

However, it appears that these changes in the age-sex mix are incapable of explaining a very large share of the slowdown (cf. Auerbach and Kotlikoff, 1998, p. 21). In some ways this is bad news; if these were the culprits, productivity would rather mechanically return to prior growth rates once labor growth returned to its prior rate and experience stabilized.

During the late 1970s and into the mid-1980s, the consensus explanation for the slowdown was the oil price spikes of the 1970s. The deep recessions across many countries were certainly consistent with that hypothesis. However, slow growth continued into the 1980s and early 1990s, even as oil prices in real terms returned to their previous levels. Nevertheless, the spike in oil prices in 2000 must be viewed as a serious threat to the recent pace of productivity gains.

Another potential explanation of slower productivity growth is the decline in the national saving rate. The average net national saving rate from NNP averaged about 11 percent from 1960 to 1974, but averaged just above 5 percent between 1980 and 1994. In closed economies where foreign trade imbalances cannot occur, a lower domestic saving rate implies a lower domestic capital accumulation rate. Slower capital deepening implies slower productivity growth through the second term in equation (3.20). New capital raises productivity in additional ways, as well. For example, new technologies are embodied in later vintages of capital so that tools become better, or more sophisticated. Further, capital accumulation may also entail economy-wide positive externalities as information about working with the new technologies spreads from plant to plant. These effects enter into (3.20) as slower multifactor productivity growth. Since slower multifactor productivity growth accounts for most of the decline in labor productivity growth, these indirect effects would have to bulk large in order for reduced capital deepening to be a principal explanation.

Further, the effect of reduced savings on productivity has been muted by increased net foreign investment in the United States. This has kept the decline in domestic investment below that in domestic savings. Historically, over long periods there is a close relationship between domestic savings and domestic investment. This suggests the costs of a reduced U.S. domestic saving rate have been deferred, boding ill for future productivity growth. On a more hopeful note, the savings of the federal government have in recent years gone from negative and large to being positive and large.

The slowdown may have been a consequence of reduced investment in the intentional creation of productive ideas, or new technologies. As stressed by the "new growth theory," firms invest in research and development (R&D) in hopes of earning a profit. Our model has stressed that technical growth is an important source of increased worker productivity. In the United States, R&D expenditures fell from over 4% in the 1960s to less than 3% in the 1970s. To the extent that this reduced the expansion of productive ideas, slower worker productivity is predicted. However, the evidence suggests that this decline in R&D had only a modest effect on labor productivity, explaining perhaps 10 to 15% of the slowdown (Griliches, 1988, pp. 9–21).

One reason to fear a long-term downward trend in productivity growth is the shift of the economy away from manufacturing toward services. In general, labor productivity grows faster in manufacturing (consider car production) than in service sectors (a back massage, anyone?). Auerbach and Kotlikoff (1998, p. 20) note that "Manufacturing's share of GDP fell from 29% in 1950 to only 18 percent in 1994. By contrast, the share of GDP produced in finance, insurance, real estate, and other services rose from 20 percent in 1950 to 37 percent by 1994."Although this reallocation of labor is no doubt part of the answer, the evidence once again suggests that most of the decline is from other sources.

In fairness, comparing productivity growth in the 1970s and 1980s with that following World War II may be akin to comparing other PGA stars with Tiger Woods. That is, it is possible that both Tiger and productivity growth during that "golden age" were unique. Taking a longer perspective, Gordon (2000) notes that multifactor productivity growth was almost as low in the period 1870–1913, at .77%, as in the period 1972–1995, when it averaged .62%. Thus, it could be that what is unusual, or in need of explanation, is the torrid 1.6% growth rate of multifactor productivity from 1913 to 1964. If the periods 1870–1913 and 1972–1995 are more the norm, there is no reason to expect a return to the rapid productivity growth of 1913–1964.

Further, Jones (2000) suggests the economy is currently benefiting from transitional growth, which cannot be expected to persist indefinitely. He notes that since the 1960s, the educational attainment of workers and the share of the labor force devoted to research have both risen substantially (even taking into account lower R&D expenditures in the 1980s). These should have placed the economy on a transition path toward a higher steady state, yielding temporarily faster growth. Once the economy reaches the new steady state, productivity growth may be expected to slow.

More optimistically, some argue that the introduction of computer technologies into the work place required substantial time investments by workers. This reduced their production and therefore wages during the investment period (Heckman, Lochner, and Taber, 1998). However, these costs have now largely been incurred by existing workers. Viewed in this light, the strong recent real wage and productivity growth may be only the start of a productivity boom. Similarly, Jorgenson and Stiroh (2000) conclude that "(p)roductivity growth in the production of information technology is responsible for a sizable part of the recent spurt" in multifactor productivity growth "and can be identified with price declines in high-tech assets and semi-conductors" (p. 43).

In conclusion, productivity growth from the 1970s until the mid-1990s was slower than in several preceding decades. Although part of this slowdown may have been illusory, due to measurement error, slow real wage growth suggests it was real and sizeable. Explanations include a reduced saving rate, increased labor force participation by inexperienced workers, a slowdown in R&D, and a shift away from manufacturing toward services. However, a longer perspective suggests that the rate of productivity growth in recent decades is close to the historical norm. There has been a modest upswing in labor productivity growth in recent years. It is hard to predict whether this faster growth will persist. An ability to maintain faster productivity growth would not only raise after-tax income growth, but could also provide tax revenues to help shore up Social Security (see Chapter 4).

3.5.1   Growth Accounting and Rapid Growth in East Asia

One of the questions posed early in the chapter was whether the extremely high rapid growth rates experienced by some countries ("Growth Miracles" in Table 3.1) are sustainable. We address this issue by applying growth accounting techniques to those newly industrialized economies. Between 1966 and 1990, GDP per capita in South Korea, Taiwan, and Singapore grew at average annual rates of better than 6.5%, and Hong Kong averaged 5.7% growth (Young, 1995, Table 1). Young details evidence showing that these "growth miracles" were a consequence of transitorily high rates of factor accumulation rather than of rapid increases in multifactor productivity growth. On average, during the interval of rapid growth, these countries experienced significant increases in the labor force participation rate, educational attainment, and investment as a share of GDP. Each of these accelerated growth in GDP per capita. However, since none of these can rise indefinitely, each may be understood as contributing to transitional growth. Consequently, the rates of per capita income growth were apparently destined to decline (and did in the 1990s). Young concludes that "Neoclassical growth theory . . . can explain most of the difference between the performance of the NICs and that of other postwar economies" (p. 675).

3.6 SUMMARY

This chapter developed the neoclassical theory of economic growth and applied that framework to address cross-country differences in labor productivity, productivity growth, and the late twentieth-century productivity slowdown in the United States. The model includes labor, capital, and output markets, which achieve general equilibrium each period. Households supply labor and capital and demand output for consumption. Firms supply output (the GDP) and demand labor and capital. Neoclassical production functions assume constant returns to scale in capital and effective labor, and diminishing returns to either alone. Capital and labor are profitable to firms until their marginal products have fallen equal to their prices in the input market. The more tools per worker, the higher is the marginal product of labor, which is the wage. The more relatively plentiful is capital, the lower is the marginal product of capital, and thus the interest rate.

The supplies of labor and capital are known at the start of any period t, meaning they are completely inelastic with respect to prices in period t: The supply of labor is just the number of young in that period; the supply of capital (or of savings) is given by the savings of the young of period t − 1. The savings of the young of a period increase with their wage earnings. The total demand for output is that for household consumption and firm investment; aggregate demand equals GDP.

The economy may or may not be on a balanced growth path (a steady state equilibrium). In steady state, capital and the wage per unit of effective labor (k and w) are constant, as is the interest rate. Countries that are away from their steady state converge to it. If k is below the steady state value, the savings of the young exceed the current stock of capital, so tools and wage per unit of effective labor are higher in the next period. Eventually k attains its steady state level, ultimately leveling off because of the diminishing returns to capital. In steady state, aggregate variables grow at the rate of technical advance plus that of population growth, or $v + n$. While n helps determine the size of the economy, the steady state growth rate of labor productivity is simply v.

The state of technology and the rate of technical advance are exogenous in neoclassical models. In the absence of human capital accumulation, the model produces counterfactual implications when it is required to explain very much growth. Augmented with human capital, the neoclassical model predicts that long-run worker productivity is determined by three variables: investment in physical capital, investment in human capital (or educational attainment), and population growth. The predictive ability of the neoclassical model has been demonstrated across broad samples of countries, with these three variables explaining perhaps 80% of the per capita income differences on average. The model performs least well among poor countries. This is unsurprising, since technology is counterfactually assumed equal across countries.

Countries grow faster the farther they are below their steady state. This principle of transition dynamics is a result of diminishing returns to capital; as the economy moves closer to the steady state, capital deepening has a smaller effect on the wage, reducing the increase in capital the following period. This principle, coupled with the fact that different countries have different steady states, gives rise to the prediction of conditional convergence. Empirically, as predicted, the growth rate of an economy depends on its relation to its steady state, not on whether it is currently rich or poor. However, the parameter values underlying claims of conditional convergence may be a function of the state of development. If this is true, there may be an increasing degree of absolute convergence in the twenty-first century.

A permanent increase in the saving rate induces an interval of capital deepening, with transitional growth above the steady state rate. However, due to diminishing returns to capital, the steady state rate of growth is independent of the saving rate. Significantly, though, output per worker is higher in the high saving rate steady state; this increase is greater the higher is capital's share of GDP. The share of GDP devoted to human capital investment is at least as large as that invested in physical capital.

Growth accounting analyzes the factors underlying growth over a specific period. The growth unaccounted for by factor accumulation is termed *multifactor productivity*. Labor productivity growths lowed in the early 1970s through the mid-1990s, largely because of slower multifactor productivity growth. A single convincing explanation of the productivity slowdown remains elusive. Nevertheless, partial explanations abound:capital deepening slowed because of faster labor growth (especially among the inexperienced) and because of a lower national saving rate; the rate of technical expansion declined due to reduced R&D and a growth in services relative to manufacturing. Recently, productivity has grown more rapidly, though the prospects for future growth are uncertain.

The framework developed in this chapter supplies answers to a variety of important questions. However, it leaves unaddressed other issues in the theory of growth. For while the rate of steady state growth was shown to depend upon the rate of technical advance, that rate was exogenous to our model. This shortcoming is partially remedied in Chapters 7 and 9, where we discuss links between human capital and technical change and between population growth and technical change. Although human capital accumulation and population growth are potentially important to growth, they were also modeled exogenously. In Chapters 6 and 7 for human capital, and Chapter 9 for population, these resources are accumulated in accordance with utility maximization. Also, little mention has been made about the potential role of government in enhancing the standard of living within an economy. This is taken up at several later junctures, beginning with the upcoming Chapter 4.

ENDNOTES

1. Conversations with Peter Rangazas significantly raised the quality of this section.

2. Entered this way, the technology variable A_t is said to be *labor augmenting* (or Harrod neutral). If technical progress had entered the production function with the same coefficient as capital, $Y_t = (A_t K_t)^{\alpha} L_t^{1-\alpha}$, it would be termed *capital augmenting,* and if knowledge entered as $Y_t = A_t K_t^{\alpha} L_t^{1-\alpha}$, technical progress would be termed *Hicks neutral.* Our choice proves consistent with the stylized fact that K/Y is roughly constant in the long run; it also eases the exposition.

3. In chapters 6 and 7 human capital decisions based on utility-maximization are examined, including their implications for economic growth. Chapters 7 and 9 each contain discussions motivating the rate of technical advance. Chapter 9 focuses on utility-maximizing fertility decisions, and the implications for economic growth.

4. This implies that effective time in equation (3.1) would need to be multiplied by $1 - v$.

5. A partial derivative is just the natural extension of the concept of a "regular" derivative to functions of more than one variable. In the calculation of a partial derivative, all other variables are held constant (then the rules for differentiation of functions of a single variable apply). Actually, the standard notation for partial derivatives employs the symbol ∂ in place of d, as in $\partial Y / \partial K$.

6. The conclusion that savings and the saving rate rise with the rates of population and income growth is an oversimplification. For faster population growth means more children to be fed, and possibly lower saving rates among the young. If this is true, and if the percentage reduction in savings per young household exceeds the percentage increase in the number of such households, faster population growth would lower savings.

The link between income growth and savings is also complex. Since equation (3.11) assumes that each person works only one period, productivity growth increases savings because the young receive a higher entry-level wage than did their parents. There is no allowance for earnings growth over the life cycle, an effect that works in the opposite direction. To see this, consider a young worker who, expecting no income growth over the life cycle, has decided upon consumption and savings when young. Now, before those plans are implemented, suppose the worker comes to expect earnings growth over the life cycle. This increases his or her estimate of human wealth, thus causing an increase in consumption and a decrease in saving. If this future earnings, or human wealth, effect dominates that of a higher entry-level salary, an increase in productivity growth would reduce savings of the young.

This effect of human wealth on current consumption depends upon the worker *expecting* increased earnings growth. For example, only if U.S. workers in 1950 had correctly foreseen the rapid growth over the next twenty years could the human wealth effect have lowered the savings rate during the 1950s. Similarly, only if workers in the early 1970s had correctly foreseen the productivity slowdown of the next two decades might the slower actual growth have translated into a higher savings rate at that time. However, if periods of unusual growth are unexpected, "fast" growth would not entail the human wealth effect on consumption while young, making it likely that growth would increase savings. In fact, the saving rate in the

United States rose in the 1950s and began declining in the 1970s. Thus, either the full increase in human wealth effect was not anticipated or other factors have been stronger. At any rate, we can appreciate that the relationship between earnings and saving rates is more complicated than we initially suggested (cf. Carroll and Weil, 1994).

7. Recall that with Cobb-Douglas utility, savings decisions when young are independent of the interest rate expected in the next period. If savings of the young in t were affected by r_{t+1}, so would be the supply of the capital-effective labor ratio in t + 1. The intersection of the supply and demand curves would still yield a well-defined equilibrium unless, as is unlikely, the supply curve were more negatively sloped than the demand curve.

8. This principle is easily demonstrated using the transition equation, repeated below

$$k_{t+1} = (1 - \theta)(1 - \alpha)k_t^\alpha/[(1 + n)(1 + v)]$$

To highlight the principle, calculate the percentage change in capital intensity between t and t + 1. This is done by, first, subtracting k_t from each side and then dividing both sides by k_t. This yields

$$(k_{t+1} - k_t)/k_t = (1 - \theta)(1 - \alpha)k_t^{\alpha-1}/[(1 + n)(1 + v)] - 1$$

Notice that the right-hand side is decreasing in k_t since it is raised to a negative power. Consequently (upon multiplying by 100), the percentage increase in capital intensity is higher the lower is the level of capital intensity; economies with lower capital intensity grow faster.

9. Recall, though, that in our model each period is roughly 30 years. If the annual interest rate now is 6.5 percent, for our 30-year periods $1 + r_1 = (1.065)^{30} = 6.614$. Then, since $r_1/r_0 = .272$, $r_0 = 24.3$. This implies an average annualized rate for that entire 30-year period of $24.3^{1/30} - 1 = 11.2\%$. However, since capital accumulation is initially quite fast, so is the decline in interest rates. This implies that the annual interest rate 100 years ago, at the start of that 30-year period, was far in excess of 11.2%.

10. In Chapter 6 we shall see that diminishing returns to human capital investments and higher foregone earnings among older students tend to reduce the rate of return as the number of years in formal schooling rises. This 10% return may thus be considered the return to the median number of years of schooling.

11. Unlike technology and population, which both grow in the steady state, years of education must be constant. Otherwise, in the long run, education would go to zero if falling, or to all of life if rising. Since u is unchanging, it "cancels out" in the numerator and denominator of k_{t+1}, which is why there is no u in the expression for k*.

12. In chapters 6 and 7 we will see that the relationship is more complex than this, since the social rate of return appears to fall at higher levels of education.

13. The following numbers are drawn from Jones (1998, tables 2.1 and B.2).

14. The relationship between this figure and the proportion saved by the young, $1 - \theta$, is inexact for several reasons. First, although saving equals investment in a closed economy (i.e., no international trade) when government savings equal zero, trade and budget imbalances break that equality. Second, our model stresses net investment, not gross. Finally, the link between $1 - \theta$ and the net saving rate depends upon the population growth rate and rate of technical change.

15. Their conclusions have been criticized on empirical grounds. They proxy human capital accumulation within a country by secondary school enrollment rates. Klenow and Rodriguez-Clare (1997) show that by adding primary school enrollment rates in the calculation of human capital, the contribution of human capital in explaining cross-country differences is significantly reduced. In turn, Topel (1999) has shown that the Klenow and Rodriguez-Clare results are not robust.

16. Communications with Peter Rangazas dramatically improved this discussion.

17. An important subtlety is illuminated using the expression above. Suppose the economy is in steady state; after one period the percentage increase in Y is n + v. Above, we saw that the stock of capital also grows at rate n + v, while labor increases n percent per period, and labor effectiveness progresses at rate v. Substituting these values into the expression yields

$$n + v = \alpha(n + v) + (1 - \alpha)n + (1 - \alpha)v$$

This reveals that capital accumulation contributed the proportion $\alpha(n + v)/(n + v) = \alpha$, or about 30%, to *steady state* growth, both per worker and in the aggregate. Thus, while there is no steady state growth in labor productivity without technical advance, part of the growth associated with the technical advance is due to additional capital accumulation. Intuitively, the greater effectiveness of labor increases the productivity of capital, providing some respite from the diminishing returns. Thus, the additional capital would not have been employed were it not for the technical advance, but the growth in income would not be as large without the additional capital accumulation.

QUESTIONS AND PROBLEMS

▶ REVIEW
QUESTIONS

1. A. What is the difference between the number of workers and the amount of effective labor? Between capital per worker and capital per unit of effective labor?
    B. What are the characteristics of a neoclassical production function? If there were constant returns to capital alone, what would the value of α need to be? Illustrate.
    C. Interpret the conditions for profit maximization in the input markets from both microeconomic and macroeconomic perspectives.
    D. Interpret α.

2. A. K is a reproducible input, i.e., can *make* more of it.
    A. Given production function (3.1), what are the returns to scale in the production of K?
    B. Assume the amount of effective labor is fixed. Plot on a graph the marginal product of capital as a function of K assuming, in turn, that $\alpha = 1$, $\alpha < 1$, and $\alpha > 1$ (As you do this do not change the exponent on effective labor; it stays the same. That is, it is no longer $1 - \alpha$, but rather some constant.)

3. A. In the steady state, at what rate do the following variables grow, and why? (a) w_t, (b) aggregate effective labor, (c) first-period consumption per worker, (d) output per worker, (e) the stock of capital, (f) GDP.
    B. In our model, if the economy is in a steady state, is it also in general equilibrium? If it is in general equilibrium, is it necessarily in a steady state?

4. Explain intuitively and show graphically the effect on steady state output per worker of an increase in the rate of population growth.

5. A. How does the neoclassical model perform in terms of predicting output per worker across countries at a given point in time? For what type countries does it perform least well? Why?

B. Does the model, including the extension with educational attainment, predict that the countries of the world will converge to a common income level? Explain, organizing your comments around the idea of *conditional convergence*.

6. Consider the model when n = v = 0, **A** = 1 and u = 0, i.e., where all the action concerns physical capital accumulation. Suppose the economy is in steady state. Now suppose that for some reason there is a *decline* in the propensity to save on the part of the young. A. Intuitively explain the implications of this for the economy's short- and long-term growth path, focusing on how and why the savings of the young are changing through time; use the transition diagram to aid your explanation. B. Why does the effect on steady state output of a change in physical savings depend upon human capital's share of GDP?

7. The "Productivity Slowdown" refers to the decrease in the growth rate of labor productivity or output per unit of labor between 1973 and 1994 (officially per hour worked).
   A. Describe the basic trends in labor productivity growth from 1948 to 1973, from 1973 to 1994, and from 1996 to the present.
   B. Briefly explain the roles of (a) labor force and experience growth, (b) R&D expenditures, (c) energy prices, (d) the change in the production mix.
   C. Discuss the importance of the choice of time period used for the basis of comparison in assessing "long-run" productivity. What are the prospects for a return to higher long-term productivity growth?
   D. Has the slowdown in productivity growth been experienced equally by all educational groups? What is the explanation given for this?

8. **A.** Is a model of transitional physical capital accumulation capable of explaining a large portion of observed economic growth without producing counterfactual implications? Explain.
   B. Why does taking into account that human capital is also a form of capital help overcome this problem?
   C. Does the effect of an increase in the saving rate depend on human capital's share of GDP? Explain.

▶ PROBLEMS

1. The time required for income per worker to double is approximately given by dividing 70 by the growth rate (×100). Suppose that currently GDP per worker is 40 in the United States and 3 in China (which roughly captures their relative incomes). Between 1960 and 1990 GDP per worker grew at an average annual rate of 1.4% in the United States. In recent years GDP per worker in China has grown extremely fast, let us say at 7% per annum. If these growth rates persist:
   A. How many years would be required for GDP to double in each country?
   B. What will be the incomes per worker in each country fifty years from now (about the time you may retire)?

2. **A.** Show that $1 - \alpha$ is equal to labor's share of GDP.
   B. Show that if each input is paid its marginal product, profits are zero.

*3. **A.** Show that $y_t = w_t + r_t k_t$.

   B. Show that output equals consumption plus investment, $Y_t = C_{1t} + C_{2t} + K_{t+1} - K_t$

4. Recall the expression for steady state output per worker for the model based on the extended neoclassical production function, which includes educational attainment. Let's use this expression to explain the relative GDPs per worker in two countries, say Brazil and Ireland, in 1990. In 1990, GDP per capita in Brazil was roughly 46% of that in Ireland. To use the formula for steady state output per worker, assume each economy is in steady state. For both suppose that the *annual* rate of technical progress is 1.1% (i.e., .011) and $\alpha = .3$. The level of technology, A_{1990}, will also be taken as equal across the two countries. We model the saving rate as $1 - \theta$, labor force grows at rate n, and educational attainment equals u. For Brazil $1 - \theta = .169$, the *annual* rate of population growth averages .021, or 2.1%, and the average educational attainment of the labor force $u = 3.5$ years of schooling. In contrast, for Ireland the saving rate is .196, or 19.6% of GDP, the annual average rate of population growth is .003, and $u = 8.0$. Did the model work better or worse for these two countries than it did for India and the United States? Why do you think this is the case?

5. Suppose the economy is in steady state in period t and that the following parameter values prevail: $\alpha = .3$, $n = 1$, $v = 1$, $\theta = .4$, $A_t = 100$, $K_t = 400$, and $L_t = 100$. Solve for k^* wage earnings per worker in t, $C_{1,t}$, K_t, and Y_t.

6. Suppose production in an economy is given by the production function:

$$Y = BK^\alpha L^{1-\alpha}$$

where B is multifactor productivity and $\alpha = 0.3$. Suppose that

Year	GDP	Capital	Labor
1990	1000	200	400
2000	2000	300	600

   A. Solve for multifactor productivity in each year. *Use the growth accounting formula* to find the percentage change in multifactor productivity.

   B. How much of output growth over this period is due to physical capital accumulation? Growth in labor? Multifactor productivity growth? Also, what are the *relative* contributions of each? (Note that totals may not sum to exactly 100 percent.)

*7. **A.** Assume that preferences are now the general CES-type of equation (2.1). Derive the period $t + 1$ supply of capital intensity equation in terms of the actual capital intensity in period t. However, assume now that θ is the coefficient on wealth in equation (2.3) of Chapter 2. Sketch the supply of capital intensity curve as was done in the text. Why do you have to know the value of σ to make a sketch? Sketch the demand for capital intensity equation for period $t + 1$. Use the sketch to come up with parameter restrictions that would guarantee a unique equilibrium exists.

B. Derive the transition equation associated with these preferences. Why can't you easily sketch the transition equation as in the text? Can you establish parameter restrictions that guarantee that a unique steady state capital-labor ratio exists? (Use a sketch.)

*8. Suppose all you know is that the transition equation takes the form $k_{t+1} = f(k_t)$. What properties must the function f have to guarantee existence, uniqueness, and dynamic stability of a steady state? Can you draw a transition diagram that gives rise to a unique steady state that is not stable? How about to multiple steady states? What required properties do these transition equations not possess?

INTERGENERATIONAL FISCAL POLICY AND CAPITAL ACCUMULATION

This chapter examines the implications for economic growth and the distribution of welfare across generations of the federal government's consumption, tax, and borrowing policies. First, though, section 4.1 considers the efficiency of a given level of capital accumulation. In section 4.2, the intertemporal link between the government's consumption and taxes is developed. A general relationship between government finance, household savings, and aggregate capital accumulation is also derived. Section 4.3 applies that framework to changes in government consumption and investment, emphasizing how those implications vary with the method of finance. The next section concerns itself with how a given stream of government consumption is financed, stressing the implications for capital accumulation of changing the assignment of taxes across generations. Section 4.5 analyzes structural aspects of the Social Security system and considers some general principles regarding reform of that system. A sixth section discusses income taxation, focusing on the efficiency issues surrounding capital income taxation. A brief summary concludes the chapter.[1]

4.1 DYNAMIC EFFICIENCY AND THE GOLDEN RULE[2]

The desirability of polices affecting savings depends upon whether current capital accumulation is appropriate. At first, suggesting that the current capital stock might be "too large" may seem peculiar. After all, Chapter 3 stressed that increasing the fraction of output saved temporarily increases the economy's growth rate, yielding steady state increases in output per person. However, accumulating additional capital requires a reduction in aggregate consumption in at least one period. Thus, steady state output gains need to be weighed against consumption losses during the transition. Also, due to population growth (and depreciation, which we continue to ignore), increases in steady state *output* per capita from capital deepening need not translate to increases in steady state *consumption* per capita. To develop these points, we assume the population grows at rate n > 0, but at first we abstract from technical change (so that v = 0 and **A** = 1).

The economy's steady state in Chapter 3 was a consequence of many independently chosen utility- and profit-maximizing decisions. To assess the efficiency of that decentralized economy, now imagine there is a benevolent social planner who chooses the economy's saving rate (and thus capital-labor ratio) so as to maximize steady state consumption per person. The resource constraint the planner faces at time t, expressed in per worker terms,[3] is (recalling the second period is devoted to retirement)

$$C_{1,t} + C_{2,t}/(1 + n) + s_t = y^w_t \qquad (4.1)$$

where s_t is savings per worker and, recall, y^w_t is output per worker. In the steady state there must be just enough savings to keep the capital-labor ratio constant. Since the population grows at rate n, so must capital. Consequently, $s_t = nk_t = nk^*$ (where, as in Chapter 3, the asterisk is used to denote the steady state value for a variable). Also from Chapter 3, equation (3.16), we saw that steady state output per worker is $(k^*)^\alpha$ when **A** = 1. Making these substitutions in equation (4.1), in steady state,

$$C_1{}^* + C_2{}^*/(1 + n) + nk^* = (k^*)^\alpha$$

so that steady state consumption per worker is

$$C_1{}^* + C_2{}^*/(1 + n) = (k^*)^\alpha - nk^* \qquad (4.2)$$

The social planner's problem is to choose k* in order to maximize the right-hand side of equation (4.2). To maximize $(k^*)^\alpha - nk^*$, consider how each term responds to a marginal increase in k. Increasing k* by one unit increases output per worker by its marginal product,

$$d(y^w)^*/dk = \alpha(k^*)^{\alpha-1} = r^*$$

(equation (3.5) shows that the derivative is equal to r*). This marginal product declines as more capital is accumulated because of diminishing marginal returns. The second right-hand-side term of (4.2) reminds us that an additional unit of capital per worker requires that an additional n units of output be put aside each period to fund the capital of the subsequent, larger generations of workers. *Thus, to maximize steady state consumption per worker, capital should be increased so long as r* > n.*

The value of k* that maximizes consumption per worker is termed the *Golden Rule*, k^*_G. Consumption per worker is graphed as a function of k* in Figure 4.1. This function is concave because of the diminishing returns to capital. When $k^* < k^*_G$. the interest rate exceeds the population growth rate, and steady state consumption could be increased by increasing savings. Such an economy is said to be *dynamically efficient*. In such an economy it is possible to increase steady state consumption per worker only by saving more

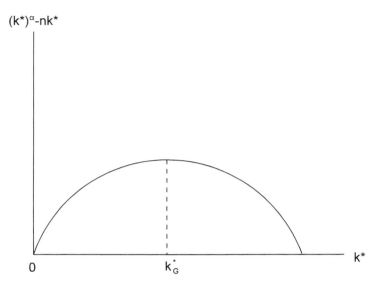

Figure 4.1 The golden rule of capital accumulation

now, which means reducing current consumption. In a dynamically efficient economy, the steady state consumption gains accruing to *each* generation in the new steady state must be weighed against consumption losses to those alive when consumption is curtailed. If each generation is weighed equally, policies that increase the saving rate should be implemented, all else the same.

If there is "too much" capital per worker so that $k^* > k_G^*$ and $r^* < n$, the economy is *dynamically inefficient*. In this case, suppose workers in t each increase consumption by one unit. Capital per worker would fall by one unit, lowering output per worker by r^* units in period $t + 1$. However, needing only to maintain this lower level of k frees up n units previously needed to maintain the old, higher, level of k. Thus, not only is consumption higher by 1 in period t, it is also higher by $n - r^*$ units in $t + 1$. In dynamically inefficient economies, *every* generation's welfare can be raised by lowering the economy's saving rate! Thus, the efficiency of perfectly competitive economies stressed by Adam Smith does not necessarily obtain when one views an economy over time. (Allowing for transitional changes in factor prices would affect only the quantitative conclusions, with the qualitative results remaining unchanged.)

Similar results obtain once long-run growth in per capita income at rate v is introduced. The *modified Golden Rule* equates r^* to the sum of population and per capita income growth, $n + v$. As before, if k^* is too large, everyone can be made better off by increasing consumption in the current period. However, when the economy is dynamically efficient, the argument in favor of capital deepening is weakened somewhat. For now the current generation that must forego consumption to increase k^* is already less affluent than those future generations whose consumption would rise.

The expression for the steady state interest rate in our model can be found by substituting the expression (3.15) for k* , repeated here,

$$k* = \left(\frac{(1 - \theta)(1 - \alpha)}{(1 + n)(1 + v)} \right)^{\frac{1}{1-\alpha}} \tag{3.15}$$

into that for the interest rate. Simplifying this produces

$$r* = \alpha(1 + n)(1 + v)/[(1 - \theta)(1 - \alpha)]$$

Estimates of these parameters for the United States were motivated in the discussion of development accounting in section 3.3; n = .31, v = .39, 1 − θ = .21, and α = .30. These figures produce an r* of 3.7, while n + v equals .7. These values, recall, are for periods of 30 years. This r* translates to an annual rate of return of about 4.5%, while the implied annual rates of population and per capita income growth are .9% and 1.1%. These numbers suggest the economy is dynamically efficient, and far below the Golden Rule. In these calculations, doubling the rate of growth in GDP per capita does little to close the gap, since this also increases the annual interest rate a bit more than 1%.

Although these numbers are suggestive at best, the majority of economists do believe the economy is dynamically efficient (cf. Mankiw, 1997). However, some economists argue that when the uncertain returns to capital are explicitly taken into account, it becomes less clear whether the economy is dynamically efficient (cf. Bullard and Russell, 1999).

Assuming the economy is dynamically efficient, fiscal policies that increase capital accumulation would increase consumption along the steady state path. Further, if those gains to future generations are viewed as outweighing the consumption losses to current generations, such policies would also increase social welfare. If economists can discern the path of consumption along the path of transition to a higher capital intensity steady state, it would be possible to identify the range of weights applied to each generation's welfare that would make such a policy desirable. This is no easy task. However, since most proposed policies are viewed more favorably if they tout increased savings, there is some sentiment in favor of increasing capital accumulation. We return to these issues in the sections that follow.

4.2 FISCAL POLICY AND CAPITAL ACCUMULATION

4.2.1 The Government's Intertemporal Budget Constraint

The federal government's current and future policies are interrelated, in a way similar to a household's life-cycle income and consumption plans. To see this, first note that the *national debt* at time t equals the debt of t − 1 plus the *deficit* of t − 1,

$$B_t = B_{t-1} + G_{t-1} - Z_{t-1} + r_{t-1}B_{t-1}$$

where B_t and B_{t-1} are the national debt at the start of periods t and t $-$ 1, G_{t-1} is government consumption, Z_{t-1} is taxes net of transfers (net taxes), and $r_{t-1}B_{t-1}$ is interest payments on the debt in t $-$ 1. Collectively, the last three terms on the right-hand side are the deficit in period t $-$ 1; government outlays on goods, interest, and transfers, minus taxes. There are comparable expressions for the debt in t $+$ 1, t $+$ 2, and so on. These expressions may all be combined by, first, substituting the above relation into that for B_{t+1}, and then that into the one for B_{t+2}, and so on. Successive substitution and rearrangement yield

$$B_0(1 + r_0) + G_0 + G_1/(1 + r_1) + \ldots = Z_0 + Z_1/(1 + r_1) + \ldots$$

which is termed the *government's intertemporal budget constraint (GIBC)*.

The GIBC states that the present value of the government's consumption, plus the initial debt and interest on it, require net taxes of equal present value. The GIBC does not require the government to balance its budget annually, or even that outstanding debt ever be repaid. At a minimum, this loose restriction does require that the debt grow no more rapidly than the aggregate economy. Otherwise, the cost of simply meeting interest payments on the debt (debt service) would eventually exceed GDP. Long before that, however, people would become leery of lending the government further amounts until it gets its house in order. (Russia put a moratorium on interest payments on its debt in the fall of 1998. Following that act, no one was anxious to lend more to that government.) The GIBC further reminds us that, even under normal fiscal conditions, there is "no free lunch." Servicing the debt into the indefinite future costs just as much—though to different people!—as paying it off immediately.

4.2.2   The GIBC and Generational Accounts

The aggregate net taxes paid in any period may be broken down into the amounts paid by the different birth cohorts or "generations" of households alive at that time. Expressed in this fashion, the GIBC helps reveal the implications of fiscal policy for different generations. As explained below, these implications prove important to assessing the impact of policies on economic growth (as well as for intergenerational equity). A relatively new method for assessing those impacts, most prominently developed by Larry Kotlikoff (cf. 1992), is termed *generational accounting*.

To appreciate this approach, consider the "average" person starting economic life in period t. Let $z_{1,t}$ and $z_{2,t+1}$ be, respectively, the taxes minus transfers (or net taxes) received in the first and second periods of life. For example, if in the second period one pays income taxes of 10 and receives Social Security benefits of 5, $z_{2,t+1} = 5$. The reduction in lifetime resources from all tax and transfer activities, termed the *generational account,* is

$$z_t = z_{1,t} + z_{2,t+1}/(1 + r_{t+1}) \qquad (4.4)$$

Since generational accounts do not take into account the enjoyment of government goods and services, they do not capture the effect on utility of the government's activities. Rather, they identify how the cost of a given amount of government goods is distributed across generations.

The calculation of generational accounts is complex, and everyone is bound to take exception with some of the underlying assumptions. The baseline calculations assume that existing tax, transfer, and expenditure policies are maintained indefinitely. In some recent years generational accounts have been included in the official budget of the United States and have been constructed for many countries around the world. Gokhale, Page, Potter, and Sturrock (2000) report recent estimates for the United States that a typical male born in 1998 faces a net lifetime present-value tax burden of \$122,100; a typical female's burden is \$61,100 (in 1998 dollars). One reason for this difference is that men have higher incomes and therefore pay more in taxes. A second reason is that since women live longer on average, they receive more years of Social Security benefits.

We now incorporate these generational accounts into the GIBC. The aggregate net taxes of a period are the sum of the net tax payments by all young and old households alive at that time. Considering any period t, we have

$$Z_t = L_t z_{1,t} + L_{t-1} z_{2,t}$$

Proceeding in this fashion for each period, the financing side of the GIBC may be written entirely in terms of the generational accounts of different cohorts,

$$
\begin{aligned}
B_0(1 + r_0) + G_0 + G_1/(1 + r_1) + \ldots \\
= L_0 z_{1,0} + L_{0-1} z_{2,0} + (L_1 z_{1,1} + L_0 z_{2,0})/(1 + r_1) + \ldots \\
= L_{0-1} z_{2,0} + L_0 z_0 + L_1 z_1/(1 + r_1) + \ldots
\end{aligned}
\tag{4.5}
$$

This expression makes clear that if one generation pays less in net taxes, at least one other generation must pay more. Below we analyze how changing the distribution of generational accounts influences capital accumulation, and thereby growth. An important finding will be that redistributing generational accounts is not a zero-sum game. Specifically, when early generations pay less tax, and so consume more, capital accumulation falls. This hurts future generations in two ways: they pay higher taxes and receive lower pre-tax wages. Before developing those points, we consider the implications of current policy for different generations.

By comparing the generational accounts of someone born in t, z_t, to life wealth W_t one can determine lifetime net tax rates, z_t/W_t. Gokhale et al. use data on previous policy and a 75-year economic and budget projection by the Congressional Budget Office (CBO) from 1999 to calculate lifetime tax rates for past and future cohorts. As examples, taking the average for men and women, this tax rate was 30.2% for the birth cohort of 1960, 23.3% for those born in 1990, and 25.6% for the cohort of 1998. Assuming current policies are maintained, they estimate as-yet-unborn generations would need to face lifetime net tax rates of 29.2% to balance the GIBC. However, other economists argue that the CBO projections are overly optimistic (cf. Auerbach and Gale, 2000). By their reckoning, the burden facing future generations will be higher.

On one hand, there is no doubt that the prospects for future generations have brightened substantially in recent years. In fact, the Gokhale et al. estimates for those unborn are *roughly half* those predicted just a few years before. As the authors note, (s)ince then, unexpectedly strong growth in both GDP and the tax share of GDP have boosted revenues, and slow growth in defense spending has reduced federal purchases as a share of GDP to a postwar low. These developments augur federal budget surpluses for at least a decade and portend a corresponding reduction in the generational imbalance. (p. 293)

On the other hand, there is legitimate concern that the CBO overestimates the size of future federal budget surpluses and neglects future shortfalls. Auerbach and Gale note that the CBO baseline forecast of July 2000 projects surpluses of at least $4.5 trillion between 2001 and 2010. This includes (off-budget) surpluses in the Social Security trust fund of about $2.4 trillion. They note that the CBO estimates assume discretionary spending will fall relative to GDP over that period—even though it is already at its lowest level since at least 1962. If it is instead assumed that the share of GDP devoted to discretionary spending remains constant, they estimate the surplus is reduced by $864 billion (including interest costs). Also, Gokhale and Kotlikoff (2000) point out that the 75-year horizon for the CBO projections understates the burden on future generations. For example, they report numbers from the Social Security trustees that the single-year deficit for Social Security for the year 2075, the last year of the 2000 CBO forecast, is $651 billion. Similarly gigantic deficits are expected in the succeeding years. Ignoring those future shortfalls understates the lifetime tax rates on unborn generations required to balance the GIBC. Gokhale and Kotlikoff estimate unborn generations face lifetime tax rates of 32.3 percent, assuming discretionary spending's share of GDP is held constant.

These estimates do not account for the Tax Relief Act of 2001, which fulfilled President Bush's promise to return part of the projected surpluses to taxpayers. The estimated revenue cost is $1.35 trillion through 2010, but the long-run costs may be much greater. Although budget rules require a "sunset" clause in all major tax legislation, the provisions are expected to be extended in 2011. And because many benefits are only gradually phased in, the costs in those later years would greatly exceed the average annual cost during the first decade.

4.2.3   Generational Accounts, Government Debt, and Capital Accumulation

This section develops relationships among fiscal policy, household savings, and capital accumulation. We continue to employ the basic OLG model in which consumers are retired throughout the second period and there is neither population nor labor-augmenting income growth. Thus, all labor income is received by the young, each cohort is the same size, and k_t is the capital-labor ratio in t.

First we integrate life-cycle net tax payments and the consumer's saving plan. Lifetime resources before net taxes are simply w_t, and resources net of generational accounts are $w_t - z_t$. With Cobb-Douglas preferences, the proportion θ of net-of-tax-and-transfer life wealth is allocated to consumption by the young. First-period consumption is then $C_{1,t} = \theta(w_t - z_t)$. Since savings of the young equal net income minus consumption, we can write

$$S_{1,t} = w_t - z_{1,t} - C_{1,t}$$
$$= w_t - z_{1,t} - \theta(w_t - z_t)$$

Now, utilizing the definition of z_t and rearranging terms, we obtain

$$S_{1,t} = (1 - \theta)w_t - (1 - \theta)z_{1,t} + \theta z_{2,t+1}/(1 + r_{t+1}) \qquad (4.5)$$

Examination of (4.5) reveals how changes in government tax and transfer policies affect saving by the young. Since $z_{1,t}$ enters (4.5) negatively and is multiplied by $(1 - \theta)$, the effect on $S_{1,t}$ is $-(1 - \theta)dz_{1,t}$. Intuitively, if $dz_{1,t}$ is positive, first-period net income and life wealth each fall by $dz_{1,t}$. First-period consumption falls by θ percent of the decline in wealth, limiting the reduction in savings to $(1 - \theta)dz_{1,t}$. Similarly, since $z_{2,t+1}$ is multiplied by $\theta/(1 + r_{t+1})$, the effect of increasing net taxes on the old is $(\theta dz_{2,t+1})/(1 + r_{t+1})$. To appreciate why, first note that life wealth falls by the present value of the increase in $z_{2,t+1}$, or $dz_{2,t+1}/(1 + r_{t+1})$. This lowers consumption by the young by θ percent of that amount, inducing an equal rise in savings. The overall effect of changing net taxes on savings on the young is

$$dS_{1,t} = -(1 - \theta)dz_{1,t} + \theta dz_{2,t+1}/(1 + r_{t+1}) \qquad (4.6)$$

Equation (4.6) captures the effect of net tax policies on household savings, but ignores government debt policy. Fortunately, it is straightforward to add government debt to our analysis.

Up to this point, all of a household's savings in t have been used as capital for production in t + 1. We now introduce a second type of asset, government bonds. Should the government need to borrow in year t, the bonds issued would necessarily be purchased by the young: the old would be dead (in this two-period story) when these bonds are redeemed! If the government runs a deficit in t, this will lead to more bonds being issued in t + 1, for that is when the bonds will be held, will pay interest, and will be redeemed. Thus, if the government needs to borrow \$x per young person at time t, debt per worker is $b_{t+1} = \$x$.

A household's portfolio now consists of government bonds and physical capital. Those savings of the young in t invested in physical capital in t + 1 are the tools per worker k_{t+1}. Altogether, private savings per young person in t equal the bonds and capital per worker in t + 1,

$$S_{1,t} = k_{t+1} + b_{t+1} \qquad (4.7)$$

Bonds and capital are assumed to offer the same riskless rate of return r_{t+1}, making the consumer indifferent between them. After the government's supply of bonds has been absorbed, all remaining funds go to physical capital.

Rearranging (4.7), the capital-labor ratio in t + 1 is

$$k_{t+1} = S_{1,t} - b_{t+1} \qquad (4.8)$$

This expression reveals that, *given* $S_{1,t}$, any increase in b_{t+1} reduces k_{t+1} the same amount. In practice only part of the U.S. federal government's several trillion dollar debt is refinanced in any year. Annual saving by the federal government was negative through the 1970s, 1980s, and most of the 1990s. Recently, budget surpluses have increased the funds available for private sector investment.

Using (4.5) and (4.6), the total effect of a fiscal policy on capital accumulation per worker in t is

$$dk_{t+1} = dS_{1,t} - db_{t+1}$$
$$= -(1 - \theta)dz_{1,t} + \theta dz_{2,t+1}/(1 + r) - db_{t+1} \tag{4.9}$$

This important relationship summarizes the effect of a fiscal policy announced at time t on capital accumulation in time $t + 1$.[4] Recall from Chapter 3 that any policy increasing k_{t+1} has the macroeconomic growth effects of increasing wages and depressing the interest rate. If the increase in the capital-labor ratio is permanent, steady state welfare will increase (assuming the economy is dynamically efficient). We now use (4.9) to assess a variety of fiscal policies.

4.3 INCREASING THE SIZE OF GOVERNMENT

In 1997, government consumption in the United States was $1.45 trillion, or about 18 percent of GDP. Government expenditures at all levels of government, which include transfer payments, are over 30 percent of GDP. Interestingly, among developed economies this is fairly low (this figure exceeds 50% in France and Sweden). How much of government consumption is at the expense of private consumption? Investment? How might the way the burden of paying for government consumption is distributed across generations affect the path of the macroeconomy? We address these and other questions using the tools developed above.

Consider an increase in government consumption, such as the growth in national defense spending during the Reagan years (as discussed below, part of such expenditure is in fact investment). Our Cobb-Douglas utility function does not include government consumption. Fortunately, this omission may be unimportant for assessing the macroeconomic implications of changing the size of government. For so long as government consumption does not affect the marginal rate of substitution between first- and second-period consumption, the implications are as if utility depends on private consumption alone.[5] For all such preferences (including Cobb-Douglas), the direct effects on private consumption follow from changes in the consumer's budget set and, therefore, generational account. If capital accumulation is affected, there will be further implications in subsequent periods from general-equilibrium changes in wages and interest rates.

To honor the GIBC, the government must levy taxes having the same present value as the new government consumption. Even the qualitative effect of the taxes depends upon how they are distributed. We first suppose the government balances its budget by taxing current generations; deficit policies are considered later.

Suppose the government expands the Medicare program, thereby increasing its consumption by g per old person in period t and every subsequent period. Let new taxes of g per young person each period balance the budget; in year t, $dG_t = L_t g$. For example, young households could face higher wage income taxation. To apply (4.9), note that $dz_{1,t} = g$, $dz_{2,t+1} = 0$, and $db_{t+1} = 0$. Consequently,

$$dk_{t+1} = -(1 - \theta)g < 0$$

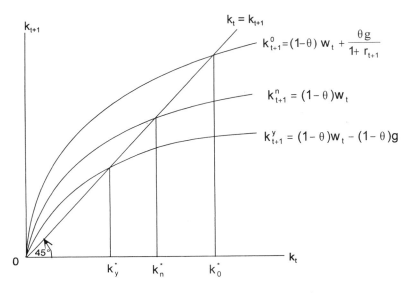

Figure 4.2 Government policies and growth

Intuitively, the life wealth of a young person is lowered by g, which reduces first-period consumption by θg. Consequently, first-period savings, the pool of funds available for capital accumulation, fall by $(1 - \theta)g$. This equals the rise in aggregate consumption per worker, with government consumption higher by g and private consumption lower by θg. In this case, increased government consumption is partially at the expense of investment and partially at the expense of private consumption. Since steady state capital intensity falls, subsequent generations also pay for the government consumption through the lower wages the decline in saving entails. This example also illustrates a point we will see often—the effects of a policy on capital accumulation need not equal those on the government's budget deficit or surplus.

This policy is illustrated using Figure 4.2. To ease the exposition, suppose there is initially no government consumption. Then the transition equation is given by $k_{t+1}^n = w_t - w_t \theta = (1 - \theta)w_t$; tools per worker in $t + 1$ are just wages minus consumption of the young in t. When the young of t are taxed, their savings equal net income, $w_t - g$, minus consumption, $\theta(w_t - g)$. Thus, tools per worker in $t + 1$ are $k_{t+1}^y = w_t - g - \theta(w_t - g) = (1 - \theta)w_t - (1 - \theta)g$. The gap between the "no-government" transition equation and the "tax young" transition equation is just the expression dk_{t+1} derived above.

Although perhaps of less historical relevance, suppose instead that the revenues to balance the budget are raised by taxing the old of each generation g. In this case, $dz_{1,t} = 0$, $dz_{2,t+1} = g$, and $db_{t+1} = 0$. Application of (4.9) produces

$$dk_{t+1} = \theta g/(1 + r_{t+1}) > 0 \qquad (4.10)$$

Perhaps surprisingly, this balanced-budget expansion of government increases capital accumulation. The reason is households young in t anticipate the higher taxes due in retirement and store up some additional funds to "spread the pain" (i.e., the reduced consumption) across both periods. From another perspective, capital accumulation rises because private consumption in t falls by more than public consumption rises. For consumption of the old in t falls the same amount as public consumption rises, g, so that the decline in consumption by the young constitutes a reduction in aggregate consumption. In terms of Figure 4.2, this policy produces the transition equation k_{t+1}^0. Tools per worker in $t + 1$ in this case are the wage earnings of a young worker in t, w_t, minus consumption, $\theta[w_t - g/(1 + r_{t+1})]$. Thus, $k_{t+1}^0 = (1 - \theta)w_t + \theta g/(1 + r_{t+1})$, so that the difference between this regime and the no-government regime is given by the vertical distance between them, given by equation (4.10).[6]

Both policies reduce the consumer's life wealth by the increase in the generational account. However, under the "tax young" policy, the generational account rises by g, while under "tax old" the increase is only $g/(1 + r_{t+1})$. Intuitively, the government raises the same revenues in each case, but with positive interest rates consumers benefit when taxes are postponed until later in the life cycle. This is called the *tax postponement effect* (see Summers, 1981). As with dynamic efficiency, these gains are positive in steady state so long as r > n. (With n > 0, taxes per old person must be n% larger.)

The benefits from this "delay" in tax payments were made possible only because the old of t paid taxes. Suppose, instead, that the policy began in t, and taxes were imposed on the old of each period *beginning in t + 1*. In this instance, the government has to borrow g per worker. Suppose this amount is never repaid, but that the bonds are simply paid off with interest and reissued in every period. Then the old of $t + 1$ would owe taxes of $(1 + r_{t+1})g$, since they pay for the current government consumption and service the newly issued debt. Their generational account is just the present value of that amount, g, so that *tax postponement without redistributing generational accounts toward the old provides no steady state gains.*

These considerations suggest steady state gains are possible from policies that shift the taxation of households from youth to old age. In fact, proposals to shift from an income to a consumption tax base have this effect: Income is highest during the working years, while consumption continues at fairly high levels later in life. (The distortionary effects of interest income taxation are probably the principal motivation behind this proposal—see section 4.6.) One problem associated with shifting taxes to late in life is that it creates an unattractive set of incentives for the old. For suppose the old believe the government is unlikely to subject them to extreme poverty. Then it might make sense for less wealthy households to spend down their wealth just before tax payments are due; not only would they be able to consume their wealth instead of giving it to the government, but the government may actually make positive transfers to them. In fact, over the past several decades net tax payments of the old have been reduced, while those on the young have been increased. The implications of this are seen clearly in the discussion of Social Security in section 4.5.

4.3.1   Further Considerations

In practice, some of what we are terming *government consumption* should instead be viewed as *government investment*. For school buildings, highways, and police cars are all durable goods, providing benefits beyond the year of acquisition. Purchases of teacher services, as another example, may also have an investment component: Teachers increase the human capital of students, and human capital affects GDP in a similar fashion as physical capital. Government investment facilitates the production of national output (winding up as multifactor productivity in a growth-accounting exercise). To the extent increased government outlays take the form of investment rather than consumption, using equation (4.9) to determine output per worker will understate future labor productivity and wages.

The results above were derived in an equilibrium setting in which the GDP produced equals "potential GDP," the maximum feasible amount given the production function and available resources. In fact, increases in government spending are at times undertaken precisely because existing supplies of resources are underutilized. Such circumstances, recall, are the basis for Keynesian economics: If the current level of the aggregate demand is too low to fully employ the economy's resources, government fiscal policies—in this case increased government consumption—can be utilized to restore the economy to full employment. Should this be the case, the short-term effect on GDP will be more favorable than described above.

Another limitation of the analysis thus far is that all taxes have been lump-sum, whereas major sources of revenue typically involve taxing some form of behavior, such as consuming or saving. Distortionary income taxation is considered in section 4.6.

4.4 IMPLICATIONS OF GOVERNMENT FINANCE

4.4.1 Changing the Timing of Taxation Within Generations

Now suppose that a given stream of government consumption has been decided upon. While the GIBC notes the present value of the associated net tax payments, it is silent regarding the implications of alternative distributions of those net tax burdens across generations. In this section we address how savings and capital accumulation are affected by the distribution of generational accounts. With current-period national income, the stock of physical capital, and government consumption fixed, a policy can have real effects only if household consumption is altered. Consumption will change only if generational accounts are affected. That is, government tax and debt policies affect capital accumulation only if they alter the distribution of net lifetime resources across generations.[7] In particular, we will stress that policies redistributing resources from younger to older generations temporarily increase aggregate consumption but permanently reduce the stock of capital.

Analysis of redistributive policies will reveal that generational accounts are superior to government deficits or surpluses as a gauge of a policy's impact on capital accumulation. The traditional view is that government deficits "crowd out" or reduce capital accumulation: If the government must borrow from households to finance its operations, less of the pool of private savings will be available for physical capital investment. This is not a general result, as it ignores any potential response of private savings to the policy. Simply put, a policy's effect on capital accumulation equals that on national saving, not public saving alone. National saving encompasses all changes in private and public saving, $dS_{1,t} - db_{t+1}$. By (4.9), this is just dk_{t+1}.

A first policy simply postpones the collection of net taxes from the generation born in t, pushing the taxes from the first to the second period of life. Specifically, the government cuts taxes of those young in t by $500, financing the resultant deficit by issuing $500 of bonds. In the notation of (4.9), $dz_{1,t} = -\$500$ and $db_{t+1} = \$500$. The policy is reversed in $t + 1$ with taxes on the old increased by $dz_{2,t+1} = \$500(1 + r_{t+1})$. These revenues are used to make interest payments on and then retire the debt issued in the previous period. (An example is a one-time reduction in Social Security taxes in period t, coupled with a one-time increase in interest income taxation—or reduction in Social Security benefits—in $t + 1$.) Notice that this policy has no effect on the generational account of those young in t; the present value of the tax hike when old just equals the tax cut when young: $dz_t = -500 + 500(1 + r_{t+1})/(1 + r_{t+1}) = 0$. Consequently, this policy changes only the *timing* of net income over the life cycle. Since life wealth is unchanged, so is consumption over the life cycle.

Those old in t are unaffected by the policy. Therefore, this policy does not affect aggregate private consumption in t. With government consumption held constant, national saving and capital accumulation are also unchanged. We verify our intuition by applying (4.9),

$$dk_{t+1} = -(1 - \theta)(-500) + \theta[500(1 + r_{t+1})]/(1 + r_{t+1}) - 500$$

$$= 500 - \theta 500 + \theta 500 - 500 = 0$$

Why doesn't the government's deficit "crowd out" private savings and capital accumulation? The government has put $500 more in the young's hands via the tax cut, only to turn around and borrow it, via the bond issue. Consequently, the policy entails no net resource flow between the government and those young in t. Private savings of the young will be higher by the tax cut in period t, in order to pay the higher taxes due in $t + 1$. On the other hand, government savings are lower by $500 in t. So there is no change in national savings.[8] This policy is peculiar in that the government is taking rather elaborate steps to do nothing of substance. Nevertheless, it clearly illustrates the importance of net resource transfers between the government and households over the life cycle.

As told, the policy just changed the timing of taxes for the one generation. However, since this policy had no effects on consumption or capital accumulation, it is easy to appreciate that this would also be true of a policy that postponed the taxes of each generation. For example, suppose it is decided to tax consumption rather than wage income. This delays some tax collections, since consumption occurs in both periods, while wage income is received only in the first period of life. As above, suppose this policy spares the old of t from paying taxes when old. The young of t are the first generation to pay lower taxes when young and also the first, in $t + 1$, to pay consumption taxes in retirement. Here, conversion from the wage to consumption tax base is accomplished without altering any cohort's generational account. Consequently, there is no effect on consumption or national savings: The government's borrowing is just offset by the young's additional saving.

Below we consider the implications of moving from wage to consumption taxation when the old of t are forced to pay consumption taxes (even though they did not benefit from the wage income tax deduction). Unsurprisingly, this alters the implications for capital accumulation. Most consumption tax proponents favor shifting from an *income* tax. As discussed in section 4.6, this has the advantage of eliminating the distortionary effects of interest income taxation.

4.4.2 Liquidity-constrained Households

Our analysis of tax postponement assumed that capital markets allow households to borrow and lend freely at the market interest rate. As discussed in Chapter 1, though, sometimes households are liquidity constrained, unable to borrow against future earnings to finance current consumption. In this case, even changes in the timing of taxation (which do not impact life wealth) will affect consumption. Consequently, widespread liquidity constraints would—in some cases substantially—alter the foregoing conclusions regarding fiscal policy. Such issues do not arise in the model above since, with the second period devoted to retirement, all households save when young.

Suppose households work in both periods and are liquidity constrained when young. Then tax postponement increases the young's consumption. Consequently aggregate consumption rises in t and capital accumulation falls. For while the government still dissaves or borrows 500 per young person, the young do not save the tax cut, but consume it. The existence of liquidity-constrained households may be one reason temporary, or "Keynesian," tax cuts are advocated as a stimulus to aggregate demand in an economic downturn. The most optimistic scenario for such a policy is that the economy will later be "booming," so the tax cut is repaid by households just when spending needs to be curtailed to keep inflation in check. As noted in Chapter 1, the vast majority of households are not liquidity constrained at any point in time. Thus, our analyses abstracting from credit market imperfections are but modestly flawed by that omission. Henceforth, we assume no households are liquidity constrained.

4.4.3 Intergenerational Redistribution

Early in the twentieth century the economic circumstance of the average old citizen was quite poor compared with that of young adults and children. By the end of the century, the relative and absolute positions of the old had improved substantially (cf. Gokhale, Kotlikoff, and Sabelhaus, 1996) . For example, the Social Security Administration reports that in 1959 fully 35 percent of the nation's elderly lived in poverty; by 1996 this figure had fallen to but 11 percent. In part, this improvement may be traced to the introduction and expansion of Medicare and Social Security. As detailed in section 4.5, the cost of these programs was not borne exclusively by the old of that period. In fact, a significant portion of the tab was deferred to future generations. Similarly, between 1987 and 1995 the U.S. national debt more than doubled from about $2.3 trillion to nearly $5 trillion. The increase in the debt over that period exceeded all the debt accumulated during the first 200 years of the nation. That buildup of debt entails obligations for future generations.

We now address the macro implications of redistributing resources from young and as yet unborn generations to those old at a point in time. To that end, consider a policy that cuts the net taxes of the old by $T in period t, only (consider the old during the "start-up" periods for Social Security and Medicare). This is a clear benefit to that generation, unambiguously increasing its welfare. There are many ways taxes could be levied on future generations to finance this tax cut. One interesting way requires each subsequent generation merely to service (i.e., pay the interest on) the debt, thereby treating all subsequent generations symmetrically. In this case, the $T of new debt per worker is simply "rolled over" every period: Those old at the beginning of a period redeem their holdings of government debt. The government finances that repayment by reissuing the same amount of debt to the young of that period. We further assume that the revenues to service the debt come from taxing the old of each period, *beginning in t + 1*. For example, the old in t + 1 are each taxed $r_{t+1}T$. The effect on their generational account is

$$dz_t = r_{t+1}T/(1 + r_{t+1}) \qquad (4.11)$$

To see the effects for capital accumulation, we apply (4.9), with $dz_{t+1} = r_{t+1}T$ and $db_{t+1} = T$. This produces

$$dk_{t+1} = \theta r_{t+1}T/(1 + r_{t+1}) - T < 0 \qquad (4.12)$$

where the fact that $\theta < 1$ ensures that the inequality obtains. Consider why this "gift" to the old of t reduces capital accumulation. Intuitively, the government borrows T from each young person. Ceteris paribus, this would lower tools per worker in subsequent periods by T. This is the second term in equation (4.12). However, the higher taxes (debt service) to be paid when one is old reduce consumption when one is young by θ percent of the reduction in net life wealth; that is, by θ percent of the present value of those taxes. This effect is captured by the first term in (4.12). Since government borrowing from the young exceeds their reduction in consumption when young, the macro economy transits to a new steady state with fewer tools per worker.

Significantly, the benefit to the old of t reduces the welfare of subsequent generations in two distinct ways. First is the direct effect of the increased taxes for the old of subsequent generations. The second is the capital accumulation effect, which leads to lower wages. There nevertheless exist justifications for such a policy. As one example, suppose each generation faces the risk of experiencing a substantial economic downturn. A policy providing tax cuts to the unfortunate generations, with higher taxes levied on luckier cohorts, would serve as a form of intergenerational risk sharing. Such considerations may have helped motivate the provision of Social Security benefits to those elderly following the Great Depression—even though they had paid in little in the way of taxes. As discussed below, the macroeconomic implications of Social Security are, in fact, quite similar to this deficit finance policy, though the full program is much more complex.

A policy with effects opposite to those above is conversion to a consumption tax base from a wage tax base in period t, when the old of t are made to pay consumption taxes—even though they paid wage taxes when young. Since the old of t pay more over their life cycle, their consumption falls and capital accumulation rises. Each subsequent generation gets a tax break and benefits from higher wages (cf. Lord, 1989 and Seidman, 1990). These results contrast sharply with those above when conversion from consumption to wage taxes was accomplished by merely postponing tax payments over the life cycle. That policy affected no one's generational account, so capital accumulation was unaffected.

There, private savings rose and public savings fell so as to leave national savings unchanged. More generally, the long-run implications of a policy are sensitive to the treatment of transitional generations.

4.5 SOCIAL SECURITY

The U.S. Social Security system is both massive and complex. The Social Security Administration's budget request for 1999 was $427 billion. There are three primary programs: old age and survivor's insurance (OASI), disability insurance, and supplemental security income (SSI). In this section we address the macroeconomic implications of OASI, which we continue to call "Social Security." The OASI program is far and away the largest, with 1999 requested outlays of $343 billion, providing $783 of average monthly benefits to 38.4 million elderly, surviving spouses, and dependent children.[9] Our focus is on the "old age" insurance aspect.

The basic features of the program at the household level are straightforward. In 1999, employees and employers each contribute 6.2 percent of the employee's first $68,400 of wage earnings; wages above the cutoff (which is indexed for inflation) are not subject to tax. Benefits increase with contributions, but at a much slower rate, introducing a strong measure of progressivity to the system (which is muted by the lower life expectancy among the poor).

There is well-founded concern on the part of younger households that the Social Security system works to their disadvantage and may fail to honor fully its future commitments to them. As discussed below, the rate of return from participation in Social Security for successive birth cohorts has fallen appreciably, a trend that is expected to continue for some time. Further, although it is almost unimaginable that the government would eliminate Social Security, it may well "redefine" its basic obligation.

This section focuses on the *intergenerational* redistribution Social Security has entailed and the implications this has for capital accumulation (*intra*generational redistribution is considered in section 1.4). Feldstein (cf. 1974, 1982) argues that Social Security has significantly reduced—by perhaps 40 percent—the rate of private saving. His conclusions are controversial and most economists believe the impact to have been much smaller. Whatever the magnitude, the intuition as to why Social Security may reduce savings is easily developed.

When considering Social Security programs, an important distinction is between *fully funded, unfunded,* and *partially funded* programs. A fully funded program has assets on hand equal to the present value of promised future benefit payments. In contrast, an unfunded system has sufficient monies on hand to meet only the obligations to current beneficiaries. This means that the benefit payments promised to current workers upon their retirement must be raised by taxes on future workers. Unsurprisingly, a partially funded system has some reserves, but not enough to fulfill all of its future obligations. Historically, the Social Security system in the United States (and in most other countries) has been unfunded. However, since the 1980s the U.S. system has become partially funded, although the unfunded liabilities remain in the trillions of dollars.

4.5.1   Fully Funded Social Security

We first consider the central features of a fully funded Social Security system, ignoring any intragenerational redistributive goals such programs may pursue. The fundamental setup is for the government to "tax" workers on their earnings, deposit the proceeds into individualized accounts *earning the market rate of return*, and "transfer" the proceeds back to the workers during their retirement years. (These features are also central to recently discussed proposals to *privatize* Social Security. However, as stressed below, there is a crucial difference between starting a private program from scratch and privatizing the current largely unfunded program.) Further, for fully funded programs nothing is lost by abstracting from economic growth, so we continue to assume there is neither population nor income growth (n = v = 0, and **A** = 1).

Let the fully funded program start in t, with the government taxing each (identical) young person $dz_{1,t}$ = \$T. Since there is no corresponding government outlay in that period, there is a surplus of \$T, so that db_{t+1} = −\$T. When old in t + 1, each retiree receives a transfer, or Social Security benefit, from the government of B = \$T(1 + r_{t+1}) = −$dz_{2,t+1}$. Since there is neither income nor population growth, T and B are constant across generations. Recall that those old in t neither contribute to nor receive benefits from the fully funded system. For all subsequent generations, the present value of the benefits equals (in absolute value) the taxes paid when young, so that a fully funded program is simply a speeding up of the timing of tax payments over the life cycle.[10] Above we saw that such policies have no effect on anyone's generational account or, consequently, on consumption. Thus, there are no effects for capital accumulation, as may be verified by applying (4.9)

$$dk_{t+1} = -(1 - \theta)T - \theta T(1 + r_{t+1})/(1 + r_{t+1}) - (-T)$$
$$= -(1 - \theta)T - \theta T + T = 0$$

Although this policy does not affect national saving, the composition between private and public saving is altered. Households, noting the effect of Social Security benefits on retirement resources, reduce their savings in stocks, bonds, savings accounts, and so on. The effect of promised Social Security benefits on *private* savings is termed the *asset or wealth substitution effect:* The magnitude of that effect is just the present value of benefits B/(1 + r_{t+1}), here T, since that is the amount of savings required to yield resources of B in retirement. *Public* saving per worker, on the other hand, has increased by T as the government "invests" the taxes by repurchasing government bonds. The offsetting changes in private and public saving explain why national saving is unaffected.

A fully funded program does not appear to be of much inherent interest. As constructed here, all it does is introduce a series of government taxes and transfers that have no real effects at either the micro or macro level. The program might be of value if consumers would otherwise undersave for retirement. This could be an issue even among far-sighted households if they believe the government would help support them in retirement should they become destitute.

The effect of Social Security on life resources is often termed net *Social Security wealth*, SSW. Recalling that generational accounts measure the *reduction* in life-cycle resources due to government tax and transfer activities, SSW = $-dz_t$. Thus, if the average member of a birth cohort had a present value benefit, net of taxes, from participation in Social Security of $5,000, the effect on his or her generational account would be $dz_t = -\$5,000$ and the SSW would equal $5,000. Since a fully funded program affects no one's generational account, SSW is zero for every generation. As stressed below, SSW differs from zero in unfunded systems.

4.5.2   Unfunded, or Pay-As-You-Go, Social Security

Consider now an unfunded or pay-as-you-go Social Security program similar to the U.S. system during its first fifty years. First we discuss the theory of such programs, both upon inception and in long-run equilibrium. Then we look at the program experience of different birth cohorts in the United States and the outlook for the system's future financing, including reform proposals.

Effects on Capital Accumulation

Suppose this unfunded program begins in period t, paying benefits B to each old person *beginning in period t*. This policy is financed by payroll taxes of $T on the young of each generation, also beginning in period t. An immediate and crucial difference between this and the fully funded system is the treatment of those old in t, when the program begins. In the funded system, recall, old individuals in the first period of the policy do not receive benefits (nor do they make contributions). In the unfunded system, those retired in t receive benefits without having made contributions. This obviously makes those old in t better off under the unfunded system. To be addressed are the implications for capital accumulation and for the welfare of subsequent generations.

Assume the program is truly "pay as you go," with no annual deficits or surpluses. Then the aggregate benefits paid to retirees each period equal the total payroll tax receipts. With no income or population growth, benefits per retiree equal taxes per worker. Consequently, for those starting economic life in period t or later, benefits received when old equal the taxes paid when young, B = T. This makes the program's rate of return *zero*, compared with r_{t+1} in the fully funded case. Below we see that per capita income and population growth increase the return from zero, but first the macro implications are developed in the no-growth environment.

This program increases the generational account of those young in t and all subsequent generations. For someone young in t, since B = T,

$$dz_t = T - T/(1 + r_{t+1}) = [T(1 + r_{t+1})/(1 + r_{t+1})] - T/(1 + r_{t+1})$$
$$= r_{t+1}T/(1 + r_{t+1}) \tag{4.13}$$

where movement to the second equality entailed multiplying and dividing the first T term by $1 + r_{t+1}$. In the final expression, the numerator is the interest income that is foregone, since participants just get back what they contributed, rather than contributions plus interest. The denominator converts this interest foregone to its present value. For generations young in $t + 1$ or later, the same expression applies (with the obvious changes in subscripts). The generation old in t is the overall beneficiary, as its old-age consumption rises by T per member. In summary, the generation old in t enjoys positive Social Security wealth while all subsequent generations suffer negative SSW. You may recall that the policy of cutting the taxes of those old in t, with subsequent generations servicing the debt, had *exactly* the same effect on generational accounts (see equation (4.11)). Discussing the reasons for this equivalence below yields an important insight.

Since unfunded Social Security shifts resources to the old from the young and as yet unborn, aggregate consumption rises, reducing national savings and capital accumulation. The effect on capital accumulation is seen from (4.9) to be

$$dk_{t+1} = -(1 - \theta)T - \theta T/(1 + r_{t+1}) = -T + \theta T - \theta T/(1 + r_{t+1})$$

This expression is usefully simplified by multiplying the top and bottom of the first θT term by $1 + r_{t+1}$ and then rearranging. This produces

$$\begin{aligned} dk_{t+1} &= -T + (\theta T + r_{t+1}\theta T - \theta T)/(1 + r_{t+1}) \\ &= r_{t+1}\theta T/(1 + r_{t+1}) - T < 0 \end{aligned} \tag{4.14}$$

Whereas fully funded Social Security had no effect on capital accumulation, an unfunded program lowers accumulation. Why the difference? Both programs reduce private saving. However, in a funded program, the monies diverted from private saving constitute an increase in public saving, so there is no effect on capital accumulation. In contrast, national saving falls in the unfunded case as the monies diverted from private saving are used to finance consumption by the elderly, rather than to increase public saving.

The effect of an unfunded program given by equation (4.14) is identical to that from cutting taxes on those old in t by T with subsequent generations servicing the resulting debt (see equation (4.12)). The fact that these policies have the same effect on capital accumulation derives from their identical effects on generational accounts discussed above.

How can these programs be fundamentally equivalent, given that they entail such different patterns of net tax payments over the life cycle? To lay bare the intuition, we now show that unfunded Social Security entails the same pattern of net tax payments as the following two policies combined: (1) the fully funded Social Security program beginning in t and (2) the debt-financed tax cut to those old in t, with the debt serviced by the old of each subsequent generation. Recall, however, that the fully funded program affects neither the generational accounts nor capital accumulation. Therefore, combining it with the debt-finance policy will alter only the timing of net taxes, producing the pattern under unfunded Social Security. This is shown in Table 4.1. Viewing the table, under a fully funded program the old of t receive nothing, whereas they get T with both unfunded Social Security and the tax cut plan. For them, the debt-financed tax cut and unfunded Social Security are clearly the same. What about those young in t, including when they are old in $t + 1$? When young they pay T under both unfunded and fully funded Social Security (and have no interchange under the debt-finance policy). When old in $t + 1$ they receive T with unfunded Social Security. Under a fully funded system they receive $T(1 + r_{t+1})$; however, they pay $r_{t+1}T$ under the debt-finance policy. On net, under the combined policy they receive T, just as with the unfunded program.

Table 4.1

	THE OLD OF t	THE YOUNG OF t	
		when young in t	when old in t + 1
Unfunded Social Security	+T	− T	+ T
Combination policy			
Fully funded Soc. Sec.	0	− T	+ T(1 + r_{t+1})
Debt-finance policy	+T	0	− r_{t+1}T
	+T	− T	+T

In summary, the overall implications of unfunded Social Security are as with the debt-finance policy alone. Indeed, economists have long emphasized the equivalence between the actual policy of tax-financed transfers and a hypothetical one using debt. Feldstein (1974) was the first to carefully construct a measure of the unfunded liability of the Social Security system, indicating how large the debt would be under the equivalent debt-finance policy. A recent estimate by Murphy and Welch (1998) places the unfunded liabilities—essentially unofficial government debt—at $2.5 trillion; Gokhale and Kotlikoff (2000) believe the unofficial debt may be twice that.

Although the debt-finance and unfunded Social Security policies have the same effect on capital accumulation, unfunded Social Security has a balanced annual budget, whereas the debt-finance requires additional government borrowing. As seen before, federal budget deficits or surpluses are an imperfect guide to the capital accumulation effects of government activities. These effects are conveyed more reliably through analysis of the generational accounts. Policies that push the burden of net tax payments from older to younger and as-yet-unborn generations reduce capital accumulation because the old consume any net tax breaks received.[11]

Economic Growth and Social Security Wealth

Economic growth is central to the long-run welfare effects of unfunded Social Security. To appreciate why we now allow for population growth and technical advance at rates n and v. Steady state aggregate income now grows at rate n + v. Aggregate Social Security taxes and benefits would grow at that same rate, assuming a flat Social Security tax rate on wage earnings. This means the benefits that someone young in i receives when old will be (n + v) percent greater than were that person's contributions when young; $B_{i+1} = T_i(1 + n + v)$. Thus, in the presence of growth, n + v is the steady state rate of return to Social Security. While this return is more favorable than the zero rate implied when we abstracted from growth, it remains unattractive to steady state participants. For notice that

$$SSW_i = (1 + v + n)T_i/(1 + r_{i+1}) - T_i = [(1 + v + n)/(1 + r_{i+1}) - 1]T_i$$

This is negative unless $n + v > r_{i+1}$ (i.e., it is positive only if the economy is dynamically inefficient in the sense of section 4.1). While there is some debate about the exact value for the interest rate to be used in such calculations, most economists believed that it exceeds n + v, so that Social Security wealth is negative in a fully mature system.[12]

However, the welfare losses to steady state generations enabled gains for the "start-up" generations. For those retiring during the early years, or start-up phase, taxes paid were small or zero while the benefits were often substantial. Consequently, Social Security wealth was positive and large for those retiring in the late 1930s and early 1940s. As time passed, retirees naturally had participated in the system for more years, which increased their contributions. However, at inception, only a small proportion of the work force was covered by Social Security. While coverage was expanding to include virtually the entire labor force, the number of contributors was growing at a rate above n. Also, the tax rate has increased from 1 percent of the first $3,000 of earnings for both employees and employers to 6.2 percent each on the first $68,400 of earnings (in 1999). For these reasons, revenues per contributor initially grew above rate v. These start-up features allowed benefits to become more generous even into the 1970s, so that SSW remained large. Thus, the transfer of resources from young and unborn to the currently old was not limited to the 1930s; indeed, policies with that effect were regularly instituted into the 1970s. Note that with positive SSW, transitional participants received a rate of return on their contributions in excess of the private rate of return, r_i. Their additional wealth increased consumption, further reducing capital accumulation.

Social Security and Post-World War II Americans

Gokhale and Kotlikoff (1999) assess how Social Security treats post-World War II cohorts, both under existing legislation and under proposals designed to eliminate the long-term actuarial imbalance of Social Security. Their calculations rely on a large microsimulation model that combines historical and household-level data to generate the characteristics of households populating the economy into the twenty-second century. The Social Security taxes and benefits of these households are then calculated in a fashion that captures most features of the Social Security system. Their calculations include the contributions of employers as well as employees.

Under existing legislation, they find that most post-World War II birth cohorts have suffered negative SSW equal to roughly 5% of the cohort's life wealth. These "net tax rates" are higher among the more affluent of a birth cohort—those with the highest life wealth. Consider, for example, those born between 1965 and 1969. They find that the most affluent quintile of households will experience negative SSW equal to 5.2% of life wealth, compared with but 2.8% among those in the least affluent quintile. Expressed differently, the poorest quintile may expect a 3.8% rate of return from participation in Social Security, compared with but 1.2% for the most affluent quintile. These rates are appreciably below the 5% rate Gokhale and Kotlikoff employ in calculating the net tax rates.

Gokhale and Kotlikoff (1999) stress that the calculations associated with the existing legislation ignore the fact that the present value of currently legislated benefits greatly exceeds that of taxes. They determine that "the immediate and permanent tax hike required to . . . eliminate the OASI budget imbalance is 4 percentage points or 38% of the post-2000 OASI tax rate of 10.6 percent" (p. 17). This imbalance is twice that reported by the Social Security trustees. The reason for the discrepancy is that the trustees' report covers "only" the next 75 years, whereas the annual deficits in the following years are projected to be massive. Another policy that would eliminate the long-term imbalance would be a 25% benefit cut beginning in 2000.

Obviously, either the tax hike or benefit cut would increase the Social Security net tax rates of postwar Americans. However, the treatment of birth cohorts differs appreciably under the two proposals. "Clearly, earlier generations fare better under the tax hike because they have limited remaining labor earnings that are subject to the higher payroll tax rate. In the case of the benefit cut, all generations are similarly hurt because none has yet begun to receive social security benefits" (Gokhale and Kotlikoff, 1999, p. 21). For example, the tax hike would raise the net tax rate only from 5.3 to 5.7% of life wealth for those born between 1945 and 1949; in contrast, for those born between 1995 and 1999 the net lifetime tax rate would rise from 5.4% under existing legislation to 8.4%.

Empirical Estimates of the Effect of Social Security on Private Savings

Due to the wealth substitution effect, a Social Security system yielding exactly the private rate of return is predicted to reduce private savings by one dollar for each dollar of contributions made. During the start-up phase of unfunded Social Security, returns from participation exceeded the private rate of return, generating a windfall gain. Ceteris paribus, this gain would increase consumption, further depressing savings. In the steady state, there is negative net Social Security wealth (a windfall loss), predicted to cushion the decline in savings.[13] However, our discussion has ignored many complications arising, as examples, from the presence of uncertainty, the existence of liquidity-constrained households, retirement incentives, and intergenerational transfers. To assess the overall effect of Social Security on private savings in light of these influences we now consider empirical analyses of this relationship.

There are now many cross-sectional studies, based on household-level data, that analyze the effect of Social Security wealth on private savings. Most such studies first calculate rest-of-life net SSW for each member of their sample. A second step estimates how private savings are changed per dollar change in net SSW. To illustrate, suppose someone age 50 is projected to receive benefits, in present value to age 50, taking into account life expectancy, of $100,000. If it is estimated that the person will pay an additional $20,000 in payroll taxes before retirement, again in present value, the net SSW is $80,000. By the wealth substitution effect, if we assume the person will have neither windfall gains nor losses over the life cycle (i.e., taxes to that point in "age-50" dollars are $80,000), his or her private savings should be $80,000 lower at age 50 than had he or she not participated in Social Security. Suppose, though, it is found that the person has reduced savings at age 50 by "only" $20,000. This means that on average he or she reduces private savings by 25 cents for each dollar of rest-of-life Social Security wealth. A cross-section estimate is the average of these propensities to save from SSW over everyone in the studies' sample.

Page (1998) reviews this empirical literature and concludes that "the cross-section evidence suggests that each dollar of Social Security wealth most likely reduces private wealth by between zero and 50 cents, with the most likely estimate lying near the middle of that range" (p. 11). This implies that the wealth substitution effect based on the simple life-cycle model appreciably overstates the negative impact of Social Security on savings. Nevertheless, the mid-point estimate implies a significant reduction in savings. In an economy below the Golden Rule capital intensity, these reductions in capital accumulation adversely affect steady state consumption and welfare.

The Trust Fund

The eventual retirement of the baby boomers poses a substantial threat to the viability of the Social Security system, as the number of retirees per worker will be much higher than in earlier periods. The number of workers paying into Social Security per beneficiary equaled 5.1 in 1960 but is projected to fall to 2 in 2045 (Gokhale and Kotlikoff, 1999, p. 4). In anticipation of the actuarial problems associated with the large baby boom cohort, several steps were undertaken in 1983 to solidify the future of Social Security. These steps included raising the age of retirement with full benefits to 67 and increasing taxation of Social Security benefits.

Central to our discussion was the creation of the Social Security trust fund. The deposits into the fund result from the fact that the payroll contributions of the baby boomers are more than enough to meet the commitments to the relatively smaller generation of current retirees; the excess of contributions is put into the fund. Then, when the boomers retire, the trust fund will augment the payroll contributions of the smaller work force. In this way, it is hoped, the Social Security system can honor its commitments to the boomers without creating too large of a burden on the next generation of workers (the boomers' kids). There is skepticism on the part of many whether the trust fund will achieve this desirable and important objective. According to the Social Security Administration, the fund had reserves of about $700 billion in 1999 and will grow to about $4 trillion over the next 20 years. However, it is expected that the fund will drop to zero about 2032. Beyond this there will be a structural shortfall of perhaps 25 percent of benefits pledged.

These projections are based on labor productivity growth rates below those enjoyed in the late 1990s. Should that higher recent productivity growth be sustained, the structural deficit will decline. Faster productivity growth increases the ratio of young people's life wealth compared with their elders'. Since legislated benefits to the old and taxes paid by the young are tied to life earnings, higher income growth increases the size of the tax base compared with the benefit base. Rapid productivity growth in the late 1990s also contributed to the emergence of sizeable federal budget surpluses. In the 2000 presidential campaign, then Vice President Albert Gore proposed that some portion of those budget surpluses be employed to reduce the national debt. A lower outstanding debt would relieve somewhat the strains on the bond market when the government begins financing the boomer's retirement benefits.

There is some concern that the trust fund deposits may not support benefits as intended once the current annual surpluses become deficits, as they will long before the fund's balance goes to zero. The trust fund would seem to be most successful if the proceeds were invested in physical capital, with the associated profits reinvested. Then this capital could be sold off as needed when the baby boomers retire. How are things different if, as is ostensibly the case, the trust fund is used to increase government saving (or decrease government dissaving)? In some ways the story need not be much different. In this case, the current surpluses are invested in government bonds. By reducing the amount of government bonds held by the private sector, less private sector investment is crowded out. Again the private sector capital stock is larger than it would have been without the trust fund. Now, when the boomers retire, the government will have to issue more government bonds, transferring the proceeds to the retired boomers.

There is also concern about the ability of affected markets to absorb these big swings in government bond offerings. Interest rates may rise as boomers retire, as the government issues new debt to finance their benefits. These higher rates may in turn depress corporate stock prices. Another issue is that policymakers may see the positive in-flows from Social Security currently and decide to increase government spending on transfers, or other noncapital purchases, or cut taxes. Such actions would increase national consumption, reducing physical capital accumulation. This concern led to the removal of Social Security from the "official" federal budget several years ago. Otherwise, reported surpluses would include monies already committed to future beneficiaries.

Privatization of Social Security

Because of the low rates of return to future beneficiaries anticipated under current Social Security legislation, and the fact that currently legislated taxes will not support promised benefits in the future, several reforms to Social Security have been proposed. In addition to the tax hike and benefit cut proposals discussed above, others involve some sort of *privatization*. By privatization is meant that (at least some) contributions are placed in personal accounts. For example, in the presidential campaign of 2000, presidential candidate George W. Bush proposed that 2 percentage points of each worker's total Social Security tax payments each year be deposited into a private account. The level of retirement assets associated with those contributions would be determined by the performance of the markets in which those assets were invested. Although many privatization proposals stress the ability to invest in risky assets with high expected returns, we initially abstract from uncertainty, keeping the returns on private assets and public debt equal; risky assets are discussed below.

Consider a reform proposal designed to (1) honor the obligations of the present system and (2) completely privatize the system from this point forward. Unfortunately, honoring the more than $2.5 trillion in unfunded liabilities under the current system makes conversion to a private system decidedly different from starting a private program from scratch (cf. Murphy and Welch, 1998). Recall, a "from scratch" program is identical to the fully funded Social Security programs discussed above (which engaged in no intra-generational redistribution). We now consider the implications of such a reform in our model of completely unfunded Social Security, where $n = v = 0$. Specifically, suppose the young of period 0, and each subsequent period, have all their social security taxes T_0 placed in a personalized account, yielding the same return r_1 as other assets. This makes their retirement benefits $B_1 = T_0(1 + r_1)$, as opposed to just T_0 when the system is unfunded. However, the existing Social Security deficit of $T = T_0$ per old person must also be financed. This may be accomplished in many ways. To spread the burden, suppose that each generation simply services that deficit, paying taxes of rT per person when old. What are the gains to generation 0? Nothing! Relative to the unfunded system, they now receive an extra rT on their Social Security contribution, but pay an extra rT to finance the existing burden.

The policy illustrated above differs from the Bush proposal in two ways. First, as previously noted, Bush suggests diverting only a portion of current contributions to private accounts. Second, and more worrisome for those currently middle-aged, is that Bush's proposal did not explicitly address the funding of transitional generations. With a portion of tax payments put into private accounts, the trust fund will not grow as fast and will be depleted sooner. With the young already having "personal accounts," they may be reluctant to support large amounts of government borrowing or increased taxes to meet the currently legislated benefits of the boomers. Instead, they may be likely to prefer reductions in non-privatized benefits, with such cuts falling more heavily on boomers.

In this way, calls for privatization put great pressure on the intergenerational social contract. Further, if all contributions are put into personal accounts, the progressivity and insurance aspects of the current system must be abandoned or financed out of general revenues. Abstracting from the financing of transitional generations, such a privatized system may be superior to no system at all, in that it provides an income floor for retirees who may otherwise have needed government transfers to support retirement consumption.

One virtue of privatization, it is claimed, is that contributions may be invested in higher yielding securities, raising the rate of return. However, higher average yields are associated with greater variability. Thus, the return for a given cohort from investing in the stock market could be below that of investing in government bonds, even. For example, the Dow Jones Industrial Average first crossed 1,000 in 1968, but did not stay above 1,000 until 1982. Of course, it was above 10,000 in 2000! If a cohort has poor investment luck, would the government be compelled to assist them? If so, might that encourage "too much" speculation?

A related alternative to complete privatization is to invest part of the trust fund in the stock market instead of in government bonds. With higher expected yields on the trust fund, smaller increases in taxes or reductions in benefits may be necessary to make the system solvent in the long run (Seidman, 1999). However, assuming the value of financial assets equals the value of the underlying real assets, investing the trust fund in the stock market may not succeed in creating additional societal wealth. Instead, there may simply be a shuffling of household portfolios. To see this, suppose a household had optimally chosen its retirement portfolio, including its risk characteristics, under the current policy. If the trust fund is withdrawn from relatively safe bonds and invested in relatively risky stocks, that household's exposure to risk has increased. It may choose to sell stocks and purchase bonds to restore portfolio risk to its optimal level. Nevertheless, by reducing Social Security's long-term deficit, investing some or all of the trust fund in the stock market may reduce the political tensions associated with making Social Security solvent.

Of course, many low and moderate income households own little, if any, stock. Abel (2001) argues this is because fixed costs of entering the stock market make stocks attractive only to those who can make sizeable investments—the affluent. For this reason, he argues, investing Social Security in the stock market (without incurring the fixed costs) would increase the wealth of less affluent households. Consequently, their consumption would rise and capital accumulation would fall.

We have considered several options to reform Social Security. Each must confront the fact that the start-up cohorts received a windfall that must be paid by subsequent cohorts.

4.6 INCOME TAXATION

This section analyzes income taxation, focusing on the efficiency implications of interest or capital income taxation. An income tax applies to wage income and capital income. In the framework of this chapter, all capital income consists of the interest earned by old households on their savings from the first period of life. All wage income accrues in the first period, since the second period is devoted to retirement. Further, since there are no alternatives to work in the first period (leisure or schooling are ignored), the supply of labor is completely inelastic. Thus, wage taxes are lump-sum, or unavoidable, in our model. The only decision margin for households in our framework is that between consumption when young and when old. A tax on interest income at rate τ raises the price of second-period consumption from $1/(1 + r)$ to $1/[1 + r(1 - \tau)]$. Since the tax on interest affects the relative price of consuming at different points in time, and since households may avoid the tax by not saving, the tax harms efficiency by distorting behavior. Below, we first address the partial equilibrium efficiency cost of capital income taxation. Then we see how these conclusions are affected by general-equilibrium considerations.

The marginal rate of substitution (MRS) is the subjective rate at which consumers are willing to trade off second- for first-period consumption. The marginal rate of transformation (MRT) is the increase in resources next period from investing a unit of output in the current period. The MRT is simply $1 + r$; investing an additional unit of output increases output the following period r units, and the total nonlabor resources (output plus capital) by $1 + r$ units. Economic efficiency requires that for any two goods MRT = MRS. Thus, in the absence of capital income taxation, utility maximization where the MRS = $1 + r$ is efficient.

The introduction of a capital income tax drives a wedge between the MRT and the MRS. For this reason, the tax imposes a cost on consumers over and above the amount of tax revenues raised. We now examine this loss in efficiency, termed the *excess burden*. In the presence of a tax on interest income at rate τ, the consumer maximizes utility where MRS = $1 + r(1 - \tau) <$ MRT. To appreciate the inefficiency, suppose the MRT is 2 whereas the MRS is only 1, so that $\tau = 1$, or 100 percent. This wedge between the MRT and the MRS means some socially profitable investments in physical capital are not privately utility maximizing. For example, reducing C_1 by 1 unit (to increase investment) would increase second-period resources by MRT = 2. Since the consumer just requires 1 unit of C_2 to compensate for the unit of C_1 foregone, social welfare would be higher by the extra, or second, unit of C_2. However, this investment opportunity is not exploited since the tax on interest, by distorting the relative price of C_2, eliminates the private incentive to undertake it. The excess burden is a dollar measure of those lost opportunities.

Recall from Chapter 1 that, with Cobb-Douglas utility, the first-period consumption (and therefore the saving decision) is independent of the net-of-tax interest rate. However, by changing the price ratio, the tax does affect the ratio of first- to second-period consumption. The excess burden of the tax on interest is developed graphically in Figure 4.3 for our Cobb-Douglas case. The pretax budget line Hw_1 has slope of $-(1 + r)$. The after-tax budget line's slope is $-[1 + r(1 - \tau)]$. The vertical distance between those bud-

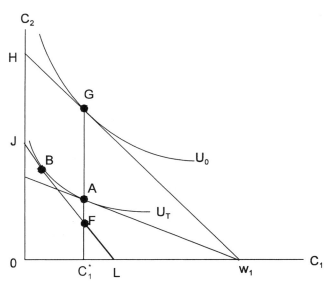

Figure 4.3 Excess burden of the tax on interest

get lines is the amount of tax revenues raised at the corresponding level of C_1 consumption. For example, at C^*_1, which maximizes utility both before and in the presence of the tax, interest income taxes are the distance GA.

Imposition of the tax on capital lowers utility from U_0 to U_T. To translate that loss into dollars, first note that that same reduction in utility could instead have been achieved by a lump-sum tax. Such a hypothetical tax would produce budget line JL. This budget line is tangent to U_T at B, and parallel to the initial budget line Hw_1 (since the lump-sum tax doesn't affect relative prices). Notice that the lump-sum tax equals HJ units of C_2, the vertical distance between the initial budget line and that with lump-sum taxation. Viewed at C^*_1, that same magnitude is GF. Significantly, the lump-sum measure of the decline in welfare exceeds the amount of tax revenues raised, GA. The excess GF − GA = AF is the excess burden of the tax. Such an excess burden arises for any reasonable preferences, not just for our Cobb-Douglas case.

Boskin (1978) and Feldstein (1978) both compute the efficiency cost of capital income taxation under the partial-equilibrium assumption that the wage and pretax interest rate are unaffected.[14] Assuming a 40% tax on capital income and, as above, no response of savings to the interest rate, Feldstein estimates an efficiency loss equal to about 20% of first-period savings. Using a 50% tax rate and assuming a compensated elasticity of saving with respect to the net interest rate (i.e., based on the substitution effect alone) of .4, Boskin estimates capital income taxation imposes a welfare loss equal to about 25% of first-period saving. However, partial-equilibrium analysis may well seriously understate the true efficiency cost if capital income taxation lowers capital accumulation. For this reason, more recent analyses have been conducted in a general-equilibrium context.

Summers (1981) conducted tax reform experiments in a general-equilibrium overlapping-generations life-cycle model with fixed labor supply. Unlike the framework of this chapter, though, he allowed for many periods (or years) in each life cycle. The fact that labor supply is fixed implies that, as in our model, both wage and consumption taxes are lump-sum. As such, they do not distort any choices or entail any efficiency costs. Summers first calibrated the initial steady state in his computer simulation model using realistic values for existing tax rates and for production and utility function parameters. He then examined the implications for steady state consumption and welfare associated with eliminating capital income taxation. In one case, the economy converts to reliance on wage income taxation, so that the revenues on interest income are obtained from increasing the tax rate on wage earnings. As a second-regime change, both interest and wage income taxation are replaced with consumption taxes.

Summers finds huge steady state welfare gains. He writes that "a complete shift to consumption taxation might raise steady state output by as much as 18 percent, and consumption by 16%. The long-run welfare gain from such a shift would for plausible parameter values exceed $150 billion annually" (p. 1). Somewhat smaller, but still large, gains are associated with a switch to a wage income base. His estimates dwarfed previous welfare estimates. One reason that output, consumption, and welfare rise so much is that his model (unlike ours) has a very high interest elasticity of savings. This high elasticity results from the human wealth effect discussed in Chapter 2: When the interest rate rises, the present value of future earnings falls, reducing consumption of the young and increasing savings. His results revealed how large that effect can be when the consumer is discounting many years of future earnings.[15] Consequently, when the tax on interest is eliminated—raising the after-tax return—there is a large increase in savings. And, since the initial steady state in his economy is far below the Golden Rule capital intensity, these higher savings produce large consumption gains.[16]

He also found conversion to a consumption tax base increased savings by appreciably more than did switching to complete reliance on wage taxation. One reason is that in realistic life-cycle models having several years of pure retirement, consumption taxes accrue later in life, on average, than wage taxes. Consequently, households have to save more when young to pay for the taxes on consumption when retired. Since government saving is restricted to be equal (and in fact zero) under each regime, the higher private savings under consumption taxation lead to greater capital accumulation.

The fact that consumption taxes occur later in life than wage taxes also increases welfare in a second fashion. This mechanism is the tax postponement effect discussed in section 4.3: The government has kept annual revenues constant while delaying taxes until later in the life cycle. This reduces the present value of taxes due, increasing consumer welfare.

For at least two reasons, Summers' estimates overstate the gain from elimination of interest income taxation. First, since Summers' model assumes household labor supply is fixed, both the wage and consumption tax alternatives to interest income taxation are lump-sum. Subsequent research allows leisure consumption to respond optimally when the tax regime changes (cf. Auerbach and Kotlikoff, 1987; Lord, 1987). These models produce lower welfare gains because now increased wage or consumption taxation further distorts the allocation of time between market work and leisure. That is, in Summers' framework, eliminating interest income taxation reduces the partial-equilibrium welfare loss to zero. In contrast, when labor supply is endogenous, reducing one partial-equilibrium distortion is possible only if another decision margin is further distorted. (Recent examinations of income taxation that model human capital decisions are discussed in Chapter 7.)

A second caveat relating to the Summers' estimates above is that they are based on comparison of steady states, thereby ignoring the implications for transitional generations. This is especially misleading in the case of consumption taxation. To appreciate why, first note that those retired when the income tax is replaced by a consumption tax do not benefit from the removal of the tax on wages. However, they now must pay the tax on consumption goods (which exceeds the tax relief from eliminated interest income taxation). Thus, Summers' consumption tax dramatically increases the generational accounts of the currently old. As seen earlier in this chapter, shifting the tax burden to early generations allows for greater capital accumulation, higher wages, and also lower taxes on future generations.

Auerbach and Kotlikoff (1987) implement a sophisticated compensation scheme to compute the efficiency or welfare changes for future generations associated with tax reform, holding constant the welfare of generations alive when the tax change is introduced. In this way, they explicitly take transitional considerations into account (as well as the labor-leisure choices mentioned above). For each tax reform they calculate the percentage change in lifetime wealth for all future generations that would make them indifferent to the tax change. They find that conversion to complete reliance on wage income taxation may well reduce welfare, while moving to a consumption base produces small welfare gains, typically below 1.5 percent of life wealth (pp. 77–78). And, recall that, unlike in the Summers' model, these pure efficiency gains arise even though the labor-leisure choice is endogenous.

More recently, Altig et al. (2001) extend the simulation model of Auerbach and Kotlikoff in two important ways. First, they incorporate many significant details about the tax system, such as personal exemptions, the standard deduction, and the ability to itemize, which the Auerbach and Kotlikoff model ignores. Second, they allow for substantial earnings heterogeneity *within* birth cohorts. One policy they consider is conversion from the existing progressive tax system with its many exclusions to a proportional consumption tax with a standard deduction of $9,500; they refer to this as a "flat tax." As in other models, steady state capital accumulation and income are higher under a consumption base. They find the reform increases steady state utility for those at every level of earnings. The long-term gains are greatest for those at the extremes of the earnings distribution. The poorest households in a birth cohort pay little in taxes under either regime, but benefit from the higher level of wages under the flat tax. The most affluent households benefit greatly from the reduction in marginal and average tax rates.

Middle-earners face quite similar tax rates under either regime and enjoy the smallest steady state utility gains. Average-income classes also fare least well during the transition. Middle-earners who enter the labor force about the time of the reform face high tax rates on earnings, since capital accumulation has not yet raised pretax wages. Further, with few assets, they benefit little from the elimination of interest income taxation. While Altig et al.'s analysis does not definitively answer whether the gains to winners outweigh the losses to losers, by considering both intergenerational and intragenerational equity these authors afford a more complete picture of the policy's effects.

4.7 SUMMARY

This chapter examined the implications of government's tax, consumption, and transfer policies on capital accumulation and intergenerational welfare. The level of capital that maximizes consumption is called the Golden Rule. That capital intensity is achieved where the net of depreciation marginal product of capital equals the growth rate of output. Most evidence indicates capital accumulation in the United States is well below the Golden Rule level, so the economy is dynamically efficient. This means the consumption of future generations may be increased only by reducing the consumption of earlier generations.

Fiscal policy can raise capital accumulation by reducing the rate of aggregate consumption. In the first period of any policy change the capital stock and output levels are fixed. Thus, a policy that suppresses the rate of aggregate consumption will lower consumption levels in the short run to free resources for the capital accumulation needed to raise the level of output and consumption in the future. This is true of policies transferring resources from the old to the young.

In practice, many government policies have instead reduced capital accumulation by shifting tax burdens from the old to the young. An important example is unfunded or pay-as-you-go Social Security. Steady state generations not only receive a rate of return from the program that is below that on private assets, but may also face lower wages on the basis of reduced capital accumulation. Significant reform of the Social Security system is hampered by the existing unfunded liabilities. Faster productivity growth would alleviate some of the stress on Social Security.

When the government raises taxes in other than lump-sum fashion, relative prices are altered. By distorting incentives, such taxes entail efficiency losses. Eliminating capital income taxation may increase steady state welfare by reducing the distortionary effects on the timing of consumption and moving the economy closer to the Golden Rule capital intensity. The steady state gains may be sizeable following conversion to a consumption base. One reason is that consumption taxation is significant even late in the life cycle, causing households to save more while young. Since these steady state gains typically need to be weighed against losses for transitional cohorts, it remains difficult to know if such reforms are desirable.

This chapter has pursued the effects of fiscal policy on capital accumulation in a model where consumers choose only between present and future consumption. We reconsider many of these issues in later chapters, in the light of transfers to dependents, human capital accumulation, and fertility.

ENDNOTES

1. The topics of this chapter are treated at a higher technical level by Ihori (1996). Auerbach and Kotlikoff (1998) address similar questions, emphasizing numerical computation of the transition between steady states.

2. This section was improved as the result of conversations with Peter Rangazas.

3. Aggregate consumption in t is $L_t C_{1,t} + L_{t-1} C_{2,t}$. To get consumption per worker c_t, we divide through by the number of workers in t, L_t ($= (1 + n)^{t-1}$).

4. Equation (4.9) is *quantitatively* accurate when consumers do not expect the interest rate to change between t and t + 1 (so-called static expectations) and when the policy does not affect capital accumulation. More generally, this equation provides quantitatively accurate responses only for small policy changes in the absence of any preexisting policies. To understand the difficulty, suppose there is in place a policy that entails net taxes of $x in the second period of life. Now suppose a new policy is introduced in t and is expected to alter capital accumulation, and therefore the interest rate, in period t + 1. This change in the interest rate induces an additional wealth effect by altering the present value of the original $x of second-period net taxes; this, in turn, would alter $C_{1,t}$. Nevertheless, the *qualitative* conclusions of (4.9) should obtain for larger policies in the presence of preexisting programs. A tractable alternative would be to abstract from the role of consumption smoothing, by having all consumption occur in period 2 (cf. Auerbach and Kotlikoff, 1998). For our purposes, it is preferable to stress the intuition regarding consumption smoothing. Large simulation models of fiscal policy systematically account for preexisting policies (cf. Lord and Rangazas, 1998).

5. Government consumption that substitutes for or complements private consumption at a particular age in life has more complicated effects. Thus, government provision of higher quality or quantity of public education may reduce the supplemental outlays of young parents; see Chapter 5. Similarly, government outlays on Medicare benefit the old. In a larger sense, the effect of government consumption on utility very much affects the size of government in democracies: If the marginal utility of government consumption is high for the median voter, "bigger government" candidates are more likely to be elected.

6. One may wonder why the taxes levied on the old of period t do not affect capital accumulation in period t + 1. The reason derives from the assumption that people die penniless. As a consequence, any monies brought into the start of old age are dissaved. Whether savings are spent on consumption or paid to the government certainly affects the welfare of those old in t, but not their dissavings. Clearly, the old in t are made worse off when they are hit by the tax.

7. Actually, this is true only of nondistortionary, or lump-sum, polices. Any policy affecting economic incentives, such as the tax on interest income examined in Chapter 1, could affect capital accumulation—even if generational accounts are not affected. Our current discussion is limited to nondistortionary policies.

8. Similarly, in t + 1 the government takes extra taxes of $dz_{2,t} = \$500(1 + r_{t+1})$ from the now old households, but gives them back the same amount via interest payments on and repurchases of the debt issued in t. In t + 1, the increased government saving, or surplus, of $500 is offset by $500 of increased *dis*saving by old households, again leaving national savings unchanged.

9. The preceding numbers, and many of the ones to follow, come from on-line publications at the Social Security Administration's web site, www.ssa.gov.

10. More explicitly,

$$dz_i = dz_{1,i} + dz_{2,i+1}/(1 + r_{i+1})$$

$$= T + -B/(1 + r_{i+1}) = T - T(1 + r_{i+1})/(1 + r_{i+1}) = 0 \text{ for } i = t, t + 1, t + 2, \ldots$$

11. In Chapter 9 we note that household fertility choices may be altered by Social Security; if so, the implications of Social Security for growth are less clear.

12. Negative SSW lowers first-period consumption, but does not alter the conclusion that unfunded Social Security lowers savings. To appreciate this, first recall that if SSW = 0, private saving per young person falls by T. For a given T, to make the overall effect on the young's savings positive, negative SSW would need to reduce C_1 by more than T. Due to consumption smoothing, however, C_1 will definitely fall by less than T. For even if B = 0 so that SSW = −T, C_1 would fall by only θT. (Of course, B = 0 with T > 0 is the fear of many young workers.)

13. A different perspective suggests that these windfall gains and losses may not affect *aggregate* savings. Intuitively, if parents enjoy a windfall gain from Social Security but expect their children to suffer a windfall loss, parents out of altruism may compensate their children by increasing their bequest to children. In essence, parents save (and bequeath) every dollar "paid in for them" by their children. Likewise, children reduce savings by a dollar for each dollar they "pay in for their parents." This effect of windfalls on savings is termed the *bequest effect*. By this reasoning, parents increase their savings relative to an actuarially fair program and children reduce theirs, but in the aggregate, windfalls don't matter—only the wealth substitution effects remain. Altruistic transfers are modeled in Chapter 5.

14. This summary of their findings is based on Davies and St. Hilaire (1987, p. 54).

15. However, as discussed later in Chapter 2, if future earnings are uncertain, the magnitude of the human wealth effect is reduced.

16. Seidman and Lewis (1999) have shown that in a model quite similar to that of Summers', the increase in *steady state* capital accumulation is independent of the interest elasticity of savings. That elasticity is, however, important to capital accumulation during the transition between steady states.

QUESTIONS AND PROBLEMS

▶ REVIEW
QUESTIONS

1. What is a generational account? Why is such an account greater for males than females? How could a current policy decision affect the generational accounts of unborn generations?

2. **A.** What is the Golden Rule level of capital intensity? How does the desirability of increasing the saving rate depend upon whether the economy is dynamically efficient or dynamically inefficient? How does the desirability of initiating unfunded Social Security depend upon whether the economy is dynamically efficient?

   B. Use a graph to illustrate the effect of an increase in k* on the consumer's budget constraint and utility. Depict this effect both when the economy is dynamically efficient and dynamically inefficient.

3. Suppose there is no steady state economic growth. How does the amount of taxes to be paid to satisfy the GIBC depend upon when the taxes are paid (which generations)?

4. **A.** Explain the difference between the tax postponement and income timing effects of changing from taxation of the young to taxation of the old.

   B. Why do simulated efficiency costs of conversion from income taxation vary between models including and excluding labor-leisure choices?

5. Intuitively explain the implications for national savings in period t of a policy that
   A. increases government spending by g per old person only in t and also increases taxes by g per old person only in t. (The policy is announced at the start of period t.)
   B. increases government spending in each period by g per young (or old) person and also increases taxes on each young person by g each period, beginning in t. Use the transition diagram to illustrate the implications of this policy for the macroeconomy.

C. increases government spending by g per young person in period t, only. The government imposes no new taxes in t. But, beginning in period t + 1, it will service (i.e., pay interest on) the debt in each period i by taxing the old $r_{t+i}g$ (that is, $r_{t+1}g$ in t + 1). Use the transition diagram to illustrate the implications of this policy for the macroeconomy.

6. Suppose it is decided to reduce wage income taxes (occurring in the first, young, period of life only) and increase consumption taxation (paid both when young and when old). Suppose this is to be done in such a fashion that no generation's generational account is affected. Assume no one is liquidity constrained before or after the policy change. *Intuitively*, what will be the implications of this policy for capital accumulation and for the composition of national savings? Now assume that some households are liquidity constrained before the tax change. Again address the implications for capital accumulation and for the composition of national savings.

7. **A.** What is an unfunded Social Security liability? What is the cause of the current liability? What must happen to remove the liability? Does the liability have to be removed?
   B. Under the currently legislated tax/benefit schedule, how will actual labor productivity growth over the next few decades affect the solvency of the Social Security system?

8. What does "privatizing" Social Security mean? Under the assumptions of our model, is privatization a better way to address the long-term structural deficit than simply raising payroll taxes?

9. **A.** Explain why the relationship between r and n + v is more important to unfunded than to fully funded Social Security systems.
   B. Why was SSW positive for several generations during the start-up phase but is now becoming negative (and eventually will become a large negative)?
   C. Why are the effects on national saving different between unfunded and fully funded Social Security systems? In the preparation of your answer assume (counterfactually) that r = n + v.
   D. Why and how has the Social Security program moved away somewhat from a pay-as-you-go system?
   E. Reforming the Social Security system will prove to be the proverbial "free lunch." Comment.

10. Consider an unfunded Social Security program in long-run equilibrium in the absence of economic growth (n = v = 0).
    A. Derive the effects on k_{t+1} using the expression (4.9) for changes in capital accumulation and intuitively explain the sign.
    B. Show that a policy giving a tax cut of T to the old of t that is financed by having the old of each subsequent generation service the debt has exactly the same effects for capital accumulation. (Hint: To make the expressions comparable, simplify the expression from A) by getting a common denominator for all the θT terms.

C. Show that unfunded Social Security has the same implications for net transfers between households and government each period as does the *combination* of fully funded Social Security and the policy described in B.

D. Given your answers to A–C, is the budget deficit a very reliable guide to a policy's effect on capital accumulation? Explain.

▶ PROBLEMS

1. Suppose that $r = 1$, $E_1 = 20$, and $E_2 = 30$. Draw an initial budget line. Now suppose $z_{1,t} = 10$ and that $z_{2,t+1} = -20$. Determine the generational account and the effects on the budget line. Now suppose second-period net taxes are instead zero, with first-period net of transfer taxes remaining 10. Again determine the generational account and the implications for the budget line.

2. **A.** Suppose that $r = 1$, $w\mathbf{A} = 40$, and $B = T(1 + r) = 20$. Illustrate the asset-substitution effect of Social Security graphically.

   B. Now suppose when young, Social Security taxes are $T = 50$, and when old, benefits are $B = 80$. Also, $r = 1$. What is the generational account associated with this program? What is Social Security wealth?

3. Consider a policy of increasing taxes by T on each old person of period t. The proceeds are used to retire government debt. Suppose the tax savings of this policy from reduced debt service are to be spread equally across future generations, with the old of each generation beginning in $t + 1$ receiving the tax cut.

   A. How large will the tax cut be?

   B. Analyze the welfare implications of this policy, addressing both the redistributive impact effects and the macroeconomic effects.

4. Suppose $\theta = .4$ and $r_{t+1} = 1$.

   A. Suppose the government announces at time t that it will reduce transfers to the old by 10 in each period, beginning in period t in order to finance additional government purchases of 10 each period. By how much will $C_{1,t}$, $S_{1,t}$, $C_{2,t+1}$, and $C_{2,t}$ change? (For your response to how $C_{2,t+1}$ will change, ignore any change in the interest rate in $t + 1$.) Provide the intuition also.

   B. What will be the *quantitative* implications of this policy for the number of tools per worker in period $t + 1$? The *qualitative* implications for the wages of workers in $t + 1$ and for the interest rate?

5. Suppose $\theta = .4$ and $r_{t+1} = 1$.

   A. Suppose the government announces at time t that it will increase taxes on the young by 10 in each period, beginning in period t in order to finance additional government purchases of 10 each period. By how much will $C_{1,t}$, $S_{1,t}$, $C_{2,t+1}$, and $C_{2,t}$ change? (For your response to how $C_{2,t+1}$ will change, ignore any change in the interest rate in $t + 1$.) Provide the intuition also.

   B. What will be the *quantitative* implications of this policy for the number of tools per worker in period $t + 1$? The *qualitative* implications for the wages of workers in $t + 1$ and for the interest rate?

Chapter
5 | INTERGENERATIONAL FINANCIAL TRANSFERS

"Households acquire wealth from two sources: they save out of income they have earned, and they receive transfers from other people."
—GALE AND SCHOLZ, 1994, P. 145

The resources devoted by parents to their children are important to the welfare of off-spring, the distribution of well-being across families, and economic growth. In developed economies, even after children achieve economic independence most transfers continue to flow downstream, from parents to their adult children or grandchildren. For example, data indicate that over 83 percent of transfers exceeding $3,000 between families are made by parents.[1] However, when elderly parents are disabled, children have been found to provide over 7 hours of care per week, on average.[2] Understanding the reasons behind voluntary private transfers is crucial to the assessment of many public policies—such as Social Security and welfare—that redistribute resources across and/or within generations. Reflecting on the reasons for transfers is also interesting in its own right, as it provides insights into the nature of close social interactions.

A natural and useful distinction arises between transfers designed to further a child's development during his or her years of economic dependency and those occurring after the child has "left the nest." These latter transfers may take the form of either end-of-life *bequests* or *inter vivos gifts* (occurring while the parents are still alive). Aggregate private financial transfers are quite large. Gale and Scholz (1994) report that bequests in 1986 were $105 billion, while inter vivos transfers were $63 billion, or $98 billion if parental expenditures on children's college education are included. The Survey of Consumer Finances data they employ inquired only about prior-year transfers in excess of $3,000, implying that the inter vivos transfers are substantially underestimated. After adjusting for underreporting, they estimate inter vivos transfers to be about 43% of total transfers between households (more than 50% if one includes college outlays).[3] This chapter addresses the motivations behind private financial transfers from parents to children, in addition to their magnitude, timing, and implications for policy. Chapter 6 examines the investments of parents in dependent children.

While transfers to dependents are intentional and most probably altruistically motivated, transfers to adult children are more difficult to characterize. As explained in Chapter 2, many households leave unintentional bequests. Such accidental bequests arise simply because the length of life is uncertain, which makes it difficult to consume all of one's wealth *and* be prepared should life continue. However, the sheer size of large estates indicates that some (often wealthy) parents fully intend to bequeath wealth. All inter vivos transfers are intentional. Intentional bequests and inter vivos transfers may well be motivated by altruism, for even casual observation suggests that parents, on average, love their children deeply. However, other motives such as exchange and family insurance arrangements are also plausible. This chapter develops the theoretical implications associated with these transfer motives and evaluates them in light of the evidence.

Section 5.1 develops the theory of altruistically motivated financial transfers from parents to adult children. The implications of this framework are then evaluated in the light of evidence in section 5.2. The model of altruistic transfers proves incapable of explaining some important stylized facts concerning financial transfers. This motivates our discussion in section 5.3 of several prominent alternatives to the altruistic formulation. The evidence regarding transfers is reevaluated from the perspectives of these competing hypotheses. Section 5.4 considers the relative contributions of life-cycle savings and intergenerational transfers to aggregate wealth holdings. The next section is devoted to policy issues surrounding intergenerational transfers. Section 5.6 contains a brief summary.

5.1 THEORY OF ALTRUISTICALLY MOTIVATED FINANCIAL TRANSFERS

5.1.1   Total Transfers Under Altruism[4]

As in the seminal contributions of Barro (1974) and Becker (1974b), parents feel altruistic toward their children, and this motivates parents to make financial transfers to them. That is, parents care about their children's economic well-being, in particular their consumption of market goods and services. Other attributes of the child's well-being, such as consumption of lesiure, will be discussed less formally. This section assumes that parents and children are each economically active for only one period (the only overlap occurring when the children are economically dependent). Children do not become independent economic agents until immediately upon the parent's death. This assumption simplifies the story considerably with little apparent cost when the focus, as now, is on total transfers. Obviously, allowing for an overlap between the economic lives of parents and their *adult* children is necessary to explain the timing of transfers to adult children. This generalization is taken up below to develop the relationships among inter vivos gifts and end-of-life bequests.

We first model total financial transfers from parents to their children over the parents' life cycle, thereby including gifts to young adults and end-of-life bequests. Initially, we imagine there is but one child whose earnings as an adult are fully known to parents. The parents are assumed to maximize a utility function depending upon their own consumption C_p and, reflecting parental altruism, the consumption of their child when she or he is an adult C_c. As developed below, the adult child consumes all of her or his resources or wealth W_c. For this reason, the utility function of parents may be written in terms of either child consumption or child wealth. That is,[5]

$$U_p = U_p(C_p, C_c) \tag{5.1}$$

and

$$U_p = U_p(C_p, W_c)$$

where U_p is the utility of parents. As in Chapter 1, economic intuition is furthered by adopting the Cobb-Douglas utility function, so that

$$U_p = C_p^\theta C_c^{1-\theta} = C_p^\theta W_c^{1-\theta} \tag{5.2}$$

Notice that, with the obvious exception of subscripts, (5.1) is identical to the two-period life-cycle model's utility function, equation (1.1).[6] As we shall see, many features of these two models are formally identical.

A more rigorous (and complicated) version of altruism models parents' utility as depending upon the child's *utility*, which in turn depends upon the grandchild's utility, and so on. Our formulation provides the useful simplification of limiting attention to two generations. And, for several important issues, the "wealth" and "utility" specifications are equivalent in terms of *qualitative* implications about behavior (quantitative differences are possible). In those instances where the simplification of (5.1) and (5.2) hinders understanding, the intuition behind the "utility" model will be developed.

The life wealth of parents W_p consists of their earnings E_p and any financial transfers I_p received from *their* parents, $W_p = I_p + E_p$. The financial transfers I_p will be referred to as an inheritance, even though they may include inter vivos gifts received by the parents while the grandparents were alive. Parental resources are spent on own consumption C_p and transfers to the child. For now, all transfers are called bequests B_p, even though they also include any gifts made by parents to their adult children (the distinction between bequests and inter vivos transfers is emphasized below). Thus,

$$W_p = E_p + I_p = C_p + B_p \tag{5.3}$$

Formally, resources are received and consumption and bequest decisions are made at the start of parents' adulthood.

Similarly, the resources of the adult child are the sum of his or her earnings and any inheritance (including inter vivos gifts) from parents, $W_c = E_c + I_c$. As the model is set up, parents die just as their children achieve adulthood. Consequently, the inheritance is received exactly one period after the bequest decision is made, so that $I_c = B_p(1 + r)$. To focus on transfers between the two generations, it is assumed that the child is concerned only with own consumption C_c.[7] For this reason the child's budget constraint may be written

$$W_c = E_c + B_p(1 + r) = C_c \tag{5.4}$$

This equation reveals that child earnings are an important consideration for altruistic parents deciding how much to consume and how much to transfer to their child.

Consolidating equations (5.3) and (5.4) enables us to express the parents' utility maximization problem in standard form. To do so, solve (5.3) for B_p and then substitute into (5.4). Some rearrangement then yields the *dynastic* budget constraint

$$C_p + C_c/(1 + r) = W_p + E_c/(1 + r) = Z \qquad (5.5)$$

where Z is dynastic, or extended family, wealth. The parents' utility maximization problem is to maximize (5.2) subject to (5.5), by choice of C_p and B_p.

As stressed below, parents can't appropriate child resources for their own use. Nevertheless, for parents planning transfers, dynastic wealth—including child earnings—is the relevant resource constraint. For it is the combination of child earnings and parental transfers that determines C_c. Assuming parents know—or have a good sense of—the child's earnings prospects, parents effectively choose C_c when they decide on the level of financial bequests B_p. Notice the formal similarity of maximizing (5.2) subject to (5.5) and the consumer's life-cycle consumption problem of maximizing (1.2) subject to (1.5).

You may have noticed that there is no attempt to decompose expenditures by parents, C_p, into goods and services they personally consume and those consumed by their *dependent* children (while still in the nest). In Chapter 6 we do isolate those expenditures by parents on the human capital development of their dependent child, which contribute to the consumption of the child after leaving home.

Recall from Chapter 1 that when preferences are Cobb-Douglas, the exponent on a good in the utility function equals the fraction of wealth spent on that good. The same results obtain here, so that parents devote θ% of dynastic wealth to C_p, with the remainder supporting C_c

$$C_p = \theta Z \qquad (5.6a)$$

and

$$C_c = (1 - \theta)Z(1 + r) \qquad (5.6b)$$

Notice that since child consumption occurs in the next period (generation), it exceeds the portion of dynastic wealth not consumed by parents by the interest factor $1 + r$.

It is both easy and good practice to solve the model numerically. For example, suppose that $W_p = 10$, $E_c = 10$, $r = 1$, and $\theta = .6$. Using (5.5), $Z = W_p + E_c/(1 + r) = 10 + 10/2 = 15$. Then each generation's consumption is determined by (5.6); $C_p = \theta Z = (.6)(15) = 9$ and $C_c = (1 - \theta)Z(1 + r) = (.4)(15)(2) = 12$. Further, the bequest is $B_p = W_p - C_p = 10 - 9 = 1$, so that the inheritance becomes $I_c = B_p(1 + r) = (1)(2) = 2$.

The model and this numerical example are illustrated in Figure 5.1. Point A is the resource endowment for the extended family and point Z is dynastic wealth. The budget constraint has slope $-(1 + r) = -2$, as that is the reduction in C_c required to increase parental consumption by one unit. U_p^0 is the parents' indifference curve achieved when utility is maximized subject only to dynastic wealth. The utility-maximizing consumption

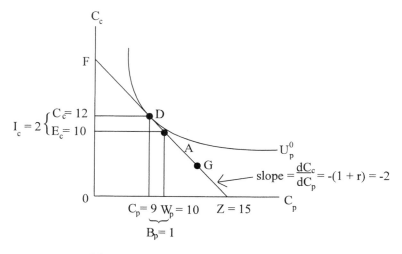

Figure 5.1 Parental bequests under altruism

bundle D produces the positive bequest shown on the horizontal axis. Consequently, child consumption exceeds child earnings by the inheritance, as shown.

In the two-period life-cycle model of Chapter 1, savings of the young are the difference between income and consumption. The bequest may be thought of as intergenerational savings. The relative contributions of life-cycle and intergenerational savings to total savings is a controversial topic, addressed later in this chapter.

Bequests may be readily expressed in terms of parental wealth and child earnings. Recall that bequests are the difference between parental resources and consumption; $B_p = W_p - C_p$. By (5.6a) we can substitute θZ for C_p. Then, using the definition of Z from (5.5) we obtain an expression for desired bequests in terms of family resources alone,

$$B_p = W_p - \theta Z = W_p - \theta[W_p + E_c/(1 + r)]$$
$$= (1 - \theta)W_p - \theta E_c/(1 + r)$$

(5.7a)

We consider the intuition associated with (5.7a) in a moment. First, though, note that there is nothing in our current specification that prohibits bequests from being negative. In fact, if parents' relative preference for own consumption is large (a high θ) and child earnings are large relative to parents', a negative desired bequest is to be expected. However, in practice, parents cannot force children to transfer resources to them. And, as noted before, significant financial flows from adult children to their parents are relatively uncommon. Further, creditors would not allow parents to go into a position of negative net wealth on the basis of vague promises from parents that children, in the absence of legal coercion, would make good on debts left by parents at death. For these reasons, if (5.7a) entails negative desired bequests, *actual* bequests will be zero. In this case, parents are said to be *transfer constrained*. (The economics literature also refers to such households as bequest constrained or intergenerationally borrowing constrained.)

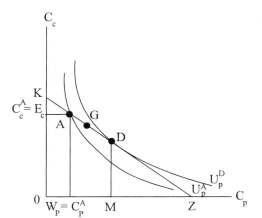

Figure 5.2 The transfer constraint

The solution for transfer-constrained parents is illustrated in Figure 5.2. If parents were free to maximize utility subject only to dynastic wealth, they would choose point D, which entails the negative bequest MW_p. Since negative bequests are not permitted, parents must choose from that portion of the budget line where transfers are nonnegative. They are thus restricted to the segment AK, since at all points below A parents' consumption exceeds their wealth. Maximizing utility along AK leads to parents and children each consuming exactly their own resources, at the endowment point A.

What determines whether the transfer constraint is binding? Intuitively, the higher are child earnings, the greater must parental wealth be before a positive bequest is desired. This is confirmed in (5.7a). Similarly, the more "selfish" are parents (the higher is θ), the wealthier they must be to make a transfer. For given child earnings and parental preference for own consumption, desired bequests rise with parental wealth, remaining negative until the constraint ceases to bind beyond some wealth level, call it W_p^*.[8]

In summary, our bequest rule is (as above)

$$B_p = (1 - \theta)W_p - \theta E_c/(1 + r)$$

if $W_p > W_p^*$, otherwise

$$B_p = 0 \tag{5.7b}$$

Bequest function (5.7) is depicted in Figure 5.3. Supposing child earnings are E_c^0, then actual transfers are zero—and desired bequests negative—until parental wealth exceeds W_p^{*0}. Bequests then rise $(1 - \theta)$ cents on each additional dollar of parental wealth. That is, for parents making positive transfers, $1 - \theta$ is the marginal propensity to bequeath, dB_p/dW_p. Should the wealth of altruistic parents planning positive transfers rise $1,000, they would increase their own consumption by $\$\theta(1,000)$ and their bequest by $\$(1 - \theta)(1,000)$. (Referring back to Figure 5.1, an increase in W_p would shift the budget line outward in parallel fashion.)

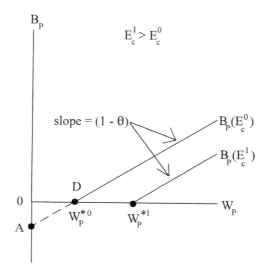

Figure 5.3 The bequest function

Equation (5.7a) also reveals that the higher are child earnings E_c, the lower is the bequest. For parents care about own as well as child consumption; if child earnings go up, parents will share in the good fortune by increasing C_p, which lowers their bequest. The marginal propensity to bequeath from child earnings, dB_p/dE_c, is therefore negative. Since an increase in E_c of \$1 increases dynastic wealth Z by $\$1/(1 + r)$, parents would increase C_p by $\theta/(1 + r)$. This reduces the bequest that same amount, so that $dB_p/dE_c = -\theta/(1 + r)$, the coefficient premultiplying E_c in (5.7a). In Figure 5.3 an increase in child earnings from E_c^0 to E_c^1 shifts the bequest function downward by the marginal propensity to bequeath from child earnings, times the change in child earnings. This prediction that transfers are inversely related to child earnings proves important to the evaluation of the altruistic model, as discussed below.

Since bequests fall as the earnings of the child increase relative to those of the parent, an increase in the rate of expected economic growth, which would make children relatively more affluent, should reduce transfers to children. This is pursued further in Chapter 6, where we see that growth may also alter the composition of transfers between investments in children's human capital and other transfers.

Holding constant the expected earnings of the adult children, transfers are predicted to increase with parental wealth. From another perspective, looking at a cross section of parents with the same wealth, children with lower expected life earnings (or "permanent income" in the parlance of Chapter 1) should receive higher total transfers. The evidence related to these propositions is reviewed shortly.

5.1.2 More Than One Child

This model of altruistic transfers is readily extended to families with more than one child. The two-child case is sufficiently general to illustrate the additional implications for transfers. Assume parents have equal concern for each child, so that the wealth or consumption of each enters the parents' utility function symmetrically,

$$U_p = U_p(C_p, W_c^1, W_c^2) \tag{5.8}$$

where $W_c^i = E_c^i + I_c^i$, for $i = 1,2$.

Suppose first that parents are unconstrained, making positive transfers to each child. The implications of this context flow immediately from the insight that utility maximization by the parents requires the marginal utility of child wealth to be equalized across the children. Since each child's wealth enters the parents' utility function symmetrically, this requirement implies *transfers should completely compensate for all differences in child earnings so as to equalize child wealth*. There are two possibilities. First, if the children have equal earnings, the total financial transfers received by each should also be equal (in present value). Alternatively, suppose that child 1 has greater earnings than child 2. In this case, the parents are predicted to make additional transfers to the low-earning child, equal to the earnings differential. Another possibility is that the parents are *partially* constrained. This occurs if the earnings differential between children exceeds the aggregate of planned transfers. Then, parents are predicted to make all transfers to the lower earning child, effectively "disinheriting" the other. In this instance, the higher earning child would still have higher wealth. For this reason, the parent would *like* to transfer funds from the high-earning child to the lower earning one.

5.1.3   The Timing of Transfers

Continuing to take the earnings of the child as given, we now consider *when* financial transfers are given, the timing of transfers. It is difficult to predict or "pin down" this timing with precision, since several influences are operative. As a starting point, note that if financial transfers of $1 in present value were of equal value to the parent and child regardless of when given, both would be indifferent between an inter vivos gift of $1 and a bequest of $(1 + r)$ one period later. However, for a variety of reasons, the value of the transfer differs through time to either the child or parent.

Adult children may prefer to receive the transfer as early as possible. Young adults desire durable goods such as cars and televisions, may need a down payment to purchase a home, have few assets, may need to service existing school debts or to accumulate more, and expect earnings to rise in the coming years. Consequently, young adults are often liquidity constrained in the sense of Chapter 1: They are unable to borrow against future earnings (or potential inheritances) to finance current consumption. Liquidity-constrained children would prefer inter vivos transfers to a bequest of equal present value (cf. Cox, 1990). An altruistic parent who has already chosen some positive present value of post-dependency transfers would naturally make transfers inter vivos, at least until the child's liquidity constraint is relieved. Of course, if the amount needed to relax the constraint exceeds in present value the total planned transfers, the child will remain (perhaps appreciably less) liquidity constrained. Also, then, the planned financial bequest would be zero.

However, a parent may not have decided upon the total postdependency transfer and, for that reason, would not be indifferent between an inter vivos gift and an estate. The parent may be hesitant because he or she is uncertain about his or her own future prospects and/or the child's future earnings. In the first case (cf. Feldstein, 1988), when the adult child is just starting out the parent may have several years of labor market work left (leading to earnings uncertainty); will not know whether he or she will incur large, uninsured medical expenses; and cannot rule out the possibility that retirement resources will have to finance an unexpectedly long life. Thus, unless accumulated resources are sufficient to cover most such contingencies, the parent may prefer to wait before transferring. Also, it is possible the child's earnings will prove unexpectedly high, with the marginal utility of the child's consumption (to the parent) falling below that of the parent's own consumption (cf. Altonji, Hayashi, and Kotlikoff, 1997). Once again, the parent prefers to delay the timing.

As another transfer timing consideration, suppose the parent's uncertainty about earnings and health outlays is so favorably resolved that the parent concludes a bequest will be subject to taxation. In 2002, the first $1,000,000 of an estate will be tax free. This is scheduled to rise to $2 million in 2006 (with Tax Relief Act by 2010 there's complete elimination). Transfers to spouses are not taxed. However, estates in excess of the exclusion are subject to graduated and high taxation. There is also some potential to evade the estate tax by use of inter vivos transfers. Under the annual gift exclusion, each parent may give inter vivos up to $10,000 per recipient, per year, without taxation. Thus, a moderately wealthy parent with several children and grandchildren may "spend down" via gifts in order to avoid estate taxation. The theory thus predicts that the wealthy will make tax-driven inter vivos transfers, or "early bequests," once they become convinced that their eventual estate will be taxable. (Estate taxation is considered separately in section 5.5.)

In summary, the timing of financial transfers under altruism depends upon a comparison of the value (to parents) of money for liquidity-constrained children with the "option" value of retaining monies in case parents would later value their own consumption, at the margin, more than their child's. These issues prove important to the effects of several public policies, as discussed in section 5.5.

5.2 IMPLICATIONS AND EVIDENCE

5.2.1 Total Financial Transfers and Parental Wealth

The theory of altruistic financial transfers is now evaluated by considering how the model's qualitative predictions fare empirically. Consider first the implication that total financial transfers should rise with parental wealth, the earnings of the adult child being held constant. Families differ in many ways besides parental wealth and child earnings, including family size and degree of altruistic sentiment. Given this underlying heterogeneity, the theory suggests that both the probability of a transfer and the magnitude of the transfer should increase with parental wealth, child income held constant. The ideal data set to test this implication would contain information concerning the annual gifts to children by a parent, the bequest, and the annual incomes of parents and children. Although such complete transfer records do not exist, there is a good deal of point-in-time information on the relationships between parental wealth and bequests, and also between inter vivos transfers and parent and child earnings.

We first consider evidence relating to inter vivos transfers, which is largely supportive. Altonji et al. (1997) examine inter vivos transfers using data from the 1988 Panel Study of Income Dynamics (PSID). The PSID has followed the same households, and the split-offs formed as children establish separate households, since 1968. Most of the analysis of Altonji et al. is based on 3,402 parent-child pairs, including 687 pairs with positive inter vivos transfers. In addition to reliable income data on parents and children, the 1988 PSID supplement also inquired about the magnitude of "loans, gifts, or support" in excess of $100 received from parents in the prior year. In their Table 3 Altonji et al. provide the probability of a transfer being made as a function of the relative *permanent*, or several year average of, incomes of the parents and children. To illustrate the tendencies, consider children who are in the middle, or third, permanent income quintile. The probability of such an adult child receiving an inter vivos transfer rises from 11.4% when the parent is in the lowest permanent income quintile to 33% when the parent is in the highest quintile. The average transfer increases from $1,035 to $4,214, again moving from the lowest to top income quintile. Thus, consistent with the framework, *the probability of children receiving a transfer and the size of transfer rise with parental resources, child earnings held constant.* McGarry (1997) and McGarry and Schoeni (1995) confirm this pattern using different data.

Large bequests are concentrated among the wealthy. Menchik and David (1983) exploit paired income tax and probate (i.e., estate) records to determine the strength of that tendency. They use measures of household's life earnings and bequests to estimate how the share of earnings devoted to bequests varies with earnings. This "bequest share" is found to be quite small (or close to zero), and largely independent of wealth, for the poorest 60% of households. However, among the 20 percent of most affluent households, bequest shares are roughly 10 percent. These large bequests of the affluent must be intentional. Unsurprisingly, inheritances are also rather concentrated; it has been estimated that the 20 percent of families receiving the largest inheritances receive 74 percent of all inheritances (Davies, 1982).

This evidence relating bequests and parental life wealth appears consistent with a model that combines length-of-life uncertainty and altruism: Most everyone dies with some assets due to life span uncertainty. However, the *intentional* bequest motive becomes operative only at high levels of parental life wealth. Although this evidence is not inconsistent with altruism as the motivation behind intentional bequests, it does suggest that most middle-class estates are accidental. Of course, altruistic parents derive satisfaction from the fact that children will benefit from their estate. If they are transfer constrained, though, they would prefer to have consumed those resources themselves.

The altruism model also requires that, for given parental wealth, total transfers should be negatively related to the permanent income of children. Laitner and Juster (1996) examine data from a survey of retirees who had been employed by colleges or universities, including faculty, staff, and administrators (participants in the TIAA-CREFF retirement programs). Their results suggest that those households intending to leave bequests behave altruistically, as they have greater asset accumulation the lower is their assessment of children's likely earnings. Consistent with their intention to bequeath, their retirement age net worth was several hundred thousand dollars higher than that of households not interested in leaving a bequest. *However*, the identity of households intending bequests is only weakly predicted by the relative wealth of parents and children: While parents expecting their children to be worse off than themselves were somewhat more likely to express a bequest motive, this pattern was not statistically significant.

Similar results were obtained by McGarry (1999) using data from the Assets and Health Dynamics Study of the Oldest Old (AHEAD) survey. AHEAD samples people born in 1923 or earlier, who were therefore at least 70 years old when first surveyed in 1993. The survey data include the household income of adult children (as reported by their parents), income information for respondents, and their plans regarding bequests. Specifically, respondents are asked to report the probability of leaving any bequest, and if positive, the probability the bequest will exceed $10,000, and the probability the bequest will exceed $100,000. As expected, the probability of leaving a bequest is greater among wealthy parents. Also, as in Laitner and Juster, the probability of leaving a bequest is little affected by children's permanent income. The probability is positively related to children's education (another proxy for life earnings), and this effect is statistically significant. Wilhelm (1996) likewise finds the earnings of children have little effect on whether a bequest will be left. Thus, our model does a good job explaining the magnitude of bequest, given the expectation of positive bequests. The model does a poor job, however, in terms of ascertaining the probability of bequest.

Accidental bequests may help explain the results of McGarry (1999) and of Laitner and Juster (1996) in a manner consistent with altruism being the motivation behind *intentional* bequests. To appreciate this, first note that accidental bequests may be proportional to parental life wealth for all except the most affluent of households. Add to this that, as developed in Chapter 6, the earnings of children and of their parents are positively and highly correlated. Combining these points, one expects a positive correlation between expected accidental bequests and the permanent income of children. Consequently, even if intentional bequests are altruistically motivated, it may be unsurprising that bequests (which may or may not be intentional) and child income are not strongly and negatively correlated.

Another potential reconciliation of altruism and the lack of influence of child earnings on the probability of bequest is *heterogeneity across households in the strength of altruistic sentiment*. We saw in Chapter 1 that there appears to be a large degree of variability among households in preferences for present and future life-cycle consumption. There may be similar amounts of dispersion among parents in their taste for own versus child consumption. One reason for such heterogeneity is offered by Laitner and Juster, who suggest that the taste for bequest may be higher among parents who received an inheritance themselves (their footnote 8). Whatever the source of heterogeneity, note that a highly altruistic parent with a strong intention to bequeath late in life also would have made large transfers to, or investments in, children when young. Such investments presumably increase the child's human capital, and therefore earnings later in life (see Chapter 6). This reasoning suggests that altruism could be driving much bequest behavior, but that preference heterogeneity substantially weakens the correlation between bequests and child income found in the cross section of households with similar parental wealth. That is, preference heterogeneity introduces a lot of "noise" into the relationships among parental wealth, bequest, and child earnings.

Thus, regarding the prediction that total transfers should increase with parental wealth, child earnings held constant, the evidence is mixed. For inter vivos transfers the support is strong and favorable. For bequests, the evidence is inconsistent with a simple model of altruism in which everyone has the same preferences and the length of life is known with certainty. However, once one allows for accidental bequests and preference heterogeneity, it becomes harder to dismiss altruism as the motivation underlying intentional bequests. Some alternatives to the altruism hypothesis considered in section 5.3 also prove consistent with bequests that are only weakly predicted by the relative earnings of parents and children.

5.2.2 Compensating Financial Transfers Within Families

The basic model of intergenerational altruism implies that financial transfers from parents should fully compensate for income differences among children, so long as the parents are completely unconstrained (making positive transfers to all children). There is no evidence that transfer differentials are of that magnitude. Behrman (1997) reports that average annual earnings differences across male (female) siblings exceeded $9,000 ($6,800) over the period 1982 to 1987 in the PSID. These values imply that if child wealth is to be equalized using only inter vivos transfers, then annual differences in transfers would need to average about that amount. They don't.

McGarry (2000) examines this issue using data from the Health and Retirement Survey (HRS). The HRS is a relatively new panel survey that samples individuals born between January 1, 1931, and December 31, 1941, with the first interviews beginning in 1992 and a second wave in 1994. The survey asks whether parents transferred to children more than $500 (1992 survey), or $100 (1994 survey) in the previous year. It also contains respondents' reports of child income, education, and home ownership, in addition to information about parents, such as their income and wealth. Unfortunately, child income is poorly measured, grouped as below $10,000, between $10,000 and $24,999, and at least $25,000. On the plus side is the fact that the HRS contains transfer information within a family for more than one year. As a consequence, we now know that there is considerable variation in the identity of recipients of transfers across time: "Fifty-nine percent of children who received a transfer in wave 1 did not in wave 2 . . . and 55 percent of those who received a transfer in wave 2 had not received one in wave 1" (p. 9). With multiple observations per child, McGarry is better able to control for unmeasured differences across children, such as unobserved ability, that may impact transfers.

McGarry employs these data to estimate the effect of earnings differentials among children within a family for amounts transferred. She finds that children "in the lowest income category are 4 percentage points more likely to receive a transfer than children in the highest category, and the expected value of the transfer is only $145 greater . . ." (p. 16). These figures are similar to those obtained by Behrman, Pollack, and Taubman (1995) using data from the PSID. McGarry notes that a child in the top income bracket must have income at least $15,000 more than a sibling in the lowest bracket (i.e., $25,000–$9,999). Therefore, annual differences in expected transfers make up less than 1% of the earnings differences. Assuming these current-year income differences are even modestly related to differences in permanent income suggests that although inter vivos transfers are compensatory, they do not *begin* to fully offset earnings differentials. Consequently, if child wealth is to be equalized, bequests would have to be much larger for lower earning children.[9] They aren't.

Menchik (1988), Wilhelm (1996), and McGarry (1999) all find that wills of decedents typically provide for equal division amongst the surviving children. Menchik, in a survey of the wills of decedents, finds exactly equal division in 84.3% of cases. Similarly, using estate tax return information, Wilhelm finds "approximately equal" division in 88% of cases. Respondents in the AHEAD data exploited by McGarry, who are therefore at least age 60, expect to leave about equal estates in 84.3% of cases. Further, in Wilhelm's sample, "in approximately half of the 259 families where unequal division occurs, earnings differences are reinforced by larger bequests to children with higher earnings" (p. 887). McGarry also finds that "(d)ifferences in the incomes of children do not affect the probability of equal bequests" (p. 23).

5.2.3 The Distribution of Income and Consumption in Extended Families

Another implication of altruism concerns how parents respond to changes in own or child resources. Recall that *so long as parents intend to make positive transfers to children*, they maximize utility by choosing consumption levels for themselves and the child, subject only to dynastic wealth. In this case, the relative incomes of parents and children determine only the amount of transfer necessary to achieve this consumption plan. Consequently, if the relative incomes of the parents and children change, but dynastic wealth is unaffected, there will be no effect on the consumption of either generation, only in the amount transferred. This intergenerational analog to the life wealth hypothesis of Chapter 1 may be referred to as the *dynastic wealth hypothesis:* The consumption of extended family members who are connected via positive transfers from parents is independent of the distribution of family resources.

Altonji, Hayashi, and Kotlikoff (1992) test the importance of altruism in extended families. They employ data from the PSID on the incomes and consumption of extended family members to examine whether the distribution of extended family income affects the distribution of extended family consumption. They (overwhelmingly) find that it does. That is, if John's household enjoys a higher income than his brother Tom's, John's household will also have higher consumption. This is true even when they restrict the sample to relatively affluent parents and relatively poor children, a sample more likely to correspond to our "unconstrained" households above. On the other hand, they also find evidence against the life-cycle hypothesis that own consumption is determined solely by own resources; extended family resources do contribute modestly to one's own consumption.

A corollary of the dynastic wealth hypothesis is that changes in the incomes of extended family members *that leave dynastic wealth intact* should not affect anyone's consumption. To illustrate, suppose there is one child, one parent, an overlap in their adult lives, and that the parent is currently making transfers to the child. Now, if child resources fall by \$1 and at the same time parental resources rise by \$1, the altruistic model predicts that the parent will increase the transfers to the child by exactly \$1 (cf. Cox, 1987):

$$dT/dE_{pt} - dT/dE_{ct} = 1$$

where T is the inter vivos transfer.

This "transfer derivative test" also applies when the changes in income occur at different points in time. In that case, holding dynastic wealth constant means that any \$1 change in parents' resources must be offset by a change of $\$(1 + r)$, in the opposite direction, in child resources. Of course then the transfer will also change by $\$(1 + r)$. To see this, refer back to Figure 5.1. The resource endowment point moves along the budget line from A to G, say, when parental wealth is increased by \$1 and child wealth is reduced by $\$(1 + r)$. However, parent and child consumption does not change. Rather the transfer increases by \$1, which increases the bequest by $\$(1 + r)$. In terms of the propensities to bequeath, recall that $dB_p/dW_p = 1 - \theta$ and $dB_p/E_c = -\theta/(1 + r)$. So, if parents' wealth rises by \$1 and child earnings fall by $\$(1 + r)$, the effect on the transfer is

$$dB_p = (1 - \theta) - \theta/(1 + r)[-(1 + r)] = 1$$

As discussed in section 5.5, this implication has been stressed in discussions of policies, such as Social Security, that transfer resources intergenerationally.

Altonji et al. (1997) test this restriction using a subsample of PSID extended families for which transfers are observed to be positive, perhaps because children are liquidity constrained. Their tests reveal that such an income redistribution increases the transfer only about 13 cents, much less than the \$1 required by the altruism model. However, their results do indicate some altruistic response. Further, transfers received are known to be underreported in the PSID. Fuller reporting of transfers would increase the estimated transfer derivative.[10]

5.2.4   Implications for Macroeconomic Utility Functions

Formal treatments of altruism view the utility of parents as depending upon the *utility* of children, whose utility depends upon the utility of *their* children, and so on. This implies parents derive utility from the consumption of descendants of descendants, alive in the indefinite future. *If* these successive generations are also linked by positive altruistically motivated transfers, parents decide on transfers taking into account the implications for consumption by distant descendants. Such reasoning lies behind the assumption in many long-term macroeconomic models of *infinitely lived agents*, who maximize utility from consumption from the present into the indefinite future. This assumption is valid only if changes in the timing of income across generations have no effect on any generation's consumption. However, the evidence described above reveals that the consumption of extended family members is very much affected by who receives the income. This finding raises serious questions about the implications in infinitely lived agent models of policies that redistribute net of tax income across generations. These implications, termed *Ricar-*

dian equivalence, are discussed in section 5.5. If each generation's consumption is determined by its own net income, the overlapping generations model of Chapter 4 is more useful for addressing intergenerational fiscal policy.

5.2.5   Evidence Concerning the Timing of Transfers

Recall that liquidity-constrained young adults prefer inter vivos transfers, while parent's uncertainty regarding their own needs encourages them to delay transfers. Also, parents anticipating taxable estates have an incentive to disperse assets to children inter vivos (since yearly gifts below $10,000 per recipient are not taxed).

Cox (1990) and McGarry (1999) both find that young households with low current income receive significant gifts, with the probability of receiving a transfer falling rapidly with the age of the potential recipient. Transfers to young adults to help finance schooling are quantitatively important. For example, Gale and Scholz (1994) report that in 1986 roughly $35 billion was spent by parents on their children's college education. Such transfers clearly help alleviate liquidity constraints. Another group of young households likely to be liquidity constrained are those who have not yet purchased a home, perhaps because they lack the down payment. Consistent with this, McGarry finds that the probability that parents will make a transfer to any children in a year is reduced about 4 percentage points if all children "own" a home. This evidence is consistent with altruistic parents timing gifts when they are of greatest value to children. (As noted below, theories of exchange-motivated transfers are also consistent with this pattern.)

The evidence for tax-driven gifts is less compelling. Poterba (2001) reports that among households headed by someone between the ages of 65 and 74, with net worth exceeding $2.4 million, only 38.2% made inter vivos gifts totaling $10,000 or more within the last year to anyone living outside the household. If parents make equal gifts to children in a year, those gifts may be made to reduce net worth below the estate tax exclusion. Consistent with tax-driven gifts, McGarry (1999) finds that the probability of equal gifts among parents with net worth above the estate tax exclusion is almost twice that of parents with lower net worth. Thus, parents with large estates are more likely to make sizeable, equal gifts, but most do not transfer the amount consistent with minimizing the estate tax burden.

5.2.6   Extensions of the Standard Model

The evidence above shows that simple models of altruism cannot explain the prevalence of equal bequests or the fact that compensatory transfers within families are far too small to equalize the resources of children. Some reasonable variations on the altruistic theme prove more consistent with these findings.

Bernheim and Severinov (2000) present a theory of altruistic transfers in which equal division of bequests is a plausible (though not unique) outcome. To the standard model developed above, they add two further assumptions. First, "each child's perception of parental affection directly affects his or her subjective well-being" (p. 4). Second, children are unable to observe directly the altruistic sentiments of parents. Instead, children infer these sentiments from parental actions, such as the division of their estate amongst the children. Under these assumptions, equal division proves consistent with a range of parameter settings, making their altruistic formulation consistent with the observation that most estates are divided equally. Further, Bernheim and Severinov's model is also consistent with the unequal distribution of inter vivos gifts observed in practice. This is because those transfers are not public information and may therefore be unequal without hurting the feelings of any child.[11] Although this theory has not yet been tested empirically, the reasonableness of the underlying assumptions makes for a convincing story. However, the theory does not explain why inter vivos transfers are not more fully compensating.

However, supposing parents care about the *utility* (rather than wealth) of offspring, there are several reasons that less than fully compensating transfers may be expected. First, the wealth one earns and the wealth one could potentially earn (potential wealth) are not the same: some earnings differentials reflect differences in job amenities across occupations, or so-called compensating differentials. For example, if one child is a professional writer earning much less than a lawyer sibling, but both appear equally happy to the parents, there may be no altruistic basis for "equalizing" transfers. Similarly, wealth differences may reflect differences in leisure consumption.

More generally, parents may be unable or unwilling to judge how children's earnings "map" into utility: Children have different propensities to be happy, have personal lives (marriage, children, health) that differ, and so on. Alternatively, children's utility may be lowered if they believe parents are "meddling" or if large transfers are viewed as a signal by parents that the child has "failed." Parents may take these sentiments into account and curb transfers accordingly. As a final possibility, altruism may require parents to "let go" of children, so they may establish independent lives. Along these lines, and consistent with the American ethos of equal opportunity, Wilhelm (1996) suggests that "parents may desire to equalize the opportunity sets (bequests, inter-vivos gifts and human capital investment) of their children. Subsequently, the decisions of the children lead to unequal outcomes, but these are not routinely redressed by parents unless they are perceived to arise because of events outside the children's control" (p. 890). These counterarguments not withstanding, compensating transfers appear to be much smaller than those required by simple models of altruism.

Some of the evidence and the several reasonable extensions to the basic model enable someone who wants to believe in the primacy of altruism to do so. However, the weak empirical support for some implications of altruism have led researchers to develop alternative, nonaltruistic explanations of financial transfers. The more prominent among these are developed below.

5.3 COMPETING EXPLANATIONS OF TRANSFERS

5.3.1 Exchange-motivated Transfers

Altruism is not the only possible motive for intentional transfers. Even if parents do not want to give money to their adult children outright, they may well enjoy their company—and be willing to compensate the children for its provision. An important example of such exchange-motivated transfers may be the passing on to a child the family business, provided the child works in the business alongside the parent-owner until control is relinquished. The provision to an adult child of a free airplane ticket to the parents' home over the holidays is another straightforward example. Similarly, when elderly parents need help, they may prefer to receive it from their children as opposed to a nonrelative, if not a stranger. Desiring help, they may be willing to compensate (perhaps quite indirectly) the child at a rate beyond that normally paid for market-provided domestic help. More generally, we assume parents are willing to compensate the child's performance of "child services," which take a variety of forms, from housecleaning to following the "correct" lifestyle. Altruistic transfers to young, dependent children need to be accompanied by parental control and authority. Given two decades of "knowing what is best" for the child, even parents who believe they are acting altruistically toward adult children may, in fact, place conditions on transfers. Quite elaborate models of exchange have been developed (cf. Cox, 1987; Davies, 1996; Lord, 1992). However, the crucial empirical prediction of exchange models may be derived from the following simple framework.

As opposed to when parents are altruistic, parents' utility is now increasing in the amount of child services s, but is independent of child consumption. Since parental utility U_p continues to increase with parental consumption C_p, the utility function becomes[12]

$$U_p = U_p(C_p, s) \tag{5.9}$$

Many child services do have somewhat substitutable market counterparts (domestic help, nurse aides, "handy" men, psychologists, etc.). Due to these market substitutes, the quantity of child services demanded will be decreasing in their "price." Further, the demand for child services is expected to be normal, in the sense that it increases with parental wealth W_p. Figure 5.4a illustrates the downsloping demand curve, and how it shifts outward when parental wealth increases. Of course, the demand curve will be more elastic the closer substitutes are market services for child services. Thus, Figure 5.4a assumes that relatively close market substitutes are available; Figure 5.4b reflects a situation with only poor market substitutes.

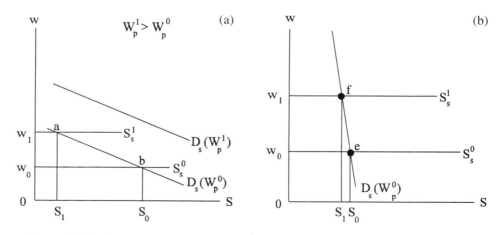

Figure 5.4 Exchange-motivated transfers (a) with elastic demand (b) with inelastic demand

Adult children are assumed to care only about their own consumption C_c. Consumption goods may be acquired by working in the labor market at wage rate w, or by providing—for compensation—services to parents. For simplicity, we assume that provision of child services requires time, time that the children would otherwise devote to the labor market. If there is no other "emotional charge" to the provision of services, positive or negative, a child is willing to supply child services so long as he or she is paid at least w per hour. Thus, the price of child services to parents is simply the child's wage, w. Graphically, the supply of child services is therefore perfectly elastic at w, as shown by the horizontal supply curves in Figure 5.4a. Should the child wage—and thus child earnings—rise, the supply curve will shift upward. If a parent has more than one child, the services of higher earning children will be the most expensive.

This model is obviously a caricature of parent-child interactions. However, visits and the like surely do require time, and the value of the adult child's time may be expected to increase with the child's wage. Consequently, the model assumptions appear qualitatively consistent with reality. Further, we now show that this simple framework lays bare the crucial behavioral difference between simple models of altruistic and exchange-motivated transfers.

Exchange-motivated transfers may be inter vivos or a bequest. One reason for inter vivos transfers is that liquidity-constrained children will have a lower supply price for services if the money is delivered when most needed. Bequests also make sense, especially if the control parents are purchasing must be continued until the parent's death. Examples include retaining of the family business and the service of phoning and visiting regularly.[13]

Recall that in the altruistic model, transfers increase with parental wealth but are lower at higher levels of child earnings. The exchange model also predicts that an increase in parental wealth W_p will increase transfers: Higher W_p increases the demand for s, increasing total transfers ws. However, under exchange, an increase in child earnings—from a higher w—may lead to higher or lower transfers, depending upon the price elasticity of demand for child services. In Figure 5.4a, an increase in the wage from w_0 to w_1 reduces total expenditures on services, and thus total transfers, from w_0bS_00 to w_1aS_10. With an elastic demand, transfers fall, just as in the altruism model. However, as in Figure 5.4b, transfers *rise* with w in the presence of an inelastic demand for child services. Since this is in direct contrast to the prediction under altruism, it affords a potential test of the motive for transfers. That is, if transfers fall when the child's wage rises, we cannot on this basis infer whether the transfers are altruistically or exchange motivated. If, however, parental transfers rise with the child's wage (or more generally child wealth), this would refute altruism, lending support to the exchange hypothesis.

Cox (1987, 1990) finds that current recipient income and the size of inter vivos transfers are positively correlated. However, later studies using better data (cf. Altonji, Hayashi, and Kotlikoff, 1992; McGarry, 1999) have found a negative relationship between current income and the probability of receiving a transfer. Cox (1990), along with McGarry and Altonji et al., finds that recipients of inter vivos transfers have lower *permanent* incomes than nonrecipients. Since transfers are negatively related to the child's income (both current and permanent), the evidence is consistent with both altruism and exchange.

In support of exchange, Bernheim, Schleifer, and Summers (1985) find that in families where adult children have provided significant child services, such as visits and phone calls, the parents tend to leave larger estates. Also, Cox (1996) notes that the exchange motive may be consistent with equal division of estates. To appreciate why, suppose the utility function of parents under exchange is Cobb-Douglas and includes separate arguments for each child's services. Now, recall from Chapter 1 that the exponent on a good in a Cobb-Douglas utility function is that good's share of total outlays. This means that we could observe equal division under exchange even though the price of child services differs across children. An exchange motivation for bequests also helps explain why parents retain assets in nonliquid forms, such as real estate, even into old age (cf. Davies, 1996). Such holdings provide evidence to children that the parents aren't planning to renege on promised, and from the child's perspective earned, end-of-life transfers.

Also, Wilhelm notes that in the small proportion of cases where bequests are unequal, differences in bequests are bigger if the decedent had a closely held business. This may imply larger transfers to children who exchanged economic freedom for economic security. Similarly, McGarry finds that the probability of unequal bequest is increased if the respondent is in poor health. This suggests primary care givers are compensated (though perhaps not fully). We summarize the evidence about nonaltruistic theories at the end of this section.

5.3.2   The Family as an Incomplete Annuities Market

An additional explanation of financial bequests lies between exchange and altruism. According to Kotlikoff and Spivak (1981), observed bequests may often be the outcome of an extended family self-insurance arrangement. These authors begin with the observation, stressed in Chapter 2, that the end-of-life annuities available in the marketplace are quite unfair, actuarially. Families may respond to this with an implicit contract between adult children and their parents. Under this agreement, parents will save enough to support themselves should their life spans fall in the normal range. If they die at a "young" age, children will inherit the estate. If, on the other hand, they live to a ripe old age, outliving their accumulated wealth, children will provide for them during their remaining years. Kotlikoff and Spivak demonstrate that this arrangement can be quite beneficial to both children and parents, especially compared with market alternatives. The altruism among and proximity of family members partially alleviates many of the problems—such as fraud, moral hazard, and adverse selection—that contribute to the high premiums for market annuities. This approach can explain equal bequests, however, only if parents believe that each child will stand in equal readiness to give support should parents' lives prove long.

5.3.3   Warm Glow Giving and Impure Altruism

Consider two situations. In each, the parent consumes 100 and the child consumes 100. In the first context, though, the parent has made a gift of 50 to the child. In the second, the parent had made no such gift. In the model of pure altruism, where all that matters to the parent are the consumption levels of the child and of the parent, these situations are comparable. Andreoni (1989) suggests that the parent prefers the case where she or he contributed more. The idea is that, in addition to caring about the utility or consumption of the child, the parent also gets a "warm glow" from making transfers. This dash of egoism means that transfers are motivated by *impure altruism*.

The parent's utility function is now written

$$U_p = U_p(C_p, T, C_c)$$

where T is the amount of the transfer given to the child. The child's consumption is

$$C_c = E_c + T$$

The parent's budget constraint is

$$W_p = C_p + T$$

Warm glow preferences alter the parent's response to resource redistributions between the parent and child, reducing the transfer derivative below 1.[14] To see this, suppose some policy transfers $10 from the parent to the child. With pure altruism, the parent will simply reduce the amount of the gift by $10, and everyone's consumption is unaffected. With impure altruism, however, there is a utility cost associated with reducing the size of the transfer. Therefore, although the transfer from the parent will fall, the decline will be less than $10.

A special case of the warm glow model dispenses with the concern for children's consumption, so that parental utility depends only on parental consumption and the amount transferred or, equivalently, the wealth at death (cf. Seidman, 1983, or Carroll, 2000). In Carroll's formulation wealth provides utility, perhaps by conferring power or status.

5.3.4   Behavioral Responses By Children

So far we have implicitly assumed that children take transfers from parents as given, or outside of their control. However, it may be more realistic to suppose that children alter their actions in light of the parents' altruism—and that parents will likewise take the potential response of children into account. We consider two examples.

The Rotten Kid Theorem

Suppose there are several children and that the parent makes positive transfers to each. Further, assume that the parent can observe each child's consumption, but not necessarily the source of the income. Under these conditions the *Rotten Kid Theorem* of Becker states that each child, no matter how selfish, maximizes the family income of the parent, and thereby fully accounts for all effects of his or her actions on the other children (1981, p. 183).

To illustrate, consider a family consisting of one parent, a rotten son Johnny, and his sister Sally. Suppose Johnny has the opportunity to steal and then trade Sally's $140 bike to a kid from another neighborhood for a $20 baseball glove (which he would claim to have received as a gift, say). By the Rotten Kid Theorem Johnny will not exploit the opportunity, even though he has no regard for Sally's welfare. For Johnny realizes that the parent will note the absence of the bike and the presence of the glove and will appreciate that family income is lower by $120, Sally worse off by $140, and Johnny better off by $20. Since each family member's consumption is a normal good to the parent, Johnny knows that the consumption of each will fall with family income. That is, the parent would reduce subsequent transfers to Johnny by more than $20, leaving Johnny worse off. Appreciating these dynamics, Johnny would not steal and then trade his sister's bike—for less than fair value.

This cheery result (albeit derived from a quite dreary view of child nature) may be overturned in a variety of circumstances. Most obviously, after parental transfers have ceased, there is no further incentive for "good" behavior. Thus, the parent must have the "last word" (Hirshleifer, 1977).

Samaritan's Dilemma

Another issue confronting an altruistic parent during the years of overlap is the so-called Samaritan's Dilemma (cf. Lord and Rangazas, 1995). In this context, the child knows the parent is prepared to make compensatory transfers if the child's resources prove low. Obviously, the adult child can influence the probability of low resources occurring by work effort and saving behavior. For if the child incurs the "cost" of reduced leisure, say, the chances of experiencing low earnings are reduced. Similarly, the child may improve the prospects for adequate future resources by curtailing current consumption. Aware of the parents' willingness to "bail him or her out," the child has an incentive to be lazy and overspend. A savvy parent considers the child's potential response when planning total transfers and how they will vary with child resources. For this reason compensatory transfers may depend on how much control the child has over her or his own resource level. For example, parents may be willing to transfer a large amount if their child suffers a long debilitating illness. In contrast, if they have a child in a field where compensation is tied closely to effort, as for a real estate agent, they may not increase transfers much in years when the child's income is low.[15] However, we saw above that compensatory transfers are small in relation to income differences between children. This suggests that children's ability to manipulate the parent's transfers is also limited.

5.3.5   Summary

There are yet other interesting formulations of transfer motives (including an evolutionary perspective). However, despite much creative work, it remains difficult to draw strong conclusions regarding the motivation(s) underlying transfers. Perhaps a large proportion of bequests are the unintentional consequence of life span uncertainty. Many inter vivos transfers are surely altruistically motivated. However, existing models of altruism overstate the role of relative incomes on transfer levels. Exchange is no doubt also of importance. Parents probably do "bribe" their grown children to pay them more attention by, for example, making sure they have a "great visit" when they come home. That such considerations explain the bulk of private transfers is harder to believe. Similar remarks apply to the other theories proffered above. It is difficult to imagine that the data required to allow powerful tests of subtle differences between transfer models could soon be available. However, if progress is as swift in the next decade as in the past one, a basic understanding of transfer motives may be achieved sooner rather than later.

5.4 THE CONTRIBUTION OF INTERGENERATIONAL TRANSFERS TO WEALTH

Chapters 1 and 2 developed the life-cycle theory of savings. In that framework, households save from their own labor earnings for retirement, but also to self-insure when faced with earnings, health expenditure, or length of life uncertainty. The budget constraint equates the present value of consumption to that of earnings. Nobel Laureate Franco Modigliani (cf. 1988) argues that the vast majority of aggregate wealth (perhaps 80%) derives from life-cycle, especially retirement, saving motives. In contrast, this chapter notes that many households receive substantial transfers from their parents. Such households do not accumulate their wealth holdings "from scratch," as the life-cycle model suggests. This section assesses the relative importance of intergenerational transfers and life-cycle savings in aggregate savings and wealth.

Kotlikoff and Summers (1981) use U.S. historical data on earnings and consumption, and on the flow of transfers, to decompose total wealth into life-cycle wealth and transfer wealth. They conclude—in sharp contrast with Modigliani—that perhaps 80% of all wealth is the result of intergenerational transfers rather than of retirement savings. Thus, for them, life-cycle wealth is but 20 percent of the total.

Before commenting on these divergent estimates, note that the origins of wealth holdings are of more than academic interest. For as developed in Chapter 3, labor productivity, wages, and long-run (or steady state) welfare are increased by wealth—and thus capital—accumulation. The best policies to stimulate saving presumably vary with the reason for saving. Further, one's views regarding the distribution of wealth across households may be sensitive to whether the wealth was saved from earnings or received from others.

To develop intuition regarding the relative importance of life-cycle and transfer wealth, consider again the simple life-cycle model of Chapter 1 (i.e., no financial transfers). The wage earnings, assets, and consumption of a representative household are shown in Figure 5.5. People in this household gain economic independence at age 20 and earn

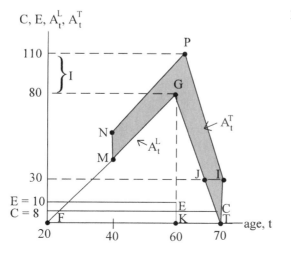

Figure 5.5 Transfer and life cycle wealth

E = 10 per year until retirement at 60; death occurs at age 70. To ease the exposition we assume the interest rate is zero. In this case, life wealth is 10 times the 40 working years, or 400. Consumption C is assumed to be constant during each of the 50 years. An equal spreading of the life wealth supports consumption of C = 400/50 = 8. In preparation for retirement, households accumulate "hump wealth," as illustrated by the age-asset profile, A^L_t. Under our assumptions, savings in each year of work are E − C = 10 − 8 = 2. Thus, at the start of retirement the household will have 40 years of savings, or 80. Assets are run down to zero at death.

In the absence of transfers, aggregate *life-cycle wealth* is found by summing across the wealth holdings of all households of each age. Consider the simple case of zero population and income growth, so that all age groups are the same size and households differ only by age. Then, if each cohort has one household, life-cycle wealth is just the area under the asset profile, or FGT. To ease calculation, break FGT into the two right triangles, FGK and KGT. Then life-cycle wealth of FGT = (1/2)(40)(80) + (1/2)(10)(80) = 2,000.

Now consider how intergenerational transfers augment wealth. Initially, suppose all transfers are in the form of bequests. Further, assume the economy is in a steady state in which each generation of households receives identical inheritances. Specifically, let each household receive an inheritance I_c of 30 at age 40 and likewise, bequeathe at death B_p = 30 to every adult child. In our simple case with no population growth and an interest rate of zero, the inheritance does not increase the recipient's consumption, since it is all bequeathed. Thus, the inheritance will just be held by the household from receipt at age 40 until death at age 70, increasing the asset profile by the inheritance (30) at each of those ages. The asset profile that includes transfer wealth is labeled A^T_t (or FMNPIT). The area between the pure life-cycle and bequest asset profiles is the amount of *transfer wealth*. This is just the inheritance of 30, times the 70 − 40 = 30 years the inheritance was held, or 900. Total wealth is the sum of life-cycle and transfer wealth, or 2000 + 900 = 2900. The share for life-cycle wealth is 2000/2900, or about 69 percent. The share for transfer wealth is 900/2000, so that about 31 percent of all wealth in this example derives from intergenerational transfers.

If all transfers are inter vivos instead of bequests, little is changed: Households receive the transfer at an earlier age but give the money to children before death. Since the transfer is held for the same interval, the implications at the household level are as above. Suppose, though, that the *reason* the transfers are made inter vivos is to relieve liquidity constraints. Consumption will be raised when the transfer is received but, continuing to assume the young recipient households pass along the same amount to their children, must be reduced later on.

Thus far we have ignored the fact that interest rates are positive and that the interest or capital income earned on inheritances is significant. Much of the difference between the estimates of Kotlikoff and Summers and those of Modigliani hinges on how the interest on inheritances and transfers is treated. According to Kotlikoff and Summers, life-cycle wealth is the difference between earnings and consumption, accumulated at the interest rate. In their view, interest earned on inheritances is part of transfer wealth. In contrast, Modigliani prefers to calculate the life-cycle component as the sum of income (earnings plus interest) minus consumption in each year, which moves the interest earned on inheritances into the life-cycle column. If life-cycle wealth is meant to reflect the accumulation that would occur in the absence of bequests, the Kotlikoff and Summers measure is more appropriate. This difference in semantics accounts for almost half of the gap between their estimates.

A more substantive omission from our simple story arises from the fact that the interest rate r exceeds the population growth rate n. With r > n, if the inheritance and interest earnings were left untouched, the estate would exceed (perhaps by a large amount) the sum necessary to leave each child the same inheritance received by the parent. In our example from above, suppose the inheritance of 30 grows with interest to 120 by death. However, if there are two children the parent will leave an estate of only 60. Thus, when r > n, there remains "net-of-bequest inheritance wealth," which is used to increase life-cycle consumption. This increased consumption reduces our current (earnings minus consumption) measure of life-cycle wealth. Conceptually it is preferable to measure life-cycle wealth as that which would occur in the absence of bequests. Thus, life-cycle wealth should be based on the lower consumption that would be observed were bequests somehow eliminated. This requires an upward adjustment to the earnings-minus-consumption measure of life-cycle wealth. Accounting for this bias, Kotlikoff and Summers adjust their estimate of life-cycle wealth upward, so that their "full" estimate of transfer wealth is reduced to about 50 percent.[16]

Careful readers may have noticed that life-cycle savings and intergenerational transfers contain some overlap. For, as discussed in Chapter 2, households interested only in their own consumption, who are forced to self-insure against low consumption if life proves long, typically leave accidental bequests. In practice, it is difficult to identify which portion of an estate is accidental and which part is intentional. Even if accidental bequests could be deleted from the intergenerational transfers column, so that only intentional transfers remain, much of the difference between the Kotlikoff and Summers and Modigliani estimates may remain. For although the findings of Menchik and David (1983) suggest that only the richest quintile of families intentionally leave bequests, their large estates are the lion's share of total bequests. Nevertheless, the difficulty in distinguishing between accidental and intentional bequests has led some researchers to focus on inter vivos transfers, all of which are intentional.

Using this approach and data from the Survey of Consumer Finances, Gale and Scholz (1994) find that inter vivos transfers, excluding payments for childrens' college, are at least 20 percent of total wealth. They note that the share may be much higher. First, their data include only cash transfers in excess of $3,000, so that smaller cash gifts and all in-kind transfers (such as furniture) are excluded. Significantly, their estimate does not include college payments made by parents on behalf of their children. Such payments, accumulated across cohorts, account for an additional 12 percent of wealth. Although their focus is on the clearly intentional inter vivos transfers, it is interesting to note that bequests, intended or accidental, account for an additional 31 percent of wealth in their data. They do not estimate the share of bequests that is intentional.

The simplest versions of the life-cycle model cannot explain a large share of capital accumulation. Extending the life-cycle framework to account for life span uncertainty still fails to account for the quantitatively important intentional bequests and inter vivos transfers. The preceding sections therefore complement the theory of life-cycle savings developed in Chapters 1 and 2 in important fashion. However, the life-cycle model featuring life span uncertainty, liquidity constraints, and precautionary savings may not be a bad approximation for the median household. For intentional transfers increase with parental wealth, and some rich decedents leave huge estates. Consequently, even if aggregate intentional transfers are quantitatively important, life-cycle motives may account for much of the wealth accumulated by the median household.

5.5 POLICY APPLICATIONS

5.5.1 Ricardian Equivalence

The nineteenth-century economist David Ricardo suggested that there may be little difference between a government policy of increasing current taxes and an alternative deficit policy, once it is appreciated that current borrowing entails higher future taxes. Barro (1974) formalized the equivalence of deficit and current tax policies in a model featuring operative altruistic links across generations. In his framework, if the government attempts to redistribute tax burdens across generations, the policy is neutralized by voluntary private transfers flowing in the opposite direction. More generally, *Ricardian equivalence* occurs whenever fiscal policies are completely offset and their effects nullified by private sector responses. We emphasize the issues surrounding Barro's application to deficit policy.

A fundamental implication of the pure life-cycle model of Chapter 1 (i.e., no credit market imperfections or bequest motive) was the life wealth hypothesis, LWH: Consumption over the life cycle depends only upon life-cycle wealth and is therefore independent of the timing of income over the life cycle. Under the LWH, a policy changing the timing of taxes over the life cycle would cause households to reshuffle their saving plans, but would not affect their consumption.

Similarly, when transfers are positive and motivated by altruism, changes in the timing of intergenerational income will not affect any generation's consumption. For example, suppose a government policy increases parental net wealth by $x and lowers child net earnings by $x(1 + r) the following period. Since the present value of the child's loss just equals (in absolute value) the gain to parents, dynastic wealth is left unchanged. As there is no change in the feasible set of parent and child consumption opportunities *facing the parent*, the same consumption levels for parents and children will be chosen. This change in intergenerational income timing would manifest only as an increase in transfers, or intergenerational savings: The tax cut to parents increased their net income by $x, but this is just funneled back to children as a higher bequest. Consequently, children's inheritance increases by $x(1 + r), just enough to repay the debt plus interest and leave their consumption at the prepolicy level. This is the most famous Ricardian equivalence result.

Graphically, this policy induces a movement along the intergenerational budget line that, so long as there are no "intergenerational borrowing constraints," leaves the utility and consumption of both generations unchanged. If Ricardian equivalence holds, attempts by the government to alter the distribution of generational accounts across generations are futile, having no effects on anyone's welfare or on capital accumulation. In terms of Figure 5.1, the policy moves the net-of-tax endowment point from A to some point further down the budget line, such as G. Point D continues to maximize parental utility.

These theoretical results have significant implications for several major policies. For example, those retired during the early years of the Social Security system received more in present value than they paid in, while the opposite will be true for future retirees. Similarly, the Reagan policies of the early 1980s were heavily debt financed, and future generations have to pay interest on, or service, the larger national debt or, if recent budget surpluses persist, retire some portion of it. On the surface, the combined effect of these policies is an implicit transfer of thousands of dollars per current "young" person to each current, or recently deceased, "old" person. However, if Ricardian equivalence holds, these policies do not affect anyone's consumption! Those "old" beneficiaries of the government polices would simply increase (or have increased) their bequests.

Obviously not all family lines are affected in exactly the same way by intergenerational policies. For example, extended families where earnings are low in both generations may have dynastic wealth increased by the introduction or expansion of Social Security, since it affords higher returns to low earners. Similarly, the same policy may lower the dynastic wealth of affluent families. Thus, consumption will rise in the "poor" extended family and fall in the affluent one. Nevertheless, Ricardian equivalence could be a good approximation in the aggregate, if not in each family. Obviously, whether Ricardian equivalence holds, even approximately, is of substantial importance to policymakers, not to mention to those currently young.

Ricardian Equivalence and the Transfer Constraint

Perhaps unsurprisingly, the same sorts of complications that caused the LWH to break down also lead to the failure of Ricardian equivalence. Remember that the LWH fails if the consumer is liquidity constrained prior to the change in the timing of income. For then current consumption changes by the full amount of the change in current income. The intergenerational parallel is the constraint prohibiting negative bequests, which makes some parents transfer constrained. Among such families, the tax cut policy discussed above has dramatically different implications. Transfer-constrained parents would be happy to increase their consumption at the expense of their children's (at least at the margin). Consequently, they spend the $x tax cut on their own consumption, while children's consumption falls by $x(1 + r)$.

Recall Figure 5.2 where the transfer-constrained optimum occurred at the endowment point A. This policy moves after-tax incomes down the budget line to point G, say. Since parents would prefer to consume at point D, they happily take advantage of the opportunity to consume at G. (If the policy is so large that it moves the endowment point to the right of D, the household is no longer transfer constrained and consumption bundle D will be chosen.)

Consequently, whether households are transfer constrained is important for understanding fiscal policies, such as budget deficits and Social Security, that transfer resources across generations. Recall, though, that perhaps only the 20 percent most affluent households intend to leave positive bequests, although a larger percentage of households are connected by bequests or inter vivos transfers. Many parents do not desire to make transfers to their adult children, and not all transfers are motivated by altruism. Consequently, policies that redistribute resources toward the old will increase aggregate consumption, and thereby reduce capital accumulation, as found in Chapter 4. However, the existence of households linked by altruistic transfers implies that the policy conclusions of Chapter 4 may overstate the extent to which redistributive policies change consumption and capital accumulation.

Ricardian Equivalence and Earnings Uncertainty

The LWH also fails in the life-cycle model when there is uninsured earnings uncertainty (see Chapter 2). Barsky, Mankiw and Zeldes (1986) extend this reasoning to the intergenerational setting. They consider parents old enough that most uncertainty regarding their own life-cycle resources has been resolved. Their remaining uncertainty is whether children's income will prove to be "high" or "low." This creates a "precautionary bequest motive" for parents, who save in case child earnings (and thus child consumption) prove unsatisfactorily low. In this context a change in intergenerational tax timing will not be neutral. To see this, consider a balanced-budget policy that cuts the taxes of each adult by $1,000. These cuts are to be paid for by higher taxes on the children's generation. To capture the fact that taxes rise with income, suppose adult children pay taxes only if income proves high. Let the probability of high income be .5. If each parent has one child and the interest rate equals zero, taxes on high-income adult children need to be $2,000, to finance the $1,000 tax cut.

This policy reduces the riskiness of second-generation income. For since bad "state" income is not reduced at all, the difference between good and bad state income is reduced. Consequently, parents increase their consumption, so that their bequest rises by less than $1,000. Ricardian equivalence fails. Nevertheless, bad state consumption of the child is higher. This policy shifts consumption from the child's high-income state to the parents and the child's low-income state, something the parents desire but could not do on their own.

A related reason Ricardian equivalence may fail is developed by Feldstein (1988). He considers altruistic parents in the first half (or period) of economic life with uncertainty concerning their *own* earnings in the second half of life. If parents' earnings in period two prove to be "high," the parent will leave a bequest. If future earnings are low, parents are transfer constrained and leave nothing.

In this environment, parents would like to insure against the possibility of low earnings later in life by shifting earnings from the good to the bad state *or* by being able to use some of children's resources (i.e., make a negative bequest). Since neither of these is feasible, the parent engages in precautionary savings in period one, self-insuring in case second-period income proves low. This lowers first-period consumption and bad-state second-period consumption compared with if one could fully insure against earnings uncertainty. Preferably, first-period consumption could be increased at the expense of second-period good-state consumption and the bequest.

Now suppose parents' taxes are cut $1,000 during the first period. Assume the government bonds financing the tax cut are to be retired, including interest due, by the children's generation. Parents can now increase first-period consumption and second-period bad-state consumption, simply by saving less than the full amount of the tax cut. Should the good state occur, however, consumption and bequest will be reduced. Since first-period consumption is increased, the policy is nonneutral.

Until the analyses of Barsky et al. (1986) and Feldstein (1988) it was commonly believed that Ricardian equivalence would hold *at the family level* whenever altruistically motivated bequests were made, but would fail in transfer-constrained families. However, these studies reveal that even if bequests are observed following the imposition of a policy, it is still quite possible that the policy will alter consumption across generations (see also Chakrabarti, Lord, and Rangazas, 1993).

Ricardian Equivalence and Liquidity-constrained Children

In the life-cycle model, changes in the timing of income are not neutral among liquidity-constrained households. For example, a tax cut when young will be entirely consumed upon receipt, so that consumption when old must fall by the corresponding tax increase. Interestingly, Altig and Davis (1989) show that if adult children are liquidity constrained, policies altering the timing of taxes across generations will not affect consumption, so long as parents are making altruistically motivated transfers.

To appreciate this, first recall that many inter vivos transfers appear timed to alleviate liquidity constraints. Now consider an adult child who *remains* liquidity constrained, despite having received altruistically motivated transfers. That is, the transfers received were insufficient to completely overcome the liquidity constraints. In this context, a government policy benefiting parents at the expense of children may be neutral, as parents would simply increase transfers to undo the policy. However, for Ricardian equivalence to obtain, the policy effects must be absorbed by the child during the liquidity-constrained years. Suppose instead the government will increase the child's taxes after the liquidity constraints are no longer binding. Then the child would consume the increase in parental transfers during the constrained years and Ricardian equivalence would fail.

Exchange, Warm Glow, and Ricardian Equivalence

Ricardian equivalence also fails if bequests are motivated by exchange. For since parents then care only about their own consumption, government redistributions from children to parents would be entirely consumed by the parents. Ricardian equivalence also fails under the impure altruism of warm glow preferences, although the deviation is smaller. In this case, a redistributive policy does not directly affect the utility arising from warm glow transfers. Consequently, a redistribution of wealth toward parents does not increase the marginal utility of transfers so much as when altruism alone operates. For this reason, parental transfers would rise by less than the amount redistributed to them.

This discussion makes clear that Ricardian equivalence is not a general result. In the examples considered, policies shifting resources from children to parents increased parents' consumption at children's expense. There are yet more stories producing a failure of Ricardian equivalence, a couple suggesting parents could *more than offset* redistributive policies via transfers. Nevertheless, the microeconomic evidence, both theoretical and empirical, overwhelmingly suggests that policies that shift resources between generations lead to consumption changes in the same direction. It should be mentioned that the macroeconomic evidence is more favorable to Ricardian equivalence (Seater, 1993). However, many economists question the strength of tests using aggregate data (cf. Poterba and Summers, 1987).

5.5.2 Taxation of Bequests Under Altruism

In the United States, only about 2 percent of all decedents' estates are subject to estate taxation, since the first $675,000 of an estate in 2000 is tax free (Gale and Slemrod, 2000). Further, estate and gift taxes account for less than 2 percent of federal tax revenues. However, since sizeable inheritances provide an easier economic life fate for recipients, increased taxation on such inheritance is perhaps attractive on equity grounds. Another rationale for estate taxes is important for both equity and efficiency: Most large estates contain assets that have appreciated in value but were not sold prior to death. The unrealized capital gains on those assets therefore escaped income taxation. Many would view it as unfair if those gains escaped taxation entirely; the estate tax therefore serves to close that "loophole." Also, if only unrealized gains could avoid taxation, the portfolio decisions of households would be distorted. However, the effective tax rate on *realized* capital gains that are part of an estate is quite high, reflecting the combined impacts of income and estate taxation.

In 1995 a donor could transfer $10,000 per recipient per year under the unified estate and gift tax without incurring tax (thus a couple could transfer $20,000 per recipient per year). This increases the total amount that may be transferred without tax far beyond $675,000. Mulligan (1997) illustrates this point with the following example:

> Consider a couple with three children; suppose the father dies a few months before the mother. In each of the twenty years prior to their death, the couple transfers $20,000 to each child. At the husband's death, another $200,000 is bequeathed to each child (in the name of the husband). Finally, the wife dies, leaving $200,000 to each child and the remainder of her estate to charity. This family pays no estate or gift taxes, even though $800,000 was transferred to each child for a total of $2.4 million in financial transfers. (p. 152).

These considerations suggest that many estates large enough to be subjected to estate taxation are probably, at least in part, not accidental. Figure 5.6 shows how an estate tax affects behavior, assuming the estate is motivated by altruism. For simplicity, parents receive no inheritance, so that $W_p = E_p$. With negative bequests ruled out, in the absence of estate taxation the effective budget line extends from the endowment point B to point A. Utility is maximized at C, and the bequest is B^0_p. Imposition of an estate tax rotates the budget line down through the endowment, with the new constraint given by BD. The posttax budget line is flatter because the price of transferring $1 to the next generation has increased from $1/(1 + r)$ to $(1 + t_b)/(1 + r)$.

Unsurprisingly, since a bequest is just intergenerational savings, there are the same sort of effects that a tax on interest income has in the life-cycle model. The fact that the tax increases the price to parents of child consumption creates a substitution effect favoring increased parental consumption (a lower bequest) and less child consumption. However, since the tax constricts the opportunity set, the income effect dictates lower consumption by the child and parent (the latter increasing the bequest). These conflicting income and substitution effects indicate that the effect on the *gross-of-tax* bequest is ambiguous. However, both effects favor reduced child consumption, so the *net-of-tax* inher-

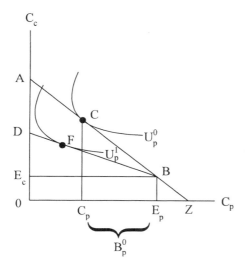

Figure 5.6 Estate taxation

itance unambiguously falls. Thus, an estate tax saps parental ability to transfer resources intergenerationally.

Changes in the estate or gift tax exclusions may alter the timing of transfers in order to minimize tax burdens. For example, suppose the estate exclusion is lowered to $300,000 but the gift exclusion is raised to $15,000 per year per recipient. In the example of Mulligan from above, the timing of transfers would change to match the new tax exclusions but would leave the total amount transferred equal to $2.4 million.

5.5.3 Private Responses to Public Assistance Programs

Whether private transfers are motivated by exchange or altruism affects the implications of government policies providing social insurance, such as the various types of welfare programs. Consider first a public transfer program targeting benefits to poor adults. Examples of such programs include food stamps, cash benefits or "welfare" (including TANF, formerly AFDC), and Medicaid. Suppose a program beneficiary also receives transfers from parents. Now assume there is a reduction in government aid, as has happened in recent years with AFDC.

A common way to assess the impact on the welfare of the recipient is to subtract the reduction in program benefits from the recipient's pre–policy-change total income. Such a calculation does not take into account any response of private transfers. However, if the parents' transfers are altruistically motivated, the parents would increase their giving, partially offsetting the reduction in government transfers. Consequently, simply subtracting the reduction of public transfers overstates the policy's harmful effect on recipient income. More generally, increases (decreases) in public assistance programs may crowd out (crowd in) private giving. Under simple altruism, when program recipients are receiving private transfers, public assistance effectively provides *extended family insurance*, rather than for the recipient alone. However, if small families are exposed to large risks, such as having a severely handicapped child, risk spreading through the public sector may confer important advantages. Suppose, instead, that the private transfers from parents to adult children are motivated by exchange. Then a reduction in public assistance would not increase parental transfers.

Cox and Jakubson (1995) conduct an empirical analysis of the response of private transfers to changes in public transfers in the United States. They conclude that private transfers respond very little to changes in public transfers. This evidence is more consistent with exchange than with altruistically motivated private transfers. It also means that changes in public transfer levels cause roughly equal changes in recipient's total income (earnings plus private and public transfers).[17]

Cox, Hansen, and Jimenez (1996) find substantial evidence of altruistic inter vivos transfers in the Philippines. They estimate that reductions in recipient income induce large increases in private transfers, just as the altruism model suggests. They note that unlike the United States, the Philippines have a quite limited social safety net. This, they argue, explains the presence of altruistic responses in the Philippines' data and the apparent lack of it in U.S. data sets. By this interpretation, large public sector transfers in the United States have largely crowded out private transfers, pushing most families into the exchange regime. By contrast, in the Philippines, a perhaps similar degree of altruism manifests as positive private transfers, for the assistance provided by the government is much smaller. More generally, in developed economies with large social insurance networks, marginal changes in public transfers appear to have little effect on private transfers. It is unclear whether recent welfare reductions in the United States are large enough to stimulate altruistic private sector compensation.

In addition to public sector redistributive transfers, numerous privately funded charities and churches provide monies to those in financial distress. Other charitable contributions benefit colleges, museums, and the arts. In 1992, individuals recorded charitable tax deductions of $54.1 billion (Rosen, 1995, p. 375). In this light, consider a reduction in public funding for causes helped by charities, with the savings passed along as tax cuts to the more affluent. If private donations to charity are motivated by simple altruism, donors would increase their contributions, effectively neutralizing the policy.

The potential interaction between public transfers and exchange-motivated private contributions appears much weaker. After all, beneficiaries are not providing yard services to those making charitable contributions. Nevertheless, "egoistic" satisfactions may accrue; those making contributions may enjoy being recognized for their philanthropy. Along these lines, recall the warm glow model of Andreoni in which people care not only about the welfare of the recipients, but also about how much they personally, voluntarily, give. With "impure" altruism, changes in public transfers need not be neutralized by private responses. For example, if the government taxes a warm glow donor an additional $1 to increase public sector giving, his or her voluntary giving will fall by less than $1. Ironically, the more egoistic are givers (recall, the warm glow is independent of the *effects* of giving on the recipient), the less will increases in public sector transfers crowd out private transfers. Andreoni points out that the empirical evidence suggests much less than complete crowding out: Each additional dollar of public sector giving may crowd out private sector giving by perhaps a dime.

5.6 SUMMARY

This chapter examined patterns of intergenerational financial transfers and the motivations behind them. Since transfers account for a large share of aggregate wealth, policies designed to increase national savings must account for the response of private transfers. Also, policies such as Social Security redistribute wealth across generations, and thereby across members of extended families. The extent to which private transfers may offset these public redistributions has enormous implications for the effectiveness of such polices.

The most natural and most extensively analyzed motive for private transfers is altruism, in which parents care about the economic well-being of their offspring. Simple altruistic models predict that if transfers to adult children are positive, income redistributions between family members will be completely offset through changes in transfers. However, the best evidence indicates that a $1 redistribution produces only a 13 cent offset. Another implication of altruism is that among families leaving *intentional* bequests, the present value sum of inter vivos transfers and bequests should equalize the wealth across children. However, although inter vivos transfers do tend to be compensatory, differences in transfers across children with large income differentials are insignificant. Further, bequests are most usually divided equally. Consequently, compensatory transfers do little to reduce income inequality across grown siblings. However, simple altruism does prove consistent with the timing of inter vivos transfers, and transfers, though small, are compensatory. Further, more sophisticated versions of altruism are available which are consistent with many of the transfer patterns. However, model variations associated with other transfer motives may also be consistent with the data, making it hard to determine which is the "true" model.

Other theories don't fare any better. An exchange model is capable of "predicting" equal bequests, but only under restrictive assumptions about the parent's utility function (it must be Cobb-Douglas). Even then, it leaves unanswered why children would be content to wait until the parent's death to receive their money. Informal family arrangements that function as an annuities market may be part of the explanation behind the small, "accidental," bequests of the middle class.

Presumably all of the motives discussed in this chapter are operative at times in various families: Parents obviously do care about their children. It is almost as certain that they want (expect) certain things from them. Most everyone enjoys the boost to their self-image from being acknowledged (by self or others) as generous. The vast majority of elderly are seriously concerned about outliving their resources. Unfortunately, data limitations (and perhaps ingenuity) so far have limited our ability to determine precisely the roles of these many considerations. As better data and more refined theories become available our understanding of transfers should improve.

The following chapter extends the model of altruism to include investments by parents in the human capital development of their dependent children. A unified model of human and financial transfers is used to examine economic inequality. A further extension of the altruism model is found in Chapter 9, where parents also decide upon the quantity of children (through fertility choices) in addition to the quality (as discussed in Chapter 6). Another role for inherited wealth is the effect on labor supply, as discussed in Chapter 8.

ENDNOTES

1. These finding are reported by Gale and Scholz (1994) employing data from the Survey of Consumer Finances between 1983 and 1985.

2. Further, among those children designated as the primary care giver, the average was 28.9 hours per week (Sloan, Picone, and Hoerger, 1997). And, before the advent of Social Security, children were often an important source of retirement income (cf. Becker, p. 8, 253, 1981).

3. Similarly, Cox (1987) and Cox and Raines (1985), on the basis of data from the 1979 President's Commission on Pension Policy Survey, find that 60 to 70% of all transfers are inter vivos.

4. The basic theoretical development follows that of Davies and St. Hilaire (1987).

5. When children are produced within a marriage, and that marriage remains intact throughout the child's years of dependency, it is reasonable to assume parents possess a single agreed upon utility function. In Chapter 9 we consider how and why transfer behavior changes when parents divorce.

6. Another popular formulation of intergenerational preferences is

$$U_p = \ln C_p + \ln W_c/(1 + m)$$

where m is the intergenerational rate of time preference or discount rate. This expression is just a monotonic transformation of the Cobb-Douglas function. To see this, first take the natural log of the right-hand side of (5.2), dividing the result by θ. Recall from Chapter 1 that the rate of time preference m in the Cobb-Douglas case is given by $1 + m = \theta/(1 - \theta)$; making that substitution yields the expression above.

7. Allowing the child to care about her or his children's consumption would complicate the story without offsetting insights. Further, since almost all transfers go from parents to children, we abstract from altruism on the part of children toward their parents.

8. Setting the expression for desired bequests, (5.7a), equal to zero and then solving for parental wealth yields the wealth threshold above which bequests are positive; $W_p^* = \theta E_c/[(1 - \theta)(1 + r)]$.

9. The altruistic model predicts that in many families, at least one child will be completely disinherited. This happens whenever parents' total desired financial transfers are fairly small, at least compared with the earnings differentials amongst the siblings. In this case, the low-earning child is predicted to receive everything transferred, yet wealth is still not equalized.

10. McGarry (2000) imagines children are liquidity constrained in the current period and have future incomes that are positively correlated with current income. She shows that the transfer derivative restriction does not hold if observing a child's current year income alters parent's expectations of the child's future income prospects. For example, suppose a daughter's current income falls because she did not make partner at a national accounting firm and, upon being "counseled out," assumed lower paying employment at a local firm. This lowers parent's beliefs regarding her "permanent" income. In this case, McGarry shows the predicted transfer derivative should be below one. Intuitively, the expectation of *future* transfers rises, which induces parents to postpone some transfers as a precaution against the need for high future transfers. Also, when the parents have uncertainty regarding the child's *current* income, it can be shown that the transfer derivative under altruism falls below 1. Along these lines, McGarry (1997) reports lower transfers to children when parents do not know their children's current income. Nevertheless, the combination of underreporting of transfers, uncertainty over current child income, and a theoretical transfer derivative somewhat below 1 seem incapable of reconciling the prediction of fully compensating transfers with the 13-cent estimate of the transfer derivative.

11. Behrman, Pollack, and Taubman (1982) present a model which implies equal bequests. They assume parents' utility depends separately on the earnings and financial transfers to children

$$U_p = U_p(C_p, E_c^i, B_p^i) \; i = 1,2$$

Parents equate their marginal utility of financial transfers to each child. If a given level of transfers brings the same satisfaction for any child, such transfers are equalized across children. Although more consistent with the financial bequest data, this formulation may have somewhat less intuitive appeal. Behrman motivates the separability assumption as follows: "parents value a dollar that their children earn in the labor market more (or at least differently) than a dollar received from assets because, for example, a person may be valued more who 'earns his or her own way'" (1997, p. 138). Also, this formulation has some distinctly nonaltruistic aspects, unless children also value earnings and transfers in the same differential fashion.

12. In the framework of Cox (1987), for example, parents continue to care about child consumption as in (3.1). However, the main contribution is analysis of the "exchange equilibrium" in which parents would prefer more services from the child without increasing transfers but the child will not supply more without compensation. This exchange regime, where further services are obtained at a price, is exactly what our model captures.

13. Davies (1996) stresses that simple exchange models of bequests have difficulty explaining why children would be willing to wait so long (until parent's death) for payment for services. More generally, Davies shows that there are important intertemporal aspects to exchange behavior which may best be viewed as a "repeated game" between parent and child.

14. This is true even in a static or single-period setting where the issues raised by McGarry do not arise; see note 10.

15. The story told above implicitly assumed that parents make only one transfer decision. However, if parents and children play a "repeated game," the difficulties of the Samaritan's Dilemma may be somewhat mitigated. For example, parent's could send a signal of low support in the crucial early years, so as to maximize child effort.

16. Employing stylized facts regarding bequest shares, Lord and Rangazas (1991) conduct theoretical simulations to measure the contribution of bequests to wealth, assuming bequests are motivated by altruism. Their general-equilibrium framework determines the interest rate endogenously. They find a partial-equilibrium contribution of bequests similar to that estimated by Kotlikoff and Summers. However, large net-of-bequest inheritance wealth increased consumption so much that bequests did little to raise the general-equilibrium saving rate above that found in the life-cycle model. Lord (1992) showed that this conclusion also obtains when bequests are motivated by exchange.

17. Such extended family considerations are not restricted to welfare but concern any program with clearly targeted benefits. Consider an increase in public school funding financed by an increase in property taxes. Here, grandparents' higher property taxes reduce the extent to which parents must supplement the human capital accumulation provided by the school system. Will grandparents reduce transfers, either to their children or grandchildren?

PROBLEMS AND QUESTIONS

▶ REVIEW
QUESTIONS

1. **A.** What is the difference between an accidental and an intentional bequest?
   B. How could one determine whether most bequests are accidental or intentional?
   C. Why might the existence of credit markets that do not permit borrowing against future earnings affect the proportion of transfers made inter vivos, as opposed to in the form of bequests?

2. Consider the two-period model of intergenerational altruism with Cobb-Douglas preferences. Show graphically, and explain intuitively, how a tax cut of $1 given to parents, which parents fully realize will be repaid with interest by their children, will affect bequests and each generation's consumption when:

   A. the parents plan to leave a positive financial bequest prior to the tax cut. In this case, also develop your argument algebraically. In what sense is Ricardian equivalence similar to the life wealth hypothesis of Chapter 1 (that consumption over the life cycle depends only upon life wealth, not upon when it is received)?

   B. parents are transfer constrained.

3. Suppose the estate tax is removed.

   A. Discuss and graph the implications for the bequest and inheritance under the assumption that bequests are altruistically motivated. What are the implications for the distribution of wealth across and within families? What is the maximum amount the survivor of a married couple could disperse to their four children before paying estate taxes?

   B. If all bequests are accidental, how might the response differ from the altruistic case of part A? In this case how would wealth distribution be affected?

4. Provide an example of (a) an inter vivos transfer to a dependent, (b) an inter vivos transfer to an adult child motivated by altruism, (c) an inter vivos transfer to an adult child motivated by exchange, (d) a bequest motivated by altruism, (e) a bequest motivated by exchange, (f) an accidental bequest.

5. **A.** Why might changes in the fertility rate affect the extent to which families operate as an "informal annuities market"?

   B. Suppose the government increases food stamp transfers to an adult child who is also receiving substantial private transfers from her parents. What will be the total effect on recipient income if private transfers are motivated by altruism? By exchange?

6. **A.** Suppose transfers are motivated by altruism. Why might the contribution of transfers to aggregate wealth vary with the size of the welfare state?

   B. How might the contribution of transfers to aggregate wealth be affected by the existence of widespread liquidity constraints?

7. Compare and contrast the comparative statics response of transfers to parental wealth and the adult child's wage for altruistically and exchange-motivated transfers.

▶ PROBLEMS

1. Consider the two-period model of intergenerational altruism with Cobb-Douglas preferences, where the earnings of the child are exogenous. Suppose the intergenerational interest rate is $r = 1$, $\theta = .5$, $E_p = 10$, $E_c = 10$, $I_p = 2$. As you work through this problem notice the many parallels with the two-period life-cycle model, when borrowing constraints are not, and when they are, binding.

   A. Determine W_p and dynastic wealth Z. Graph the intergenerational budget line, showing magnitudes for axis intercepts. Determine and interpret the slope of the budget line.

B. Calculate the equilibrium values of C_p, C_c, B_p, and I_c. Draw an indifference curve consistent with this solution on your graph from part A and depict the solutions on the graph.

C. What is the marginal propensity to bequeath from I_p? From E_c?

D. Suppose now that there is growth in real wages thru time and that $E_c = 20$. (You could think of this real wage growth as either being a macroeconomic phenomenon, or reflecting higher earnings for your child, only.) How does this affect C_p and B_p? Graph the new budget constraint, showing axis intercepts.

E. Suppose again that $E_c = 10$, but now let $\theta = .8$. What would desired and actual C_p and B_p be? In what sense is this similar to being liquidity constrained? In what sense is "transfer constrained" different?

2. Use the bequest equation (5.7a) to show that a tax cut of $x to parents coupled with a tax increase of $x(1 + r) to the child increases the bequest by $x, as required for Ricardian equivalence. Use (5.6a) and (5.6b) to show that there is no change in either the parent's or the child's consumption.

3. Assume that children have altruistic feelings toward their parents, so that there is "two-sided" altruism. How might this affect the conclusions regarding Ricardian equivalence when parents are transfer constrained (ignoring uncertainty, liquidity constraints, etc.)? Why is the growth rate of the economy important in terms of which direction transfers would flow?

Chapter 6

FAMILY INVESTMENTS IN CHILDREN, CHILD EARNINGS, AND ECONOMIC GROWTH

"If one were to summarize the main message of the extensive scientific litera-ture dealing with family influences, a single line would suffice: it pays to choose one's parents."

—GAVIRIA, 1999, P. 3

What determines the distribution of earnings within and across generations? How has the expansion of education contributed to economic growth? This chapter examines the eco-nomic role of families in these processes. To this point, the earnings of workers have been outside the control of individual or family decision-making. Earnings were exogenous in the models of Chapters 1, 2, and 5. In Chapters 3 and 4, worker productivity and earn-ings were determined by macroeconomic variables, such as capital accumulation, techni-cal change, and fiscal policy. In contrast, the remaining chapters all model the earnings of workers as being determined, in part, by the utility-maximizing choices of individuals or their parents. This chapter extends the model of altruistic financial transfers of Chap-ter 5 by incorporating parental investments in the earnings capacity of their offspring. Chapter 9 extends this discussion to include the fertility decisions of households. Chap-ters 7 and 8 emphasize how the decisions of adults affect their own earnings potential. Each chapter contains applications to policy and to economic growth.

It is now explicitly recognized that each worker was once a child who grew up in some family environment. Section 6.1 motivates and develops a theory of family invest-ment in children's human capital development. In the following section, the implications of that framework are evaluated in the light of evidence. Section 6.3 examines the link between educational investments in children and U.S. macroeconomic growth. Section 6.4 considers policy implications, including how family investments in children's human capital affects the Ricardian equivalence proposition discussed in Chapter 5. A brief sum-mary concludes the chapter.

6.1 A MODEL OF HUMAN CAPITAL BEQUESTS[1]

6.1.1 Motivation

The family may affect the economic well-being of children through several channels. Families differ in their economic resources, genes, education, marital structure, size, school district, race, luck, and so on. Before attempting to disentangle some of these influences, we show that *some* aspect(s) of family background must be important to child earnings.

One direct test of family influence compares the dispersion or variability in earnings across all individuals with that among children belonging to the same family, that is, siblings. Solon (1999) reviews the empirical literature concerning the correlation of earnings among siblings. If family background does not help predict the earnings of children, the correlation is zero; if it provides the entire explanation, the correlation is 1. Solon concludes that the correlation of average (log) earnings among American brothers is about .4.[2] He notes that "If that is right, about 40 percent of permanent earnings inequality so measured is attributable to family and community origins, and 60 percent is due to factors not shared by brothers" (p. 17). Thus, families do matter a good deal, but why?

Of course, there is greater genetic similarity between siblings than between nonsiblings, so the role of families may be "in the genes." At the extreme, if the sole determinants of earnings are genetics and "luck," the role of economics in explaining earnings would be primarily limited to economic theories of marriage markets.[3] It may never be possible to ascertain the precise contributions to life outcomes of "nature" and "nurture." However, suggestive evidence comes from comparing the overall sibling earnings correlations with correlations among fraternal twins and among identical twins. Fraternal twins have the same genetic variability as siblings who are not twins, but experience less variability in other aspects of family background (such as parent's age at the child's birth and neighborhood of residence). Identical twins have no genetic variability and their experience variability in the family environment is similar to that of fraternal twins. Solon reports a substantially higher earnings correlation among identical twins (between .58 and .64) than among fraternal twins (estimates of their correlation averaging somewhat more than for nontwin siblings), suggesting a substantial role for genetics.

However, there is also evidence indicating a prominent role for environment. As one provocative example, Solon reports "that most estimates of the IQ correlation between identical twins reared apart are about .70 or a bit higher. The correlation between identical twins raised together is even higher at about .85, suggesting a role for common environment" (p. 21). Further evidence is associated with the economic effects of schooling decisions. Children of poor families will be seen to obtain fewer years of education than children of more affluent parents, and earnings increase with years of education. Apparently, genes are not the only aspect of families of origin important to child earnings.

We pay particular attention to how differences in the economic resources of families affect the amount invested in the development of children's human capital, and therefore earnings. More affluent parents will be predicted to have better educated, higher earning children. The earnings of parents and their children are, in fact, positively and significantly related. Several recent examinations of that relationship in the United States have utilized the Panel Study of Income Dynamics (PSID) and National Longitudinal Surveys (NLS). Both data sets began with national probability samples in the late 1960s and have followed the children in the sampled families throughout dependency and as they established their own households This has made it possible to relate the children's earnings as adults to their parent's earnings, with both generation's incomes self-reported contemporaneously.[4] Solon has also reviewed these studies. He concludes that the intergenerational elasticity in long-run earnings for men in the United States is probably about .4. That is, assuming everything else is the same, if one father has earnings that are 10% higher than another's, we would expect his son's earnings to be about 4% higher than those of the other son. This suggests a good degree of persistence in earnings across generations, yet also a fair amount of regression of child earnings back toward the mean of earnings.

Thus, the earnings or more generally resources of parents are important to children's earnings prospects. But why? We develop a story in which high-income parents are better able to undertake the efficient investments in their children's human capital. Intuitively, even if poor parents devote a "large" share of their life wealth to child development, the investments will fall short of the child's capacity to utilize developmental resources efficiently. We also consider the possibility that, in addition to differential investments, earnings are correlated across generations because the genetic or cultural traits that contributed to the parent's high earnings are passed along to the children. Below, human capital investments are embedded within a model of altruistically motivated human capital *and* financial transfers to children developed by Becker and Tomes (1986). Viewing both types of transfers enables a rich discussion of the transmission of economic inequality.

6.1.2   The Model

An important building block of our model is what we assume motivates parents to invest in their children's development. As with the financial transfers to adult children examined in the preceding chapter, the motives of parents for these investments may be more complex than simple altruism. For example, parents may live vicariously via the child's experiences and accomplishments, both of which may be embellished by greater investment. Nevertheless, Becker and Tomes consider altruism the most obvious motivation; parents invest in their children because they receive utility from the children's wellbeing. As in the Chapter 5 discussion of altruistic financial transfers, the preferences of parents are given by

$$U_p = U_p(C_p, W_c) \tag{6.1}$$

so that parents care about own consumption and the wealth or consumption opportunities of their child. As in Chapter 5, it will sometimes be more appropriate to think of the utility rather than wealth of the child. This will allow us to address differences in leisure consumption or job amenities (i.e., compensating differentials in wages).

Parents can augment the resources of their children in two ways. They may make financial transfers after the child has "left the nest"; they may also invest in the child's human capital to increase the child's earnings during adulthood. Parents allocate their wealth

W_p between own consumption C_p, human capital investments (or "human capital bequest") B_p^h, and possibly a financial bequest B_p. That is,

$$W_p = C_p + B_p^h + B_p \qquad (6.2)$$

For ease of exposition, we assume there is no overlap in the *economic* lives of parents and their adult children. Any financial bequest put aside at the start of parent's economic lives will produce a financial inheritance for the child of $I_c = B_p(1 + r)$, received at the start of the child's adulthood (r being the intergenerational money interest rate).

For most parents, the principal transfers to children are the investments of time, energy, and money in their development while they are economically dependent. Parental time inputs include holding a baby, reading to a preschooler, helping the young student with homework, and discussing life's complexities with the adolescent. The time parents devote to children is drawn from market and housework, sleep, and leisure. If the mother, say, stays home full- or part-time while the father works full-time (what used to be called the traditional family), time devoted to children comes mainly from "mom's" depressed labor market activity. If both parents work full-time, time with children reduces leisure, sleep, and housework. Examples of goods inputs include purchased child care services (daycare), books, music lessons, summer camp, computers, and health and nutrition products.

Schooling inputs account for a good portion of the developmental resources invested in older children. Some home inputs are presumably complementary to and others substitutable with schooling inputs. Clearly, though, parents have many options when choosing the amount by which they augment formal schooling investments. Both because it is reasonable and it simplifies the analysis, we first model the parents' choices as if parents also *directly* choose the spending per pupil at the public or private primary and secondary school(s) attended by their children. In the United States, local schools have traditionally been financed by local property taxes. This makes expenditures per pupil sensitive to the tax rate and average property value. The link between school inputs and outputs is discussed further below. For now, though, allow that there is an economically efficient level of educational inputs, which may be expected to vary with child ability. For example, the level and pace of curriculum can be higher for more able children (holding "readiness" constant). Although ability tends to regress to the mean across generations, more successful parents tend to have more able children. Affluent parents are willing to purchase the efficient amount of schooling outlays. Consequently, they will migrate to or "sort into" school systems that set the curriculum and property tax rate to achieve the efficient expenditures per pupil. Thus, affluent families will tend to congregate in homogeneous neighborhoods. Their children's schools will be efficiently financed and, as in Garrison Keillor's mythical Lake Woebegone, all children will be above average. Less affluent households may be unable to afford the efficient level of schooling. For this reason, among less affluent households (school districts), schooling expenditures will increase with average neighborhood income.[5] The assumption that parents choose schooling expenditures is not appropriate in all contexts. Fortunately, most results continue to apply when parents choose non-schooling outlays, taking schooling expenditures as given. Further, section 6.4 addresses issues associated with statewide as opposed to local school finance.

The relationship between parental time and goods inputs and the human capital produced by the child is formalized by a human capital production function. Consider, for example, the production function

$$h_c = x^\theta (sh_p)^\lambda \tag{6.3}$$

Here, h_c is the child's human capital in adulthood, x is the goods inputs, and s is the time parents devote to the child's development, h_p is the parents' human capital, and θ and λ are parameters affecting the productivity of the inputs. As argued above, x includes formal schooling inputs as well as supplemental inputs (including, for example, any premium in the purchase price of a house due to its location in a good school district). The human capital of the parent is included, as more educated parents are perhaps better able to teach (and monitor) their children. This formulation excludes the child's time devoted to learning. Indeed, an important use of the parent's time input is to monitor and direct the child's allocation of time. (In some ways this is the crucial distinction between this and the next chapter. There, time investments of young adult students/workers are included, but the time input of their parents is not.) Notice that the same exponent applies for parental time and human capital, which implies that an increase in the human capital of parents raises the effective time input sh_p by the same proportion.

Two other potentially important determinants of human capital production are taken up later in the chapter, but should be mentioned now. First is the ability of the child(ren). For the time being, we simply note that equation (6.3) refers to a child of given ability. Second, the broader environment in which human capital is accumulated may play an important role. Some "spillover" effects associated with the level of human capital in the economy are discussed by Borjas (1995) and in section 6.3. (However, since parents in a school district are largely homogeneous, the role of neighbors' human capital could be approximately captured simply by increasing the exponent on h_p.)

Investment costs are the sum of the amount of goods (whose per unit price is 1) and the earnings foregone by the parent to assist the child. In practice, the amounts of goods and time inputs are not chosen independently. For example, if both parents work full-time while the child is young, parental time inputs are depressed while goods outlays (on daycare) are increased. Similarly, among less affluent or single parents, the mix of time and goods may depend upon the work disincentives of welfare programs or on early schooling subsidies like Head Start. More generally, *parents choose the mix of goods and time inputs so as to minimize the cost of producing any level of child human capital.* The amount invested by the parent is

$$B_p^h = x + wsh_p \tag{6.4}$$

where w is the wage per unit of human capital (perhaps determined by macro-level factors as in Chapter 3). The relationship between the human capital investments B_p^h and the child's human capital h_c is portrayed in Figure 6.1.

The fact that we have drawn the production function to be concave implies there are diminishing returns to scale in the goods and time inputs (taking parent's human capital as given). The exponent on an input in this production function equals the elasticity of output with respect to that input (see Chapter 3). For this reason the sum of θ and λ are

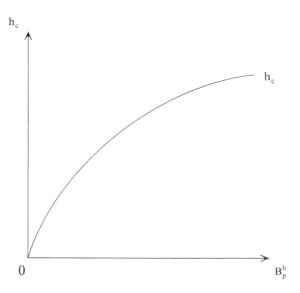

Figure 6.1 The effect of investments on human capital

the total returns to scale in production. In equation (6.3), if $\theta + \lambda = .4$, say, a 10% increase in both goods and parents' time would increase the child's human capital by 4 percent. So long as $\theta + \lambda$ is below 1, there are diminishing returns to scale. Diminishing returns seem reasonable, as some of the important inputs, such as the child's innate capacity and some features of the environment, are essentially fixed. Thus, a declining rate of return on investments in children is but a slight variation on the law of diminishing marginal returns.

6.1.3 Evidence of Diminishing Returns to Investments

A great deal of empirical evidence supports the assumption of diminishing returns to investments in the quantity or quality of schooling. Somewhat less is known about the productivity of investments at home. Our discussion draws heavily from a review by Rangazas (2000a). We begin with schooling, then address home investments.

Returns to schooling may be viewed along quality and quantity dimensions. The *quantity* margin corresponds to more schooling time of a given quality. There is general agreement that earnings increase with years of schooling. For example, Angrist and Krueger (1991) estimate that an additional year of schooling due to compulsory education laws raises earnings on the order of 7.5%. Using data on identical twins, Ashenfelter and Krueger (1994) find appreciably higher returns to an additional year's schooling.[6] Returns in this neighborhood exceed those on *safe* financial assets. However, human capital investments are not riskless, and these returns appear roughly comparable to those on similarly risky financial assets. There is also evidence of diminishing returns to education. For example, the *marginal* return to education both in the United States and elsewhere is found to fall as one goes from primary to secondary to college education (Psacharopoulos, 1985). The returns to high school and college education are examined in Chapter 7.

A higher *quality* of education refers to the application of better or more inputs to a given amount of student time. Higher quality education may result from teachers with better training, more computers and teachers per child, or better curriculums, as examples. Economists have examined the relationship between school quality and student performance on standardized tests, and between school quality and the child's earnings in adulthood. In an influential literature review, Hanushek (1986) finds little link between school expenditures per student and school quality, as measured by the cognitive achievement of students. *If* his assessment is correct and *if* test performance really captures human capital accumulation, there would not only be diminishing returns to schooling inputs, but zero returns!

In contrast, several recent studies employing better data and statistical techniques have found that raising the teacher-student ratio improves performance. Notably, Finn and Achilles (1990) and Krueger (1999) report that student test scores increased with the teacher-student ratio in a controlled experiment (called STARS) in Tennessee. Lower class size improved the test scores of kindergartners the most, with the gains showing persistence over the next few grades for which data are available. We will argue more generally that resources appear to matter most at young ages.

Positive effects from reducing class size on student outcomes have also been found by other researchers (cf. Case and Deaton, 1999). It also appears that reducing class size has a positive effect on both high school and college graduation rates (cf. Card and Kreuger, 1996). Unfortunately, reducing class size is very expensive. For this reason, current results may not be definitive or sizeable enough to justify further reductions. Even granting that lower class size improves student performance, this literature suggests quite low *marginal* returns to schooling expenditures *at recent funding levels*.

Researchers focusing on the relationship between schooling resources and the subsequent *earnings* of children often find greater effects than those discussed above. Card and Krueger review this literature stressing several studies in which a 10% reduction in the average pupil-teacher ratio, or a 10% increase in the mean spending per student, increases wages or weekly earnings by, on average, somewhat less than 1%. However, these studies often have little information about family background. This raises serious questions about interpretation, since wealthier families tend to invest more in their children at home and to live in communities with better funded schools.

The racially segregated South circa 1920 provides an interesting "experiment" in which schooling resources differed appreciably across groups for reasons other than family resources. Card and Krueger show that as funding disparities between blacks and whites narrowed through time, so did their educational attainment and earnings. This suggests that when quality is quite low, as it was for segregated blacks in the Carolinas early in the twentieth century, substantial quality improvements may lead to substantial gains in human capital. Similarly, cross-country comparisons indicate higher returns to quality when average expenditures were lower than in the modern-day United States (cf. Barro and Sala-i-Martin, 1995). Thus, there are diminishing returns to at least primary and secondary school expenditures on quality, and marginal returns appear to be quite low at current expenditure levels. Also, returns to education appear higher at lower years of schooling. Consequently, earlier in U.S. history when schooling expenditures and educational attainment were much lower, the productivity of investments may have been much greater. In section 6.3 we examine whether human capital deepening from rising educational investments may explain much U.S. growth over the past century or so.

Home investments include time parents spend with children on developmental activities and expenditures on educational goods. Little is known about the productivity of home goods inputs, and there remains much uncertainty regarding the role of parental time inputs. Stafford (1996, p. 232) reviews previous studies and concludes that greater maternal child care time leads to better school performance as measured by educational attainment in years of schooling or teacher assessment of grade school performance. Similarly, the ratio of parents to children may affect child development. Hanushek (1992) finds that the average reading test performance of children within a family declines with family size. Middle children of large families, who *always* have to compete with siblings for parental attention, fare least well. In general, the more children there are, the less adult time there is per child, and the less developed is the child. This result is similar to the effects of class size and quality discussed above. The effects of family size may be stronger, though, because the resource differences occur when the child is young and therefore most responsive to nurturing.

Stafford also reports that better educated mothers spend more time on child care, with more of that time having an educational component. This helps explain the frequent finding that the educational attainment of children is strongly and positively related to the mother's education. An important question is whether parental human capital has an *independent* effect on the return to human capital investments, or if the principal influence is through greater parental earnings leading to greater investments. The production function of equation (6.3) presumes such an independent effect.[7] Rangazas (2000a) believes much of this link is due to educated parents somehow instilling a stronger taste for education among their children. (This link is reminiscent of the possibility discussed in Chapter 5 that parents who received an inheritance have a stronger taste for leaving bequests.)

Having examined the connection between investments and human capital, we now link investments, transfers, and the wealth of children more formally. The life resources of the child are the sum of earnings and financial inheritance and may be written

$$W_c = (1 + r_h^a)B_p^h + (1 + r)B_p = wh_c + (1 + r)B_p$$
$$= E_c + I_c \tag{6.4}$$

Here r_h^a is the *average* rate of return on human capital investments and w is the wage per unit of human capital faced by children in adulthood. In Figure 6.2, curve AW_p is derived from the human capital investment function (Figure 6.1), and shows how parental investments are transformed into child earnings. It has slope $-(1 + r_h)$, where r_h is the *marginal* rate of return on human capital. Because of the assumed diminishing returns, r_h falls as investments rise.

Efficiency requires that each successive or marginal dollar of the total bequest be transferred in the form—human or financial—where it produces the largest increase in child wealth. Crucial to this portfolio choice are the assumptions that the return on financial bequests is constant at r, while r_h falls as the human bequest is increased. Thus, at first all transfers will be in the form of human bequests; it makes little sense to take on a second job to finance a trust fund for an infant if there is no time left to read to her. At some investment level, point B on the graph, r_h will fall to equal r. Then, any further transfers would be in financial form, since additional human capital investments offer a return below r. Straight line segment BK, with slope $-(1 + r)$, reflects parent's ability to save money at rate r for financial transfers the following period.

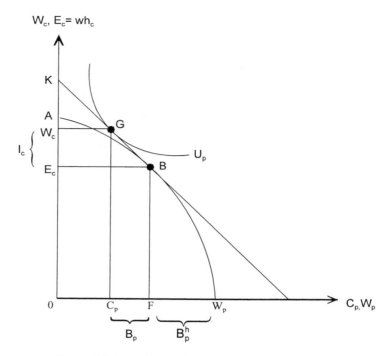

Figure 6.2 Parent's transfer decisions and child earnings

We can now state the parent's utility maximization problem: Parents must choose levels for own consumption C_p, human bequest B_p^h, and financial bequest B_p to maximize utility function (6.1) subject to the human capital production function (6.3), and the life wealth constraint (6.2).[8] In Figure 6.2 parents have maximized utility where the MRS = $1 + r$, at point G. In this case, the efficient human bequest (where $r = r_h$) and a financial bequest are made. B_p^h and B_p are read off the horizontal axis and the contributions to C_c of I_c and E_c are found on the vertical.

6.1.4 The Transfer Constraint

Parents having less wealth than in Figure 6.2 would make smaller total transfers to their children. To the extent possible, this occurs via reduced financial transfers. However, we noted in Chapter 5 that most families leave little in the way of a planned financial bequest, nor do they make sizeable ongoing inter vivos transfers. If r_h remains above r after sizeable investments *and* parental wealth is modest, the household may *desire* a combination such as point J in Figure 6.3. That is, parents would make the efficient investment in their children at point D and then choose consumption bundle J along the budget line MN. This strategy would maximize dynastic wealth, the sum of parental wealth W_p and the "profits" from child investments for which $r_h > r$. Notice, though, that this makes parent's consumption equal to OK, even though their own resources net of the human bequest are only OA. The only way their consumption can equal OK is if the child trans-

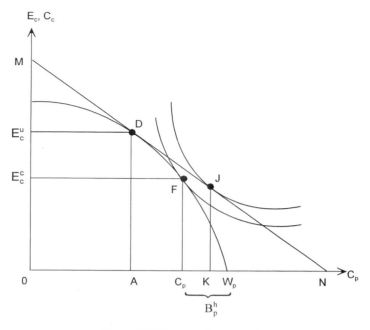

Figure 6.3 The transfer constraint

fers back to them the amount AK, plus interest. Since, as discussed in Chapter 5, adult children may not be legally compelled to make good on parent's debt, parents may be reluctant to choose point J.[9] In the language of Chapter 5, such parents are transfer constrained. Constrained parents would like to increase child investments by making financial transfers become negative. Most investment decisions, however, have to be made while the child is a minor and thus unable to enter into legally enforceable contracts. Further, the absurdity of discussing with an elementary school child whether a tutor should be hired, for which the child, as an adult, would compensate the parents, is clear. At any rate, since children are not liable for parents' debts at death, negative transfers are not a viable option.[10]

Since a dollar's investment in human capital raises child earnings by $\$(1 + r_h)$, parents can buy an additional unit of child earnings, and therefore child consumption, by foregoing $1/(1 + r_h)$ units of own consumption. This exceeds the price to unconstrained parents, which is $1/(1 + r)$. The price of child consumption is therefore endogenous to constrained parents; as investments rise, the return falls, and the price of increasing child consumption increases.

Transfer-constrained parents maximize utility subject to the additional constraint that financial transfers are nonnegative. In Figure 6.3, this restricts the effective budget line to W_pDM. The transfer-constrained point of utility maximization is F, where the MRS = $1 + r_h$. Recall, when unconstrained parents have maximized utility, their MRS = $1 + r$. Since $r_h > r$, the utility-maximizing MRS for constrained parents exceeds that of affluent ones. Since convex indifference curves entail diminishing MRS, transfer-constrained households actually have a *higher* ratio of child to parent consumption (than unconstrained parents with the same preferences). The consumption of constrained parents equals their net-of-investment resources, whereas the child's consumption or wealth equals the child's earnings. The figure shows the positive human bequest B_p^h and the absence of a financial bequest.

The transfer-constrained solution is inefficient. For suppose parents could extend human capital investments somewhat above the constrained solution and have children, upon reaching adulthood, repay them with interest at rate r on that further investment. Such a "loan" would make children better off. On an additional $b investment, child earnings would increase by $b(1 + r_h), leaving $b(r_h − r) for increased consumption by the child. Since repayment keeps parental consumption intact and makes children better off, the "loan plan" also increases parental utility. Thus, such a policy expands the intergenerational consumption set (Drazen, 1978), making it a *potential* Pareto improvement.

This theory has interesting implications for local school finance. First, we should expect little variation in expenditures per student across unconstrained school districts. (Rich districts may, of course, be expected to have more consumption amenities per student.) Across constrained school districts, expenditures should fall with neighborhood income. Second, if states legislate minimum funding levels for schools, parents in the poorest school districts may be at a corner, wishing they could convert some of the schooling expenditures on their children into family consumption. (Some implications of statewide or centralized finance are considered in section 6.4.3.)

In Chapter 5 we learned that most parents don't leave much in the way of an *intentional* financial bequest. Further, at least some inter vivos transfers are probably motivated by exchange. This suggests the nonnegativity constraint on transfers may affect a large share of families. Indeed, Gaviria (1999) cites evidence suggesting that perhaps 40% of households are transfer constrained. Further, the fact that adults have difficulty borrowing against their *own* earnings makes it easy to understand the difficulty of arranging loans based on the future earnings of children: The future earnings of a 5-year-old boy are surely riskier than those of a 30-year-old man.

A partial solution to liquidity constraints in some families is for parents to make inter vivos transfers to young adult children. Were it not for such transfers by unconstrained parents, the proportion of young households that are liquidity constrained would surely be higher. These considerations may underlie the prevalence of "targeted" transfers from grandparents to finance grandchildren's college education. Constrained parents are less likely to receive inter vivos transfers themselves, since inter vivos transfers are received with greater frequency and in larger amounts from affluent parents (whose well-educated children are less likely to be constrained as adults). Thus, transfer-constrained parents may be forced to compound overall low investments with less than optimal timing for those investments that are made. That is, liquidity constraints may often be layered onto transfer constraints.[11]

It is easy to identify the conditions under which the transfer constraint is likely to bind (cf. Lord and Rangazas, 1993). Perhaps most important is if the parents have low earnings. The lower are parental resources, the lower are desired transfers, and the more likely it is that desired transfers fall short of the efficient investment level. Secondly, the more able is the child, the more resources the child can efficiently utilize (ability is discussed below). Finally, the more selfish or less altruistic are parents, the smaller is the share of resources devoted to children's development.

How much harm is associated with the nonnegativity constraint on financial transfers, and who suffers it? Viewing Figure 6.3, the transfer constraint eliminates the set of opportunities to the right of point D, above the earnings transformation curve, and below the market borrowing line, or W_pDN. Suppose we hold constant the shortfall of actual investment from the efficient investment. Then the reduction in child earnings is greater the more rapidly diminishing are the returns on investments. Intuitively, when returns fall off rapidly, the *average* return on the foregone investments is high, which makes for a large reduction in child earnings.

Relative to the unconstrained solution, imposition of the transfer constraint entails both wealth and substitution effects (similar to those from a change in the interest rate discussed in Chapter 1). The wealth effect arises because the budget set has been curtailed. Ceteris paribus, this reduces both investment and parent consumption. The substitution effect occurs since the constraint decreases the price of child consumption. That is, along the unconstrained budget line, the price of increasing child consumption one unit is $1/(1 + r)$ units of parental consumption. However, when facing the transfer constraint, this price is $1/(1 + r_h)$, which is lower since investments are more productive than market loans, $r_h > r$. The substitution effect favors increased investment and reduced consumption by the parents. Both the wealth and substitution effects imply reduced consumption by parents. However, these effects conflict for the child, making it unclear how the transfer constraint affects the child's well-being.

Now, if parents view child consumption as a poor substitute for own consumption, the lower price of child consumption has little impact on consumption or investment. If parents have L-shaped indifference curves, they always choose the same ratio of parent and child consumption, regardless of their relative prices. In that case, only the wealth effect operates—the substitution effect is zero. Consequently, both investments (or child consumption) and parental consumption fall so as to keep the relative consumption of parent and child unchanged.

If indifference curves are much flatter, so that parent and child consumption are close substitutes, the substitution effect is strong. In response to the lower price of child consumption, this parent can greatly limit the utility loss by substituting less expensive child consumption for own consumption. In Figure 6.3 the substitution effect dominates, so that child consumption exceeds what parents would choose if they could impose debt on children. The closer substitutes are own and child consumption, the more parents' consumption is reduced by the transfer constraint, but, ironically, the less their utility falls because they are better able to take advantage of the "price reduction."

Summarizing, if returns to scale are only slightly decreasing, the transfer constraint has only modest effects on investments (and child consumption) and the consumption of parents. If returns diminish rapidly, effects can be substantial. In general, the utility and consumption of parents is unambiguously lowered by the inability to impose debt on children to further their education. On the other hand, whether the child's wealth is lowered depends upon the parent's willingness to substitute child consumption for own consumption. If parents view these as close substitutes, parental consumption (but not utility) will decline appreciably, investments won't fall much, and the child may be better off since he or she no longer has debt to repay. (We assume the child doesn't care about parent's consumption).

We previously presented evidence that the returns to human capital investments at current investment levels are rapidly diminishing. Empirically, what do we know about the substitutability to parents of child consumption for own consumption? There is some direct evidence. Hurd (1989) estimates the parameters of a utility function that includes bequeathable wealth. Lord and Rangazas (1993) note that his estimates imply an intertemporal elasticity of substitution across generations in excess of 1. Other indirect evidence concerns the willingness to substitute own future consumption for current consumption, and the willingness to substitute charitable giving (the consumption of others who, though unknown, one cares for) for own consumption. Recent estimates of the elasticity of substitution over the life cycle tend to exceed .5 (with some approaching 1). Similarly, the price elasticity of demand for charitable giving appears to be in excess of 1, implying a large elasticity of substitution. If charitable giving is motivated by altruism, that elasticity may be below the intergenerational one, because consumption of parent and child are presumably closer substitutes than those of parent and stranger. Altogether, the limited evidence indicates that parent and child consumption are fairly substitutable, suggesting that parent consumption is reduced by the constraint.

Children *may* have higher consumption in the presence of the constraint. If this is the case, relaxing the constraint may harm children. In section 6.4 we address the implications for equity and efficiency of policies that relax the transfer constraint by redistributing tax burdens from parents to children (such as with deficit policies).

6.1.5   Comparative Statics for Affluent and Constrained Households

When both financial and human bequests are made, changes in parental or child resources have an effect quite similar to that found in the model abstracting from human bequests. Thus, an increase in W_p would increase both C_p and C_c as children share in parents' good fortune via an increased financial bequest. Similarly, should expectations of E_c be revised upward, parents would withdraw some financial support from children, with the smaller bequest allowing for increased C_p. Thus, small changes in either parent or child resources in unconstrained families are reflected in an altered financial bequest, which serves to smooth consumption over the generations. It is important to appreciate that, for households planning a financial bequest, (small) changes in resources leave the human bequest at its efficient level.

Unlike marginal changes in either parents' resources or child's exogenous finances, changes in the interest rate *do* affect the human capital accumulation of unconstrained households. Suppose, for example, that there is a reduction in the rate of taxation of interest income so that the net-of-tax interest rate r rises from r_0 to r_1. This is shown in Figure 6.4. The effective budget line before the increase in r was ABD; afterwards it is RTD. The efficient human bequest is reduced, since those investments with return below r_1 are now inefficient. Nevertheless, as we now explain, the children may be expected to benefit from the higher return to financial assets.

An increase in the interest rate lowers the price of increasing child consumption through financial transfers. The *substitution effect* associated with this price change favors increasing the now relatively less expensive child consumption at the expense of parents' own consumption. Further, the new budget line lies above the old one, so that parents are made better off (after all, there was a tax cut). Parents will want children to share in their good fortune. Thus, the *wealth effect* favors increased C_c and C_p. Both effects therefore serve to increase C_c. With the human capital bequest smaller and C_c higher, the

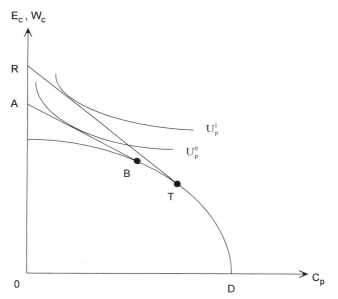

Figure 6.4 The effect of changing r

financial inheritance I_c must have risen. We *can't* say what will happen to financial bequests, though. With a higher r, even a *smaller* B_p could be consistent with a higher I_c. Since human capital transfers dominate financial ones, a marginal increase in the interest rate does not impact the transfers of constrained households.

We now consider *constrained* households. If there is an increase in parents' resources, parents will allow children to share in their good fortune. The least-cost, or most efficient, way to increase C_c is by increasing the human bequest, leaving financial bequests at zero. For the cost of increasing C_c by $1 is $1/(1 + r)$ via financial transfers, which exceeds that via human bequests, $1/(1 + r_h)$. Thus, *for transfer-constrained parents, the marginal propensity to bequeath is positive for human bequests, but zero for financial bequests.* This implies that an increase in the wealth of transfer-constrained parents should increase the quantity and quality of developmental resources.

Other aspects of the environment may also affect the rate of return on human capital investments. In particular, *skill-biased technical change* raises the return to skills. With the returns to financial transfers unaffected, among unconstrained parents this creates a portfolio effect whereby human investments are substituted for financial transfers. For constrained parents, the higher return on human capital investments makes child consumption less expensive (the substitution effect) and enlarges the opportunity set (the wealth effect). Both effects serve to increase child consumption (and therefore earnings). However, these effects conflict for parental consumption, and therefore for the human capital bequest.

6.1.6 Ability

The relative importance of nature (ability) and nurture (environment) in determining a child's life fate remains controversial. Child A is said to be of greater ability than child

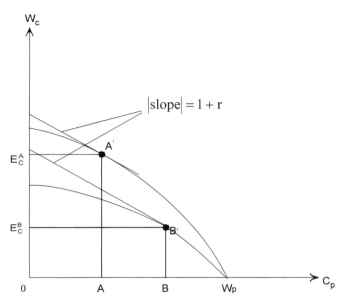

Figure 6.5 Child ability and unconstrained parents

B if A's productivity or earnings exceed B's productivity or earnings, when A and B receive equal developmental investments. More able children are assumed to assimilate schooling more easily, which raises their rate of return to education. Thus, our primary focus is on mental ability or intelligence, although physical endurance, attractiveness, and social aptitude are obviously important as well.

Figure 6.5 shows how an unconstrained parent's investments in a child depend upon the child's ability. The steeper earnings transformation curve is associated with more able child A, reflecting a greater marginal return on investments. Note that the efficient human bequest is greater for the more able child ($AW_p > BW_p$), since greater input productivity implies r_h will fall to equal r only at a higher investment level. For this reason, the more able child's earnings are larger both because of greater ability (higher earnings when investments are equal) and the larger human bequest. Since an increase in child ability makes investments more profitable, the budget set available to parents is expanded. This positive effect on dynastic wealth increases both child and parent consumption. The share of financial transfers in the portfolio of transfers may fall as parents substitute toward higher yielding human capital investments.[13]

Figure 6.6 shows how resource allocation in constrained families depends upon the abilities of their children. The steeper curve is for more able children. Therefore, a more able child expands the budget set confronting parents. This wealth effect implies, ceteris paribus, more consumption for the parent and child (than if the child were slow). Having a child with greater ability reduces the price to parents of increasing child consumption, inducing a substitution effect away from parental consumption. Both the wealth and substitution effects favor increased child consumption. However, they conflict for parental consumption, which makes the effect on the human capital bequest ambiguous: The human bequest equals parental wealth minus parental consumption; since the effect on con-

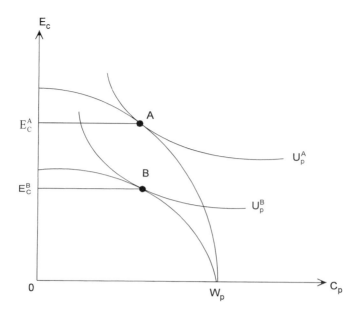

Figure 6.6 Child ability and constrained parents

sumption is ambiguous, so is the effect for investments. Nevertheless, greater child consumption means the human capital inheritance has increased.

In unconstrained families, ability alone determines schooling, with the marginal return equal to that on (equally risky) financial assets. For children of constrained households, r_h exceeds r. For this reason, comparing two children with equal education, the one from the constrained household is expected to have the higher earnings (cf. Mulligan, 1997). More generally, the fact that the returns to education depend on both ability and the amount invested presents serious problems for those attempting to estimate the return to schooling. In particular, there is long-standing concern that part of the estimated returns to schooling should in fact be attributed to "genes." That is, if able people get more education and earn more, how much of the additional earnings is due to ability, and how much to schooling? Numerous studies have attempted to "control" for ability and family background in order to determine the "true" contribution of schooling to earnings. This literature is examined in Chapter 7. For now, though, we simply note that the returns to schooling noted above are representative of studies that do control for (or purge the effects of) ability.

There is substantial evidence that cognitive ability is positively correlated across generations, as are other "endowments" such as height, weight, and athleticism. However, there appears to be appreciable regression to the mean in "endowments." That is, although Bobby Bonds and Ken Griffey Sr. may have been expected to have athletic children on the basis of their own highly successful professional baseball careers, few would have predicted the athletic success of their children, Barry Bonds and Ken Griffey Jr.

More formally, if the ability of a parent of generation t is denoted a_t, then the ability of his or her child is

$$a_{t+1} = \mathbf{a} + z(a_t - \mathbf{a}) + e$$

where **a** is average ability in the population, z is the degree of heritability, or persistence, of ability, and e is a random variable with mean of zero. Because of the random element e, it is possible (though unlikely) for dull parents to have brilliant children, or for brilliant parents to have dull children. Gaviria (1999) writes that all "the available evidence concerning both genetic and cultural transmission of endowments suggests a value" for the degree of persistence of endowments z "much smaller than 1.0, and probably smaller than 0.6" (p. 6). Limited heritability implies that the ability of children from unconstrained families may on average be less than that of their parents, while ability in constrained households may rise. For the affluent child, earnings relative to their parents' earnings would fall from both lower investments and a lower return on those investments. However, this would induce affluent parents to increase their financial transfers, limiting the decline in child consumption (see Chapter 5).

6.2 EMPIRICAL IMPLICATIONS AND EVIDENCE

6.2.1 Intergenerational Mobility of Earnings and Education

This Becker-Tomes theory of altruistic transfers has important implications for both the extent of intergenerational mobility and the amount of inequality within families. Solon (1999) provides an intuitive illustration of the links between intergenerational mobility and overall inequality: Contrast two societies with the same distribution of income and therefore the same degree of inequality. In society A one's relative position in the earnings distribution is exactly inherited from one's parents. That is, if your parents were in the 80th (20th) percentile of earnings in their generation, you will be in exactly the 80th (20th) percentile of earnings in your generation. "As far as earnings are concerned, society A is an extreme caste society" (p. 1). In contrast, members of society B experience complete intergenerational mobility: The children of parents who were in the 80th (20th) percentile of earnings will themselves have the same distribution of earnings as children whose parents were in the 20th (80th) percentile.

Under what conditions is a society more like A than B? For now, suppose everyone receives the optimal investment (we won't worry about the transfer constraint). First imagine there is no market luck, that ability and tastes are completely inherited, and that the earnings transformation curve is unchanging across generations (no economic growth). This case corresponds to a caste society such as A in which the distribution of income, wealth, consumption, and so on, is the same as the distribution of ability. In contrast, suppose that there is no tendency for ability to be inherited, there exists substantial market luck, and there is no inheritance of financial earnings. Such a society would, like B, have perfect intergenerational mobility. It may be that mobility makes people more tolerant of inequality, so that even more inequality could prove acceptable if it were accompanied by greater mobility.

What are the implications of the Becker-Tomes framework for intergenerational mobility? Recall that in affluent households investments in children are determined by efficiency (and therefore ability) alone; investments stop when the return to investments falls to equal that on financial assets. For such households, there is no marginal *direct* effect of parental earnings on child earnings (the marginal propensity to investment from parental wealth is zero). However, there is an indirect effect due to the positive correlation between the ability of parents and their children. Affluent parents are more likely to have had high ability, which contributed to their high achieved schooling and high earnings. Their children, due to regression to the mean, tend to have lower ability than their parents, though still above average. Since investments among such families are determined by efficiency alone, investments fully adjust to the now lower, efficient level. (Parents are predicted to partially cushion the decline in child consumption by increasing financial transfers.)

Conversely, the children of parents with low earnings enjoy greater ability, on average, than did their parents. There is also a direct effect of parental earnings on investments in constrained households (the marginal propensity to bequeath human capital is positive). This dependence of investments on parental wealth implies sluggishness in the regression to the mean, which is absent in affluent households. Therefore, the Becker-Tomes framework implies that *earnings are predicted to regress to the mean less quickly among poor or constrained families than among affluent or unconstrained families.* That is, the transfer constraint increases the extent to which the society is more like type A than type B.

Gaviria (1999) notes that

> The additional sensitivity of children's earnings to parental earnings in 'poor' families can be interpreted as a measure of inequality of opportunity. If there were equal access to education, all families would invest the efficient level of human capital, and earnings would regress to the mean at similar rates for both "rich" and "poor" families. Without equal access, family wealth matters and children from "rich" parents enjoy a clear advantage in their quest for socioeconomic success. (p. 9)

There are important policy implications associated with the presence of the constraint and the degree to which it binds. With no constraint, the intergenerational transmission of earnings is driven entirely by the inheritance of endowments and market luck. Suppose one makes the additional assumption that cognitive ability is the crucial endowment, as do Herrnstein and Murray in their book *The Bell Curve* (1994). Then, policies aimed at increasing access to education for the children of poor families could be *detrimental* to efficiency, so an equity objective may be better served by other types of redistribution. Equity and efficiency implications of policies in the *presence* of the transfer constraint are taken up in section 6.4.

Several economists have attempted to test empirically for the presence of transfer-constrained households. Such tests can be explained in terms of the simple model

$$\ln E_{t+1} = c + \beta \ln E_t + \text{other terms}$$

where β measures the persistence of earnings across generations. Expressing the relationship in terms of log earnings makes for easy interpretation, since β is then the elasticity of a child's earnings with respect to a 1% change in parent's earnings. For example, suppose that $\beta = .4$ and consider a father whose earnings are 10% above the (log) mean of earnings. His child's earnings would then be predicted to be $\beta(10\%)$ or 4% above the mean. Since they would have regressed $(1 - \beta)$ or 60 percent of the way back to the mean, $1 - \beta$ is a measure of intergenerational mobility, while β measures the persistence of earnings.

The Becker-Tomes model predicts greater persistence of earnings (higher β) among transfer-constrained families. Precise and unbiased estimates of β require good measures of the earnings of successive generations and a proper sorting into constrained and unconstrained households. The PSID now has observations on earnings for several years of parents and children, enabling fairly good estimates of the average or permanent earnings for each generation (cf. Solon, 1999). How the sample is partitioned between constrained and unconstrained family types is less straightforward in practice, if not in theory. Since unconstrained households make the fully efficient investments in their children's development, theory suggests that that group be selected on the basis of provision of inter vivos gifts or bequests (assuming these are motivated by altruism). However, inter vivos transfers have been measured in only one wave of the PSID and, as McGarry (1997) shows, there is substantial changeover across years in the recipients. Further, many of the parents remain alive, so some planned transfers have not yet been made.

Mulligan (1997) partitions households into the constrained and unconstrained camps on the basis of whether children *expect* to receive an inheritance in excess of \$25,000. Intuitively, if children expect at least a modest bequest, Mulligan concludes that the parents must be intending to bequeath and were therefore unconstrained during the investment years. With this method of splitting samples he finds little difference in the extent to which "constrained" and "unconstrained" families regress to the mean. However, his expected inheritance criterion is suspect on a couple of grounds. Most important, young adults may have little understanding of how much their parents will leave behind. Indeed, Gaviria (1999) reports that the "correlation coefficient between expected and actual inheritances in the PSID is either -0.05 or 0.08 depending upon whether inheritances smaller than \$25,000 are taken into account" (p. 20, fn 11). Since expected inheritances are essentially unrelated to actual inheritances, there is little reason to expect that grouping households by expected inheritance correctly identifies constrained and unconstrained families. Clearly, we should like to know whether Mulligan's results prove robust to alternative ways to classify households.

Gaviria tackles this issue, again employing data from the PSID but using different criteria for inclusion in the "rich" families subsample: Children must have reported *receipt* of inheritances worth \$10,000 or more in the previous five years (from 1989) *or* they must have parents who reported a net worth in excess of \$100,000 in 1988. While one may quibble with these selection criteria, they have the obvious virtue of being based on magnitudes received (rather than amounts expected in the perhaps distant future).

Unlike Mulligan, Gaviria finds strong support for the greater persistence of earnings among less affluent households. Consider his findings based on the most nationally representative subsample of the PSID for fathers and sons. Then, averaging across the three estimation techniques he employs, β equals .41 for his constrained sample but only .22 among those designated as unconstrained. Thus, Gaviria finds almost twice as much persistence of earnings among transfer-constrained households! Not only do his results offer strong support for the predictions of the Becker-Tomes framework, they also suggest a potential role for government policies that provide developmental resources for children of poor parents, if not for the parents themselves (see section 6.4.2). However, even if one believes that the classification system of Gaviria is superior to that employed by Mulligan, there is a clear need to learn whether Gaviria's results are robust (to yet more convincing selection criteria and alternative data sets).

In the Becker-Tomes framework, once parental wealth becomes high enough to induce the efficient investment, further increases have no impact on schooling (abstracting from the consumption benefits from schooling). On the other hand, among constrained households, years of completed schooling is predicted to rise with parental wealth. This is just a rephrasing of the result that the marginal propensity to bequeath human capital is positive among the constrained, but zero among the unconstrained. There is modest support for this prediction.

First, Tomes (1981) found that the correlation between an adult child's educational attainment and his or her parent's income is positive and stronger for children not receiving a financial inheritance. Among families leaving a bequest, family income was found to have no significant effect on years of schooling in his probate sample (i.e., using information about the estates of the deceased). This issue was also addressed by Mulligan in the study discussed above. Consistent with the findings of Tomes, Mulligan finds that there is greater sensitivity of education to parental income among those households he identifies as being constrained than among the unconstrained. However, once again there are questions about whether Mulligan has in fact correctly identified constrained and unconstrained households.

Even if one concludes that the predicted correlation does obtain, this does not *necessarily* imply that it is due to the borrowing constraint. For example, Cameron and Heckman (1998) argue that the less affluent may acquire less college education because they face lower returns to schooling rather than because they are unable to borrow in financial markets. If these lower returns are due to lower ability, transfer constraints may be unimportant. If they are due to poor preparation (low investments) at young ages, then transfer constraints are implicated. The financing of college involves parents, adult children, government, and sometimes employers. Cameron and Heckman's arguments are pursued further in Chapter 7 where college education is discussed.

Overall, the implications of the Becker-Tomes framework regarding greater persistence of earnings among the poor and also greater sensitivity of investments (schooling) to parental wealth among the poor are supported. Although the findings of Gaviria are yet to be replicated, the available empirical evidence adds to the intuitive appeal of the framework.

6.2.2   Distribution within the Family

The Becker-Tomes model also has interesting implications for the distribution of earnings within affluent and transfer-constrained families. Generalizing to two children enables us to make the new points. As in Chapter 5, parental preferences are now given by

$$U_p = U_p(C_p, W_c^1, W_c^2)$$

where now the wealth of child 1 and child 2 enter separately. Also as in Chapter 5, parents have equal concern for each child, so that the marginal utility to parents of child wealth is the same for each child (when each child has the same wealth). Assuming diminishing marginal utility of child wealth, parents have some innate aversion to inequality. The implications of this aversion differ between constrained and unconstrained families.

Among unconstrained households, the model predicts that neither efficiency nor equity is compromised. If each child is of equal ability, each receives equal investments and (if market luck is unimportant) equal financial transfers. Suppose instead that child 1 is more able. Then, child 1 is predicted to earn more because of both higher ability and completion of more schooling. However, the parent is predicted to equalize wealth across the children through greater financial transfers to child 2.

Now consider constrained families. If child 1 is more able, there is a fundamental tension between equity and efficiency. For suppose the parent pursues efficiency alone, equating r_h^1 to r_h^2. Then the earnings of the more able child may be much greater than those of the less able sibling, because the ability differential is amplified by greater investments. Instead, let the parent value only equity. Then the earnings of each child will be equalized, but at the expense of efficiency: the marginal return on investments is greater for the more able than for the less able child (and above r for each). Since the parent is by assumption at least somewhat risk averse, we expect a compromise, with the more able child having greater earnings, but also a greater earnings loss on the last dollar of investment *not* made. Stafford (1996) discusses evidence concerning the equity-efficiency trade-off when children are young. He reports that parents increase the time spent aiding children upon learning they are performing poorly in grade school. Further, studies of families with a Down's syndrome child suggest an "equity tax": higher investments in this child come partly at the expense of higher ability siblings.

The theory also predicts greater earnings inequality among siblings in affluent than in constrained families. This arises because the full implications for earnings of ability differentials are allowed to play out in unconstrained families, with financial transfers equalizing wealth. In contrast, in constrained households ability differentials are partially muted because of the inability to use financial transfers to equalize wealth.[14] Assuming that years of schooling constitute a good proxy for human capital investments, the model also predicts greater schooling inequality for affluent than for poor households.

Gaviria (1999) also tests these implications of the Becker-Tomes model, using criteria to classify rich and poor households similar to those used in his analysis of intergenerational mobility. Here the results are in general *not* supportive. He finds that inequality in earnings and in schooling within families is largely independent of family wealth.

Given our discussion in Chapter 5, this refutation of the implications for *within*-family distribution is not terribly surprising. By Becker-Tomes, financial transfers, whether inter vivos or bequests, are altruistically motivated and used to increase and equalize child wealth. However, recall that for the most part bequests are evenly divided among children. Further, although inter vivos transfers are disproportionately awarded to lower earning children, the magnitude of those transfers is far too small to offset earnings differentials. Since unconstrained parents do not plan to equalize wealth via financial transfers, it is unsurprising that they may curb schooling differentials implied by efficiency alone.

Gaviria (p. 28) notes that there are many stories that could be spun (or theories developed) that would prove consistent with the observed patterns of earnings and schooling. Here is one such story. Suppose parents care about the *potential* wealth or utility rather than simply actual life wealth of children (as briefly discussed in Chapter 5). Children with similar potential wealth may have unequal earnings due to different choices regarding leisure consumption and/or compensating differentials in earnings due to unequal job amenities. Further, parents may be reluctant to pass judgment either on the ability of children, when making investments when the children are young, or on the level of childrens' well-being (utility), when deciding on financial transfers. In this expanded conception of altruism, investments and transfers would be similar across children, in spite of modest differences in their ability and even more significant differences in their earnings.

6.3 THE CONTRIBUTION OF EDUCATION TO U.S. GROWTH FROM 1870 TO 1970

The average growth rate of per capita income in the United States over the last century has been about 1.8% and has shown but modest fluctuation about that trend. This suggests to some observers that the U.S. economy has been at or close to its steady state path over this period. However, steady state growth is by definition "balanced," so that investment shares from GDP, for example, are unchanging (see Chapter 3). In fact, though, the period from 1870 to 1970 was a period of dramatically increased investment of time and money in the accumulation of human capital. For example, Goldin and Katz (1997) find the high school graduation rate rose from less than 5% to almost 80% between 1910 and 1970.

With such rapidly rising investments in human capital, it seems unrealistic to view this as an interval of steady state growth. Another interpretation of the relatively steady growth from 1870 to 1970 is that the steady state growth rate is below 1.8%, but that increased human capital accumulation has made the interval look like a steady state. By this story, diminishing returns to physical capital have been offset by increased skills per worker, with these skills complementary to physical capital. A similar argument is made by Jones (2000) concerning the United States since 1960. He points to transitional increases in college enrollments and the share of scientists and engineers (R & D workers) in the labor force.

The relative contributions of transitional and steady state growth to observed growth was initially considered in Chapter 3. There, we first developed a neoclassical growth model based on *physical* capital accumulation. In that model steady state growth in income per capita was driven solely by exogenous technological change. However, living standards could also advance due to transitional dynamics, when a low capital to labor ratio induces faster than steady state capital accumulation. Theoretical simulations by King and Rebelo (1993) were cited showing transitional physical capital accumulation incapable of explaining much growth in the United States between 1870 and 1970. Requiring substantial transitional growth based on physical capital alone produced counterfactual implications for interest rates (i.e., the marginal product of capital) and capital accumulation. For example, King and Rebelo note that "if the initial capital stock is very low so that accumulation is important for growth, then its initial marginal product is correspondingly very high" (p. 909).

They suggest that growth theorists shift their attention to either human capital accumulation or endogenous technical progress. Chapter 3 briefly considered a formulation that included human capital. However, human capital was assumed to rise mechanically with income, rather than being based on optimizing behavior by households. In that framework, significant transitional growth did not have counterfactual implications for the interest rate. It is unclear, though, whether similar results obtain when human capital is accumulated by households actively maximizing utility. We now consider whether an empirically grounded version of the Becker-Tomes framework developed earlier in this chapter can, once joined to a model of the macro economy, contribute much to our understanding of longer term U.S. growth.

Rangazas (2000b) constructs a neoclassical growth model employing household foundations similar to those of section 6.1. After calibrating that framework using the available empirical findings, he simulates the model to ascertain whether the increase in the quantity and quality of primary and secondary education in the United States is capable of explaining much of the growth between 1870 and 1970 without entailing counterfactual implications. Viewing human capital deepening as arising from family investments is appropriate for the period from 1870 to 1970, which includes the end of the rise of primary education, the "high school movement" of the early twentieth century, and the beginnings of a similarly revolutionary college movement. The increase in college enrollment and graduation rates continued beyond 1970 (and may be ongoing still). However, some portion of undergraduate training, and much of graduate training, may better be viewed as investments in self undertaken by young, economically independent adults. To that extent, an explanation of the expansion of college requires a model of human capital accumulation in adulthood, as developed in Chapter 7.

Suppose the rise in family human capital investments was important to growth over that period. Are those investments best viewed as having been on average efficient, as in households making financial transfers, or inefficiently low, due to a binding transfer constraint? Rangazas models the transition under both assumptions, allowing the simulations to suggest the answer. His macroeconomic framework is similar to that developed in Chapter 3, with the addition of endogenous human capital.[15] The aggregate production function is Cobb-Douglas, with constant returns to scale in physical capital K and effective labor H. Thus, in period t

$$Y_t = K_t^{\alpha} H_t^{1-\alpha}$$

or, in intensive form

$$y_t \equiv (K_t/H_t)^{\alpha} = k_t^{\alpha}$$

where y and k are output and capital per unit of effective labor. As in Chapter 3, output per unit of effective labor increases with the ratio of capital to effective labor. The parameter α determines the shares of GDP received by capital (α) and labor ($1 - \alpha$), and the elasticity of output with respect to each.

Adults are assumed to work (full-time) for two periods. Letting $L_t(L_{t-1})$ be the number of young workers entering the labor force in period $t(t - 1)$ and $h_t(h_{t-1})$ be the number of units of human capital a worker entering the labor force in $t(t - 1)$ has, the aggregate effective labor supply in period t may be written

$$H_t = L_t h_t + L_{t-1} h_{t-1}$$

Input markets are perfectly competitive, so that physical capital is paid its rate of return, the interest rate r_t, while the wage per unit of effective labor is w_t. The wage is positively related to the capital to effective labor ratio, while the interest rate is negatively related. (Chapter 3 develops the theory of factor market equilibrium in detail).

On the basis of the empirical literature, Rangazas supposes human capital accumulation is produced in the following manner:

$$h_{t+1} = (B_{pt}^h)^a h_{t,avg}^b D_t^{1-a-b}$$

where B_{pt}^h is the goods purchased by parents as inputs in their dependent child's human capital development, $h_{t,avg}$ is the *average* stock of human capital in the parent's generation, and D_t is the stock of disembodied technical knowledge available at time t (which is assumed to grow at a constant percentage rate). The average human capital of the parents' generation is a spillover effect that boosts the productivity of goods inputs.[16] The exponents indicate that there are constant returns to scale in technical knowledge, goods inputs, and the average human capital of "teachers."

However, there are diminishing returns to goods and human capital taken together. For this reason, there is no steady state growth in per capita variables unless exogenous technological advance is positive. Therefore, this is not a model of *endogenous* steady state growth. From his review of the literature, Rangazas considers both a "high returns" case where a = .15 and b = .25 and a "low returns" case, with a = .10 and b = .20. The fact that the sum of returns to reproducible inputs, equal to a + b for goods and human capital, is *far* below 1 implies *rapidly* diminishing returns. This severely constrains the potential for increasing per capita income through human capital deepening provided by the family.

Each generation is economically active for three periods, consuming in each, though retired in the third. Parents maximize a standard three-period utility function by choosing consumption in each period, investments in the child's development B_{pt}^h, and perhaps a financial transfer. As motivated earlier in the chapter, B_{pt}^h explicitly incorporates schooling expenditures.

As in King and Rebelo, Rangazas requires transitional growth to explain only half of the observed growth between 1870 and 1970. This demands transitional growth to be quantitatively important, but also acknowledges the significance of steady state growth. Rangazas presents several stylized facts any model explaining growth as resulting from the expansion of human capital should be able to explain. First is the rapid rise in the quantity and quality of primary and secondary education over this period. For example, the ratio of primary and secondary education spending to GDP rose from a bit less than 1% to about 3.5% over that period. This was associated with spending per child that in 1970 was 14.5 times that in 1870 (in real terms). Also, there has been little trend in the output to capital ratio or the interest rate over that period.

There are three possible regimes in his framework. The first is essentially the King-Rebelo model of physical capital accumulation. This is obtained by setting a = b = 0 in equation (6.5), which eliminates any role for human capital. The results of this framework are the "straw man" with which the versions with human capital are compared. A second model assumes efficient human capital investments by parents in their children. Unlike the unconstrained households that undertake the efficient investments earlier in this chapter, here the efficient investments are undertaken *even if financial transfers are required to be negative.* The final case respects the transfer constraint. This may prohibit some or all generations of parents from making efficient investments in their children. We are especially interested in whether it proves important to acknowledge the transfer constraint when assessing if human capital bequests are consistent with significant, noncounterfactual, transitional growth.

Modeling the transition as a function of physical capital deepening alone (regime 1) is unsuccessful. As found by King and Rebelo, requiring physical capital accumulation to explain a substantial portion of growth produces counterfactually high interest rates at the beginning of the transition analysis. Rangazas' calibrated model produces an (average annualized) interest rate of 17.2% for the start of the transition, far in excess of the 6.5% steady state rate, and far above what is known of the marginal product of capital at that time.

The first human capital case assumes human capital investments in children are made at the efficient level. Even though human capital is efficient, its rate of growth exceeds that in the steady state due to a transitorily high spillover effect, as explained below. Since the capital to effective labor ratio grows rapidly during the transition, the potential earnings of children greatly exceed the actual earnings of parents. For this reason, the efficient investment level of 1870 would imply *negative and substantial* financial transfers. In recent years large positive financial transfers *from children to parents* are rare. However, in earlier times in-kind repayments by children (such as shared housing and personal care) were more prevalent. In any event, in the general-equilibrium model, the promise of financial repayments by children keeps parent's savings and overall capital accumulation low. Therefore, once again the interest rates early in the transition are counterfactually high, *averaging* more than 10% over the period from 1870 to 1890.

Nevertheless, this is an improvement relative to regime 1, where the interest rate averaged 13.4% over that same interval. Intuitively, since human capital now contributes part of the transitional growth, less is required of physical capital. For this reason there can be more physical capital and a lower interest rate at the start of the transition than when physical capital deepening alone had to account for the transitional growth. This consideration more than offsets the fact that large investments in children, and the promise of positive transfers from them later in life, lowers savings when parents are young.

The high interest rate early in the transition corresponds to a low wage per unit of human capital. As physical capital accumulates, the interest rate falls and the wage rate rises. Both of these encourage additional human capital accumulation. Further, as investments rise between periods, so does average human capital, so that the spillover limits the decline in the productivity of the goods input. This also induces larger investments. Nevertheless, efficient human capital investments result in too little of an upward trend in the expenditure share from GDP. Similarly, expenditures per student rise to only six times the initial level (compared with over 14 in the data).

The third regime, where human capital is inefficiently low, proves the most satisfactory. As Rangazas notes, the transfer constraint is more likely to bind when the current generation's *actual* earnings are sufficiently low relative to the *potential* earnings of the next generation. Since parents cannot safely lend to children, financial transfers equal zero (not negative as in regime 2) and child investments are lower. Compared with the case with efficient investments, this increases the savings of young parents, making for a lower interest rate early in the transition. In fact, over the period 1870–1890 the interest rate is quite close to its steady state value of 6.5%. Thus, the counterfactual implications for interest rates of the physical capital model are essentially eliminated.

The transfer-constrained regime also outperforms the efficient human capital version with respect to educational investments. Expenditure shares from GDP now rise more rapidly, more than doubling over the course of the transition. As when investments were efficient, the anticipation of rising wages per unit of human capital for children encourages more investment. However, unlike the efficient human capital regime, the investments by constrained parents increase as their income rises (which relaxes the transfer constraint). The rising expenditure share is reflected in the increase in spending per student, which for one set of parameters rises a bit more, and for another a bit less, than the 14.5 times seen in the data.

The transfer-constrained model performs quite well in these simulations. Therefore, it appears as though neoclassical human and physical capital accumulation can explain a significant share of U.S. growth between 1870 and 1970 without producing counterfactual implications for interest rates, or for primary and secondary school spending. However, it proves important to take seriously the nonnegativity constraint on financial transfers. Also, in the simulations of Rangazas, human capital investment levels in dependent children had become close to their efficient levels by 1970. This suggests that future transitional growth must arise from other sources. One natural candidate is increases in post-dependency human capital accumulation. In fact, college attendance and graduation have both risen significantly in recent decades. However, as explained in the next chapter, the opportunity cost to adults of attending college includes greater foregone earnings than is the case for primary and secondary students (whose foregone earnings were ignored above). Thus, it *may* be difficult for further educational deepening to temporarily raise growth rates far above the steady state level. We return to this in Chapter 7.

6.4 POLICY APPLICATIONS

6.4.1 Ricardian Equivalence and Human Capital Bequests

In Chapter 5 we noted that it is necessary to take private transfer responses into account when assessing government policies that redistribute resources across generations. For example, among extended families where parents are making altruistically motivated financial transfers to their adult children (and there is no uncertainty), changes in transfers completely offset any redistribution of resources imposed by the government. This is the Ricardian equivalence result. However, among households unconnected by altruistic money transfers, the consumption of parents and their adult children would change by the same amount as, and in the same direction of, the government redistribution. Do the theoretical implications of such policies change when the earnings of children are determined endogenously by parental investments?

Ricardian equivalence does continue to obtain for households connected by financial transfers over and above the efficient human capital bequest. For such households, intergenerational redistribution simply moves the net-of-tax endowment point along the *linear* portion of the parent's budget constraint. Since neither the feasible consumption set nor preferences have changed, parents choose the same levels of consumption for themselves and their child as before. In this case, bequests change so as to neutralize the redistribution introduced by the redistributive policy.

However, the results among transfer-constrained parents are affected by the inclusion of human capital bequests. To appreciate why, consider a $b tax cut to the parent financed by a $b(1 + r) tax increase on the child in the next period. Such a policy constitutes a *potential* Pareto improvement: Parents *could* maintain own consumption and invest $b in the child's human capital, while the increased child earnings would allow the child to pay the $b(1 + r) in additional taxes and still increase consumption by $b(r_h − r).

However, the policy has an additional effect, which is to increase the price of child consumption. That price increases as investments are expanded (and r_h falls) in response to the policy. Thus, policies that relax the transfer constraint introduce both wealth *and* substitution effects. The wealth effect, due to the expanded opportunity set, increases child consumption. The substitution effect, though, serves to reduce the now more expensive child consumption.

Lord and Rangazas (1993) assess the effects of a marginal relaxation of the transfer constraint. To do so, they calibrate a general-equilibrium simulation model consisting entirely of transfer-constrained households, employing information on parent time and goods expenditures on children, as well as preference and production function parameters. They then conduct the type of government "loan" or tax policy discussed above. The strength of the substitution effect depends on two factors. First is the extent of the "price" increase, which is greater the lower are the returns to scale in the production of child human capital. Second is the parent's sensitivity to this price increase, which is greater the closer substitutes are parent and child consumption in the parent's utility function. The wealth effect is stronger the more r_h exceeds r in the absence of the policy. This difference is greater the faster returns to investments fall and the greater the shortfall of the initial to the efficient investment.

Lord and Rangazas' simulation results reveal that the most probable outcome of such a policy is for child consumption to *fall*. Investments and child earnings do increase, but not enough for the child to maintain consumption after paying the additional tax. Thus, although the policy is a *potential* Pareto Improvement, parents allow their consumption to rise at the expense of their children. As in Chapter 5 among transfer-constrained households where child earnings were exogenous, Ricardian equivalence fails such that children suffer from programs such as unfunded Social Security, expansions to Medicare, and federal budget deficits.

6.4.2   Intragenerational Redistribution

Government also redistributes *intra*generationally through its social insurance, or "safety net," programs such as welfare (formerly AFDC), food stamps, Medicaid, and some features of the Social Security system. This subsection examines the equity and efficiency implications of a simple government redistribution from an unconstrained to a transfer-constrained household.

Suppose both households have identical preferences and children of equal ability. Then the difference in their transfer behavior arises from the greater life wealth of the unconstrained household. Inequality in the parents' generation spills over into the children's generation as children from "poor" families receive lower human capital bequests and no financial transfers.

One efficiency measure of this policy's impact is the change in dynastic wealth across all families. In each family, dynastic wealth exceeds parent's wealth W_p by the "profits" from investing in child human capital. These profits equal the present value of child earnings minus the investment in human capital. In unconstrained families, the efficient human bequest where $r = r_h$ is undertaken, so dynastic wealth is maximized in the absence of policy. Among constrained households, investments cease where $r_h > r$, so that wealth could be increased by further investments. (Such parents don't expand investments because their own consumption is low, making its marginal utility high.)

Now suppose an affluent household is taxed $b in lump-sum fashion, with the proceeds transferred to a transfer-constrained household. This policy certainly reduces inequality in the parents' generation. Less clear are the implications for inequality in the children's generation and for overall economic efficiency. In unconstrained families, parents' wealth falls by $b, the amount of the tax increase. These affluent parents will cushion the effect of the tax on own consumption by reducing their *financial* transfer. The human bequest and earnings of the child are unaffected. Consequently, dynastic wealth falls by $b in the unconstrained household. Parental wealth rises by $b for constrained parents, part of which they share with their child. Since they are transfer constrained, they increase their human bequest. But with $r_h > r$, dynastic wealth is increased by $[b + fb(r_h - r)/(1 + r)]$, where f is the portion of the transfer invested in the child.

Since dynastic wealth of the constrained family rises by more than it falls in the unconstrained family, the policy enhances efficiency (cf. Becker, 1991). This conclusion is in sharp contrast to the traditional notion of a trade-off between equity and efficiency; that in the process of making the shares of the economic pie more equal, some (perhaps sizeable) crumbs are lost.[17]

The results may be much different if this policy is expected to be "permanent" rather than "temporary" (cf. Rangazas, 1991). To appreciate why, suppose now parents expect this transferring of $b from the "rich" to the "poor" will be repeated when the children are adults. Now, current transfer-constrained parents appreciate that their children, upon reaching adulthood, will receive a $b transfer, just as they did. This will induce current parents to *reduce* the human bequest relative to when parents thought their generation alone was receiving a transfer. Consequently, for a permanent policy there may be little effect on the human bequest, and thus much of the efficiency gain associated with the "temporary" policy is lost. Similarly, unconstrained parents will revise their planned financial bequest upward in appreciation that their children will also be taxed. Thus, there also may be little effect on financial bequests when both generations are taxed. Overall, the "permanent" policy continues to reduce inequality, but may have only modest efficiency effects.

6.4.3 Education Finance, Inequality, and Economic Growth

Economists have recently begun to combine discussions of school finance, inequality, and economic growth. Of particular interest are the implications for equity, efficiency, and economic growth of converting from a system of local school finance to one of state (or national) finance. These issues are important, since in recent times opponents of local school financing of public schools have successfully challenged the constitutionality of such financing in 16 states (Murray, Evans, and Schwab, 1998). We mention only a few results from this recent, yet rapidly growing, literature (cf. Benabou, 1996, and Glomm and Rvikumar, 1992).

As noted in section 6.1, the financing of local schools through local property taxation encourages parents to sort into school districts on the basis of income: Affluent parents spend more on their children, both because they can afford the efficient level of financing and because their on-average high-ability children make that efficient level high. Transfer-constrained parents desire lower property taxes and school expenditures because they cannot "afford" even the lower efficient level of expenditures associated with their on-average lower ability children.

Sorting into homogeneous neighborhoods is further encouraged if there are important positive spillovers from classmates and these spillovers are positively correlated with the parental income of classmates. For example, a given student may benefit more from interacting with a bright student whose affluent family has provided him or her with rich experiences than from interacting with an average student. The most affluent parents would then desire their children to have as classmates the children of other equally affluent households. Further, the mixing of students of different economic backgrounds, and therefore on average different ability, could impose a drag on efficiency in human capital production: With heterogeneous students, the "curriculum" may be too slow for able students and too fast for those less able. Summarizing, local school finance may result in parents sorting into school districts by income, with students from affluent families receiving large, efficient investments based on their parent's wealth and on their own and their classmates' high ability. Differential schooling investments, compounded by differences in ability and in peer effects, may produce appreciable income inequality when the students become adults.

In this context, consider a movement to statewide financing of local schools that equalizes spending across school districts. Suppose taxes to finance schooling increase with household income. This increases the price of schooling to affluent parents, since some of their tax monies now support the education of less affluent students. Likewise, this lowers the price of schooling to constrained parents, who now receive greater schooling expenditures per tax dollar than before. Equalizing schooling expenditures should reduce the inequality in educational outcomes. It also reduces the benefits of residential segregation by income. The efficiency effects are less clear. On one hand, efficiency is raised by better schooling for students from transfer-constrained families. On the other hand, the benefits from fine-tuning the curriculum and from complementarities in classmate ability are compromised if diversity increases within school districts.

However, inequality in schooling outcomes may also have implications for efficiency in production. To understand why, suppose that all education and therefore skill levels are complementary in aggregate production. "This complementarity captures the idea that poorly educated, insufficiently skilled production or clerical workers will drag down the productivity of engineers, managers, doctors, and so on" (Benabou, 1996, p. 587). If complementarities in production are quite strong, the homogenizing effect on skill attainment of statewide school financing may be growth enhancing. Clearly, though, the effects of school financing on efficiency, growth, and inequality will depend upon the relative strength of these various interactions in schooling and production. Benabou models many of the elements discussed above, using explicit functional forms and incorporating "market luck." He finds that movement from local to state financing may slow growth in the short run. However, when complementaries are relatively strong in production, growth will be faster in the long run. At this point, theory is sufficiently ahead of our empirical knowledge to prohibit meaningful policy conclusions. The importance of the issues involved suggests this literature may progress rapidly.

6.5 SUMMARY

Families play a large role in the determination of their offspring's economic life fate. To analyze this role, we presented a model due to Becker and Tomes, evaluated its implications, and considered extensions to economic growth and public policy. In their framework, the earnings of children are strongly affected both by the genetic and cultural inheritance the children receive from parents and by the investments parents make in children's development. With diminishing returns on investments, there is an efficient level beyond which financial transfers are more productive than development investments. Affluent parents desire to spend more on their children than the efficient investment costs, so they supplement with financial transfers. Since parents can't commit their children to repay them if they increase investments to the point of efficiency, "poor" parents are transfer constrained. In such households, children receive too little education and parents sacrifice by devoting a smaller share of parental wealth to parental consumption. Ability is assumed to regress to the mean across generations. The model implies that children born to poor parents experience less upward mobility, due to the transfer constraint, than children born to affluent parents exhibit downward mobility. In general, the empirical evidence appears to support this contention.

The fact that many households apparently are transfer constrained currently, in spite of dramatically higher wealth and educational expenditure levels, suggests that transfer constraints may have been of great importance earlier in U.S. history. Rangazas shows that the expansion of primary and secondary education in the United States over the period from 1870 to 1970 may help explain a sizeable portion of U.S. growth over that period. In his framework, rising family income in the presence of inefficiently low educational investments allowed for an interval of transitional growth above the longer term growth potential. Applications of the Becker-Tomes Model were also made to both intragenerational and intergenerational redistributive policies.

One-time intragenerational policies were shown to enhance both equity and efficiency. If a policy is instead "permanent" (becomes institutionalized), the efficiency gains largely disappear. Assuming transfer constraints are pervasive, policies that shift the nation's tax burden from older to younger and to as yet unborn households have the potential to increase the welfare of all generations. In practice the policy may not have this effect. Since the policies saddle children with higher future taxes, parents must invest more in children to bequeath any level of after-tax earnings. However, due to diminishing returns on investments, the price to parents of increasing children's after-tax earnings is raised. The discouraging effect of this on investments apparently leads parents to increase investments by less than the amount necessary to offset the higher tax burden: Deficit policies may increase parent's consumption at the expense of children's consumption (though by less than if the generations were not altruistically connected).

Subsequent chapters extend this discussion in various directions. Chapter 7 develops the theory and evidence of human capital investments by young adults in themselves, after they have become economically independent. Chapter 9 extends the theory of parental altruism to fertility decisions, so that parents care not only about the earnings of each child, but also about the number of children they bear.

ENDNOTES

1. My thoughts about these issues and the style of presentation were strongly influenced by Davies and St. Hilaire (1987) and Solon (1999), and especially by conversations with Peter Rangazas. See also the survey by Behrman (1997).

2. There is also a similar correlation between the earnings of sisters. The correlation between the earnings of brothers and sisters is a bit lower, perhaps reflecting the effect on hours and years worked of sisters assuming greater family responsibilities.

3. Gokhale, Kotlikoff, Sefton and Weale (1999) present simulations showing that marital sorting is a more important source of inequality than is differential transmission of financial bequests.

4. Solon (1999) argues that these richer data sets overcome substantial problems associated with many earlier studies. First, much previous work needed to rely on parent and adult child income measures for a single year only, which is a poor measure of the long-term average, or permanent, incomes of each. By mismeasuring permanent incomes, these studies understated the correlation between the incomes of parents and their children. Second, earlier research was often based on data sets that were more homogeneous than is the general population. In such data there is less underlying variability to begin with, because other family background determinants of income are unusually similar. Once again, this biased downward the correlation between earnings across generations. Intuitively, in a homogeneous sample in which even unrelated families resemble each other, the resemblance among generations will appear less striking. Becker and Tomes' (1986) review of this earlier literature led them to say, "The point estimates for most of the studies indicate that a 10% increase in father's earnings (or income) raises son's earnings by less than 2%." This corresponds to an intergenerational earnings elasticity of .2, about half of that found in more recent studies.

5. These arguments draw heavily from Rangazas (2000a). Of course, parents (like economists) may not know the efficient level of expenditures per child! Parents are also risk averse, which may offer a different explanation for the efforts of affluent parents to be in "safe" schools (perceived as ones devoid of children from poor family settings). The existence of private schools complicates the "neighborhood sorting" model discussed above, without overturning its primary implications. Similarly, an increasing number of states have moved *incrementally* toward central financing, or expenditure equalization. Since such financing stands in relation to individual ability to pay, this has the effect of increasing the price to affluent parents of voting for better financed schools. Even where this is prevalent, PTA and other parental fund-raising efforts offer opportunities for affluent families to supplement centrally legislated budgets.

6. There is additional international evidence suggesting that the quantity margin is productive. For Asian students perform better than U.S. students on international achievement exams, but also spend more hours per week in school or studying. Thus, it is estimated (Stafford, 1996) that the average total time devoted to studies by senior high school students—time at school plus homework—is 30 hours per week in the United States, 60.5 in Japan, and 61.4 in Korea.

7. Rangazas (2000a) reviews the literature and concludes that the main contribution of mother's education comes from the higher family income and child investments it helps ob-

tain. Behrman (1997) reviews many studies that find a positive, but modest, effect. Of course, if "education" is measured poorly, then part of the "direct" effect of education might be inappropriately attributed to earnings.

8. We could obtain an explicit solution if we also employed a specific functional form for parent's utility function. However, because of the transfer constraint discussed below, full explicit solutions are cumbersome. In Chapter 7, however, we do derive an explicit solution for human capital investments in adulthood.

9. Of course, parents may anticipate some degree of altruism on the part of children toward them. However, they may be uncertain about either the strength of that altruism or whether the earnings of the child (which we have modeled as certain) will in fact materialize. These issues are analyzed by Chakrabarti, Lord, and Rangazas (1993).

10. A different perspective is offered by Mulligan (1997), who argues that intergenerational borrowing takes the form of care giving (instead of cash) by adult children to elderly parents. He cites the prevalence of care giving by children for elderly parents as an important example of repayment. However, if such care giving is repayment for investments, why is care most often provided by a low-earning daughter rather than the highest earning son? Also, when uneven bequests are made, it is often when one child has provided more care giving. This suggests that the parent believes he or she has incurred a "debt" that must be discharged, rather than that the care giving constituted a repayment (from the perspectives of those involved). Further, some evidence indicates that adult children provide more attention to wealthier parents—the ones least likely to borrow intergenerationally (see Chapter 5). Finally, how parents can feel assured that investments in toddlers would be repaid in this fashion is unclear.

11. For example, suppose a liquidity- and transfer-constrained parent works overtime while the child is young in order to raise the down payment on a house. For this reason little time is spent with the child until the house is acquired. The same aggregate time investment may be more efficient if spread evenly over the childhood years.

13. Another possibility is that the only effect of "ability" is to increase exogenous earnings. Graphically, exogenous earnings mean that the earnings transformation curve begins at a positive level of child wealth. High ability shifts this wealth level upward. In this case there is only a wealth effect, which lowers the human capital investment. Examples of this type of "ability" with respect to earnings capacity might include gender, race, or physical attractiveness.

14. See Behrman, Pollak, and Taubman (1995) for a discussion of "somewhat affluent" families who make financial transfers to some but not all of their children.

15. His framework is somewhat more general than that of Chapter 3, including three periods of adulthood and more general preferences as examples.

16. Although Rangazas stresses the role of other adults in a parents' generation, if one prefers to view the human capital spillover term as including the effect of parent's human capital, the intuition of the framework is little affected.

17. In this model the taxes and transfers do not affect labor supply decisions. In Chapter 8 we revisit the equity and efficiency effects of redistributive policies when labor supply is allowed to vary.

PROBLEMS AND QUESTIONS

▶ REVIEW
QUESTIONS

1. Consider a transfer-constrained household when parents can make human and/or financial transfers.

    A. Since $r_h > r$, is dynastic wealth maximized? Explain.

    B. Suppose the government were to cut taxes by \$1 on parents' generation, with the understanding that children will have to pay an extra $\$(1 + r)$ in taxes. Explain how this could expand dynastic consumption opportunities.

2. Consider an unconstrained household that makes both the efficient human bequest and leaves a financial bequest. Would Ricardian equivalence hold if the economy were entirely composed of such households? How would a government redistribution toward parents affect the portfolio of transfers?

3 **A.** For an unconstrained household making human and financial bequests, how and why does a permanent change in r affect the efficient human bequest?

    B. Would a reduction in r affect the human bequest for a transfer-constrained household? Show graphically.

    C. What is the effect on child's human capital accumulation of an increase in W_p when parents are transfer constrained? Are unconstrained?

4. Consider a two-child family. Assume parents have "equal concern" for each child and that child wealth is what affects parent utility. Describe utility-maximizing transfers under the following conditions:

    A. The parents are unconstrained and the children are of equal ability.

    B. The parents are unconstrained and child 1 has greater ability than child 2.

    C. The parents are transfer constrained and the children are of unequal ability.

5. **A.** For a transfer-constrained household, what is the effect on B_p, B_p^h, C_c, and C_p of a ceteris paribus increases in W_p? What is the effect on economic efficiency? Explain.

    B. For an unconstrained household, what is the effect on those variables of a *decrease* in W_p? What is the effect on efficiency? Explain.

    C. What is the effect on equity and efficiency of a lump-sum tax on the "rich" (unconstrained) given to the "poor" (transfer constrained)?

6. Explain why the rate of regression to the mean in earnings across generations is expected to differ between poor and affluent families. Discuss the evidence of Gaviria related to this prediction.

7. Why are the welfare implications for parents and children from imposing a binding transfer constraint ambiguous? On what parameters do these implications depend? What is the available evidence?

▶ PROBLEMS

1. Suppose parents have Cobb-Douglas utility as in Chapter 5, $U = C_p^\theta W_c^{1-\theta}$ (recall that with Cobb-Douglas preferences, the exponent on a good is the proportion of the relevant wealth amount devoted to that good). Further, assume there are constant returns on investments, so that the marginal rate of return is constant at $r_h > r$ (we don't need to worry about the specific production function). Finally, assume households cannot enforce repayment of loans to children, that is, there is legal constraint prohibiting negative bequests. Set up the utility maximization problem faced by altruistic parents and determine (graphically if you want) the optimal solution.

Do parents maximize dynastic wealth? Are any parents unconstrained? Does this example make it seem plausible that there are constant (private) returns to human capital investments in children? Explain.

2. Consider the private response to public programs that redistribute intragenerationally toward those with low income. Assume that *human bequests* to dependents are always altruistically motivated.
   A. Suppose the government starts a new preschool program, similar to Head Start, spending $2,000 per participating child from transfer-constrained families. How (qualitatively) will this affect the human bequest?
   B. Suppose instead the $2,000 were given to the parents. Is the parental response the same as in part A?

3. In section 6.3 we addressed the role of education in U.S. economic growth between 1870 and 1970.
   A. What problem do models based on physical capital accumulation alone have when used to explain a substantial portion of growth over this period?
   B. How does the version of Rangazas' model based on efficient human capital investments improve the simulations compared with the model without human capital? What shortcomings remain?
   C. What further improvements are associated with the model that employs the transfer constraint?
   D. Explain the role of changes in the average human capital during the transition.
   E. What role is played by exogenous growth in technology in Rangazas' model? That is, how might the transition paths for human capital differ were there no exogenous technical growth, both in the unconstrained and constrained cases?

*4. A. Suppose the production function for human capital is $h_c = zx^\alpha$. Suppose the price per unit of goods inputs is p_x and that w is the wage per unit of human capital in both parent's and child's generations. r is the generational interest rate. (a) Determine the dynastic wealth-maximizing quantity of human capital investment, and the level of child human capital. Hint: One way to solve this is to equate the marginal benefits MB and marginal costs MC of investment. First write the expression for investments. Then solve the production function for x and use this result to express investments in terms of output. Take the derivative of this expression with respect to h_c to find MC. Equate this to the MB of another unit of h_c, then solve for h_c. (b) Algebraically assess the comparative statics of optimal x and h_c to changes in p_x, w, and z. Discuss the intuition behind the results.
   B. Now suppose the production function for human capital is $h_c = zs^\alpha$. Suppose there are now no longer any goods inputs and that w is the wage per unit of human capital in both parent's and child's generations. r is the generational interest rate and s is the proportion of parent's time devoted to human capital investments. Determine the dynastic wealth-maximizing quantity of human capital investment, and the level of child human capital. Algebraically assess the comparative statics of optimal x and h_c due to changes in w and z. Discuss the intuition behind the results. Contrast the comparative statics of parts A and B.

Chapter 7 | SKILL ACQUISITION, INEQUALITY, AND GROWTH

"The most valuable of all capital is that invested in human beings."
—ALFRED MARSHALL, *PRINCIPLES OF ECONOMICS* (1890)

Chapter 6 analyzed family investments in dependent children. This chapter complements that discussion by examining human capital investment decisions in adulthood. Section 7.1 develops a model of human capital accumulation in adulthood. Empirical implications of that model are evaluated in section 7.2. Section 7.3 employs human capital theory to explain recent trends in earnings inequality. The fourth section assesses several mechanisms by which human capital accumulation may affect economic growth. Section 7.5 examines the microeconomic and macroeconomic implications of taxation for human capital accumulation. A short summary concludes the chapter.

7.1 HUMAN CAPITAL ACCUMULATION IN ADULTHOOD

As children age, parent's knowledge and time inputs become less important to the children's development. In turn, the time input of the dependent child ceases to be determined by the parent and instead becomes a matter of choice to the young adult. This section develops a theory of the human capital investments adults make in themselves, including vocational and liberal arts college education, graduate school, and postschooling on-the-job training (OJT). Of course, children are not instantaneously transformed from being completely dependent upon their parents economically to being completely independent. As seen in Chapter 5, even after high school some young adults continue to receive significant transfers of money and goods (including housing) from parents. The children of more affluent parents presumably enjoy more support and later into the life cycle than children from less affluent families. An important question is whether the adult children of poor families forego valuable training opportunities because of a lack of funds. Though we address this below, we begin by assuming human capital decisions are not constrained by an inability to borrow against future earnings. The story is first developed in a two-period setting, then extended to a more realistic many-year perspective. The framework abstracts from labor-leisure choices and household production, which are taken up in Chapter 8.

7.1.1 A Two-Period Model

Consumers live two periods, maximizing a life-cycle utility function that depends on the amounts consumed in each period (and that has convex indifference curves).

$$U = U(C_1, C_2)$$

Notice that the consumer derives no utility or disutility from human capital aside from its use in obtaining market goods. The consumer is interested in acquiring human capital only if it increases consumption.[1]

During the first period, the individual divides her or his or his time between the labor market and human capital investment. In the second period, all time is devoted to market work. In the *absence* of adult human capital investments, wage earnings are assumed constant over the two periods and equal to $E = wh_1$, where h_1 is the human capital brought into the first period of life and w is the rental rate or wage *per unit of human capital*. This earnings potential reflects parental human capital investments in the child, genetic factors, other environmental influences, and with respect to w, macroeconomic conditions. To the consumer, w is a parameter that, for now, is assumed to be constant over time.

Human capital produced in period one, q_1, is available for use in the labor market in period 2. Thus, the stock of human capital in period 2, h_2, is

$$h_2 = h_1 + q_1 \tag{7.1}$$

Earnings in the second period are therefore $E_2 = wh_2$.

Human capital investments typically involve both time inputs (entailing foregone earnings) and goods inputs (out-of-pocket expenditures on books, tuition, supplies, etc.). The skills and knowledge the "student" brings into the learning situation—the initial stock h_1—are also important. The input *mix* of goods and time would be chosen efficiently, so as to minimize the costs of production. Fortunately, the core intuition may be obtained from a setup that abstracts from goods inputs. We begin with such a model, though the role of goods inputs is fully recognized wherever appropriate.

As a special case of the investment model developed by Ben-Porath (1967), our production function for human capital takes the form,

$$q_1 = zs_1^\lambda h_1^\lambda = z(s_1 h_1)^\lambda \tag{7.2}$$

where s_1 is the proportion of the first period devoted to human capital investments. z is an efficiency parameter, assumed to be larger for more able individuals.

It is easy to appreciate why time s_1 must be devoted to mastering a new computer manual, for example. Equation (7.2) further states that human capital brought into adulthood h_1 increases the productivity of subsequent learning efforts. Prominent human capital theorists support this position: Nobel Laureate Gary Becker stresses that the mastery of lower levels of material is a prerequisite to assimilating more advanced knowledge. Similarly, Nobel Laureate James Heckman argues that "learning begets learning."

The product of time and human capital, $s_1 h_1$, is the *effective* time devoted to human capital production. Since time and the existing stock are both raised to the power λ, an increase in h_1 increases by the same proportion the effective time in human capital production and the market value of time.

Browning, Hansen, and Heckman (1999) review estimates of the parameters of the Ben-Porath model. In some studies the exponents on time and human capital are restricted to be equal, while in others they are allowed to differ. Even where the exponents are free to differ, it is typically not possible to reject the hypothesis that, as in (7.2), they *are* equal. Altogether, those studies suggest λ is close to .8. It is easily shown that λ is the elasticity of human capital production with respect to time s_1 or the initial stock h_1. Thus, since $\lambda < 1$, there are diminishing marginal returns to s_1 or $s_1 h_1$. However, since λ is not far below 1, the marginal product of effective time does not fall off quickly.[2] Of course, doubling both s_1 and h_1 would quadruple effective time, which, given λ, would more than double production. Since h_1 is fixed as of period one, the individual's choice of s_1 determines the investment of effective time.

The production function is illustrated in Figure 7.1. Reflecting diminishing returns in s_1, the function is concave. The production function is higher the larger is h_1, since human capital increases the marginal product of efforts to learn. Although not depicted, the function increases with the efficiency parameter z.

Labor market earnings in the first period are the difference between potential earnings E and the human capital investment, equal to earnings foregone. Thus,

$$E_1 = E - ws_1 h_1$$

$$h_1^1 > h_1^0$$

Figure 7.1 The human capital production function

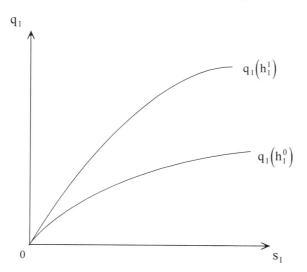

Therefore, observed earnings are less than the marginal product of a full-time worker.

For now, we assume the individual may borrow or lend at rate r, subject only to a constraint that limits the present value of consumption over the life cycle to that of earnings over the life cycle (life wealth). This allows the consumer to maximize utility in two steps. First, he or she chooses q_1—and thereby s_1—to maximize life wealth. Then, as in chapters 1 through 4, he or she chooses consumption in each period to maximize utility, subject to the life wealth budget constraint. The consumer's problem is to

$$\text{maximize } U = U(C_1, C_2)$$

subject to

$$W = E_1 + E_2/(1 + r)$$

and

$$q_1 = z(s_1h_1)^\lambda$$

Figure 7.2 depicts the basic model. DF is the earnings possibility curve, which is concave reflecting the diminishing returns to human capital investments portrayed in Figure 7.1. The earnings frontier has slope with absolute value of $1 + i$, where i is the *marginal rate of return* on adult human capital investment

$$i \equiv dE_2/(-dE_1) - 1$$

Because of diminishing returns, i declines as investment increases.

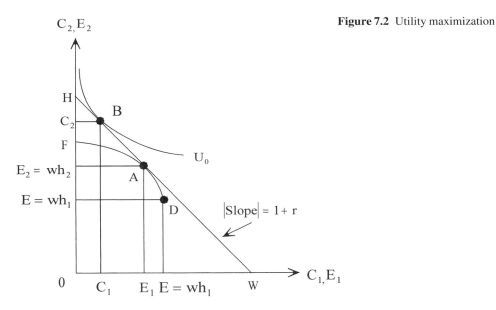

Figure 7.2 Utility maximization

How much investment is optimal? The effect on life-cycle wealth of a marginal investment is

$$dW = dE_2/(1 + r) + dE_1 \qquad (7.3)$$

Thus, for the marginal investment to be profitable, that is, $dW > 0$, the discounted increase in earnings (the marginal benefits) must exceed the marginal cost of investment. By definition, for a marginal investment, $dE_2 = -dE_1(1 + i)$. Making this substitution in (7.3) and rearranging, a profitable investment requires $-dE_1(1 + i)/(1 + r) > -dE_1$, or $i > r$ (note that $-dE_1$ is positive). If $i > r$, one could borrow a dollar, invest it in human capital, increase period-two earnings by $1 + i$, pay back the dollar plus interest $(1 + r)$, and still increase second-period consumption by $i - r$.

In Figure 7.2 the consumer is endowed with the earnings capacity shown as point D. The human capital investments that maximize life wealth occur at point A, where i has fallen to equal r. Human capital investment equals the reduction in first-period earnings from E to E_1. This investment increases second-period earnings by $E_2 - E$ (recall that E is the earnings the person would obtain if human capital remains h_1). The earnings stream entitles the consumer to choose consumption from along the budget constraint HW. Utility is maximized at point B. The average rate of return on the human capital investment is given by the slope of the (unpictured) straight line between points D and A.

Saving when young has both human capital $(E - E_1)$ and conventional savings $(E_1 - C_1)$ components. These are not independent. Human capital investments increase life wealth W and therefore consumption in both periods. Consequently, human capital investments reduce conventional savings in two ways: reducing first-period earnings and increasing first-period consumption. An unresolved issue is whether the expansion in human capital investments over the past several decades may provide a partial explanation of the reduction in the personal saving rate documented in Chapter 1.

Human Capital Decision in the Ben-Porath Model

Equating the marginal benefits MB and marginal costs MC of investment enable us to determine the optimal production level q_1. The MB of an additional unit of human capital is just the present value of its contribution to wealth. Increasing q_1 by one unit increases second-period earnings by w and wealth by $w/(1 + r)$. Thus,

$$MB = w/(1 + r) \qquad (7.4)$$

The expression for marginal costs is a bit harder to come by. To derive MC, first note that total investments I equal the earnings foregone:

$$I = wh_1 s_1 \qquad (7.5)$$

However, to find the marginal cost of *output*, we need to reexpress investment in terms of q_1. This is accomplished by first rearranging the production function to solve for s_1 and then substituting this result for s_1 into the investment function. So, from (7.2),

$$s_1 = (q_1/z)^{1/\lambda}/h_1$$

Substituting this result into (7.5) yields

$$I = wh_1(q_1/z)^{1/\lambda}/h_1 \qquad (7.5')$$
$$= w(q_1/z)^{1/\lambda}$$

Finally, since MC is just the rate of change or derivative of investments with respect to q_1,

$$MC = dI/dq_1 = (q_1)^{1/\lambda - 1}(w/\lambda)z^{-1/\lambda} \qquad (7.6)$$

Due to diminishing marginal returns ($\lambda < 1$), the exponent on q_1 is positive, so that MC rises as q_1 is increased. MC also increases with w and is lower for those more talented (higher z).

It is now easy to determine the optimal q_1; equate the MB from equation (7.4) with the MC from equation (7.6), then solve for q_1. This yields

$$q_1 = z^{1/(1-\lambda)}[\lambda/(1 + r)]^{\lambda/(1-\lambda)} \qquad (7.7)$$

We now discuss important, straightforward implications of this solution.

7.1.2   Comparative Statics in the Two-Period Model

This subsection examines how optimal production varies with the model's parameters. The evidence relating to these predictions is considered in section 7.2, after we develop a many-period version of the Ben-Porath framework.

Notice that the current stock of human capital h_1 does not appear in (7.7). That is, *the optimal quantity of human capital produced is independent of the initial stock.* This perhaps surprising result is a consequence of our assumption that h_1 increases effective time at work and human capital production by the same proportion: Although a high initial stock increases the cost of time devoted to investments, it also increases the productivity of that time. Altogether, MC is independent of h_1 (see 7.6). Intuitively, suppose a business employee has mastered the intricacies of a new spreadsheet software package. This knowledge improves the employee's productivity at work as a bookkeeper, but also increases his or her ability to analyze cases in corporate finance courses at school.

This neutrality proposition has an interesting implication: Suppose two people have the same ability z.[3] However, one attends a good high school and the other a poor one. For this reason the "good school" graduate brings a larger stock of human capital into adulthood. By the neutrality proposition, they each produce the same quantity q_1. However, the "good school" graduate is able to devote a lower fraction of first-period time s_1. Consequently, he earns more in the first period. This story assumes individuals work at least part-time. However, Davies and St. Hilaire (1987) note that some students are at a corner, devoting all time to schooling. For such students, the marginal return i in a schooling year exceeds r.[4] To appreciate the implications of this case, suppose these two students now attend school full-time. Since the stock of human capital increases the productivity of time, the student who began with more human capital will also acquire more.

As before, students from "good high schools" earn more. Here, though, the earnings differences are magnified by the equal time investments.

Now consider two individuals who bring equal initial stocks into adulthood, but one has more ability. Assume these individuals are *not* at a corner. By (7.7), the "high z" individual produces more human capital and has higher life wealth.[5] Intuitively, a higher ability person faces a lower MC of human capital, so MC = MB at a higher level of production. In practice, distinguishing whether high-earning individuals begin economic life with more ability or higher amounts of human capital is difficult. It proves important to policy, however, and we examine the issue in sections 7.2 and 7.3.

Interestingly, the wage per unit of human capital w does not appear in (7.7), meaning that optimal production is independent of w. This result relies on our assumption of no out-of-pocket investment costs. Since the only costs are foregone earnings, an increase in w raises MC the same percentage as MB, leaving production unaffected.

In practice goods inputs (tuition, books, computer, etc.) can be an important component of educational costs. Imagine they are 20 percent of the total and, for purposes of illustration, that there is no ability to substitute between goods and own time in the production of human capital. Then a 10 percent wage boost increases investment costs by only 8 percent, while the benefits rise by the full 10 percent. Thus, in the presence of goods inputs, higher wages increase the benefits more than the costs, so human capital is predicted to rise. (However, since instructional costs are the primary portion of tuition, tuition may rise at about the same rate as wages in the long run. This limits the positive effect of wage growth on human capital.)

Expected growth in w over the life cycle is predicted to increase training. To see this, again assume foregone earnings are the only cost. In the presence of economic growth, the wage *per unit of human capital* rises through time at rate v, say. This increases the MB to

$$MB = w(1 + v)/(1 + r) \qquad (7.4')$$

However, marginal costs are unaffected. Consequently, fully anticipated economic growth results in more human capital accumulation than in the "no-growth" economy. If this higher growth rate remains constant across generations, production of human capital will remain at the higher level in each generation. To get ongoing increases in human capital across generations would require an increasing growth rate. (If out-of-pocket expenses are important and rise less rapidly than wages, even a constant rate of labor productivity growth would translate to higher human capital production levels.) We return to this issue in section 7.3.

Finally, suppose there is an increase in the rate of return on financial assets, r. From the perspective of maximizing life wealth, this makes human capital less attractive since the benefits (higher earnings) are now discounted more heavily. Put differently, suppose the household is viewed as choosing a portfolio of assets when young to provide for second-period consumption. An increase in r induces substitution away from human capital to financial investments. This intuition is confirmed by equation (7.7), which reveals that higher r discourages human capital. One may also infer this from Figure 7.2. An increase (not shown) in the slope of the budget line would move the wealth-maximizing investment from A down toward D.

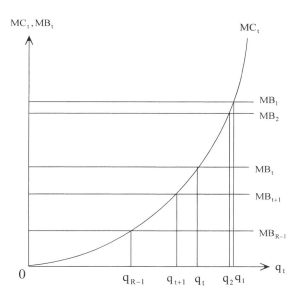

Figure 7.3 Optimal investment in human capital over the life cycle

7.1.3 Human Capital over the Life Cycle

To better match earnings over the life cycle with our theory, we extend the framework to many years, or an annual basis. To that end, suppose an individual works R years. The human capital production function in each period retains the same form as that for q_1 in the two-period model. Then marginal cost remains the same basic function of output. That is, the expression for MC in period t differs from (7.6) only by having a t subscript on the amount produced.

$$MC_t = (w/\lambda)(q_t)^{1/\lambda - 1}z^{-1/\lambda}$$

If an eighth unit of human capital costs $100 in the fifth period of adulthood, say, it would also cost $100 in the twenty-fifth period. MC_t is portrayed in Figure 7.3.

The extension to many years affects marginal benefits in several ways. First, the human capital produced in year one, q_1, will be useful not only in year two, but in every year until retirement at the end of year R. Thus, the present-value calculation for marginal benefits now includes the contribution to potential earnings in all future working years. *As the consumer ages, there are fewer working years over which to reap benefits, which reduces MB.* For example, the MB of learning computer skills is greater for someone entering the work force than for someone on the verge of retirement. Assuming human capital does not depreciate (more below), the marginal benefit of a unit of human capital produced in year one MB_1 is

$$MB_1 = w/(1 + r) + w/(1 + r)^2 + \cdots + w/(1 + r)^{R-1} \tag{7.8}$$

In year two it would be[6]

$$MB_2 = w/(1 + r) + w/(1 + r)^2 + \cdots + w/(1 + r)^{R-2}$$

Each year's MB expression has one fewer term, so that in year R the marginal benefit is zero (since human capital produced in R would not be available until the following year, when the consumer would be retired). The marginal benefit in each year t of work, MB_t, is also illustrated in Figure 7.3. At young ages, benefits decline slowly between years because the effect of distant amounts on present value is low. As the horizon nears, MB_t falls more rapidly.

7.2 EVALUATING THE BEN-PORATH MODEL

7.2.1   Earnings, Education, and Experience over the Life Cycle

The life-cycle profiles of investment and earnings are now readily developed. The intersection of the declining MB_t with the fixed MC_t schedule traces the optimal investment profile, q_1, q_2, and so on, where the stock in t is now $h_t = h_{t-1} + q_{t-1}$. This profile is depicted in Figure 7.4, which reveals that additions to the stock are predicted to decline as the consumer ages.

Above, we assumed skills do not depreciate. However, especially when technical change is fast, skills accumulated at one age may become less useful in future years, or depreciate. For the average person, the reading, writing, and arithmetic skills developed during the early years of dependency may not depreciate. This is less true of some more

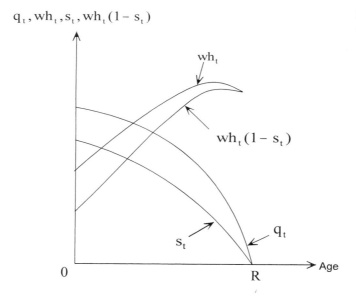

$q_t, wh_t, s_t, wh_t(1 - s_t)$

Figure 7.4 Earnings and investment profiles

wh_t

$wh_t(1 - s_t)$

s_t

q_t

0   R   Age

advanced skills. As examples, word-processing packages and communications, payroll, and inventory systems change, and the skills associated with operating a specific type of capital equipment are less useful when the software or equipment is upgraded. Therefore, depreciation is an additional force that lowers the benefits of accumulating human capital.[7] Heckman, Lochner and Taber (1998) estimate the rate of depreciation to be close to zero, while other researchers find somewhat greater depreciation.

Potential earnings wh_t equal the amount a worker would earn if no time were devoted to human capital production. For now, we treat economic age and potential work experience as the same concept. The predicted age profile of potential earnings is displayed in Figure 7.4 (q_t, s_t, and wh_t are not drawn to scale; their shapes are best viewed in isolation). At first, additions to the stock are large while depreciation is small, so that the stock and potential earnings increase rapidly with age. However, as the retirement horizon approaches, production of new skills declines. Further, a large current stock entails greater depreciation, which makes the net of depreciation additions to the stock smaller yet. Toward retirement, new investments are low and depreciation is high, so that the stock of skills falls. Thus, the *potential earnings* profile is concave, with a peak toward the end of the working years.

Because some potential earnings are foregone as investment, actual earnings $wh_t(1 - s_t)$ in Figure 7.4 are below potential earnings. Consequently, observed earnings do not reflect the individual's earnings capacity or full-time marginal product. The wedge between actual and observed earnings is greatest during the early years when investments are large. The time input s_t declines with age, both because investment $wh_t s_t$ falls and because the higher stock makes time investments more costly. This narrows the gap between potential and observed earnings, which become equal only in the last year of work.

Our development of the Ben-Porath model implies that investments decline smoothly with age. However, formal full-time schooling, the most obvious fashion in which human capital is acquired, ends abruptly and is accompanied by a large jump in earnings. Figure 7.3 could be amended to allow for this pattern. Beyond the production level achieved when all time is devoted to schooling, the MC schedule would become vertical. This vertical segment would shift rightward each year as the production capacity grows with the stock of human capital. After some age, MB would equal MC when less than all time is devoted to schooling. This is the case depicted for each year in Figure 7.3.

General and Specific Training

Education and human capital accumulation are, to varying degrees, now a lifetime process. Workers receive training on the job, and they return to school for further vocational training. Becker (1975) identified two types of on-the-job training. Some training provides *general* human capital, which raises the worker's marginal product in many firms. Other training is *firm specific*, useful only to the current employer. Either type requires time by the worker that otherwise could have been devoted to current production, along with costs for trainers and materials. The exact results from the Ben-Porath framework apply only in the case of general training.

Becker points out that workers must pay the whole cost of any general human capital. To see why, again consider our two-period framework. General human capital investments in period one entail period-one costs while boosting productivity in period two at the current *or any other firm*. To retain the worker in period two, the firm must pay a wage equal to the worker's marginal revenue product at that time. Otherwise, the employee will migrate to another firm that will. Therefore, anything the firm pays for the training is lost (since it is unable to recoup the outlays by paying less than the marginal revenue product in period two). On the other hand, since the worker receives the benefits via higher future wages, he or she is willing to incur the cost of worthwhile training.

For example, consider someone who upon completion of an accounting degree joins one of the "Big 5" accounting firms. The pay in the first few years is about what a small local firm might pay. However, the hours worked may be appreciably greater, leading to a *lower* hourly wage. Yet such a position is much harder to obtain than one at a local firm. Becker's explanation would be that the worker at the national firm is exposed to many different jobs or accounts and must learn a variety of skills: More general human capital is acquired at the national firm. Since the worker could quit that firm and be compensated for those skills elsewhere, the firm is unwilling to subsidize acquisition of those skills. Thus, the worker implicitly pays for training by accepting an hourly wage below what would be paid elsewhere where all of his or her time would be devoted to current production. Nevertheless, the expected life wealth is higher at the national firm.

In contrast, Becker argues that firms and employees must split the cost of firm-specific training. On one hand, the employee is unwilling to pay for all the training in period one because there is some chance he or she will be laid off in period two. On the other hand, the employer is unwilling to pay all of the expense because there is some chance the worker will quit before period two. If each pays part of the training cost, the probability of worker separation is greatly reduced, making both parties amenable. In this case, the worker receives less in the first period than he or she would at an alternative firm, but is paid more than at an alternative firm in the second period. Also, the firm wants to retain the worker in period two, because his or her contribution to revenues would exceed the wage.

Figure 7.5 illustrates the implications for earnings of OJT in the many-period context. The flat line shows the marginal revenue product (MRP_t) and annual earnings E_t in the absence of training. Now allow for training and assume there is the same amount, with the same effect on productivity *at the given firm*, whether the training is general or specific. The steepest schedule depicts the MRP profile in the presence of either type of training. If the training is general, that profile also indicates worker earnings at each amount of experience. For specific training, the age-experience profile is given by the intermediate profile. In both cases, in the early years the employee accepts less than in the absence of training, but earns more later in the work cycle than if untrained. The fact that earnings for the specifically trained worker fall short of the MRP in the later years ensures that the firm will want to employ him or her at that time.

Several studies indicate that such implicit "lifetime employment contracts" may be common even in the United States, since a sizeable proportion of employees ultimately work for the same employer 20 or more years. There is also, though, evidence that wages across workers doing the same job in the same firm differ much less than their productivities, a phenomenon known as *wage compression*. Acemoglu and Pischke (1999) show that in the presence of wage compression, the predictions of the Becker model can break down. In particular, as the wage structure becomes more compressed, workers pay a lesser fraction of the costs of general training.

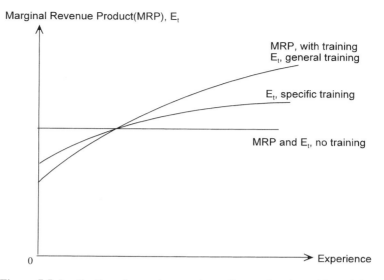

Figure 7.5 Implications for worker earnings of general and specific training

Returns to Education

How do observed earnings over the life cycle vary with training? Figure 7.6 presents age-earnings profiles of year-round, full-time workers by gender for college and high school graduates in 1998 (Bureau of Labor Statistics). These age-profiles are obtained by looking at a cross section of workers at a point in time, rather than following a cohort of workers over their life cycle. Assuming economic growth, members of successive cohorts earn more at each age, which means a cohort's life-cycle profile would be steeper than in these cross sections. Thus, in contrast to what is shown in the figure, earnings near retirement may decline less rapidly.

Viewing Figure 7.6, several facts stand out. First, holding gender constant, college graduates earn appreciably more than high school graduates. Second, holding education constant, men earn appreciably more than women. Third, earnings rise during the early years of work. Less definitively, the rate at which earnings rise is greater for college workers between age 35 and age 45 than for high school graduates.

Of course, the positive correlation between education and earnings is exactly as the Ben-Porath model suggests. We would like to know more about the strength of that relationship: Specifically, what is the rate of return to educational investments? The Ben-Porath model requires the return on the *last* dollar invested in each period i to equal the interest rate r. However, since there are diminishing returns within periods, the average rate of return will exceed i. Reviewing Figure 7.3, the within-period marginal returns on the first units produced are always the highest, with initial units especially profitable during the early years. This suggests that the average return on investments should fall as the consumer ages.

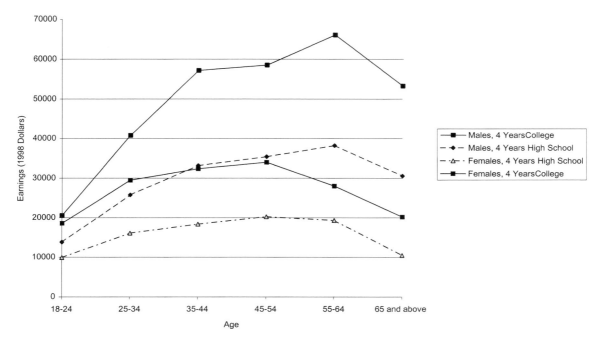

Figure 7.6 Age-earnings profiles of year-round, full-time workers by gender and education, 1998 (1998 dollars)

The return to schooling may be affected by differences across education levels in the ability to invest in OJT. Unfortunately, the *size* of investments in OJT are notoriously hard to measure. There is more information about the duration and frequency of postschooling investments, and we consider their effects on earnings below. First, though, we consider the many studies and issues that arise when little direct attention is afforded postschooling investments.

Mincer (1974) developed an influential statistical model to estimate the returns to education that does not require direct OJT information. The simplest form of the Mincer earnings function regresses the log of an individual's earnings at a given age E_t on years of schooling for the individual S_t, experience X_t, and experience squared,

$$\log E_t = a + bS_t + cX_t + dX_t^2 + e_t \tag{7.9}$$

where e_t is an error term, reflecting omitted and random factors. The idea is that since OJT increases with experience, controlling for experience leaves just the effect on earnings of education (we return to this below). However, in many data sets (most notably the Current Population Survey, or CPS), information on experience is also unavailable. For this reason, it is often approximated by *potential experience*, equal to age minus years of schooling minus 6 (the age when schooling usually begins). The squared or quadratic term on X_t allows for the possibility that the earnings function is concave in X_t (as the Ben-Porath model suggests). Estimates of this basic Mincer equation are calculated using ordinary least squares (OLS), which determines the values of the parameters a, b, c, and d that make (7.9) fit the data best.

Using the log of earnings makes for easy interpretation of b. For b then provides the change in the log of earnings associated with an additional year of schooling and, for small changes, the change in the log of a variable (times 100) equals the percentage change. Thus, b (times 100) becomes the percentage change in earnings from an additional year of schooling. For this reason, b is typically considered to be the rate of return to schooling (this interpretation implicitly assumes that students do not work, there are no out-of-pocket expenditures for schooling, and the retirement horizon is far away).[8]

Significantly, the Mincer function (7.9) does not control for ability. This is troublesome since both educational attainment and earnings are affected by ability. As Card (1999) notes, "it is very difficult to know whether the higher earnings observed for better-educated workers are *caused* by their higher education, or whether individuals with higher earning capacity have chosen to acquire more schooling" (1999, p. 1). For this reason many economists believe that estimates of b based on the simple Mincer model are biased upward, attributing some of the effect to schooling that is actually due to ability.

Separating the roles of schooling and ability in the determination of earnings is important to a variety of policy issues, as discussed below. Consequently, many economists have addressed this question. The state of the art is surveyed and deepened by Card, who tackles ability bias from several theoretical and empirical perspectives. He concludes, as have others, that education does indeed cause higher earnings. Further, he finds the bias from use of the simple Mincer model is quite small (about 10% of the estimated b).[9]

One procedure for eliminating the ability bias examines the relationship between the education and earnings of identical twins who differ by years of schooling completed. Since genes are conveniently held constant by nature, the resulting estimates of the return to schooling are essentially free of ability bias. Ashenfelter and Rouse (1998) examine 340 pairs of identical twins using earnings data for three years. Controlling for twins' education, race, gender, and age they estimate the return to an additional year of schooling to be roughly 10 percent. As predicted by the Ben-Porath model, they find evidence of declining returns to additional years of schooling. Their results indicate that the returns to schooling decline from about 0.12 at 9 years of schooling to 0.08 at 16 years of schooling. The twins literature is not without controversy. Some researchers wonder why "identical" twins would receive different amounts of education. If "something happened" to one twin that accounts for the difference in training, and this "something" is not controlled for, the estimated returns may be biased.

Other approaches attempt to hold constant, or control for, ability when estimating b. One extension to the basic Mincer model controls for or "nets out" ability by adding an ability variable to the list of explanatory variables. For example, the National Longitudinal Survey of Youth includes individuals' performance on the Armed Forces Qualifying Test (AFQT), which is designed to measure the ability of recruits to perform various tasks. However, as discussed below, there is some debate whether the AFQT is a measure of ability, z, or human capital at the age of maturity, h_1. It is also common to use the education of other family members as an instrument for ability. If these latter variables are only weakly correlated with ability, the extent to which ability is truly controlled for is limited, so an upward ability bias remains. Overall, the evidence seems to suggest private returns to education of between 6 and 10% (cf. Acemoglu and Angrist, 2000).

The range of estimates of the rate of return and the fact that returns vary with worker characteristics make it difficult to determine how good an investment education is. If the average return to training were equal to that on financial assets, training would steepen the age-earnings profile but would *not* increase the present value of life earnings. Training increases life wealth only if the rate of return exceeds that on financial assets. Suppose the return to an additional year of education is 10%, a figure in the range of estimates discussed above and a popular ballpark response among economists. Whether 10% is a "good" return depends upon the return on equally risky financial investments. Recently, Cocco, Gomes, and Maenhout (1999) consider portfolio choices over the life cycle. To implement their simulations, they estimate the variability of labor earnings and of equity (the stock market). They conclude that even though labor income is risky, it is a closer substitute for risk-free asset holdings than for equities. Assuming that human capital investments increase the mean and variance of earnings proportionately, this suggests that human capital investments are less risky than investments in stocks.[10] The stock market over long periods has done only slightly better than 10% per year on average. Thus, the average returns to education and stocks are comparable. Since labor earnings appear to be less risky than stock returns, we may conclude that adjusted for risk, human capital offers a better return. In this sense, human capital appears to be a good investment.

There may also be nonpecuniary benefits from higher education. For example, the work done by college graduates may be more interesting, cleaner, and less dangerous than that performed by high school graduates. If this is true, the full return to college exceeds that based on monetary calculations alone.

It is important for policy purposes to distinguish between the social and private (or individual) rates of return to education. For example, if all of the returns to education are private and if people are not denied training because of borrowing restrictions, there would be no need for the government to intervene in the education market. In fact, the role of government in education is quite large, which introduces a wedge between social and private returns. To illustrate, consider junior high school. Foregone earnings are quite low among students of that age. Further, from the perspective of the student (or the parents), public education is "free" in the sense that the property taxes supporting the schooling must be paid independent of attendance. For these reasons, private costs may be close to zero. Social costs are much larger, with per pupil annual expenditures at public elementary and secondary schools exceeding $5,000 in most states. For this reason, in the absence of externalities, social returns are below private returns. Among high school students, foregone earnings become significant, lowering both the private and social returns. More generally, Psacharopoulos (1994) finds social returns to education fall at higher levels of training. However, whereas public subsidies to education are relatively easy to assess, externalities associated with education are difficult to measure. For this reason there remains substantial debate about whether human capital investments are appropriately subsidized. We return to this in section 7.4.

The return to education may be expected to change through time. Autor, Katz, and Krueger (1998) use supply/demand analysis to examine the consequences of the educated baby boom for the relative reward to college education. This *college wage premium* is measured as the ratio of wages of college to high school graduates. They partition the work force into high school equivalents and college equivalents. "College equivalents" are defined as workers with 16 or more years of college (typically a B.A. degree or more), plus half of those with some college. High school equivalents include those with 12 or fewer years, plus half with some college. Not only was the baby boom cohort large, it was also well educated. Autor et al. calculate that the relative supply of college equivalents grew at an average annual rate of 4.99% between 1970 and 1980. In contrast, the demand for college equivalents grew at less than 4%. They show that this is consistent with a decline in the college wage premium from about 46 percent in 1970 to approximately 39% in 1980. As explained below, the college premium rose appreciably in the latter part of the 1980s into the 1990s.

Extensions to the Ben-Porath Framework and OJT

Heckman, Lochner, and Taber (1998) (henceforth HLT) criticize the Ben-Porath assumption that all human capital is the same, so that hourly earnings depend only upon the *quantity* of human capital brought to the market. They stress that occupations are not distinguished merely by different amounts of the same skill. Rather, auto mechanics and bookkeepers, for example, possess quite different skills. Also, different skills may not be readily substitutable in the production process. Further, individuals may be expected to sort among the various skill types according to comparative advantage. Thus, the mechanic may have chosen to become a mechanic precisely because he or she is good at working with his or her hands and "seeing" solutions to mechanical problems. The failure to account for differences in types of skills makes it difficult to explain changes in earnings between groups of workers, such as managers and manual laborers. This observation motivates HLT to generalize the Ben-Porath model in several directions. Significantly, they allow for potential differences in the Ben-Porath postschooling investment functions across educational groups. Also, since schooling decisions are discrete choices, they allow for ability differences within schooling groups. Without introducing the full complexity of their model, we employ their insights to address OJT.

Marcotte (2000) examines the incidence of *formal* postschooling investments by education in the National Longitudinal Survey (NLS). The NLS follows the same individuals over a period of several years. Marcotte studies the original cohort, which ran from 1966 to 1981, and a more recent one, interviewed between 1979 and 1994. He limits his analysis to samples of young white men. NLS participants are asked about work experience and the types, amounts, and location (at work, community college, etc.) of training engaged in after completion of formal schooling. Such relatively formal training occurs frequently, with over 70% in the earlier sample and almost 65% in the later cohort reporting training. He finds quite high payoffs from participation in such training. "For the first cohort, continuing learning resulted in an average earnings premium of 14.0 percent and, for the second, 10.5 percent" (p. 14). This premium is observed several years after the training, so the complete wage dynamics of training are unreported. Also, it is unclear what portion of training is firm specific and to what extent general training was depressing current wages. Nevertheless, since these programs are typically much shorter than a school year, and since paychecks continued to be earned, such training appears to be appreciably more lucrative than an additional year of college.

Of course, much training occurs informally. While one may take an initial workshop on use of a computer software package, the trial and error associated with becoming proficient occur informally. This sort of "learning-by-doing" occurs frequently. Models of learning by doing typically assume that each unit of time spent working (or gaining experience) imparts knowledge that allows the worker to perform better in the future. This suggests experience *costlessly* increases productivity—and that the Ben-Porath model is therefore inapplicable to informal OJT. However, Browning, Hansen, and Heckman (1999) argue that allowing for differences across jobs in the opportunities to learn makes the learning-by-doing framework indistinguishable from the Ben-Porath model. Specifically, workers would be willing to accept lower pay for positions where more learning (additions to human capital) is coupled with work experience. This insight suggests that learning by doing is not a "free lunch," but is a costly activity. Consequently, if informal and formal investments are positively correlated, the rates of return implied from viewing formal investments alone are biased upward.

OJT provides one explanation for the positively sloped age-earnings profiles observed in Figure 7.6.[11] Further, if there is some complementarity between formal OJT opportunities and schooling investments, such training could provide an explanation for the greater steepness of the age-earnings profiles of college graduates. However, there is little support for this contention from the formal training reports in the NLS. Especially in the period from 1966 to 1981 there is little difference in the training participation rates of high school and college graduates. Also, Marcotte reports that college graduates have a somewhat *lower* return to formal postschool training. Thus, the relative steepness of the profiles is not well explained by differences in relatively formal training programs. Significantly, this does not rule out complementarity between *in*formal OJT opportunities and formal schooling. For example, skilled employment (college grad jobs) may well provide more opportunities for learning by doing than repetitive unskilled jobs. Further, the higher "ability" that leads to greater schooling among the college educated may also increase the returns to, and investments in, less formal OJT. Unfortunately, systematic evidence about informal training is unavailable.

The human capital model accurately predicts that those with higher schooling earn more. But is the human capital model a large part of the story regarding the distribution of earnings? According to Card (1999), basic human capital models consistently explain 20 to 35 percent of the variation in observed earnings data.

7.2.2 Family Background and Earnings (Again)

Human Capital Accumulation and Liquidity Constraints

Heckman and Klenow (1997) examine the relationship between college participation among young adults and parental income between 1970 and 1994. They find that 40 to 45% of high school graduates (aged 18–24) whose parents were among the poorest 25% of families participated in college. In contrast, children from families in the top half of the income distribution had participation rates between 70 and 80 percent. One potential explanation of this pattern is that children from poor families may be unable to finance otherwise profitable college training due to an inability to borrow. Surely, such considerations have been important for the enactment of policies expanding public expenditures on education at all levels, including student loan programs for college students.

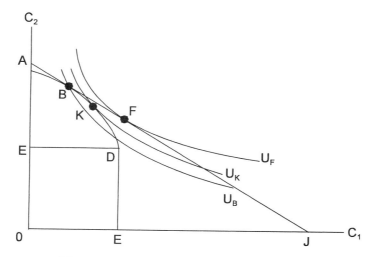

Figure 7.7 Human capital and borrowing constraint

Households are liquidity constrained if they desire to borrow against future earnings to finance current consumption or investments, but are unable to do so. For such households, section 7.1's two-step procedure of, first, investing to maximize life wealth and, second, choosing consumption subject only to life wealth, is not feasible. In this case, investments and consumption must be chosen simultaneously. For this reason liquidity-constrained consumers must weigh the costs of low current consumption against the advantages of higher future earnings and consumption.

In Figure 7.7 the wealth-maximizing human capital investment occurs at point B, where i = r. In the absence of borrowing restrictions, the consumer can choose any consumption path along budget line AJ to maximize utility. If it is not possible to borrow, points along BJ are not feasible. The household can *lend* at rate r, however, so the points along segment BA are attainable. Notice the household may also locate along the earnings transformation curve between D and B. There, first-period resources are exactly divided between C_1 and investments in skills, so that financial assets equal zero. Consequently, if the consumer cannot borrow, the budget set is DBA.

Now consider a consumer who desires a point such as F, which is efficient but would require borrowing to finance the desired C_1. Since the consumer can't borrow, C_1 and/or investments must be reduced until the need to borrow is eliminated. One option is to make the wealth-maximizing investments as before, letting C_1 equal net-of-investment resources. Utility is then given by the indifference curve passing through B, U_B. However, utility may be raised by moving to point K where more C_1 is obtained by reducing investments. At the liquidity-constrained solution, the indifference curve U_k is tangent to the earnings possibility frontier. This tangency implies equality between the MRS and the slope (in absolute value) of the earnings frontier, 1 + i. Whereas i = r when the wealth-maximizing investment is undertaken, i > r at point K. Compared with the wealth-maximizing solution, young liquidity-constrained households consume and invest less, but earn more in period 1. The present value of consumption is decreased, since life-cycle wealth does not reach its maximum.

Young adults from affluent families are less likely to be liquidity constrained.[12] In Chapters 5 and 6 we saw that the resources transferred by altruistic parents to grown children increase with parental income. If the adult child would otherwise be liquidity constrained, efficiency dictates those transfers be used to alleviate the constraint (bequests or earlier further investments in young children having less impact on child wealth and utility). However, even poor or transfer-constrained parents may be willing to make *loans* to children to finance advanced schooling. The risk to such parents may be small since even selfish children have incentives to repay. First, there is the threat of disinheritance if repayment is not made. For with uncertain life span, some (accidental) bequest is expected even among relatively poor families. Also, the parental disapproval that would accompany failure to repay presumably enters negatively into the utility functions of most children.

Cameron and Heckman (cf. 1998) point out that if liquidity constraints limit students' educational attainment, the probability of attending college should increase with parental family income *controlling for student ability or prior scholastic achievement*. To determine the impact of family resources, and thus liquidity constraints, they utilize a data set that includes student performance on the Armed Forces Qualifying Test, the exam used to determine the placement of potential military recruits. Students take the exam between ages 14 and 21. Cameron and Heckman find that, controlling for AFQT scores, the positive effect of family income on college enrollment rates largely disappears.

Heckman and Klenow (1997, p. 33) write,

> If a student's probability of attending college were .50, increasing this family's income by $10,000 would only raise that probability to .52. . . . This lends support to the view that long term factors like ability, family structure, neighborhood effects, and the quality of primary and secondary schools an individual attends may be more important than short-term credit constraints in determining who goes to college.

Less affluent families are less likely to make gifts to children, so that marginal increases in parental income need not lead to them helping to finance education. However, an extra $10,000 of annual family income constitutes a significant relaxation of the family budget constraint. Hence, that such an increase has little effect on college attendance among students with a probability of attending of .50 indeed suggests that credit constraints are not very important.

While family income does not much affect the probability of college attendance, Cameron and Heckman find that it strongly influences the choice between community college and a four-year institution. This makes good sense. Community colleges have lower tuition than their four-year counterparts *and* community college students may more often continue to live in their parent's home, saving on dormitory outlays. Further, Kane and Rouse (1995) find that the economic return to community college credits is similar to that from four-year institutions. Significantly, these investigators are able to control for ability and family background (using data from the National Longitudinal Survey of the class of 1972). Their results indicate that the rewards to credits among students who do not complete their degree are quite similar for both types of institutions. Thus, the fact that more affluent students tend to attend better institutions may have larger implications for consumption benefits during and after college than for productivity after graduation. Similar results have been obtained by Dale and Krueger (1998) with respect to attending selective or "elite" instead of less selective four-year colleges. They have earnings data on students who were admitted to selective and less selective institutions, with some attending each type of institution. The earnings of students attending the less selective schools were found to be roughly equal to those attending the elite colleges.

One potential explanation of the weak effect of parental income is that government-sponsored student loan programs, loan subsidies, and tax credits for educational outlays leave few students with insufficient access to funds (see also section 7.5). Indeed, the findings of Heckman and Klenow bring into question the need for expansion of such programs, at least as tools to overcome liquidity constraints. Nevertheless, government loan and subsidy programs may have been important contributors to the expansion of schooling earlier in the twentieth century (the so-called high school movement, as well as the rise of college education).

For some reason, when family income is low, so (on average) is performance on the AFQT. Further, it is whatever these AFQT scores represent, rather than liquidity constraints, that retard college attendance among the children of poor households. Perhaps unsurprisingly, there is considerable debate about whether the AFQT scores measure ability z or scholastic achievement h_1. What is measured by AFQT has important policy implications. One possibility is that AFQT measures the stock of human capital rather than ability, and that children of poor families possess less human capital at the time the test is taken. Intuitively, affluent parents may send their children to better (or at least more resource-laden) primary and secondary schools, summer camps, and richer after-school activities. Affluent parents may also provide a richer education culture for preschoolers. However, interpreting the AFQT as representing the stock of human capital—rather than ability—appears somewhat inconsistent with the empirical evidence.

Recall that in the Ben-Porath model, current accumulation is independent of the existing stock of human capital. However, the higher is that stock, the less time is required to increase the stock. Let's apply this logic to two otherwise identical students except that the first has higher h_1, having come from a more affluent family. The high-capital student will have higher earnings at each point in the life cycle, both because more (less) time is devoted to current production (investment) and because of the higher initial stock. However, by this story the poor, or low h_1, student is predicted to invest more time, or engage in more schooling. This is at variance with the evidence shown above that children of more affluent families acquire more schooling. This suggests that AFQT must not reflect h_1 *alone*.

In the human capital model, high parental income is positively related to high parental schooling and ability. Even though ability, especially as related to genes, tends to regress to the mean, children of wealthy parents may also be more able than average. This could account for their higher AFQT scores. In this story, more affluent children have a higher return to schooling, accounting for the greater amount of schooling completed. If poor parents have less "able" children, their lower observed years of schooling could reflect optimal investments in the face of lower returns. *If* lower AFQT scores reflect inferior genes (as proposed in *The Bell Curve* by Hernstein and Murray, 1994), increasing subsidies at any point in the life cycle is inefficient, but may reduce inequality.

An emerging perspective is that, even if there are "ability" differences between affluent and poor children, they may be *primarily* the result of low income and investment rather than of genes. That is, low investments in the early years may lead to low child *ability*. This is most obviously true with respect to prenatal investments: The incidence of cigarette smoking, excessive drinking, drug abuse, and inadequate nutrition among pregnant women are all higher at low levels of income. Such behavior is known to affect the fetus adversely. Further, low income is associated with higher rates of out-of-wedlock child bearing, which greatly limits the nurturing and perhaps medical resources available to the newborn. Poorly educated poor parents may also make too low and/or inappropriate investments in the child during the early years when the neurological system is developing. (The pliability of the neurological system is purportedly illustrated by the "Mozart" effect, which claims laudatory effects on child *intelligence* of early exposure to classical music). More generally, some poor parents may invest less in the child both before the child is born and during the crucial early years, lowering z in the process.

This perspective suggests there may be an *efficiency* rationale for increasing support for government programs targeted to low-income pregnant women and their young children. This window of opportunity may be narrow: Currie and Thomas (1999) find that test scores as early as age 7 significantly impact future educational and labor market outcomes. On the other hand, increasing government support for *advanced training* among the poor may reduce inequality but would be inefficient. Such policies should therefore compete with other policies designed to mitigate inequality.

Heckman and Klenow argue that the returns on government investments appear to be larger the earlier in the life cycle they are targeted. In particular, they conclude that substantive government interventions on behalf of young disadvantaged children may be quite worthwhile. The Perry Preschool Program is an extensive intervention program, with much more contact with parents and children than, say, Head Start. They report that studies of the Perry program (featuring random assignment) have found that participants have "higher earnings and lower levels of criminal behavior in their late 20s than do comparable children randomized out of the program. . . . Measured through age 27, the program returns $5.70 for every dollar spent" (p. 38). On the other hand, they write that "adults past a certain age and below a certain skill level achieve poor returns to skill investment" (p. 50). Overall, their policy recommendation is to reallocate funds from investment in the old and less skilled toward the young.

Human Capital and Women

Altonji and Blank (1999) examine wage differences among men and women, employing data from the CPS, the monthly household survey that serves as the official source of U.S. labor force data. They find that men earned about 44% more than women in 1980; the gap had fallen to 29% by 1995. We argue that the human capital model can explain much of the wage gap and the change in that gap. Nevertheless, other factors, such as discrimination or differences in tastes, also appear to play a role.

Gender differences in earnings are partially explained by the fact that among older cohorts, women have less education than men. However, recalling Figure 7.6, this cannot be the whole story since, holding education constant, women earn less than men. Nevertheless, that earnings differential is smaller among younger workers, consistent with the decline in the gap noted above. Significantly, these profiles do not capture potentially important gender differences in postschooling experience (and therefore OJT) or in the types of human capital acquired in formal schooling. Both of these prove important.

Men and women differ in the amount of market work they plan to do per week and in the number of years they anticipate working over the life cycle. Further, the amount of market work women anticipate has changed through time. Young American women early in the twentieth century (i.e., early 1900s) expected—correctly—to work outside the home only until marriage, after which they would specialize in homemaking. Over the course of that century the market presence of women increased dramatically. In fact, the labor force participation rate (LFPR) of married women increased from 5.6% in 1900 to 59.9% in 1996 (Goldin 1990 and CPS). Substantial differences remain in the work weeks of men and women. Women's total market work per week in 1981 averaged 23.9 hours, compared with 44 hours per week for men (Juster and Stafford, 1991). Despite increases in the experience of women compared with men, an experience gap also remains. For example, among whites in 1996, 78.3% of men but only 63.2% of women worked during the year. Similarly, among those working in 1996, 86.3% of men worked full-time, compared with 69% of women (CPS, March 1998).

Such differences in market orientation may affect, and be affected by, human capital investments. The basic human capital model suggests that the returns to the acquisition of a skill increase with the amount of time that skill is employed. Consequently, the less time one expects to work in the market, the lower are the marginal benefits to the acquisition of market-oriented human capital, including OJT. This shows up clearly in estimates of the returns to education. Card (1999) finds that in "the U.S. labor market in the mid-1990s, about two-thirds of the measured return to education observed in annual earnings data is attributable to the effect of education on earnings per hour, with the remainder attributable to the effects on hours per week and week per year" (p. 9). Thus, the fact that women work less than men helps explain lower returns to education among women than men. Similarly, the fact that women now work more than before helps explain the increased return for women compared with men in recent years, and the rise in women's educational attainment compared with that of men.

How significant are these effects in terms of explaining the relative increase in women's earnings? Blau and Kahn (1997) find that increases in education and experience among women relative to men reduced the earnings gap from 34% in 1979 to 22% in 1988. Nevertheless, they find that changes in the wage structure worked against women: The relative wages of skilled workers have risen, and women continue to be employed in less skilled professions, on average. Without these changes in wage structure, they predict the relative wages of women would have risen an additional 7% over this period. Also, as women have increased their market work, they have chosen higher paying majors while in college. Altonji and Blank (1999) note that women now receive large fractions of the law, D.D.S., M.D., and M.B.A. degrees granted. They also report that between 1968 and 1991 the fraction of women among business majors increased from 8.7 to 42.7%.

Further increases in education and experience should continue to narrow the earnings gap between men and women, at least over the next several decades. For although educational attainment is lower among older women than older men, a higher proportion of women than men now complete at least a bachelor's (bachelorette's?) degree. Among those 25 to 29 years of age in 1998, 30.4% of white females had completed at least a B.A., compared with only 26.5% of males. Among blacks, the comparable numbers were 17 and 14.2% (CPS, March 1998). Second, the recent trends of greater experience among women and more market-oriented education are not yet fully reflected in the labor histories of older women.

Although the human capital model accurately predicts that men have earned more than women historically, a substantial gender gap remains after accounting for differences in human capital variables. Women, like blacks, were not allowed to vote, own property, attend certain universities, and so on, until rather recent times. No doubt vestiges of that discrimination continue to depress the earnings of women. Also, women have historically assumed greater responsibility for the rearing of children. This rewarding task may reduce the energy for and commitment to market work. We emphasize this issue in Chapters 8 and 9.

7.3 WAGE INEQUALITY AND SKILL-BIASED TECHNICAL CHANGE

7.3.1 Trends in Earnings Inequality

Inequality in wage earnings increased significantly from the mid- to late 1970s to the mid-1990s. Measures of that change typically contrast some aspect of the distribution of earnings among workers at two points in time. Since earnings data are often "top-coded," earnings at the top of the distribution are understated. Other measurement problems arise at the bottom of the income distribution. For these reasons, inequality is often assessed some distance from the tails. One common comparison is the percentage change in the *ratio of earnings* of workers in the 90th to with those in the 10th percentile. Katz and Autor (1999) calculate this measure using data from the CPS. They determine that the 90-10 weekly wage differential rose about 19% between 1979 and 1995 among full-time, full-year workers.

Also over that period, women's earnings rose about 15% more than men's. Since women's earnings continue to lag behind men's, their relative gains served to depress the overall rise in inequality. In fact, inequality among women and inequality among men each rose more than 25%. Since this was a period of low average wage growth, these gains by women imply real wage losses by men. In fact the real wages of male high school graduates—no college—remained below those in 1979. Katz and Autor report little change in overall inequality during 1963–1971 or 1971–1979, though average earnings rose about 20 percent in the earlier period and fell slightly in the latter period.

The rise in inequality may also be phrased in terms of the human capital model. Between 1979 and 1987 the earnings of those completing high school but not attending college fell roughly 6%, while earnings of college graduates rose over 5%. This increase in the relative reward to college—*the college wage premium*—continued into the mid-90s. Altogether, whereas in 1979 college grads earned roughly a third more on average than high school grads, by 1995 the college premium had risen above 50 percent (Katz and

Autor, 1998). This contrasts sharply with the period from 1971 to 1979, when earnings of high school grads rose 1.3% while earnings for those with a college degree *fell* by 7.1%. Annual average earnings in 1997 among those with high school only was $22,895, but those with only a bachelor's degree averaged $40,478 (CPS, March 1998).

Comparisons between educational groups fail to illuminate important experience effects. For example, between 1979 and 1987 those with 12 years of schooling (high school grads) and 5 years of experience saw their earnings decline about 18%, while earnings of college grads with 5 years' experience rose about 8%. Over the entire 1979–1995 interval, college grads with 25–35 years of experience had little change in their real earnings, while high school grads with the same experience saw earnings decline about 11 percent. In contrast, there was a decline of college premium for those with 5 years' experience from 1971 to 1979.

These figures relate to changes in inequality "between groups" of workers, with group membership entailing similar education and experience. Equally important has been the increase in earnings inequality "within groups" of workers, that is, among those possessing the same education and experience. The rise in within-group inequality accounts for more than half of the total increase. Autor and Katz conclude that the rise in within-group inequality for men in the 1980s consists of approximately equal increases in permanent and transitory factors. Here transitory inequality arises from year-to-year earnings fluctuations, which have become more volatile. Netting out these transitory fluctuations, "permanent" or life-cycle inequality within and between groups rose by similar amounts.

Summarizing, there were roughly equal increases in between-group and permanent within-group inequality. Further, the average of earnings over the 1970s, 1980s, and early 1990s was relatively flat. This reflects the productivity slowdown documented in Chapter 3. Any convincing explanation of the changes in inequality documented above must be consistent with this slow average growth. Below, we consider the role of human capital in the increase in the college wage premium, the changing returns to experience at different educational levels, the rise in within-group inequality, and the productivity slowdown.

7.3.2   Technical Change and Human Capital

The interaction of technical change with human capital accumulation decisions has implications for the distribution of earnings as well as for economic growth. An appreciation of these interactions follows from generalizing the Ben-Porath framework along the lines of HLT, discussed above.

Recall that the Ben-Porath model envisions only one *type* of human capital, with productivity varying across workers who possess different amounts of this generic skill. Thus, a worker with x units of human capital is x times more efficient or productive than a worker with but one unit. For a moment, suppose all workers have one of only two levels of human capital. Then, in this efficiency-units framework, the aggregate effective labor supply in period t is given by

$$L_t = N_{1t}h_{1t} + N_{2t}h_{2t} \tag{7.10}$$

where h_{1t} and h_{2t} are the efficiency units embodied in type 1 and type 2 workers, respectively. These are weighted by the numbers of each N_{1t} and N_{2t}. Formulation (7.10) implies perfect substitutability; if $h_{1t} = 2$ and $h_{2t} = 1$, then one type-1 worker is a perfect substitute for two type-2 workers. Aggregate labor could then be joined with an aggregate production function, say of the Cobb-Douglas form

$$Y_t = K_t^\alpha L_t^{1-\alpha}$$

where Y is output and K is physical capital. With competitive markets, the wage per unit of effective labor is then the marginal product of labor, or $w = dY/dL$ (see Chapter 3 for details). Consequently, the earnings of type 1 are wh_{1t} while those of type 2 are wh_{2t}.

In efficiency-units models, technical change is skill neutral and therefore cannot affect between-group inequality. Further, that framework requires the elasticity of substitution between skilled and unskilled workers to be infinity. However, empirical estimates of that elasticity are around 1.4 to 1.5 (cf. HLT and Katz and Murphy, 1992).

In practice, a large variety of skills are embodied within workers and employed in the economy at any point in time. These skills are not perfectly substitutable: x auto mechanics are not equivalent to one dental hygienist. Relatedly, individuals are better at some tasks than others and decide which skills to accumulate on the basis of comparative advantage. For these reasons, we now consider the implications of skill gradations that are imperfect substitutes.

Given skill diversity and comparative advantage, technical change is unlikely to reward all skills equally; it is not necessarily skill neutral. For example, the movement from artisans to mass production reduced the returns to skill and resulted in a deskilling of the work force. Conversely, the computer/information revolution has apparently increased the returns to skill, and perhaps to ability as well. To allow for more general effects of technical change, suppose now that there are two *imperfectly substitutable* types of skills in the economy. Specifically, let high school graduates possess "unskilled" human capital, while those with a college education embody "skilled" capital. Following Autor, Katz, and Krueger (1998) (henceforth AKK), we aggregate skilled and unskilled human capital using the constant elasticity of substitution function[13]

$$L_t = [\pi_t(a_t N_{ct})^\rho + (1 - \pi_t)(b_t N_{ht})^\rho]^{1/\rho}$$

In this expression, the elasticity of substitution between the two skill types is $1/(1 - \rho)$. Here a_t and b_t reflect the state of technology affecting the two skill types. If technical change is skill neutral, the ratio a_t/b_t will not change. If technical advance is *skill biased*, that ratio rises. π indexes the share of work activities performed by skilled workers, and it may also vary through time. For example, skill-biased technical change may lead to an increase in π. N_{ct} (N_{ht}) is the number of college educated (unskilled) workers.

Combining this framework with the assumption of perfectly competitive factor markets makes it possible to analyze relative wage changes in terms of changes in the supplies of and demand for each skill type. For example, the relative wage of skilled labor decreases following an increase in its relative supply. Further, the higher is the elasticity of substitution between skill types, the smaller is the effect on between-group inequality of a change in relative supply.

It is widely believed that technological change over the past several decades has been skill biased, implying complementarity between technical change and educated workers. A convincing piece of evidence concerns the sustained increase in the relative supply of more highly educated workers. Recall that AKK partition the work force into "college equivalents"—workers with 16 or more years of college, plus half of those with some college—and high school equivalents—those with 12 or fewer years of education, plus half those with some college. They calculate from 1940 census data that the employment share of college equivalents was 9.6%. By 1996, using CPS data, they find the relative supply of college equivalents in the work force had risen to 42.7%. If technical change over that period had been skill neutral, raising the demand for all skill/educational types equally, the relative wages of college graduates should have fallen, with those of high school dropouts soaring. In fact, though, this has not occurred; the premium paid to college-educated workers, though volatile over this period, has risen. This suggests that technical change must be increasing the relative demand for educated/skilled workers at least as rapidly.

AKK argue that another reason to view technical change as skill biased is the growing prominence of computers. By making information more plentiful, computers may increase the value of those information-processing skills associated with higher education. They find that "women, more highly educated workers, whites, white-collar workers, and full-time workers are more likely to use computers. The groups that experienced the greatest increases in computer use between 1984 and 1993 are also more likely to have experienced relative wage gains" (p. 1187). Conversely, "direct substitution of computers for human judgment and labor is likely to have been more important in clerical and production jobs than in managerial and production jobs" (p. 1186).

In the Ben-Porath model, investments may be perfectly calibrated so that incrementally higher ability translates into incrementally greater training. Consequently, that model includes no mechanism by which one can understand within-group inequality, let alone changes in such inequality. HLT point out that full-time schooling often ends abruptly (following completion of high school or college), at which time earnings jump dramatically.[14] To account for this, they model the decision to attend college as a discrete choice. By making formal educational investments lumpy, people with somewhat different ability levels will end up with the same education. This breaks the perfect correlation between ability and human capital in the Ben-Porath framework, providing one route by which within-group inequality may arise. HLT also allow the human capital production functions for OJT to differ between educational groups. Skill production continues to follow the basic Ben-Porath model of equation (7.2) (extended to many periods), except these authors allow z and λ to vary across educational groups. We now apply their framework to recent trends in earnings inequality.

HLT embed these features in a general-equilibrium, perfect-foresight simulation growth model, otherwise similar to that of Chapter 4. Their paper details how the model is numerically calibrated in accordance with available estimates of its parameters. As do others, HLT point to 1974 as a watershed year for modern technology. They assume that skill biased technical change (SBTC) begins at that time and continues for 30 years.[15] That is, over 30 years the demand for skilled labor shifts out to the right, while that for unskilled labor shifts inward.

The model yields implications for the supplies of each skill type, experience level, and age. First consider young workers who have already left school. The higher demand for skilled workers increases their skill prices and therefore potential earnings. However, since perfect foresight informs them that this trend will continue for some time, the marginal benefits of additional investment rise significantly.[16] Higher benefits induce young skilled workers to increase the time devoted to OJT. For this reason, the hours they supply and their earnings *fall* at first. Reduced supply gives a further upward boost to the skill price. In contrast, older skilled workers invest little before or after the SBTC starts; they are nearing retirement and have few years to recoup new investments. Consequently, their earnings rise along with the wage paid to skilled labor. Thus, during the first few years, the slope of the age-experience profile for skilled workers is predicted to steepen.

Young *unskilled* workers foresee the decline in their skill prices and reduce their current training before their wage falls further yet. Thus, their supply, and even earnings, rise at first. This serves to flatten the experience profile among unskilled workers during the early years of the SBTC.

These training effects reduce the college wage premium among workers with little experience in the first few years of SBTC. This prediction enjoys some empirical support: We noted above there was a decline of college premium for those with 5 years' experience from 1971 to 1979 (recall SBTC is *assumed* to have begun in 1974). Another point stressed by HLT is that changes in earnings may differ significantly from changes in earnings *potential* (i.e., human capital stocks or full-time earnings in the absence of training). The empirical literature, they note, typically focuses on the former, sometimes mistaking increased investment as reduced earnings capacity.

Within just a few years the supply movements reverse. The supply of skilled workers begins to increase both because each worker's stock of skill has increased and because the initial increase in training begins to taper off. Also important, the higher price for skilled labor induces a larger proportion of young people making the one-time schooling decision to enter college and become skilled. For these reasons the skill price increases at a slower pace than in the first years. Similarly, the supply of unskilled labor begins to fall because fewer young people choose to remain unskilled. As predicted, college enrollments have risen, increasing from 46.7 percent of recent high school graduates in 1980 to 57.8 percent in 1990.

The wage for skilled labor rises throughout the 30 years of SBTC. Notice that when the wage is expected to be rising, investment will be high: Whereas the marginal costs depend on the current wage only, the marginal benefits reflect the higher wages anticipated. As time passes, future wages are no longer expected to rise so much (because of the supply response), reducing OJT among the college educated compared with the large initial increase. For this reason, in this latter phase of the transition, the experience-earnings profile (in the cross section) flattens among the college educated. Conversely, as the future wage for unskilled labor is no longer expected to fall, young unskilled workers begin to undertake more training. For them, the experience-earnings profile is predicted to steepen in this second phase.

Katz and Autor (1998) present evidence consistent with this. For those with 16 or more years of schooling (i.e., those college educated) between 1971 and 1979, earnings fell almost 13% among those with 5 years of experience, but earnings were essentially unchanged for those with 25–35 years of experience. In the period 1979–1987, the earnings of those with less experience rose faster than those with 25–35 years, flattening the experience-earnings profile. Among high school graduates, the experience-earnings profile became steeper in both periods, though the steepening was more pronounced in the latter period. Also, Marcotte (2000) finds that formal postschooling investments did increase among the unskilled in this latter period, as predicted.

Unsurprisingly, the model predicts an increase in the college wage premium from the episode of SBTC. The thirty-year rise in the demand for skilled labor, and the decline for unskilled, is not nearly offset by the supply responses. This important prediction of increased between-group inequality matches the stylized fact discussed above; between 1979 and 1987 the college wage premium rose from about one-third to about one-half.

What about within-group inequality? Consider first new entrants among skilled workers. Two factors tend to increase inequality in this group in the first portion of the transition. First, since college graduates now include less able workers than before, skill dispersion is higher among recent graduates. Second, more able workers can also benefit more from OJT opportunities associated with SBTC. While the wage for skilled labor is expected to be rising, those most able invest and benefit the most. This prediction is in accordance with the empirical evidence discussed above: within-group inequality increased at least as much as did between-group inequality. During this early period, the converse is predicted for those of lower ability: While the wage for unskilled labor is expected to be falling, no one invests much, including the most able of high school grads. Further, the most able of those who would previously have attended high school only, now go to college. This reduces the dispersion of ability.

During this first phase, then, within-group inequality is expected to rise for the young college educated and fall for those with high school only. In fact, HLT report that the rise in wage inequality between 1979 and 1987 was largest for new entrants among skilled workers. The model predicts that during the second phase of the transition, during which there is little further change in wages expected, within-group inequality will decrease among the skilled. As of the late 1990s, there is little evidence that this has begun to happen. In this second phase, training is predicted to recover among high school graduates, increasing within-group inequality there. Altogether, applying the HLT model to explain the rise in inequality as a consequence of SBTC provides a rich set of theoretical predictions. Many of these are borne out.[17]

7.3.4 Another View

In the HLT framework, technologies reward skilled and unskilled workers differentially. However, in their view jobs are not technology specific. If they were, a change in technology would make some existing skills largely obsolete, forcing workers to switch to the new technology. (In contrast, HLT estimate that the rate of depreciation of human capital is essentially zero.) A complementary approach to understanding the rise in inequality by Galor and Moav (2000) stresses the link between vintages of technology and vintages of skill. Although Galor and Moav focus on *ability-biased* technical change rather than SBTC, their intuition is similar to that of HLT.

Galor and Omar argue that new technologies depreciate previously acquired human capital among some workers in some sectors. As examples, word-processing packages lowered the value of pure typing skills, and spreadsheets devalued the ability to add quickly in one's head. The same is true of nonmarket human capital. The ability to make clothes and cakes "from scratch" is worth less in the presence of mass production technologies.

Galor and Moav suppose that jobs are technology specific. When a new technology arrives, workers must either remain with their current technology or switch entirely to the new regime. Switching technologies makes more sense for younger workers for two reasons: First, they have more years to recoup the investment costs associated with the switch, and second, the opportunity cost of switching is lower since they have less experience and therefore they forego fewer earnings while investing. As in the HLT model, young workers who make the switch may experience an earnings decline during the years they acquire the new skills.[18]

This suggests that during the switch period there may well be a productivity slowdown. For although the same number of hours are *reported* as being worked, more time is withdrawn from current production to invest in the new technologies. *If* we had accurate measures of investment in OJT we might well see a decline in hours worked when technical change is rapid. However, the hours-worked measure employed for productivity calculations is not reduced by OJT. Thus, although output per hour worked (rather than devoted to training) *increases* with the onset of technical change, *measured productivity declines*. These considerations raise the possibility that the productivity slowdown detailed in Chapter 3 was an artifact of mismeasurement: Although growth in output per full-time worker declined, output per hour actually worked may have been rising faster than normal.

Similarly, an episode of SBTC could also slow productivity growth. Johnson (1997, p. 50) notes that with SBTC,

> The wage of skilled workers rises, but the wage of unskilled workers falls. The average wage in the economy rises due to extensive skill-biased technological change, but it does not rise by very much, for the increased efficiency associated with skilled workers performing their new jobs more efficiently than unskilled workers used to is at least partially offset by the decrease in employment in the initially skilled jobs and by the lower productivity of unskilled workers in the jobs that remain for them. . . . The introduction of personal computers, for example, *may* have increased the efficiency of skilled workers in their initial jobs, but it is clear from the various empirical studies that it caused an increase in the fraction of jobs normally performed by skilled workers. A lot of research and development expenditure over the past twenty years probably went into figuring out ways that various repetitive functions could be computerized. This should have increased the relative demand for skilled labor, but it would not necessarily have increased output per person-hour very much.

The relationship between human capital investment and income growth is important and controversial. In the next section we consider those links from a different perspective.

7.4 HUMAN CAPITAL AND ECONOMIC GROWTH

Real per capita income growth, when averaged over several decades, has been fairly constant over the last 130 years in the United States. This has been accompanied by dramatic increases in human capital accumulation as measured by years of schooling completed. As recently as 1940, only 24.1 percent of adults age 25 or over had completed high school. By 1993, this figure had risen to 80.2 percent. In Chapter 6 we argued that the "high school movement" may have been an important contributor to economic growth in the first two-thirds of the twentieth century. In recent decades college enrollments have also risen. Thus, while but 4.6 percent of adults over age 25 had completed college as of 1940, this figure was 23.8 percent in 1997 (Filer, 1996, and CPS).

This section considers the role of human capital accumulation *among adults* in producing economic growth. Topel (1999) reviews the empirical literature linking human capital and growth. He concludes that researchers "find little evidence that growth of human capital is associated with growth of output, but a higher *level* of education per worker . . . is associated with a higher rate of economic growth" (p. 17). Qualitative results developed below are consistent with these findings. We first note significant reasons that the contribution of college education or OJT to growth may be smaller than the contribution of primary and secondary education. However, we then address other mechanisms that make advanced training uniquely important to growth.

7.4.1   Expanding Human Capital When Private and Social Returns Coincide

Human capital directly affects the aggregate supply of effective labor and has indirect effects on conventional savings and, therefore, physical capital. This suggests that the acquisition of human capital will affect the level, and perhaps growth, of aggregate income. To address these issues we (loosely) extend the overlapping-generations model of Chapter 3 to include human capital. For now, we abstract from either population growth or technical change. We also assume that the social return to human capital equals the private return; all costs and benefits accrue directly to the worker. Later we allow for benefits that are not captured by the individual.

At any time there are two overlapping generations of economically active individuals. Individuals work in both periods of adult life. Initially, suppose there is no investment in human capital. This may be due to credit market imperfections, for example, but the reason is not important for the issues at hand. However, for whatever reason, beginning in t = 1 young households invest $x *via foregone earnings*, increasing earnings when old by $x(1 + i^a), where i^a is the average rate of return. With diminishing returns, the average return i^a exceeds the marginal rate i. For a moment, though, we abstract from diminishing returns to envision the simple case where i^a = i = r. The interest rate r represents the return on financial investments and on physical capital.

With i^a = r, human capital and conventional savings are perfect substitutes in a household's portfolio. This investment does not affect life wealth but simply postpones the *timing* of income over the life cycle. Since life wealth is unchanged, neither is consumption in any period. However, since earnings while the household is young are lower by $x, so too are financial savings. Then, when the household is old, the increase in labor income of $(1 + r)x (using the fact that i^a = r). This just offsets the decline in savings of $x and interest income of $xr, to leave old age resources unchanged. This policy has no welfare implications for those young in t = 1.

We now consider the implications for aggregate income (assuming a constant wage and interest rate). Aggregate income in a period is the sum of the labor income of the young, the labor income of the old, and the capital income of the old. In period $t = 1$, wage earnings of each young worker fall by \$x. Neither the labor supply of the old nor their interest income in $t = 1$ is affected. Consequently, GDP falls by \$x per young worker in $t = 1$.

How does GDP at $t = 2$ compare with that in $t = 0$? The young of $t = 2$ again invest \$x via reduced labor earnings. The old's labor income is higher by $x(1 + r)$. Since their financial savings are lower by \$x, interest income is lower by \$rx. Thus, adding the changes in income across sources and cohorts, aggregate income is unchanged compared with when no investments were made ($-x + x(1 + r) - rx = 0$). During the transition, $t = 1$, output falls by x per young worker, while at $t = 2$ there is no change. Pushing earnings later into the life cycle entails an interval of reduced income, and has no effect on long-run income or anyone's welfare.

Let us see how these results generalize, first allowing for population growth at rate n. Setting the number of young workers at $t = 1$ equal to 1 (billion?), there are $1 + n$ young workers at $t = 2$. As above, in $t = 1$ human capital investment reduces aggregate income and conventional savings each by \$x per young worker.

What about aggregate income at $t = 2$? As without population growth, the old in $t = 2$ have labor income that is higher by $x(1 + r)$ and \$xr less interest income. However, since there are $1 + n$ young at $t = 2$, their labor income falls by $(1 + n)x$. Summing the income changes across cohorts, "long-run" income is lower by \$nx: Income falls because the young who make investments are more numerous than those who reap the benefits of (past) investments, the old. With population growth, aggregate income falls in both the transition ($t = 1$) and subsequent periods. As when $n = 0$, there is no effect on anyone's consumption.

Of course, the foregoing failed to acknowledge that the average rate of return exceeds the marginal, and so exceeds r. Acknowledging that $i^a > r$ reduces the drag to growth. However, only if $i^a - r$ exceeds n will such human capital investments increase the *level* of aggregate income in the long run. (Actually, with $i^a > r$ there is a wealth effect that increases first-period consumption. This lowers conventional savings even more; for this reason an even larger average return is required for growth). Introducing investments does not affect the long-run growth *rate* in this story; GDP will grow at rate n as before. Nevertheless, if $i^a > r$, the human capital investments increase household wealth, consumption, and welfare.

Finally, suppose (labor-augmenting) technical change occurs at rate v, allowing per capita income to rise at that rate in the long run. In this context, the investment costs of human capital reduce long-run income by $(n + v)x$, since the young are not only more numerous but more productive as well. Thus $i^a - r$ must now exceed $n + v$, if long-run income is to rise.

Population growth and technical change alter the incentives to produce human capital, and the foregoing mechanical discussion abstracted completely from those complications. These thought experiments were designed to illustrate that an increase in the rate of human capital investments *need not* increase transitional growth, or even long-run income. This result contrasts sharply with that of section 6.5, where the rise in primary and secondary education was argued to be a driving force of early twentieth-century growth.

What assumptions account for the difference in growth effects? In the model of human bequests, all investment was in the form of goods inputs. In particular, we abstracted from the foregone earnings of young teens associated with schooling. Parents financed the expansion of education by reducing consumption and, to a lesser extent, financial savings. The small decline in savings did not affect output until the newly educated workers could boost output. Further, since investments were inefficiently low at the start of the transition, the expansion of primary and secondary education may have had a large impact on labor earnings. Most probably, the foregone earnings of teens did dampen growth somewhat relative to the story of Chapter 6. However, the greater foregone earnings and larger declines in physical capital associated with adult investments make it harder for adults to boost growth, supposing the story we have told above is otherwise complete. However, that may not be a reasonable assumption, for reasons we explore below.

7.4.2   Human Capital Externalities and Growth

The discussion above assumed that the social and private rates of return on human capital investments are equal. However, human capital externalities and government subsidy and tax policies make this unlikely. An interesting possibility is that human capital externalities are large, so that human capital accumulation significantly encourages growth. One possible source for externalities is that high human capital workers may raise the productivity of those around them, in a way that markets are unable to internalize. If so, the social rate of return exceeds the private rate, and the likelihood of human capital contributing to growth is enhanced.

That person A can benefit from the knowledge of person B is obvious. Who doesn't want a person in the next office with better computer skills, a broader knowledge of some relevant literature, or state of the art quantitative training? More generally, since people pay to be taught by high human capital people in formal schooling settings, it is reasonable to assume that they derive benefits from associating (or mentoring) informally at work with more knowledgeable colleagues or being mentored by them.

However, Heckman and Klenow (1997) point out that such benefits make a contribution to growth *beyond* private returns only if they are not internalized through differential compensation. And, at the level of the firm, they argue that such compensation is likely. For low human capital workers "would accept lower wages in return for the opportunity of working around high human capital workers from whom they can learn more. Firms will compete for high human capital workers on these grounds, so that the high human capital workers are compensated for what they teach other workers" (p. 19). More generally, at the firm level we *expect* inputs to be complementary; when they are, this is not evidence of an externality.

For an externality to exist, workers must benefit the higher is the human capital of workers at *other* firms. As one example of such effects, Foster and Rosenzweig (1996) find that educated farmers are more likely to adopt new, efficient seed technologies, and that farmers in general are more likely to adopt a technology after a neighbor has used it. In this example, an increase in education hastens the adoption of advanced technologies (we return to this below). However, there is no estimate of the quantitative significance of such effects.

Technical knowledge is nonrival; one person's use of Windows 98 does not detract from another's ability to use it. However, technical knowledge is often excludable through, as examples, patent and copyright protection. To the extent that it is *not* excludable, the creation of new technology may generate beneficial externalities that are not internalized. Further, the line between human capital accumulation and technological progress is often blurred (a doctoral dissertation, for example, is often both human capital accumulation and an advancement of general knowledge).

Private sector scientists, and the companies that employ them, are able to accrue many of the benefits of their innovations as a consequence of patent and copyright law. Nevertheless, evidence suggests that the social rate of return on R&D investment is exceedingly high, and substantially above the private return. Recently, Jones and Williams (1998) find social returns of *at least* 30% on R&D! They conclude that even a conservative estimate of the social return "indicates that optimal investment in R and D is more than two to four times actual investment" (p. 1134).

Ultimately, whether externalities raise the contribution to growth beyond private returns is an empirical question. Unfortunately, current data make empirical assessment difficult. In one recent study, Acemoglu and Angrist (2000) find external returns to education of perhaps just 1%. Even if convincing evidence of externalities is uncovered, the implications for policy are unclear. As Heckman and Klenow note (1997, p. 3),

> Evidence for externalities at some base level is not evidence that subsidies to human capital should be boosted from their current levels. Existing subsidies may have already eliminated a gap between social and private returns. We estimate that, to justify the current level of subsidies to public college instruction in the U.S., the social marginal product of the human capital gained from college education has to be about 30% higher than the private marginal product. If externalities are positive but not sufficiently large, then existing subsidies are actually too generous, at least on efficiency grounds.

7.4.3 "Teachers" and Rapid Development

Topel (1999) notes a puzzle in economic growth is that while some countries remain trapped in a low-growth state, other countries rise quickly from underdevelopment, accumulating physical and human capital along a path of rapid output growth. He notes that Becker, Murphy, and Tamura (1990), among others, take a broader view of human capital production to shed light on that issue.

The key insight builds on the notion that, in formal schooling (or OJT), an important input is teachers (or mentors), and in particular, their human capital. To simplify, suppose that "teachers" are adults in their second period of life. To illustrate the positive effect of teachers' human capital we supplement the Ben-Porath production function of equation (7.2) as follows

$$h_{2t+1} - h_{1t} = q_{1t} = z(s_{1t+1}h_{1t})^{\lambda}(h_{2t})^{1-\lambda} \qquad (7.11)$$

Subscripts have been added to variables to keep track of time.

Dividing both sides of (7.11) by h_{1t} we obtain the proportionate growth in human capital over the life cycle

$$(h_{2t+1} - h_{1t})/h_{1t} = z(s_{1t})^\lambda (h_{1t})^{\lambda-1}(h_{2t})^{1-\lambda}$$
$$= z(s_{1t})^\lambda (h_{2t}/h_{1t})^{1-\lambda} \qquad (7.12)$$

This equation reveals that the growth rate of human capital is higher the more knowledgeable are teachers (i.e., second-period adults) relative to students.[19]

Now, suppose there is some "shock" that increases the human capital of teachers in t. For example, an international development agency may supplement the teaching corps with external scientists and engineers in that period, only. This raises the productivity of time investments by students, lowering their marginal cost of acquiring skills. Viewing equation (7.12), with both time investments by students and "teacher intensity" having risen, the average human capital of older adults or teachers may rise as rapidly between t and t + 1 (than between t − 1 and t when the foreign teacher increased the average). To simplify, suppose the ratio of teacher to student human capital in t + 1 is exactly the same as that in t. Then there would be no further change in time investments. However, time investments and the growth rate of human capital are both *permanently* higher. The initial temporary shock to human capital transformed the country from one of slow growth to a developed, rapidly growing economy. More realistically, there may be decreasing returns in human capital production, rather than the constant returns assumed in equation (7.11). Even then, the temporary shock would produce several periods of fast economic growth, before diminishing returns to human capital restored the economy's initial growth rate.

7.4.4 Assimilating Technology

It is widely acknowledged that technical progress becomes embodied in physical capital so that, holding investment constant, the productivity of physical capital rises. Similarly, advances in knowledge are embodied in successive "vintages" of workers so that, holding investment constant, the productivity of workers rises.

Children learn from parents, neighbors, peers, and teachers at school. The usefulness of such learning may increase with the state of knowledge, or technology, when children are young. Then the human capital of young adults in t would increase with the stock of general knowledge in her childhood, $\mathbf{A}_{t-1}$. That is

$$h_{1t} = h_{1t}(\mathbf{A}_{t-1})$$

Similarly, the knowledge imparted by teachers of young adults is positively related to "best practice," meaning the technology of the current period. For this reason, the human capital of mentors in t increases with $\mathbf{A}_t$

$$h_{2t} = h_{2t}(\mathbf{A}_t)$$

Incorporating these ideas into the Ben-Porath function (7.11) yields

$$q_{1t} = z[s_{1t}h_{1t}(\mathbf{A}_{t-1})]^\lambda[h_{2t}(\mathbf{A}_t)]^{1-\lambda}$$

so that dividing through by h_{1t}, growth in human capital is given by

$$(h_{2t+1} - h_{1t})/h_{1t} = z(s_{1t})^\lambda[h_{2t}(\mathbf{A}_t)/h_{1t}(\mathbf{A}_{t-1})]^{1-\lambda}$$

This expression reveals that the faster is technical change (the growth in $\mathbf{A}$), the higher is the knowledge of teachers compared with that of young adults. As above, this makes the time of students more productive, raising the return to education and time investments. It also illustrates how even constant technical growth may lead to ongoing increases in human capital (but constant time investments). For example, due to the ongoing expansion of knowledge, current college training in economics utilizes better economic theory, empirical knowledge, and quantitative methods than those used in, say, the 1970s—even though instruction is and was predominantly performed by Ph.D.s in both periods. This transmission of superior knowledge may improve the skills and raise the productivity of economics graduates. More generally, with an expansion of ideas, each generation of college graduates obtains a better education and is more productive than their parents. Similarly, the same time devoted to OJT training or learning-by-doing results in more productive knowledge being acquired.

Topel argues that the role of human capital in assimilating technology may be an important contributor to economic growth. This role is one reason growth regressions typically indicate that the *level* of human capital *is* important to growth. Topel reports research of Barro and Sali-i-Martin, who find perhaps unbelievably large positive effects of the level in a cross section of countries: They find that roughly a 1-year increase in average years of secondary education raises the average annual growth *rate* of a country by 1.5% per year! Even if, as argued by Topel, the effect is much smaller, it may be significant.

7.4.5   Effects of Human Capital on Technical Progress

Above we considered how exogenous technical change may affect human capital accumulation. Equally important is whether, and if so how, human capital affects the rate of technical change. An economy's rate of technical advance is positively related to the number of workers whose human capital is close to the frontier of knowledge, for both supply and demand reasons. On the supply side, there are more people who are most capable of extending knowledge. On the demand side, in recent times new technologies have required, or been complementary to, educated workers. Thus, a more educated work force increases the demand for new technology, providing a further incentive for its creation. We address these in turn.

Among developing economies, technical progress often derives from technology transfer, whereby technologies developed elsewhere are assimilated domestically. However, technical advances are not of equal value to each country (cf. Basu and Weil, 1998). In general, the adoption of new technologies presupposes a work force capable of using them (possessing some threshold level of human capital). For example, in a country where literacy is not prevalent, personal computers contribute little to most firms. This suggests that increased human capital accumulation within a developing economy may allow the adoption of more sophisticated technologies, at least temporarily raising the rate of technical progress.

In "leading edge" economies, technical progress entails the creation of entirely new ideas. The generation of advanced technologies is often a product of explicit research and development activity. Perhaps especially in R&D, the ability to substitute unskilled for skilled labor is limited. This makes the advancement of technology responsive to the distribution across workers of skills or human capital. Thus, in both "assimilating" and "leading edge" economies, workers closer to the economy's technical frontier (i.e., with more training) have a higher marginal product with respect to knowledge creation.

In the spirit of Jones (1998) and Datar and Rangazas (1999), we model a "discovery function" for new ideas, paying particular attention to the role of human capital. Assume workers far below the economy's technical frontier are less likely to advance technology. To capture this idea in a tractable way, assume that only those workers with sufficiently high human capital relative to the "state of the art" contribute to $\mathbf{A}$. Let R_h be the number of such workers. The ability to advance knowledge may also be sensitive to the current level of knowledge. This suggests a discovery function of the form

$$\mathbf{A}_t = \mathbf{A}_{t-1} + gR_h^\beta \mathbf{A}_{t-1}{}^\Theta \qquad (7.13)$$

where g is a positive constant. Following Jones, suppose that $0 < \beta < 1$. As noted above, $\beta > 0$ because more researchers mean more ideas. Intuitively, $\beta < 1$ because the more knowledge workers there are, the more duplication of effort or "stepping on toes" there will be: Several researchers may be working on related designs for a better mousetrap simultaneously. If $\Theta > 0$, the more ideas that have already been created, the more opportunities there are for combining and/or extending ideas. Then, the higher is the existing stock, the more productive are research efforts. Or, in the words of Isaac Newton, "If I have seen farther than others, it is because I was standing on the shoulders of giants." This effect is a positive externality to other researchers. Newton did not capture all the benefits to society associated with his contributions to the development of calculus. (On the other hand, it could be that the easiest ideas are discovered first, so that more effort is required to produce ideas the greater is the stock; this is the "fishing out" effect and occurs if $\Theta < 0$. The large returns to R&D discussed above suggest $\Theta > 0$.)

Whether Θ is greater, less than, or equal to 1 is important to the prospects for increasing growth through human capital deepening. To appreciate why, divide both sides of (7.13) by $\mathbf{A}_{t-1}$ to yield the growth rate for technology v_t:

$$v_t = (\mathbf{A}_t - \mathbf{A}_{t-1})/\mathbf{A}_{t-1} = gR_h^\beta \mathbf{A}_{t-1}^{\Theta-1} \qquad (7.14)$$

If $\Theta = 1$, the right-hand side of (7.14) simplifies to gR_h^β, so technical growth increases with R_h. If $\Theta > 1$, technical growth accelerates even when R_h is constant. In the most probable case, $\Theta < 1$, so that the growth rate of ideas slows as a society progresses; although new ideas continue to be developed, their number declines relative to the existing stock of ideas (cf. Jones, 1998, Ch. 5).

Earlier we argued that assimilation of technical change by students may increase human capital, even when the time devoted to training is constant. Suppose individuals' knowledge *relative to the frontier* depends only upon the quantity of training, and therefore is independent of the level and growth of technology. Then growth in **A** wouldn't affect R_h. Even in this case, R_h may increase as a consequence of population growth. In this way, population growth could produce *scale effects* in economic growth, with larger economies growing faster. However, in Jones' model, in the likely case where $\Theta < 1$, long-run per capita income growth increases only when the *rate* of population growth is higher. Diminishing returns to the stock of ideas means that the *size* of the economy does not affect long-term growth.

More generally, as technology expands, additional training may be required to maintain the same relative distance from the research frontier (even if a high school science class is more informative now, for example). Then a combination of technical growth and constant population would cause R_h to fall. Uncertainty regarding the degree of assimilation when schooling is held constant makes it difficult to know how much the dramatic increase in education in the twentieth century increased the *proportion* of workers who are "close to the frontier." Nevertheless, rising education and rising population may be expected to increase the number of workers most capable of advancing knowledge. In fact, Jones finds that the number of scientists and engineers engaged in R&D in the United States quintupled between 1950 and 1990. However, worker productivity did not gain speed over that period. This suggests that incomplete assimilation and stepping on toes, $\Theta < 1$, may both be important.

Acemoglu (1998) argues that there is a distinct mechanism by which an increase in the number of educated workers contributes to technology growth. By this link, increases in the supply of skilled workers create a larger market for skill-biased technologies. That is, developers of new technologies anticipate a larger profit when there is a larger pool of potential users of the technology. In particular, the entrance into the labor market of the well-educated baby-boom cohort, beginning in the late 1960s, entailed a rapid outward shift in the supply of skilled workers. These workers constituted a large, ready market for new skill-biased technologies. In this light, it may be unsurprising that the rate of SBTC increased just a few years later.

7.5 TAXATION AND HUMAN CAPITAL ACCUMULATION

The importance of human capital accumulation to earnings, inequality, and growth underscores the need to understand how tax policy affects skill accumulation. Our analysis of these issues begins with a discussion of the incentive effects of taxes on worker behavior. This partial-equilibrium analysis proves to be quite misleading on some counts, as explained in our extension to general equilibrium (which allows for feedback effects of factor prices through capital accumulation).

7.5.1 Microeconomics of Taxation and Human Capital

Human capital and financial assets are alternative ways for households to carry resources into the future. Tax policy alters the optimal asset portfolio of households by affecting the returns to either type of capital. In practice, tax codes are complex. Nevertheless, we gain substantial insight through study of the primary tax instruments. In turn, we consider wage income taxation, interest income taxation, and, finally, a general income tax.

Consider a *proportional* tax on wage income, so that all labor earnings are taxed at the constant rate t_w. Recall that the marginal return on investments i is determined by the ratio of marginal benefits to marginal costs. Clearly, a proportional tax reduces the marginal benefits (higher wages) of investment by t_w percent. The effect on costs is less straightforward. Suppose, initially, that investment costs consist of $1,000 of foregone earnings. In this case, the tax reduces those costs by t_w percent: foregoing $1,000 of pre-tax earnings now reduces net income by only $1000(1 − t_w)$. Since the tax reduces benefits and costs equiproportionately, there is no effect on the return i, the time invested, or skills acquired. Therefore, a proportional wage tax is neutral when there are no out-of-pocket costs of training (as with general OJT). Of course, there *are* important out-of-pocket expenses for college tuition, books, and so on. We consider below the tax implications of out-of-pocket expenses.

The neutrality of wage taxation when all costs are foregone earnings is overturned if wage taxes are *progressive* in the sense that marginal tax rates rise with income. In the United States, for example, low-earning individuals pay no income tax, while the marginal tax rate rises to 38.6% among high-income individuals.[20] Since investments are typically made during the early years when income is low, progressive taxation tends to hit the benefits more heavily than the costs. This reduces i at any investment level, discouraging accumulation.

To see this explicitly, let unimproved earnings (i.e., those in the absence of first-period investments) be equal in the two periods. Now, since human capital accumulation reduces first-period earnings and increases those in the second period, progressive taxation hits income in period 2 at a higher rate (t_w^2) than in period 1 (t_w^1). The rate of return in the presence of the tax, i', may be expressed in terms of the no-tax return (at a given investment level) as

$$1 + i' = dE_2(1 − t_w^2)/[−dE_1(1 − t_w^1)] − 1 < dE_2/(−dE_1) − 1 = 1 + i$$

Since $t_w^2 > t_2^1$ the rate of return on any unit of human capital is reduced by progressive taxation, $i' < i$. This reduces human capital accumulation relative to the no-tax or proportional tax level. Since the tax reduces the private return (based on net earnings and costs) below the social return (based on gross earnings and costs), accumulation is made inefficiently low.

Finally, consider again proportional wage taxation, but now recognize that there are often substantial out-of-pocket expenses associated with human capital accumulation, such as tuition, books, and computers. Even in this case, if the out-of-pocket expenditures are tax deductible, the tax remains nondistortionary. For example, if $1,000 is spent before taxes, tax relief of $1,000t_w$ lowers the net cost to $1,000(1 − t_w)$, just as if the cost had been foregone earnings (see above). When expenses may not be deducted, the tax does not affect the cost of out-of-pocket outlays. For this reason costs decline by less than t_w percent, falling by a larger percent the greater is the share of foregone earnings in total costs. As before, the tax reduces benefits by t_w percent. Since benefits decline more than costs, the accumulation planned in the absence of the tax now proves too large, so accumulation declines.

Recent legislation in the United States allows for tax *credits* from educational expenses. The Hope Credit reduces taxes dollar for dollar on the first $1,000 of eligible expenses in the first two years of college, and 50% of the next $1,000 of expenses. The credit may be claimed by parents on each dependent student, or by independent students. In 2000, the Lifetime Learning Credit is 20% of up to $5,000 of eligible expenses within a year, and may be taken in any year of undergraduate or graduate training. (A 20% tax credit is the same as a full tax deduction for someone in the 20% tax bracket.) Both credits are phased out for adjusted gross income from $40,000 and $50,000 for singles ($80,000–$100,000 for couples filing joint returns). More generally, Heckman and Klenow (1997) present figures suggesting that close to 90 percent of the *instructional* costs of attending public institutions, including community colleges, are paid from public funds. These provisions would seem to be large enough to ensure that outlays for community college are treated at least as well as foregone earnings. They may leave a significant portion of private college tuition without tax relief. Even here, though, other provisions such as Education IRAs may afford significant tax savings for some families.

Since human capital and financial investments are alternative ways to save, changes in the return to money investments may affect saving in the form of human capital. To see this, consider the taxation of interest income at rate t_r, which depresses the net-of-tax return to financial savings to $r(1 - t_r)$. Now, at the pretax investment level, $i > r(1 - t_r)$, so that further human capital investment is encouraged. Thus, the taxing of financial assets induces a portfolio shift toward human capital.

It is interesting that a tax on earnings does not lower the return to human capital, but a tax on interest does lower the return to physical capital. The reason is that, whereas wage taxation reduces benefits and costs proportionately, the tax on interest doesn't: The benefits to saving (higher future consumption) are taxed, but the cost of saving (reduced current consumption) is not tax deductible. Notice that a *consumption* tax would treat savings in that symmetrical fashion; increased savings would lower current taxes but increase future taxes.

Davies and St. Hilaire (1987) point out that in the important case where students or their parents borrow to finance education, the stimulative effect of interest taxation for human capital accumulation relies on interest expense being tax deductible. If not, the borrowing rate would remain r and interest income taxation would not affect human capital accumulation. In the United States in 2000, up to $1,500 per year of interest paid on educational loans in the first 60 months of scheduled loan repayments is tax deductible. More generally, *all* interest expense on home mortgages is tax deductible for those homeowners who itemize (which is the majority). About two-thirds of U.S. households are homeowners.

Analysis of a proportional income tax simply combines the interest and wage income taxation results. Since the interest income tax encourages human capital while the wage tax (with goods inputs) decreases human capital, the overall effect is ambiguous. The fact that tax rates are progressive increases the likelihood of an adverse effect on accumulation. Further complications arise once it is acknowledged that the returns to human capital accumulation are uncertain (cf. Lord and Rangazas, 1998).

An empirical examination of the effects of taxes on human capital requires the researcher to take account of households' expectations concerning future wages, interest rates, and tax policy. This may prove difficult to do in a convincing fashion. Further, since human capital affects the economy broadly, such partial-equilibrium assessments would be of dubious value. For this reason, the impact of taxes on human capital has often been assessed using general-equilibrium simulation models. We now consider such models and some results of tax reform simulations.

7.5.2   Macroeconomics of Taxation and Human Capital

We extend the discussion of human capital taxation to a general-equilibrium growth framework, similar to that employed in Chapters 3 and 4. Several modifications are required, though, to allow for the endogenous accumulation of human capital. Our approach follows most closely Lord (1989) and Davies and Whalley (1991), both of whom develop aggregate versions of the Ben-Porath model developed in section 7.1.

Consumers live, work, and consume for two periods. In the first period, time is allocated between the labor force and the accumulation of human capital. The effective supply of labor in this economy at time t is

$$L_t = (1 - s_1)h_{1t}N_{1t} + h_{2t}N_{2t}$$

where $N_{1t}(N_{2t})$ is the number of workers who are young (old) in period t.

Let the economy's output be produced in accordance with the Cobb-Douglas production function

$$Y_t = K_t^\alpha L_t^{1-\alpha}$$

Dividing both sides by effective labor, output per effective worker y_t is expressed in terms of the capital-effective labor ratio k_t,

$$y_t = k_t^\alpha$$

This is a neoclassical production function, with constant returns to scale overall and diminishing returns to capital or effective labor alone. Assuming a perfectly competitive economy, the wage per unit of effective labor equals its marginal product and is positively related to k_t (see Chapter 3). Similarly, the interest rate or rental rate on capital equals its marginal product, which falls as capital becomes relatively more plentiful.

Suppose human capital is produced in accordance with the Ben-Porath function of equation (7.2),

$$q_1 = z(s_1h_1)^\lambda$$

so that, for now, we abstract from goods inputs.

Imagine consumers have Cobb-Douglas utility, $U_t = C_{1t}^\theta C_{2t+1}^{1-\theta}$. For two reasons there will be a positive relationship between savings and the interest rate. First, since a portion of labor income is earned in period 2, an increase in the interest rate expected in t + 1 reduces life wealth and, therefore, C_{1t}. (This is the human wealth effect of Chapter 2). Second, at higher interest rates, investment in human capital is lower, so that conventional saving is higher.

In Chapter 4, tax policies were seen to have important implications for capital accumulation even in the absence of incentive (i.e., relative price) effects. For example, policies that postpone taxes until later in the life cycle increase private savings, as households set aside monies while young in anticipation of the additional taxes when old. We begin by abstracting from tax-timing considerations in order to isolate the household-level incentive effects for capital accumulation. To this end, suppose tax revenues are redistributed to households in lump-sum fashion in that same period (cf. Lord and Rangazas, 1995).

Suppose the economy is initially in a no-tax steady state when the decision is made to impose a proportional tax on labor and capital income (i.e., an income tax). How might this affect the accumulation of human capital? Remember that at the household level, a proportional tax on wages does not affect human capital when, as here, there are no goods inputs. Since lowering the net interest rate makes human capital relatively more attractive, the partial-equilibrium effect (i.e., taking factor prices as given) is an increase in accumulation.

However, there are also general-equilibrium effects to consider, since the tax alters the capital-effective labor ratio. Recall from Chapter 3 that in a two-period overlapping-generations framework, the supply of capital in t + 1 equals the aggregate savings by those young in t. Before the tax is imposed, the savings of a young person in t are wage earnings minus consumption

$$S_{1t}^0 = w_t h_{1t}(1 - s_1^0) - C_{1t}^0.$$

In the presence of the tax, recalling that tax revenues are redistributed in lump-sum fashion, first-period savings become

$$S_{1t}^1 = w_t h_{1t}(1 - s_1^1)(1 - t_w) - C_{1t}^1 + t_w w_t h_{1t}(1 - s_1^1)$$
$$= w_t h_{1t}(1 - s_1^1) - C_{1t}^1$$

Since the tax revenues are returned in lump-sum fashion in the same period they are paid (as seen in the third right-hand-side term in the first line), the payment of taxes by itself does not affect savings. However, the incentive effects that increased human capital accumulation do alter savings. First, the higher investment increases the time investment, $s_1^1 > s_1^0$, reducing earnings when young. Second, the lower after-tax interest rate increases first-period consumption, since the present value of earnings is higher (the human wealth effect). Both of these effects serve to decrease saving.

The supply of effective labor is also altered. As discussed in section 7.4, the expansion of human capital time investments will reduce effective labor supply at time t: the labor supply of the old of t is unchanged, while the young work less to invest more. However, beginning in t + 1, aggregate effective labor supply will rise so long as the increase in the human capital of the old exceeds the decline in earnings among the young. This is true so long as the marginal rate of return exceeds the rate of population growth (i > n), as seems likely. Consequently, by the second period following the tax imposition, the capital-effective labor ratio k will have fallen, reflecting both lower saving when young and increased effective labor. In general equilibrium, falling k means rising r and falling

w. The increase in r serves to reduce the positive partial-equilibrium effect on human capital. Thus, the general equilibrium effect would be positive, though smaller, than that in partial equilibrium.

Allowing for nontax deductible goods inputs complicates the story, since wage taxation then reduces human capital in partial equilibrium. Thus, compared with the previous case, there is either a smaller partial-equilibrium increase in human capital investments or, theoretically, even a decline. Nevertheless, if savings are very responsive to the interest rate, taxing interest income lowers k as before. However, with goods inputs, the fact that falling k reduces the wage implies a negative general-equilibrium effect (lowering benefits of human capital more than costs). This effect was not present in the absence of goods inputs. Also, falling k pulls the net interest rate back up toward the taxless rate, discouraging human capital investments. Thus, general-equilibrium factor price movements reduce human capital.

Trostel (1993) employs a large simulation model to capture these various effects quantitatively. He calibrates the initial steady state of the model on the basis of the existing tax treatment of income, paying special attention to goods inputs. From this baseline, he reduces the tax rate on income slightly, returning taxes in lump-sum fashion.[21] Adverse general-equilibrium effects in conjunction with limited deductibility of out-of-pocket expenses lead to a large negative effect of income taxation on human capital accumulation. He concludes that "a one-percentage point increase in the income tax rate causes the long-run stock of human capital to decline by .97 percent under the most plausible set of parameters" (p. 328). Especially if human capital contributes to growth via the other mechanisms discussed in section 7.4, negative effects of this magnitude are quite disconcerting.

More recently, Lord and Rangazas (1998) also address the effects of income taxation on human capital in a general-equilibrium simulation model. They employ an overlapping-generations framework that includes income uncertainty, making the returns to human capital investment uncertain as well. In their model, tax proceeds are redistributed in lump-sum fashion equally to everyone in the economy. This is consistent with the findings of Browning and Johnson (1984), who find the redistributive component of the U.S. tax system effectively operates in this fashion. Significantly, this aspect of the tax system provides a measure of insurance. Specifically, while income taxation reduces the benefits of human capital as in Trostel's model, it also reduces the *variability* of the returns to human capital. An unlucky (low-income) worker receives more from redistribution than he or she pays in taxes, and so is helped by the income tax. Since uncertainty tends to lower investments by risk-averse agents, the insurance effect of taxation can increase investments. In their simulations, Lord and Rangazas find the insurance component largely offsets the negative effects highlighted by Trostel, so that the overall effect of income taxation on human capital accumulation is minimal.

Many interesting tax reform proposals are concerned with switching from one tax base to another. Such reforms typically alter savings by changing the timing of taxes over the life cycle. For example, assuming consumption exceeds income later in life, conversion from an income to a consumption tax base postpones tax payments until later in life. This aspect of the reform would increase private and national savings (so long as there is no change in government savings). Higher savings increase capital intensity, raising the wage and lowering the interest rate. In a thoughtful analysis, Davies and Whalley (1991) examine that reform in a model where human capital is produced using time, only, and there is no uncertainty. They find that in general equilibrium there is very little change in the after-tax interest rate, as higher capital accumulation offsets the lower tax rate on interest.[22] Consequently, they find little effect on human capital of this fundamental reform. Taber (1999) finds their results also obtain when the progressivity of taxes is taken into account and human capital decisions are modeled as in HLT, detailed in section 7.3.

The effects of taxation on human capital are difficult to gauge empirically. Most carefully calibrated simulation models find neither income taxation nor proposed fundamental tax reforms have large long-run effects on human capital accumulation. Future modeling should account for externalities and the implications for technical change.

7.6 SUMMARY

This chapter examined consequences of utility-maximizing human capital accumulation for earnings over the life cycle, earnings inequality, economic growth, and tax policy. Expenditures on human capital appear to be most productive when the current level of expenditures is low and are made at an early stage of the life cycle. The qualitative predictions of the Ben-Porath model of human capital accumulation prove consistent with behavior. However, human capital variables alone appear incapable of fully explaining the high wages of men relative to women. An extension to the Ben-Porath model by Heckman, Lochner, and Taber, when simulated, is largely successful in explaining the recent rise in inequality.

Human capital accumulation may impact economic growth through a variety of channels. However, the costs of increasing accumulation in adulthood exceed those in youth, which limits the extent to which output growth in developed economies may be increased by further investment. More needs to be learned about the relationships among human capital, technology, R&D, and growth. The tax system affects human capital in a variety of ways. Nevertheless, most simulation models find only modest long-run general-equilibrium effects of the tax system on human capital accumulation. However, simulations are a poor substitute for empirical knowledge. Once more is known empirically about the role of advanced human capital in the creation of technical knowledge, simulation models may be usefully extended in that direction.

ENDNOTES

1. Education may increase appreciation of literature, politics, or music. Inclusion of such benefits would not affect the qualitative implications of the model, though the benefits would encourage greater human capital accumulation at any level of monetary benefits.

2. If λ equals 1, the marginal product of effective time is independent of the quantity of effective time invested. If $\lambda = 0$, so is the marginal product of effective time.

3. λ may also reflect ability: The higher is λ the larger is the percentage increase in q_1 from increasing investments. For the most part, we envision that λ does not vary across people, so that variation in ability is summarized by z.

4. They note that students may be able to increase goods inputs enough to equate i and r. We ignore this possibility.

5. The high-ability person is also predicted to devote more time to education. This may be seen by substituting the optimal q_1 from equation (7.7) back into that for s_1, and differentiating with respect to z.

6. Note that these are the marginal benefits discounted back to period *two*. To find the impact on life wealth one needs to discount this magnitude back to the first period. Our approach is to compare the MB and MC in each period.

7. In the presence of depreciation at a constant annual rate d, the marginal benefits of a unit of human capital produced in year one, for example, become $MB_1 = w/[(1 + r)(1 + d)] + w/[(1 + r)^2(1 + d)^2] + \cdots + w/[(1 + r)^{R-1}(1 + d)^{R-1}]$. Also, the net increase in the stock each year is the amount newly produced q_t minus depreciation. In later working years, net of depreciation investment can easily be negative if there is very much depreciation at all.

8. This interpretation makes sense because the investment in going to school an extra year is E (the foregone earnings) and the return is dE. So, dE/E, i.e, the rate of change of earnings (which is captured by b), is the return to the investment—ignoring the fact that the investment will stop paying off when the individual retires.

9. The small overall bias associated with the Mincer equation is not evidence that ability bias is quantitatively unimportant. Rather, a countervailing bias arises, since studies typically must rely on survey data in which amount of education is self-reported. Unsurprisingly, there is evidence that reported and actual amount of schooling often differ. Even if the measurement error is random (no "resume" padding), this introduces a *downward* bias. Intuitively, the greater is measurement error, the less of reported or observed variability is explained by true changes in schooling. In practice, the extent to which the ability bias exceeds the bias from measurement error may be small.

10. They estimate that compared with college grads, high school grads face somewhat higher transitory shocks to earnings but somewhat lower permanent shocks (see their Table 3).

11. Other, not mutually exclusive, explanations have been provided. Perhaps most prominent are theories of internal labor markets. Briefly, firms may pay employees less than their marginal product in early years and more later in the employee's service to the firm. This reduces the probability that the employee will steal or shirk during the early years.

12. Other factors that increase the probability of being liquidity constrained include high time preference, high ability, and little access to other resources.

13. A Cobb-Douglas function would restrict the elasticity of substitution between skill types to be exactly one. Since that elasticity appears to exceed one, simply extending the Cobb-Douglas function to allow for different types of human capital would be inappropriate.

14. In his paper, Ben-Porath explicitly—and in some detail—developed the case of corner solutions, where all time may be devoted to schooling in the early years.

15. In particular, they assume that $\log((1 - \pi)/\pi)$ declines 3.6 percent per year.

16. Marginal benefits of investment rise appreciably for young workers. However, investments then begin to fall back, rather than continue to rise with the demand. The reason is that, as detailed in the text, the supply of skilled labor rises through greater skill acquisition among workers and also from increased college enrollments. When supply and demand are both shifting outward, the effects on price are reduced.

17. Other explanations of the increase in inequality include deteriorating neighborhoods among the poor, increased immigration of low-skill workers, greater outsourcing of manufacturing jobs overseas, and increased sorting of students by ability in schools. Although these other factors may play a role, many economists believe skill-biased technical change is the most important factor.

18. Relatedly, Ren and Rangazas (2000) argue that faster technical change induces earlier retirement. With a shorter time to recoup skills, new investments are not profitable, even though productivity with the outdated technology may fall quickly.

19. Equation (7.12) implies that the long-run rate of growth of human capital is positive, as in Lucas (1988). Consequently, human capital can be an engine of long-run growth in per capita incomes. Constant returns in human capital are unrealistic in practice, but simplify making the point that the relative human capital of teachers is important.

20. The top official tax bracket is 38.6%. However, there is a range of income over which the itemized personal exemptions are phased out, which increases the effective marginal rate. Also, it is appropriate to view at least some portion of the payroll tax for Social Security as a tax on labor (as opposed to a "loan" to the government).

21. Trostel relies on an infinitely lived agent model, rather than the overlapping-generations context (for this reason tax-timing issues *cannot* arise in his framework).

22. Seidman and Lewis (1999) also find the net-of-tax interest rate to be essentially independent of the rate of capital income taxation, in a model without human capital.

QUESTIONS AND PROBLEMS

▶ REVIEW
QUESTIONS

1. Consider the two-period Ben-Porath model.
   A. In what two ways do adult human capital investments affect financial savings of the young?
   B. How is the marginal rate of return calculated? Why are social and private rates of return different for, especially, primary education?

2. Explain the effect on optimal investment in the two-period model of an increase in w
   A. in the absence of goods inputs.
   B. in the presence of such inputs.

3. Suppose credit markets are perfect so that the life wealth-maximizing investment in human capital is undertaken. On a graph similar to Figure 7.2, depict the effect of an increase in the rate of interest income taxation on the efficient amount of human capital investment, assuming (a) Interest expense is tax deductible, (b) Interest expense is not tax deductible.

4. Suppose there are constant returns to scale in human capital production, $\lambda = 1$. What is the relationship between the marginal and average return to human capital in this case? Draw a budget line assuming there is no possibility to invest in human capital; another with $i > r$. If $i > r$, and all costs are foregone earnings, what would determine the amount of investments? If $i > r$ and all costs are out-of-pocket expenditures, what is the optimal investment? Why doesn't this make sense? Now suppose that one can invest and that $i = r$. What effect would this have on the budget set?

5. In what ways does the Heckman, Lochner, and Taber model generalize that of Ben-Porath? For each way, provide an example of an interesting new question that can be addressed.

6. A. How and why might an individual's rate of time preference affect the amount of human capital investment undertaken?

B. With prohibitions against borrowing, how might parental wealth condition human capital accumulation? What is the evidence relating to this?

C. If borrowing constraints aren't keeping relatively poor children from attending college, what factors produce that result?

D. Evaluate briefly the evidence relating to the possibilities mentioned in part C.

E. Consider a training program that further subsidizes college or vocational training in hopes of increasing participation in such training. How do the implications for equity and efficiency of such programs depend upon why the targeted population wouldn't otherwise undertake the training?

7. Consider the two-period model of adult human capital accumulation.

   A. If the only costs are foregone earnings, how and why will a proportional wage tax affect human capital accumulation?

   B. If the only costs are foregone earnings, how and why will a progressive wage tax affect human capital accumulation?

   C. If there are direct costs (e.g., tuition) in addition to foregone earnings, how and why will a proportional wage tax affect human capital accumulation?

   D. If there are direct costs (e.g., tuition) in addition to foregone earnings, how and why would a subsidy to direct costs (e.g., making tuition free) affect human capital accumulation?

   E. How will an interest income tax affect human capital accumulation when schooling is financed from savings?

   F. How will an interest subsidy on school loans affect human capital accumulation?

   G. How will an interest income tax affect human capital accumulation when schooling is financed through government loans and interest expense is *not* tax deductible?

8. How well does the human capital model explain the difference in earnings between men and women? How well does it explain the decline in that difference in recent decades? What does it predict about the future of the earnings gap?

9. Provide an example of (a) skill-biased technical change, (b) ability-biased technical change, (c) deskilling technical change, (d) skill-neutral technical change (which increases the returns to all skill levels equiproportionately).

10. In the "discovery function" for new ideas, what are the "standing on the shoulders of giants," "fishing out," and "stepping on toes" effects?

▶ PROBLEMS

1. How would figures 7.3 and 7.4 differ: If there is a higher interest rate? If there is the expectation of an increasing wage per unit of human capital over time at rate v, say?

2. Suppose that $q_1 = z s_1^\alpha h_1^\beta$ where $\alpha > \beta$. What implications does this have for the relationship between the stock of human capital h_1 and the marginal costs of production? Do empirical studies shed any light on the relative values of α and β? If so, explain the findings of those studies and their implications.

3. **A.** Heckman, Lochner, and Taber model a 30-year period of SBTC. Describe the short- and medium-term effects of this SBTC for (a) the wage-experience profile for skilled, unskilled, (b) between-group inequality at 5 and 25–35 years of experience, (c) within-group inequality for skilled and unskilled.

   B. Continuing to use the HLT model, now assume that there is a 30-year period of skill-neutral technical change (i.e., change that increases the returns to all levels of skill equiproportionately). Answer parts (a), (b), and (c) from above for this experiment. Which results are the same, and which differ? Which do you think is the better way to think of technical change in recent decades? Why?

4. In section 7.4, using a two-period model we derived a set of relations between the rate of return to human capital, to physical capital, to population growth, to rate of technical change, and to output growth. To what extent do these results hinge on the "period structure" of the model? That is, if consumers worked for 4 periods, say, how and why might the conclusions change? Suppose $r = i^a = 0$, and that $n = v = 0$.

*5. In the two-period model, suppose that $q_1 = zx^\lambda$, where x is a goods input and $\lambda < 1$. Suppose the price of the goods input is p_x.

   A. Determine the MC, MB, and optimal amount of human capital.

   B. What are the comparative statics effects on q_1 of r, w, z, and p_x. Present your answers both analytically and intuitively.

Chapter 8

THE ALLOCATION OF TIME BETWEEN HOME AND MARKET OVER THE LIFE CYCLE

The allocation of time across activities and over the life cycle is a fundamental aspect of economic life. This chapter focuses on how the economic environment affects this allocation. It examines changing patterns in the supply of market labor, the consumption of leisure, and household production over the life cycle. This chapter complements Chapters 6 and 7, which discussed time devoted to increasing the productivity of future time through human capital investments. The allocation of time is also important to economic growth. Changes in the labor force participation rate, retirement age, and normal hours worked directly affect aggregate labor supply and GDP. Further, these changes affect fertility and educational decisions, which are also important to resource accumulation.

In practice, an expenditure of time may simultaneously accrue several types of benefits. For example, gardening may yield tomatoes and flowers, while also being a form of leisure. Nevertheless, the following nonoverlapping categories prove useful. Clearly enough, *market labor* is time devoted to creating value for others in exchange for material compensation. Market labor differs in how interesting, meaningful, or pleasant it is. Differences in job amenities may be reflected in the wages paid to occupations. If so, pleasant jobs (like university professor) would pay less than dangerous, unpleasant tasks, with training or ability held constant. The wage difference across job amenities is called the *compensating differential*.

Leisure is an expenditure of time that directly provides utility. Sometimes the benefits of leisure are largely independent of market goods, for example basking in the sun. At other times leisure consumption is complementary to goods, for example sailing on one's boat. Retirement obviously involves a large increase in leisure, but age, gender, marital status, and children also influence leisure consumption. *Household production* time involves the creation of goods or services, such as a clean house or child care, in the home for personal consumption. In this chapter we are especially interested in home products for which there exist close market substitutes. For example, one may clean one's own house, or hire a maid. Similarly, one may hire professional child care instead of provid-

269

ing direct parental care. Chapter 9 broadens the notion of household production to include home-produced "goods" for which there are no close market substitutes, such as children and marital intimacy.

Time allocation changed tremendously during the twentieth century: The workday shortened; time spent in retirement lengthened; years of education increased, which delayed entry into the labor force; and the sharp division of labor where men worked in the market and married women worked in home production largely disappeared.

For example, Costa (2000, p.156) reports that the typical worker in the 1880s labored 10 hours per day, 6 days per week. By 1940 this had fallen to 8 hours per day, 5 days per week. Since then, time worked per day has fallen little, but vacation, holiday, and sick and personal leave days all have increased. Elsewhere, Costa (1995, p. 297) reports that in 1880, 78% of men age 65 or older were in the labor force, whereas only 25% were working in 1980. This figure is now below 20%. Similarly, Costa notes nonparticipation has risen among somewhat younger men. At the turn of the twentieth century (i.e., circa 1900), the labor force participation rate of men aged 55 to 64 was 86%, a figure that had fallen to 71% by 1980. Also, over the twentieth century the average young adult's educational attainment expanded from completion of primary school to some postsecondary school participation. Because of the delayed entry into the work force associated with education, earlier retirement, and fewer hours worked per week, the average man works only half as many hours over his lifetime in the market today as a century ago. Significantly, the work performed currently is less physically arduous and, on average, more interesting than that of a century before. These improvements in the welfare of male workers are not reflected in the roughly seven-fold increase in GDP per capita that occurred over this same period.

Women, by contrast, increased their participation in and attachment to the labor force during the twentieth century. This of course is not to say women work more now: According to Goldin, farm housewives in 1920 performed about 65 hours of housework per week (1990, p. 226). Strikingly, whereas but 3.2% of white married women were in the labor force in 1900, this figure had risen to 55.8% by 1988 (these figures were 26 and 64% among nonwhites). In 1996, 59.9% of all married women were employed (Current Population Survey). Single women have always participated more, and thus their increase has been somewhat less pronounced: In 1900, 41.5% of white single women were in the labor force, whereas 68.6% worked for money in 1988. (Among nonwhite single women, participation *fell* slightly, from 60.5 to 56.4%.) As women's market work has increased, there have been reductions in their nonmarket labor and a modest reallocation of time from market to home by men. Despite these homogenizing changes in the allocation of time, men on average have continued to perform more market work and much less household work than women. Thus, although gender differences in the allocation of time between the home and market sectors have fallen, significant differences remain (especially among older cohorts).

This chapter examines economic factors contributing to these patterns, along with their aggregate implications. Section 8.1 develops the theory and evidence regarding labor supply based on single-period or "static" labor-leisure choices. Also in section 8.1 we analyze labor-leisure choices over the life cycle. Sections 8.1 and 8.2 then extend the analysis to include nonmarket, or household, production. This requires some discussion of the division of labor within the household, and therefore of marriage, divorce, and children.

In section 8.4 we briefly address the role of increased market participation by women in twentieth-century economic growth. Section 8.5 employs the tools developed earlier in the chapter to analyze important policy issues. A brief summary concludes the chapter.

8.1 THE DEMAND FOR LEISURE AND THE SUPPLY OF LABOR

In this section we assume consumers derive satisfaction both from the consumption of market goods, as in Chapter 1, and from time spent away from work, called *leisure*. There are other similarities with Chapter 1. There we were primarily interested in the consumer's savings. However, the direct objects of choice were consumption over the life cycle. Given consumption, we easily determined saving from income. Similarly, although we are here mainly concerned with labor supply, consumers will directly choose the amount of leisure to consume; labor supply will be time not devoted to leisure.

8.1.1 Preferences

Suppose consumers derive utility U from the consumption of goods C and leisure L so that, for some representative consumer,

$$U = U(C, L) \tag{8.1}$$

Equation (8.1) suggests that market work provides neither pleasure nor displeasure; the sole motivation for market work is the monetary compensation it imparts. In fact, surveys report that many people derive significant satisfaction from their work (cf. Juster and Stafford, 1991, p. 496). Fortunately, such psychic benefits do not affect the *qualitative* implications of our framework, so long as the *net* effect of switching time to leisure from work is to increase utility (goods being held constant).

Thus, while not denying that work is sometimes pleasurable, we assume that the marginal utilities of leisure U_L and goods U_C are positive. For this reason the indifference curve U^0 in Figure 8.1 is negatively sloped; greater leisure must be associated with fewer goods if utility is held constant. At any point along U^0 the (absolute value of the) slope is the marginal rate of substitution of leisure for goods. This $MRS_{L,C}$ is the demand price for leisure, indicating the maximum C one would forego for an additional unit of L. It is equal to the ratio U_L/U_C. If the $MRS_{L,C} = 2$, the consumer likes the marginal unit of L twice as much as that of C. Indifference curves are convex, exhibiting diminishing $MRS_{L,C}$. This means C and L are not perfect substitutes: a consumer with lots of money, but little time to enjoy it, values additional leisure more than if he or she were equally happy but enjoyed high leisure and few goods.

A stronger relative preference for L would increase the $MRS_{L,C}$ at every level of L consumption, producing steeper indifference curves. If L and C were closer substitutes than shown, the $MRS_{L,C}$ would not fall as rapidly and the indifference curves would be flatter; less substitutability would increase the rate at which the $MRS_{L,C}$ falls. It is plau-

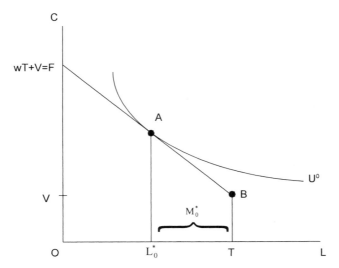

Figure 8.1 Interior solution

sible that preferences over work and leisure change over long periods of time: Perhaps because of technical advances, jobs become less physically taxing but more mentally stimulating. Similarly, the advent of, and advances in, the television and the Internet, as examples, may have made leisure more attractive through time. Preferences are stable when the time frame is short or if these changes balance out so that the marginal rates of substitution are constant.

In general, the marginal utilities of leisure and goods depend upon the amounts of both goods and leisure consumed. That is, $U_L = U_L(C,L)$ and $U_C = U_C(C,L)$. For now we simply note that diminishing $MRS_{L,C}$ imposes no *independent* requirements regarding the substitutability of L and C.[1] In section 8.15, we'll see that the extent of substitutability is important to understanding leisure and market work over the life cycle.

8.1.2   Opportunities

We now describe the budget the consumer must respect when attempting to maximize (8.1). The consumer is assumed to possess a total of T units of time, say hours per day, which he or she apportions between market work, M, and leisure. Therefore,

$$T = L + M \tag{8.2}$$

with M and L nonnegative. The worker's efforts command a wage of w per hour, taken to be outside the worker's control. A more complete model would integrate work, leisure, and human capital decisions, making the wage endogenous (cf. Heckman 1976).

We initially assume that there are no restrictions on hours worked (one could supply M = 17.63 hours, if desired). This assumption is reasonable for the self-employed and for those in many types of sales (real estate, telemarketing) and service (waitress or hair stylist jobs). This may also hold approximately for many other workers, once occupational choice and multiple jobs are taken into account.

With flexible hours, one can choose between earning $w or taking another hour of leisure. This crucial observation reveals that w is not only the wage, but also the price of leisure. When there are restrictions on hours worked, or when $M = 0$, the value of L may differ from w. The distinction between nominal and real wages is not central to our deliberations. Consequently, units are chosen for C such that the price is 1. For this reason C is both the units of and expenditures on C. Thus, the real wage and relative price of leisure both equal the amount of C that must be foregone when another unit of L is consumed. In turn, with competitive labor markets, w is also the worker's marginal product.

Other nonlabor resources the consumer may have, such as savings and the associated interest earnings, home equity, gifts, and inheritances, are denoted by V. This resource position may be negative, as for a recent graduate with college loans to repay. Expenditures on goods are constrained by the sum of wage and nonlabor resources:

$$C = wM + V$$

This is more readily graphed if we substitute for M from (8.2) and rearrange to yield

$$C = w(T - L) + V = wT - wL + V$$

so that

$$C = wT + V - wL \tag{8.3}$$

Equation (8.3) produces the budget line FBT in Figure 8.1. The slope of segment FB is $-w_0$, the rate at which goods must fall as L rises. Vertical segment BT, of height V, reminds us that even if the consumer does not work at all, she or he will still be able to consume nonlabor resources. An increase in V would lengthen the vertical segment but not alter the slope. Conversely, an increase in w would steepen the slope but not affect the vertical segment.

It is useful to rearrange (8.3) so as to isolate the *uses* of income, including expenditures on leisure, on one side of the budget constraint, with the *sources* of income or wealth on the other:

$$C + wL = wT + V \equiv F \tag{8.4}$$

The right-hand side of (8.4) is the consumer's endowment F, or "full income." F is the sum of the market value of the consumer's time endowment wT (her maximum potential wage earnings) and nonlabor income V. The left-hand side shows the uses of full income, treating "expenditures" on leisure wL and outlays on goods symmetrically. Expenditures on goods and leisure are limited to full income.

8.1.3   Whether and How Much to Work

The consumer maximizes the utility function (8.1) subject to (8.4) and the restriction that M cannot be negative. The optimality condition requires that

$$MRS_{C,L} \equiv U_L/U_C \geq w \tag{8.5}$$

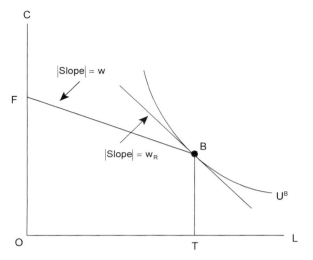

Figure 8.2 Corner solution

When equation (8.5) holds with equality, hours worked are positive. Such an *interior solution* is given by point A in Figure 8.1. This solution equates the subjective willingness to trade C for L with the ability to trade C for L afforded by the market. At A, L_0^* units of leisure are demanded, so that $M_0^* = T - L_0^*$ units of the time endowment are supplied to market work.

For those not working, or "at a corner," $MRS_{L,S} > w$ even when $M = 0$. A *corner solution* is illustrated in Figure 8.2. This occurs at point B, where the indifference curve U^B is tangential to the budget line FBT. However, at some sufficiently high wage the consumer may be induced to perform market work. The wage rate that draws a nonparticipant into the labor market is termed the *reservation wage,* w_R. This reservation wage is the value of the $MRS_{L,C}$ when $M = 0$ and goods consumption C equals V. Graphically, it is the slope (in absolute value) of the line tangent to U^B at point B.

Given the consumer's preferences, the optimal consumption bundle depends on the budget line, the position of which is determined solely by w and V. More generally, then, the utility maximizing choices are functions of w and V; $L^* = L^*(w, V)$ and $C^* = C^*(w, V)$. We now address how leisure demand and labor supply respond to changes in opportunities, as determined by w and V.

8.1.4 Comparative Statics

The Effect of Nonlabor Income on Labor Supply

Suppose leisure is a normal good, as is indicated by the empirical evidence discussed below. Then an increase in nonlabor income increases leisure consumption and depresses labor supply. (Imagine the labor supply response of a sanitation worker to winning the lottery.) This is illustrated in Figure 8.3. Budget lines F_0BT and F_1ET are parallel, each having a slope of $-w$. Constraint F_1ET is the higher, reflecting additional nonlabor income of BE. The effect of a change in V on L, and thus M, is termed the *income effect*. Assuming leisure is normal, the income effect on leisure is unambiguously positive. Con-

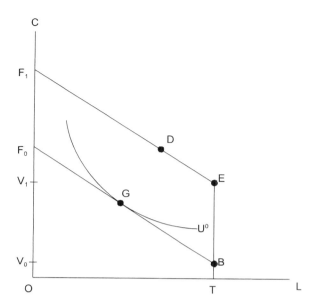

Figure 8.3 Increasing nonlabor income

sequently, the income effect on labor supply is unambiguously *negative*; higher nonlabor income is predicted to reduce labor supply. This may take the form of a reduction in hours worked, as when the worker chooses point D after the increase in income (new indifference curve not pictured). Alternatively, the consumer could be induced to exit the labor force, choosing point E.

Empirical studies find that leisure is a normal good. For example, Holtz-Eakin, Joulfaian, and Rosen (1992) measure labor force participation rates for individuals and couples before and after the receipt of an inheritance. They find that the higher the inheritance, the greater the likelihood of the person(s) exiting the labor force. Thus, whereas 4.6% of single individuals receiving inheritances smaller than $25,000 had exited the labor force within three years of the inheritance, over 23% receiving inheritances above $150,000 had exited three years hence. Similar results obtained for married couples. These authors also found that among workers remaining in the labor force, those receiving larger inheritances experienced slower earnings growth. This less conclusive evidence suggests that hours of work among those continuing to work fell by more the larger the inheritance.[2]

In a married household, it may be reasonable to view changes in the wage earnings of one spouse as a change in the nonlabor income of the other. However, the rise in the divorce rate during the 1970s and 1980s surely limits the extent to which either spouse is willing to view a spouse's earnings as "own" income. For this reason, the effect of one spouse's earnings on the other's employment may have fallen over time. Juhn and Murphy (1997, p. 92) report evidence consistent with this intuition using matched husband-wife pairs from the Current Population Survey. They find that "(c)ontrolling for the presence of children, we estimate that a $1,000 decrease in husband's earnings would have increased the wife's employment rate by 0.7 percentage points in 1968–1970 and by 0.4 percentage points in 1988–90." We shall have more to say of the interrelationships be-

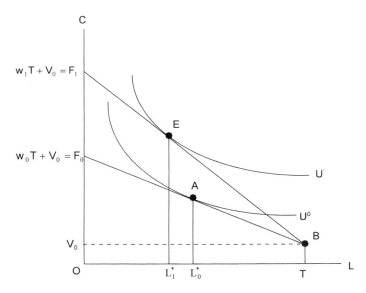

Figure 8.4 An increase in the wage

tween husband and wife's supplies of labor in section 8.3. Now, though, we consider the effects of an individual's own wage on the individual's labor supply behavior.

Uncompensated Leisure Demand and Labor Supply Curves

Figure 8.4 illustrates the effect on a current worker of an increase in the wage. As the wage rises from w_0 on budget line F_0BT to w_1 on F_1BT, the worker alters his or her consumption bundle from point A to point E. As drawn, $L_1^* < L_0^*$. However, as we explain below, the relationship between w and L* among current workers is in general ambiguous. Figure 8.5 shows that a wage increase may induce a nonworker to enter the labor market. When the wage is w_0, the consumer is at the corner of nonparticipation, point B. The new wage w_1 is in excess of the reservation wage, inducing her or him to locate at point I, so that hours of work become positive. Graphically, the relationship between the wage and leisure produces the ordinary, or uncompensated, demand curve for leisure (not shown). This is often written $L^* = L^*(w; V)$ to stress that nonlabor income V is held constant in this schedule's construction.

Since $M^* = T - L^*$, knowledge of $L^*(w; V)$ allows immediate derivation of $M^*(w; V)$, the ordinary or uncompensated labor supply schedule. Figure 8.6 depicts this relationship. At wages below the reservation wage w_R, hours worked are zero. At higher wages, hours are positive. Since, among those working, the effect of changing w on L* is ambiguous, so is the sign of the slope of M*. There has been an enormous amount of empirical work devoted to assessing the shape of M* and how it depends upon worker characteristics such as age, gender, marital and parental status, and wealth. We review some such evidence below. To properly do so requires first explaining a decomposition of a wage change into income and substitution effects.

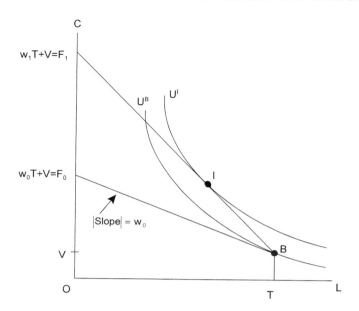

Figure 8.5 Entering the labor market: effect of a wage increase

The Substitution Effect, Compensated Leisure Demand, and Labor Supply Curves

A wage change alters both utility and the price of leisure. Conceptually, the effects on leisure may be separated into (a) that of changing the price of leisure, holding utility constant, and (b) that from altered utility, holding the wage constant. Adding the effects of (a) and (b) produces the *full effect* when relative prices and welfare vary simultaneously.

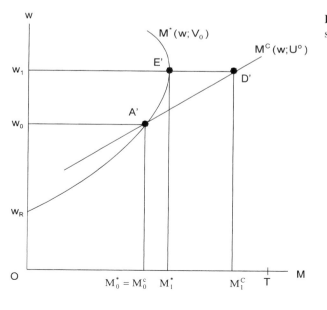

Figure 8.6 Ordinary and compensated labor supply

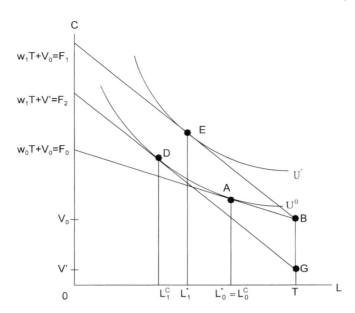

Figure 8.7 Substitution effect on leisure of change in income

That sum is what we typically observe in practice and is the basis of the ordinary leisure demand and uncompensated labor supply curves considered above. In standard terminology, the full effect of a wage change can be decomposed into the substitution effect (a) and the income effect (b). This decomposition clarifies and isolates the influences of w on labor supply.

Figure 8.7 again depicts the increase in the wage from w_0 to w_1 that produced the movement in the consumer's chosen bundle from A to E, as in Figure 8.4. In this context, the substitution effect is the movement up along initial indifference curve U^0. For such a (hypothetical) movement to occur, V must be adjusted to keep utility unchanged. In Figure 8.7 the substitution effect is the movement along U^0 from A to D. Point D lies on budget line F_2GT, whose slope reflects the new, higher wage w_1. For this reason, F_2GT is parallel to the true post-wage-increase budget line F_1BT. Compared with F_1BT, budget line F_2GT is based on the (hypothetically) lower nonlabor income, V', which returns the consumer to the initial indifference curve, U^0.

Graphing the relationship between L and w keeping utility equal to U^0 produces the *compensated demand curve* for leisure L^c (not shown). L^c reflects only the substitution effects on leisure of changes in w. Due to diminishing $MRS_{C,L}$, the substitution effect of an increase in w on L is always negative: Since optimality requires that the $MRS_{L,C} = w$, a higher w increases the optimal $MRS_{L,C}$ along U^0, so that L is lower (and C higher). Consequently, compensated leisure demand schedules are *unambiguously* negatively sloped.

Figure 8.6 portrays the compensated labor supply curve $M^c(w, U^0)$ obtained from $M^c = T - L^c$. *The substitution effect is always positive for labor supply. Since M^c reflects only the substitution effect, it is unambiguously upsloping.* Notice that the closer substitutes are goods and leisure, the flatter are indifference curves, the greater is the substitution effect, and the more elastic are L^c and M^c. Family considerations were associated with historical differences in the size of the substitution effect across men and women. This is taken up in section 8.3.

The Income Effect of a Wage Change

By reducing V to hold utility constant, the substitution effect of an increase in w unambiguously reduces leisure. In practice, V is not reduced to maintain U^0 when w rises. Thus, an increase in w increases utility or real income. This increase in real income would be the increase in V necessary to move the worker from U^0 to U^1, holding the wage constant at w_1, its new, higher level. It is the maximum amount one would pay to obtain the pay raise and is called the *compensating variation*. Figure 8.7 shows this to be $F_1 - F_2 = V_0 - V'$, with $w = w_1$. The *income effect* is the change in leisure this additional nonlabor income would produce.[3]

Because leisure is a normal good, the income effect is positive for leisure but negative for labor supply. The income effect on leisure is the movement from D to E or from L_1^c to L_1^* in Figure 8.7; the negative income effect on labor supply is the reduction from D' to E', or M_1^c to M_1^*, in Figure 8.6. The full effect on uncompensated labor supply M^* in Figure 8.6 combines the positive substitution effect A' to D' with the negative income effect D' to E'. Clearly, if the income effect had been drawn to be stronger, leisure consumption could have increased and labor supply could have fallen.

The positive income effect when the price of leisure w rises contrasts sharply with the negative income effect that accompanies an increase in the price of a *normal* good or service (such as clothing). These qualitatively different income effects are the reason the (uncompensated) demand curve for normal goods and services is unambiguously negatively sloped, whereas the uncompensated leisure demand and labor supply curves are of ambiguous slope. Why does the income effect of a price change differ between the fixed-income goods and services model and the labor supply model? In both models, an increase in the price of a good (whether a market good or leisure) affects the *uses* of income, how much it costs to purchase goods. In the labor supply model, there is an additional effect on real income because the wage rise boosts the *sources* of income. The value of the time endowment rises by the increase in the wage times the time endowment T, or $(w_1 - w_0)T$. The conventional (or uses) and endowment (or sources) income effects are of opposite qualitative sign. However, the endowment effect *must* dominate since only a portion of the appreciated endowment is spent on leisure, L < T.

Less abstractly, real income rises with w because more is now earned at any given amount of labor supply. For with labor supply held constant, C can rise by the increase in w times the number of hours worked, $(w_1 - w_0)M$. *Consequently, the greater is labor supply, the more the post-wage-increase budget line exceeds the initial one, and the larger is the income effect.* Obviously, there is *no* increase in real income or utility if M = 0 both before and after the increase in w. Because the increase in real income and the income effect rise with M, uncompensated labor supply curves may be backward bending. If the individual is working very little, the income effect is small and is probably dominated by the substitution effect. As M rises, so does the income effect. At some M the income effect may dominate, causing labor supply to *fall* as w increases. Thus, at high w and M the uncompensated labor supply curve M^* may assume a negative slope, or be backward bending.

Figure 8.6 reflects these considerations. Recall that the compensated labor supply schedule M^c contains only substitution effects, whereas M^* incorporates both income and substitution effects. The horizontal distance $M^c - M^*$ captures the income effect for wage increases from w_0. As w rises, $M^c - M^*$ increases, reflecting the greater income effect. At w_1, the uncompensated schedule M^* is almost vertical, as the income effect has come to equal the substitution effect. At a somewhat higher wage, M^* declines with further increases in w.

Empirical Evidence

Casual inference from aggregate data on the wages and employment of men through time, or time series analyses, suggests the predominance of the income effect. For, while real wages increased dramatically during the twentieth century, hours worked per week and age at retirement both fell substantially. Thus, the labor supply schedule may be expected to be backward bending for men through much of that century. Further, as men's hours have declined through time, so has the expected magnitude of the income effect. This suggests that the uncompensated labor supply schedule would become less backward bending and perhaps forward bending through time. However, such a cursory examination confounds the effects of wage increases with other substantial changes potentially having similar effects on men's labor supply. Important examples (discussed later) include the much greater coverage of workers by private pension plans and Social Security as well as the rise in women's employment.

Similarly, the fact that women's LFPRs and hours worked per week have risen through time suggests that for them the substitution effect has been dominant, leading to a forward sloping uncompensated labor supply schedule. Also, though, as their hours worked have risen, the income effect should become stronger, so that their uncompensated labor supply schedules should become less elastic through time. Once again, other factors, such as changes in fertility and the marriage contract, make such casual inferences of limited value.

Due in part to the difficulties with time series analyses, many studies of labor supply have been cross-sectional, sampling workers at a point in time. Recent estimates have been obtained by Pencavel (1997, 1998) employing data from the Current Population Survey over the period from 1975 to 1994. These surveys contain many of the personal characteristics one would like to account for. Pencavel finds (1998) that women facing 10% higher wages have an 8% higher employment probability and work about 1.3 more hours per week, an extra 0.5 week per year, and 1.8% additional hours per year. This translates to a wage elasticity for annual hours of 0.18, so the uncompensated labor supply curve is upsloping, but inelastic. Pencavel's results are similar to those of many other studies, which find that although the substitution effect dominates, both the income and substitution effects are relatively low in recent years among those currently employed. Young women (who are more likely to have young children present), are more responsive to the wage. For example, he finds the elasticity with respect to annual hours to be 0.301 for those aged 25 to 30.

Consistent with our distinction between interior and corner solutions, the empirical literature stresses differences in the responsiveness to wages of those employed and those induced to enter or exit the labor force. Historically, this distinction has proven more important for females, who have had a more fluid relationship with the market than men. Decisions to enter the labor force depend upon substitution effects alone (recall that if M = 0 there is no income effect). In earlier periods when women's LFPRs were much lower, estimates of the substitution effect that included the participation response were routinely found to exceed 1. As women's LFPRs and life-cycle attachment to the labor force have risen, this substitution effect has fallen (cf. Goldin, 1990, especially Table 5.2).

Although there exists a range of estimates regarding the wage elasticity for men, Borjas (1995) concludes "there is some consensus that a 10 percent increase in the wage increases hours of work by about 1 percent because of the substitution effect, but that it also leads to a 2 percent decrease because of the income effect" (p. 59). This implies a "consensus" uncompensated elasticity of -0.1, so that the labor supply curve is slightly backward bending. This would be consistent with the longer term decline in hours and increase in early retirement among male workers observed in the twentieth century. However, in a recent study, Pencavel (1997) estimates wage elasticities of men for annual hours of about 0.2. If the substitution effect has come to dominate for men in recent years, this would be consistent with an income effect that has fallen along with annual hours worked. In summary, the wage elasticities for men and women workers are (in recent years) similar, relatively small, and, at least for women, positive.

There is a final piece of information concerning hours worked that merits attention. Costa (2000) finds that in the 1890s those men and women working the longest hours on average faced the lowest wages. For example, she reports that in the 1890s hourly male workers in the lowest wage decile worked 11.14 hours per day, compared with 8.88 hours among those in the top 10% of the wage distribution. In contrast, by 1991 the converse was true: men in the bottom decile labored 8.05 hours while those among the top 10% worked 8.72 hours. This suggests that those choosing more education are simultaneously choosing to raise the return on educational investments by working longer hours. Since Costa also finds that this trend of high earners working more has continued beyond 1973, the increase in individual earnings inequality in recent decades chronicled in Chapter 7 may overstate changes in welfare. Relatedly, Juhn and Murphy (1997) report that the wage elasticity is higher for higher earning, and therefore better educated, men.

8.1.5 Life-Cycle Implications of the Labor-Leisure Model

We argued in our Chapter 7 discussion of human capital accumulation that an individual's wage rate is likely to increase for several decades as productivity rises due to training and experience. Toward the end of the working years, however, real wage rates may fall as one's existing skills depreciate more rapidly than new skills are acquired. What effect will this pattern of wages have on labor-leisure choices over the working years? The basic theory is straightforward and receives modest empirical support. The retirement decision is treated separately.

Suppose the life-cycle utility function takes the form

$$U = u(C_1, L_1) + u(C_2, L_2) + \ldots + u(C_T, L_T) \tag{8.6}$$

Equation (8.6) expresses life-cycle utility as the simple sum of utilities from each period, where the period utility functions u are the same each year. The additivity of (8.6) means the marginal utility of leisure (goods) in a period depends only upon the amounts of leisure and goods consumed in that period. Then, for example, the car one owns in 1978 is assumed to have no effect on the marginal utility of leisure in 2003 (or 1977). We also assume that there is diminishing marginal utility for leisure and goods within a period.

Let u_{Lj+1} and u_{Lj} be the marginal utilities of leisure in periods $j + 1$ and j. The core intuition regarding life-cycle leisure consumption and labor supply flows from the simple case where the utility from L and C within a period are independent. In this case u_{Lj} just depends upon the amount of leisure consumed in period j. So, if $L_j = L_{j+1}$, so also equal are the marginal utilities of leisure in the two periods.

Assume the individual knows, at time 1, what his or her wage will be at each age. To focus on the issues at hand, assume the interest rate and nonlabor income are each zero, $r = V = 0$. Individuals live exactly T periods, having one unit of time in each of the R working years to allot between L or M; $L_t + M_t = 1$. With these assumptions, lifetime full income is simply

$$F = w_1 + w_2 + \ldots + w_R$$

Expenditures on market goods and leisure over the life cycle are constrained to be less than or equal to life wealth,

$$C_1 + C_2 + \ldots + C_T + w_1L_1 + w_2L_2 + \ldots + w_RL_R \leq F \qquad (8.7)$$

The consumer's problem is to maximize life-cycle utility (8.6) subject to the budget constraint (8.7). Assuming an interior solution in each year, utility maximization requires that the MRS, or ratio of marginal utilities, between any two "goods" equal the ratio of their prices. This holds for all of the T market goods and R leisure goods, L_t and C_t. Significantly, the ratio of marginal utilities of leisure in adjacent periods j and $j + 1$ must equal the wage ratio for those years,

$$u_{Lj+1}/u_{Lj} = w_{j+1}/w_j \qquad (8.8)$$

Assuming the wage is higher in $j + 1$ so must be, by (8.8), the marginal utility of leisure. Given diminishing marginal utility and that the utilities from C and L within a period are independent, this implies *lower* leisure consumption in $j + 1$ than in j.

More generally, in years when wages are high, less leisure is predicted. Intuitively, we are expected to buy less leisure when it is most expensive. Real wages increase until the mid-40s, peak, and then decline. And, as discussed in the next section, the structure of (especially private) pensions may mean that the real wages of men in their 60s and 70s are lower than when calculated on the basis of earnings alone. This suggests that leisure consumption should be high when young, fall through middle age, then rise again. This age profile for leisure L_t is depicted in Figure 8.8. Similarly, in a cross section of workers, we would expect labor force participation rates $LFPR_t$ to be positively correlated with wages over the life cycle—and thus inversely related to leisure. This profile is also depicted in Figure 8.8.

The empirical evidence suggests that intertemporal substitution effects on leisure are weak among those who are in the labor force, but they appear stronger when effects on

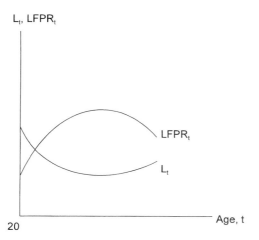

Figure 8.8 Life-cycle leisure and labor force participation

participation are taken into account. Considering hours among those working, Card (1994) looks at hours worked in a cross section of workers. He notes that between the ages of 30 and 50, wages rise rapidly among college-educated men, especially when they are compared with less educated men of those ages. Under the assumption that these wage gains were perfectly anticipated at the start of economic life, hours worked by the college educated should have risen by more than those of the less educated. However, he finds the hours profiles are similar.[4] More generally, Costa (2000) notes that the variation by age in daily hours is small over the entire period 1890–1990. She suggests that "if there is intertemporal substitution, it takes the form of exit from the labor force" (p. 177).

Indeed, the relationship between age-participation rates and the age-wage profile is striking. In 1992 the LFPR of men rose from about 45% among those aged 16 to 17 to almost 90% for those in their mid-40s, then fell to around 10% for those older than 65. Similarly, although there is not much variation in the workday among those employed, Costa finds great variability by age in total hours worked averaging across those in and out of the labor force: In 1991, total hours averaged 1,896 among men aged 45 to 54. This number fell to 1,291 among men 55 to 64, and to 313 among older men.

Thus, there is evidence of wage-induced intertemporal substitution effects. These effects appear relatively weak among those who remain in the labor force, perhaps because of limited ability to choose hours. However, men are much more likely to be employed at those ages when their wages are highest.

The theory of life-cycle leisure consumption provides an additional explanation for the close tracking over the life cycle of earnings by market goods consumption, first discussed in Chapter 1 (see Figure 1.9). To appreciate this, suppose that goods and leisure are substitutes for one another, with the marginal utility of goods in a period falling when leisure rises in that same period. Now, in years when wages are high, leisure is low. This raises the marginal utility and consumption of market goods. Further, if $w_{j+1} > w_j$, leisure is predicted to fall between j and $j + 1$, with goods consumption rising. Notice that when wages are high, earnings will be high both because of the high wage and also because leisure is low. Consequently, if goods and leisure are very substitutable, goods consumption and earnings will tend to track each other over the life cycle. However, Deaton's

(1992, p. 59) review of the literature leads him to conclude that the factors discussed in Chapter 2, precautionary savings and liquidity constraints, provide better explanations of the strong correlation between contemporaneous income and consumption.

Retirement

Through the nineteenth century, workers typically retired only when their health was bad or they found it difficult to find new employment when "let go" at an advanced age. Further, if relatively poor, retirees often had to rely on children for support. In fact, Costa (1998, p. 110) reports that in 1880, 46% of retired men lived with their children (compared with 5% in 1990). There has been a pronounced trend toward earlier retirement since the nineteenth century. Costa finds that "among men older than age sixty-four, participation rates fell steadily, from 78 percent in 1880 to 65 percent in 1900. By 1930 the figure had dropped to 58 percent and in 1990 to less than 20 percent" (1998, p. 7). This subsection addresses the retirement decision and asks why the age at retirement has fallen.

The intertemporal substitution effects discussed above indicate that leisure should increase in later years as the real wage falls. However, they do not predict the *instantaneous* transition from full-time employment to retirement that occurs in about 75% of all retirement sequences (cf. Costa). Sudden transitions may be associated with fixed costs of labor force participation, coupled with pension plans that punish work at older ages.

Fixed costs of employment (independent of the number of hours worked per day or week) may be as straightforward as the costs of commuting, buying parking passes, and maintaining a work wardrobe. Other costs are more subtle, such as being unable to commit to being the grandchildren's babysitter on snow days, or to being the "fourth player" in a bridge club or tennis group that meets irregularly. Clearly, the magnitude of fixed costs varies across workers. Several hours of work per week may be required simply to recoup the monetary value of these costs. However, these hours themselves entail additional costs in the form of foregone leisure. In the presence of such costs, working a "few" hours per week is not worthwhile.

To see this more explicitly, consider the (somewhat artificial) problem of someone entering the last period of life T: this person must decide whether to take retirement or to devote part of this period to work.[5] Imagine that he or she brings total assets of A_T into the period, which include financial assets, housing equity, and accumulated Social Security benefits. If the consumer retires in T, leisure $L_T = 1$ and $C_T = A_T$, yielding some utility of U_R, say. This combination of leisure and goods is given by point R and indifference curve U_R in Figure 8.9.

If the consumer instead works part-time in T, his or her wage is w and fixed costs are Z. Consequently, he or she views budget line JB1. Suppose preferences are such that if he or she works utility will be maximized at point E on indifference curve U_R. According to Figure 8.9, the consumer receives the same utility whether working quite a bit or if retired; the extra goods from working $1 - L_E$ units just offsets the loss of leisure. Clearly, if fixed costs were slightly higher, the preference for leisure a bit stronger, assets at the start of retirement a bit higher, or the wage a bit lower, retirement would be assured.

Figure 8.9 also depicts retirement under a lower wage: The budget line is NB1, and if working, the consumer would choose point K. One may wonder why the lower wage

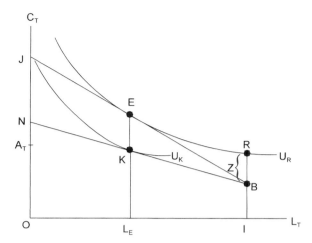

Figure 8.9 The retirement decision

didn't produce an ambiguous implication for retirement from conflicting income and substitution effects. The reason is that one is choosing between retirement yielding utility of U_R and point K. Obviously, the lower wage reduces utility from working to below U_R. Since the consumer was indifferent between retirement and working when the wage was higher, retirement is preferred at the lower wage.

That a lower wage induces retirement has important policy implications. As recently as 1998 each \$1 of earnings (beyond a low threshold) reduced Social Security benefits by 50 cents for workers aged 62 to 64.[6] The benefit reduction rate was one-third for those aged 65 to 69. Many have speculated that this explains why so few of those claiming benefits at age 62 work at all. Recently, Friedberg (1999) estimated that eliminating the earnings penalty (or "earnings test") would raise average hours worked by 5.3% for those earning more than the threshold. Further, she finds that the cost to the government would be quite small. Earnings tests were eliminated in 2000. It remains to be seen how much work behavior will change among those receiving Social Security.

Other innovations in pension plans also may have contributed to earlier retirement. Current formulas for determining private pensions in defined benefit plans typically provide an incentive to continue work until age 60, say. Beyond that age, the annual additions to the present value of expected benefits decline, or are even negative. Social Security also punishes retirement beyond age 65, in the sense that the present value increase in monthly benefits from deferring retirement another year does not offset the loss of benefits during that year. Anderson, Gustman, and Steinmeier (1999) attribute about a quarter of the trend toward earlier retirement by men in their early 60s from 1970 to the mid-1980s to the combined effects of private pensions and Social Security.

Consider a more realistic multiyear setting, and suppose that the marginal utility of leisure is independent of the consumption of market goods. Each year of work raises lifetime earnings and therefore the height of the age-consumption profile. Higher consumption lowers the marginal utility of goods. With the marginal utility of leisure unchanged, the relative attractiveness of retirement rises with years worked, and therefore with age. Similarly, the higher is life wealth, the lower is the marginal utility of goods and the more attractive is retirement.

Costa (1995) examines a unique data set of Union Army pensioners whose pensions varied with their health status, to the extent that the infirmity was traceable to the Civil War. Union Army pensioners were more likely to retire the larger was their pension, controlling for health status. Her results offer some confirmation that the retirement elasticity of income was positive around the turn of the twentieth century. If so, the approximately sevenfold increase in GDP per capita over the last 100 years may explain much of the trend to earlier retirement.

Also, cable television, the Internet, the rise of retirement communities, golf, and many other leisure activities may all have increased the relative desirability of retirement. (In terms of Figure 8.9, the argument would be that the indifference curves have become steeper through time at older ages.) Costa argues further that the relative price of recreational goods has fallen.

Poor health presumably raises the marginal utility of leisure. Therefore, adverse changes in health status should reduce the age at retirement. In this light, it is important to appreciate that the secular trend toward earlier retirement has taken place in the context of *improving* health in old age and jobs that are less taxing physically. Thus, the effects on retirement age of rising income, the evolution of pension policies, and more attractive leisure options, more than offset the effects of improving health.

This section discussed static and life-cycle labor-leisure choices, including retirement. However, it is inappropriate to regard all time not devoted to the labor market as time devoted to leisure. The next section acknowledges that appreciable economic output is produced outside the context of market employment.

8.2 HOUSEHOLD PRODUCTION

Some time away from the labor market is utilized in *household production,* when goods and services are produced in the home. This does not refer to time spent in "cottage industries," where quilts, for example are produced at home and then sold. Rather, in this context, household production refers to the creation of goods and services that are consumed at home. Goldin (1990) notes that American housewives worked in the home about 65 hours per week at the turn of the twentieth century. Although time spent in home production has fallen, it remains appreciable.

This section considers the implications of the home sector for time allocation. The *household production function* approach, pioneered by Nobel Laureate Gary Becker (1965), views the household as a small factory, combining household members' time with market goods to produce a variety of "basic" commodities. A basic commodity such as a "clean house" can be produced in numerous ways, such as hiring a maid, making the kids vacuum the rugs, personally scrubbing the bathtub with cleanser, and so on. The clean house is the output, while the maid, children, vacuum cleaner, own time, and cleanser are all inputs. Since the inputs do not yield utility directly, the demand for inputs derives from the demand for the underlying basic good. The technological relationship between the inputs and output is summarized by the household production function, described below.

The general model of household production is both flexible and cumbersome.[7] To sharpen our focus we allow several simplifying assumptions. First, rather than consider separately the many different basic goods, such as "clean house," "supper," and "entertainment," we imagine a simple aggregate of household goods, whose quantity is denoted G. Similarly, the aggregates of time and goods inputs allocated to household production are H and X.

Another concession is that market inputs X will be regarded as fixed, enabling us to focus on time allocation. Thus, X may be conceived of as a stock of durable consumer goods that is neither augmented by additional purchases nor diminished through depreciation. Over a span of a few years, this is reasonable for the house itself and for major appliances such as washing machines, refrigerators, and dishwashers. For food, cleaning supplies, and many other inputs, such a view is clearly unrealistic. More generally, for basic goods that are quite time intensive and/or for which substitution between goods and time inputs is difficult, the quantitative effect of fixing goods is small. And, for the questions we address, the qualitative implications for time allocation are not affected by the simplification. The framework provides insight into the substitution of market goods and services for household production time, as with market daycare; the effects on time allocation of technological improvements in the *quality* of the fixed home input; and changes in the relative productivity of market versus home production time (such as when wages rise).

The household production function is written

$$G = G(H; X)$$

where time H is a variable input and X is fixed in amount. Of course, the marginal products of the time (G_H) and goods inputs are positive. Further, due to the existence of fixed X, it is natural to assume that there are diminishing marginal returns to the time input.

To simplify the analysis, we assume that goods produced at home G and those purchased in the market C are perfect substitutes. This may in fact be a pretty good approximation for Chinese food prepared at home or purchased as carryout. However, a gift of a handmade sweater differs appreciably from a store-bought one in the consumer's preferences (although the sweaters might be equivalent to a disinterested third party). More generally, we previously aggregated all market goods into one composite good, and all household goods into another. Those aggregations proved useful, and it is no further great leap of faith to aggregate these two composites. For now, we also abstract from leisure consumption, so that maximizing utility is the same as maximizing C + G. The analysis is later generalized to include leisure.

Since the worker allocates time between the labor market and household production, the time constraint is H + M = T. In contrast to the diminishing returns in household production, each hour of market work is rewarded with w units of the market good C. The consumer's problem is to maximize C + G, subject to the time constraint, the household production function, and the requirement that expenditures on market goods not exceed labor earnings (assuming no nonlabor income). Optimizing behavior requires that each hour be spent where it makes the largest contribution to C + G. The model is illustrated in Figure 8.10, where C + G is measured on the vertical axis and labor market time M is measured on the horizontal. The household production function is given by TZ. Its (absolute) slope is G_H, which declines due to the diminishing returns to H. If all time is devoted to household production, C + G will consist entirely of home-produced goods G, in the amount of vertical distance OZ.

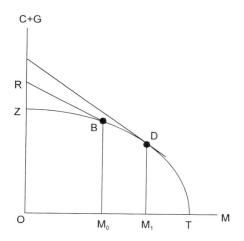

Figure 8.10 Time allocation, home and market production

As drawn, at first the marginal product of household production time, devoted to washing dishes and taking the trash out, say, is quite high, exceeding the market wage. At point B though, G_H has fallen to equal w. Consequently, the remaining time is devoted to market work. Thus, the output (and utility)-maximizing allocation of time is M_0 units of market work and $H_0 = T - M_0$ units of household production time. Total output is given by height R.

An increase in w raises the productivity of labor market time but leaves unaffected the productivity of time in home production, G_H. Consequently, following a wage increase, the number of hours previously worked in home production is too high, since w > G_H. To maximize the C + G, time must be shifted from the household to the labor market until the productivity of time in the household rises to the new wage. The reduction (increase) in H associated with an increase (decrease) in w is termed the *production substitution effect*. This effect follows from technological efficiency. In contrast, the consumption substitution effect between market goods and leisure, discussed earlier, involves market wages (which depend on technology) and preferences. In Figure 8.10 an increase in w moves the point of tangency below B, to D, inducing a reallocation toward the market and away from home of magnitude $M_1 - M_0$. A slight generalization of this framework is now employed to help understanding of a couple's division of labor between market and home work.

8.2.1   Household Division of Labor Between Home and Market

Until recent times women specialized in home production, men in market labor. Becker (1981) argues that this resulted from women's special role in childbearing. When families were large, women were pregnant often. Especially when market work requires a lot of brawn or energy, pregnancies, child birth, and recuperation time all disrupt market performance. Further, while wet nurses were available to the affluent, and "formula" is affordable to most now, mothers alone can breast feed. The effect on time allocation of women's modest biological advantage in home production was amplified by a second rationale for specialization: the returns on human capital investment increase with the utilization of those skills. Thus, the investments by women in learning how to make clothes, preserve foods (canning), cook from scratch, and so on, were more worthwhile when those activities were undertaken frequently. Similarly, the acquisition of market skills by men led to a concentration in that realm. Thus, most families achieved an "equilibrium" characterized by complete specialization of men in market work and women in home production. This section further develops the origins of this equilibrium, and also why it has broken down in recent decades.

Historically, men have enjoyed an absolute advantage in market work (higher wages) and women an absolute advantage in home production (breast-feeding, baking, etc.). For our purposes, we emphasize the effects of women's (men's) historical *comparative* advantage in home production (market work). Taking these comparative advantages as given, let us see how they help explain historical trends in female time allocation. Suppose for simplicity that men and women are perfect substitutes in household production but that men earn more per hour w_m than do women w_f. This captures the wage differential and comparative advantage, but obviously abstracts from the historically considerable skills of women in sewing, canning, and cooking, important to the earlier period we wish to explain. (Allowing for women's absolute advantage at home would complicate, but not alter, our qualitative results).

Suppose each spouse has a time endowment of 50 hours per week and that the couple desires to maximize the aggregate, or family, C + G they can produce. Since they are perfect substitutes in household production, each has the same marginal product for the nth hour of combined hours worked in household production. That is, if 34 hours have been worked in the household sector, all by the wife, the marginal product for the next hour worked there would be the same for the wife (her 35th) or the husband (his 1st). To understand historical changes in the allocation of time, suppose that the labor market demand for workers rises through time, increasing wages. Also we suppose, for now, that the structure of relative wages between men and women remains constant. Finally, we assume that there is no change over time in the productivity of time spent in household production. Many of these assumptions are relaxed later.

The reservation wages that induce market employment are easy to discern. For the husband, this is the marginal product of the 100th hour devoted by the couple to household production (since his wage exceeds hers). If $G_H > w_m$ when both husband and wife work full-time, there is no incentive for him to enter the labor force. Similarly, the reservation wage of the wife is the marginal product of the 50th hour devoted to household work—all of which would have been supplied by her. Suppose market wages are initially so low that the marginal product of the 100th hour spent in household production per week does exceed w_m. Then both husband and wife devote all time to household production, "living off the land."[8] Imagine that wages later rise to a point such that $w_m = G_H$ when total time in household production is somewhere between 50 and 100 hours, say 80 to be concrete. Then, C + G is maximized with the wife specializing in household production and the male devoting 30 hours to work at home, with the remaining 20 worked for market wages. As market productivity, and thus wages, continue to climb, the wages of women will come to exceed the marginal product of the 50th hour of household work, inducing the woman to enter the labor market. As w_f continues to rise, her market hours continue to rise at the expense of household production time.

This simple story does a surprisingly good job of explaining the changing patterns of the allocation of work effort. Initially, home-based agriculture predominates, with perhaps small cash crops grown to procure those few items not produced at home. Then the movement of men from home-based agriculture to market work begins, with women continuing to specialize in household production. In time, women enter the labor force in larger numbers, but work fewer hours in the market than men. Women continue to perform all of the declining home production.

8.2.2   Interrelationships with Marriage, Divorce, Schooling, and Fertility[9]

The framework also provides insight into some sources of the economic gains to marriage—as well as why those gains have fallen in recent decades, and the divorce rate has risen. Economic gains to marriage arise from a variety of sources. As discussed above, the division of labor in accordance with comparative advantage increases the size of the marital pie and consequently the attractiveness of marriage. In addition, economies of scale occur, since doubling the number of people in a household less than doubles the costs of maintaining the household. Also, public goods in marriage—in particular the enjoyment of children—raise the benefits of expenditures on those goods. Further, marriage enables the sharing of certain risks. For example, average earnings uncertainty is reduced with two earners. Finally, in *committed* marriages, it makes sense for couples to undertake marriage—specific human capital investments, and then divide labor in accordance with comparative advantage. We consider interrelationships between the erosion of comparative advantage and the decline of commitment to marriage.

To that end, suppose an unmarried man and woman maintain separate households, each facing identical household production functions. We continue to assume they are perfect substitutes in household production. Let the man's wage be $w_m = \$40$ and the woman's $w_f = \$20$ per hour. Suppose the maximization of the single man's total goods $C + G$ requires him to work 30 hours in the labor market and 20 hours at home (at which time G_H equals w_m). Since the woman's market wage is lower, she works at home longer, until G_H falls to equal her wage of $20. We'll assume this happens after she has devoted 20 hours to the market, 30 to the home.

Now let these two marry. Suppose the household production functions in the joint household are just as if the married couple maintained separate households. That is, we abstract from economies of scale in household production (which would only strengthen our argument). Their time allocations as singles are no longer optimal now that they are married. As discussed in the previous section, aggregate $C + G$ can be raised by having the wife specialize in home production and the man in market work. Here, having the wife work 20 more hours at home and the man 20 additional hours in the market, combined market earnings rise by $(w_m - w_f)20 = \$400$ per week—with no change in household production. How these gains are split between the couple may depend upon conditions in the marriage market, which we do not have space to consider. Clearly, though, as long as the marriage is otherwise neutral, both can benefit.

These gains arising from specialization have declined as gender differences in wages and in skill levels in home production (which we ignored) have fallen. In fact, the wages of women relative to men increased appreciably, if not steadily, over the twentieth century. Goldin concludes that the "ratio of female to male earnings in the economy as a whole rose from 0.46 to 0.56 during the period 1890–1930, but was virtually stable from 1950 to around 1980" (1990, p. 63). Further significant advances have occurred in recent years. According to the Current Population Survey, the relative earnings of full-time woman rose from 0.63 in 1979 to 0.76 in 1998. Among workers 20 to 24 years old, the earnings ratio in 1998 was 0.894. This erosion of men's comparative advantage in the marketplace constitutes one source of reduction in the gains to marriage.

Another important feature of the equilibrium in which men specialized in market work, women in housework, was that divorce was rare. With divorce rare, or the commitment to marriage great, the risk from making large relationship and sector-specific human capital investments was relatively low. In that context, women could rather safely specialize in the largely marriage-specific investments of rearing children.[10] Also, before the coming of fully stocked supermarkets, microwaves, and mass-produced clothing, the amount of domestic human capital associated with canning, cooking, and sewing was substantial. The large investments required to acquire that human capital increased comparative advantage, which increased the attractiveness of the union relative to divorce. These interactions helped make the equilibrium with complete specialization stable.[11]

Conversely, if marriages are unstable, it is quite risky for one spouse to specialize in nonmarket production, or for either spouse to make marriage—specific investments. For a late entrant into the labor market has fewer years to work, making subsequent market human capital investments less profitable. Late entrants also may not fare as well with respect to private pensions, many of which greatly reward tenure. Similarly, children are not in general as valuable to nonbiological parents, reducing the public goods benefits of children upon divorce. And, until recent times, mothers retained full custody of children upon divorce, while fathers often reneged on court-ordered child support (perhaps in anger over the limited visitation privileges that were then common). This lack of postdivorce child support also made marital investments in children risky for the mother. Thus, an equilibrium in which women specialize in nonmarket work is tenable only when marriage is a lifetime contract.[12]

An increase in the aggregate frequency of divorce may reduce the perceived long-term stability of individual unions. This may cause individuals to insure more heavily against the possibility of divorce, which makes divorce less unappealing, which may increase the probability of any specific marriage failing. A primary way to insure against the event of divorce is to increase general human capital at the expense of marriage-specific capital, including children.

Thus, young women, aware that marital prospects are uncertain, obtain more marketable skills prior to marriage. Recall from Chapter 7 that not only have college attendance rates risen for females, but women now major in business, law, and medicine more than when divorce was rare. The rise in the market income of women increases the wife's divorce-state income. Johnson and Skinner (1986) find more evidence of such "defensive investments"—women in troubled marriages increase their labor force participation in anticipation of divorce.

Women currently have roughly half the number of children, on average, borne by women a century ago. Since own children are a durable public good within marriage (both parents enjoy, say, Sarah's enthusiasm for life), the reduction in marital fertility has also reduced the gains from marriage. Also, this lower fertility within marriage improves subsequent prospects should divorce occur, perhaps increasing the frequency of divorce. Similarly, this higher probability of divorce makes children riskier, reducing desired fertility. Empirically , the presence of children within a marriage does lower the probability of divorce. However, if divorce occurs, children increase the time until remarriage and reduce the probability of remarriage. The relationship between children and marriage is both complex and important. An in-depth discussion of fertility is undertaken in Chapter 9.

The sharp increase in divorce in the 1970s and 1980s is certainly consistent with the increase in women's relative wages. In a recent empirical analysis, Hoffman and Duncan (1995) find that higher husband earnings reduce divorce, just as the model predicts. The findings for the wages of women are more subtle. Weiss and Willis (1997) find that increases in women's wages that were anticipated at the start of a marriage are not destabilizing. However, wage increases for wives that were unanticipated at the time of marriage do increase the probability of divorce. Apparently, reductions in the *current* gains from marriage consistent with the original implicit marriage contract are not destabilizing. However, if rising women's wages reduce not only the current but also the long-term gains from marriage (breaking the original marriage contract), divorce becomes more likely.

Lee and Casterline (1996, p. 9) comment that as a result of the changes discussed above, there

> has been a shift from the unstable equilibrium of the traditional family to a new stable equilibrium in which the nuclear family is less common and/or in which there is less division of labor and less difference between the marketable skills of men and women. In the first, unstable equilibrium, families are large; in the new equilibrium, children are costly and few, and the cost is not only in the day-to-day present, but also in a reduction in future options and an increased exposure to the risk of economic adversity following divorce.

Obviously, the presence of children also affects the allocation of time between home and work; it is to those issues we now turn.

8.2.3   Children and Household Production Time over the Life Cycle

Infants would be happy to have 100 percent of their parent's attention at all times. Many teenagers might be happy to have close to 0 percent of their parent's attention at all times. While neither of those allocations are in the child's best interest, it is certainly the case that older children have less need of parents' time and energy than young ones: As children evolve they no longer need to be carried, fed, dressed, have their diapers changed, have endless new situations explained to them, and so on. Here we consider the implications of child development for the allocation of time to household production over the life cycle.

To focus on the care giver, suppose the other spouse's labor supply (historically the husband's) is largely independent of the age and number of children in the household. To further isolate issues, assume the wage rate for the "flexible" spouse is constant over the

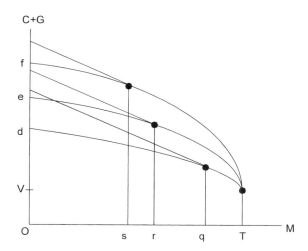

Figure 8.11 Children's age and home productivity

life cycle. Also suppose that hours of work at each age M_t are positive and may be freely chosen. Then at each age t, $w = G_{Ht}$.

When there are no children in the household, this condition may be met at a low level of household production time; H_t will be small. When a first child is born, at say age t = b, the marginal product of housework efforts rises dramatically: feeding, coddling, and bathing an infant are all important, or high G_H, tasks. This is illustrated in Figure 8.11. Household production frontier dT prevails before children. The function becomes steeper when young children are present, as shown by fT. Such a steepening increases the reservation wage. Thus, the birth of a child may induce some previously employed women to exit the labor force. For those continuing employment, household production time is predicted to rise. Women specializing in household production before the birth of the child are expected to continue to do so. As children grow older, productivity at home falls, as reflected by production frontier eT. Housework H is qT before children and after they leave home, rises to sT when children are young, and is rT when children are older but still dependent. Holding leisure constant, M_b is predicted to fall and H_b to rise until G_{Hb} falls to again equal w. This is another application of the production substitution effect; time is allocated between M and H so as to maximize C + G.

Additional children further increase the productivity of home work and thus the reservation wage. As the (last) child ages, the G_{Ht} profile falls—and H_t along with it—until the child achieves parental independence. Consequently, H_t is low until children are born, increases substantially upon birth of the first child, and then falls gradually to the initial level as children become less dependent. These predicted H_t and M_t profiles are illustrated in Figure 8.12 for the flexible parent who remains in the labor force at every age of the children. (Again, the market work profile depends on the assumption that leisure time is fixed).[13]

Thus, our framework predicts that LFPRs and hours worked by participants will rise with the age of the youngest child and decline with the number of young children. Even this highly stylized model has rough correspondence with empirical knowledge. Hotz and Miller (1988) estimate the time parents spend on child care falls roughly 12% per year

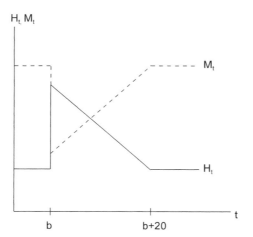

Figure 8.12 Children and the allocation of home work

from the peak commitment during the first year. The model also correctly predicts that the LFPR of mothers rises as children age. For example, in 1996, 55.9 percent of married mothers with children under the age of 1 were employed, compared with 63.4% of married mothers with children 2 years of age (Bureau of Labor Statistics). These participation rates for mothers are much higher than even a few decades before. Thus, in 1948 only 10.8% of married mothers with children under the age of 6 were in the labor force, compared with 26% of those with children between the ages of 6 and 17 (Jacobsen, 1998, Table 4.1).

Several factors have contributed to the rise in market work by mothers with young children. Obviously important is the continuing rise in women's wages, which increases the opportunity cost of staying home. We noted that as successive cohorts of young women have come to expect greater market involvement, their premarket human capital accumulation has risen. This increases their shadow wage (i.e., wage if employed), inducing earlier reentry into the labor force.

Another important consideration is that until recent times the degree of substitutability between market daycare and mother care was very uncertain, because experience with daycare was uncommon. As young mothers began to enter the labor force in large numbers, there was appreciable concern that market daycare may be a poor substitute for mother, making mother's absence from the home detrimental to children's intellectual and emotional development. Presumably, one can purchase different qualities of market care, with price and perceived quality rising with factors such as staff-child ratio and staff education. Since parents are particularly risk averse regarding their children's well-being, they may act as if the most pessimistic relationship between market inputs and child quality is correct. In this case, that market care that is perceived to be largely comparable to mother's would be very expensive. Consequently, the real wage of young mothers (i.e., their nominal wage deflated by a price index heavily weighted by the price of quality daycare) remained low. In this way, the combination of uncertainty and risk aversion kept young mothers out of the labor force. Evidence supportive of this contention is found in Goldin (1990). She reports that older mothers entered the labor market in large numbers following World War II. Mothers with young children did not begin to enter the labor force in large numbers until the 1960s, even though younger cohorts of women had higher education and would have had more years to benefit from any human capital acquired on the job.

Although knowledge of the degree of substitutability between daycare and mother care remains imprecise, this uncertainty has been reduced appreciably over the past twenty years or so. Blau, Ferber, and Winkler (1998, p. 291) summarize this relationship as follows[14]:

> The general consensus among researchers is that children between the ages of two and four tend to do better in center day care both intellectually and emotionally than children cared for entirely at home. For infants and toddlers the evidence is more mixed. . . . The impact on school-aged and older children when mothers are successful in their paid work appears to be overwhelmingly favorable.

Findings such as these have served to reduce the uncertainty over the effects of daycare and have shown the worst-case scenarios to be unfounded.

This reduction in the uncertainty facing risk-averse parents effectively constituted an additional rise in the real wage, giving further impetus to the LFPR of young mothers. Also, as women following childbirth have returned earlier and in larger numbers to the labor market, institutions have begun to accommodate. For example, the Family Leave Act requires employers to provide some unpaid leave time to a new parent without loss of employment. These reasons help explain why gender differences in labor market participation have narrowed in recent times.[15]

In this section we have discussed several issues affecting the allocation of time between market and home work, holding leisure constant. In section 8.1 we analyzed choices between market work and leisure, abstracting from household production. Unsurprisingly, some issues are best illuminated by viewing leisure, home production, and market work simultaneously. These considerations are the subject of section 8.3.

8.3 MARKET WORK, HOME PRODUCTION, AND LEISURE

Combining the labor-leisure and household production models provides further insights. Since the individual likes both leisure and goods, the utility function becomes

$$U = U(C + G, L)$$

Naturally, the marginal utilities of leisure and goods are positive and the indifference curves convex.

The budget constraint is illustrated in Figure 8.13. The allocation of time must be consistent with the time available, $T = L + M + H$. As a consequence of unearned income V_0, this constraint is vertical from the time endowment to A. Segment AS is the household production function. Its slope at each point is $-G_H$. AB is the portion of that

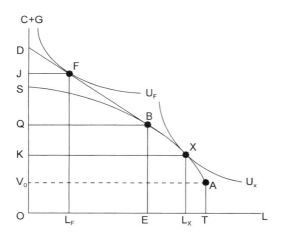

Figure 8.13 Leisure, market work, and housework

function for which $G_H > w$, while the wage is greater along BS. Any time not devoted to leisure will be allocated to maximize the sum $C + G$, flowing to where it has the greatest marginal product. For this reason, only segment AB is relevant to the constraint, for if $G_H < w$, any additional time devoted to $C + G$ production will be worked in the labor market. Therefore, that part of the constraint associated with market employment, BD, emanates from B where $w = G_H$. Of course, the market labor segment BD has slope of $-w$. Thus the entire constraint is TABD.

This budget constraint readily applies for a single head of household. When the household includes a married couple, the graph depicts the decision-making for only the flexible spouse. Since we continue to address the increase in women's labor force participation during the twentieth century, we shall call the decision-maker the wife. (For contemporary applications, the decision-maker may be of either gender, of course.) Since one adult's home production time substitutes (perhaps imperfectly) for the other's, the wife's household productivity is lower the more housework performed by the husband. Similarly, the higher are the husband's market earnings, the greater is the couple's command over market goods.[16]

Two points can be made with reference to efficiency alone: Since at zero hours of work $G_H > w$, the first hours allotted to $C + G$ production occur in home production. Further, since G_H falls to equal w at point B, TE hours is the maximum time one would devote to household production. If total work time $M + H < TE$, $M = 0$; if $M + H > TE$, $H = TE$.

More generally, utility maximization also depends upon the consumer's preferences. There are two fundamental equilibria to consider; one where the consumer engages in market work, and a second where the wife is out of the labor force. Point F, where indifference curve U_F is tangent to the market labor portion of the budget constraint, illustrates the "market" equilibrium. At F, $MRS = w$ and leisure consumption is OL_F. Since the consumer simultaneously chooses H so as to equate w and G_H, when labor market participants have maximized utility, $MRS = w = G_H$. The time *not* devoted to leisure L_FT is spent in the production of $C + G$. Of this, $M = L_FE$ is applied to market work. Housework time is the maximum that efficiency allows, $H = TE$. With respect to the OJ goods consumed, V_0 units are the result of nonearned or spousal income, V_0Q units are produced at home, and QJ are purchased using own market earnings.

The second type of equilibrium is combination x on U_x where the consumer divides her time between household production and leisure. At x, $M = 0$ and the individual is unemployed. In this equilibrium, the indifference curve is tangent to the production function so that $MRS = G_H$. Since the individual is choosing not to work, w is below the reservation wage; at point X, the $MRS > w$. Since work is not being done in the market, increasing L by one unit would reduce H by one unit, lowering goods by G_H. Thus, the opportunity cost or price of L is G_H. Recall that in the labor-leisure model the price of an additional hour of leisure was w units of C, no matter how much leisure was currently consumed. Here, due to diminishing returns, leisure's price G_H rises with L (or falls as H rises). Thus, for those voluntarily out of the labor force, $MRS = G_H > w$. The time allocation is $H = L_XT$, with $L = OL_X$. V_0 market goods derive from nonearned or spousal income; additional consumption derives from the home production of V_0K units of G.

In general, one expects most single individuals living under their own roof to be in the first type of equilibrium, with $M > 0$. Those single heads of households who are out of the labor force must have some combination of "high" V and "low" w. Welfare recipients typically face a low w, which may make the rather small transfer payments, here V, sufficiently attractive for them to withdraw from the labor force. Also, those fortunate enough to have received a large inheritance or gifts from parents may be able to afford so much leisure that market labor is not undertaken.

8.3.1 Comparative Statics

Nonlabor Income

V has no effect on the productivity of time worked at home or in the market. For this reason an increase in V entails an income effect on leisure, but no substitution effects. Since time spent on leisure is normal, it rises with V. The model also specifies where the leisure time is withdrawn from. For someone in the labor market both before and after a rise in V, the increase in leisure time is predicted to come entirely at the expense of market work. That is, since changing V doesn't affect the productivity of time at work or at home, $w = G_H$ at the same amount of housework as before. Thus, if $M > 0$, an increase in V is predicted to leave H unchanged and to reduce M by the increase in L. Leisure time is also predicted to increase for those initially out of the labor market. In this case there is still a reduction in work effort, but now it is limited to the home sector.

Do these model predictions square with the facts? There is some evidence to the affirmative. As discussed in section 8.1, higher nonlabor income does appear to reduce market work. What about the interesting prediction that higher nonlabor income reduces H for the unemployed but not for the employed? Some time back, Gronau (1977) found that an increase in nonlabor income of $1,000 per year leads to a reduction of 44 hours in the annual time spent in household work by white married women who are not employed. However, this effect was not found for employed white married women. His study therefore lends support to the model's predictions.

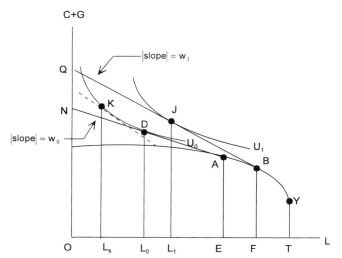

Figure 8.14 Effect on leisure of a wage increase

Own Wage Rate, w

We next consider an increase in w. For someone not working, this will have no effect, *unless* the higher wage matches or exceeds the reservation wage. In that case the person would enter the labor market. There are three distinct effects of an increase in w for someone currently employed: the income and consumption substitution effects on leisure, and the production substitution effect. These effects operate in combination no differently than they operate in isolation. Nevertheless, the benefits of viewing all effects simultaneously merit a brief discussion.

The wage increase is portrayed in Figure 8.14. The consumer initially maximizes utility at point D, along the labor market segment of the budget line NAYT. Production efficiency is at point A, where $w_0 = G_H$. Thus, at the initial optimum, $L = L_0$, $M = L_0 E$, and $H = ET$. Once the wage rises to w_1, efficiency requires a reduction in H. Household time falls to FT, where G_H has risen to w_1. Thus, the production substitution effect is the reduction in H of EF units.

The consumption substitution effect reduces the now relatively more expensive leisure. Efficiency dictates that the increase in work occurs in the market. This effect is the movement along the initial indifference curve from D to K, which increases M by $L_0 L_s$. The increase in well-being allowed by the wage increase entails a positive income effect for leisure, which comes at the expense of market work. Graphically, this is captured by the movement between indifference curves, from K to J, which increases leisure by $L_s L_1$.

Notice that the model is unambiguous in its prediction that home production time will decline. In contrast, the income and consumption substitution effects conflict as in the labor-leisure model. This makes for ambiguous effects of a wage increase on L and M. However, allowance for the production substitution effect increases the likelihood that the uncompensated labor supply curve is up-sloping, compared with the labor-leisure model. Unfortunately, most empirical analyses have not distinguished between H and L, effec-

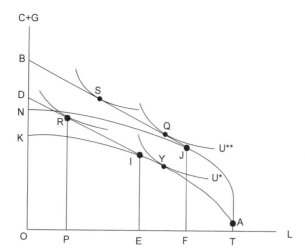

Figure 8.15 Effect of advances in home technology on home production

tively treating household production time as leisure. Gramm (1974) and Gronau (1977) are two (now dated) empirical studies that explicitly incorporated the production substitution effect. Gram found that the time spent cooking and cleaning by married women fell as their wage rose. Gronau found that annual hours of housework declined significantly among employed married women in response to higher wages. Thus, both studies indicate a role for production substitution effects.

Improvements in Home Technology

Through time the quality of home appliances (the "fixed" goods input X) has risen dramatically. Obvious examples are conventional and microwave ovens, refrigerators, clothes washes and dishwashers, garbage disposals, and vacuum cleaners. These innovations decrease the time required to produce a given amount of G. Thus, over at least some interval of time, there is a higher marginal product of time spent in household production G_H. This is illustrated in Figure 8.15, where better technology expands the household production frontier from TAK to TAN. However, if the standard chores such as cooking and cleaning can now be completed faster, the marginal product of the "extra" time may begin to fall quickly. To illustrate this possibility, TAN has a lower G_H near the vertical axis than in the original frontier. For example, if at high H the most important remaining task is that of repolishing the silver that had been polished just last week, G_H would be below its value when technology was cruder. Although average home productivity would be higher if the original amount of time spent in home production were to remain the same, marginal productivity would fall.

How might such innovations affect time allocation? As with a change in the wage, enhanced technology entails both income and production substitution effects. Also, for women remaining housewives after technology advances, there is a consumption substitution effect.

Imagine that the initial household appliances gave rise to household production frontier TAK. Suppose a consumer maximizes utility at point R, working in the home and market. The maximum efficient H is ET at point I, where $w = G_H$. Labor supply is $M = PE$ and total work time, $M + H$, is PT. When technology advances, w in general will no longer equal G_H at the same H as before. The resulting reallocation between M and H, with total hours worked being held constant, is another version of the production substitution effect.

Figure 8.15 is drawn to reflect the interesting case where, at the initial allocation of time to home production, $H = ET$, G_H is lower with the new than with the old technology. The maximum efficient H falls to FT at point J. The production substitution effect is the reduction in the H, or increase in M, of EF. This effect is another factor helping to explain the increase in women's hours of work over the past several decades. It is often argued that technological progress embodied in market physical capital displaces market workers from specific tasks. Analogously, technological advances embodied in the household's stock of physical capital reduce the demand for household production time.

Better household technology may also help explain the increase in women's labor force participation rates. To see this, suppose that utility is initially maximized at point Y, so that all work time occurs in the home. Following the technological improvements, the efficient H falls such that the woman is now employed, maximizing utility at point Q on U**. In other words, this technical change lowered the housewife's reservation wage below her market wage. In contrast, higher wages increased participation when they came to exceed a given reservation wage. In combination, improvements in household technology and rising women's wages provide a powerful explanation of the increase in labor force participation rates and hours of market labor.[17]

Additionally, there is an income effect that unambiguously increases leisure consumption. Following the technological improvement, the new budget constraint TAJB is everywhere above the initial one TAID. For those in the labor market both before and after, moving between points like R and S, the increased leisure consumption is at the expense of labor supply. If the production substitution effect reduces H, the overall effect will be to increase L and reduce H, with the change in M ambiguous. For someone who is a housewife both before and after the innovation, the positive income effect reduces H and increases L. There is also a consumption substitution effect as leisure consumption adjusts to equate the MRS to G_H.

Not every technical advance served to reduce housework, however. In fact, despite the growing mechanization of household activities, there is evidence that the number of hours devoted to housework *by the housewife* did not fall much between the dawn of the twentieth century to the late 1960s, before declining appreciably in recent years (Mokyr, 1997).[18] One reason is that, among modestly affluent families, the use of house servants declined from the nineteenth into the twentieth century, reducing the *total* time devoted to housework (and implying that the housewife's output per hour was increasing). Mokyr argues that another important explanation of persistently high levels of housework was the spread and acceptance of the germ theory of disease throughout the nineteenth and into the twentieth century.

> In short, homemakers spent more time cleaning, nursing, laundering, cooking, and looking after their children because they had become convinced that the health of the members of their household was under their control and part of their responsibility, and because they had

been persuaded that wholesome food, clean clothes and bed sheets, and a hygienic environment were crucial variables in the determination of good health and longevity. (p. 22)

That is, new scientific theories of the origin of disease increased the perceived marginal product of household production time. Fears about undercleaning may have led to overcleaning; "in the presence of uncertainty, a certain margin of unnecessary cleaning may be regarded as an insurance premium against low-probability but high-cost events" (p. 22, ftnt. 34). This household war against infectious disease diminished appreciably following the introduction of antibiotics in the 1940s.

8.4 INCREASED FEMALE LABOR FORCE PARTICIPATION AND ECONOMIC GROWTH

U.S. census reports indicate that labor force participation by females tripled from 19.6% in 1890 to 59.8% in 1998. Most dramatically, only 4.6% of married women were in the measured labor force in 1890, a figure that rose to 59.9% by 1996. These figures raise the question of how much of the rise in twentieth-century income per capita can be attributed to this transitional rise in the labor force participation rates of women.

Goldin (1986) calculates the partial-equilibrium increase in wage income per capita attributable to increased LFPRs by women between 1890 and 1980 (ignoring any effects on the wages of men or on capital accumulation). Using census data, her accounting approach shows that total labor earnings per capita rose by about 28% more than did male earnings per capita. In Chapter 3 we noted that labor's share of GDP has shown little change from .7 over the past century. The relative constancy of this share suggests that (partial-equilibrium) GDP per capita also rose by about 28% more than if female participation rates had not changed. Given that GDP per worker has increased roughly sevenfold over this period, an alternative phrasing is that GDP per capita in 1980 would have risen about 200 percent above that of 1890 as a consequence of the increase in women's labor force participation alone. These figures require a variety of adjustments.

Goldin adjusts for census undercounts of female agricultural workers and boardinghouse keepers. However, in combination these lower the contribution of females no more than 3 or 4%. A more significant bias occurs because of the decline in household production between 1890 and 1980. That is, as women moved their productive efforts from home to market, some goods formerly produced at home were now purchased in the market. Most important among these goods, according to Goldin, was the making of clothes and baked goods. She estimates that 9 hours per week, from a total of 65 hours of housework per week, were devoted to these activities (above current levels for baking). She corrects for this by attributing 9/65, or 14 percent, of the time of 1890 homemakers to the labor market of 1890. In combination, these corrections reduce the partial-equilibrium contribution of women to between 15 and 19%.

Goldin found that most of the contribution occurred between 1950, when the LFPRs of *married* women began to rise rapidly, and the end of the interval she studied, 1980. Since 1980 the LFPR of mothers with *young* children has risen sharply. However, their market work has moved much child care from the home to commercial daycare. These daycare outlays need to be considered when assessing the contributions of these mothers to output. The 1980s through the early 1990s was also a period of substantial increase in the ratio of women's to men's wages (see Chapter 7). As the demand for labor and skill upgrading continue to raise women's wages, the contributions of women to income per capita should also continue to rise.

Goldin's accounting procedure omits some potentially important indirect behavioral changes. Most famously, Becker (1981) argues that as women have worked more, they have chosen to have fewer children but to invest more in the human capital of each.[19] Relatedly, Carter (1986, p. 598) remarks that "in the absence of women willing to teach for low wages it is plausible that mass education would have been too costly to be politically feasible." These considerations imply that some of the increase in men's education, and therefore wages, over the twentieth century may not have occurred had women continued to specialize in home production and to have many children. Men now complete about 13 years of school on average, compared with roughly 8 years at the start of the century. Suppose the private return to an additional year's schooling is 10%. Raising men's schooling by 5 years, with each year increasing wages 10%, implies a compounded wage increase of about 61%. Clearly, though, a substantial part of the rise in men's education may be a consequence of other factors, such as skill-biased technical change. Nevertheless, even attributing a couple of years of schooling to indirect effects of women working suggests a larger contribution of women to growth.

However, increased market work by women may entail important general-equilibrium effects, such as slowing the growth in market wages of men and/or affecting the accumulation of and returns to other inputs, such as capital. Goldin (1986) briefly addresses general equilibrium considerations (pp. 558–559), but does not allow for the important feedback effects of changing factor prices on behavior. Galor and Weil (1996) provide such a discussion, based on changing demands in production for "brains" and "brawn," with women having a *comparative* advantage with respect to brains. Their analysis focuses on fertility as well, and we postpone our discussion of their model until Chapter 9.

The increased labor market participation of women, especially married women, in the twentieth century increased GDP both directly and indirectly. There remains substantial uncertainty regarding the extent of that contribution. Going forward, as women's wages continue to rise in importance compared with the foregone household production, so should also the contribution of women to growth. Conversely, if higher earnings by women increase the divorce rate and reduce investments in children, the effect on growth may be muted.

8.5 POLICY APPLICATIONS

8.5.1 Producer's Surplus and the Compensating Variation

Recall the compensated labor supply curve, $M^c = M^c(w; U^0)$, discussed in section 8.1 and depicted in Figure 8.16. This schedule may be used to measure the welfare effects on a consumer from a wage change. The height of M^c is the supply price, or minimum w, the

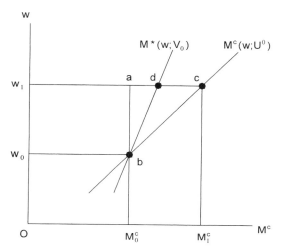

Figure 8.16 Producer's surplus and excess burden

worker must receive to maintain the utility U^0 associated with the initial, or anchoring, wage w_0. Suppose one were to move up along M^c between b and c, *receiving the supply price for each additional unit of labor supplied.* The increase in labor supply to M_1^c would lead to additional income of $M_0^c bcM_1^c$. This amount would exactly compensate the consumer for the leisure foregone, leaving utility at U^0.

Suppose, as is more common, that the increase in labor supply is instead associated with an increase in the wage from w_0 to w_1 *for each unit of labor.* Total wage income on M^c will increase by the area $w_0 w_1 cM_1^c M_0^c b$. Recall, the amount $bcM_1^c M_0^c$ is required to keep utility at U^0. The remaining portion $PS = w_0 w_1 cb$ constitutes payments beyond those necessary to induce the additional $M_1^c - M_0^c$ units of labor. This monetary measure of the increase in welfare from facing w_1 rather than w_0 is the addition to *producer's surplus.* This producer's surplus obtained from the compensated supply curve should and does equal the compensating variation $V_0 - V'$ derived from the indifference curve analysis in section 8.1: Each yields the same monetary measure of the increase in welfare from facing w_1 instead of w_0.

What if producer's surplus is measured using the more readily observed ordinary labor supply curve $M^*(w; V_0)$? We can see from Figure 8.16 that the same increase in the wage induces movement along the uncompensated demand curve from b to d. Use of M^* to calculate the surplus yields a measure of $w_1 dbw_0$, thereby understating the true surplus gain by bdc. Notice that the bias in surplus measurement is larger the greater is the income elasticity of labor supply (since the income effects are what make M^* and M^c differ). In section 8.1 we noted that income effects appear to be relatively weak. Therefore the bias from use of M^* may be small.[20]

8.5.2   Evaluation of Training Programs

Welfare reform over the past decade has consistently moved in the direction of helping recipients shift from welfare to paid employment. This "help" is typically some combination of stick (reduced eligibility after an interval of participation) and carrot (providing job training to make recipients more employable). Welfare policies are discussed in a subsequent application. Our current concern is the appropriate evaluation of training programs, which raise the human capital and thus the wage of participants. Consider someone previously out of the labor force who, upon graduation from a job-training program, commands a wage in excess of his or her reservation wage. The person will commence paid employment. We now know that total earned income is not the appropriate dollar measure of the increase in the person's welfare, since part of those earnings are necessary to compensate for the leisure a person loses when working. In fact, the compensating variation or increase in producer's surplus may be *much* less than the increase in earnings. However, program directors often tout the full increase in earnings as a measure of the program's success. This may not reflect misunderstanding on the part of the director but rather conscious use of an alternative, perhaps social, utility function that puts less weight on the leisure consumption of the poor than do the poor themselves.

8.5.3   Efficiency Costs of Wage Taxation

When taxes are levied on outcomes that economic actors can influence, economic behavior is distorted. Such taxes result in costs to the economy that exceed the revenues they generate. These efficiency costs, or *deadweight losses*, from taxation are an important consideration when labor income is taxed. We first illustrate this in a partial-equilibrium context where we assume the gross-of-tax wage rate is fixed and where there are no other taxes.

Consider Figure 8.16 where w_1 is the wage before the imposition of any tax. Now, suppose a tax is levied at rate t_w, reducing the net wage to $w_0 = w_1(1 - t_w)$. This tax generates government tax revenues of w_1abw_0. Notice, though, that there is also a reduction in producer's surplus equal to w_0cbw_1 (after one subtracts the value of the increased leisure from the reduction in wage income). Now, suppose workers value each dollar of government revenues and of net income equally (vbg). Then, workers are made worse off by $w_0bcw_1 - w_1abw_0 = abc$. Stated differently, part of the reduction in wage income went to the government, part of it was "used" to increase leisure consumption, but part of it (abc) went to no one. For this reason abc is also often termed an *excess burden*.

Assuming the supply curve is linear, this deadweight loss triangle is just one-half the base times the height, or $\frac{1}{2}(w_0 - w_1)(M_0^c - M_1^c)$. This measure is typically expressed in terms of the elasticity of the *compensated* labor supply schedule with respect to the wage, call it e, where

$$e \equiv (M_0^c - M_1^c)w_1/[(w_0 - w_1)M_1^c]$$

(Recall that the subscript 1 corresponds to the initial wage, 0 to the posttax wage.) Using the fact that $w_0 = w_1(1 - t_w)$, along with the definition of e, one finds after some rearrangement that

$$abc = 1/2t_w^2ew_1M_1^c \tag{8.9}$$

Although there is some uncertainty regarding the size of e, a value of .2 is not unrealistic for a married male. For illustrative purposes consider John, who works 2,000 hours per year in the absence of taxes (50 weeks at 40 hours per week). Suppose John's pretax wage is $25 per hour and that a tax rate of 30 percent is now imposed on John's earnings. Substituting these values into (8.9), the excess burden is about $450. Additional perspective is afforded by computing the deadweight loss as a percentage of revenues raised. With e = .2, the tax reduces the compensated labor supply to 1,880 hours. Since $25(.3) = $7.50 is collected per hour, total receipts are $14,100. Consequently, the excess burden is roughly 3.2 percent of the new revenues. Notice that this efficiency loss will arise even if there is no change in uncompensated labor supply (i.e., if the income effect just offsets the substitution effect).

The 3.2% figure was the *average* efficiency cost per dollar of revenues raised. Of perhaps greater interest is the *marginal* efficiency cost associated with raising further revenues. This is much greater, because as seen in equation (8.9), the excess burden rises with the *square* of the tax rate. For example, increasing the tax rate from .30 to .31 increases the deadweight loss from $450 to $480, so that the marginal excess burden per dollar of revenues is about 7%. Meaningful assessments of the efficiency cost of wage taxation differ in important respects from the partial-equilibrium calculations described above.

First, a dynamic general-equilibrium setting should be employed, so that the effects of the tax on capital accumulation and therefore on the gross wage and interest rate are considered. Second, if the government has given obligations to finance, changes in the tax rate on wage earnings must be reflected in other taxes so as to keep constant aggregate government revenues. Structural tax reforms along these lines were analyzed in Chapter 4.

Feldstein (1999) argues that tax avoidance is another reason the partial-equilibrium procedure discussed above is incorrect. Feldstein points out that adjusting hours of work is not the only way taxpayers respond to higher taxes. They also respond, he argues, by working less hard and by taking compensation in the form of nontaxed benefits (such as employer-provided health insurance). Similarly, a household may respond to higher taxes by choosing to own rather than to rent (and thereby receive the mortgage interest tax benefits). Using a random sample of 100,000 tax returns, Feldstein found the deadweight loss of income (not just wage) taxes to be about 30 percent of the total personal income taxes collected. Further, the marginal deadweight loss of increasing tax revenues was found to exceed 1! His results are controversial and most other estimates of the deadweight loss are appreciably lower. For example, Jorgenson and Yun (1991) estimate the deadweight loss to be about .30.

8.5.4   Poor Female Family Heads and Welfare Policy

Until recently, the major form of welfare for female family heads was Aid for Families with Dependent Children, or AFDC, which began in the 1930s. At that time, divorce was rare, out-of-wedlock childbirth shameful, and married mothers with young children rarely worked. Thus, the program was small, and beneficiaries were often widows with young children or in some other somewhat "tragic" circumstances. There was only modest concern that women would seriously contemplate changing marriage, work force, and/or fertility decisions so as to take advantage of the rather meager monies AFDC afforded.

However, the world changed. By the 1980s the number of female heads of households (i.e., no husband present, dependent children under age 18) on AFDC was close to 5 million. Those on AFDC typically also received Food Stamps and Medicaid benefits, so that the total benefit package had become a real disincentive to work. In fact, Moffitt (1992) reports that in 1987 only 6 percent of AFDC recipients worked, whereas over 85 percent of female family heads not on AFDC worked. Relative to when welfare was initiated, clothes washers and dryers, dishwashers, vacuum cleaners, carry-out and frozen foods, and so on have reduced the time required to "run" a household. This (and higher wages) help explain why more than half of married women now return to work within the first year following a pregnancy (as opposed to 15% as recently as 1962). Unsurprisingly, working married mothers (and their husbands) have become less enthusiastic about paying for other mothers to stay home.

Also, adverse changes in family organization since the inception of AFDC at least loosely correspond to the period of rapid growth in welfare benefits. By the late 1980s, almost half of all marriages were expected to end in divorce, 80 percent of live births to nonwhite teenagers occurred out of wedlock, and 40 percent of all black families with dependent children were female headed (Moffitt, 1992, Fig. 4). The illegitimate birth rate among white teens was about 40% and had been rising for 25 years. Was welfare to blame? Moffitt (p. 27) notes that AFDC "provides an obvious incentive to delay marriage, increase rates of marital dissolution, delay remarriage, and have children outside of a marital union." The empirical evidence regarding the effect of welfare on "the breakup of the nuclear family" has mostly found very weak effects, though more adverse effects on out-of-wedlock pregnancy have been reported recently (see section 9.3). Even if effects on family structure are unclear, it is unsurprising that attitudes and public policy toward single female family heads have changed in recent decades.

The modern focus of welfare appears to be creating incentives for as many female family heads as possible to work, which requires keeping transfers to the unemployed low and difficult to obtain (at least long-term). The welfare reform act of 1996 eliminated the traditional federal matching of state expenditures on several types of aid, most notably AFDC. The remnants of AFDC were renamed Temporary Assistance to Needy Families, TANF. The federal government now awards predetermined dollar amounts, or block grants, to the states to help finance welfare programs. It is important to appreciate that while the *federal* matching provision has been eliminated, *states* do continue to provide cash transfers to single female family heads. However, elimination of the matching provision effectively doubles, from 50 cents to one dollar, the cost to a state of increasing recipient's transfer income. Further, these federal block grants are made contingent upon the state reducing long-term welfare dependency and increasing the proportion of recipients who "earn" their transfer. States have great latitude in how they achieve these objectives. Although there is great variation across states in program design, cash transfers have in general declined, while job search, job training, and work requirements have been strengthened. As state programs have become less generous, participation has declined.

"The end of welfare as we know it" has been accompanied by increased reliance on training programs at the state level and on the Earned Income Tax Credit (EITC) at the

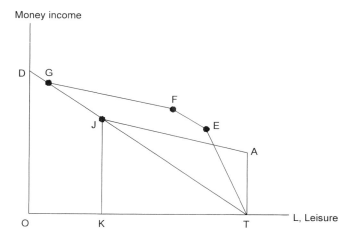

Figure 8.17 Substitution effects of welfare and the Earned Income Tax Credit on work and leisure

federal level. Both of these have the effect of raising the market wage. Here we briefly contrast the work incentives of AFDC-type programs (including the ongoing state remnants) with the EITC.[21]

The central features of the traditional welfare system (AFDC) resembled a negative income tax, NIT. Under a NIT, there is some guaranteed level of income, or maximum transfer, shown as height TA in Figure 8.17. This guaranteed annual income must not be set so low as to leave impoverished those recipients who are for some reason virtually unemployable. On the other hand, if it is set too high, program costs and case loads will be exorbitant. In the absence of the program, the potential beneficiary's wage is w, producing the earned income budget line TJD. Under the NIT, as recipient income is earned, benefits are taxed away at the benefit reduction rate (BRR). This reduces the net wage rate to w(1 − BRR) along line segment AJ. Historically, the BRR has varied between 67 and 100%. The vertical distance between the earned income line segment TJ and the NIT budget segment AJ is the amount of the transfer. This falls with hours worked from the maximum TA at zero hours to zero when TK hours are worked. Income equaling height JK is thus termed the "break-even" income level, since at that income there is no monetary gain associated with participation in the program. Because leisure is desirable, welfare and no work may nevertheless offer a *utility* gain for those otherwise working with earned income exceeding JK.

Since those eligible to participate in a NIT-type welfare program can always choose not to, participation must increase utility. Consequently, the income effect of participation on leisure consumption is positive, decreasing desired labor supply. The BRR reduces the net of transfer wage below that if not participating. Thus, leisure becomes less expensive under such programs, so that the substitution effect also increases L, reducing work effort. Therefore, unlike a general tax on wage income, a NIT has a theoretically clear effect upon labor supply, which is to reduce it. However, so long as the BRR is less than 1, the NIT offers more incentive to work than would a program that simply offers a guaranteed annual income.

The EITC works like a wage subsidy at low levels of earnings, while at higher earnings levels the tax credits are taxed away. Although the EITC is not restricted to single mothers, they receive about two-thirds of the benefits. Meyer and Rosenbaum (2000) present an example for a single mother of two children in 1996. On the first $8,890 of earnings she receives a 40% tax credit on earnings. If she earns exactly $8,890 she would receive a net transfer (negative tax) of $3,556. That transfer is unchanged through earnings of $11,610. Beyond that, the transfer declines with earnings at a rate of 21.06%. The transfer falls to zero at an earned income of $28,495.

Figure 8.17 illustrates the basic features of a budget line under the EITC, abstracting from other features of the personal income tax and transfer systems. Along segment TE the slope is $w(1 + s_1)$, where s_1 is the rate at which wages are subsidized. From E to F the tax credit is constant so that income rises with hours worked at rate w. Along FG the slope is $w(1 - s_2)$, where s_2 is the rate at which benefits are taxed away. Over the first segment, the EITC is like a wage subsidy scheme. Over the last portion it is like a NIT; as income rises, so do state and federal income tax liabilities. In fact, at higher incomes the work disincentives of EITC become as onerous as those under AFDC. Elwood (2000, p. 194) finds "the phasing out of EITC and food stamps and the phasing in of federal taxes can push marginal tax rates for people in the $15,000–$20,000 income range above 70 percent. . . ."

The NIT and the EITC both have income effects serving to reduce labor supply. However, at low incomes the substitution effects are exactly opposite one another: The NIT lowers the wage, discouraging work. The EITC increases the wage, so that the substitution effect favors increased labor. Further, the positive income effect under a NIT is highest at zero hours of work. In contrast, the income effect rises with hours worked under the EITC. The differences in these incentives seem to have substantial effects on the labor force participation of female family heads who face low wages. For example, Elwood reports that traditional welfare case loads in Wisconsin have fallen 87% since 1993. More generally, he finds that as benefits fell under AFDC and the EITC was expanded, work by unmarried women in the bottom quartile of wage earnings "rose sharply—rising from roughly 30 percent in the early 1990s to roughly 50 percent in 1997" (p. 192). His analysis of these increased LFPRs leads him to conclude that "(r)oughly 50 percent could be traced to welfare reforms, 30 percent to the expansions in the EITC and other worker supports, and 20 percent is the result of the strong economy" (p. 192).

Boadway and Wildasin note that income support programs "inherently give rise to incentive problems, because the amount of income transferred to a household must diminish as a household's income rises" (1984, p. 448). This applies to the EITC since, as earnings rise, the substitution effect reverses once the tax credits begin to fall. Thus, over the range of earnings in which credits are falling but remain positive, both the income and substitution effects serve to reduce hours worked compared with the program's absence. Since the unit of taxation is the family for the EITC, a family with one low-wage worker has little incentive to send a second low-wage worker into the market, because the effective marginal tax rate is very high. Elwood reports evidence that the EITC does reduce work by wives in some families.

Decreased reliance on NIT-type welfare programs and increased reliance on the EITC have increased the incentives for low-wage unmarried mothers to commence market employment. In fact, their LFPRs have risen dramatically. A major test of the welfare reforms will arise once the current economic expansion ends. At that time, unemployment among unmarried mothers will rise, and the costs of reduced benefits to the nonworking will become more evident.

8.6 SUMMARY

This chapter has chronicled, and attempted to explain, major shifts in the labor market behavior of men and women. Men work fewer hours per year and retire at earlier ages than in decades past. On the other hand, the LFPRs of women have risen dramatically, and hours worked among the employed have risen. Altogether, there has been a large measure of convergence in labor market participation among men and women. A backward-bending labor supply schedule appears important to understanding both lower number of hours worked and longer retirement among men. However, the labor supply curve may now be positively sloped, in part because prior reductions in hours may have reduced the strength of the income effect. Women are working more in response to higher wages, improvements in home technology, the availability of more and better market substitutes for goods formerly produced within the home (notably child care), and also the erosion of the lifetime marriage "contract." As women have worked more, market output has risen relative to home production. The increased LFPR of women in the twentieth century has contributed to the rise in living standards. In addition to the direct effect of wage earnings that exceed the value of home production foregone, indirect contributions in the form of higher schooling may also be important. Little attention was paid in the chapter to the interrelationships between increased market work by women and family structure. Chapter 9 examines the interplay among women's work, marriage, and fertility in some detail.

ENDNOTES

1. Nor does it require diminishing marginal utility for goods or leisure. The technical condition for convexity may be found in Hands (1991, pp. 84–85).

2. Of course, inheritances may not be entirely unexpected, but their timing is uncertain and, especially among middle-class households, this influences their magnitude. If inheritances were entirely unexpected, the labor supply effects might be larger.

3. When the price of a good or service rises, utility falls and the compensating variation is negative. Another dollar measure, the *equivalent variation*, instead considers the additional income required to move from U^0 to U^1 when $w = w_0$.

4. However, the interpretation of such findings is often difficult. To see why, recall that a fully anticipated wage increase has no *current-period* income effect in a life-cycle model, having already been incorporated into life wealth. In contrast, if these wage gains to the college educated were largely unanticipated, they would entail both income and substitution effects. This would make the hours response ambiguous, just as in the single-period setting. More realistically, suppose educated workers expect that across the population those more educated will experience faster earnings growth. Nevertheless, individual workers realize that their wages may not rise, because of the chance of poor health, layoffs, changing labor demand patterns, etc. If they are sufficiently risk averse, they will tend to "not count their chickens until they

are hatched," suggesting that rational, forward-looking agents may not behave in accordance with our simple perfect-foresight model.

5. The story becomes a bit more complicated if the choice is between retiring at the start of some period t and at "some time in the future." However, the qualitative implications of the factors we consider would not be affected.

6. In 1998 the threshold amount was $9,120 for those age 62 to 64. Until earnings reach that amount, the slope of the budget line is unaffected by the policy.

7. For example, it enables examination of the effect of a price change on *how* basic goods are produced (i.e., the goods-time input mix) and on the relative quantities produced of the various basic goods. Though interesting, these issues are not central to our current purpose.

8. Relaxing the assumption of perfect substitutability in household production, there would be significant specialization by gender. Men may specialize in tasks requiring gross motor skills, such as the plowing of fields, while women perform those tasks employing fine motor skills, such as sewing.

9. This section draws extensively from the insightful discussion of Lee and Casterline (1996).

10. Cultural considerations may also have slowed the entry of married women into the labor market. Goldin notes that when few married women were employed, "her paid labor outside the home was a clear and inescapable signal that her husband had failed to provide for his family" (1990, p. 133). Eventually, as women's education increased, the jobs performed by women became more interesting. As employment among educated wives came to be associated with a meaningful expression of her life, a wife's employment ceased to imply that the husband had failed as a provider. Eventually, the reservation wages of especially highly educated women were no longer affected by those cultural assessments.

11. When specialization is incomplete, some household production tasks also may be assigned on the basis of comparative advantage. For if one partner is great at household repairs and the other at cooking, efficiency is increased by the appropriate specialization of labor. The learning-by-doing associated with this specialization increases these comparative advantages through time; that is, the stocks of human capital related to these realms grow for the "one responsible" and depreciate for the partner specializing in other pursuits. While the benefits from such human capital investments are not necessarily specific to this marriage, such accumulations may be inefficient outside of the marriage.

12. Suppose marriage is risky but that it is not costly to construct a contract specifying the distribution of marital wealth under all contingencies. Then the spouse specializing in nonmarket production could ensure herself or himself "fair" compensation should divorce occur. In practice, the number of relevant contingencies is huge, making the costs of contracting prohibitively large. This is one reason, then, for the existence of "public" marriages, which provide a role for courts should the divorce be difficult to negotiate. Another is that private marriage contracts may not provide adequately for as yet unborn children in the event of divorce.

Investments within marriage also may be sensitive to the legal standard concerning divorce settlements. If a consensual divorce is required, the risk of nonmarket investments is relatively low, since the current marital share is essentially guaranteed (abstracting from the existence of spouses who become abusive until consent is forthcoming). With "no-fault" divorce, the risk is greater. Thus, by increasing the loss from divorce for women specializing in nonmarket production, the movement to no-fault divorce may reduce nonmarket specialization. Since inefficiently low investments reduce the gains from marriage, no-fault divorce may reduce the incentive to marry among women with strong comparative advantage in household production.

13. As discussed below, most mothers now continue to work close to full-time following the arrival of a newborn, in part because they are not free to choose fewer hours at the

full-time wage. With M greater than optimal, and the child's needs of great moment, time given to leisure may often fall. In practice, attempts by researchers to allocate the time parents spend with children into H and L may yield little fruit. Is time spent playing games of imagination with a child parental leisure, or is it an attempt to increase the child's human capital, more properly viewed as H in the current context? Presumably it is both, and examples of such joint production are commonplace.

14. For infants and toddlers, they report that some studies find unfavorable effects regarding an infant's attachment to the mother. However, they report, a large 1996 study by the National Institute of Child Health and Human Development found that the relationship with mother "was not affected by being in day care, the number of hours spent in day care, the age when they entered day care, or how many times the arrangement changed. Instead, the key factor was the mother's sensitivity and responsiveness to her child" (p. 291).

15. There is some controversy regarding the effect of children on the hours worked by fathers. Survey data (cf. Browning, Deaton, and Irish, 1985) suggests men work more upon the arrival of a child. Juster and Stafford (1991, p. 495), however, note that while Swedish men in surveys report higher hours of work with young children present, the *same* men's time diaries show a *reduction* in hours worked when there are children under 3 years of age.

16. For a married woman, V includes some portion of the husband's earnings and household production, and the production function faced by the wife $G(H; X, H_h)$ takes his home production time H_h as given. The more stable is the marriage, the more willing is the wife to base her labor supply decisions on husband's income, and the closer is V to the husband's earnings. Finally, the utility function depicted graphically depends upon the couple's C + G consumption and the wife's leisure; the husband's leisure is taken as given. Later, when we do comparative statics exercises related to the wage and productivity, we will not change the shape of the indifference curve. This will then imply either that the husband's leisure is unaffected, or that the wife's and husband's leisure are neither complements nor substitutes with respect to the utility function. In practice, the couple may make their consumption and time allocation decisions jointly. In that case, our graph depicts the household's utility-maximizing choices for the wife that are associated with the simultaneously agreed upon choices for the husband.

17. The result depends upon the assumption that new technology lowers G_H at the initial H. If, in fact, G_H is higher at the original H worked, the production substitution effect works in the opposite direction, serving to increase H. The combination of rising wages and home productivity would still create an overall production substitution effect—increasing labor force participation and market hours for women—so long as w/G_H rises. That is, a production substitution effect reducing H requires only an increase in the productivity of labor market time *relative* to household production time.

18. It should be noted that all housework is not equal. The pet care, gardening, cooking, and shopping, which were an important component of the time allocation in the 1960s and later, differ dramatically from the backbreaking labor performed by housewives in the nineteenth century and turn of the twentieth century.

19. Becker also stressed this point in a much-appreciated personal communication.

20. We have graphically decomposed the effect of a wage change for labor supply into income and substitution effects. When expressed in terms of the *slope* of the ordinary labor supply curve, this decomposition is termed the *Slutsky equation*

$$dM^*/dw = dM^c/dw + M_0^* \, dM^*/dV$$

The left-hand side of this expression is the slope of the uncompensated labor supply curve and is clearly a slope version of the "full effect" of a w change. The first term on the right-hand side is the slope of the compensated labor supply curve dM^c/dw, making it a slope version of the substitution effect. The last term should then be a slope analog of the income effect, but this is less obvious.

What we have is the initial labor supply M_0^* times the rate at which labor supply changes with income, dM^*/dV. It *seems*, though, as if we should have $(dV/dw)(dM^*/dV)$: the rate at which real income changes with w, times the rate at which (uncompensated) labor supply changes with income. Thus, the latter term dM^*/dV accords with our intuition and, you may recall from intermediate price theory, is the slope of the Engel curve. We now argue that $M_0^* = dV/dw$, assuring us of the sensibility of the equation.

Graphically, the income effect is the reduction in labor supply from the increase in real income (the compensating variation) that the higher w entailed. This compensating variation was shown to equal the change in producer's surplus. Consider again Figure 8.16. For a *small* increase in w from w_0, the increase in PS is just the change in the wage dw times M_0^* (the change in PS per unit of labor supplied times the number of units). Rearranging, the rate at which real income rises when w increases is $PS/dw = dV/dw = M_0^*$, justifying the appearance of M_0^* in the equation.

The Slutsky equation also reveals the indeterminancy of a wage change for labor supply. The slope of the compensated labor supply curve dM^c/dw is positive. M^*_0 is of course also positive. However, dM^*/dV is negative, leaving the overall sign of the ordinary labor supply curve dM^*/dw ambiguous.

21. Training programs are similar to a wage subsidy in that by raising human capital, the wage is increased. There are, however, important differences. Like a wage subsidy program, the wage is higher than in the absence of the program. Unlike a wage subsidy, though, the cost to the government is incurred before work commences and the cost is independent of how many hours are worked. By raising the wage, training programs have an ambiguous effect on the labor supply of those otherwise working. The positive income effect increases leisure, causing labor supply to fall. However, the substitution effect works to reduce the now relatively more expensive leisure, causing labor supply to rise. Among the unemployed, only the substitution effects operate, leading to higher LFPRs among low-wage single heads.

REVIEW QUESTIONS AND PROBLEMS

▶ REVIEW
QUESTIONS

1. When hours worked are positive, equilibrium in the labor-leisure choice model is where MRS = w. Consider instead someone not in the labor force, so that $M = 0$, $L = T$. Graph this situation and interpret the relationship between the MRS and w. How and why is the reservation wage affected by V? By changes in home technology? How have wage increases over time affected LFPRs? How might the reservation wage have been affected by higher divorce probabilities? By reduced fertility?

2. Consider the incentive effects of the classical type of welfare program: If earnings are zero there is some maximum grant, say G. Then, as earnings rise, the grant falls, or is taxed away (typically at some very high rate, but below 100%). What are the incentive effects of such programs for welfare recipients, expressed in terms of income and substitution effects?

3. **A.** Among males, the age at retirement and hours worked per week have fallen during the twentieth century, while real wages have risen. Ceteris paribus (i.e., all else held constant), what does that imply about the relative magnitudes of the

income and substitution effects associated with wage increases? Discuss how the structure of public and private pension plans and the increase in female labor force participation may alter your response to the question phrased above.

B. How might the response of labor supply to w (usually reported as wage elasticities of labor supply) differ when considering only those currently working as opposed to considering those working and not working at the time of the wage change? How does this distinction help explain why ordinary labor supply curves for the aggregate of females have traditionally been more positively sloped than for males?

4. Why do the shapes of the age-leisure and age-goods profiles depend on how close substitutes C and L are within a period?

5. Consider the full-time allocation model, $T = L + M + H$. Assume $V > 0$.
A. Why was it appropriate to interpret V as including the spouse's wage earnings when constructing an individual's initial solution, but less appropriate to interpret a change in V as arising from a change in the spouse's wage rate?
B. What happens to the efficient H when there is an increase in V? Explain.
C. Examine the implications for time allocation, and for the sources of consumption, of an increase in nonlabor income assuming (a) the individual is currently in the labor market, (b) the individual is working in the home sector only.

6. Consider again the full-time allocation model, $T = H + M + L$. Assume $V > 0$.
A. Graph the initial equilibrium for an employed individual. Referring to the graph, explain how much time is spent in each activity.

Now, suppose the tax rate on wage income is reduced, increasing the net wage. (Suppose the cut is financed by a reduction in government consumption.)
B. Show graphically how optimal time allocation changes.
C. Explain the production substitution effect and indicate it on the graph.
D. Explain the consumption substitution effect and show it graphically.
E. Explain the income substitution effect and show graphically.
F. In terms of the graph, what is the total effect on labor supply for this individual?
G. Contrast the production substitution effect of a wage change with that of introducing a child into the family. When the flexible spouse is working, the child must be in paid child care, reducing the "mother's" wage (net of child care). Graph and discuss the effects of introducing a child when paid child care reduces the "net" wage.
H. Graph the compensated labor supply curve and label the excess burden of the tax. Explain intuitively why the excess burden arises and what affects its magnitude.

▶ PROBLEMS

1. Assume utility follows the Cobb-Douglas function $U = L^\theta C^{1-\theta}$ where θ is the proportion of full income F devoted to leisure consumption L. That is, the optimal solutions are of the form $wL = \theta F$ and $PC = (1 - \theta)F$. Let $P = 2$ be the price per unit of the goods input (instead of 1 as in the text). $w = 4$ is the wage per unit of time and there is a total of T = 100 units in the time endowment. θ = .4 and non-labor income V = 0.

A. Determine C and L and depict this situation graphically.

B. Suppose w rises to 5. Again solve for C and L and graph. Graphically decompose the effect on L into income and substitution effects. How would the uncompensated and compensated labor supply schedules look?

C. Return w to its initial value of 4. Now, though, suppose that P rises to 4. What are the effects on C and L? Explain in terms of income and substitution effects.

D. Suppose that w = 4 and P = 2 as in part A, but that now V = 200. Find C and L. Compare your answers with those of part A.

E. With V = 200, again increase w from 4 to 5 and determine C and L. Again decompose the effects of the w change on L into income and substitution effects. Why, intuitively, do the effects differ for L compared with part B?

F. Return w to equal 4. But again increase P to 4. Determine the effects on C and L and compare your answer with that in part C.

2. A. Using separate graphs, illustrate preferences where C and L are close substitutes and where they are poor substitutes. (Preferences must therefore be more flexible than the Cobb-Douglas type.) Now, suppose there is a reduction in the rate of tax on wage income (financed by a reduction in government consumption, say). Graph the responses in C, L space, and then draw the compensated and uncompensated labor supply curves. Explain any differences between the two cases with respect to the income, substitution, and full effects.

B. Using separate graphs, sketch the optimum C and L for two consumers full effects. One consumer has no financial assets; the other has financial assets equal to roughly half of life wealth. Assume they each have the same full income, face the same wage, and have identical Cobb-Douglas preferences. Again suppose there is an increase in the net-of-tax wage rate. Graph the responses in C, L space, and then draw the compensated and uncompensated *leisure demand* curves. Explain any differences between the two cases regarding the relative size of the income, substitution, and full effects.

3. When former president Ronald Regan first campaigned for office, his economic platform was "supply-side" economics, by which was meant a focusing on the incentive effects of policies for factor supplies, i.e., labor and capital. A central tenet was the Laffer curve, which shows that total tax receipts rise with the tax rate at low rates and fall with tax rates once tax rates are "too" high. Supply-siders claimed pre-1981 tax rates were so high that reducing them would increase tax receipts. How would this argument work with respect to the simple labor supply model (ignoring capital income tax receipts)? Is the empirical evidence supportive? Sketch the Laffer curve and justify your sense of where the economy is on that curve.

4. A. Consider the time allocation model where there is no possibility for market work, T = L + H. Graph the consumer's initial optimum. Now suppose Robinson Crusoe finds a plot of land more fertile than that he currently farms. Using a household production function and indifference curves, explain the effect this has on the optimal choice of food (goods) and leisure. Use the language of income and substitution effects.

B. Consider the introduction of household labor-saving devices (such as clothes washers) in a model of household production that does not allow for leisure, $T = H + M$. Explain the effect for the allocation of time between market and home production, in terms of the production substitution effect. Is the sign of the substitution effect unambiguous?

5. Assume men and women each work a total of 60 hours per week between market and home, $T = 60 = M + H$. There is diminishing marginal productivity in household production, but the hourly wage is independent of hours worked.

A. Suppose women and men each face the same wage, but that for any hour worked in the home, women are twice as productive as men. A men's marginal product in home production is $G_H^M = 85 - 2H$. The wage is $25 per hour. How many hours does the man work in the market? What is the allocation of the woman's time? What is her marginal product for the last hour devoted to household production?

B. Mike and Jane are unmarried, maintaining separate households. They are perfect substitutes with equal productivity in home production. Mike's market wage is $30 per hour and he works 25 hours per week in the market when single. As a single, Jane earns $50 per hour and works 35 hours in the market. Suppose Mike and Jane marry and allocate their time to maximize the sum of aggregate market plus market production. Upon marriage there are twice as many chores as when they lived separately, with no economies or diseconomies. For example, if each person's laundry took 4 hours when single, the couple's laundry will require 8 hours. What is the output-maximizing distribution of marital work effort? What are the gains to marriage from this reallocation?

6. A. We showed how to calculate the excess burden or wage income taxation in the labor-leisure model. Graphically and intuitively, explain how the excess burden of wage income taxation is altered once it is acknowledged that some nonmarket time is allocated to household production, and that there is some ability to substitute between household and market production.

B. Discuss the calculation of the excess burden of a wage tax when the consumer works both when young and old.

*7. Assume utility follows the Cobb-Douglas function $U = L^\theta C^{1-\theta}$. The budget constraint is $F = wT + V = PC + wL$ where the price of goods, P, is not restricted to equal 1. Set up the optimization problem (using Lagrangian methods if possible). Solve for C and L in terms of the model's parameters. Compute the comparative statics effects on L and C of changes in w, P, and V. Discuss the intuition for each.

Chapter 9 | HOUSEHOLD FERTILITY AND ECONOMIC GROWTH

The average woman in the United States now bears about two children over her lifetime, or roughly half the number born to American women a century ago. Coupled with the increased labor force participation rates of women and the rise in the divorce rate documented in Chapter 8, this constitutes nothing less than a revolution in the structure and function of families. This chapter focuses on fertility, which necessitates that some attention also be paid to marriage markets and labor supply. Fertility has many dimensions, including birth control, abortion, and the timing of births over the life cycle. Although we touch on those aspects, we focus on completed fertility (the quantity of children), the investments in those children (quality), and the implications for economic growth. The introduction continues with a presentation of key stylized facts concerning fertility. Section 9.1 develops a framework in which the quantity and quality of children may be addressed simultaneously, focusing on the relationship between income and fertility among married couples. Section 9.2 models the effect of changes in women's wages on labor supply and fertility. In section 9.3 we attempt to account for the rise in out-of-wedlock childbearing, modeling marriage and fertility decisions simultaneously. A macroeconomic treatment of historical trends in fertility is presented in section 9.4, and a summary in section 9.5. Policy applications are taken up throughout the chapter.

In 1860, the average 25-year-old married or divorced white woman would eventually bear about 5.5 children.[1] By the Great Depression, the comparable group of women would bear but 2.3 children (Goldin, 1990, Fig. 5.3). The figure for comparable women today may not differ much from this latter figure, despite significant fluctuations since the depression. Other important facts concern fertility trends among all women, and fertility among different educational and income groups.

To appreciate those patterns, consider the *age-specific fertility rate,* which is the average number of children born in a year to women of a particular age. This is employed to construct the *period total fertility rate* (period TFR) for a given year, which is the sum of that year's age-specific fertility rates. Thus, the period TFR of a year predicts the fertility rate of the cohort of all women entering the childbearing years in that year. It predicts cohort fertility accurately only if the prevailing age-specific fertility rates do not change. In recent times, the period TFR peaked during the baby boom at 3.69 children over the interval 1955–1959 (Census Bureau).[2] By 1979 the period TFR had fallen to 1.76 (Vital Statistics). After that it rose gradually until the early 1990s and then leveled off; it was 2.06 in 1998. The birth rate necessary to maintain a constant population, or the replacement rate, is about 2.1. Thus, ignoring immigration, recent birthrates in the United States are roughly sufficient to maintain the current population. However, fertility in the United States remains appreciably above that in most of Western Europe which, significantly, did not experience a baby boom at the end of World War II. Fertility in Canada and Japan is also appreciably below replacement.

On average, more affluent and better educated women within a country have somewhat fewer children. In 1995, women between the ages of 35 and 44 in the United States who had graduated from high school but not attended college on average had given birth to 2.0 children. By way of contrast, women between those same ages who had a graduate or professional degree had given birth to 1.36 children on average (Current Population Reports).[3] Given the positive relationship between education and earnings, and the fact that the educational attainments of husbands and wives are positively correlated, it is unsurprising that fertility is lower at higher levels of household income. For example, consider married households in which the wife is in the labor force. In 1995, wives aged 35 to 44 with household incomes between $10,000 and $19,999 had given birth to 2.31 children on average. In contrast, when household income is at least $75,000, the average number of children was 1.73. When the wife is not employed, the average falls from 2.96 when income is between $10,000 and $19,999 to 2.27 for household incomes of at least $75,000.[4] Interestingly, despite this evidence of a negative relationship between wives' labor force participation and fertility within a country, in recent years there is a positive relationship between rates of female labor force participation and fertility across countries (cf. Rindfuss and Brewster, 1996).

Compared with the middle of the twentieth century, there is now a looser association between fertility and marriage. Marital fertility declined from 146 to 85.7 births per 1,000 married women ages 15 to 44 between 1963 and 1998. Over this same interval, out-of-wedlock births rose from 23 to 44.3 per 1,000 unmarried women of childbearing age. Consequently, the proportion of births to unmarried women in the United States increased from .06 in 1963 to .328 in 1998 (Hotz, Klerman, and Willis, 1997, p. 286, and Vital Statistics). This tendency to separate childbearing and marriage has been greatest among black women, among whom the proportion of extramarital births reached .68 in 1992. The birth rate among unmarried women has fallen modestly in recent years, with a 2% decline among teenagers between 1998 and 1999 alone (Centers for Disease Control).

The historical relationship between population and income growth is one of the central issues in economic development and macroeconomics. Galor and Weil (2000, Fig. 1) report that between 500 and 1500, the annual growth rates of output and population in Europe were essentially zero (roughly 1/10 of 1%). Gradually, the rates of growth in output and population increased.

> The growth rate of total output in Europe was 0.3 percent per year between 1500 and 1700, and 0.6 percent per year between 1700 and 1820. In both periods, two-thirds of the increase in total output was matched by increased population growth, so that the growth of income per capita was only 0.1 percent per year in the earlier period and 0.2 percent in the later one. (p. 4)

Output and population growth continued to accelerate. However, the proportion of GDP growth that manifested as higher per capita income rose, while that due to population growth diminished. "Population growth was 40 percent as large as total output growth over the period 1820–1870, but only 20 percent as large as total output growth over the period 1929–1990" (p. 5). Eventually, although population continued to rise, the total fertility rate began to decline. This *demographic transition* was both sudden and pronounced. For example, reporting findings by Wrigley, Galor and Weil note that in England live births per 1,000 women between the ages of 15 and 44 declined from 153.6 in 1871–1880 to 109 in 1901–1910. In fact, despite continued increases in aggregate and per capita income, much of Western Europe is predicted to experience *negative* population growth over the next several decades. Through time the association between income and population growth will then have gone from positive to negative.

To account for these facts we develop economic models of fertility, based largely on the pioneering work of University of Chicago economist Gary Becker (cf. 1960, 1981), Robert Willis (1973, 1999), and Oded Galor and David Weil (1996, 2000); see also the survey by Hotz et al. (1997). These theories model the demand for children in terms of prices, income, and the rate of return on children's human capital. This price-theoretic orientation is often termed the *Chicago School* approach. Some space is also accorded the Relative Income Theory of Richard Easterlin (cf. 1987). His framework emphasizes the link between the "material aspirations" of young couples and fertility, with women's labor force participation a secondary consideration. We begin with the well-articulated Chicago School approach.

9.1 INCOME AND THE QUANTITY AND QUALITY OF CHILDREN

9.1.1 Preferences

It is assumed that the household is headed by a married couple that agrees on a well-defined utility function. The probability of divorce is zero. (These assumptions are relaxed in section 9.3, where out-of wedlock fertility and divorce are considered.) Parents are economically active for one period only. They receive utility from their own consumption C_p, the number or quantity of their children n, and the quality of each child W_c. This discussion therefore extends that of Chapter 6, where parents received utility from own consumption and the quality of a *given* number of children. As in Chapter 6, we assume the quality of a child may be measured by his or her life wealth, W_c. Since a child's utility increases with life wealth, the parents may be considered to be altruistic toward children. The preferences of parents are expressed as

$$U_p = U_p(C_p, n, W_c) \qquad (9.1)$$

This utility function has the standard properties, including a diminishing marginal rate of substitution (i.e., convex indifference curves) for each pair of "goods." The number of children is not restricted to be an integer, which simplifies the analysis without affecting important results.

In Chapter 6 we carefully distinguished between investments in the human capital of children and financial transfers. Here, to maintain tractability while introducing fertility, we abstract from the portfolio decisions of parents concerning human capital and financial bequests. To this end, we assume that parents invest or bequeath an amount B_p, which leads to child wealth of

$$W_c = B_p(1 + r) \qquad (9.2)$$

where r is the rate of return on investments in child quality, whether they be in the form of human capital or financial transfers.[5] (Section 9.4 models human capital investments in children in some detail.) Under these assumptions, the price per unit of child quality (or wealth) per child is constant and equal to $1/(1 + r)$.

Following Becker (cf. 1981), we make the strong assumption that *child quality is chosen to be constant across children*. While parents may choose to have one fancy and one beat-up car, they are assumed to make equal investments in each of their children. While primarily an analytical convenience, this assumption may deviate but slightly from reality. The most important reasons for unequal investments are when some children in a family are especially gifted or particularly challenged (see Chapter 6). Our assumption may thus be interpreted as equal child ability within families.

A child is more expensive the more is invested in him or her. In this sense the price of a child is endogenous to parents. Similarly, it is more costly to make large investments per child when the family is big. These facts are reinforced by viewing the family's budget constraint

$$\begin{aligned} W_p &= C_p + nB_p \\ &= C_p + nW_c/(1 + r) \end{aligned} \qquad (9.3)$$

where W_p is the resources of the parents, and where we have substituted from (9.2) in moving to the second line.

Now consider the price π_n of having an additional child, that is, of increasing n by 1. Since, by assumption, we are requiring this child to have the same quality any other children in the family may have,

$$\pi_n = W_c/(1 + r) \qquad (9.4)$$

That is, and it is important to note, the price of quantity n is proportional to the quality per child W_c. Similarly, the cost of increasing quality by a unit, π_W, is the price per unit of quality per child $1/(1 + r)$ times the number of children:

$$\pi_W = n/(1 + r) \qquad (9.5)$$

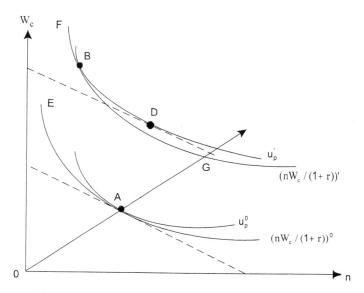

Figure 9.1 Income and the quantity and quality of children

Thus, the price of child quality is proportional to the quantity of children. For if you de-cide to send any of your children to an exclusive private school, you will send them all. These relationships among prices and quantities have several important implications.

Consider Figure 9.1, which shows the choices for n and W_c associated with a given amount of total expenditures on children $nW_c/(1 + r)$. That is, for a given amount of parental resources W_p, we are taking parental consumption C_p as given and focusing on how the remaining resources may be expended on n and W_c. One set of same-cost op-tions is given by curve E, with curve F based on higher total expenditures. Whereas tra-ditional budget lines are linear, these are convex. (In fact, they are rectangular hyperbo-las, since nW_c is a constant, given r.)

In absolute value, the slope of a budget line is the ratio of the price of the good mea-sured on the horizontal axis (here n) to the price of that on the vertical (here W_c). Thus, the budget line has slope (in absolute value) equal to the relative price of n: $\pi_n/\pi_W = W_c/n$. This makes the relative price of quantity high when W_c is large and n low, as at B, and lower when quality is relatively lower, as at D.

Becker (cf. 1981, p. 104) notes that this interaction between prices and quantities im-plies that n and W_c are not close substitutes: If they were, indifference curves would be more shallow than in Figure 9.1 and equilibrium would be at a corner (with either n or W_c equal to zero). In fact, in such a case, the point of tangency between indifference and budget lines would *minimize* utility. Only if n and W_c are less substitutable, or more com-plementary, as with indifference curve U_p^0, will equilibria with positive quantity and qual-ity be observed. Price effects are large usually when goods are close substitutes; in the case of n and W_c we shall see that price effects can be large, even though n and W_c can't be too close substitutes.

9.1.2   Income, Fertility, and Child Quality

As countries have developed and living standards have risen, fertility rates have declined. This need not mean that children are inferior goods. For there is a general consensus that total expenditures on children, including quantity and quality, have risen with income. Bryant (1990), for example, reports an income elasticity for total outlays on children of .43. However, this need not imply that the *separate* income elasticities for quantity and quality are equal, or even that both are positive. In fact, the evidence suggests that expenditures on child quality rise much more rapidly than those on quantity (cf. Bryant).

A difficulty of interpretation regarding income effects is that once either n or W_c changes, so does its price. For suppose the initial, or impact, effect of an increase in income is to raise quality proportionately more than quantity. Since the relative price of quantity is W_c/n, quantity will become relatively more expensive. Thus, a pure income increase *induces* a substitution effect. Once this indirect price effect of higher income is taken into account, it is not surprising that quantity has only a weak positive relationship with income, while quality rises more dramatically.

Historically, fathers devoted little time to direct child care. The original Chicago School models made the simplifying (if increasingly unrealistic) assumption that fathers devote *no* time to child care or housework. This implies that a change in husband's earnings has a pure income effect as its *initial* impact. As discussed below, an increase in the mother's wage has a direct, and strong, substitution effect, in addition to the income effect. In addition to being produced by changes in a father's earnings, an income effect could be produced by a change in nonlabor income, such as interest income or an unanticipated inheritance.

Consider a rise in family income due, say, to a rise in the husband's earnings. The direct income and induced substitution effects are illustrated in Figure 9.1. At the initial level of expenditures on children, $(nW_c/(1 + r))^0$, utility is maximized at point A. When total expenditures are increased to $(nW_c/(1 + r))^1$, the consumer chooses point B. A pure income effect, as when budget lines are linear and the budget is increased, is shown as the movement from A to D. This movement entails increases in both n and W_c, making n normal in this conventional sense. Since the income elasticity for quality exceeds that for quantity, an increase in income will increase W_c by more than n. However, this increases the relative price of n! This induced substitution effect is shown as the movement between D and B. While the income effect alone increases n, the induced substitution effect reduces n. As drawn, these conflicting effects roughly offset one another, so that n is similar at both expenditure levels. Moffitt (1984) finds a positive but statistically insignificant effect of income on fertility. Schultz (1994, p. 656) finds that the fertility of younger women is increased by higher husband wages. However, the effect on lifetime or total fertility is quite small.

Note that this relationship between income and the quality and quantity of children has not always obtained. For example, for many centuries formal education was unimportant among the middle and lower classes. Consequently, increases in income—and therefore in total expenditures on children—were primarily associated with rising fertility. The return to education has quite possibly risen through time, inducing optimizing parents to shift child expenditures away from quantity into the quality of children. The historical relationships among income, fertility, education, and technical change are the subject of section 9.4.

9.1.3   Policy Applications

Tax Policy

Several policies of state and federal government entail costs or benefits that are related to the quantity of children in a household. The personal exemption allowed in the personal income tax directly reduces the cost per child. In the United States in 1999 the personal exemption per child was $2,750 (it is indexed to rise with inflation). For a family in the 28-percent tax bracket, a child reduces taxes by almost $770 per year, or by over $15,000 (undiscounted) for 20 years.

More generally, allowing the lifetime tax benefit per child to be b, total expenditures on children become

$$n[W_c/(1 + r) - b]$$

The cost or price of an additional child of given quality is now the amount spent on quality per child, minus the tax benefit. So π_n becomes

$$\pi_n = W_c/(1 + r) - b \tag{9.4'}$$

This price rises with quality, as before. The price of raising child quality by 1 remains $\pi_W = n/(1 + r)$. Consequently, these benefits reduce the relative, as well as absolute, price of quantity. This entails a substitution effect encouraging more children. The income effects of the policy may have little effect on quantity but increase quality.

Milligan (2000) estimates the fertility response to a large pronatalist policy in Quebec, the Allowance for Newborn Children, which began in 1988 and ended in 1997. "When the program was in full force in 1992, the birth of a first or second child brought a $500 immediate payment. Second children also entitled the family to a second $500 payment on the child's first birthday, and a third or higher parity child brought twenty quarterly payments of $400, totaling $8,000" (p. 6). He finds that those eligible for the maximum benefit increased their fertility by a huge 25 percent (p. 4).

Using data from the United States, Whittington, Alm, and Peters (1990) also find a sizeable response of fertility to tax incentives. They estimate an elasticity of the fertility rate with respect to the personal exemption of about .2. The tax credit for children, introduced during the Clinton administration and equal to $500 per child in 1999, similarly relaxes the family's budget constraint. This increases the tax benefits per child by 500/770, or almost two-thirds, compared with the personal exemption alone. Suppose the total fertility rate was 2 children per female before the introduction of the tax credit. Using the elasticity estimate of .2, this 65% increase would raise fertility by (.2)(.65) = .3 children, to 2.3 children per female, on average. (The 2001 Tax Relief Act raises the credit to $600 through 2004, then incrementally to $1000 by 2010.)

Other policies target fertility less directly.[6] For example, public primary and secondary education in the United States has no tuition, relying primarily upon the property tax for financing. Since this tax is independent of the presence of children in a household, public education is essentially free to parents (though property values and taxes are higher in "good" school districts). Free public education lowers the price of quantity, encouraging fertility. As another example, the personal income tax code is progressive, in that the marginal tax rate rises with income. Consequently, higher earning children end up paying taxes at a higher rate, which increases the price to parents of child quality.

Intergenerational Redistribution and Ricardian Equivalence

As stressed in chapters 4 and 5, many government policies redistribute resources between generations. For example, unfunded or pay-as-you-go Social Security programs benefit members of the start-up generation but impose losses on participants in the fully mature system. Similarly, government deficit policies may take the form of cutting taxes on those currently alive, with future generations having to repay or at least service the debt. In Chapter 5 we saw that when parents are altruistic toward their children, they may undo the forced governmental redistributions through voluntary transfers in the opposing direction. This Ricardian equivalence proposition, recall, took the number of children as given (in addition to abstracting from uncertainty and capital market imperfections). Wildasin (1990), using a framework similar to the one developed above, shows that Ricardian equivalence fails when fertility is endogenous (even in the presence of perfect foresight and perfect capital markets).

To see this, suppose all parents of a generation are identical and that the government gives the parents a tax cut of T_p, financed by issuing government debt, paying interest at rate r. On average, the children of each family must collectively repay an amount of debt plus interest equal to $T_p(1 + r)$. The tax that must be paid by each member of the child's generation (not taking any response of fertility into account) is

$$T_c = -T_p(1 + r)/n$$

If parents left fertility intact, this policy would not entail an income effect. For parents could increase the bequest to each child by T_c and obtain the same own consumption, child quantity, and child quality as before the redistribution. However, parents would *not* choose the same quantity as before. The reason is that the taxes on children raise the price of quantity to $\pi_n = W_c/(1 + r) + T_c$. With the price of quality unchanged, there is a substitution effect away from quantity toward quality. For this reason, intergenerational redistribution away from children, as with unfunded Social Security, reduces fertility. More generally, endogenous fertility is but one more reason that Ricardian equivalence is not expected to obtain. Interestingly, children end up better off, that is, child quality rises, since the increase in the bequest per child exceeds that in taxes.[7] Wildasin notes that empirically the presence and size of Social Security programs seem to adversely affect fertility. He cautions, though, that these empirical studies have typically not controlled for how the program is financed. Since the theory predicts that the financing scheme should be quite important, it is best to regard the empirical link between fertility and debt policy as yet to be firmly established.[8]

9.1.4   Other Factors Affecting the Prices of Quantity and Quality

Changes in Birth Control, Including Abortion

The link between desired and actual fertility, in terms of timing and completed fertility, is imperfect: Some desired conceptions never occur, while other pregnancies are unwanted. A large number of unwanted pregnancies end in abortion. In 1997 there were 1,184,758 legal abortions performed in the United States, making the ratio of legal abortions to live births about 0.3. This constitutes an appreciable decline since 1990, when 1,429,577 abortions were reported, the most ever (Centers for Disease Control). Nevertheless, legal abortions remain appreciably above the number in 1973, when the Supreme Court legalized abortion (*Roe* v. *Wade*).

The decriminalization of abortion reduced the psychic, physical, and monetary costs of terminating unwanted pregnancies. Similarly, the introduction in the early 1960s of the birth control pill (the Pill) and of the intrauterine device (IUD) reduced the cost of averting pregnancies. These technological changes made it easier to keep completed fertility from exceeding desired levels, and thereby contributed to the decline in fertility. And, as stressed above, an initial decline in fertility reduces the relative cost of child quality, inducing parents to increase quality at the expense of yet lower quantity.[9]

Akerlof, Yellen, and Katz (1996) argue that the majority of the increase in out-of-wedlock childbearing is due to the decline in "shotgun marriages," in which premarital conception entails social pressures resulting in marriage before the child's birth. They argue that the norm of shotgun marriages has weakened because of the decriminalization of abortion and the advent of contraception that, while effective, only modestly reduces the pleasure from sex. They describe two mechanisms by which this increases out-of-wedlock childbearing. First, those women willing to rely on abortion or conscientious use of effective contraception now have less incentive to precondition sexual relations with a promise of marriage in the event of pregnancy. This increases pressure on all women to have premarital sex without that promise. Second, they argue that "(t)he sexual revolution, by making the birth of a child the *physical* choice of the mother, makes marriage and child support a *social* choice of the father" (p. 281). In section 9.3 we emphasize other changes in marriage markets and gender inequality that have contributed to the rise in out-of-wedlock childbearing.

The Role of Declining Infant and Child Mortality

Until recent times many children died before the end of the first year of life (infant mortality) due to miscarriage during pregnancy, death in childbirth, or complications during the first year. More children were lost to now easily treatable illnesses, such as pneumonia. Galor and Weil (1999) cite evidence that much of the decline in mortality is attributable to improved nutrition, made possible by rising per capita income. Reduced infant and child mortality affects the demand for quantity and quality in several ways. First, there are costs associated with the carrying and delivery of a child that are essentially unrelated to child quality. These costs per surviving child are reduced when fewer total births are required to achieve a "target stock" of living children. This effect serves to reduce the price of quantity. Second, the expected return on investments in child quality rises when the probability of a child surviving rises. This reduces the relative cost of child quality, inducing substitution away from quantity toward quality.

Galor and Weil suggest another route by which lower mortality reduces fertility. They argue that parents are risk averse with respect to the number of surviving children. That is, to ensure they have an adequate number of surviving children, they engage in a certain amount of "precautionary childbearing." (Precautionary motives are discussed in Chapter 2. The technical requirement is that the marginal utility of a surviving child be convex in the number of survivors.) Then as mortality improved, uncertainty regarding the relationship between births and surviving children declined. As a result, there was a decline in precautionary childbearing.

Due to interactions between the prices of quantity and quality, shocks to either induce further substitution effects. We now consider arguments that the rise in women's wages has resulted in a substitution of quality for quantity.

9.2 THE VALUE OF WOMEN'S TIME, WORK, AND FERTILITY

In Chapter 8 we argued that the rise in women's wages through time has increased the labor force participation rate of women, especially for young mothers. In this section we argue that this same increase in wages and participation in market work helps explain the significant decline in fertility that occurred in the twentieth century. We also argue, though, that this effect has declined in importance in recent years.

Historically, women have assumed primary responsibility for the rearing of children. And, according to the Chicago School, raising children is a very time-intensive undertaking. That is, the ratio of mother's time to market goods is greater in the production of "child services" than in the production of other goods, such as housing services. Whether children are especially intensive of mother's time over the entire period of dependency is not entirely clear, but there is little doubt that children are especially time intensive during the early years of life. For example, Hotz and Miller (1988) estimate that after the child's initial year of dependency, the time devoted by parents to child care declines geometrically at about 12 percent per year. On the other hand, they could not reject the hypothesis that the *goods* input has a constant time profile. All else constant, as the market wage obtainable by mothers has risen over time, the relative time intensiveness of young children implies increasing tension for the mother between caring for young children and working in the labor market.

For much of the twentieth century, female wages and rate of labor force participation rose, and the fertility rate declined. In fact, mothering an infant and participating in the labor force were almost mutually exclusive in 1900, when less than 5 percent of all married women were employed. By 1994, the proportion of married women with children *under age 1* who were employed was 58.8% and almost identical to the labor force participation rate of *all* wives, 60.6 percent. Also between 1900 and 1994, the total fertility rate fell from about 4 to 2. Although motherhood now has little effect on the labor force participation of wives, market work continues to lower lifetime fertility. Thus, for women aged 35 to 44 in 1995, the average number of children was 1.78 among those in the labor force, but was 2.34 among those not employed (Current Population Reports, June 1995, Update, Census Bureau).

To develop the link between wages, work, and fertility in more depth requires that women's fertility and labor supply decisions be modeled simultaneously. This was achieved in an influential paper by Willis (1973). We now sketch and evaluate a version of his model.

9.2.1 Preferences

In section (9.1) parents maximized the utility function,

$$U_p = U_p(C_p, n, W_c)$$

in which own consumption, the quantity of children, and child quality all entered as separate arguments. Willis considers a special case of these preferences in which the quantity and quality of children enter multiplicatively and are termed *child services*. Since we measure quality by life wealth, child services are simply the aggregate wealth of children, $S \equiv nW_c$. Since the well-being of children increases with their wealth, we may again view parents as altruistic (so that child services might be relabeled child well-being). Then utility may be written as

$$U_p = U_p(C_p, S) \tag{9.6}$$

where C_p remains parental consumption. This utility function has the normal properties; it is increasing in both arguments and has convex indifference curves. Collapsing quantity and quality into a single variable enables Willis to introduce labor supply decisions in a tractable fashion. However, the modeling trade-off is that it becomes more difficult to decompose any changes in S into quantity and quality.

9.2.2 The Production of Child Services

Willis assumes that consumption goods and child services are both produced via household production functions as in Chapter 8. However, we may retain his intuition and save on notation by assuming that all consumption goods aside from child services may be purchased directly in the market. The quantity of such goods is simply C_p as in equation (9.6). In contrast, the production of child services requires both mother's time t_S and market goods G_S,

$$S \equiv S(t_S, G_S) \tag{9.7}$$

This production function is assumed to have constant returns to scale in both inputs. The marginal products $dS/dt_S \equiv S_t$ and $dS/dG_S \equiv S_G$ are positive, with diminishing marginal productivity for each. Further, the inputs are complementary in the sense that the marginal product of time is greater when it is combined with more market goods. Similarly, the marginal product of market goods rises when more of the time input is utilized.

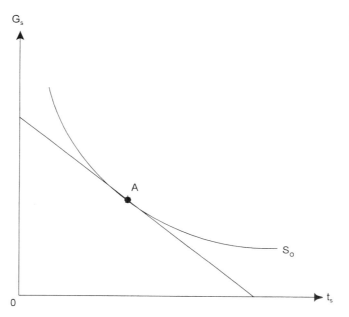

Figure 9.2 Isoquant for child services

An isoquant for S is depicted in Figure 9.2, showing all combinations of time and goods that produce the level of child services S_0. The marginal rate of technical substitution MRTS is the rate at which the goods input may be substituted for mother's time, leaving S unchanged. Consequently, the MRTS equals the ratio of the marginal products; MRTS = S_t/S_G. Graphically, the MRTS is the (absolute) slope of an isoquant at a point. Our neoclassical production function for S implies diminishing MRTS, making the isoquants convex to the origin.

To minimize the cost of producing a given level of S, input proportions are adjusted so that the ratio of the marginal products, or MRTS, equals the ratio of the input prices. With the price of market goods equal to 1 and assuming, for now, that the cost of the time input is the mother's wage w_m, the input price ratio is w_m. The MRTS = w_m at point A in Figure 9.2. With constant returns to scale, the marginal cost of S is constant so long as the input prices are unchanged.

Turning attention to resources, the father is assumed to work full-time with earnings of E_f. We abstract from any nonlabor income. Assuming there is one unit of time available, mother's market work equals $1 - t_S$, so that her earnings are $w_m(1 - t_S)$. Family income is exhausted between own consumption and goods inputs for child services. Consequently, the budget constraint facing the couple may be written

$$E_f + w_m(1 - t_S) = C_P + G_S \qquad (9.8)$$

Parents maximize utility by choosing C_p and S (and ultimately the amounts of time and goods for S) in order to maximize the utility function (9.6) subject to the budget constraint (9.8) and the production function for child services, equation (9.7). The parents' problem is depicted graphically in Figure 9.3.

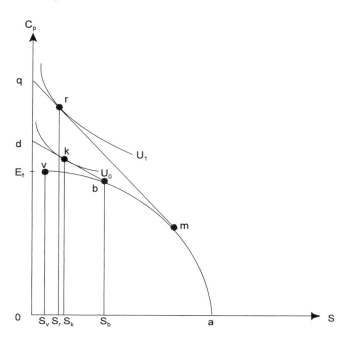

Figure 9.3 Mother's wage and child services

If there is no possibility for mother to perform market work, the family's budget constraint is given by production possibilities frontier va. At each point along va all of mother's time is devoted to S production. At point v, no market goods are used in the production of S: Consequently, C_p equals the husband's earnings and, due to diminishing returns for mother's time, S is low. Increases in S beyond S_v are obtained by increasing the goods input. With diminishing returns, the amount of market goods required to produce each additional unit of S rises. Equivalently, the cost of S in terms of C_p foregone is increasing, explaining why the slope of va becomes steeper. (The slope of va at a point is simply $1/S_G$, in absolute value.)

Even if the mother's time is not traded in the labor market, we may still price it in accordance with its value in production. This "shadow price" equals the additional goods required to keep S constant should her time input be reduced a small amount. However, this is just the MRTS when all time is devoted to S production. As S is *increased*, it must be produced in a more-goods-intensive fashion. With diminishing returns, this raises (lowers) the marginal product of time (goods), causing the MRTS to increase.

We now incorporate the ability of mother to earn wage rate w_m in the labor market. Efficiency requires mother to allocate each hour of time where it is most valuable. At high levels of S production, the shadow wage is high, exceeding w_m, and the mother is a housewife, engaging in no market work. However, at some lower S, the shadow wage falls equal to the market wage, and the mother will work part-time if S is any lower. The shadow price equals wage w_m^0 at point b in Figure 9.3.

When mother is employed, the marginal value of her time is w_m and the marginal cost of S expressed in terms of C_p foregone is constant: S is produced using the input proportions generating a MRTS = w_m. And, with constant returns to scale, each additional unit of S requires the same withdrawal of mother's time from the market and the same amount of market goods; C_p falls by the reduction in earnings plus the market goods per unit of S. This cost—the marginal rate of transformation, MRT—is the slope (in absolute value) of the linear portion of the budget constraint, db. At point d, the mother works full-time in the market and no S is produced. Market work declines as S is increased. When S production has risen to S_b, the shadow wage has increased to equal the market wage and market work ceases. Altogether the budget constraint is given by dba when the wage is w_m^0. Utility maximization occurs at point k, indicating the mother works part-time in the labor market.[10]

Suppose now the wage rises to w_m^1. S will be produced in a more-goods-intensive fashion when mother is working; input proportions are adjusted to where MRTS = w_m^1. Nevertheless, the cost of child services to the working mother is increased, producing the new, steeper budget line qma. As drawn, the couple maximizes utility at point r, with S having fallen and C_p having increased. However, this need not be the case. Specifically, since the budget line shifts out in addition to becoming steeper, the wage increase entails both income and substitution effects. Since utility (real income) has risen, the income effect serves to increase S and C_p assuming, as we do, that both are normal. The substitution effect arises because the wage increase raises the price of time-intensive child services; this increases the relative price of S (since the price of market goods is unchanged). This induces substitution away from S, toward C_p. Thus, C_p is expected to rise, while these effects in combination make the response of child services ambiguous.

9.2.3   Decomposing the Reduction in S into n and W_c

Historically, women's earnings were not a large share of family income. For this reason, an increase in women's wages may have increased family resources by a smaller percentage than it increased the price of S. With a relatively small income effect, the Chicago School argues that the substitution effect dominates, so that child services fall. Supposing S falls, it remains to determine the individual effects on quantity and quality. As a mechanical first approach, simply assume that the quality per child is held constant. With quality fixed, a reduction in S means reduced quantity. We now consider less contrived routes by which the rise in women's wages during the twentieth century lowered fertility (and increased child quality).

A first explanation is that the same rise in education that contributed to rising wages for women in the twentieth century also raised the return to quality of children relative to quantity. Consistent with this, measures of child quality such as health and educational attainment are positively related to the mother's education (cf. Lam and Duryea, 1999). Apparently, more highly educated mothers provide better nutrition and hygiene and are better at introducing reading skills and scientific and cultural understanding. In other words, the productivity of mother's time in these quality-related endeavors increases with her education. In contrast, education may not increase the productivity of many activities primarily related to the quantity of children—such as washing dishes and clothes; picking up; conception, delivery and recovery from childbirth; and breast-feeding. Because of this asymmetry, increasing mother's education raises the productivity of time in producing quality relative to quantity. Therefore, as mother's education (and therefore market wage) rises, there may be substitution away from quantity toward quality. This is one explanation for why higher mother's education and wages reduce fertility.

Lam and Duryea study these interactions among mothers in Brazil, where amount of education remains low but has increased rapidly in recent years. They find that as number of years of education of mothers rises from zero to eight, the mothers' fertility falls substantially while child outcomes (quality) improve. Interestingly, these quantity-quality adjustments are observed even when education levels of mothers do not induce increased labor force participation. In their interpretation, when amount of education is low, increases in the amount raise the shadow price of mother's time in producing child quality at least as rapidly as they increase the wage. For this reason labor force participation remains low, even though the wage premium on early schooling is quite high. Thus, their explanation is a bit different from that of Willis: For them, the decline in fertility rate is driven by increases in education which raise the value of women's time at least as much in home production as in the market (for early years of education). Further, the value of time increases asymmetrically across home production activities, with relatively large increases observed for time devoted to raising the quality of children.

A second reason increased wages for mother lower quantity follows from the claims of Becker and Barro (1988) and Mulligan (1997) that altruism toward children is endogenous. Becker and Barro assume that parental altruism *per child* falls as family size increases. Intuitively, more children typically result in fewer interactions between the parent and each child. And, such relationships may be an important building block of endogenous altruism. Along these lines, Mulligan views altruism per child as increasing with the "child-oriented resources" devoted by parents to children. He writes that "(t)ime spent with children is the most important example of child-oriented resources" (p. 3). Not all time is equal in this regard; for example, the additional cleaning and cooking a child entails contributes less than time spent on family outings. He concludes that altruism per child is lower in families where wages are higher because parents conserve on the very time intensive child-oriented resources.

Mulligan's analysis for the most part ignores the relationship between labor market participation and investments in child-oriented resources. This relationship may, however, be important. To see this, consider two families with the same preferences, income, and level of child services. In family A, the father's earnings are high and the mother is a housewife. In family B, the mother and father each work full-time to achieve the income of family A. Since the mother in family B is away from her children all day, she has invested fewer child-oriented resources. Consequently, by this theory, she cares less about each child than does the mother in family A, receiving less satisfaction from the same level of child services. If the mix of parental consumption, child-oriented resources, and child services is optimal in family A, it will not be in family B. Without setting up the optimization problem, it is clear that in family B there is too little altruism per child and too much child services.[11]

The question is how will family B adjust so as to improve its allocations? Reducing the quality of children would certainly reduce child services S but may reduce further the altruism per child (since child quality is itself relatively time intensive for parents.) Conversely, reducing the number of children reduces S while allowing an increase in child-oriented resources and altruism per child. This informal reasoning suggests that families in which the mother works will have fewer children than families with the same income in which the mother stays at home. This prediction is borne out in the data, as noted in the introduction. For example, in 1995 among families where total family income falls between $35,000 and $49,999, wives aged 35 to 44 have had 2.41 children when the mother doesn't work, but only 2.01 when she does (Current Population Survey, June 1995).

However, the same insight is perhaps more usefully applied to explain why fertility has fallen over time as the labor force participation rate of mothers has risen. As mothers have been drawn into the labor market by higher wages, they desire fewer child services under our maintained assumption, following Willis, that the substitution effect dominates. For a given number of children, working mothers have less time and a weaker bond with each. To maintain loving relationships, reductions in S are more likely to take the form of reductions in the quantity of children. For recent cohorts of women, market participation, including hours worked, approaches that of men working full-time and may not rise much further. For this reason, further increases in women's wages may not entail further reductions in fertility.

The Chicago School, Fertility, and Growth

Economic growth increases the wages of men and women. The effect of an increase in income (or men's earnings) on fertility is positive, but moderate, since the larger impact on quality increases the price of quantity. In contrast, the Chicago theory suggests that rising women's wages reduce quantity. Thus, as the wages of both men and women have grown, the overall effect would be consistent with lower fertility. Reduced fertility is not here the result of an absence of parental altruism toward children, for the quantity and quality of children enter explicitly into the utility function. Rather, fertility falls because young children are very time consuming, and they become more expensive as the opportunity cost of time (market wages) increases.

In Chapter 5 we discussed the effects of higher expected earnings for children in adulthood on parental investments in child quality. The response of fertility to increased opportunities for children is also of interest, and important to economic growth. This issue is considered in section 9.4 (see *Parent's Problem*).

The Weakening Substitution and Strengthening Income Effect

We have assumed that rising women's wages reduce S because the substitution effect dominates the income effect. However, in recent years the income effect of a wage increase for mothers may have increased and the substitution effect may have weakened. Consider first the income effect. Mothers work more hours on average and contribute a larger share of household income than in prior times (see Chapter 8). Intuitively, the more hours one works, the greater is the benefit from a wage hike and, since women's share of family earnings has risen, the larger is the percentage increase in family income. As a result, increases in the wages of women now entail a larger income effect. We now consider why the substitution effect may have weakened.

In the Chicago School, the asymmetry between the effects of men's and women's earnings on fertility was based on the assumption that mothers rather than fathers were responsible for child care. An additional implicit assumption was that the presence of preschool age children in the home was incompatible with mother's market work. As mother's potential wages rose, it would pay her to have fewer children, closer in age, so as to reduce her time away from market work. However, as women's wages continued to rise, the tension between mother's care of children and market work grew. One way to relax those tensions was to replace mother's care of preschoolers with paid daycare. However, there was substantial resistance to this "solution," based on fears that children would suffer from the reduced contact with mothers. Lee and Casterline (1996) note that these concerns "have changed substantially in the last 25 years. For example, from 1970 to 1991 the proportion of married women of childbearing age who thought that a child suffers if the mother works fell from 73 percent to 34 percent. . . ." Less clear is whether this change in perceptions was a response to the rather benign research findings concerning the relationship between mother's employment and child outcomes (see Chapter 8), or a rationalization of sorts. In any event, the reliance on child daycare grew to the point that about 60 percent of mothers with children *under the age of 1* are now employed.

Greater willingness to employ child care increases the elasticity of substitution between market goods and mother's time in the production of child services. This reduces the link between the cost of children and mother's wages. First, as a consequence of increased reliance on paid child care, the time intensiveness of children has fallen. And, the less time intensive are children, the smaller is the substitution effect. Also, although higher income families hire higher quality daycare, the relationship between mother's wages and daycare outlays is presumably concave (rather than linear).

Changing Cost of Children over Time

The monetary costs of children have of course risen over time. Craig (1993) estimates the net cost of children in 1860—total costs minus the value of output produced by children. In the Midwest, he finds "children between 7 and 12 contributed about $28 and teenage girls about $40 . . . the equivalent of 1.5 to 2 months' wages of a hired man" (p. 79). Overall, Craig finds that "the net present value of a child at birth in antebellum northern agriculture was probably between negative $100 and negative $200" (p. 91). Thus, net money outlays on children, using the figures above, constitute 5 to 10 months' wages of a hired man. Using data from the 1970s, Lazear and Michael (1988) find that a two-adult household with two children and annual average income of $50,000 spends $57,600 in present value per child. When income is $15,000, outlays are $23,000. This suggests outlays per child in recent times are between 13 and 19 months' of *family* income. Supposing women contributed about one-third of family earnings in the early 1970s, this translates to about 18 to 30 months of a mans' earnings. However, costs per child fall as family size increases, and these figures are based on a family with two children, whereas antebellum families averaged around five children (cf. Craig). Even adjusting for family size, it appears as though the monetary cost of children in terms of the husband's wage has risen over time. And, given that output per worker rose about sevenfold over this period, real expenditures per child may easily be ten times those of 150 years ago.

It is likely that both the absolute and relative time intensiveness of children rose during much of the nineteenth century into the twentieth century, before declining in recent decades. When most families lived on farms and years of education were few, older daughters contributed a great deal to housework, including the care of younger children. In this respect, older daughters were "time saving." However, Goldin (1986) reports that between 1900 and 1930, as years of schooling rose, the share of young women not in the labor force who were "at home" fell from two-thirds to less than 10%. She writes that the "increase in formal education exactly offset the time devoted to home production by young single women" (p. 564). Thus, as education years rose, the time intensiveness of young children was no longer offset by the contributions of older daughters, increasing the time intensiveness of children for mothers.

These declining contributions by daughters, especially, may help explain falling fertility even among housewives. For when older children were around the house and available to help as needed, household production excluding child care did not need to fall much upon the arrival of a newborn.[12] As older children enrolled in school for additional years, the cost of a baby—in terms of foregone cooking, cleaning, mending, gardening, and care of other young children—rose. And this increased cost could be avoided by bearing fewer children.

The greater time intensiveness of children increased the substitution effect among working mothers. In recent years, as working mothers have increasingly relied on paid child care, the relative time intensiveness has fallen, and the substitution effect along with it. This suggests the negative effect of women's wages on fertility may have risen for much of the twentieth century, but fallen (perhaps to roughly zero) in recent decades.

9.2.4 Empirical Evidence about the Effect of Men's and Women's Wages on Fertility

There have been numerous attempts to estimate empirically the effect of men's income and women's wages on fertility. Due to data availability, most studies have focused on the second half of the twentieth century. Early examinations were quite supportive of the underlying theory, as revealed by this statement of Cigno (1991): "The evidence on the relationship between birth and wage rates is unequivocal. Econometric estimates for the USA put the elasticity of fertility to the average female wage rate at -1.73, and the elasticity of the same to the average male wage rate at $+1.31$" (p. 112). These particular estimates are those obtained by Ward and Butz (1980) in a well-known study of aggregate fertility between 1948 and 1974. They argued that these results could also explain the volatile pattern of fertility over that period. "Our empirical results indicate that the 'baby boom' of the 1950's can be explained as a response to rising male income, whereas the baby bust of the 1960's was due primarily to increases in female wages and income" (p. 318). Empirical work based on micro data was also supportive of the theory (cf. Heckman and Walker, 1990).

However, the empirical support for the inverse relationship between mother's wages and fertility has weakened in recent years. First, although the Ward and Butz results explained fertility trends over their sample period, the explanation has since performed poorly. Commenting on her own earlier research, Macunovich (1996) notes that when the Ward and Butz estimates are used to predict fertility for just the first few years beyond their sample (from 1976 to 1983), actual fertility is underpredicted by 24% for women aged 25 to 34 and by over 30 percent for women aged 20 to 24! Macunovich also finds that when micro data are used instead of the aggregative data employed by Ward and

Butz, the results even for *their* sample period are substantially weakened. Further, Lee and Casterline (1996) note that "over the past two decades women's wage rates have been rising relative to men's . . . and women's labor force participation has been growing rapidly, yet fertility rates have remained nearly unchanged and have recently even risen somewhat" (p. 5). Given the convergence of men's and women's labor market participation rates and hours, it is perhaps unsurprising that the wage effects are now weak and ambiguous.

Also troublesome for the Chicago theory is that across OECD countries there is now a positive correlation between fertility and the labor force participation rates of women (cf. Rindfuss and Brewster, 1996). This is somewhat surprising given that in the United States, for example, there remains a modest negative relationship between participation and fertility. One potential reconciliation is if countries with the highest female LFPRs are also leaders in employer accommodation of women's child-rearing responsibilities. This is plausible since the need to accommodate may be greater when employers have to attract a high proportion of females as employees. Such accommodation would ease the balancing of children and work, increasing both.

Given the declining substitution effect and rising income effect, the price of women's time and fertility may no longer be negatively linked. Consequently, though mother's wages are expected to rise through time, it is unlikely that fertility rates will be driven to an extremely low level. As Lee and Casterline write,

> It is plausible that we have entered an era in which observed temporal and cross-sectional variation in fertility behavior will have little to do with observed variation in female labor force participation. Prevailing levels of women's market work probably preclude a return to the total fertility rates of the baby boom era. In this sense, women's work may contribute greatly to the explanation of fertility in the West in the last decades of the twentieth century. Nevertheless, variation in women's work may offer comparatively little insight into short-term . . . variation. (p. 5)

Nevertheless, the rise in women's wages and labor force participation may well have played a substantial part in the demographic transition. A model of this longer term process by Galor and Weil (1996) is discussed in section 9.4 (see 9.4.6 "The Role of Gender Differences"). Their model is in the tradition of the Chicago school, as it also stresses the roles of prices, income, and technology. We now turn to an alternative formulation of the relationships among male earnings, female labor force participation, and fertility, due to Easterlin.

9.2.5 The Easterlin Hypothesis: Is a Synthesis Possible?

Richard Easterlin (cf. 1987) developed a less formal framework for the analysis of fertility in which income and female labor force participation again play a large role. However, in his framework it is not an increase in absolute income that raises fertility but rather in income relative to the income of one's parents. Easterlin's *relative income theory* views "movements in both fertility and young women's labor force participation as effects of a common cause, the income status of young adults relative to that of their parents, the latter proxying the material aspirations of the young" (1996, p. 151).

Certainly, the satisfactions from one's standard of living may be conditioned by the material conditions of one's upbringing. (This part of the story is similar to that of habit formation in consumption, discussed in Chapter 2, section 2.4). Also, when relative income is low, couples may delay beginning a family a bit in order to "get established." And, to some extent, fertility postponed may become fertility foregone. In writings related to the nineteenth century, Easterlin stresses parents' desire to provide their children with as good a start in life as they had. This also potentially explains why there may be greater downward flexibility for the quantity than for the quality of children.[13]

Easterlin views relative cohort size as a primary determinant of relative income. Intuitively, workers of different ages are imperfect substitutes in production, so that a large cohort confronts relatively poor employment and compensation prospects. As Macunovich describes the full set of interactions,

> a large birth cohort meets unfavorable labor market conditions which reduce the earning potential of young males relative to their aspirations. In an attempt to close the gap between income and aspirations, members of such a cohort will tend to make a number of adjustments including increased female labor force participation and delayed/reduced marriage and child-bearing. Thus in this formulation the driving force behind both increased female labor force participation and reduced fertility, is the desire of a large cohort to improve relative economic status, with parental income as the measure of that cohort's material aspirations. (1996, p. 95)

Because they fail to account for these mechanisms, Macunovich argues that most empirical examinations of the Chicago model are seriously flawed. She points out that findings of a negative *correlation* between fertility and mother's wage *explain* the variation in fertility only if the female wage is exogenous. In fact, though, she argues, most empirical studies have employed wages that are in part endogenous. The problem is that such studies do not control for increases in women's experience and education, which have contributed to the increase in female wages (see the discussions in Chapters 7 and 8). And, educational attainment and work experience may be (and in Easterlin's theory *are*) an endogenous response by females to low male earnings. For this reason, unless an exogenous wage is used, a negative correlation between fertility and the mother's wage may also be interpreted as evidence in favor of the Easterlin hypothesis.

The Easterlin model, like the Chicago model, is capable of explaining the baby boom and subsequent baby bust. Young men at the end of World War II obtained good, steady employment, which increased their income relative to that of their fathers (whose work lives encompassed the Great Depression). For this reason fertility was high, generating the baby boom. However, the children of boomers constituted a very large cohort, which depressed their wages. As a consequence, marriage was delayed, and young women received more education in anticipation of working longer. Since relative income was lower than it had been for their parent's generation, the baby bust ensued.

However, fertility did not rise among the potential mothers of the baby bust cohort as their small numbers led relative income theorists to predict. In response to a degree of failure on the part of both the Chicago and Easterlin models to predict fertility in the 1980s, Macunovich proposes a merging of the two. In her formulation, fertility increases with the income of males relative to their household of origin. Fertility then increases with son's income, as in both the Chicago and Easterlin models, and is lower at higher income in the household of origin. She finds empirical support for both assertions. The income effect of female wages is predicted to be inversely related to male earnings: When male incomes are "low," female earnings are very important to the meeting of material aspirations, making the income effect large. The substitution effect of women's wages works as in the Chicago School. However, there is explicit acknowledgment that it may decline with increased availability and acceptability of paid child daycare. The combined model performs well over her sample period through 1991. However, in the remainder of the 1990s, income and relative income growth have both been strong, yet there has been no further increase in fertility.

If labor productivity growth remains at the relatively high level of the late 1990s, relative income will rise appreciably. The Easterlin model's logic would then predict fertility approaching that obtained during the baby boom. However, the extent to which young women have oriented themselves to the labor market in recent years (attending college in greater numbers than males, for example) makes it unlikely that married couples will on average again bear four children any time soon.[14] Given the lower substitution and higher income effects now observed among women, an update of the price-theoretic Chicago School would also predict that fertility should rise with income.

However, neither the Chicago theory considered thus far nor the Easterlin theory may be sufficiently rich to predict future fertility with much accuracy. This is because they were largely formalized before the relatively recent increases in divorce and out-of-wedlock childbearing. Some of the complications these phenomena introduce are analyzed in section 9.3. Additionally, both theories may suffer from insufficient attention to factors influencing the relative benefits of quantity versus quality of children. Section 9.4 considers a macroeconomic model that extends the Chicago theory by accounting for technical change and its implications for the return on investments in child quality.

9.3 FERTILITY AND MARITAL STATUS

In 1998 almost one-third of all births in the United States were to unwed women. Also, compared with the 1960s, a smaller proportion of women now marry after having a first birth out of wedlock (Current Population Reports Census Bureau). Many other children have parents who have divorced. Single parenthood is often associated with low resource investments in children, which impairs their human capital development. Also, unwed teenage mothers tend to acquire less human capital themselves and to receive a lower rate of return on their investments (cf. Klepinger, Lundberg, and Plotnick, 1999). These facts underscore the importance of generalizing our earlier discussion that considered the fertility decisions of married couples in committed unions. Relaxing those assumptions requires a model in which fertility and marital status are determined endogenously. After discussing some results from the marriage market literature, we develop the model of Willis (1999), which focuses on the high rates of out-of-wedlock childbearing among poor minority women. His framework is extended to encompass incentives surrounding custodial rights. The section closes with a discussion of divorce and child quality.

9.3.1 Sorting in Marriage Markets

Becker (1973, 1974a) developed an ingenious theory of the marriage market to explain the sorting into marriages of all market participants. In his model, searching for a partner is costless, information is perfect, and marital output can be aggregated into a single private good. Under these conditions, Becker shows that marriage market equilibrium results in the total output across *all* marriages being maximized. Otherwise, it would be possible to determine an alternative assignment of partners so that at least one couple is better off, and no one is worse off. In practice, the marriage market is not that efficient, and later work by Becker, Landes, and Michael (1977) relaxes the assumptions of perfect information and costless search to provide an economic analysis of divorce.

In Becker's original framework, a person's contribution to marriage differs across potential marriages because of, as examples, complementarities between the traits of prospective partners and comparative advantage. For this reason, the theory does not predict that each person will be in the marriage that maximizes the *output* of his or her individual marriage; it is the overall *gains* to the marriage that prove decisive. In Becker's model, when men and women differ only in their productive capacities at home and in the labor market, there will be a *negative* sorting of prospective partners into marriages in accordance with these productive capacities. For example, assuming equal productivity at home and higher wages for men, the gains within and across marriages are maximized when high-wage men (compared with all men) marry low-wage women. In Chapter 8 we saw that until modern times this meant total marital output (home and market) was maximized when men specialized in the market and women performed most of the housework. However, as this comparative advantage has declined, so has the extent of specialization and the associated gains to marriage.[15]

That Becker's model assumes all goods are private in nature limits its usefulness in joint discussions of fertility and marital decisions. For many of the investments by parents in children produce benefits, such as high academic or athletic performance, which are enjoyed by both parents; mom's enjoyment does not diminish the enjoyment available for dad. For this reason children, especially within marriage, have many public goods attributes. Lam (1988) shows that when marital goods are public rather than private, the gains to marriage are maximized by a *positive* sorting across mates with respect to productive traits, here income.[16]

To appreciate Lam's result, consider a man and a woman with identical preferences, but allow the woman to have the higher income. Upon marriage, each spouse's "marital share" would consist of his or her own private good consumption, plus the jointly consumed child quality. Given child quality and the parental incomes, marital shares vary with consumption of the private good. As in Becker's model, the discipline of the marriage market establishes minimum shares for each spouse. That is, to be viable, the marriage "contract" has to dominate the utility both from remaining single and from marriage to the best alternative prospect. This limits the extent to which one spouse can free-ride off the other's public goods contribution. For if one partner contributes more to the public good, that partner can expect to be compensated with greater consumption of the private good. This leads to conflict, though, when preferences are identical and incomes are unequal: An affluent woman not only desires to contribute more to the public good (child quality) but, given her "outside" options, can demand a larger contribution toward child quality than a poor man would find acceptable. For if he met her minimum marital share, he would be left consuming so little of the private good that his marital share would fall below his minimum. Similarly, if the poor man gets to choose an equal-matching level of public good provision, the rich woman would have "too much" of the private good and too little of the public good. Her utility would be higher if she were matched with a partner whose income is more similar to her own—who will thus have a similar demand for the public good.

9.3.2 Choices of Mothers

Willis (1999) builds on these insights to model the marriage market and fertility simultaneously. The choices confronting men and women are first discussed separately, setting the stage for an analysis of the marriage market. Willis assumes that women and men both derive utility from their own private consumption of market goods and from the quantity and quality of children. For mothers,

$$U_m = U_m(C_m, n, W_c) \qquad (9.9)$$

where U_m is the mother's utility and C_m is her consumption of the private good; n and W_c remain the quantity and quality of children. Notice that no characteristics of potential husbands appear in her utility function. As seen below, this implies that the only benefits from a spouse derive from his material contributions to child quality. Although unrealistic, this assumption helps keep the model tractable and focused on the relationship between fertility and marriage.

Since the focus of the analysis is whether or not to have children, Willis limits the options of females to remaining childless (n = 0) or having one child (n = 1). He abstracts from the labor market considerations of the prior section by assuming that the incomes of females and males are exogenous. For this reason, there are no gains to marriage from the division of labor, only from the publicness in consumption of children. Thus, the results of Lam apply and there will be a positive sorting of partners into relationships on the basis of income.

To simplify, Willis assumes that the production of child quality requires goods inputs only (time inputs are considered below) so that

$$W_c = W_c(G_m, G_f) \qquad (9.10)$$

where G_m (G_f) are expenditures on child quality by the mother (father). The inputs are subject to decreasing returns. Under marriage, W_c will simplify to $W_c(G_m + G_f)$.

Women need not be married to bear children, and Willis models this option of single motherhood. Since children are a discrete choice, 0 or 1, and child quality competes with own consumption, Willis argues that single women with low incomes will not have a child. Intuitively, no child is preferable to a very low-quality, perhaps "problem," child. However, a single woman with a sufficiently high income will be better off giving birth to a child, even without any support from a father (or the government). Of course, as discussed below, she may be even better off if married with a child.

The budget constraint facing the single woman is

$$E_m = C_m + nG_m \tag{9.11}$$

The problem confronting a single mother is to maximize (9.9) by choice of C_f, n, and W_c subject to the budget constraint (9.11) and the production function for child quality, (9.10).[17]

9.3.3   Choices of Fathers

Potential fathers also enjoy high-quality children, so that their utility function is

$$U_f = U_f(C_f, n, W_c)$$

Aside from the obvious difference in subscripts, the utility functions of men and women may differ in other ways. For example, women may value the welfare of children more highly. Willis supposes that men enjoy parenthood whether or not they have custody or were ever married: any shame from fathering out of marriage is exceeded by the benefits of progeny.[18] And these benefits increase with child quality. Since women can bear but one child, a *married* man can father but one. However, an unmarried man may father any number of children, by the same number of women.

Since males value child quality (i.e., have a positive marginal rate of substitution between child quality and own consumption), both a man and a woman could be made better off if, given that there is a child, the child's quality exceeds what a single woman would provide. For this reason, if a man may father a child by only one woman, he would choose marriage and positive support of the child's development to "walking away from the child."

The contributions of a married father to his child follow from Willis' conception of marriage as an institution that enables the efficient coordination of investments in child quality. Central to an efficient allocation is that child quality benefits both parents. This publicness in the consumption of child quality increases the couples' demand compared with that for ordinary, or private, goods. For private goods, such as workday lunches, an extra dollar of expenditures provides benefits to the consuming spouse alone. In contrast, efficient provision for the public good child quality is at that level where the *sum* of the marginal benefits of the parents equals the marginal cost, or price (the "Samuelson conditions"). If, for example, on the fifth unit of child quality the father's enjoyments are 10 and the mother's 12, altogether a fifth unit would provide benefits of 22. Within marriage, the close coordination of efforts by the partners enables the efficient level of child quality to be provided.[19] In this case, the demand for child quality is a function of the sum of the incomes of the mother and father (given the price of child quality, and thus the productivity of the goods input).[20]

$$W_c = W_c(E_m + E_f)$$

Marriage, by increasing child quality over what the single mother would choose, also is preferred by the mother.

In contrast, according to Willis, the father's incentive to provide support for children declines precipitously when the child lives with the mother only.[21] The difficulty is that since the father is absent, he cannot monitor the mother's outlays on the child. For this reason, he concludes that any child support he pays will be treated by the mother as "general family income," so that the mother's marginal propensity to spend *on the child* from child support transfers is less than 1. Willis notes that this effectively increases the price of child quality to the father. For example, if the mother spends 50 cents of each dollar of her resources on the child, the father's price for increasing child quality by $1 rises to $2. With a downsloping demand for child quality, he purchases fewer units than if each dollar transferred increased expenditures on the child by a dollar. Consequently, the child suffers. From an efficiency perspective, the problem is that the mother does not take the father's benefits into account when deciding upon child expenditure levels. For this reason, children, mother, and father are all harmed by an absence of marriage.

More formally, the father takes the relationship between his contributions and the mother's expenditures on the child into account when making his child-support and own-consumption choices. The father's problem may be stated as

$$\max U_f(C_f, W_c)$$

subject to

$$C_f + G_f = E_f$$

and

$$W_c = W_m = W_m(E_m + G_f)$$

where W_m is the child quality chosen by the mother and the second constraint is the mother's investment function. The utility-maximizing conditions require the marginal rate of substitution between quality and consumption to exceed the price ratio, in recognition that part of any transfer is consumed by the mother. (The solution to problems with this general structure is called a *Stackelberg equilibrium*.) This solution reduces transfers compared with if the father could directly influence expenditures on the child, again taking the transfers of the mother as given. And, in each instance, child quality is lower than the efficient allocation with marriage.

9.3.4   Equilibria in the Marriage Market

The foregoing makes clear that if mother and father are to have one child with one partner and may choose only between being married or not cohabiting, they will marry—otherwise some gains associated with efficient spending on child quality are foregone. Such marriages are consistent with marriage market equilibrium under certain circumstances. For example, suppose there is an equal number of men and women and that members of each gender differ only by income. Then the results of Lam apply, so that the highest income male will marry the highest income female, the second richest male marries the second richest female, and so on, through the poorest male and female. In this context, everyone marries, has children, and provides the efficient level of child quality.

This "traditional" marriage market—where biological parents are married, and each parent is married to only one spouse—can also arise when there are unequal numbers of men and women. If men outnumber women, for example, some men will remain unmarried and women will be able to appropriate the lion's share of the gains from marriage. However, equilibrium in the marriage market may in fact be consistent with other outcomes.

Willis notes that an equilibrium in which some women bear children out of wedlock can arise when women outnumber men and women are affluent both absolutely and also relative to men. In turn, we consider this option from the perspective of men, women, and the marriage market. Above we saw that if a man may father children by only one woman, he will do so within marriage, and the efficient level of child quality will be provided. Imagine, instead, that there is an alternative of fathering children with several different women, making low or zero contributions to the quality of each. If the number of women he can impregnate is "large enough" and if the women are sufficiently affluent that they would provide at least his minimally acceptable level of child quality given little if any support from him, this option could dominate marriage to a single partner.

To understand how this outcome may arise, assume that if a man fathers children by more than one mother he must forego marriage and cohabitation.[22] Since child quality is a normal good, it will increase with mother's income (holding constant any transfers by the father). Higher transfers by the mother, though, will reduce the transfer amount from the father: higher maternal transfers increase the ratio of child quality to father's consumption, thereby lowering his demand price for child quality (i.e., his marginal rate of substitution of child quality for own consumption). This suggests that should the mother's income prove sufficiently high relative to the father's, his contributions could be driven to a corner. And, if he is able to father enough children at little or no cost to himself outside of marriage, this can dominate marriage and a more efficient investment in child quality.[23] Willis (1999, p. 46) notes that, ironically, "(a)lthough out-of-wedlock fatherhood . . . increases the marginal cost of child quality from the father's point of view, it may reduce or even eliminate the 'cost of fatherhood,' as measured by the total transfer from the father to the mother."

Women who have sufficient income to bear children on their own are, in Willis' model, never made worse off by establishing paternity (rather than choosing a sperm bank); they are strictly better off if the father contributes anything toward child quality. This explains why women may choose out-of-wedlock childbearing, even if it may turn out after the fact that the father contributes no support. Becker and Willis stress that the gains accruing within marriage are a consequence of the marriage market equilibrium. Willis shows that an equilibrium in which some men and women choose out-of-wedlock childbearing can arise when (1) women have incomes that are absolutely and relatively high and (2) women are in excess supply. Their absolutely high incomes make them demand children even if single; their relatively high incomes drive men's contribution when unmarried to low levels (possibly zero); their greater numbers ensure that men capture most of the gains from parenthood. Further, the portion of the marriage market selected into out-of-wedlock childbearing is those men and women with relatively low incomes: Given positive sorting by income, those most affluent have the greatest gains from marriage (since the gains are associated with the publicness of child quality, which is high for them).

Willis' model seems to explain certain features of fertility and marriage in the contemporary United States, especially aggregate differences between whites and blacks. As noted, out-of-wedlock motherhood is much higher among blacks than whites. According to the model, this means that the incomes of black men should be lower relative to those of black women, especially in the lower tail of the earnings distribution, than is the case among whites; they are. Also, there should be an excess supply of black women. Willis, and many others, argue this is true because of the high rates of incarceration and unemployment among black men.

It is important to appreciate that the Family Support Act of 1988 required states to establish paternity for all births and obligates fathers to make child support payments for the first 18 years of a child's life. Such payments are to increase with the father's income. Consequently, the zero to low paternal support equilibrium we have discussed is not a *legal* option (though actual support remains appreciably below court-ordered magnitudes on average). Further, even for low-income fathers such payments would constitute a significant burden. For example, Willis notes that a median-income black male who fathers a child out of wedlock is required to pay $167 per month until the child's eighteenth birthday. This has clear implications for the marriage market equilibrium developed by Willis. He notes that "(i)f legal paternity is established and collection of child support were strictly enforced, our theory suggests that the attractiveness of nonmarital relative to marital fatherhood would decrease and the equilibrium fraction of children born out of wedlock would be reduced" (p. 62). The birthrate among unmarried women, especially black teenagers, has fallen in recent years. It is unclear how much of this decline is due to passage and enforcement of the Family Support Act, including increased efforts to collect court-ordered child support from delinquent fathers.

9.3.5 Welfare and Out-of-Wedlock Fertility

In the 1960s through the mid-1990s, AFDC (now TANF) benefits encouraged most participants to refrain from much if not all work. Even including associated benefits from food stamps and Medicaid, the total benefit package from AFDC participation did not necessarily exceed what a mother would earn if she did not participate in welfare (see Chapter 8). However, once one takes account of the extra time available for the home production of child services, participation in welfare presumably did increase the potential to consume. By increasing this real income of low-income single mothers, both absolutely and relative to poor men, AFDC would be predicted to raise the proportion of women who bear children out of wedlock.

Recent empirical support for this proposition comes from Rosenzweig (1999). He utilizes individual-level data on young women (from the National Longitudinal Survey of Youth (NLSY)). His data include whether a woman experienced a nonmarital birth by age 22, a measure of income in the woman's family of origin, and the average AFDC benefits to which she was exposed during adolescence. The NLSY also contains each woman's score on the Armed Forces Qualifying Test, widely used as a measure of ability. Ability may be an important signal of both potential wages and the ability to attract a mate. Rosenzweig finds a large, statistically significant effect of AFDC on out-of-wed-lock childbearing among young women from poor families. He reports that "among women with poor parents, a mere 10% rise in welfare benefits increases the probability of a woman having a nonmarital birth by age 22 by 12 percent and decreases the probability of having no children by age 22 by 2.3 percent. The effects on the fertility behavior of the non-poor are almost nil" (p. 6). Compared with other studies, those effects on nonmarital child-bearing are quite large.[24] One reason for Rosenzweig's seemingly large effects is that he focuses on women from poor families, who are likely to be poor themselves. This is exactly the segment of the marriage market Willis identifies as most likely to have non-marital children. Rosenzweig concludes that "women who bear children outside of and prior to first marriage are less able to attract high-endowment mates" (p. 31).[25]

Policymakers have become more sensitive to the fertility incentives of welfare. Consequently, the amounts received for an additional child have been reduced in many states, as have the number of years a mother can receive this state support. The marked decline in premarital childbearing among black teens since the mid-1990s may be a consequence of welfare reform—both in work requirements and benefit reductions. However, other explanations have also been proposed. These include increased condom use as an AIDS preventive, greater use of oral contraceptives (especially those shown to decrease acne), improved earnings prospects for young black men, and, as discussed earlier, better efforts to collect court-ordered child support payments.

9.3.6 Custodial Rights and Relationship Capital

Edlund (1998) notes that legal custody of a child automatically reverts to the biological mother in the absence of marriage. An important implication is that when women marry, they surrender some portion of legal custody. Edlund argues that women trade custodial rights for paternal resources. Thus, whereas in Willis' model a mother prefers marriage if the husband would invest in the child at all, Edlund's insight is that the benefit of increased investment must more than offset the cost of custody foregone. Her analysis predicts that couples marry only if the earnings of the man are sufficiently high relative to the woman's to warrant the transfer of custodial rights.

Edlund tests her model using data on 700 Swedish married and unmarried couples (who are cohabitants) with at least one of the partners 25 to 35 years of age. In general, her results are supportive of the theory. She finds "that a higher male earnings share raises the probability that a couple is married, which . . . supports the claim that marriage amounts to a transfer of custodial rights from the woman to the man" (p. 7). Willis argues that black men don't marry because they can father a more attractive mix, to them, of quantity and quality of children out of wedlock. In contrast, Edlund would argue that men who may be incarcerated or unemployed are not affluent enough to buy their way into a custodial relationship.

In Willis' model, a father's investments in a child are determined by marital status and the relative incomes of the biological parents. Marital status is important only because of an inability, if unmarried, to monitor the mother's expenditures on the child, which raises the price to the father of making transfers to the child. We now argue that paternal investments are also affected by the interaction between endogenous altruism and the legal assignment of child custody.

To apply endogenous altruism when the association with the child may change, we model altruism as increasing in the stock of *relationship capital*. Relationship capital summarizes the current status of the historical bond between parent and child. Its value at time t, R_t, equals investments in child oriented resources in $t - 1$, I_{t-1}, plus the undepreciated portion of the stock of $t - 1$,

$$R_t = I_{t-1} + \delta R_{t-1}$$

where δ is 1 minus the per-period rate of depreciation. We additionally suppose that enjoyment of child quality at time t increases with time spent in t with the child. That is, time with the child is complementary to both child quality and relationship capital. For this reason, the expected return on current investments in child quality and relationship capital increase with the time one *expects* to spend with the child in the future. The ability to choose freely the time spent with the child, however, may be limited for a parent with less than full legal custody. The interactions between custodial rights and relationship capital produce interesting implications.

Mothers retain legal custody in cohabiting relationships, which fail with greater frequency than marital relationships. Fathers in such unions may invest less in their children; the lack of custody rights and the high probability that the union will falter reduce the return to investments in relationship capital.[26] Similarly, relationship capital potentially explains why father's involvement postdivorce is larger the longer was the marriage. Furstenberg, Hoffman, and Shrestha (1995) use data on parents and their adult children from the PSID to see how transfers of time and money from parents are conditioned by divorce. They find that among fathers divorcing while children are still dependents (less than age 18), the probability that the father makes transfers to the children when they are adults is higher when the children are older at the time of divorce. In our interpretation, the higher transfers are a consequence of the greater relationship capital prevailing between fathers and children older at the time of divorce. On the other hand, the probability of monetary transfers from mother is lower when children are older upon the parent's divorce. One possible reason is that, with greater paternal relationship capital, the mother can free-ride somewhat on the father's larger transfers.[27] More generally, relationship capital suggests that the resources devoted to the child's development may differ appreciably between children born out of wedlock, children of divorce living with a sole custodian, and children of divorce whose parents share joint physical custody.

9.4 FROM SUBSISTENCE TO MODERN GROWTH

The relationship between income and population is one of the central issues in economic development and macroeconomics. There has been a great deal of high-quality work on the macroeconomics of fertility in recent years (cf. Kremer, 1993; Becker et al., 1990;

Jones, 2000). We emphasize a model by Galor and Weil (2000) because it addresses the relationship between income and population employing mechanisms we have deemed important in this and earlier chapters. Brief attention is also afforded an earlier model of theirs (1996), for similar reasons.

Galor and Weil (2000) partition the historical relationship between income and fertility in Europe into three conceptually distinct regimes. First is the *Malthusian* regime during which population and income per capita are essentially constant. In this regime, as originally described by Thomas Malthus at the end of the eighteenth century, an increase in income leads to population growth, thereby eroding any gains to income per capita. During the *Post-Malthusian* regime, there continues to be a positive relationship between income and population. Now, though, not all of the increase in GDP is associated with population, so that both population and living standards rise. Finally, the *Modern Growth* regime is characterized by steady growth in per capita income, perhaps faster than in the Post-Malthusian regime. In the Modern Growth regime, increases in income per capita are associated with lower fertility than the Post-Malthusian regime, leading to low (and potentially negative) population growth. Galor and Weil model these changing relationships among income, income growth, and population as a function of advances in technology and increases in education. They stress that the framework does not apply to currently undeveloped economies, which are able to import preexisting production and health technologies. We now describe their modeling of these mechanisms in some detail.

9.4.1   Production and Factor Prices

In Galor and Weil's formulation, aggregate production at time t follows the Cobb-Douglas function

$$Y_t = H_t^\alpha (A_t X_t)^{1-\alpha}$$

where H_t is the aggregate stock of human capital measured in efficiency units, A_t is the state of technology, and X_t is land. The product $A_t X_t$ constitutes *effective resources*. We immediately notice that one simplification is the exclusion of physical capital from the analysis. Galor and Weil argue that inclusion of physical capital would obscure important interrelations among population, human capital, and technology without much altering the conclusions.[28]

Land is assumed to be fixed in supply, which was crucial to the analysis of Malthus. The production function is neoclassical, with constant returns to scale in human capital and effective resources, and diminishing returns to either alone. Notice that, unless technology improves, the diminishing returns to human capital greatly limit its role in growth. Technical growth is necessary in order for the returns to human capital to remain high in the presence of human capital accumulation.

Galor and Weil focus on the intensive form of the production function, expressing output and resources per worker as

$$y_t = h_t^\alpha x_t^{1-\alpha} = y_t(h_t, x_t)$$

where $x_t \equiv A_t X_t / L_t$ and $h_t \equiv H_t / L_t$ are effective resources and human capital per worker, respectively. As another concession to tractability, they assume that there are no property rights over land; it is nonexcludable, and therefore free. However, the fixed supply of land is sufficiently small that, even when it is fully utilized, its marginal product remains positive. The fixed nature of land proves important because it constrains the productivity of workers and, in early stages of development, population.

Since labor is the only input receiving a positive return, all output accrues to labor. Consequently, laborers receive their *average* product. The wage per unit of human capital is therefore

$$w_t = y_t / h_t = (x_t / h_t)^{1-\alpha} \equiv w_t(h_t, x_t) \tag{9.12}$$

This wage increases with effective resources but, due to diminishing returns, falls as human capital per worker increases.

9.4.2   Parent's Problem: No Subsistence Constraint

Each generation lives for two periods. In the first, they are children and economically dependent on their parents. In the second, they are parents. As in section 9.2, altruistic parents derive utility from own consumption C_{pt}, and from the aggregate earnings or wealth of children (child well-being or services). The potential life wealth of the child is

$$W_{ct+1} \equiv w_{t+1} h_{t+1}$$

where h_{t+1} is the human capital, or number of efficiency units of labor, the worker brings to the labor market as an adult. The fact that there are no financial transfers implies that issues pertaining to an efficient composition of human and financial bequests do not arise. The Cobb-Douglas utility of parents of time t is

$$U_{pt} = C_{pt}^{1-\gamma}(n_{t+1} w_{t+1} h_{t+1})^{\gamma} \tag{9.13}$$

The potential income of parents, $W_{pt} = w_t h_t$, is the labor earnings associated with devoting all time to the labor market. Potential income is allocated between own consumption and the rearing of children. To simplify the analysis, Galor and Weil assume that expenditures on children are limited to time only. This feature captures the relative time intensiveness of children stressed in section 9.2. Notice, though, that since all adults are identical, the results would not be affected if adults other than the parents are hired at the going wage to impart child quality. Each child requires τ^n units of time independent of the quality of the child: This time includes trips to the doctor during pregnancy; actual delivery and recovery; and bonding with, feeding, dressing, bathing, and changing diapers of young children. Further, parents may enhance the human capital of children by educating them. To increase the education of a child, e_{t+1}, by one unit requires τ^e units of time. Total time investments in children are then equal to $n_t[\tau^n + \tau^e e_{t+1}]$. Normalizing the parent's endowment of time to equal one unit, $n_t[\tau^n + \tau^e e_{t+1}] \leq 1$. Since this time may otherwise have been employed in the labor market, the total (foregone earnings) cost of raising children is $W_{pt}n_t[\tau^n + \tau^e e_{t+1}]$. We may write the parent's budget constraint as

$$C_{pt} + W_{pt}n_t[\tau^n + \tau^e e_{t+1}] \leq W_{pt} \qquad (9.14)$$

An individual's human capital depends not only on the educational investments by parents, but also on technology. Specifically, technical change is assumed to erode or depreciate human capital. Skills learned in one technical environment are less productive in a different one: "when technology is changing rapidly, the knowledge gained from observing the previous generation will be less valuable and the trial-and-error process, which led to a high degree of efficiency under static conditions, will not have had time to function" (Galor and Weil, 2000, p. 810). Thus, new technology creates a demand for the ability to analyze and evaluate new production possibilities. They argue that this ability increases with education so that *the return to education increases with the rate of technical change*. An implication is that if technical progress is slow, the return to education will be so low that all child expenditures are devoted to raising the quantity of children (i.e., $\tau^e = 0$).

This production technology is depicted in Figure 9.4. In the absence of any formal education, if technology is stagnant, human capital is h(0). Human capital then rises with education, though at a decreasing rate (reflecting diminishing returns to education). When technical progress proceeds at some particular positive rate, human capital in the absence of education is h(1), recalling that technological progress depreciates human capital. Once again human capital rises with education, but now at a faster rate (reflecting the assumption that technical progress increases the return to education). At high enough education,

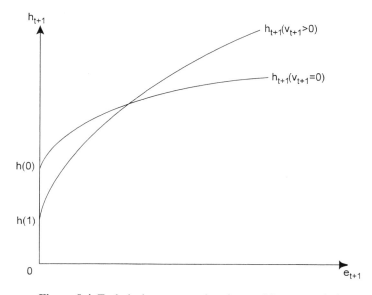

Figure 9.4 Technical progress, education, and human capital

human capital will be greater at the faster rate of technical change. The human capital production function is written

$$h_{t+1} = h_{t+1}(e_{t+1}, v_{t+1}) \qquad (9.15)$$

where

$$v_{t+1} \equiv (\mathbf{A}_{t+1} - \mathbf{A}_t)/\mathbf{A}_{t+1}$$

is the rate of technical progress foreseen between periods t and t + 1.

To model the Malthusian regime, an additional constraint is imposed that requires consumption to be at least equal to some subsistence level, C^s. This restriction prevents households from devoting so many resources to their children that parent's own survival is compromised. The utility maximization problem of parents may now be stated as

$$\text{Max } U_{pt} = C_{pt}^{1-\gamma}[n_{t+1}w_{t+1}h_{t+1}(e_{t+1},v_{t+1})]^{\gamma}$$

by choice of n_{t+1}, e_{t+1}, and C_{pt} subject to

$$C_{pt} + W_{pt}n_t[\tau^n + \tau^e e_{t+1}] \leq W_{pt}$$

and

$$C_{pt} \geq C^s$$

where the production function for human capital has been substituted for h_{t+1} in the utility function.

Solving this problem is easier than one might think. Let's first consider the solution in the absence of the subsistence constraint (or assuming the subsistence constraint is not binding). At several previous junctures in the book we have shown that the exponents of a Cobb-Douglas function (which sum to 1) represent the share of total resources devoted to that variable. For example, in Chapter 1 the exponent on first-period consumption was seen to equal the share of life wealth devoted to it. Similarly, in Chapter 3 the share of GDP paid to labor is equal to its exponent. The same is true here, though we will not pursue the messy algebra. Thus, as derived in their paper, the proportion $1 - \gamma$ of parental wealth is devoted to own consumption, with the proportion γ allotted to expenditures on children.

$$C_{pt} = (1 - \gamma)W_{pt}$$

and

$$W_{pt}n_t[\tau^n + \tau^e e_{t+1}] = \gamma W_{pt} \qquad (9.16)$$

Notice that dividing (9.16) through by potential income, we obtain the simple result that

$$\gamma = n_t[\tau^n + \tau^e e_{t+1}]$$

Thus, so long as the subsistence constraint is not binding, the fraction of time devoted to the raising of children is simply γ.

To appreciate the underlying intuition, suppose the wage of parents, w_t, rises, while no change is anticipated for w_{t+1} (perhaps a series of good weather conditions has made some traditionally unusable land temporarily suitable for cultivation by parents). The income effect from the higher wage encourages parents to increase both own consumption and aggregate child wealth. However, the higher wage also entails a substitution effect, as the time required to raise children is now relatively more expensive. This substitution effect increases parental consumption at the expense of children's earnings. The combined income and substitution effects increase parental consumption, but conflict concerning aggregate child earnings. However, in the Cobb-Douglas case, the income and substitution effects offset exactly, so that aggregate child earnings (or services) are unaffected. This contrasts with section 9.2 where the substitution effect was assumed to dominate. Other mechanisms discussed below account for the rise in quality and decline in quantity in this model.

With Cobb-Douglas preferences, parents would spend γ percent of those higher potential wage earnings on children. The allocation of time between home and market would not change though, since potential earnings and the price of time inputs rise proportionately. Further, since the relative returns to n_{t+1} and e_{t+1} are unaffected, neither is the mix between them.

An expected increase in the wage rate for children also entails income and substitution effects. As in the discussion of altruistically motivated transfers in Chapter 5, parents desire to consume part of the additional income of children, so the income effect increases both child wealth and parental consumption. Since higher wages for the child make it less expensive to increase child wealth, the substitution effect serves to increase child wealth at the expense of parental consumption. The income and substitution effects on parental consumption exactly offset in the Cobb-Douglas case. However, with C_{pt} unchanged, the parent's budget constraint tells us that expenditures on children must also be unchanged. The wealth of children rises because of higher wages, not because of higher investments.

These comparative static results for child and parent wage rates in combination reveal that economic growth need not affect the time investments in children. In sharp contrast, an increase in the *pace* of technical change asymmetrically raises the marginal benefit of quality compared with quantity. This higher return on investments in child education increases time devoted to that purpose, while reducing time allotted to quantity (reducing fertility).

9.4.3   Parent's Problem: Subsistence Constraint Binding

The optimal choices for quantity and quality, and how they respond to changes in income, differ when the subsistence constraint is binding. In this case, the potential income of parents devoted to children is

$$W_{pt}n_t[\tau^n + \tau^e e_{t+1}] = W_{pt} - C^s$$

The subsistence constraint binds when countries are poor and, as seen below, where technology grows quite slowly. So long as the rate of technical change is below some threshold, say v^e, the return to education does not justify investments in quality. In that context, then, all expenditures on children go to increasing their numbers. Consequently, as parental wealth rises, so does the proportion of wealth spent on children. Beyond some wealth level the subsistence constraint no longer binds, and the share of expenditures devoted to children is simply γ. Also, when the rate of technical change exceeds the threshold v^e, expenditures on children are no longer exclusively on quantity.

9.4.4 The Rate of Technical Change

The final building block of the model links the rate of technical change to the size of the population and to the level of education. That is,

$$v_{t+1} \equiv v_{t+1}(L_t, e_{t+1})$$

Similar mechanisms were discussed in Chapter 7. First, holding constant the probability that a given individual will make a contribution to technology, the larger is the population, the more new ideas will be discovered in the aggregate. Second, the more highly educated are individuals, the greater is the probability that a given person will invent something valuable. These model features are now utilized to explain the path of development from the Malthusian regime, to the Post-Malthusian regime, through the demographic transition, and on into the Modern Growth regime.

9.4.5 From the Malthusian to Modern Growth Regime

In the early stages of economic development, the economy is in the Malthusian regime where the population is small and the subsistence constraint is binding. The small population keeps the rate of technological change below the threshold v^e, so parents have no incentive to provide education to their children. If there is *no* technical change, any population growth will reduce effective resources per person x_t, which by equation (9.12) lowers the wage w_t. With human capital unchanged, a lower wage per unit of human capital means lower parental wealth W_{pt}. In the Malthusian regime this results in lower fertility. Similarly, negative shocks to population, like the Black Death, would be reflected in only temporarily higher wages and temporarily faster population growth. Thus, the Malthusian regime is stable in that following temporary shocks to population, the economy will return to the initial equilibrium.[29] Notice that the longer term constancy of wages and population imply aggregate income is constant as well.

However, even with a small population, some trivial advance in technology occurs. This serves to glacially increase aggregate effective resources and, were population constant, output per worker. However, any income beyond subsistence is still spent on a larger quantity of children, limiting any rise in effective resources *per worker*. Income per capita remains essentially constant, while population and aggregate income rise.

As the population continues to grow, so does the rate of technical change. At some point, technical growth is fast enough to induce parents to begin investing in their children's education. This may occur before the subsistence constraint ceases to bind. In this case, it is possible for both population and quality to grow, as the share of potential income that is devoted to children continues to rise with potential income. However, at some point in time, the subsistence constraint ceases to bind. Although incomes continue to rise, the share of potential income allocated to children becomes constant. This impact of population on the pace of technical growth signals the end of the Malthusian regime.

Galor and Weil note that in the subsequent Post-Malthusian regime, "the Malthusian mechanism linking higher income to higher population growth continued to function, but the effect of higher population on diluting resources per capita, and thus lowering income per capita, was counteracted by technological progress, which allowed income to keep rising" (p. 808). As education becomes positive, education and rising population both serve to increase the rate of technical advance. This, in turn, raises the return to education so that a virtuous circle develops: higher human capital increases technological progress which, in turn, raises further the return to education.

Recall that the proportion of parental wealth allocated to children is constant at γ once the economy leaves the Malthusian regime. Since parental wealth derives exclusively from wage income and the cost of children is exclusively foregone earnings, higher time inputs into education in the Post-Malthusian regime imply a reduction in fertility. Eventually, the demographic transition ensues; the return to education continues to rise, population growth declines, and per capita income rises. Galor and Weil report findings that the decline in fertility during the transition was accompanied by a rapid rise in schooling; "the average number of years of schooling in England and Wales rose from 2.3 for the cohort born between 1801 and 1805 to 5.2 for the cohort born 1852–56 and 9.1 for the cohort born 1897–1906" (p. 809).

The demographic transition is followed by the Modern Growth regime. In this regime, resources per capita rise, as technological progress produces growth in effective resources which outstrips population growth. The model makes no firm prediction about what the rate of population growth will be in the Modern Growth regime (except that it will be below that in the Post-Malthusian regime). If the growth rate of population is zero, the rate of technological progress will tend to stabilize, and there will be no further substitution of education per child for family size. This case would produce a constant growth rate for effective resources x, and therefore a long-run steady state equilibrium with constant growth in per capita income. Alternatively, if the rate of population growth is positive, for example, the rate of technical progress will continue to accelerate, and education will continue to rise.[30]

The Role of Gender Differences

This model of the long process of evolution from a positive to negative relationship between income growth and fertility invokes several plausible mechanisms. However, it abstracts from the differences between men and women that were so important to the analyses of, especially, sections 9.2 and 9.3. Galor and Weil (1996, 1999) emphasize such gender differences in a different general-equilibrium framework which is also capable of explaining the long transition from the Malthusian to the Modern Growth regime.[31] We briefly consider those results as well. These are complementary (not opposing) mechanisms to the story developed above.

Males and females are assumed to have identical mental capabilities, whereas males have more physical strength than females. Mental and physical labor are both important to production. For this reason, the wages of men always exceed those of women. How-ever, Galor and Weil argue that physical capital accumulation and technical progress re-duce the premium to the physical strength advantage of males: Intuitively, physical cap-ital complements mental labor more so than physical labor. For this reason, the relative wages of women rise with physical capital accumulation and technological progress.

As in Galor and Weil (2000), there is a fixed quantity of land utilized in production and the rate of technological progress is positively related to the size of the population. With land fixed, population growth that is unaccompanied by capital accumulation or technical progress leads to lower wages.

Parents derive utility from own consumption and from the quantity of children (they abstract from financial transfers and educational investments in children that would af-fect child quality). Men and women are equally productive in child rearing, but the higher wages of men mean that only women raise children (we ignore the possibility that quan-tity is so large that both men and women are required). Child rearing requires time, but not goods, and the productivity of *that* time does not increase with capital accumulation or technical progress. For this reason, as in the models above, higher relative wages for women raise the cost of children. This reduces the fertility of women and increases their labor supply. In contrast, higher wages for men have a pure income effect, increasing fer-tility. Since child rearing reduces the labor earnings of women, it reduces retirement sav-ings and, in the aggregate, capital per worker.

Suppose the economy is initially in the Malthusian regime. Technical advance is slow while the population is low, but advances more rapidly as population grows. Although the land to labor ratio falls, wages can eventually increase when the effect of better tech-nology dominates. As their wages increase, so do savings and capital accumulation. In the early stages of development, the relative wages of men are quite high—even though their absolute wages are not. Then, as wages rise, the income effect of males' wages dom-inates family planning and fertility rises. The economy is in the Post-Malthusian regime. However, greater capital accumulation increases the relative wage of women. At some point, the substitution effect of females' wage increases dominate family planning. Then, women reduce fertility and increase labor force participation, and the economy experi-ences a demographic transition.[32]

9.5 SUMMARY

This chapter examined the economic determinants of fertility, including why they may have changed over time. The price theoretic approach of the Chicago School stresses the roles of income, prices, and technology. Early microeconomic models (cf. Becker, 1981) emphasized that interactions between the quantity and quality of children could induce a negative relationship between income and fertility, even though children are a normal good. Since the price of quantity increases with the quality of children, a higher income elasticity for quality than quantity meant that higher earnings by men would induce sub-stitution away from quantity.

Since young children are relatively time intensive, higher wages for mothers entail a substitution effect as well as an income effect. Assuming the substitution effect domi-nates, fertility is predicted to fall as female wages increase (cf. Willis, 1973). Recent willingness to utilize paid child care has reduced the time intensiveness of children, weakening the link between mother's wages and fertility. Nevertheless, the increasing value of women's time may have played an important role in both the demographic transition and U.S. fertility through the mid-1980s (cf. Galor and Weil, 1996). The relative income theory of Easterlin suggests that the demand for children increases with the material affluence of young adults compared with that of their parents. Although the Easterlin model appears consistent with both the baby boom and baby bust, it, like the Chicago School, has had little success predicting recent fertility movements.

Out-of-wedlock childbearing has risen in recent decades, especially among blacks (cf. Willis, 1999). Contributing factors include rising relative wages for black women and declining relative numbers of black men. These trends reduce the relative contribution of men to marriage and increase the willingness of women to raise children on their own.

Over the longer horizon, in the model of Galor and Weil (2000), population growth has sped technological change, leading to rising per capita incomes. This faster pace of technical change increases the return to children's education. Consequently, it reduces the relative return to child quantity. In this way, rising population and the associated technical change interacted to produce the demographic transition. In the Modern Growth regime, per capita incomes can continue to rise, while fertility would fall further only if the technological advance quickens.

Existing fertility models have enjoyed little success in forecasting fertility trends. As models capture population heterogeneity better, this may improve. The demand for children should continue to change with the economic environment. However, the degree to which women are now entrenched in the labor market may preclude a near-term return to very large families.

ENDNOTES

1. Two genealogical samples analyzed by Wahl (1986) indicate that fertility in earlier periods was higher yet. Bourne finds the period total fertility rate, defined below, from 1750 to 1759 was 7.2.

2. During the boom, women not only had more children, but also had them earlier in the life cycle. This speeding up of the life-cycle timing of births meant that the period TFR overestimated the number of children young women of the time would eventually bear.

3. This comparison exaggerates somewhat the completed fertility between these groups, as those more educated tend to delay childbearing.

4. The inverse relationship between income and fertility and education and fertility has weakened in recent years. For an earlier time Bryant (1990, p. 196) reports that in 1979 births per thousand women (aged 18–44) was 94.3 for women in families with incomes of less than $5,000 but only 48.5 in families with incomes above $25,000. Similarly, this measure was 91.9 for women who did not complete high school but only 52.1 for women with five or more years of college.

5. The constancy of the rate of return implies that human capital production is characterized by constant returns to scale. In Chapter 6, as investments rose, the return on human capital (there r_h) fell.

6. The inclusion of these policies was suggested to me by Jim Davies.

7. Wildasin obtains this result under the assumption that each child of a given quality makes the same contribution to parent's utility; he terms these "utilitarian preferences." By distorting the structure of relative prices the policy makes parents worse off; the rise in child

quality does not fully compensate for the reduction in fertility and associated change in first-period consumption.

Of course, many such policies do entail income effects when the analysis is limited to but two generations. For example, the net benefits enjoyed by the "start-up" generations of Social Security may entail costs for many subsequent generations. Nevertheless, under versions of the altruism model in which parents derive utility from the utility of children (rather than simply life wealth), the same results obtain (cf. Becker and Barro, 1988). Thus, theoretical reasoning suggests that if parents are altruistic, both Social Security and deficit policies reduce fertility.

8. If parents have children to provide for support in old age, as may be true in many developing countries, there may be even larger negative effects of Social Security on fertility (cf. Zhang and Zhang (1995). Consider the start-up period. Intuitively, parents would receive retirement support even without children, while any children they have would be less able to provide support because they must fund the program.

9. The decriminalization of abortion may have provided some unexpected social benefits. Donohue and Levitt (2000) argue that this decriminalization may account for half of the decline in crime rates since the early 1990s. Intuitively, those children who were aborted were unwanted and disproportionately disadvantaged. Had they been permitted to live, they would have been at high risk of criminal behavior.

10. Note that one cannot read the time and goods inputs for S and G from the graph. However, these may be obtained given S, G, and the efficiency condition MRTS = w_m^0, from the production functions.

11. More realistically, the combined earnings in two-earner households may be larger. With higher income, parents may produce other household goods in a relatively goods-intensive fashion. Consequently, the proportion of time devoted to children in the evenings that is "relationship enhancing" may be greater in type B families.

12. As supporting evidence, Tiefenthaler (1997) finds that Philippine girls aged 6 to 12 in the early 1980s contributed only 4.2 hours per week between child care and housework when there were no children under age 5. However, upon the introduction of a newborn, hours increased appreciably, totaling 12.7 hours per week fourteen months postnatal. The Phillippines in the 1980s is relevant to the current story, since formal education was low.

13. In the nineteenth century, a good start depended upon land and financial assets. A further reason for relatively greater downward rigidity for quality in modern times is the diminishing returns to human capital production, and thus child quality, stressed in Chapter 6; each dollar withdrawn from child quality would decrease child wealth by a larger amount.

14. Also, the relative income theory cannot explain the decline in fertility that has taken place since the nineteenth century, given the manyfold rise in income over that longer period. In fairness, Easterlin did not view his model as applicable until immigration was restricted early in the twentieth century: when immigration was open, the effect of a small cohort on wages would be reduced by increased immigration.

15. Becker's theory predicts a positive sorting across potential mates with respect to *consumption* traits—"likes marry likes." He (1981, p. 75) presents evidence that the simple correlations between intelligence, education, race, age, nonhuman wealth, religion, ethnic origin, and many other traits of spouses are positive and strong.

16. Lam (1988) works out a relatively general case in which time is required for household production, thereby combining the specialization story from Becker's formulation with the "similar demands" mechanism of the public goods story. Unsurprisingly, this results in an indeterminate sorting on the basis of wages. Suffice it to say that under reasonable conditions, positive assortative mating results in which the low-wage spouse specializes incompletely in household production, working some in the labor market but less than the high-wage spouse. Thus, the correlation between spousal wages is an empirical matter.

Most studies report a positive simple correlation between the wages of husbands and wives. However, a fundamental empirical difficulty arises in that, even if negative assortive mating is common, it may be difficult to detect. As Becker notes, comparing the wages of working couples will bias the findings in favor of positive assortive mating. For the married women who are *not* in the labor force, and thus omitted from the estimation, are expected to have lower wages. Thus, without imputing the unobserved wages of housewives it is difficult to accurately estimate the direction of sorting. However, Behrman, Rosenzweig, and Taubman (1994) use data on twins to control for ability and therefore potential labor market earnings. They do find some evidence of negative sorting on potential earnings. Summarizing the literature, Lam (1997, p. 1031) writes that recent "trends in family income inequality are in fact suggestive that there has been an increase in the tendency toward positive assortive mating, an increase that may be economically important in its effect on the distribution of family income."

17. This problem is similar to that developed in section 9.1, used to discuss the relationship between income and fertility. However, since in this version mothers may have but one child, the trade-off between child quantity and quality does not arise *for mothers*.

18. Like women, men may have a minimum level for child quality that is acceptable to them. As it turns out, for our purposes we need to assume only that that level is no higher than the level for women.

19. This type efficiency concerns the externality, or public goods, aspects of child quality. This differs from the efficient child quality provision level discussed in Chapter 6, which prescribes investment where the marginal rate of return on human capital equals that on financial assets. The current framework does not distinguish between human capital and financial transfers, so issues of "portfolio" efficiency do not arise.

20. Actually, this simple demand function also presupposes that there is transferable utility between the parents. For current purposes, this means expenditures on quality are independent of the relative magnitudes of the couple's income. In fact, there is growing evidence that expenditures on children rise with mother's share of family income.

21. This discussion is closely related to that of Weiss and Willis (1985), who consider voluntary transfers by noncustodial, divorced fathers. Divorce increases the price to fathers of child quality for exactly the same reason out-of-wedlock fatherhood does: The father recognizes that the mother will treat his child support transfers as family income, which reduces to below 1 her propensity to spend from them on the child.

22. Obviously, one may cohabit without marriage, as is quite common in Sweden, for example. We consider cohabitation in the absence of marriage below.

23. To retain tractability, our model assumes that only one child may be conceived within marriage. However, suppose a couple within marriage can choose any number of children. Then, for a given number of children, a man would have higher utility within marriage than outside marriage with multiple mothers, because of the coordination issues discussed above.

24. Until recently, most empirical evidence suggested that AFDC had only a small positive effect on out-of-wedlock fertility (cf. Ellwood and Bane, 1985). For the most part, these studies did not include estimates of unemployed women's wage rates *were* they employed, or of mens' earnings *were* they married. Willis' model views the wages of women and of their potential husbands as important determinants of equilibrium within the marriage market. To overcome this misspecification, Schultz (1994) constructs measures for these unobserved wages. He finds a *negative* effect of AFDC on *aggregate* fertility. This may occur if AFDC reduces the probability of marriage, since unmarried women have smaller families than married women. However, when Moffitt (1994) controls for unobserved wages *and* differences across states which may be correlated with AFDC benefits, he finds only weak effects of AFDC on fertility.

25. Since his study employs both an attractive methodology and good data, his findings have attracted considerable attention. Hoffman and Foster (2000) replicate and extend the

Rosenzweig analysis using individual panel data from the PSID. The PSID sample is somewhat smaller, but this is compensated for by better information on state of residence throughout the sample period and the capture of more nonmarital births than the NLSY. In general, Hoffman and Foster's results are supportive of the magnitudes found by Rosenzweig. They report that the effects are especially large on women in their early 20s; effects on teens are quite weak.

26. On the other hand, if the father desires marriage, he has an incentive to understate his true preferences for own consumption relative to child quality in an attempt to win custodial rights through marriage. After marriage he may reduce his contributions. Thus, among fathers of children born out of wedlock, there may be large differences in the propensity to spend on the child between those who eventually marry, and those who never marry *while the mother and father remain a couple.*

27. Relationship capital also provides a natural explanation for the rise in joint physical custody among divorced parents. As women have spent more time at work, men's relative relationship capital has grown. If relationship capital is also important for the child, and the court has the interests of the child in mind, a husband whose wife works may be more likely to be awarded joint physical custody upon divorce.

28. In an earlier version of their paper which they cite, physical capital is incorporated.

29. Also in this Malthusian regime, any differences in technology across countries would be reflected in population density; they would not impact living standards.

30. Jones (cf. 1995) argues that models that link the rate of technical advance to the *level* of population counterfactually imply ever-increasing rates of growth in per capita income. Thus, it is important to note that Galor and Weil argue that their results largely carry through when technical advance is instead linked to the *rate* of population growth. Under that assumption they can be more precise about the modern regime. There would be "a steady-state modern growth regime, in which the growth rates of population and technology would be constant. Further, such a steady state would be stable: if population growth fell, the rate of technological progress would also fall, inducing a rise in fertility" (2000, pp. 825–826, ftnt 23).

31. Their 1996 paper models explicitly the Post-Malthusian regime, Modern Growth regime, and the transition between them. The 1999 paper contains a description of a hybrid model that incorporates elements of the 2000 paper discussed above into the 1996 paper. The hybrid model potentially explains the entire transition of fertility, beginning with the Malthusian regime. Our discussion is a loose, and not entirely faithful, sketch of the hybrid model.

32. This story produces a U-shaped labor force participation trajectory for women. Galor and Weil (1996, p. 384) note that substantial evidence is consistent with this prediction.

REVIEW QUESTIONS AND PROBLEMS

▶ REVIEW
QUESTIONS

1. Why might the income elasticities of quantity and quality of children be expected to differ?

2. How do the Relative Income and Chicago theories, respectively, explain the baby boom and baby bust? What would each have predicted for the early 1990s, and then for the late 1990s through early 2000s?

3. **A.** In Willis' model of out-of-wedlock childbearing, if a woman would prefer marriage to a man who makes positive financial contributions to her child, why would she ever choose to be impregnated out of wedlock by a man she knows will not contribute to her child?

B. How and why would Edlund's custody arguments affect the conditions from the Willis model under which a mother will marry a father?

4. **A.** In what ways is the relationship between income and fertility of section 9.1 similar to that in section 9.4? In what ways are those mechanisms different?

B. In what ways is the relationship between mother's wage and fertility in section 9.2 similar to (different from) that between wages and fertility in the Galor-Weil (2000) model? The Galor-Weil (1996) model?

5. Suppose the Easterlin model is correct. Also suppose that the relatively higher rate of labor productivity growth that began in the mid-1990s persists indefinitely. Women currently of childbearing age made their educational choices under the assumption that labor productivity (and thus wage) growth would be lower, as it had been since the early 1970s. Their female children, when young women, will accurately predict future wages when they make their educational choices. Discuss how imperfect foresight may lead to different fertility choices between the two generations of young women.

6. **A.** How and why does the relationship between income and fertility change from the Malthusian to Post-Malthusian to Modern Growth regimes?

B. How and why does the relationship between technical change and educational investments change from the Malthusian to Post-Malthusian, to Modern Growth regimes?

7. Recall our version of the Willis model in section 9.2. Explain why the marginal cost of S in terms of C_p is constant when mother is in the labor market, but is increasing when she is a full-time housewife.

▶ PROBLEMS

1. Compare and contrast the roles of female labor force participation in explaining fertility in the relative income and Chicago models. What empirical results would allow one to distinguish between the Relative Income and Chicago theories about the causes and effects of the rise in women's wages? Keep the Macunovich criticisms of many empirical examinations of the Chicago theory in mind as you develop your answer.

2. Suppose

$$U_p = C_p^\gamma n^{1-\gamma}$$

A. Let family wealth be exogenous and equal to $W_p = wT$, where w is the wage and T is the time endowment. Suppose children cost π_n units of goods per child (i.e., child quality is exogenous) and that the price of goods is 1. Graph the parent's utility maximization problem and depict the solution. Graphically illustrate the comparative statics results for C_p and n of changes in w and π_n. Discuss these results in terms of income and substitution effects.

B. Now suppose income is endogenous and that "the" parent can earn w per each of his T units of available time he devotes to the labor market. That is, $W_p = wT$ is now potential wealth. Children are now assumed to require no goods inputs, but each requires τ units of the parent's time. State and graph the utility maximization problem. Graphically illustrate the comparative statics for n and C_p with respect to w and W_p. Discuss the answers in terms of income and substitution effects. Compare and contrast intuitively the effect of a change in π_n on n (from part A), with that of a change in w on n from B).

*3. (This problem is just a more analytic version of problem 9.2.) Suppose

$$U_p = C_p^\gamma n^{1-\gamma}$$

A. Let family wealth be exogenous and equal to $W_p = wT$ where w is the wage and T the endowment of time. Suppose children cost π_n units of goods per child (i.e., child quality is exogenous) and that the price of goods is 1. Set up the parent's utility maximization problem and solve for C_p and n. Compute the comparative statics results for C_p and n of changes in w and π_n. Discuss these results in terms of income and substitution effects.

B. Now suppose income is endogenous and that "the" parent can earn w per each of his T units of available time he devotes to the labor market. Potential wealth is $w_p = wT$. Children are now assumed to require no goods inputs, but each requires τ units of the parent's time. Again set up and solve the optimization problem. Compute the comparative statics for n and C_p with respect to w. Discuss the answers in terms of income and substitution effects. Is the effect of w on n the same as in the model of section 9.2?

*4. Consider the financial contributions by a noncohabiting father to a mother, intended for his child's benefit. The father knows that the utility function of the mother is

$$U_m = C_m^\gamma W_c^{1-\gamma}$$

and that her budget constraint is

$$W_m + T = C_m + B_m$$

and that the child's wealth is $W_c = B_m(1 + r)$, where T is the transfer from the father and B_m is the investment made by the mother in the child. The father's utility function is

$$U_f = C_f^\beta W_c^{1-\beta}$$

and his budget constraint is

$$W_f = C_f + T$$

A. How and why do the prices of transferring \$1 of wealth to the child differ between the mother and father? What are these prices?

B. Solve for the mother's investments in the child, the father's transfers, and child wealth.

C. Compute the comparative statics of these solutions with respect to mother's wealth W_m and father's wealth W_f.

D. How would the solutions in part B differ if the parents were married with the utility function $U_p = C_p^\beta W_c^{1-\beta}$?

REFERENCES

Abel, Andrew B. (2001). "The Effects of Investing Social Security Funds in the Stock Market When Fixed Costs Prevent Some Households from Holding Stocks," *American Economic Review* 91(1):128–148.

Acemoglu, Daron. (1998). "Why Do Technologies Complement Skills? Directed Technical Change and Wage Inequality," *Quarterly Journal of Economics* 113(4):1055–1090.

——— and Joshua Angrist. (2000). "How Large Are Human Capital Externalities? Evidence from Compulsory Schooling Laws." Mimeo.

——— and Jorn-Steffen Pischke. (1999). "The Structure of Wages and Investment in General Training," *Journal of Political Economy* 107(3):639–672.

Akerlof, George A., Janet L. Yellen, and Michael L. Katz. (1996). "An Analysis of Out-of-Wedlock Childbearing in the United States," *Quarterly Journal of Economics* 111(2):277–317.

———, Alan J. Auerbach, Laurence J. Kotlikoff, Kent A. Smetters, and Jan Wallister. (2001). "Simulating U.S. Tax Reform. *American Economic Review* (in press).

Altig, David and Steve J. Davis. (1989), "Government Debt, Redistributive Fiscal Policies, and the Interaction Between Borrowing Constraints and Intergenerational Altruism," *Journal of Monetary Economics*, July, pp. 3–29.

Altonji, Joseph G. and Rebecca Blank. (1999). "Race and Gender in the Labor Market," in Orley Ashenfelter and David Card, eds., *Handbook of Labor Economics*. Amsterdam: North Holland Publishers, vol. 3C.

———, Fumio Hayashi, and Laurence J. Kotlikoff. (1992). "Is the Family Altruistically Linked? Direct Tests Using Micro Data," *American Economic Review* 82 (December):117–198.

———, ———, and ———. (1997). "Parental Altruism and Inter Vivos Transfers: Theory and Evidence," *Journal of Political Economy* 105(6):1121–1166.

Anderson, Patricia M., Alan L. Gustman, and Thomas L. Steinmeier. (1999). "Trends in Male Labor Force Participation and Retirement: Some Evidence on the Role of Pensions and Social Security in the 1970s and 1980s," *Journal of Labor Economics* 17(4):757–783.

Andreoni, James. (1989). "Giving with Impure Altruism: Applications to Charity and Ricardian Equivalence," *Journal of Political Economy* 97(6):1447–1458.

Angrist, Joshua D. and Alan B. Krueger. (1991). "Does Compulsory Schooling Attendance Affect Schooling and Earnings?," *Quarterly Journal of Economics* 106:979–1014.

Arrow, Kenneth J. (1962), "The Economic Implications of Learning By Doing," *Review of Economic Studies* 29(June):153–173.

Ashenfelter, Orley and Alan Krueger. (1994). "Estimates of the Economic Returns to Schooling from a New Sample of Twins," *American Economic Review* 84:1157–1173.

——— and Cecilia Rouse. (1998). "Income, Schooling and Ability: Evidence from a New Sample of Identical Twins," *Quarterly Journal of Economics* 113(1):253–284.

Attanasio, Orazio P. and Martin Browning. (1995). "Consumption over the Life Cycle and over the Business Cycle," *American Economic Review* 85(5):1118–1137.

———— and Guglielmo Weber. (1995). "Is Consumption Growth Consistent with Intertemporal Optimization? Evidence from the Consumer Expenditure Survey," *Journal of Political Economy* 103(6):1121–1157.

Auerbach, Alan and William G. Gale. 2000. "Perspectives on the Budget Surplus." Working paper.

Auerbach, Alan J. and Laurence J. Kotlikoff. (1987). *Dynamic Fiscal Policy*. Cambridge: Cambridge University Press.

————. (1998). *Macroeconomics: An Integrated Approach*. 2d ed. Cambridge, Mass.: MIT Press.

Autor, David H., Lawrence F. Katz, and Alan B. Krueger. (1998). "Computing Inequality: How Have Computers Changed the Labor Market?," *Quarterly Journal of Economics* 113(4): 1169–1213.

Barsky, Robert, N. Gregory Mankiw, and Stephen P. Zeldes. (1986). "Ricardian Consumers With Keynesian Propensities," *American Economic Review* 76(4):676–691.

Barro, Robert. (1974), "Are Government Bonds Net Wealth?," *Journal of Political Economy* 82:1095–1117.

————. (1997). *Determinants of Economic Growth: A Cross-Country Empirical Study*. Cambridge, MA: MIT Press.

———— and Xavier Sali-i-Martin. (1992). "Convergence," *Journal of Political Economy* 100(2): 223–251.

————. (1995). *Economic Growth*. New York: McGraw-Hill.

Basu, Susanto and David N. Weil. (1998). "Appropriate Technology and Growth," *Quarterly Journal of Economics* 113(4):1025–1054.

Becker, Gary S. (1960). "An Economic Analysis of Fertility," in *Demographic and Economic Change in Developed Countries*, Universities-National Bureau Conference Series No. 11. Princeton, N.J.: Princeton University Press, pp. 209–231.

————. (1965). "A Theory of the Allocation of Time," *Economic Journal* 75(299):493–517.

————. (1973). "A Theory of Marriage: Part I," *Journal of Political Economy* 81(4):813–846.

————. (1974a). "A Theory of Marriage: Part II," *Journal of Political Economy* 82 (2, part 2): S11–S26.

————. (1974b), "A Theory of Social Interactions," *Journal of Political Economy* 82:1063–1093.

————. (1975). *Human Capital*. 2d ed. New York: National Bureau of Economic Research.

————. (1981). *A Treatise on the Family*. Cambridge, Mass.: Harvard University Press.

———— and Robert J. Barro. (1988). "A Reformulation of the Economic Theory of Fertility," *Quarterly Journal of Economics* 103(1):1–25.

————, Elisabeth M. Landes, and Robert T. Michael. (1977). "An Economic Analysis of Marital Instability," *Journal of Political Economy* 85(6):1153–1189.

———— and Casey B. Mulligan. (1997). "The Endogenous Determination of Time Preference," *Quarterly Journal of Economics* 112:729–758.

————, Kevin M. Murphy, and Robert F. Tamura. (1990). "Human Capital, Fertility and Economic Growth," *Journal of Political Economy* 98(5):S12–S37.

———— and Nigel Tomes. (1986). " Human Capital and the Rise and Fall of Families," *Journal of Labor Economics* 4(3):S1–S39.

Behrman, Jere R. (1997). "Intrahousehold Distribution and the Family," in Mark R. Rosenzweig and Oded Stark, eds., *Handbook of Population and Family Economics*. Amsterdam: Elsevier Science, vol. 1A, pp. 125–182.

————, Robert A. Pollack, and Paul Taubman. (1982). "Parental Preferences and Provision for Progeny," *Journal of Political Economy* 90(1):52–73.

———— ———— ————. (1995). *From Parent to Child: Intrahousehold Allocations and Intergenerational Relations in the United States*. Chicago: University of Chicago Press.

————, Mark R. Rosenzweig, and Paul Taubman. (1994). "Endowments and the Allocation of Schooling in the Family and in the Marriage Market: The Twins Experiment," *Journal of Political Economy* 102(6):1131–1174.

Benabou, Roland. (1996). "Heterogeneity, Stratification, and Growth: Macroeconomic Implications of Community Structure and Finance," *American Economic Review* 86(3):584–609.

Ben-Porath, Yoram. (1967). "The Production of Human Capital and the Life Cycle of Earnings," *Journal of Political Economy* 75(August):352–365.

Bernheim, B. Douglas. (1991). "How Strong Are Bequest Motives: Evidence Based on Estimates of the Demand for Life Insurance," *Journal of Political Economy* 99:899–927.

———— and Sergei Severinov. (2000). "Bequests as Signals: An Explanation for the Equal Division Puzzle." NBER Working Paper no. 7791.

————, Andrei Shleifer, and Lawrence H. Summers. (1985). "The Strategic Bequest Motive." *Journal of Political Economy* 93:1045–1076.

Bils, Mark and Peter J. Klenow. (2000). "Does Schooling Cause Growth?," *American Economic Review* 90(5):1160–1183.

Blau, Francine D., Marianne A. Ferber, and Anne E. Winkler. (1998). *The Economics of Women, Men, and Work*. 3d ed. Upper Saddle River, NJ: Prentice-Hall, Inc.

Blau, Francine D. and Lawrence M. Kahn. (1997). "Swimming Upstream: Trends in the Gender Wage Differential in the 1980s," *Journal of Labor Economics* 15(1):1–42.

Boadway, Robin W. and David E. Wildasin. (1984). *Public Sector Economics*. 2d ed. Boston: Little, Brown and Company.

Borjas, George J. (1995). "Ethnicity, Neighborhoods, and Human-Capital Externalities," *American Economic Review* 85(June):365–390.

Boskin, Michael J. (1978). "Taxation, Saving, and the Rate of Interest," *Journal of Political Economy* 86(1):3–27.

Browning, Edgar K. and William R. Johnson. (1984). "The Trade-off Between Equality and Efficiency," *Journal of Political Economy* 92(2):175–203.

Browning, Martin, Francois Bourguignon, Pierre-Andre Chiappori, and Valerie Lechene. (1994). "Incomes and Outcomes: A Structural Model of Intrahousehold Allocation," *Journal of Political Economy* 102(6):1067–1096.

————, Angus S. Deaton, and Margaret Irish. (1985). "A Profitable Approach to Labor Supply and Commodity Demands Over the Life-Cycle," *Econometrica* 53:503–544.

————, Lars Peter Hansen, and James J. Heckman. (1999). "Micro Data and General Equilibrium Models," in John Taylor and Michael Woodford, eds., *Handbook of Macroeconomics*. Amsterdam: North Holland Publishers, vol. 1A, part 2.

Brady, Dorothy S. (1972). "Consumption and the Style of Life," in Lance E. Davis, Richard A. Easterlin, and William N. Parker, eds., *American Economic Growth: An Economist's History of the United States*, New York: Harper and Row, pp. 61–89.

Bryant, Keith W. (1990). *The Economic Organization of the Household*. Cambridge: Cambridge University Press.

Bullard, James and Steven Russell. (1999). "An Empirically Plausible Model of Low Real Interest Rates and Unbacked Government Debt," *Journal of Monetary Economics* 44(3):477–508.

Cameron, S. and James J. Heckman. (1998). "*Should College Education Be Further Subsidized to Reduce Rising Wage Inequality?*," in Marvin Kosters, ed., *Financing College Education: Government Policies and Social Priorities*. Washington: American Enterprise Institute Press.

Card, David E. (1994). "Intertemporal Labor Supply: An Assessment," in Sims, ed. Advances in Econometrics, Sixth World Congress. New York: Cambridge University Press, pp. 49–78.

————. (1999). "The Causal Effect of Education on Earnings," in Orley Ashenfelter and David Card, eds., *Handbook of Labor Economics*. Amsterdam North Holland, vol. 3A, Ch. 30.

———— and ————. (1996). "School Resources and Student Outcomes: An Overview of the Literature and New Evidence from North and South Carolina," *Journal of Economic Perspectives* 10(4):31–50.

Carroll, Christopher D. (1994). "How Does Future Income Affect Current Consumption?," *Quarterly Journal of Economics* 109(1):111–148.

———. (1997a). "Death to the Log-Linearized Consumption Euler Equation! (And Very Poor Health to the Second Order Approximation)." National Bureau of Economic Research Working Paper 6298.

———. (1997b). "Buffer-Stock Saving and the Life Cycle Permanent Income Hypothesis," *Quarterly Journal of Economics* 112(1):1–56.

———. (1999). "Precautionary Saving and the Marginal Propensity to Consume Out of Permanent Income." Manuscript, Johns Hopkins University.

———. (2000). "Why Do the Rich Save So Much?" In Joel B. Slemrod, ed., Does Atlas Shrug?: *The Economic Consequences of Taxing the Rich*. Cambridge, Mass.: Russell Sage and Harvard University Press, pp. 465–484.

———, Jody R. Overland, and David N. Weil. (2000). "Saving and Growth with Habit Formation," *American Economic Review* 90(3):341–355.

——— and Andrew A. Samwick. (1997). "The Nature of Precautionary Wealth," *Journal of Monetary Economics* 40(1):41–71.

——— and ———. (1998). "How Important Is Precautionary Saving?," *Review of Economics and Statistics* 80(3):410–419.

——— and Lawrence H. Summers. (1991). "Consumption Growth Parallels Income Growth: Some New Evidence," in B. Douglas Bernheim and John B. Shoven, eds., *National Savings and Economic Performance*. Chicago and London: University of Chicago Press, pp. 305–347.

——— and David N. Weil. (1994). "Saving and Growth: A Reinterpretation," *Carnegie-Rochester Conference Series on Public Policy* 40:133–192.

Carter, Susan B. (1986). "Comment" on Goldin, in Stanley L. Engerman and Robert E. Gallman, eds., *Long-Term Factors in American Economic Growth*. Chicago: University of Chicago Press, pp. 594–599.

Case, Anne and Angus Deaton. (1999). "School Inputs and Educational Outcomes in South Africa," *Quarterly Journal of Economics* 114(3):1047–1084.

Cebeddu, Luis and José-Víctor Ríos Rull. (1997). "Marital Risk and Capital Accumulation," Working Paper.

Chakrabarti, Subir, William A. Lord, and Peter Rangazas. (1993). "Human Capital Investment with Uncertain Two-Sided Altruism," *American Economic Review* 83(4):994–1002.

Cigno, Alessandro. (1991). *Economics of the Family*. Oxford: Clarendon Press.

Cocco, Joao, Francisco J. Gomes, and Pascal J. Maenhout. (1999). "Consumption and Portfolio Choice Over the Life Cycle." Manuscript, Harvard University, Cambridge, Mass.

Costa, Dora L. (1995). "Pensions and Retirement: Evidence from Union Army Veterans," *Quarterly Journal of Economics* 110(2):297–320.

———. (1998). *The Evolution of Retirement*. Chicago: University of Chicago Press.

———. (2000). "The Wage and the Length of the Work Day: From the 1890s to 1991," *Journal of Labor Economics* 18(1):156–181.

Cox, Donald. (1987). "Motives for Private Income Transfers," *Journal of Political Economy* 95(June):508–546.

———. (1990). "Intergenerational Transfers and Liquidity Constraints," *Quarterly Journal of Economics* 105(February):187–217.

———. (1996). "Comment on James Davies', "Explaining Intergenerational Transfers," in Paul Menchik, ed., *Household and Family Economics*. Boston/Dordrecht/London: Kluwer Academic Publishers, pp. 83–90.

———, Bruce Hansen, and Emmanuel Jimenez. (1996). "How Responsive Are Private Transfers to Income: Evidence from a Laissez-Faire Economy." Mimeo.

——— and George Jakubson. (1995). "The Connection Between Public Transfers and Private Interfamily Transfers," *Journal of Public Economics* 55(1):129–167.

——— and Fredric Raines. (1985). "Interfamily Transfers and Income Redistribution," in Martin David and Timothy Smmeding, eds., *Horizontal Equity, Uncertainty, and Economic Well Being*. Chicago: University of Chicago Press.

Craig, Lee A. (1993). *To Sow One Acre More*. Baltimore, Md.: Johns Hopkins University Press.

Currie, Janet and Duncan Thomas. (1999). "Early Test Scores, Socioeconomic Status and Future Outcomes." National Bureau of Economic Research Working Paper 6943.

Dale, Stacey Berg and Alan B. Krueger. (1998). "Estimating the Payoff to Attending a More Selective College: An Appplication of Selection on Observables and Unobservables." Princeton University Industrial Relations Sector Working Paper 409.

Datar, Ashlesha and Peter Rangazas. (1999). "Long-run Effects of Initial Conditions Despite Diminishing Returns." Working Paper, Indiana University-Purdue University at Indianapolis.

Davies, James B. (1981). "Uncertain Lifetime, Consumption, and Dissaving in Retirement," *Journal of Political Economy* 89:561–577.

———. (1982). "The Relative Impact of Inheritance and Other Factors on Economic Inequality," *Quarterly Journal of Economics* 47(August):471–498.

——— (1996). "Explaining Intergenerational Transfers," in Paul Menchik, ed., *Household and Family Economics*. Boston/Dordrecht/London: Kluwer Academic Publishers, pp. 47–82.

——— and Frances St. Hilaire. (1987). "Reforming Capital Income Taxation in Canada." Economic Council of Canada.

——— and John Whalley. (1991). "Taxes and Capital Formation: How Important Is Human Capital?," in B. Douglas Bernheim and John B. Shoven, eds., *National Savings and Economic Performance*. Chicago and London: University of Chicago Press, pp. 163–200.

Deaton, Angus S. (1991). "Saving and Liquidity Constraints," *Econometrica* 59:1221–1248.

———. (1992). *Understanding Consumption*. Oxford: Clarendon Press.

Diamond, Peter A. (1965). "National Debt in a Neoclassical Growth Model," *American Economic Review* 55:1126–1150.

Donohue, John and Steven Levitt. (2000), "The Impact of Legalized Abortion on Crime." National Bureau of Economic Research Working Paper 8004.

Drazen, Alan. (1978). "Government Debt, Human Capital, and Bequests in a Life-Cycle Model," *Journal of Political Economy* 86(June):505–516.

Dynan, Karen E. (2000). "Habit Formation in Consumer Preferences: Evidence from Panel Data," *American Economic Review* 90(3):391–406.

———, Jonathon S. Skinner, and Stephen P. Zeldes. (1996). "Do the Rich Save More?" Manuscript, Board of Governors of the Federal Reserve System.

———, ———, and ———. (2000). "Do The Rich Save More?" Manuscript, Board of Governors of the Federal Reserve System.

Easterlin, Richard A. (1987). *Birth and Fortune*. 2d ed. New York: Basic Books.

———. (1996). "Fertility and Fertility Research: Where Are They Going? A Comment on the Macunovich Paper," in Paul L. Menchik, ed., *Household and Family Economics*. Boston/Dordrecht/London: Kluwer Academic Publishers, pp. 151–157.

———. (2000). "The Worldwide Standard of Living Since 1800," *Journal of Economic Perspectives* 14(1):7–26.

Edlund, Lena. (1998). "Custodial Rights and the Rise in Out-of-Wedlock Fertility." Mimeo.

Ellwood, David T. (2000). "Anti-Poverty Policy for Families in the Next Century: From Welfare to Work—and Worries," *Journal of Economic Perspectives* 14(1):187–198.

——— and Mary Jo Bane. (1985). "The Impact of AFDC on Family Structure and Living Arrangements," in Ronald Ehrenberg, ed., *Research in Labor Economics*. Amsterdam: JAI Press, pp. 137–207.

Engen, Eric M. (1992). "Precautionary Saving and the Structure of Taxation." Mimeo, April.

——— and William G. Gale. (1997). "Debt, Taxes, and the Effects of of 401(k) Plans on Household Wealth Accumulation." Mimeo, October.

———— and ————. (2000). "The Effects of 401(k) Plans on Household Wealth." Mimeo.

————, ————, and John Karl Scholz. (1996). "The Illusory Effects of Saving Incentives on Saving," *Journal of Economic Perspectives* 10(Fall):113–138.

Feldstein, Martin S. (1974). "Social Security, Induced Retirement, and Aggregate Capital Accumulation," *Journal of Political Economy* 82(5):905–926.

————. (1978). "The Welfare Cost of Capital Income Taxation," *Journal of Political Economy* 86(2):S29–S52.

————. (1982). "Social Security and Private Saving: Reply," *Journal of Political Economy* 90(3):630–642.

————. (1988). "The Effects of Fiscal Policies When Incomes Are Uncertain: A Contradiction to Ricardian Equivalence," *American Economic Review* 78(1):14–23.

————. (1999). "Tax Avoidance and the Deadweight Loss of the Income Tax," *Review of Economics and Statistics* 81(4):674–680.

Filer, Randall. (1996). *The Economics of Work and Pay.* 6th ed. New York: Harper Collins.

Finn, Jeremy D. and Charles M. Achilles. (1990). "Answers and Questions About Class Size: A Statewide Experiment," *American Educational Research Journal* 27(Fall):557–577.

Foster, Andrew D. and Mark R. Rosenzweig. (1996). "Technical Change and Human Capital Returns and Investments: Evidence from the Green Revolution," *American Economic Review* 86(4):931–953.

Friedberg, Leora. (1999). "The Labor Supply Effects of the Social Security Earnings Test." National Bureau of Economic Research Working Paper 7200.

Furstenberg, Frank F., Saul D. Hoffman, and Laura Shrestha. (1995). "The Effect of Divorce on Intergenerational Transfers: New Evidence," *Demography* 32(3):319–333.

Gale, William G. and John Karl Scholz. (1994). "Intergenerational Transfers and the Accumulation of Wealth," *Journal of Economic Perspectives* 8(Fall):145–160.

Gale, William G. and Joel B. Slemrod. (2000). "Rethinking the Estate and Gift Tax: Overview." Mimeo, Brookings Institute and the University of Michigan, Ann Arbor. Forthcoming in William G. Gale, James R. Hines, and Joel B. Slemrod, eds., *Rethinking Estate and Gift Taxation.* Brookings Institute.

Galor, Oded and Omer Moav. (2000). "Ability-Biased Technological Transition, Wage Inequality, and Economic Growth," *Quarterly Journal of Economics* 115(2):469–498.

Galor, Oded and David M. Weil. (1996). "The Gender Gap, Fertility, and Growth," *American Economic Review* 86(3):374–387.

———— and ————. (1999). "From Malthusian Stagnation to Modern Growth," *American Economic Review* 89(2):150–154.

———— and ————. (2000). "Population, Technology and Growth: From Malthusian Stagnation to the Demographic Transition and Beyond," *American Economic Review* 90(4):806–828.

Gaviria, Alejandro. (1999). "Intergenerational Mobility, Siblings' Inequality and Borrowing Constraints." University of California-San Diego Discussion Paper 98–13.

Gloom, Gerhard and B. Ravikumar. (1992). "Public versus Private Investment in Human Capital: Endogenous Growth and Income Inequality," *Journal of Political Economy* 100(4):818–834.

Gokhale, Jagadeesh and Laurence J. Kotlikoff. (1999). "Social Security's Treatment of Postwar Americans: How Bad Can It Get?" Manuscript.

———— and ————. (2000). "Medicare, Social Security, and the Calm Before the Generational Storm." New York: Third Millenium.

————, ————, and John Sabelhaus. (1996). "Understanding the Postwar Decline In Saving: A Cohort Analysis," *Brookings Papers on Economic Activity* 1:315–390.

————, ————, James Sefton, and Martin Weale. (1999). "Simulating the Transmission of Wealth Inequality via Bequests." Working paper.

————, Benjamin Page, Joan Potter, and John Sturrock. (2000). "Generational Accounts for the United States: An Update," *American Economic Review* 90(2):293–296.

Goldin, Claudia. (1986). "The Female Labor Force and American Economic Growth, 1890–1980," in Stanley L. Engerman and Robert E. Gallman, eds., *Long-Term Factors in American Economic Growth*. Chicago: University of Chicago Press, pp. 557–604.

Goldin, Claudia. (1990). *Understanding the Gender Gap*. New York: Oxford University Press.

———— and Lawrence F. Katz. (1997). "Why the U.S. Led in Education: Lessons from Secondary School Expansion." National Bureau of Economic Research Working Paper 6144.

Gordon, Robert J. (2000). "Does the New Economy Measure up to the Great Inventions of the Past?," *Journal of Economic Perspectives* 14(4):49–74.

Gourinchas, Pierre-Olilver, and Jonathon Parker. (1999). "Consumption Over the Life Cycle." Manuscript, Princeton University, Cambridge, Mass.

Gramm, William L. (1974). "The Demand for the Wife's Nonmarket Time," *Southern Economic Journal* 41:124–133.

Griliches, Zvi. (1988). "Productivity Puzzles and R&D: Another Nonexplanation," *Journal of Economic Perspectives* 2(4):9–22.

————. (1994). "Productivity, R&D, and the Data Constraint," *American Economic Review* 84(1):1–23.

Gronau, Reuben. (1977). "Leisure, Home Production, and Work—The Theory of the Allocation of Time Revisited," *Journal of Political Economy* 85(6):1099–1123.

Gross, David B. and Souleles, Nicholas. (2000). "Consumer Response to Credit Supply: Evidence from Credit Card Data." Manuscript, University of Pennsylvania, Philadelphia.

Gustman, Alan L., Olivia S. Mitchell, Andrew A. Samwick, and Thomas L. Steinmeir. (1999). "Pension and Social Security Wealth In the Health and Retirement Study," in James Smith and Robert Willis, eds., *Wealth, Work and Health, Innovations in Measurement in the Social Sciences*. Ann Arbor: University of Michigan Press, pp. 150–208.

Hall, Robert E. and Frederic S. Mishkin. (1982). "The Sensitivity of Consumption to Transitory Income: Estimates from Panel Data on Households," *Econometrica* 50:461–481.

Hands, D. Wade. (1991). *Introductory Mathematical Economics*. Lexington, MA: D.C. Heath and Company.

Hanushek, Eric A. (1986). "The Economics of Schooling: Production and Efficiency in Public Schools," *Journal of Economic Literature* 24:1141–1177.

————. (1992). "The Trade-off Between Child Quantity and Quality," *Journal of Political Economy* 100(1):84–117.

————. (1996). "Measuring Investment in Education," *Journal of Economic Perspectives* 10(Fall):9–30.

Heckman, James J. (1976). "A Life-Cycle Model of Earnings, Learning, and Consumption," *Journal of Political Economy* 84(4):S11–S44.

———— and Peter Klenow. (1997). "Human Capital Policy." Mimeo.

————, John Lochner, and Christopher Taber. (1998). "Explaining Rising Wage Inequality: Explorations with a Dynamic General Equilibrium Model of Labor Earnings with Heterogeneous Agents," *Review of Economic Dynamics* 1(1):1–29.

———— and James R. Walker. (1990). "The Relationship Between Wages and Income and the Timing and Spacing of Births: Evidence from Swedish Longitudinal Data," *Econometrica* 58(6):1411–1442.

Herrnstein, Richard J. and Charles Murray. (1994). *The Bell Curve: Intelligence and Class Structure in American Life*. New York: The Free Press.

Hirshleifer, Jack. (1977). "Shakespeare vs. Becker on Altruism: The Importance of Having the Last Word," *Journal of Economic Literature* 15(2):500–502.

Hoffman, Saul and Greg J. Duncan. (1995), "The Effect of Incomes, Wages, and AFDC Benefits on Marital Disruption," *Journal of Human Resources* 30(1):19–41.

Hoffman, Saul D. and E. Michael Foster. (2000). "AFDC Benefits and Non-Marital Births to Young Women," *Journal of Human Resources* 35(2):376–391.

Holtz-Eakin, Douglas, David Joulfaian, and Harvey S. Rosen. (1992). "The Carnegie Conjecture: Some Empirical Evidence," *Quarterly Journal of Economics* 108:413–435.

Hotz, Joseph V., Jacob Alex Klerman, and Robert J. Willis. (1997). "The Economics of Fertility in Developed Countries," in Mark R. Rosenzweig and Oded Stark, eds., *Handbook of Population and Family Economics*. Amsterdam: Elsevier Science B.V., vol. 1, pp. 275–342.

———— and Robert A. Miller. (1988). "An Empirical Analysis of Life Cycle Fertility and Female Labor Supply," *Econometrica* 56(January):91–118.

Hubbard, R. Glenn and Jonathan S. Skinner. (1996). "Assessing the Effectiveness of Saving Incentives," *Journal of Economic Perspectives* 10(4):73–90.

————, ————, and Stephen P. Zeldes. (1995). "Precautionary Saving and Social Insurance," *Journal of Political Economy* 103:360–399.

Hurd, Michael D. (1989). "Mortality Risk and Bequests," Econometrica 57(July):779–814.

————. (1997). "The Economics of Individual Aging," in Mark R. Rosenzweig and Oded Stark, eds., *Handbook of Population and Family Economics*, Amsterdam: Elsevier Science B.V, Vol. 1B, pp. 891–966.

————. (1999). "Mortality Risk and Consumption by Couples." National Bureau of Economic Research Working Paper 7048.

Ihori, Toshihiro. (1996). *Public Finance In an Overlapping Generations Economy*. New York: St. Martin's Press.

Jacobsen, Joyce P. (1998). *The Economics of Gender*. 2d ed. Malden, MA: Blackwell Publishers.

Johnson, George E. (1997). "Changes in Earnings Inequality: The Role of Demand Shifts," *Journal of Economic Perspectives* 11(2):41–54.

Johnson, William and Jonathon Skinner. (1986). "Labor Supply and Marital Separation," *American Economic Review* 76(3):455–469.

Jones, Charles. (1995). "R&D-Based Models of Economic Growth," *Journal of Political Economy* 103(August):759–784.

————. (1998). *Introduction to Economic Growth*. New York: W.W. Norton and Company.

————. (2000). "Sources of U.S. Growth in a World of Ideas." Working paper.

———— and John C. Williams. (1998). "Measuring the Social Return to R&D," *Quarterly Journal of Economics* 113(4):1119–1136.

Jorgenson, Dale W. and Kevin Stiroh. (2000). "Raising the Speed Limit: U.S. Economic Growth in the Information Age." Mimeo.

———— and Kun-Young Yun. (1991). "The Excess Burden of Taxation in the United States," *Journal of Accounting, Auditing and Finance* 6(4):487–508.

Juhn, Chinhui and Kevin M. Murphy. (1997). "Wage Inequality and Family Labor Supply," *Journal of Labor Economics* 15(1, part 1):72–97.

Juster F. Thomas, Joseph Lupton, James P. Smith, and Frank Stafford. (1999). "Savings and Wealth; Then and Now." Working paper, October.

———— and Frank P. Stafford. (1991). "The Allocation of Time: Empirical Findings, Behavioral Models, and Problems of Measurement," *Journal of Economic Literature* 29(2):471–522.

Kane, Thomas J. and Cecilia Elena Rouse. (1995). "Labor Market Returns to Two- and Four-Year College," *American Economic Review* 85(3):600–614.

Katz, Lawrence F. and David H. Autor. (1998). "Changes in Wage Structure and Earnings Inequality," in Orley Ashenfelter and David Card, eds., *Handbook of Labor Economics*. Amsterdam: North Holland, vol. 3, pp. 1463–1555.

———— and Kevin M. Murphy. (1992), "Changes in Relative Wages, 1963–1987: Supply and Demand Factors," *Quarterly Journal of Economics* 107:35–78.

King, Robert G. and Sergio T. Rebelo. (1993). "Transitional Dynamics and Economic Growth in the Neoclassical Model," *American Economic Review* 83(4):908–931.

Klenow, Peter J. and Andres Rodriguez-Clare. (1997). "The Neoclassical Revival in Growth Economics: Has It Gone Too Far." *NBER Macroeconomics Annual*, pp. 73–102.

Klepinger, Daniel, Shelley Lundberg, and Robert Plotnick. (1999). "How Does Adolescent Fertility Affect the Human Capital and Wages of Young Women?," *Journal of Human Resources* 34(3):421–448.

Kotlikoff, Laurence J. (1988). "Intergenerational Transfers and Savings," *Journal of Economic Perspectives* 2(2):41–58.

———. (1992). *Generational Accounting*. New York: Free Press.

——— and Avia Spivak. (1981). "The Family as an Incomplete Annuities Market," *Journal of Political Economy* 89:372–391.

——— and Lawrence H. Summers. (1981). "The Role of Intergenerational Transfers in Aggregate Capital Accumulation," *Journal of Political Economy* 89(4):706–732.

Kremer, Michael. (1993). "Population Growth and Technical Change: One Million B.C. to 1990," *Quarterly Journal of Economics* 108(3):681–716.

Krueger, Alan B. (1999). "Experimental Estimates of Education Production Functions," *Quarterly Journal of Economics* 114(2):497–532.

Laitner, John and F. Thomas Juster. (1996). "New Evidence on Altruism: A Study of TIAA-CREF Retirees," *American Economic Review* 86:893–908.

Lam, David. (1988). "Marriage Markets and Assortative Mating with Household Public Goods: Theoretical Results and Empirical Implications," *Journal of Human Resources* 23:462–487.

———. (1997). "Demographic Variables and Income Inequality," in Mark R. Rosenberg and Oded Stark, eds., *Handbook of Population and Family Economics*. Amsterdam: Elsevier Science, vol. 1A, pp. 1015–1059.

——— and Suzanne Duryea. (1999). "Effects of Schooling on Fertility, Labor Supply, and Investments in Children, with Evidence from Brazil," *Journal of Human Resources* 34(1):160–192.

Lawrance, Emily C. (1991). "Poverty and the Rate of Time Preference: Evidence from Panel Data," *Journal of Political Economy* 99(1):54–77.

Lazear, Edward P. and Robert T. Michael. (1988). *Allocation of Income Within the Household*. Chicago: University of Chicago Press.

Lee, Ronald D. and John B. Casterline. (1996). "Introduction," in John B. Casterline, Ronald D. Lee, and Karen A. Foote, eds., *Fertility in the United States*. Supplement to *Population and Development Review* 22:1–15.

Lord, William. (1987). "Welfare Effects of Capital Income Taxation Under Variable and Fixed Labor Supply," *Southern Economic Journal* 54(July):48–54.

———. (1989). "The Transition from Payroll to Consumption Receipts with Endogenous Human Capital," *Journal of Public Economics* 67(1):53–74.

———. (1992). "Saving, Wealth and Exchange Bequest Motives," *Canadian Journal of Economics* 25:743–753.

——— and Peter Rangazas. (1991). "Savings and Wealth in Models with Altruistic Bequests," *American Economic Review* 81(1):289–296.

——— and ———. (1992). "Tax Reform in Models With Altruistic Bequests," *Public Finance* 1:66–81.

——— and ———. (1993). "Altruism, Deficit Policies, and the Wealth of Future Generations," *Economic Inquiry* 31:609–630.

——— and ———. (1995). "Uncertainty, Altruism, and Savings: Precautionary Savings Meets the Samaritan's Dilemma," *Public Finance* 3:405–419.

——— and ———. (1998). "Taxation and Capital Accumulation in a General Equilibrium Model with Risky Human Capital," *Journal of Macroeconomics* 20(3):509–531.

Lucas, Robert E., Jr. (1988). "On the Mechanics of Economic Development," *Journal of Monetary Economics* 22(July):3–42.

———. (2000). "Some Macroeconomics for the 21st Century," *Journal of Economic Perspectives* 14(1):159–168.

Lundberg, Shelly and Robert A. Pollak. (1996). "Bargaining and Distribution in Marriage," *Journal of Economic Perspectives* 10(4):139–158.

Lusardi, Annamaria. (1997). "Precautionary Saving and Subjective Earning Variance," *Economics Letters* 57:319–326.

Macunovich, Diane J. (1996). "A Review of Recent Developments in the Economics Of Fertility," in Paul Menchik, ed., *Household and Family Economics*. Boston/Dordrecht/London: Kluwer Academic Press, pp. 91–137.

Mankiw, N. Gregory. (1997). *Macroeconomics*. 3d ed., New York: Worth Publishers.

————, David Romer, and David A. Weil. (1992). "A Contribution to the Empirics of Economic Growth," *Quarterly Journal of Economics* 107(2):407–438.

Marcotte, Dave E. (2000). "Continuing Education, Job Training, and the Growth of Earnings Inequality," *Industrial and Labor Relations Review* 53(4):602–623.

McGarry, Kathleen. (1999). "Inter Vivos Transfers and Intended Bequests." *Journal of Public Economics* 73(3):321–351.

————. (2000). "Testing Parental Altruism: Implications of a Dynamic Model," National Bureau of Economic Research Working Paper 7593, March.

———— and Robert F. Schoeni. (1995). "Transfer Behavior Within the Family: Results From the Asset and Health Dynamics Survey." National Bureau of Economic Research Working Paper 5099.

Mehra, Rajnish and Edward C. Prescott. (1985). "The Equity Premium: A Puzzle," *Journal of Monetary Economics* 15(March):145–161.

Menchik, Paul L. (1988). "Unequal Estate Division: Is it Altruism, Reverse Bequests, or Simply Noise?," in Denis Kessler and Andre Masson, eds., *Modelling the Accumulation and Distribution of Wealth*. New York: Oxford University Press, pp. 105–116.

———— and Martin David. (1983). "Income Distribution, Lifetime Savings, and Bequests," *American Economic Review* 83(4):672–690.

Meyer, Bruce D. and Dan T. Rosenbaum. (2000). "Making Single Mothers Work: Recent Tax and Welfare Policy and Its Effects," National Bureau of Economic Research Working Paper 7491.

Milligan, Kevin. (2000). "Subsidizing the Stork: New Evidence on Tax Incentives and Fertility." Working paper.

Mincer, Jacob. (1974). *Schooling Experience and Earnings*. New York: Columbia University Press.

Modigliani, Franco. (1988). "The Role of Intergenerational Transfers and Life-Cycle Saving in the Accumulation of Wealth," *Journal of Economic Perspectives* 2(2):15–40.

Moffitt, Robert. (1984). "The Estimation of Fertility Equations on Panel Data," *Journal of Human Resources* 19(1):22–34.

————. (1992). "Incentive Effects of the U.S. Welfare System," *Journal of Economic Literature* 30(1):1–61.

————. (1994). "Welfare Effects on Female Headship with Area Effects," *Journal of Human Resources* 29(2):621–636.

Mokyr, Joel. (1997). "Why Was There More Work for Mother? Knowledge and Household Behavior, 1870–1945." Mimeo.

Mulligan, Casey B. (1997). *Parental Priorities and Economic Inequality*. Chicago: University of Chicago Press.

Murphy, Kevin M. and Finis Welch. (1998). "Perspectives on the Social Security Crisis and Proposed Solutions," *American Economic Review* 88(2):142–150.

Murray, Sheila E, William N. Evans, and Robert M. Schwab. (1998). "Education-Finance Reform and the Distribution of Education Resources," *American Economic Review* 88(4):789–812.

Page, Ben. (1998). "Social Security and Private Saving: A Review of the Empirical Evidence." Congressional Budget Office memorandum.

Pencavel, John. (1997). "Changes in Male Work Behavior and Wages." Mimeo.

————. (1998). "The Market Work Behavior and Wages of Women, 1975–94," *Journal of Human Resources* 33(4):771–804.

Poterba, James M. (2000). "Stock Market Wealth and Consumption," *Journal of Economic Perspectives* 14(2):99–118.

————. (2001). "Estate and Gift Taxes and Incentives for Inter Vivos Giving in the United States," *Journal of Public Economics* (in press).

———— and Lawrence Summers. (1987). "Finite Lifetimes and the Effects of Budget Deficits on National Savings," *Journal of Monetary Economics* 20(September):369–392.

————, Steven F. Venti, and David A. Wise. (1996). "How Retirement Saving Programs Increase Saving," *Journal of Economic Perspectives* 10(4):91–112.

Psacharopoulos, George. (1985). "Returns to Education: A Further Longitudinal Update and Implications," *Journal of Human Resources* 20:583–604.

————. (1994). "Returns to Investment in Education: A Global Update," *World Development* 22:1325–1343.

Rangazas, Peter. (1991). "Redistribution and Capital Formation," *American Economic Review* 81(3):674–682.

————. (2000a). "The Human Capital Production Function." Mimeo.

————. (2000b). "Schooling and Economic Growth: A King-Rebelo Experiment with Human Capital," *Journal of Monetary Economics* 46:397–416.

Ren, Liqian and Peter Rangazas. (2000). "Retirement Saving and Development Traps." Mimeo.

Rindfuss, Ronald R. and Karin L. Brewster. (1996). "Childrearing and Fertility," in John B. Casterline, Ronald D. Lee, and Karen A. Foote, eds., *Fertility in the United States.* Supplement to *Population and Development Review* 22:258–289.

Romer, David. (1996). *Advanced Macroeconomics.* New York: McGraw-Hill.

Romer, Paul. (1990). "Endogenous Technical Change," *Journal of Political Economy* 98(October):S71–S102.

Rosen, Harvey S. (1995). Public Finance. 4th ed. Chicago: Richard D. Irwin.

Rosenzweig, Mark R. (1999). "Welfare, Marital Prospects, and Nonmarital Childbearing," *Journal of Political Economy* 107(6), part 2:S3–S32.

Samuelson, Paul A. (1958). "An Exact Consumption-Loan Model of Interest with or without the Social Contrivance of Money," *Journal of Political Economy,* 66:467–482.

Samwick, Andrew. (1998). "Discount Rate Heterogeneity and Social Security Reform," *Journal of Development Economics* 57(October):117–146.

Sandmo, Agnar. (1970). "The Effect of Uncertainty on Savings Decisions," *Review of Economic Studies* 37(July):353–360.

Schultz, T. Paul. (1994). "Marital Status and Fertility in the United States: Welfare and Labor Market Effects," *Journal of Human Resources* 29(2):637–669.

Seater, John J. (1993). "Ricardian Equivalence," *Journal of Economic Literature.* 31(March):142–190.

Seidman, Laurence. (1983). "Taxes in a Life Cycle Growth Model with Bequests and Inheritances," *American Economic Review* 93:437–441.

————. (1990). "Is a Consumption Tax Equivalent to a Wage Tax?" *Public Finance Quarterly* 18(1):65–76.

————. (1999). *Funding Social Security.* Cambridge: Cambridge University Press.

———— and Kenneth A. Lewis. (1999). "The Consumption Tax and the Saving Elasticity," *National Tax Journal* 52(1):67–78.

Skinner, Jonathan. (1988). "Risky Income, Life Cycle Consumption, and Precautionary Saving," *Journal of Monetary Economics* 22:237–255.

Sloan, Frank A., Gabriel Picone, and Thomas J. Hoerger. (1997). "The Supply of Children's Time to Disabled Elderly Parents," *Economic Inquiry* 35(2):295–308.

Solon, Gary. (1999). "Intergenerational Mobility in the Labor Market," in Orley Ashenfelter and David Card, eds., *Handbook of Labor Economics*. Amsterdam: North Holland Publishers, vol. 3A, Ch. 29.

Solow, Robert M. (1956). "A Contribution to the Theory of Economic Growth," *Quarterly Journal of Economics* 70(February):65–94.

———. (1957). "Technical Change and the Aggregate Production Function," *Review of Economics and Statistics* 39(August):312–320.

Souleles, Nicholas S. (1999). "The Response of Household Consumption to Income Tax Refunds," *American Economic Review* 89(4):947–958.

Stafford, Frank P. (1996). "Early Education of Children in Families and Schools," in Paul Menchik, ed., *Household and Family Economics*. Boston/Dordrecht/London: Kluwer Academic Press, pp. 219–242.

Summers, Lawrence. (1981). "Capital Taxation and Accumulation in a Life Cycle Growth Model," *American Economic Review* 71:533–544.

Taber, Christopher. (1999). "Tax Reform and Human Capital Accumulation: Evidence from an Empirical General Equilibrium Model of Skill Formation." Mimeo.

Thaler, Richard H. (1994). "Psychology and Savings Policies," *American Economic Review* 84(2): 186–192.

Tiefenthaler, Jill. (1997). "Fertility and Family Time Allocation in the Philippines," *Population and Development Review* 23(2):377–397.

Tomes, Nigel. (1981). "The Family, Inheritance, and the Intergenerational Transmission of Inequality," *Journal of Political Economy* 89(5):928–958.

Topel, R. (1999). "Labor Markets and Economic Growth," in Orley Ashenfelter and David Card, eds. *Handbook of Labor Economics*. Amsterdam: Elsevier Science B.V., vol. 3A, pp. 2943–2984.

Trostel, Philip. (1993). "The Effect of Taxation on Human Capital," *Journal of Political Economy* 101(2):327–350.

Venti, Steven F. and David A. Wise. (2000). "Choice, Chance, and Wealth Dispersion at Retirement." National Bureau of Economic Research Working Paper 7521.

Wahl, Jenny Bourne. (1986). "New Results on the Decline in Household Fertility in the United States from 1750–1900," in Stanley L. Engerman and Robert E. Gallum, eds., *Long-Term Factors in American Economic Growth*. Chicago: University of Chicago Press, pp. 391–438.

Ward, Michael P. and William P. Butz. (1980). "Completed Fertility and Its Timing," *Journal of Political Economy* 88(5):917–940.

Weiss, Yoram and Robert J. Willis. (1985). "Children as Collective Goods and Divorce Settlements," *Journal of Labor Economics* 3(3):268–292.

——— and ———. (1997). "Match Quality, New Information, and Marital Dissolution," *Journal of Labor Economics* 15(2) part 2:S293–S329.

Whittington, Leslie, James Alm, and H. Elizabeth Peters. (1990). "The Personal Exemption and Fertility: Implicit Pronatalist Policy in the U.S.," *American Economic Review* 80(2):545–556.

Wildasin, David E. (1990). "Non-Neutrality of Debt with Endogenous Fertility," *Oxford Economic Papers* 42:414–428.

Wilhelm, Mark O. (1996). "Bequest Behavior and the Effect of Heirs' Earnings: Testing the Altruistic Model of Bequests," *American Economic Review* 86(4):874–892.

Willis, Robert J. (1973). "A New Approach to the Economic Theory of Fertility Behavior," *Journal of Political Economy* 81(2) part 2:S14–S64.

———. (1999). "A Theory of Out-of-Wedlock Childbearing," *Journal of Political Economy* 107(6) part 2:S33–S64.

Young, Alwyn. (1995). "The Tyranny of Numbers: Confronting the Statistical Realities of the East Asian Growth Experience," *Quarterly Journal of Economics* 110(August):641–680.

Zhang, Junsen and Junxi Zhang. (1995). "The Effects of Social Security on Population and Output Growth," *Southern Economic Journal* 62:440–450.

INDEX